CONTENTS

FOREWORD

LOIS ZACHARY HAS done it again. In *The Mentee's Guide: Making Mentoring Work for You*, she and her colleague Lory Fischler have added a much-desired third volume of wisdom, direction, and inspiration about mentoring to round out a troika of books providing essential wisdom and practice. This new book joins Zachary's acclaimed two volumes *The Mentor's Guide* and *Creating a Mentoring Culture*. *The Mentee's Guide* mentors you through the process, and it practices what it preaches.

Mentoring is a well-recognized concept in today's world, but it is frequently interpreted in different ways by different people. When individuals use the term very loosely to describe a variety of activities and outcomes, often without much attention to specifics, they may easily think they are clearly communicating their needs and expectations when in fact these may be interpreted quite differently by someone else. By defining *mentoring* as a relationship, breaking it down into distinct parts, and identifying specific aspects that are associated with effective mentoring, the book provides flexible but direct guidance to support mentees and other readers in their quests to learn and find new insights and awareness.

In 2009, more than ever, individuals benefit from the learning that mentoring can provide as they develop as professionals and as global citizens. Though a massive infusion of publicity has increased awareness of the potential benefits of providing mentoring for youth, especially those considered "at risk," there is also an increasing appreciation in the United States of the value of mentoring throughout individuals' lives. It is this benefit to adult learning that Zachary and Fischler know and impart with such passion, clarity, and precision to their readers. As we move through rapid social and economic changes wrought by technological development and resulting globalization of markets, former employment practices and expectations related to professional and career development have all but vanished. It's up to the individual to determine how to navigate these unfamiliar waters.

Although the documented benefits of mentoring accrue to organizations, society, and to the individual mentors themselves, as Zachary's previous two books have so well detailed, it is the *mentee* in the end who is likely to gain the most from an effective mentoring relationship. Now, at last, we have a guide for those who would like to be proactive in developing a powerfully productive mentoring relationship. Taking the initiative, as the adult seeking mentoring should do in driving a mentoring relationship, is likely to bring more useful benefits more efficiently. This book provides the insights and inspiration for the mentee to do so. Truly effective learning requires adult learners to take charge of their learning experiences and own them. They need to be open to new ideas but also test those ideas' authenticity and power to expand their own knowledge against their experiences and current understanding. Ongoing interactive communication with a mentor helps develop that process.

The Mentee's Guide provides a comprehensive overview, with guideposts along the path from selecting a mentor to transitioning into the role of mentor. Although the guide primarily focuses on mentoring related to work and professional development, its wisdom is applicable to personal mentoring as well. It is comprehensive, accessible, and illustrated with real-life examples from those who have experienced powerful mentoring relationships.

An internationally renowned consultant and expert, Dr. Zachary is well known for her wisdom and experience in developing leaders and her prominent use of mentoring in doing so. Her approach is simultaneously compassionate and challenging, thoughtful and clear-minded. It can help us take charge of envisioning and realizing our futures, leading to better lives, more rewarding and valuable work, and an improved world.

Carol B. Muller
Palo Alto, California

• • •

Carol B. Muller is the founder of MentorNet, the E-Mentoring Network for Diversity in Engineering and Science (www.MentorNet.net), *and served as its chief executive from 1997 until 2008.*

Preface

MY CONNECTION to mentoring began before I was born. My maiden name was actually Menter (pronounced the same as mentor), so perhaps it was not coincidental that my work focuses on mentoring. What is certain is that my introduction to mentoring began as a Menter.

My mother seemed to be everyone's informal mentor. She was a leader in a host of community organizations, and people would frequently call on her to share her leadership secrets, bolster their confidence, and support their good intentions. Sometimes she would be gentle, sometimes a bit stern, but she always balanced candor and compassion. Those who were privileged to call her "Mentor Menter" knew that she was there for them and believed in them and the power of their possibilities. To this day we hear stories of how enduring her impact had been and how, in her own special way, she didn't transform those she mentored but helped them transform themselves.

My personal mentoring stories are many. I marvel at how my mentors raised the bar for me, modeled the way, pushed me beyond my personally defined limits, encouraged me to enlarge my thinking, and believed in me even when I was unsure of myself. I was grateful for their time, their stories, and their commitment to my growth. I recall one mentor in particular who always seemed to open doors of possibility for me. She saw something in me I didn't see in myself. To be honest, I was sure that I was going to be overwhelmed as each door opened, but with her support I was able to rise to the challenge, consolidate the learning, and move onto the next one. Before I knew it, I had developed competencies that I'd never imagined. Another mentor stood alongside me as I took on a major leadership role in my community. He was there to support me, help me through the political minefields, and make sure I kept the big picture at the forefront of my thinking.

Although most of my experiences were positive, there were a few that could have gone better. I had no clue then that there were things I could have done, said, asked, and tried that would have allowed me to make the most of my mentoring relationships. I didn't realize that as a mentee I had an instrumental role to play in shaping and defining the outcomes of the relationship.

AN INVITATION TO EXERCISE YOUR VOICE

My experience is not unique. Some mentees engage in formal and informal mentoring relationships—personal and professional—just so they can "sit at the foot of the master." As result, they don't find their own voice to ask for what they need from a mentoring relationship but settle on what they get instead.

The Mentee's Guide: Making Mentoring Work for You is an invitation to exercise your voice with full resonance and not to settle for anything less than what you need. Whether you are just starting out in your career, seeking personal or professional development, transitioning to new responsibilities, retiring, or re-careering, it is important to understand what it means to be a mentoring partner and to fully engage in the relationship.

To that end, *The Mentee's Guide* presents a simple, straightforward practical approach to help you make the most of your mentoring relationship. Although there are many books for mentors, there are fewer for mentees and even fewer that focus specifically on empowering mentees to take an active, creative, and self-authored role in their own mentoring relationships. *The Mentee's Guide* fills that gap. Not only a book chock full of stories, practical tools, tips, and exercises, *The Mentee's Guide* is also an invitation to learning. As we take the journey together, I will guide you through the process step by step, offering straightforward and practical exercises so you can choose what works best for where you are now and where you want to go.

This book is an extension of our work at Leadership Development Services. It reflects what we've heard, observed, and learned in our work with thousands of individuals engaged in mentoring. The idea for the book started when six people approached me after a presentation at Google several years ago and asked me when I was going to write a book for mentees. I asked them what questions they would want such a book to address, and therein lies the inception of the process.

An important part of the process of shaping this book was undertaken by my colleague, Leadership Development Services' Senior Associate Lory

Fischler. Lory interviewed over thirty people of different ages from an array of settings—corporate, educational, nonprofit, and small business. We were interested in getting their on-the-ground candid stories and digging deeply into the day-to-day realities of a mentoring relationship, with all its exhilarations and frustrations.

The stories in this book are based on those interviews and on the experiences of individuals Lory and I have encountered in multiple settings over the years. We've changed many of the details to protect the privacy of the individuals, but the essence of their experiences has been preserved.

HOW TO USE THIS BOOK

If you are new to mentoring, I would encourage you to read chapters one through six before you do any of the exercises provided in the book. This will give you an overview of the entire mentoring process and help you fully appreciate the purpose of each phase. If you've had a mentor before, however, or are already engaged in a mentoring relationship, skim through the book and start out where you are right now. You can dip in and out of other chapters as needed. If you are considering making the transition from mentee to mentor, be sure to work through the exercises in Chapter Seven. If you'd like to dig deeper into the topics presented in each chapter, I've included an annotated bibliography in the Appendix for your reference. Also, I invite you to visit my Web site: www.leadershipdevelopmentservices.com.

My goal is to help you make *excellence* in your mentoring relationship a personal priority and be more reflective about your own role in that relationship. I hope you will accept my invitation to delve more deeply into understanding your role in a mentoring relationship and how you can make mentoring work for you.

ACKNOWLEDGMENTS

STORIES have the ability to stir and teach us. Reading about them often awakens something deep within us that gives us pause to reflect on our own story. Writing *The Mentee's Guide* created its own story, a story enlivened by the generosity of many people.

Lory Fischler, friend, associate, and storyteller extraordinaire—Your wisdom, talent, sense of humor, patience, and dedication enriches our partnership and collaboration every day and made this book exciting and fun to do. Know that I appreciate you and your many gifts.

Story Sharers (you know who you are)—Thank you for taking the time to candidly share your mentoring stories with Lory. Your experiences illuminated the everyday concerns, struggles, and satisfactions involved in mentoring and created the master story for this book.

Paula Stacy, my "book mentor"—You guided me in shaping and bringing to life the story I wanted this book to tell. With your quiet wisdom, attentive ear, and guiding hand you helped me zero in on what was important. I applaud you.

David Brightman, senior editor—We've worked together before, and now again. It only gets better. Thanks for honoring my work and encouraging me to write about it.

Marge Smith—My "critical friend," who always asked deep probing questions and kept encouraging me to bring more of my own story to the book.

Mentors, mentees, friends, and family—You are part of my continuing story. I am very grateful for that indeed.

Lois J. Zachary
Phoenix, Arizona

THE AUTHORS

LOIS J. ZACHARY is an internationally recognized expert in mentoring and leadership. She is president of Leadership Development Services, LLC, a Phoenix-based consulting firm offering leadership development, consulting, coaching, education, and training for corporate and nonprofit organizations.

Zachary is the author of *The Mentor's Guide: Facilitating Effective Learning Relationships* (Jossey-Bass, 2000), a best-selling book that has become the primary resource for mentors who are looking to deepen their mentoring practice. Her second book on mentoring, *Creating a Mentoring Culture: The Organization's Guide* (Jossey-Bass, 2005), provides a comprehensive resource for promoting organizational mentoring sustainability. In addition to books on mentoring, Zachary has written numerous articles, columns, and monographs about mentoring, leadership and board development, staff development, consulting, and adult development and learning. She is the coeditor of *The Adult Educator as Consultant* (Jossey-Bass, 1993) and the coauthor (with Lory Fischler) of *Creating and Sustaining Collaborative Partnerships* (Leadership Development Services, 2002).

Zachary was selected by *Leadership Excellence: The Magazine of Leadership Development, Managerial Effectiveness, and Organizational Productivity* to its "2007 Excellence 100" list as one of the 100 "best minds" in the field of organizational leadership.

Zachary received her doctorate in adult and continuing education from Columbia University. She holds a master of arts degree from Columbia University and a master of science degree in education from Southern Illinois University.

• • •

LORY A. FISCHLER, Leadership Development Services' senior associate, is a facilitator par excellence. In her role as the company's program-development specialist, she builds client-customized mentoring and leadership training programs. She is also the creator of Leadership Development Services' unique Effective Meeting Model©, as well as a work style inventory that promotes self-understanding and team interaction. In addition to collaborating on the publication *Creating and Sustaining Collaborative Partnerships*, Fischler and Zachary developed a series of Mentoring Excellence Pocket Toolkits.

Fischler is a graduate of Lake Erie College and has studied at the University of Grenoble, Boston University, and Boston State University. She is a Master Instructor for Motorola University, and in 1991 she was the first person to receive Motorola University West's Instructor of the Year Award.

THE MENTEE'S GUIDE

CHAPTER 1

The Power and Process of Mentoring

WHAT EXACTLY IS a mentor? Because *mentor* is often used loosely to refer to various learning relationships, it is important as you set out on your path as a mentee to understand just what mentoring is and what it isn't. We can gain some insight by considering the origins of the word. *Mentor* is a Greek word stemming from the name of a character in Homer's *Odyssey*. Mentor was an elderly man, whom Odysseus asked to watch over his son Telemachus when Odysseus set off to fight in the Trojan War. We don't know much about the interactions between Mentor and Telemachus; few conversations are recounted in the story. But at one point the goddess Athena takes the form of Mentor and guides Telemachus in his quest to find his father, and the brief description of this suggests what sets mentoring apart from other learning relationships. Unlike a teacher or even a coach, who is focused on helping us learn and practice a particular set of skills, a mentor acts as a guide who helps us define and understand our own goals and pursue them successfully.

Of course, mentors in today's world may not have a goddess's supernatural powers to help us negotiate our struggles, but they have something else, something that I would argue is just as powerful. They—and you, as a mentee—have access to insights and research about what helps create strong mentoring relationships and what helps adults learn and grow. In the past fifteen years, as mentoring has grown more pervasive and popular and as the field of adult learning has expanded, we have learned a great deal about what both mentors and mentees need to do to build and maintain the kind of relationships that change lives.

WHAT WE KNOW ABOUT GOOD MENTORING RELATIONSHIPS

Good mentoring depends on effective learning. We now know that the best learning occurs when there is a mix of acquiring knowledge, applying it through practice, and critically reflecting on the process. This means that the model of mentoring popular in the 1980s, in which an older, more experienced adult passed on knowledge and information to a younger, less experienced adult, is being replaced by a new model, one that is similar to the one that I first described in *The Mentor's Guide* (Zachary, 2000). The new model emphasizes the value of the mentees engaging actively in their own learning and critically reflecting on their experiences.

Good mentoring therefore depends on a reciprocal learning relationship between you and your mentor. Together you form a partnership to work collaboratively on achieving mutually defined goals that focus on developing your skills, abilities, knowledge, and thinking.

To be successful, this relationship must have the following elements: reciprocity, learning, relationship, partnership, collaboration, mutually defined goals, and development. Let's look more closely at each of these elements:

Reciprocity This means equal engagement on the part of you and your mentor. Both of you have a responsibility to the relationship and a role to play, and both have much to gain from the relationship as well, not just the mentee. Although mentees often wonder what the mentor has to gain from the relationship, there is more than you might expect. Mentors say that they receive a great deal of satisfaction from sharing their knowledge and experience. Their own perspectives expand as a result of engaging in a mentoring relationship. Often the experience reaffirms their own approaches or suggests new ones. It helps them reconnect to the people in their organization and become reenergized. As a mentee, it is important that you keep this in mind. If you see yourself only as a grateful receiver of help and advice you may be reluctant to ask for what you need.

Learning The purpose, the process, and the product of a mentoring relationship is learning. Your relationship may be a good one, but without the presence of learning there is no mentoring. By *learning* we mean more than simply acquiring knowledge, which, though important, is but one aspect of learning. The learning that goes on in a mentoring relationship is an *active* learning: the mentee gains expanded perspectives; knowledge about the ins and outs of the organization, field, or profession; an understanding of what works and doesn't work; and, most important, a deepened self-knowledge and self-understanding. The process of critical reflection enables the mentee to transform and apply learning in new ways. Because mentoring is so learner-focused, it is important to understand yourself as a learner and what you bring to the relationship. Because not everyone learns in the same way, it is useful for both you and your mentor to be aware of the how you learn best. In Chapter Two, on preparing yourself for mentoring, you will find some tools for helping you better understand your own learning style.

Relationship Relationships don't occur by magic. They take time and work to develop. Working at the relationship is part and parcel of effective mentoring. It is difficult to learn if you don't feel secure in the relationship. Hence it is critical that mentoring partners work at establishing and maintaining trust. Without trust a good mentoring relationship is impossible. Without trust mentoring partners tend to take things personally and make false assumptions or start blaming. They end up going through the motions of mentoring rather than the process of mentoring. This underscores the importance of having authentic and honest conversations, being committed to the relationship, and following through on commitments.

Partnership In the past, mentoring relationships were driven by the mentor. The mentor was an authority figure who took the mentee under his or her wing; the mentee was there to receive the wisdom of the mentor and be protected, promoted, and prodded. The current paradigm calls for more involvement of both partners in a mentoring relationship. Just as in any other partnership, mentoring partners establish agreements and become knowledgeable about and attuned to each others' needs. Each mentoring partner is unique and that uniqueness includes all of the experience, history, diversity, and individuality they bring to the mentoring relationship.

Collaboration As with any partnership, the work in a mentoring relationship involves collaboration. Mentor and mentee engage in sharing knowledge and learning and building consensus; in the process they mutually determine the nature and terms of the collaboration. You and your mentor each bring your own experience to the discussions that take place. It is this give and take that contributes to shared meaning, and something greater emerges because of this process. Collaboration requires openness on the part of both mentoring partners.

Mutually defined goals It is hard to achieve a goal that has not been defined. It may be defined in your mind but unless it is mutually defined with your mentoring partner you may be working at cross purposes or on different goals. Clarifying and articulating learning goals is critical to achieving a satisfactory mentoring outcome because mentoring partners must continuously revisit their learning goals throughout the mentoring relationship to keep it on track. Without well-defined goals, the relationship runs the risk of losing its focus.

Development The focus in a mentoring relationship is on the future, that is, developing your skills, knowledge, abilities, and thinking to get you from where you are now to where you want to be. Mentoring thus differs from coaching, which is more oriented toward boosting performance and specific skills in the present.

THE POWER OF MENTORING

What can mentors help you achieve? Our research at Leadership Development Services reveals multiple reasons for individuals seeking mentors. Some are looking for a safe haven, a place to go where they can vent or get candid feedback. Others are seeking a sounding board to test ideas. Many say they don't get the support that they need in their jobs, at school, or in their organizations to manage their productivity.

Within organizations, mentees we've interviewed say that mentors were invaluable in helping them navigate the organization and learn about what works and what doesn't in the organizational culture. Many report increased confidence, risk-taking, and competence in key areas. Others report more visibility in the organization and expanded networks and opportunities. Gen-Xers and Gen-Yers clamor for mentoring, and it is a drawing card for organizations looking to recruit them. What mentees gain from a mentoring relationship has a lot to do with how open they are to learning. Let's turn to Kendra's story and what happened for her as a result of her informal mentoring relationship.

Kendra's Story

Kendra had been having a hard time at her new job as manager of customer service at a large retail chain. She sought this job to escape from a very toxic situation in her previous workplace, where there was little communication or information sharing and information was used more as a weapon than as a tool for cooperation. At the time, she had assumed that everything that was going wrong in her previous job was her fault in some way. If, for example, someone refused to share information with her, she assumed it was because that person wanted her to fail. On top of this she believed that anyone in a senior position was probably smarter and more competent that she was. As a result, she became overly cautious, untrusting, and lost all self-confidence.

Even though the culture of the new organization was completely different from that of her old job, she was finding it difficult to shake the old feelings, suspicions, and self-doubt. Kendra had brought the defensive and ineffective behaviors she learned at the old job to the new one, and it wasn't working for her. Although the new job had a culture of collaboration and openness, Kendra assumed that people were withholding information and didn't want her to succeed. Instead of trying to function effectively in her new workplace, Kendra's strategy was to focus on impressing everyone and making herself look as good as she could. To this end, she took a very top-down approach, quickly implementing a series of changes and dictating new policies. She managed to alienate her colleagues and the people who reported to her in very short order.

Kendra was lucky, however, because Sandra, the HR manager took notice. She saw that Kendra was struggling and invited her to lunch one day to talk. Sandra made it clear to Kendra that she believed in her and offered to meet with her regularly to give her feedback and direction. Sandra saw, for example, how Kendra's lack of confidence was causing her to make decisions without consulting and working cooperatively with her colleagues and reports. At one meeting, Sandra said, "You need to take credit for your ideas. I would like to see the day when your confidence catches up with your ability. You have good ideas, but you aren't leading." That comment made a big impact on Kendra. She realized that it was OK to admit to yourself and even show others that you are good at something. She started very slowly and tentatively to switch her tactics. Instead of pushing her agenda on others, she began to enthusiastically and straightforwardly present her ideas. As she did, other people began to see value in her work and to see her differently.

Sandra helped Kendra realize exactly what she needed to do to be successful. She was able to make concrete suggestions for ways to approach meetings, influence some tough department heads, and resolve conflicts with her peers. When Kendra saw the results from her first performance review (which involved 360 degree feedback from those she reported to, worked with, and managed) she was overwhelmed by the praise from her colleagues and direct reports. Kendra had left her previous position feeling like a failure. Sandra's help allowed her to change how she behaved, as well as her view of herself and the world around her. Kendra observed, "With Sandra's help I was able to turn myself around."

Although Kendra was not involved in a formal mentoring program, she was engaged in an informal mentoring process with Sandra which allowed her to develop confidence and success at a very critical time in her career. All this came about because Sandra had approached her and essentially offered to informally mentor her at a time when she needed it most.

The profound influence of a mentor's candid in-person feedback can dramatically transform one's personal perspectives and worldview, build self-confidence, and add to one's professional competence.

Some mentees say that mentoring gives them exposure to people and ideas they would never have encountered on their own. Others find that their mentor's belief in them gives them strength and bolsters their courage in taking risks. Some report that mentoring helps demystify their profession, organization, or job. Still others find the benefit of mentoring a way to jump-start their learning process in new and unfamiliar areas.

THE PROCESS OF MENTORING

Mentoring occurs every day in many places and spaces. Mentoring relationships can look very different depending on the people involved. Although spontaneous and informal mentoring can have great results, in this book we focus on a way to intentionally find and nurture mentoring relationships that will help you achieve specific and satisfying results.

As already mentioned, research has taught us a lot about how adults learn best and what makes good mentoring. The bar on mentoring practice has risen considerably over the years as a result. We now know, for example, the kind of preparation and work that both mentor and mentee need to engage in to develop a good relationship, set goals, work to achieve them, and create a satisfying result to their work together. This knowledge has been shaped into a four-stage model, which I first introduced in *The Mentor's Guide,* and provides a framework for managing the life cycle of a mentoring relationship.

Do you really need a model? Does it seem artificial? Sometimes working with a model can seem awkward or unnatural. If you are concerned about this you are not alone. A number of the people we interviewed explained that although they were initially wary of using a model, they found that it provided them with the fundamentals and a solid structure that made a dramatic difference in the outcomes of the mentoring and helped them derive more satisfaction and learning from their relationships.

The model I presented in *The Mentor's Guide* sets out four phases of the mentoring relationship: (1) preparing (getting ready), (2) negotiating (establishing agreements), (3) enabling (doing the work), and (4) coming to closure (integrating the learning and moving forward). The phases build on one another to form a predictable developmental sequence that varies in length from one relationship to another. These stages often merge into one another, and as you work together with your mentor you may be unaware that you have progressed from one phase to another.

The Four-Stage Mentoring Cycle

Here are the four stages in more detail.

Preparing

This is the *getting ready* phase. It involves preparing yourself for mentoring and preparing the relationship. This phase therefore occurs individually and then jointly. Each partner examines his or her motivations and engages in self-reflection to determine what he or she is expecting from the relationship. Partners then enter into a dialogue and explore these issues together. For mentees, it is especially important at this phase that you honestly examine what you want to learn and how you learn best. The more self-knowledge you have the more prepared you will be to approach the job of defining appropriate and realistic goals. You will be able to come to the relationship with your mentor as a full partner with an agenda of your own. This phase is discussed in Chapters Two and Three.

Negotiating

This is the *establishing agreements* phase, in which mentoring partners discuss details and agree upon goals, processes, and ground rules. The work that takes place during this phase lays the foundation for the relationship. An important aspect of this phase is establishing trust, and to that end it is important that mentoring partners discuss confidentiality. Another issue that should be addressed during this phase is setting realistic boundaries for your time together to ensure that your work is not derailed by discussions of personal issues. Finally, this is the time in which you set up the logistics of your work, agreeing on questions such as: How often will we meet? Where and for how long? What are target dates for achieving specific goals? You will learn more about this phase in Chapter Four.

Enabling

Enabling may be a hard word for you to swallow in this context. Because the term is emotionally loaded, I want to make my intention clear. I use this word to describe this phase in its most positive sense. It is the *implementation* or *work* phase of the partnership. Most of the learning occurs during this period. It is therefore the longest phase. During enabling, partners work toward achieving the mentee's learning goals and communicate regularly about their progress and how well they are meeting goals and objectives. This phase requires much attention and care. There are likely to be setbacks as well as successes. Issues may arise that will need renegotiating. You may find that you need to change the frequency or duration of your meetings. Questions about trust can surface and resurface and should be addressed and resolved quickly or the relationship will suffer. It is challenging, but both mentee and mentor need to stay focused not only on the mentee's learning goals but also on the relationship. This phase is described in depth in Chapter Five.

Coming to Closure

This is the *integration and moving forward* phase. It entails consolidating the learning, evaluating the partnership, and celebrating successes. Both partners reflect upon the relationship, their personal and professional growth, and how they can each leverage their learning. There is a temptation to dismiss this phase as unimportant—after all, the real work is over, the learning has occurred; it's time to move on, right? Wrong. One thing we have learned from our work with mentees is that if this phase isn't handled well (if, for example, a mentor leaves suddenly at the end for a new job), it can leave both mentor and mentee frustrated and dissatisfied. If mentees don't feel good about the relationship it can adversely influence how they feel about their learning. Chapter Six explains how to ensure that this phase goes well.

Different Kinds of Mentoring

Mentoring relationships come in all shapes and sizes and include multiple modes (informal and formal) and models (one-to-one and group) in diverse and disparate organizational types and settings. The following are common types of mentoring:

One-on-One Mentoring

One-on-one mentoring is the traditional and most common model of mentoring. It involves two people working together to help the mentee achieve specific goals. The mentor can be a peer, a more senior person, or a person with specific expertise and experience. The relationship can be informal or formal. An informal relationship may occur without your even being aware of it at first. For example, you may find yourself seeking and receiving advice from a trusted colleague, a manager, or anyone really who has something to offer. A good example is Lory Fischler's relationship with her tennis coach, Ed, which we describe below. Lory didn't set out to be mentored but found herself receiving advice not just about tennis but also about lots of areas of her life. She never formalized the mentoring side of this relationship but continued to reap the benefits of listening to and knowing Ed. In formal mentoring relationships, on the other hand, mentees and mentors are typically involved with a program within an organization. Still, anyone can decide to formalize a mentoring relationship whether in a program or not. Formalizing a relationship would simply mean following many of the steps in this book—identifying goals, negotiating the terms of your relationship with your mentor, and following through to closure.

Group Mentoring

Group mentoring is a type of social networking that honors and shares the knowledge and expertise of the individuals within a group. It typically involves a small number of people who have similar job functions, experiences, interests, or needs and so form a self-directed group to learn from each other. The group is self-managed and takes responsibility for crafting its own learning agenda and managing the learning process to meet members' learning needs. These groups can be part of a formal mentoring program or you can set up your own; this is what I did when I first moved to Phoenix. I had been meeting people who were truly inspiring and interesting and I wanted to stay connected to them. Despite my desire, I was finding it difficult to find the time to connect with them all. I invited them to a first meeting and asked them whether they found the same value in each other as I did, and, if so, whether they would want to form a peer mentoring group in which we could engage in good conversation, share best practices, and support one another. Most of them said yes, and our group was formed. When we met again we invented a peer mentoring structure that worked for us. The format varied over the years. We took turns presenting to each other on our area of expertise. From time to time we invited experts to meet with us. Some years we had a theme and a retreat. We orchestrated our own learning and supported each other in our development.

Reverse Mentoring

Reverse mentoring has become more popular in recent years, growing out of a mutual need for learning. People in senior positions learn from individuals with expertise within their rank and file and at the same time those in junior positions learn from the senior leaders of their organization. It often works like this: a senior person is mentored by someone who has specific technical knowledge they need to learn. That individual, in exchange, is mentored by the senior executive, who offers the big organizational picture and perspective.

Mentoring Board of Directors

In the mentoring board of directors model, a group of hand-picked mentors functions as a personal board of directors to help facilitate an individual's achievement of a clear and specific learning goal. The board has the advantage of providing multiple perspectives and diverse feedback to a mentee by clarifying, pushing, and expanding the mentee's thinking, promoting personal reflection, and functioning as a sounding board. Typically in the personal board of directors' model it is the mentee who seeks out and recruits multiple mentors to help her achieve specific goals. The mentors meet together with the mentee at regular intervals; the mentee manages the learning process, calls meetings and hosts them together with her mentors, and shares accountability for the learning process and achievement of desired results.

Informal versus Formal Mentoring

The model outlined in this book provides a framework for mentoring excellence that is relevant to mentors and mentees whether they are participating in a mentoring program or acting on their own agree to formalize their relationship as mentor and mentee. Thus, those who find themselves in informal mentoring relationships can draw on this model as well. What does informal mentoring look like? Kendra's story is a good example of informal mentoring. Sandra, her mentor, approached her and agreed to give her feedback, and what followed was a process that evolved as Kendra's needs arose. There were no formal agreements or commitments, just two people committed to learning and a mentee who was motivated and open to change. Informal mentoring occurs every day in various settings. It can last a week, a number of months, or it can last a lifetime. The more you know about yourself, what you want to learn, and how to form a good relationship with your mentor, the more you will benefit, no matter how spontaneous or informal your work is.

More Praise for The Mentees' Guide

"Lois Zachary and Lory Fischler's book confirms the importance of providing newly appointed leaders the support and tools they need to maximize the learning opportunities available through a mentoring relationship. Principals and vice principals in Ontario currently value Zachary's books on creating a culture of mentoring and her guide for mentors in facilitating effective relationships. This new resource completes the collection and provides a comprehensive resource for establishing successful mentoring programs."
—Joanne Robinson, senior consultant, Education Leadership Canada

"Lois Zachary understands the essence of mentoring. Her new book, written with her associate, Lory Fischler, is another great tool for me as a leader, working with mentoring everyday, always looking to make the relationships more effective. Successful mentoring is not about a cup of coffee now and then; it is a real, committed relationship with clear expectations on both sides."
—Pernille Lopez, president, IKEA US

"A leading authority on mentoring, Lois Zachary writes with the clarity of purpose and generosity of spirit that animate successful mentoring relationships. Based on solid research, her book presents useful exercises and juicy, real-life examples that will help you make your time as a mentee wonderfully productive and affirming."
—Sheila Grinell, president and CEO emeritus, Arizona Science Center

"This easy-to-read, highly practical and reliable book teaches lessons that lead to successful mentoring in cross-cultural and international environments."
—Eric Ng, president, ESSN International Pte Ltd, Training & Consultancy Services

THE MENTEE'S GUIDE

Making Mentoring Work for You

Lois J. Zachary

with Lory A. Fischler

JOSSEY-BASS
A Wiley Imprint
www.josseybass.com

Published by Jossey-Bass
A Wiley Imprint
One Montgomery Street, Suite 1200, San Francisco, CA 94104-4594—www.josseybass.com

The materials that appear in this book (except those for which reprint permission must be obtained from the primary sources) may be reproduced for educational/training activities. We do, however, require that the following statement appear on all reproductions:

The Mentee's Guide by Lois J. Zachary.

This free permission is limited to the reproduction of material for educational/training events. Systematic or large-scale reproduction or distribution (more than one hundred copies per year)—or inclusion of items in publications for sale—may be done only with prior written permission. Also, reproduction on computer disk or by any other electronic means requires prior written permission. Requests for permission should be obtained through payment of the appropriate per-copy fee to the Copyright Clearance Center, Inc., 222 Rosewood Drive, Danvers, MA 01923, 978-750-8400, fax 978-646-8600, or on the Web at www.copyright.com. Requests to the publisher for permission should be addressed to the Permissions Department, John Wiley & Sons, Inc., 111 River Street, Hoboken, NJ 07030, 201-748-6011, fax 201-748-6008, or online at www.wiley.com/go/permissions.

Readers should be aware that Internet Web sites offered as citations and/or sources for further information may have changed or disappeared between the time this was written and when it is read.

Limit of Liability/Disclaimer of Warranty: While the publisher and author have used their best efforts in preparing this book, they make no representations or warranties with respect to the accuracy or completeness of the contents of this book and specifically disclaim any implied warranties of merchantability or fitness for a particular purpose. No warranty may be created or extended by sales representatives or written sales materials. The advice and strategies contained herein may not be suitable for your situation. You should consult with a professional where appropriate. Neither the publisher nor author shall be liable for any loss of profit or any other commercial damages, including but not limited to special, incidental, consequential, or other damages.

Jossey-Bass books and products are available through most bookstores. To contact Jossey-Bass directly call our Customer Care Department within the U.S. at 800-956-7739, outside the U.S. at 317-572-3986, or fax 317-572-4002.

Jossey-Bass also publishes its books in a variety of electronic formats. Some content that appears in print may not be available in electronic books.

Library of Congress Cataloging-in-Publication Data
Zachary, Lois J.
    The mentee's guide : making mentoring work for you / Lois J. Zachary ; with Lory A. Fischler.
        p.   cm. — (The Jossey-Bass higher and adult education series)
    Includes bibliographical references and index.
    ISBN 978-0-470-34358-6 (pbk.)
      1. Mentoring in business.   2. Corporate culture.   I. Fischler, Lory A., 1947-   II. Title.
    HF5385.Z33 2009
    650.1—dc22
                                                                                    2009011952

Printed in the United States of America

FIRST EDITION

PB Printing

10 9 8 7

MENTORING CAN HAPPEN ANY TIME AND ANY PLACE

My colleague Lory Fischler tells the following story about her mentor and tennis coach Ed. It is a great example of how mentoring can happen at any time and any place. Here is the story of Ed in Lory's own words:

Lory's Story

I had been playing tennis most of my life and at the age of forty was on a tennis team. We played in USTA sponsored tournaments and met weekly to practice. One day during practice we saw another team on the courts who looked like they were having a blast. We thought, "Hey, we'd like to do it that way." So, we hired their coach and thus began my relationship with Ed, tennis coach and mentor.

Ed didn't look much like your typical tennis coach, five feet eight, a bit overweight, and scruffy—and not inclined to show us a lot of deference. But what was clear to me from the beginning was that his whole orientation was to my being the best at my game. My game. And that is where the mentoring began.

Ed started every lesson with, "How've you been playing? What do you need to work on?" Even when I would tell him about some wonderful victory, where I finally beat someone who had been kicking my butt, he would say, "On your best day, you are never as good as you think you are. And on your worst day, you are never as bad as you think you are." He forced me to stay focused on my goal. Ed taught me a lot about tennis, but more important, he taught me about life. It wasn't good enough to bask in past victories; it was important to keep moving forward and stay focused on my goals.

Another big Ed lesson: One day after I dunked a ball into the net, he asked me, "What were you thinking?" I replied, "Nothing . . . I was just trying to hit it back." He responded, "On every shot, at every moment, you need to go in with a plan. Even if it doesn't work, always have a plan." I have taken that lesson to heart and whenever I feel stuck or stressed, I summon up Ed's words like a mantra, "Always have a plan." While this doesn't always result in a long-term solution or a winning shot, it puts me in control. Without a plan I'm just throwing things against a wall and seeing what sticks. If something did work I wouldn't even be able to identify what it was. With a plan, even if it doesn't work, I can look back on it, reflect on why it didn't work, and actually learn something.

More Ed wisdom: "Play your bread and butter shots." Mine is a down the line shot. He always advised me, "Know what you have that you can rely on. That is what is going to win you games, when you play your best and most consistent shots." In tennis, as in life, it is important to play to your strengths. This doesn't mean you don't work on stretching your game, practicing other shots to use in a pinch, but if you try to make your fundamental game about doing what is hard for you, you will lose games. I learned to know my strengths and rely on them.

Ed was my teacher for twenty years. That adds up to a lot of life lessons.

"Put a positive message in your head," he told me one day when I was working on serving after coming back from shoulder surgery. "Don't tell yourself not to double fault. Instead," he reminded me, "tell yourself to throw the ball higher, or out more or reach for it. Give yourself a positive not negative message."

When I was struggling with my ground strokes one year, he asked me what I was thinking about in trying to correct my stroke. I listed about five things. "Work on only two things at a time," he challenged me. "That's about all the brain can handle at once. Especially your brain," he said, smiling.

I am without Ed now on the tennis court. He died rather suddenly last year after a short illness. But he died living all those life messages he had been passing down to me over the years. And because of him I am living those messages too. He told me, "I have had a great life. I have made great friends, played a game I love, with people I care about. What could be better?"

Knowing Ed, as a mentor and as a friend, what could be better?

P.S. I wasn't the only person who was mentored by Ed. At his memorial service with only twenty-four hours notice over sixty people showed up. When the time came to share Ed stories, after an initial silence there suddenly came a flood of stories of things Ed had told people, what they had learned, how they would be forever influenced by his words, wisdom, and teaching.

Ed's job title was tennis coach, but his work went way beyond coaching. What made him a mentor was what he asked of people and how they responded. He cultivated mentoring relationships when he asked his students to create goals, know and challenge themselves, reflect on their practice, and grow and learn. He nurtured his relationship with his students consciously. It was this relationship that served as a vehicle through which learning happened. Although natural mentors like Ed may not be typical—he knew instinctively what good mentoring involved—the learning that resulted from his mentoring, his effect on those he mentored, can happen anywhere. People can learn to be good mentors and mentees. All that is necessary is for people to come to the process with an open mind, learn about the fundamentals of good mentoring, and put these fundamentals into practice. That is what this book is all about.

IS MENTORING RIGHT FOR YOU?

The people mentored by Ed were mentored successfully because they were ready to receive what he had to offer. In much the same way, Kendra was also ready when her mentor stepped forward at a very teachable moment. She was open to learning and professional development. Because she had a mentor who created a safe climate, she was able to be open with herself and her mentor. She learned how to listen to and respect critical feedback and convert those lessons learned into action. Mentoring was right for her. Before moving on to the next chapters about the mentoring process, it may be useful take a moment and consider how ready you are.

Here are some questions for you to think about:

- Do I have a sincere interest in learning?
- Am I willing to commit time to developing and maintaining a mentoring relationship?
- Am I willing to work on my own growth and development?
- Am I willing to be open and honest with myself and another person?
- Am I willing to listen to critical feedback?
- Can I participate without adversely affecting my other responsibilities?
- Am I committed to being an active mentoring partner?

Although these are important questions to consider, don't worry if you can't unequivocally answer each with a resounding, Yes! Learning to be a mentee can take time. Still, it is useful to go into the process with an awareness of aspects that you might find particularly challenging. The next chapter on preparing yourself for mentoring will give you an opportunity to explore just how ready you are and address these areas of challenge before you move forward.

CHAPTER 2

PREPARING YOURSELF TO MAKE THE MOST OF MENTORING

A DESIRE TO grow and learn is a great start for a mentee, but if you really want to get the most out of your mentoring relationship you have to prepare for it. This is true whether you are in a formal mentoring program or are on your own looking for someone who can give you some guidance. Whatever your situation, if you have decided that you would benefit from mentoring, you may be eager to jump in, find or meet your mentor, and start getting the help you need. But as I described in the previous chapter, the mentoring process doesn't begin with you and your mentor; it begins with you. Before you can engage with a mentor, you need to do some serious and focused preparation that will help you know better what you want to achieve, how you learn best, and what kind of mentoring relationship might work well for you.

Let's look at an example that clearly underscores the need for preparation before we get started.

Ian's Story

Ian had always been very ambitious. As a freshman in college he used to tell everyone that he planned to become an entrepreneur and run his own company. He was impressed with stories he had heard in the media about entrepreneurs and liked the idea of a life on his own terms. Other than that, he didn't know much about business in general and didn't have an interest in any particular kind of business. His ambition was fueled more on image than on knowledge. After graduation he decided not to go to business school. Instead he took a job with a pharmaceutical supply company to get some business experience. He hoped to have a chance to learn the ropes and that his energy, confidence, and brains would single him out for more training and development.

According to plan, it wasn't long until he was approached by his boss's boss, who was impressed with his work and wanted to hear more about his career goals. They agreed that it would be a good idea for Ian to find a mentor in the company. After getting some names from his boss, Ian took the initiative and made contact with Marcus, senior vice president of sales. He assumed Marcus had the contacts, connections, skills, savvy, and experience that he needed. Marcus was happy to work with Ian, and in that first meeting they set up monthly lunches for the next six months. Then Marcus recommended that Ian read Jim Collins's book Good to Great *so that they could talk about it at their next meeting. Ian got the book but didn't read it. He simply skimmed it. By the time his next lunch with Marcus rolled around he had actually forgotten that it had even been assigned. Needless to say the lunch didn't go well. When Marcus asked, "Well, what did you think of the book?" Ian danced around the question hoping to hide the fact that he hadn't done his homework. He could see that Marcus was disappointed in his response, and the only thing that salvaged lunch was turning the talk to baseball, a sport they both loved. At the end of lunch Marcus suggested that Ian research other books or articles about CEOs—perhaps he might find one that would inspire him. Marcus also asked him to write out what his vision for success in five years might look like and bring it to their next meeting. Ian happily agreed.*

Every so often during the next month, Ian thought about what his vision might be but didn't carry his thinking further than the vision he had had since he was a college freshman—the vision of himself as entrepreneur. He asked some friends for recommendations for books but never did anything further with the information. On the night before his next lunch with Marcus he still hadn't done any of the research Marcus had suggested, but he thought that at least he could write the vision. He sat down in front of a piece of paper and tried to put his vision into words. Try as he might, he was stuck. Ian was unable to get beyond the words "CEO of my own company." After fifteen minutes (which seemed like hours) Ian went out to get dinner. When he got back, the paper was still on the table. Ian gave it a glance, then decided to check in on the ball game on TV. He fell asleep on the couch and the next thing he knew it was morning and he had nothing for Marcus.

Ian told Marcus that he really tried, but that he just couldn't see what being a CEO in five years might look like. Marcus looked him straight in the eye and said, "Ian, I think you have energy and you have the smarts. But you need to do this work in order to get the most out of this relationship. Nobody said it would be easy. I will stand by and when you are ready I will be happy to help you."

It is easy to see that Ian wanted to succeed but he wasn't ready to do the serious work that a successful mentoring relationship requires. Researching his vision, reflecting on his reading, and preparing for his meetings with Marcus certainly wasn't a priority. Any sincere effort at research and reflection would have been better than no effort at all. Marcus would have then had a starting place for discussion and could have drawn him out and guided him in the process.

It is all too easy to assume that because mentors have more experience in a particular kind of work, business, or field of study they know best how to help you and to structure a mentoring relationship. Although some mentors in formal programs are also receiving guidance on how to mentor and some may have mentored others successfully, they are not necessarily experts on the most important aspect of their mentoring relationship with you. They may not know how you learn best, how you communicate, or what your vision for your future is unless you make that clear. And you will be unable to make these things clear to your mentor if you have not achieved a good measure of clarity for yourself. The information and exercises in this chapter will help you develop this clarity.

Before you engage in any of the exercises read through the entire chapter and consider what you already know about yourself and what you may need to explore further. You need not do every single exercise; some may fit better with how you learn than others. But it is important to familiarize yourself with the activities and understand, if you choose not to do one, why you have made that choice. You also may also find that an exercise that seemed difficult at one time will be easier at a later date, perhaps after you have had a chance to reflect further or have completed a different activity. Finally, keep in mind that what you do here is just a start. It is likely that as you go through the mentoring process your self-knowledge will grow and sharpen. This is where it all begins.

MENTORING: A REFLECTIVE PRACTICE

Some people may regard reflection as a waste of time, but nothing could be further from the truth. You may be a person who doesn't naturally engage in reflection. You may think it seems like too much work and an inefficient way of using your time. If so, I'd like to disabuse you of that notion and invite you to make thoughtful reflection a personal habit that you engage in regularly throughout your mentoring relationship. It may feel awkward at first, but it is well worth the effort.

According to my colleague Bruce Barnett and his coauthors, who wrote about reflection in their 2004 book, *Reflective Practice: The Cornerstone for School Improvement,* "the meaning of reflection and its value are rarely made explicit in our personal and professional lives." They point out that when you combine hindsight, insight, and foresight you can make the most of your reflective powers. (Barnett, O'Mahony, and Mathews, 2004, p. 6.) Their definition of reflection closely aligns with mine. I define *reflection* in the context of mentoring as the ability to critically examine your current or past practices, behaviors, actions, and thoughts in order to more consciously and purposefully develop yourself personally and professionally. You can liken this process to pulling a rubber band back as far as you can and letting it go. The further back you pull it, the farther forward it goes. So it is with thoughtful reflection; it catapults you forward.

Reflection is an instrumental part of the mentoring experience. Taking time to reflect on your experience and your hopes for the future is critical to the success of your relationship. There is no better time to begin this habit than in the preparation phase.

Everyone has a history of experience that they bring to the mentoring relationship. These are the experiences and skills that have brought you this far in your personal and professional development. They help you make decisions, work well with others, generate plans, and get others involved— the skills that help you play a responsible and active role in your own life. Before you move into a mentoring relationship it is important that you do an honest self-appraisal of your own development and understand your personal strengths and challenges. This way you can better understand not only what areas you need to work on, but also the kind of people and experiences that best help you develop your skills.

The Personal Reflection Exercise

The Personal Reflection Exercise (PRE), Exercise 2.1, is designed to help you reflect on your personal and professional journey. This process of self-discovery will reveal personal insights and deeper meaning about how people and events in your past have contributed to your personal and professional development.

EXERCISE 2.1

Personal Reflection Exercise

1. This is a time line of your career journey. Reflect on your journey and plot the specific milestones and marker events you encountered along the way. Include important challenges, disappointments, transforming events, and so forth. Once you have completed your time line use it to inform your responses as you complete the following questions.

2. Describe three to four milestones that contributed to your *personal* development. Of these, which affected you the most and why?

3. Identify your top three personal or professional successes. Describe the role you played and why you felt each was successful. Which one are you most proud of and why?

4. What were the major personal or professional challenges you faced? Why were they particularly challenging and what specifically did you do to respond or overcome them?

5. How are you different today than you were five years ago?

6. Create a realistic balance sheet of your current personal and professional assets and liabilities.

7. What barriers are you creating for yourself?

8. What false assumptions might you have about your role, your impact, your value, and your self-confidence?

For more information see Cathy McCullough. "Developing You!" *Training and Development,* December 2007, *16*(12), 64–67.

As your write about your experiences, challenges, successes, and disappointments in response to the questions posed in the PRE you should begin to better understand what and who shaped you into the person you are today. Personal reflection will give you a starting point for moving forward. Sometimes knowing where to begin a process like this is intimidating. Give yourself a number of days to work on this. Trying to complete it in one sitting is likely to result in frustration or in a superficial exploration of your leadership history. In this exercise, you will notice that you are asked to complete a time line first. You will want to transpose the time line onto a much larger piece of paper so that you have plenty of room to write in the specific milestones and marker events you have encountered on your personal journey. Use the vertical lines as markers for specific dates and fill in your information at the appropriate time markers.

This exercise starts by asking you for some concrete details to stir your memory. You may wonder at what age you should begin the time line. Of course, that's up to you, but you may want to begin when you were in high school or even earlier, as this is when we often begin to chart our own direction, making choices about the interests we pursue and the people we seek out. Perhaps you ran for student body president in elementary school and lost, maybe you were in a play in middle school and realized that you loved being on stage, or perhaps there was a teacher in high school who recognized your talent for helping others in the classroom. In your adult life, you may have worked waiting tables and realized that you were at ease in dealing with cranky and demanding customers. Remember, you have been shaped by *all* of your experiences, so do not assume that some experiences don't count because what you did was not important. Write down everything you can think of. Don't worry if you can't remember details or if you put things in the wrong order at first. The point is to start thinking about your history.

As the examples above suggest, the remaining questions on the PRE are designed to help you reflect deeply on your personal and professional history. That means answering the questions completely and honestly. You do not have to write beautiful prose—no one will be reading this but you. You just need to make sure you are getting all of your thoughts down on paper. Here are some tips:

- Try to think back and imagine yourself at different points of your life. What were you thinking, feeling, and doing at each of those stages?
- Write about not how you should have performed, thought, or felt but about your actual experience.
- Start with the word *I*; it will make it easier to begin.

- Be as specific and detailed as you can in answering the questions.
- If you find yourself overwhelmed or drawing a blank, stop writing, take a break, and return to the PRE when you are rested and relaxed.

The following example demonstrates how to complete the exercise.

I was recently promoted to my first leadership position and my career in management is now officially launched. When I think back about the events that led me to this place in my life, I recall a small but transformational moment that occurred when I was nine years old. Up until that time, I thought of myself as like most boys my age—a prankster, fun-loving, and always looking for a good time. Then, during a Boy Scout camp overnight, a bunch of us scouts were sent to collect wood to make a fire. Before he sent us out on our mission, the scoutmaster took out a large bowie knife, housed in a leather sheath. Six of us huddled around that knife, staring at it like it was precious treasure or a deadly snake, or both. Our scoutmaster said, "I am going to give this knife to one of you to use to cut kindling. But it is dangerous, and it needs to be handled by someone who has shown me leadership and good judgment." And then an amazing thing happened! He handed the knife to me. I was stunned. I was overwhelmed. I was proud. I was in awe. And I was transformed from that moment. I had never seen myself as a leader, as responsible, as particularly special. But at that moment, someone saw something in me that I hadn't seen. And from that moment on, I wanted to be the person who deserved to carry the knife.

CREATING A PERSONAL VISION

It is hard to arrive at a destination if you don't know where you have been and even harder if you don't know where you are going. Embarking on a mentoring journey requires a sense of the destination and end goal. It will expedite your mentoring relationship and help focus your conversation if you have done the important work of exploring your own destination. The activity of creating a personal vision has proven helpful to mentees who are about to begin a mentoring relationship. Those who craft a personal vision are significantly more effective in their jobs and more likely to achieve their financial and professional goals than those who do not. It has been said, "If you can imagine it, you can achieve it. If you can dream it, you can become it." I invite you to think about the possibilities that lie ahead of you and imagine yourself realizing your full potential.

Have you ever, for example, closed your eyes and imagined yourself in another place doing something very different? Have you at some time wished you were in a different position—working in TV broadcasting, helping relief workers in a refugee camp, managing your department instead of following orders? Part of visioning is thinking about yourself in your ideal, optimal, preferred state. It focuses not where you are now but where you would like to be if the stars aligned and your best hopes and dreams were realized. A personal vision statement is not about winning the lottery or wishing that your divorced parents would reunite. It doesn't rely on outside people, events, or magic. Instead, a personal vision statement is an expression of the future you want to have. It is a vivid description and a detailed picture of your life fulfilled. It articulates the values to which you ascribe and that guide your life. Creating a personal vision statement is a risk-taking activity. You are pushing your personal envelope and imaging yourself out of your comfort zone doing something that so far has only resided in the back of your mind. By putting your vision into words you are bringing it center stage. A personal vision statement is also an act of leadership. Leaders align their behavior with their vision. They create a concrete view of the world they want to create and then work to get others on board. In leadership, the vision may be directed at the organization. In this case, it is personal.

How to Get Started

Start by getting into a relaxed state and finding a stress-free, distraction-free environment. Allow yourself at least thirty minutes of uninterrupted time to work at completing this activity. Get in front of your computer or use a notebook or pad of paper. Begin by thinking of yourself, five years from now, in a highly fulfilled and happy state. Allow yourself to dream. Remember, anything is possible, so don't censor your thoughts as they surface. To help you focus your thinking and develop a clear vision, answer the following questions. Because you are putting yourself in your future, answer the questions in the present tense:

- What job are you doing?
- How are you contributing to the success of your organization or the enterprise you are engaged in?
- What are people saying about your performance? Your contribution?
- What impact are you having on the people around you?
- In what ways have you grown, developed, or raised your skill level?

Stretch your thinking and don't settle for easily accomplished goals. If you are trying for a new position, envisioning yourself getting it and functioning in it is not enough of a reach. What's next after that? What would really "knock your socks off"? Make sure you stay positive and optimistic. If you have a smile on your face while you are writing, you are probably on the right path. Try to suspend your internal critic and your modesty as you work on your vision. This is a time to stretch. Be as descriptive as is necessary for you to see yourself in your mind's eye living the vision. Play your vision out to the end. Where does it lead? What is the legacy that you will leave behind?

Once you have fully answered the questions the next step is to put it all together into a clear statement of your vision of the future. On a separate piece of paper describe your vision as if it were real today. The purpose of this statement is to communicate to yourself and others as clearly as possible what you will be doing and what that will be like. Using the present tense is a way of giving the future an immediacy and reality. The following is an example of a vision statement. Notice that it is written in the present tense and reads as though the person writing it is actually doing the job she envisions.

Mary's Vision Statement

I arrive early to work this morning and I am eager to get started. I am working with two former coworkers at a graphic design firm doing lots of creative and interesting projects. The firm has grown in size and reputation since I have been there and I like to think that, in part, it is due to what I have contributed to building a talented team in the firm. I love the diversity of ideas that float around the table as part of the creative process and being encouraged to just "go for it" without any restrictions. I am much more open to learning and, as a result, welcome any feedback that is given to me. I am contributing to the organization by being very collaborative in my approach and bringing people into the process from idea conception to execution. I've gotten plenty of kudos from my boss and coworkers about the quality of projects delivered and my ability to meet deadlines. I feel valued and appreciated. Many clients specifically ask for my services on their project and I have developed a faithful following. I am relaxed and happy—a big change from where I was five years ago—and amaze myself with how well I am able balance work and family. I am taking creative writing courses at a community college near my home and several of my short stories are being published.

At some point, either before or after you have written up your formal statement, you will want to consult the checklist in Exercise 2.2.

EXERCISE 2.2

Beginning with the End in Mind: Visioning Checklist

Visioning Criteria	Yes	No
Will my vision require me to stretch to achieve it?		
Will I need to expand my skills and competencies?		
Does my vision excite me?		
Does my vision support my values and beliefs?		
Is my vision aligned with my development goals?		
Can I picture my vision fulfilled in very concrete terms?		
If I were to describe my vision to someone else would they be able see it?		
Will achieving the vision make me feel proud?		
Is my vision clear and to the point?		
Does my vision express hope and optimism?		
Does my vision include empowering words?		

Answering the questions in Exercise 2.2 about your vision will help you make sure that it will be truly helpful as a tool to guide you in the mentoring process. Getting feedback from friends and coworkers on your vision will also be helpful. I encourage you to talk about it and test out how it feels to speak about your goals and dream out loud. When you get feedback, listen carefully and with an open mind. Let's look at Mary's vision and see whether it meets the criteria set forth in the checklist.

Mary's vision would certainly require her to stretch. She might even need to change jobs and expand her skills in order to achieve this vision. She is obviously excited about it. We don't know for sure that her vision is aligned with her development goals, but we have the sense that it is. Her vision is realistic and she has a clear picture of what that would be like. In fact, we can see it clearly from her description. Her phrases "eager to get to work," "contributing to the organization," "getting kudos," "amaze myself," and "happy" are empowering expressions filled with hope and optimism.

One of the most important things a mentor can help you do is work toward your vision. Doing so productively, however, requires that you understand the skills required to fulfill this vision, your current level of competency in each skill, and what you need to do to improve or acquire these skills. In other words, what are the gaps in your skills that need to be addressed before you can achieve what you want to achieve? Exercise 2.3 below will help you engage in analyzing these gaps.

To help you understand this process, let's take another look at the example of Mary. Mary was excited about the person she described in her vision but she also knew that she had to get out of her own way to arrive there. She interviewed a few of her colleagues and her boss about what they saw as critical success factors for realizing her vision. As a result, she was able to identify seven competencies that she needed to develop. In Exhibit 2.1 you will find a sample of Mary's Gap Analysis that provides a list of these competencies.

Technical expertise was the first on Mary's list. She was pleased that she could rate herself high on that competency but realized that it was probably the easiest of the seven for her to develop. She was relieved as well that client relationships was fairly high but recognized that she needed to bring a stronger voice to the table when she met with clients and do more selling of ideas rather than receiving instructions. She also realized that she had work to do in terms of risk taking, initiative, confidence, time management, and conflict management, all of which had been in her way for a long time.

EXERCISE 2.3

From Vision to Goal Setting: Gap Analysis Exercise

Instructions: What gaps exist between your vision and current competency?

Competency	Current Competency Level (low) 1–5 (high)	Competencies to Be Developed (Those you want to work on)

EXHIBIT 2.1

From Vision to Goal Setting: Mary's Gap Analysis

Instructions: What gaps exist between your vision and current competency?

Competency	Current Competency Level (low) 1–5 (high)	Competencies to Be Developed("*" Those Mary wanted to work on)
Technical expertise	4	*Master the ABC 6.2 program
Client relationships	3.5	*Selling ideas rather than waiting for clients' reaction
Risk taking	2.5	*Tolerating mistakes and being out of my comfort zone
Initiative	2.5	Planning and leading a project
Confidence	2.5	Not second guessing myself and being comfortable with decision making
Time management	2	Planning the project milestones and sticking to schedules; giving up on perfectionism to meet timelines
Conflict management	2	Recognizing that we both have perspectives and it isn't personal if others see it differently. Being able to raise issues, not take positions, without fearing the conflict

As you move forward before or during your mentoring relationship, hone your vision; assess the competencies you have and the competencies you need to achieve that vision; and then identify goals that you want to work on. Your personal analysis of strengths and weaknesses and gaps in competencies is excellent preparation for your opening conversation with your mentor.

What If You Don't Have a Vision?

Coming up with a vision may be very challenging. Not everyone has a clear sense of the possibilities that exist and what it might feel like to work in a particular job. Remember Ian, who was stuck when he couldn't envision what it might be like to be a CEO of his own company? What Ian needed to do was to persevere and begin the process of thinking seriously about his vision. Even though you may feel stuck it is important that you begin the process. Your vision isn't a contract, it isn't a promise, and it isn't necessarily realistic. It is simply a point to begin a conversation with yourself and with your mentor. You might want to "try on" various visions and see what fits. Don't worry about details at first, just think about yourself at work. Are you traveling and going to meetings? Are you collaborating with various people one on one or are you in front of a group giving a presentation? Maybe you are working quietly at home by yourself and taking time to go for walks or water your garden. You may not be ready to articulate a full-fledged professional vision, but there is probably something that you can put on paper about your hopes and dreams that will give you and your mentor a starting point.

HOW YOU FUNCTION IN A MENTORING RELATIONSHIP

Another level of analysis that should be completed before moving into a mentoring relationship focuses on your previous experience being mentored. In some way all of us have had this experience, even if at the time we didn't consciously look at it as mentoring. If you look back at your life (again, consider the time line you created in your PRE) there are certainly people who gave you guidance, advice, or support. This might have been a grandparent or other family member; a teacher or coach, such as Ed, Lory's tennis coach, in Chapter One; or a boss or colleague.

Insights from Experience

Consider the following four questions to help you reflect on previous mentoring relationships or relationships you've had with others who have guided, supported, and strengthened you. Reflecting on these questions should reveal some powerful insights about what worked in the relationships, what could have worked better, and why.

1. What were the most satisfying aspects of those relationships and why?

2. What did you learn about being in a mentoring relationship?

3. What did it require from you to make the most of the relationship?

4. What lessons will you carry forward for your present mentoring relationship?

You may discover, for example, that you had a hard time asking for help or showing weakness and, on reflection, you realize you could have gotten much more from the experience had you been willing to reveal more. Or you may notice that the person who was the most helpful to you had a certain way of giving you feedback. Perhaps he used humor or was very direct and frank. Maybe you responded best to direct advice or perhaps you got the most from someone who was a great listener. These kinds of insights can help you make decisions about who would be a good mentor for you and can also be shared with a new mentor to help you both find ways to work together effectively.

Mentee Skills

Being involved in a mentoring relationship isn't something you do once and then you are launched. It is something that you learn to do and then learn to do better. You will learn as your relationship unfolds by honing your skills and thus getting more and more out of it.

Your mentoring experience can be qualitatively better if you possess and use specific skills. Prepare for the relationship by understanding what these skills are, how they can affect the mentoring process, and what your competency level is with each. Exercise 2.4 lists these mentoring skills and asks you to identify your proficiency level and what you need to work on for each. It is important to consider all of these skills so you don't simply rely on your areas of strength, using the skills you already have or are best at while neglecting others. Knowing which of your skills are weak and targeting them can help you grow in ways that are surprising as well as enormously beneficial. Before you do this exercise, let's take a moment to look closely at each of these ten skills. These are the some of the essential skills for mentees, and ones that mentees find the most challenging.

Let's examine each of the skills in Exercise 2.4 in more detail.

EXERCISE 2.4

Mentee Skill Inventory

Instructions: Evaluate your proficiency on the mentee skills listed below. Once you have identified what you need to work on (medium and low), look for ways to develop your skills. You may want to discuss your assessment with your mentor and use it to set some personal goals. Evaluate your progress as you work on increasing your proficiency level.

Number	Skill	High	Medium	Low	Developing My Skills
1.	Giving and receiving feedback				
2.	Self-directed learning				
3.	Building relationships				
4.	Communication				
5.	Goal setting				
6.	Effective listening				
7.	Follow-through				
8.	Reflection				
9.	Initiative				
10.	Valuing differences				

1. *Giving and receiving feedback.* Being able to ask for, give, receive, act on, and accept feedback effectively is a practiced skill. Most people are better at giving feedback than they are at asking for, receiving, and accepting it. You will need to use your feedback skills, especially your ability to receive, accept, and act on feedback, to get the maximum benefit from the mentoring relationship. What feedback challenges do you typically face?

2. *Self-directed learning.* At one time mentoring was based on the "sage on the stage" concept, meaning that the relationship was mentor-driven. That paradigm has shifted over time. Today, mentee and mentor collaborate to meet the mentee's learning goals. In practical terms this means that, as the mentee, you are in charge of your own learning. Together with your mentor, you define your specific learning needs, identify what it is you want to learn, formulate learning goals, identify relevant learning resources, select and implement learning strategies, and evaluate the learning that results. How proficient are you as a self-directed learner?

3. *Building relationships.* There is no magic wand that you can wave to build a mentoring relationship. It takes time to get to know one another and so it develops over time. As a mentee, you need to be authentic and open, sharing yourself and your story so that your mentor can get to know you. You need to come to the relationship with curiosity and commitment about your mentoring partner and be steadfast in working on the partnership. Does relationship building come naturally to you or do you need to work at it?

4. *Communication.* Effective communication is critical to successful mentoring, just as it is in any relationship. Good communication depends on building up a trust account so that you have enough trust deposits to encourage open and authentic communication. People who are good at this skill continuously check for understanding and clearly say what they mean and mean what they say. How well do you communicate?

5. *Goal setting.* Since setting and working toward completion of learning goals is the focus of the mentoring relationship, this is a vital skill to develop. Remember that these are your goals, not your mentor's. Your mentor can help you crystallize and clarify them, but at the end of the day they are your goals; you own them. You and your mentoring partner must each understand them since you will be measuring your progress against them. Your goals will need to be specific, measurable, action oriented, realistic, and timely. Does goal setting come easily to you?

6. *Effective listening.* Everyone listens to some extent, but do they really hear what is being said? Effective listening requires attention, intention, and retention. It is hard to be open to learning if you are hearing another melody. Mentees must be active listeners and learn to hear both what is said and what is unsaid. Can you leave behind the chatter in your own head and really focus on what someone else is saying?

7. *Follow-through.* You need to do what you say you will do and do it as promised. If you don't execute, it will eventually compromise the trust in a relationship and upend your learning progress. Follow-through includes being organized and a good time manager in order to meet commitments. What is your track record when it comes to delivering on your promises?

8. *Reflection.* Reflection, as stated before, is a significant tool for facilitating the growth and development of mentee, mentor, and the mentoring relationship. It is the springboard to action and further learning. Being comfortable with the process skill of reflection means being able to step back, evaluate, process, and consider the implications of one's own experience in informing future action. How good are you at stepping back and seeing the big picture?

9. *Initiative.* You are the driver in this relationship, which means stepping up to the plate and asking for what you need when you need it. Hoping that your mentor will tell you, lead you, and be directive is not productive in helping you sustain the learning. Are you comfortable in making the first move?

10. *Valuing differences.* One of the benefits of mentoring is the exposure to different perspectives. During the course of your relationship, you are likely to hear perspectives different from your own. There may be positional differences, generational differences, learning style differences, or gender or ethnic differences. Can you be open to those perspectives and ideas and welcome them?

Self-awareness about your skills is an important step in preparing for your mentoring relationship. Self-awareness about how you learn helps make your mentoring experience more productive. We turn now to a discussion of learning style.

KNOWING YOUR LEARNING STYLE

Learning style can have a dramatic impact on a mentoring relationship. It influences how you work with your mentoring partner. It will also help you discern what kinds of learning opportunities would work best for you. We focus on learning style because of the centrality of learning to the mentoring relationship. Knowing how you learn will not only help you in a mentoring relationship but it will also help you in other situations. For example, knowing your learning style can help you be more collaborative, solve problems more easily, build and maintain other relationships in your life, create more motivated, engaged, and productive teams, and make better decisions.

At Leadership Development Services, we are great fans of David Kolb's Learning Style model (http://www.haygroup.com/tl/Questionnaires_Workbooks/Kolb_Learning_Style_Inventory.aspx) and use it as a tool for mentoring preparation. Kolb's model focuses on four styles or ways people perceive and process information. To determine your predominate learning style think about your own learning experience and your personal strengths and challenges. Focus on how you learn now, not how you would like to learn or how you think you should be learning. Then review the following four descriptions and see whether you can recognize yourself in one of them. Keep in mind that all of us are a blend of the four learning styles and what you are looking for here is your preferred style, the one on which you rely the most when you learn.

Diverging Learners

Some people perceive information concretely and process it reflectively. They learn best by reflecting alone about what they are learning and then sharing ideas and feelings. This style, called *diverging*, describes individuals who like to explore possibilities—the more ideas the better. They enjoy brainstorming and have fertile imaginations. Visioning comes quite naturally to them. They are inclusive and place a high value on preserving harmony and consensus. Their creativity is exciting and energizing to those around them. The downside is that when too many ideas are presented at once they often become indecisive. In the name of harmony they are conflict-adverse and often forgo their personal opinions. For example:

> *Isabella was regarded by her coworkers a team player. Everyone counted on her to be there, to help and do whatever it took to get a job done. She always supported her coworkers' ideas during staff meetings to make sure everyone felt included. Everyone liked her fresh ideas and openness. Wanting to please her mentor and avoid creating tension during their meeting, Isabella avoided confronting her mentor when she really didn't agree with the goals and suggestions her mentor was making for her. Not wanting to ruffle any feathers, she called her friend afterward to complain about her feeling of being pushed in an unwanted direction.*

Assimilating Learners

Those with an *assimilating* learning style perceive information abstractly and process it by thinking things through in an integrated and rational way. Logic, order, and perfection are important to them. They have a talent for analyzing disparate facts and organizing them into coherent concepts, models, and theories. They are data-hungry and need trusted information and facts before they can make a good decision. And sometimes that decision making is slow in coming because they are still assimilating data. Such learners value procedures and systematic plans because they provide a rational order to things. They might gravitate more toward the Personal Reflection Exercise (PRE) than the visioning aspect of preparation. They are often dependent on others to provide the impetus for action. They can become too theoretical and may be seen by some as being overly cautious and more concerned with theories and models than their practicality. Often they are perceived as overly critical and skeptical.

> *Last week during their mentoring session, Carol's mentor asked her a provocative question, "If you weren't in your current job, what other route might you have chosen?" It caught Carol off guard. She immediately began to mull over the various options she might have considered. After three long minutes of thought and silence, she still hadn't spoken. Carol was trying to sort out the possibilities in her head and wanted to be sure about her answer. Questions like this were not easy to for her to answer and doing it on the fly only made her nervous.*
>
> *Her mentor tried another tactic and decided to give her some homework. He asked her to draft a plan of what career development might look for her this next year. Carol spent a lot of time thinking about what might make realistic and appropriate goals for her plan. It took her several weeks and multiple drafts. She finally came up with a detailed grid that itemized each goal, its key objectives, and detailed strategies for achieving it. She e-mailed her plan to her mentor with a note, "I am not sure that I have it right. Please excuse the typos, I am sending this from my Blackberry."*

Converging Learners

Converging learners perceive information abstractly and process it actively and quickly into a concrete solution. Their strength is practical application, strategic thinking, and planning. These doers thrive on time lines and are quick to ask about the bottom line before they tackle a problem. Sometimes they act too quickly, without enough data, and make wrong decisions or errors. They rarely change their position once they have made up their minds. They are direct and to the point but often impatient and prefer to do things on their own to make sure the job gets done.

> *Phil identified a direction he wanted to go in and, at his boss's suggestion, found a mentor to help him get there. He was skeptical as first that someone else might be able to offer him assistance. Since Phil had a very clear idea about what he needed to do and how to go about doing it, he was willing to invest some time to see if it actually paid off with results. He was pleased to find that his mentor had great contacts and set up some immediate connections that he thought would speed up his career move. However, Phil was argumentative and blunt in mentoring meetings when he disagreed with his mentor. He never backed down once he took a stand and was pretty firmly convinced that he is right. This often created tension in the room.*

Accommodating Learners

The *accommodating* learner perceives information concretely and processes it actively. The result is that such learners are accommodating to people and adapt well to new situations. They are energizer bunnies in executing plans and tasks. They are creative problem solvers and risk takers, and they invite change and like visioning even more than the diverging learners. They learn by trial and error. However, they may get bogged down in trivialities and get behind schedule. They often get bored easily and appear scattered, disorganized, and sometimes pushy and impatient.

> *Charlie was excited about working collaboratively with his mentor, a senior VP of the company. He was hopeful that it would help him get recognition and ultimately the promotion he so badly wanted. He appreciated the opportunity to share his ideas with someone from the executive team about how the company could improve their image and relationship with the customer. Recently Charlie was asked to prepare an overview of his career path for the next five years and the key goals he needed to work on to achieve those goals for a mentoring session. As it turned out, Charlie hadn't prepared anything specific. He had a lot of ideas in his head and planned on "winging" it.*

Working with Your Own and Your Mentor's Learning Styles

Many conflicts between mentoring partners arise out of lack of understanding of differences in learning styles and not significant points of disagreement. The style with which you will probably have the potential

EXHIBIT 2.2

Selected Learning Style Descriptors

Accommodating	Diverging
• Energizing people	• Motivating the heart
• Visioning	• Being imaginative
• Motivating	• Understanding people
• Taking risks	• Recognizing problems
• Initiating	• Brainstorming
• Getting things done	• Being open-minded
• Being adaptable and practical	• Valuing harmony
Converging	**Assimilating**
• Exercising personal forcefulness	• Using principles and procedures
• Solving problems	• Planning
• Making decisions	• Creating models
• Reasoning deductively	• Defining problems
• Valuing efficiency and timeliness	• Developing theories
• Being practical	• Being logical
• Setting goals and timelines	• Deciding with data

for greatest conflict is the style that is in your diagonal quadrant. If you look at Exhibit 2.2 below you can identify your diagonal quadrant.

Accommodators and assimilators are in diagonal quadrants, as are diverging and converging learners. As you review the characteristics listed under each heading you can see how people with these styles might frustrate each other. The person with a diverging style wants to think about ideas and the person with a converging style wants to get it done. The assimilator is data driven and the accommodator is driven by instinct. Even if you and your mentor do not have a good style match, being aware that you have a different style can make the difference between shutting down in frustration and working through any conflicts.

For example, you might need to think about things for a long time to make a decision (diverging style) and your mentor may be someone who likes to move quickly and have agendas and time lines in place (converging style). Conversely, you may prefer to read as much information you can (diverging style) and your mentor may only want the bulleted version (converging style). By communicating about how you learn best you will be able to make steady progress and avoid some stumbling blocks in the learning process. Knowing your mentor's style will help you in your interactions with your mentor. So, for example, if your mentor wants plans and time lines and your style is more free-flowing and conversational, you know how to adjust your interaction. The bottom line? Know your style and let your mentoring partner know how you learn best. Be aware of your mentoring partner's style. Learn to adjust your style depending on who you are interacting with.

• • •

Preparation is essential to make the most of your relationship, and it begins with you. Knowing yourself comes through honest, intentional, and focused reflection. The preparation you've done so far is going to serve you in good stead. It will position you to understand yourself and share that understanding with your prospective mentoring partner. And speaking of mentoring partner, it is now time to take what you've learned in this chapter and use it to find the right match for you.

CHAPTER 3

FINDING AND GETTING TO KNOW YOUR MENTOR

IN CHAPTER TWO you considered what you needed from a mentor and the skills, strengths, and approaches to learning you will bring to the relationship. This means you completed the groundwork to help you become a strong partner in a mentoring relationship. Now it is time to take that learning forward and consider what kind of mentor you need, given your situation. Specifically in this chapter we look at how to identify, seek, and select a mentor; ensure that you and your mentor are a good fit; and establish a relationship with a mentor.

People find mentors in a number of ways. Some formal programs make mentoring matches for mentees. Many involve mentees in some aspect of making choices that lead up to the final match. Some, while providing support and resources, leave the mentee sole discretion in seeking and selecting his or her own mentoring partner, much like in an informal mentoring relationship. If you are in a mentoring program and have been assigned a mentor, you may feel that the section in this chapter on selecting a mentor is not relevant to your situation. I encourage you, however, to read through this section anyway, as there are insights about what makes for a good learning fit between mentoring partners that you may be able to put to use in your mentoring relationship.

CHOOSING A MENTOR: A CRITERIA-BASED DECISION-MAKING MODEL

We choose our mentors or they choose us. In either case, your decision to participate in mentoring needs to be deliberate and well thought out so that you can make the most of the opportunity. Mentor selection is critical to achieving successful outcomes. The natural tendency is to zero in on chemistry when meeting with prospective mentors. If the chemistry doesn't feel right the inclination is to go no further. Rather than rely on chemistry alone, I recommend using a *criteria-based* decision-making model. It can help you make good choices and avoid those that don't support your talent and capability or are not otherwise in your best interest. Even if there are better choices, it is easy to bias our selection toward those that set us up for easy success. Without some sound criteria, our decisions can be flawed, and neither you nor your mentor is truly well-served. Often, the result is disengagement, disappointment, and wasted time. Using a criteria-based selection model helps you clarify just what you need and suggests possibilities you probably never thought about before. It keeps the focus on end results, needs, and wants. And most important, it minimizes personal bias and low-level decision making.

Exhibit 3.1 outlines the eight steps in the Criteria-Based Decision-Making Model that you can apply to help you decide which mentor is right for you.

EXHIBIT 3.1

Criteria-Based Decision-Making Steps

Step 1. Identify your goal.	Consider why you want a mentor. Define what you hope to achieve as your end result.
Step 2. Create a list of criteria.	Identify the qualities you want in a mentor.
Step 3. Determine qualities that are "must haves." (Musts)	Select those requirements that are non-negotiable from your list.
Step 4. Rank the remaining criteria. (Wants)	Rank order the remaining criteria in order of importance to you.
Step 5. List possible options.	Brainstorm a list of possible mentors.
Step 6. Eliminate options that don't meet the "musts."	Evaluate each possible mentor against the "musts." If the candidate cannot fulfill them, do not consider him or her further.
Step 7. Rate each option against "wants."	Compare how well each of the remaining options stacks up against your "wants." Assign a numeric rating (e.g., 1–10) for each potential mentor to measure how well he or she measures up against each "want."
Step 8. Make the decision.	Tally the numeric score to identify which of the candidates best meets your desired end result based on the criteria you established.

GOING THROUGH THE STEPS

Next I take you through the steps of the model, providing both instructions and examples from the experience of Will, who used the model to help him make a good choice of mentor.

Step 1: Identify Your Goal

The first step is to stand back and consider why you want to find a mentor. Having a mentor because it is the "in" thing to do is not a good reason. There is a greater purpose involved: articulate what you are seeking to learn and why it is important to you. In doing so you are building on the work you did in Chapter Two, in which you were asked to develop a personal vision and to reflect on past experiences and on previous supportive or mentoring relationships. After doing the exercises from Chapter Two you should have a better sense of what you want to achieve in the long term, information that will help you understand what you need in a mentor. It is important also to take stock of your current situation. Let's look at Will's experience of Step 1.

Will is an account executive on a sales team. He is relatively new in the business and anxious to learn. He has already shown enthusiasm, energy, and willingness to work hard. Among his peers there is a lot of competition, and very few people are willing to help him develop his skills and take an interest in his career. His boss recruited him with the promise that mentoring and coaching would be available. Unfortunately, two weeks after Will took the job, his boss was promoted and the company hadn't found someone locally to replace him. Will has decided that he needs a mentor to help guide him, develop his skills as a sales team member, and show him how to succeed in the company.

Step 2: Create a List of Criteria

Identify qualities you need in a mentor. Look at your current situation, but also reflect on your vision for the future and on what kind of support has worked for you in the past. This means building on much of the work you did in Chapter Two. To see this step in action, let's check in again on Will.

Will's current situation, since he was new to the organization, clearly indicated that he needed a mentor who was experienced and knowledgeable about this particular company. This may seem like an obvious quality that anyone might want in a mentor, but not necessarily. For many people, especially those who have experience with a company but are interested in making other changes, company-specific knowledge and experience may not be important qualities for a mentor.

When Will reflected on times that he had received truly helpful support, he remembered one person in particular who stood out. She was his supervisor on his first sales job. He had a great rapport with her from the start—they both liked joking around and he soon felt comfortable being honest with her about his ambitions. He also remembered that her door was always open, and he never felt awkward seeking her out. He realized that he needed someone who was both accessible and with whom he felt compatible. Finally, Will considered his vision for his future, which was eventually to oversee a large sales force, and he knew he needed someone who would understand and help him pursue his ambitions.

Here is the list of qualities Will developed:

- Experienced in sales
- Accessible
- Successful track record
- Knowledgeable about the field
- Compatible personality
- Committed to mentoring
- Go-getter style
- Shared interests

Step 3: Determine Qualities That Are "Musts"

Select from your list those requirements that are nonnegotiable; these are your "musts." It is important that you keep the musts to a minimum. Two or three qualities should be sufficient. If you choose more, you may significantly limit your choices down the road and inadvertently overly influence the outcome of your decision. If you think you have more than three musts, convert one or two of them to strong "wants."

When Will went through this step he came up with the following two items: (1) experienced in sales and (2) successful track record.

Step 4: Rank the Remaining Criteria ("Wants") in Order of Importance and Assign a Value to Each

First, order the criteria, putting the most important first. Then give each a value by assigning a number according to just how important it is. For example, Will assigned a value of 8 to both "committed to mentoring" and "go-getter style," which effectively gave them the same importance. He gave "shared interests" a 5 to reflect just how much lower it was in importance than those he rated as 8. You will use these values later when you measure your mentor choices against the criteria.

Here are Will's wants, ranked in order of importance:

1. Accessible (value: 10)

2. Compatible personality (value: 9)

3. Committed to mentoring (value: 8)

4. Go-getter style (value: 8)

5. Shared interests (value: 5)

6. Knowledgeable about the field (value: 4)

Step 5: List the Possible Options

In contrast to Step 3, here you will want to make sure that you do not limit your choices prematurely. In later steps you will be evaluating how the people on your list measure up against your criteria. If you don't have a roster readily available, use your networks to cast a wider net by getting referrals from both inside and outside your organization. For Will, this step was relatively easy because he had a wide pool of potential candidates from which to draw. He came up with four good possibilities:

1. Daniel, the new regional sales manager. Daniel has been warm and friendly to Will, but since he moved offices he has been swamped. He now comes to Will's office once a month for two days to work with the team.

2. Emilio, the senior account executive in the office. Emilio is a very successful sales rep, and has bragged that he will get Daniel's job because he is the top performer, and he probably will get the appointment. He has been friendly to Will but not very helpful.

3. Ana, senior sales representative who works for one of Will's suppliers in town. Ana and Will hit it off immediately when they had to work together to solve a customer problem. She is a good listener and was very helpful to Will in dealing with the problems they faced. Her calm, assertive style helped resolve the dispute.

4. Steve, a professor of Will's from college who taught sales and marketing. Steve had a lot of experience before becoming an academician. Will enjoyed his classes and learned a lot from him.

Step 6: Eliminate Options That Don't Meet the "Musts"

This can be a very powerful step. It may be frustrating to simply eliminate a number of people right away, but if you have correctly identified the qualities that your mentor must have, do not confuse your decision making by continuing to consider mentors who really can't provide what you need. In Will's case, his two musts—"experienced in sales" and "successful track record"—made him realize immediately that he probably needed to eliminate his professor, Steve, from the mix because Steve didn't meet the criteria of a successful track record. Will crossed him off the list.

Step 7: Rate Each Option Against "Wants"

You will be using a scale of 1–10 to rate how each potential mentor stands in relation to your wants. Let's look at the process Will went through to rate Emilo.

1. Accessible—Emilio was rated high because his desk was right next door. Will gave him a 9.

2. Compatible personality—Emilio didn't fare well here; Will was turned off by his cocky attitude. He got a 4.

3. Committed to mentoring—Will had to guess here, but everything he sensed about Emilio was that he was not a mentoring type of guy. He gave him only a 3.

4. Go-getter style—Will had to admit that Emilio was strong in this department. He gave him a 10.

5. Shared interests—Here, too, Will really didn't know Emilio well enough to comment so he neutralized the grade, giving him a 5.

6. Knowledgeable about the field—Emilio was strong here and scored well with a 10.

Will continued to complete the evaluation of each mentor, trying to fairly evaluate their strengths and weaknesses. The final results are shown in Exhibit 3.2. Notice that the rating each candidate received for a criterion is multiplied by the value assigned that attribute. For example, Emilio's rating of 10 for being "knowledgeable about the field" is multiplied by 4, the value that Will had assigned that attribute. Doing this allows you to factor in the relative importance of an attribute to the score each candidate will receive.

Step 8: Make the Decision

To make your decision, do the math and total each column. If you have been diligent and honest with yourself, you will have a numeric evaluation of the candidates that indicates who best serves your well-defined musts and wants. Each candidate will have an accurate rating, and the final total will pinpoint the most appropriate choice for you. This model will also allow you to move down the rankings if your first choice proves unavailable.

EXHIBIT 3.2

Using the Criteria-Based Decision-Making Model to Select a Mentor

Decision Goal: Choose a mentor who will help me be successful in sales		Option #1	Option #2	Option #3	Option #4
		Daniel	Emilio	Ana	Steve
Musts					
Experienced in sales		Yes	Yes	Yes	Yes
Successful track record		Yes	Yes	Yes	No
Wants	**Assigned Value**				
1. Accessible	10	3×10=30	9×10=90	8×10=80	×
2. Compatible personality	9	9×9=81	4×9=36	10×9=90	×
3. Committed to mentoring	8	9×8=72	3×8=24	8×8=64	×
4. Go-getter style	8	10×8=80	10×8=80	7×8=56	×
5. Shared interests	5	8×5=40	5×5=25	8×5=40	×
6. Knowledgeable about the field	4	10×4=40	10×4=40	6×4=24	×
		343	295	354	

FINAL RECOMMENDATION: Select Ana as my mentor

Will was pleased with the results. Ana's high score was a strong indicator that she had all the right qualities to function as a good mentor for Will, which confirmed his gut feeling. The model allowed him to share this analysis and comparison with others to defend why he was looking outside the company for mentoring. The process gave him confidence that choosing Ana was a wise decision. He was, however, surprised that Emilio scored as highly as he did. This made Will realize that Emilio may have more to offer than Will had been willing to admit and that he needed to be more open to learning from Emilio, even if he wasn't going to ask him to be his formal mentor.

TALKING WITH POTENTIAL MENTORS

The criteria-based decision making model is a tool for identifying a mentor, but the tool for actually recruiting a mentor is *you*. Even when you have been assigned a mentor and you don't have to do the work of actively recruiting someone, your initial conversation is important. The criteria you developed and their order of importance can inform your conversation and inquiry when you approach your mentor. Whatever your situation, you are essentially asking someone to make a big commitment of time and energy to guide you in your development. Katherine Klein, a professor of management at Wharton School of the University of Pennsylvania, observes in Wharton's online journal Knowledge@Wharton, "Once a mentor sees that you're eager, the more likely it is the mentor will want to spend the time and social capital on you, introduce you to the right people, and so on" (reprinted in MentorNet News, 2008).

An article entitled "Why Mentoring Matters in a Hypercompetitive World" in *Harvard Business Review* says it another way, "If you want a mentor, start acting like you do and you will eventually find yourself connected with [people] who are invested in your personal development" (DeLong, Gabarro, and Lees, 2008, p. 121). When you are approaching a potential or assigned mentor for the first time it is important that he see that you

- Have genuine enthusiasm for your work
- Are conscientious
- Actively show interest in your future
- Are open to feedback
- Are committed to your own growth and development, curious, and ready to learn

Take few moments to review these bullet points and ask yourself two questions: (1) Would others see me this way? (2) How do I demonstrate

Recruitment Conversations

Scenario One

Eve, a quality supervisor in a mid-size manufacturing company, felt that without an engineering degree she was at a dead-end in her current position. She was interested in getting more into the operations side of the company, where she believed she could really influence quality and outcome. When she heard the new chief operating officer tell her own story at an operations review meeting, Eve realized this was the person she wanted to choose for her mentor. After the meeting Eve worked up her courage and asked her to lunch.

Eve: "Thanks for joining me for lunch. I really appreciate the time. Ever since the ops review meeting, I have been thinking about the story you told us about your career journey. It really struck a chord with me because it is my hope to one day be doing those very same kinds of things. I know that you are very busy. I am wondering, however, if you could find some time to meet with me on a regular basis for mentoring. I'd like to take advantage of the company mentoring program. I want find a similar path that would work for me, get to know more about the field and more about the opportunities and potential in it. I could learn a lot from hearing about your struggles—especially being a woman in this male-dominated field. I want to hear about what you did to overcome the obstacles that you faced because I really want to figure out where I can make my mark. I have given a lot of thought to where my strengths and weaknesses are and I'm interested in exploring what I can do to make changes. Maybe we could decide on a schedule that works for you, meet once a month, and talk or e-mail in between. I've checked it out with my manager and he would support the time. What do you think?"

Scenario Two

Kevin, a CPA by profession and a long-standing volunteer in a local nonprofit, found himself having been talked into chairing a capital campaign even though he had never done it before. He decided he needed to look for a mentor who had the skills and experience he lacked. After contacting a number of nonprofits who had used professional fund raisers in their campaigns, Kevin was given the name of a professional fund raising consultant. He used the referral as an entrée to make the telephone call.

Kevin: "I volunteered for an assignment in a nonprofit organization and now I have been recruited to be the head of their major fundraising division. I just don't feel like I have the skills to do this job even though everyone is saying 'you can do it, you can do it.' I have to lead a group of sixty volunteers; I have a budget—which I have never managed before. I've got to lead this fund-raising effort—be responsible for bringing in a million dollars in the next twelve months—and I don't know what the heck I am doing. I know I could go to the previous campaign chair but I simply can't relate to the style of the people who have done this before. First of all, they have all been here a long time, have a lot of contacts, and were able to raise money from their friends. That is clearly not going to work for me. I need your help. I need a mentor. So I think, on one level, I am asking you to hold my hand but on another level, I need real guidance. I feel like I could really learn something from you."

Scenario Three

Carmen was struggling in her current role as an HR specialist in a small regional sales organization where she felt isolated, insecure, and unsuccessful in influencing upper management. She was seeking a mentor who held a senior position in a similar organization and who had been able to successfully overcome the hurdles she now faced. She decided to seek mentoring help from a colleague from a larger organization who she saw periodically at HR conferences. After a presentation that they had both attended, Carmen asked her out for coffee.

Carmen: "It's been great seeing you at these HR conferences. At work, I never get to see anyone in our field. My company only has fifty employees and I do all the HR functions myself. This is a new job and I hope a new career for me. I had been a teacher for many years and entered this job to make a career change. I am eager to learn what I need to do to be my best and get to the next level. My long-term goal is to work in corporate HR, heading up training and employee development. I don't feel that what I am doing right now positions me well for that. But I have watched you at these meetings and I so admire your skills, background, and experience. You are doing what I hope to be doing in a few years. So I was wondering if we could get together occasionally. I'd like to pick your brain about what I am thinking and to see if I am heading in the right direction and get your ideas and feedback."

these attributes? For those of you whose first conversation with a mentor will be a recruitment conversation, you will find examples of ways to word your request in the examples on the next page.

MAKING YOUR FINAL CHOICE: SOME THINGS TO THINK ABOUT

After you have met with prospective mentors—or if you have a mentor assigned to you, after you have had an initial meeting—ask yourself two questions: Is this a good fit? Does this person have the time, willingness, and sincere interest in mentoring me?

If you've been assigned a mentor, you may feel that you have no choice, but you do. If you suspect there may not be a good learning fit, speak up. The more preparation you have done, the greater your ability to understand whether someone is or isn't a good fit and to advocate for a change if necessary. Does your prospective mentor truly fit the criteria you set forth? If you are reasonably certain that he does, then you can launch into the serious work of preparing your relationship. But before you make a final choice, let me offer some caveats about what to avoid:

Supervisors as Mentors

To some extent, all supervisors engage in mentoring their employees. Usually this looks and feels like a series of mentoring moments or minutes and happens informally as part of their job. However, when it comes to a structured and formal relationship, there are some important things you should consider before you jump into a mentoring relationship with a supervisor. Being mentored by an immediate supervisor is a slippery slope and often limits the authenticity of the relationship. The relationship doesn't invite candor because an uneven playing field exists and risk taking is often compromised. Mentoring tends to focus more on day-to-day work issues and less on big-picture development issues.

Choices Based on Convenience

Avoid the trap of making the "easy ask" or selecting a mentor simply because she is conveniently located or you already have a relationship. If you have truly followed through on using the criteria-based model, you should be able to avoid this pitfall. Unfortunately, I have seen too many people talk themselves into a choice based on convenience (or allowed themselves to be assigned a mentor based on convenience) only to regret the choice later on because it wasn't a good fit.

Personality and Charisma

It is easy to get drawn into a relationship because someone is very charismatic and has an engaging personality. Look beneath the surface and consider your criteria or you may end up passing up an incredible learning experience with someone who is very wise and talented.

Now that you've found your mentor, it is time to get started on building the relationship. This begins by getting to know the person behind the criteria and letting her get to know you.

PREPARING THE RELATIONSHIP

If you already know the person who is mentoring you it is tempting to just jump into the business of mentoring and skip the process of preparing the relationship. Although you may be tempted, it is not a good idea. Mentoring signifies the beginning of a new kind of relationship and you need to start at ground-zero with a really robust conversation that focuses solely on this relationship as a mentoring relationship. No matter how many mentoring relationships you have had, each is a new partnership and therefore building trust in that relationship is the first order of business. One way to build trust is to come to your relationship prepared. The exercises you have completed up to now have contributed to your readiness for this conversation. Once your mentor has said yes, or your mentor has been assigned, it is time to arrange for your first meeting.

Initial Mentoring Conversation: What to Talk About

The initial conversation is an exploratory one in which you and your mentoring partner learn about each other, establish points of connection, and lay the preliminary groundwork for working together. Topics that you will want to include to enrich that conversation are itemized in Exhibit 3.3, along with specific strategies and some guiding questions.

Let's take these items one by one.

Take Time to Get to Know Each Other

You need to bring yourself to the relationship fully and completely and be open and honest. Does that mean that your mentor needs to know everything that ever happened to you? Certainly not. Your mentor needs to understand who you are as a person; your challenges, hopes, and dreams; and your past experiences. It is your responsibility to bring your mentor up to speed.

You'll also want to get to know your mentor as a person. Review what you know already and make a list of what you want to know. You might

EXHIBIT 3.3

Initial Mentoring Conversation: Preparing the Relationship

To Do List	Strategies for Conversation	Questions to Ponder
1. Take time to get to know each other.	Obtain a copy of your mentoring partner's bio in advance of the conversation. If one is not available, create one through conversation.	What kind of information might you exchange to get to know each other better? What points of connection have you discovered in your conversation? What else do you want to learn about each other?
2. Talk about mentoring.	Share your previous mentoring experiences with your mentoring partner.	What did you like about your experiences that you each want to carry forward into this relationship?
3. Share your learning and development goals.	Describe your career vision, hopes and dreams, and articulate broad learning goals and the reasons why they are important.	Why do you want to engage in this relationship? What learning goals would align with your vision of the future?
4. Determine relationship needs and expectations.	Ask your mentoring partner what he or she wants, needs, and expects out of the relationship.	Are you clear about each other's wants, needs, and expectations for this mentoring relationship?
5. Candidly share your personal assumptions and limitations.	Ask your mentor about his or her assumptions and limitations. Discuss implications for your relationship.	What assumptions do you hold about each other and your relationship? What are you each willing and capable of contributing to the relationship? What limitations do you each bring to the relationship?
6. Discuss your personal styles.	Talk about your personal styles. You may have data from instruments such as EI, MBTI, DiSC, and LSI.	How might each other's styles affect the learning that goes on in the mentoring relationship?

Adapted from Losis J.; Zachary, *The Mentor's Guide: Facilitating Effective Learning Relationships.*
San Francisco: Jossey-Bass, 2000, p. 91.

be curious about your mentor's career journey. For example, how did she begin her professional career, who was it that helped her along the way, and what were some of her challenges? The goal is to establish points of connection immediately that you can build on later in the relationship.

Talk About Mentoring

Share your personal stories about individuals who had a profound impact on your development and learning. You have previously prepared to discuss your own mentoring and learning experience by answering the four questions under the heading Insights from Experience in Chapter Two, and as a result you should be able to see more clearly what you appreciated about them, what worked for you, and what didn't. Invite your mentor to share his mentoring stories. Learn from his experience, then talk about what you each valued in your experiences and how you might bring that to bear in your mentoring partnership.

You may have been in a mentoring relationship that was disappointing. Share your story about that relationship and see whether you can identify what went wrong and why. Apply those lessons learned to your new relationship.

Share Your Learning and Development Goals

Here's another instance in which having done personal preparation pays off. Describe your career vision and what led you to that vision. Articulate your learning goals as best as you can. Broad goals will suffice; they don't need to be precise at this point. Some examples of broad goals are to learn what it takes to be a better realtor, balance work and family life, or improve communication or presentation skills.

Determine Relationship Needs and Expectations

Be honest about what you personally need in a relationship. Do you need a brain to pick? Another set of eyes? An ear to listen? A shoulder to lean on? Someone who can help you get your arms around a problem? Do you need a helping hand? A kick in the pants? Talk about what you personally need to help you be successful in this relationship.

An honest discussion about expectations for the relationship is also critical. This means explicitly asking your mentoring partner what she wants, needs, and expects out of the relationship and stating exactly what you want, need, and expect as well. Putting these on the table and discussing them is essential to arrive at consensus about what is realistic and what isn't. This ensures that both parties are satisfied with the relationship.

For example, if you have the expectation that a mentor should be a friend and confidant, you need to say so. It's better early on to know whether or not your mentor is comfortable with this. If you find out that she isn't comfortable, that doesn't mean you have to end the relationship. It does mean that you two can discuss this and determine how you can work together given that expectation.

Candidly Share Your Personal Assumptions and Your Limitations

Instead of focusing on the relationship as you did above, now you focus on *personal mentoring* assumptions, specifically the assumptions you hold about your role and the role of your mentor. Ask your mentor about his assumptions. Talk about similarities and differences, and consider how they might play out in your mentoring relationship. Talk about your personal limitations in the relationship and find out about those of your mentor.

Assumptions One of the most important items in Exhibit 3.3 is the sharing of assumptions. Our assumptions determine how and what we perceive and are a result of our past experience. They become our truths, which we convert into actions. What makes this discussion so critical is that each person in a mentoring relationship carries truths about their role (their assumptions) and these guide their behavior. If mentoring partners don't share their assumptions with each other, they end up with miscommunication, and that, in turn, can upend a relationship.

Spend time with your mentoring partner talking about your assumptions about each of your roles. It may be easiest for you to share the list of assumptions that you completed earlier in your preparation and ask your mentor how they jibe with his expectations. Does it look like you are on the same page?

How does this play out? Marisa assumes that Howard, her mentor, will be a sounding board and help her get through her day-to-day challenges, provide just-in-time answers to her questions, introduce her to his network, and advocate for her when it comes time for promotion. Howard assumes that his role as a mentor is to be a guide. In that role he is to ask questions to help Marisa find her own answers, focus on the big picture, and support her in reaching her career development goals and learning how to access the right people. Unless Marisa and Howard talk openly and frankly about these assumptions, Marisa will be looking for quick fixes, expecting answers, and 24/7 access to her mentor.

Limitations Each of us has limitations; whether personal, time-related, work-related, or physical. It is important to be up-front about any limitation that may affect the mentoring relationship.

Discuss Your Personal Styles

In addition to your learning style (see Chapter Two), you've probably taken other personality inventories or emotional intelligence instruments. Information about the results will help your mentor know more about you. For example, Kim is a pretty easy-going person and takes things as they come. She is not a worrier and is very accepting. Mark might tell his mentor that he has taken the MBTI (Myers-Briggs) and that he is an ISTJ (one of sixteen Myers-Briggs personality types) and that pretty much is how he operates. He likes structure, is not into "touchy-feely," and likes to tie up loose ends and therefore prefers to work on one goal at a time.

If You've Been Assigned a Mentor

If you have been assigned a mentor, make it a point to establish rapport and really get to know the person behind the title before you jump full throttle into the relationship. At the same time you will want to share yourself, your story, and your context. A mentor needs to be able to walk in your shoes in order to support and challenge you appropriately so that you can work toward achieving your goals.

At this point, you have laid the groundwork for your mentoring relationship by meeting with your mentor, learning more about her, and talking about your hopes, dreams, and what you want to accomplish. You have discussed mutual expectations and explored some initial opportunities for learning. With the relationship preparation work completed, you are ready to take the next step: building a foundation for your mentoring relationship to grow and flourish. The next phase of the relationship requires some negotiating with your mentor to establish agreements.

CHAPTER 4

ESTABLISHING AGREEMENTS WITH YOUR MENTOR

WHEN MENTEES PROACTIVELY establish agreements they are more likely to achieve their desired learning outcomes and experience greater satisfaction from their mentoring relationship. Whether you are engaged in informal mentoring or in a more formal mentoring relationship, establishing agreements up front will ensure that your learning and the relationship stay on track.

The process of establishing agreements requires its own conversation to clarify mutual expectations, accountability, and outcomes. The agreements made during these "negotiating conversations" become the guideposts for balancing learning and the relationship. With agreements in place, obstacles are less likely to derail you or the relationship. You are less likely to take things personally when stumbling blocks do get in the way of your learning, because you have a process in place to deal with them.

Establishing agreements will enrich and focus your mentoring experience. A mentor who isn't experienced but eager to help you may be grateful for the structure that this conversation provides.

In this chapter, the focus is on the process of establishing agreements—taking broadly stated goals from your initial mentoring conversation and refining them, putting processes in place to assure that the relationship stays on track, and creating a strategy and work plan to help you make the most of your relationship. Exhibit 4.1 lists each component of the negotiating conversation and the questions that need to be addressed for each in order to establish the agreements that will serve as a foundation for your work with your mentor. We will explore these more fully later in the chapter.

EXHIBIT 4.1

Establishing Agreements

Components	Questions Answered
Well-defined goals	What do I want to learn/accomplish as a result of this relationship?
Success criteria and measurement	How will we know if I am successful? What is our process for evaluating success?
Accountability assurances	How do we assure that we do what we say we are going to do?
Ground rules	What are the norms and guidelines we will follow in conducting the relationship? Who will be responsible for what?
Confidentiality safeguards	What do we need to do to protect the confidentiality of this relationship?
Boundaries and hot buttons	What are the not-to-exceed limits of this relationship? What hot buttons do you have that might present barriers and boundaries?
Protocols for addressing stumbling blocks	What stumbling blocks might we encounter? What process should we have in place to deal with them as they occur?
Consensual mentoring agreement	What do we need to include to ensure that this agreement works for us?
Mentoring work plan	What are the steps for achieving the goals? What are the learning opportunities?

Adapted from Lois J. Zachary, *The Mentor's Guide: Facilitating Effective Learning Relationships.* San Francisco: Jossey-Bass, 2000, p. 95.

SMART GOALS

Goal setting is probably the most challenging aspect of establishing agreements for both mentors and mentees. SMART goals frame and define the focus of the work to be done, eliminate ambiguity, provide a framework for gauging progress and measuring success, ground the learning, and set a context for mentoring. They harness and focus energy and invite action. One mentor we interviewed noted the importance of clarity regarding goals, "We were not really clear about the goals despite the fact that we had talked about it up front. We should have been more specific and concrete. Lack of it made our relationship a meandering process that was not as helpful as it could have been to each of us." If goals are left too broad, neither the mentor nor the mentee will be satisfied with the learning process, the learning outcome, or the mentoring relationship. For example, the goal of "being a more effective manager" makes it hard to focus the learning and determine what a successful outcome might be. If, on the other hand, goals are too narrow—such as completing performance reviews within two weeks—they may not challenge you. This incredibly important topic of goals requires more examination. We turn next to the difference between a SMART goal and a not-so-smart goal.

A SMART goal is Specific, Measurable, Action-oriented, Realistic, and Timely. If a goal isn't specific enough, you may find it hard to focus the learning; if not measurable, knowing whether you have accomplished it is difficult; if not action-oriented, it may not lead to visible, tangible results; if not realistic, it is difficult to accomplish and both partners may lose enthusiasm for the effort. And finally, if the goal isn't timely, you may have difficulty maintaining momentum.

The conversation that takes place between you and your mentor leading up to the formulation of your goals is a critical part of establishing a mentoring agreement. Formulating SMART goals is an iterative process that requires time and good conversation. It usually begins with discussion of a fairly broad statement of intent—as in your initial conversation described in the previous chapter—and moves from the general to the more specific and focused. Ideally, the questions your mentor will ask you will help you sharpen the focus of your goal and articulate it in written form. (If goal setting is not your mentor's strength, I would encourage you to share this information on SMART goals with your mentor to ensure that you are working together with the same approach.)

The following list represents some of the more typical "starter" goals we hear from mentees. (A *starter goal* is the goal a mentee first presents to a mentor before it develops into a mutually agreed upon SMART mentoring goal.) Although the items on this list meet some of the criteria of a SMART goal, none of them meet all five criteria and thus represent a starting point for conversation with your mentor.

- Managing office politics
- Working on work–life balance
- Advancing career development
- Promoting innovation
- Team building

- Managing up
- Moving beyond glass ceiling

"Managing office politics," while a laudable and desirable goal, is an example of a not-so-smart goal. It is too global and lacks specificity and measurability. Likewise, "advancing career development" meets none of the criteria, yet it is a worthy goal. It, too, begs for specificity in describing what it would mean if achieved.

Let's rework a few of these into SMART mentoring goals. A common goal that surfaces more and more these days is finding work–life balance. It is a very appropriate starter goal but lacks focus, measurement, and specifics. As a SMART goal, it might be articulated as, "Manage my time better so that I can be home for dinner with my family at least three nights during the week." Reworked in this format, it captures the components of SMART: it is specific, can be measured, and is action-oriented, realistic, and timely.

Let's look at another typical goal, "building a team." Framed this way, building a team is a good start. It requires you and your mentor to discuss the issue, intention, and problems that underlie your choice of this goal. But to launch the work to achieve this goal, the goal needs a SMART makeover. This goal might then look something like this: "Building a more cohesive, collaborative, and efficient team so that I can spend more time leading than managing." Although the goal as stated is not as specific and measurable as the previous one, it nevertheless implies an ability to compare before and after and identify a successful outcome.

Not all goals are appropriate mentoring goals. It is important to consider the context in which you are being mentored, as well as the experience and expertise of your mentor. For example, if you have a personal goal of writing a best-selling novel, using your mentor at work to achieve that goal would probably be inappropriate unless, of course, that person has a track record in publishing. There are some topics that are simply inappropriate for mentoring relationships. We delve into this further when we discuss setting boundaries in a mentoring relationship.

Goal Setting: An Iterative Process

It may take several meetings to turn a starter goal into a SMART mentoring goal and identify the criteria for success. We begin by eavesdropping on a goal-setting conversation between Joan, a management consultant, who is speaking to her mentor about her goals in general terms. Next we follow her progress as she and her mentor create SMART goals. Later we see how she identifies the specific criteria by which she will measure her success.

Joan initially stated her goal like this: "I've worked for a very long time on a large account and feel really good about the work that I've done because it is so vital to customer satisfaction. However, because the account is large and the client so high-profile, there are limited personal opportunities for me to actually get in front of the client and manage projects. It seems to me that the more senior consultants are the ones who get the visibility and recognition and they may be unintentionally standing in the way of my development. I'd really like to be out front on this account, in some way."

What followed was an extended series of conversations over several meetings in which her mentor posed lots of probing questions. Initially, they discussed Joan's hopes and dreams and why she was committed to this account. He challenged her on her statement that senior consultants were unintentionally standing in her way. He asked what led her to that conclusion. It was a frank and lively discussion in which he asked her to consider what she might be doing that allowed others to take over. After some soul searching and in-depth conversation Joan realized that she needed to work to increase her visibility in the company. She also had to acknowledge that she sometimes felt intimidated in the presence of the senior consultants and often didn't speak up as assertively as she should. She shared a few situations in which she had allowed herself to feel distracted and unnerved during important presentations.

Her mentor's questions helped her refine her thinking from the broad to the specific and to clarify what she really wanted to accomplish through mentoring.

The articulation of these goals served as a platform for even deeper conversation about which competencies, which accounts, and what kind of visibility would work for her. This process of exploration helped Joan formulate and prioritize her initial goals. She was ready to start turning these goals into SMART goals.

Turning Your Goals into SMART Mentoring Goals

SMART goals generally fall into two categories. The first type, "do" goals, are skill based and short-term; they integrate what you are learning and practicing. They are performance-based. For example, technical skills, mastering conflict management and communication skills are all "do" goals. Joan's goal of developing and managing accounts is an example of a "do" goal. The second type of goal, "be" goals, focus on longer-term development goals, expansion of the mentee's perspective, and the big picture. These are often amorphous and harder to articulate (for example, coping with change, empathy, patience, openness to feedback, resilience, tolerance for ambiguity). "Be" goals lead to leadership development, career development, personal development, and significant change.

Not all goals will fit neatly into this dichotomy, however. There are some goals that fit both types. For example, listening is really a skill, but the attitude of becoming more open and receptive is a quality about you and is therefore a "be" goal. Some have suggested that the "be" goals are hardest to accomplish because they make the biggest impact on development.

You may be asking yourself at this point, Which of these two kinds of goals do I want to focus on in a mentoring relationship? The answer is both. You will find that you need to develop some skills (that's the coaching part of mentoring) and to develop yourself. The former contributes to the latter. You might start with the latter and work back to the "do" goals as you talk with your mentor. If you do the preparation work of defining a SMART goal, it can help jump-start your relationship because your focus will be clear. Exhibit 4.2 is the initial draft of Joan's SMART goals. Exercise 4.1, which follows the exhibit, offers some tools to help you make a first draft of your own goals.

Now, turn to Exercise 4.2 to evaluate the "smartness" of your goals and refine your draft goals.

SUCCESS CRITERIA AND MEASUREMENT

Once you've decided on what your learning goals will be, your next conversation should focus on what those goals will look like when they are accomplished. Stephen Covey's famous catch phrase, "begin with the end in mind," is precisely what is called for here. Project yourself into the future when you and your mentoring partner are celebrating your success. What will you both agree on that you have accomplished? What will you be proudest of? What will you be able to do? How will you be different then from how you are now?

Answering these questions will help you define your criteria for success. Once you have identified the criteria, think about how you will measure your success, and create some milestones to assess your progress. Let's look again at Joan.

EXHIBIT 4.2

Joan's First Draft

Do	Be
Increase my visibility and expertise in client services Manage complex accounts Improve my presentation skills	Raise my confidence level in working with senior management Increase influence

EXERCISE 4.1

SMART Mentoring Goals Worksheet

Things to Think About
Specific
What is it I am trying to accomplish?
Measurable
In what ways can my success be measured?
Action-oriented
What results will I be able to see when my goals are accomplished?
What concrete things will I be able to do as a direct result of accomplishing these learning goals?
Realistic
Are my goals achievable?
Are there additional resources that need to be available in order to achieve my goals?
Timely
What is the time frame for accomplishing my learning goals?

Do	Be

EXERCISE 4.2

SMART Goal Checklist

When you have successfully articulated a SMART goal you should be able answer each of the questions below affirmatively. If you cannot, it means more work is required to articulate your SMART goal.	
Question	**Yes/No**
1. Is the goal clearly future oriented?	
2. Is the goal realistic?	
3. Will the goal be challenging for me? (That is, is it a stretch goal rather than a maintenance goal?)	
4. Will this goal require me to make a personal investment of time, energy, and effort?	
5. Will this goal contribute to my growth and development?	
6. Does this goal require constructive feedback and candid conversations?	
7. Is this goal achievable within the time frame of this relationship?	
8. Will I feel a sense of pride and satisfaction in accomplishing this goal?	
9. Will this goal produce tangible and measurable results?	
10. Is this goal in my best professional or personal interest?	

Joan and her mentor explored each goal, the strategies they would develop to tackle each one, and, particularly, how they would measure progress. They agreed that a clear way to measure the goal of increasing her visibility would be to identify the number of times she was able to speak in front of the senior team. Previously those opportunities had been limited to once a month. She and her mentor determined that if she was participating in or leading three presentations, that would be a sign of success. Improving her presentation skills was somewhat easier to gauge. They decided that Joan would ask a trusted colleague to work with her when she practiced her presentations and then to sit in on her formal presentation with the team. They agreed that getting feedback and working on areas of improvement should produce results over time.

The goal of raising her confidence was going to be harder to work on and to measure. Her mentor shared some of his thoughts about ways to determine success and the strategies to get there. Joan was eager to calm the butterflies in her stomach and she felt she could make a pretty accurate measurement of her comfort level. Confidence was something they would be working on and talking about over the course of their mentoring relationship.

Exercise 4.3 offers a tool for recording criteria for success, measurements, and milestones for each of your goals. Once you complete it you will want to agree on a time line to review your progress regularly with your mentoring partner.

ACCOUNTABILITY ASSURANCES

Mutual accountability plays a key role in helping mentoring partners make the most of a mentoring relationship. It begins with a candid and open conversation to create shared understanding, shared commitment to action, and working agreements about some of the "softer" issues in a mentoring relationship. In this section, we focus on four specific areas: ground rules, confidentiality, boundary setting, and hot buttons. Whether you are engaged in informal or formal mentoring relationships, having ground rules, safeguarding confidentiality, and honoring boundaries are important accountability assurances.

Ground Rules

Ground rules are the norms or rules of the road to which mentoring partners agree in order to manage expectations in a mentoring relationship. Without them you may end up spending more time managing the relationship than

EXERCISE 4.3

SMART Goals: Success Criteria, Measurements, and Milestones

Goal		
Criteria for Success	**Measurement**	**Milestone**
Goal		
Criteria for Success	**Measurement**	**Milestone**
Goal		
Criteria for Success	**Measurement**	**Milestone**

actually learning from your mentor. Ground rules will help you avoid the problems that Dave, one of the mentees we interviewed, had in his mentoring relationship with his mentor, Catherine. "You know, she was so smart and savvy about people. My only regret is that I didn't have more time with her. I could have avoided some of the people problems I did have by getting her advice and insights more often. We never actually agreed on how often we would meet. We never established a clear schedule or time line. I think if we had talked about how often formally and informally we would connect, I would have felt more comfortable dropping in during one of my crises. I was frantic, but I had just been in her office two weeks earlier, so I was worried about using too much of her time. I think now that if we had set up a more structured time to meet, and she would have also said, 'but, come by or contact me whenever you need something,' I would have avoided a few more disasters."

As you discuss ground rules, keep in mind that they should not restrict the relationship. Their purpose is to encourage and support accountability. Some of the more common mentoring ground rules include the following:

1. We will meet a minimum of once a month for an hour.

2. Our meetings begin and end on time.

3. I will be in charge of scheduling the meetings.

4. We will always have a meeting date on the calendar.

5. We will set an agenda for every meeting.

6. We will put interruptions aside.

7. We will manage our time well.

8. Each of us actively participates in the relationship.

9. Our communication is open, candid, and direct.

10. We will have a closure meeting no matter what direction our mentoring relationship takes.

Once you and your mentoring partner have decided on your ground rules, be sure to calendar some checkpoints to determine whether the ground rules are working for you and your mentor or are simply providing unnecessary obstacles.

Confidentiality

Confidentiality is a topic that is often omitted in mentoring conversations because it can be an uncomfortable or difficult subject to talk about. Although some individuals fear that such a discussion undermines trust, it actually lays a solid foundation for building it.

Tanya, a graduate student, was enthusiastically talking about her mentor, Julia, and how wonderful the year's experience had been for them. Laughing, she reported that her colleagues called her and Julia the "dream team" and she had to agree. It had been a completely enriching and growth experience for Tanya. When we asked her to identify what made it so successful she zeroed in on her initial confidentiality conversation just as the relationship was getting started. She described that Julia wanted to clarify issues regarding confidentiality right from the start. Tanya was appreciative. Tanya knew that Julia had four other students she was mentoring and she was worried about whether Julia might talk about her to the others. After their confidentiality conversation, Tanya came away relieved, knowing that Julia wasn't going to be sharing her struggles and problems with the other students or with her faculty advisor. In the conversation, Tanya and Julia had some different ideas about confidentiality, but they discussed them frankly and openly and were able to quickly come trust each other.

Then fast-forward a year. Tanya's formal mentoring relationship with Julia ended as the semester came to a close and Tanya was then assigned to Paula, a faculty member with whom she would be working for the next two years. Their first meeting couldn't have been more different from that with Julia. At the end of their meeting, when Tanya could see Paula was wrapping things up, she said, "Maybe we should talk about confidentiality." Paula replied, "OK, if you want." But Tanya could see that she really wasn't invested in the conversation and even as she nodded and said, "Sure, I agree," on each issue, she didn't show any genuine concern or interest. Knowing that Paula also was going to be mentoring four other students, Tanya felt herself immediately close down and become guarded. Even though they have been in a mentoring relationship for a full year, they never managed to develop a trusting relationship. Tanya believes they could have had one if they had been mutually committed to a conversation about confidentiality.

There are a number of ways to approach the discussion of confidentiality. For example, you might discuss what confidentiality means to you and ask your mentor the same question. Building on your responses, you might consider the types of confidentiality safeguards you would both want to put in place. If this approach doesn't feel comfortable you might use the checklist in Exercise 4.4 to begin the conversation about confidentiality. If you find, as Tanya did, that your mentor doesn't share your concern with confidentiality, it is important not to give up. Bring it up again at another meeting.

Because people have very different views of privacy, your concerns may not seem immediately important to your mentor. It is your job to push for clarity in confidentiality agreements.

Exercise 4.4 is a tool that you can use to begin a discussion about confidentiality with your mentor. You may find that all of the items work for you or none of them do. The tool itself will help focus your conversation.

Boundaries

A candid discussion about the boundaries of the mentoring relationship sustains the focus on learning, manages expectations, and ensures mutual accountability throughout the duration of the relationship. When boundaries are left undefined or personal hot buttons not discussed, they can eventually undermine the relationship by deflecting energy away from the learning focus of the relationship. Although you don't want boundaries to be so loose that they may be misinterpreted, you don't want them to be so rigid that they constrain the relationship.

Some of the instances in which boundary crossing becomes an issue include a mentor or mentee suspecting the other of a breach of ethics or honesty; inappropriate conversation, language, or familiarity; infringement of mentor's time.

Marietta had been hired as part of a corporate diversity initiative. Each new hire was assigned a mentor to help him or her acclimate successfully and understand the culture of the organization. Marietta's mentor was Jim. When Jim asked Marietta about what attracted her to the company, she told him that she had been a stay-at-home mom for the last five years, but she was recently separated from her husband and in the midst of filing for a divorce and knew she had to get back into the workforce. She told Jim that the separation from her husband had been difficult and that she anticipated an ugly proceeding. She expressed appreciation for landing a demanding job so she could focus on something more positive than what was happening at home.

After that first meeting, Jim realized that he was uncomfortable spending so much time talking about Marietta's personal problems. Jim and Marietta set up a time for their next mentoring meeting where they could explore some of the challenges Marietta anticipated, what she hoped to get out of the mentoring relationship, and the goals she needed to work on. At the end of that second meeting, after the two had established some clear goals, Jim suggested that they set some guidelines and boundaries to frame their conversations.

Jim told Marietta that he felt pretty confident that he could assist in her in achieving some of her work goals around developing her accounting

EXERCISE 4.4
Confidentiality Checklist

Instructions: After you and your mentor partner have each completed this checklist individually, come to consensus about which confidentiality protocols you want to adopt for your relationship.

Which of the following assumptions about confidentiality do you hold?	Yes	No	Not Sure
1. What we discuss stays between us for as long as we are engaged in our mentoring relationship.			
2. We can freely disclose what we talk about in our conversations with other people.			
3. After our mentoring relationship has ended, it is OK to talk about what we discussed or how we related.			
4. If there is a demonstrated need to know, we can appropriately disclose our conversations, impressions, etc.			
5. What we say between us stays there unless you give me specific permission to talk about it with others.			
6. Some issues will be kept confidential while others will not.			
7. It is OK to discuss how we relate to one another but not the content of our discussions.			
8. It is OK to talk about what we talk about as long as it is positive.			
Are there other assumptions I hold that should be added to this list?			

Adapted from Lois J. Zachary, *The Mentor's Guide: Facilitating Effective Learning Relationships.* San Francisco: Jossey-Bass, 2000.

skill, but he was definitely not on comfortable ground dealing with marital issues. He acknowledged that she was going through some difficult personal issues that might easily distract them if they became the focus of their conversations. He suggested that the company's employee assistance program might be a good resource if she needed support, and recommended that they leave her personal issues out of the mentoring conversations. Marietta agreed. In fact, she told him she appreciated him bringing it up early so she didn't jeopardize their relationship unwittingly.

Exercise 4.5 offers some questions to stimulate a frank and honest discussion about boundaries.

Despite best intentions, boundaries are sometimes crossed and the learning in the relationship is negatively affected. The best way to respond is to have a strategy in place to deal with boundary crossing if and when it occurs. Here are some potential strategies to consider when boundaries are crossed. First, let your mentoring partner know that a boundary has been crossed. Second, refer to the ground rules outlined in your mentoring agreement. Third, describe the behaviors that clearly demonstrate how the boundary was crossed. Fourth, request that the behaviors stop. If your mentoring partner acknowledges that boundaries have been crossed, let her know you appreciate the understanding. If boundaries go unacknowledged and continue to be crossed, ask your mentoring partner to stop crossing the line. Then insist that they be stopped. If that doesn't happen, bring the relationship to closure.

Hot Buttons

Andy was mentoring Suzanne for six months and really getting frustrated. Suzanne was anxious to have a forum for talking about her ideas, but every time Andy challenged her on her thinking, or suggested another course of action, she became defensive and shut down. Andy was beginning to see that she really wanted a one-way relationship—a place to get affirmation and confirmation of *her* thinking, not a place to explore the best approach or broaden her thinking. Suzanne had pushed Andy's buttons and he was losing interest in committing the time to the relationship.

Each of us has "hot buttons," things that irk us and make us react negatively to situations. Think about the hot buttons you have that might present barriers and boundaries to your relationship and share them openly with your mentoring partner. Ask you mentoring partner about his hot buttons. Hot buttons often include not showing up, being late, coming unprepared to meetings, multi-tasking, and lack of follow-through, to mention a few.

EXERCISE 4.5

Discussion Guide: Boundaries

What are examples of boundary issues that we might face in our mentoring relationship?
Are there any topics, issues, or discussions that are out of bounds?
What is our process if boundaries are crossed?
What strategies would help us prevent crossing boundaries?

PROTOCOLS FOR ADDRESSING STUMBLING BLOCKS

All relationships, at one time or another, come up against stumbling blocks, even with accountability assurances in place. In my research I have found that most mentoring partnerships face five common stumbling blocks: failure to meet regularly, unfocused goals, untested assumptions, breach of confidentiality, and lack of communication. You owe it to yourself and your mentoring partner to have a full discussion about the "what-ifs" and what you will do if they become a reality. That is, what stumbling blocks might occur, and if they do what process will you use to address them?

There are questions you will want to discuss with your mentoring partner:

1. What are some of the stumbling blocks we've each experienced in previous relationships?

2. What potential stumbling blocks might we anticipate?

3. What other internal and external factors might negatively affect the relationship?

4. What would be an indication that we've hit a stumbling block? (Answer for each of the potential stumbling blocks anticipated.)

5. What process can we agree on to deal with the "what-ifs"?

MENTORING AGREEMENT

Until now we have been looking at the individual components of the negotiating conversation. When taken together these shared understandings become the basic framework of your mentoring agreement. They fit together like the pieces of a puzzle into a coherent whole and become the repository of your conversation notes. The form your mentoring agreement takes is not as important as its content. Your mentoring agreement could be as simple as organizing your notes, or you may decide to summarize your agreements in a memo of understanding. Some mentoring partners draft a mentoring partnership agreement. This will probably be the case if you are involved in a formal mentoring program. Whatever form you ultimately choose to use, it should be user friendly and work for both you and your mentoring partner.

This mentoring agreement template (Exhibit 4.3) may suggest other forms and formats. It is important to record your mutual agreements somewhere so that you can refer to them. Documenting your agreement together helps ensure that your relationship will be a partnership. The process of

EXHIBIT 4.3

Sample Mentoring Partnership Agreement

	We have agreed on the following goals and objectives as the focus of this relationship:	Our measures for successful accomplishment of each of these objectives will be:
1.		
2.		
3.		

TO ENSURE THAT OUR RELATIONSHIP IS A MUTUALLY REWARDING AND SATISFYING EXPERIENCE, WE AGREE TO:

1. Meet regularly.

Our specific schedule of contact is as follows:

2. Look for multiple opportunities and experiences to enhance the mentee's learning.

We have identified the following opportunities for learning (e.g., projects, task forces, client teams, conferences):

3. Maintain confidentiality of our relationship.

Confidentiality for us means . . .

4. Honor the ground rules we develop for the relationship.

Our ground rules are . . .

5. Provide regular feedback to each other and evaluate our progress.

We will do this by . . .

At least once during the course of the next year, and again at the conclusion of the mentoring cycle, we agree to review this agreement and evaluate our progress and our learning. If we choose to continue our mentoring partnership, we may elect to do so, as long as we have discussed and agreed to the basis for that continuation. Should we decide to conclude the relationship earlier than we anticipate, we agree to do so with appropriate closure.

Mentor	Date

Adapted from Lois J. Zachary, *The Mentor's Guide: Facilitating Effective Learning Relationships.* San Francisco: Jossey-Bass, 2000.

creating the agreement is as important as the agreement itself. It accelerates the trust-building process and creates shared accountability. It gives you something to go back to when you hit a hitch, glitch, or stumbling block.

MENTORING WORK PLAN

Michael Watkins, author of *The First 90 Days*, makes the point that the actions you take in your first ninety days on the job largely determine your success or failure. He says, "Failure to create momentum during the first few months virtually guarantees an uphill battle for the rest of your tenure in the job" (Watkins, 2003, xi). The same might be said of a mentoring relationship. Once your mentoring agreement is complete, it is time to roll up your sleeves and create the strategy for achieving your goals. Gordon and his mentor did just that.

Gordon sought out a mentor to help him in his new position as communications director of WEBMATE, a web development company that specializes in electronic services for nonprofit organizations. He had been handed the mandate of rebranding the organization's image, products, and services for their Gen-X clients and growing business opportunities with this group. WEBMATE serviced hundreds of clients in its portfolio that included organizations as varied as one that rescued pit bulls to another that promoted the practice of quilting. Gordon didn't know where to begin.

His mentor helped him focus. He asked him a pointed question: "Why did they hire you?" The bottom line, Gordon understood, was to increase business with a specific group of clients who currently were underrepresented at WEBMATE. Together, he and his mentor determined that Gordon should begin by identifying specific clients whose target audiences were predominantly Gen-X readers. They also agreed that he needed to create ways to increase communication with and for the nonprofit leaders of these organizations whose needs and methods were vastly different than the more traditional nonprofit clients of WEBMATE. Together they created the game plan in Exhibit 4.4 to help them focus their efforts.

A solid mentoring work plan becomes a road map for momentum. Exercise 4.6 showcases a form you might use to draft a mentoring work plan. Keep in mind that it is not the form or the format that matters but the substance of the work plan. You may want to complete a separate work plan for each of your goals and then when you are done put together a comprehensive overview of work plan that includes all of your goals.

EXHIBIT 4.4

Gordon's Mentoring Work Plan

Learning Goal		Measures of Success	
To develop expertise in implementing communication and business development strategies with Gen-X nonprofit leaders and their organizations		• 25% increased revenue from Gen-X organization by year-end; • Development and implementation of a new web-page design for Gen-X newsletters; • Three new products and services that respond to Gen-X clients	
Objectives	**Steps to Completion**	**Learning Opportunities**	**Target Date**
Create new designs, approaches, information, and resources that respond to the needs and "language" of Gen-X clients	Identify 10 clients that focus on the Gen-X audience Meet with clients for feedback and survey needs Evaluate 20–30 web sites that focus on Gen-Xers and identify success components Identify technology needs and requirements Create a new model for Gen-X branding	Online classes E-letters and newsletters Interviews with target clients and other leaders	Begin interviewing clients immediately Complete survey of sites by Dec 2009 Talk with professionals in the field between now and July

First Step: Identify ten clients that focus on Gen-X.

EXERCISE 4.6

Sample Mentoring Work Plan

Learning Goal	Measures of Success		

Objectives	Steps to Completion	Learning Opportunities	Target Date

First Step:

The Steps for Completing Your Work Plan

Enter your learning goal and itemize your criteria for successful completion of that goal (your measures of success). Lay out the objectives. Objectives must be specific and measurable with visible results. They describe how to achieve the goal. A goal might be "to position myself to get promoted." An objective would be "completing three new projects that would provide me exposure to the executives in the company."

Once your objectives are identified it is time to look at "steps to completion." These are the specific steps you need to take to meet your objectives. For example, in order to "complete new projects," what will you need to do? Attend a conference? Take on a special assignment? Shadow your mentor? Make presentations? You will want to factor your learning style into designing this part of the work plan. Don't settle for low-level learning opportunities. Give due thought to learning opportunities that will be most interesting and challenging to you. Consider human as well as material resources.

Set a target date for completion of each of your objectives. Setting a deadline will keep the momentum going. Although you may need to renegotiate the time frame, knowing that you have a target date gives you a milestone by which to evaluate your progress.

• • •

In this chapter we've covered the nuts and bolts of establishing agreements. The time it takes to establish these agreements varies depending on how well defined your goals are and how well you know the person who is mentoring you. Please don't be discouraged if takes you several conversations to establish your agreements. It is essential that you formulate SMART mentoring goals. Your mentor should be able to assist you in this process and help you make sure that you are clear about your own goals. In the process you will learn more about yourself, your motivations, and the possibilities that lay before you.

Before moving on to the next and longest phase of the mentoring relationship, doing the work, make sure that all of your bases are covered.

1. Are goals are well defined and clear?

2. Will you know what success looks like when you see it?

3. Have you and your mentoring partner talked about each of your responsibilities?

4. Have ground rules have been developed and agreed to by you and your mentor?

5. Are you in agreement about how often to connect and when and who should do the connecting?

6. Have your operating assumptions about confidentiality been well articulated?

7. Have you put accountabilities in place for yourself, your mentor, and the relationship?

8. Have you developed a realistic strategy for dealing with obstacles to the relationship?

9. Have you discussed how and when the relationship will be brought to closure?

10. Does the work plan excite and motivate you?

Bases covered? Great. The real work of the mentoring is about to begin. Chapter Five offers strategies that put you in the driver's seat and help you get the most out of your relationship.

CHAPTER 5

DOING THE WORK

NOW THAT AGREEMENTS have been established, it is time to go to work *on* and *in* your mentoring relationship. As you move into this phase you are probably wondering how it is going to evolve. Will you and your mentor be compatible? Will your mentor live up to your expectations? Will you live up to your mentor's expectations? Will you be able to keep your relationship on track? Will you be able to make the most of this opportunity?

This is the time in a mentoring relationship during which you execute the work of mentoring, strengthen your relationship, and make tangible progress toward your mentoring goals, guided by your established agreements. Whether you are in an informal mentoring relationship or a formal one, you will want to ensure that you work effectively with your mentor to achieve your learning goals and that you develop and maintain a good relationship with your mentor.

Mentoring unfolds in many different ways. Each and every mentoring relationship is unique because the individuals who come to it bring their own unique personalities and contexts. In a formal mentoring relationship there are two levels of accountability, those that are internal to the relationship and those that are external—based on organizational requirements. In an informal relationship the only accountabilities are those to which you and your mentoring partner agree.

While some relationships just seem to flow, others meander. What makes the difference? The simple answer is doing the work and working the relationship. You must be self-directed in your approach and remember that you are in the driver's seat. This phase requires you to play an active role in making sure that you use your time well, the learning stays focused, the relationship grows, and you address obstacles as they occur. Before I discuss each of these three areas—time, learning, and relationship—in detail, let's look at a story that illustrates what can happen if you don't pay attention to these things.

Don was a very willing and energetic mentee and was particularly pleased that he had been matched with Saul as his mentor. Saul was the firm's champion of the mentor program and in everyone's eyes, including Don's, *über*-supportive. They spent considerable time in the first two meetings just getting to know one another and were delighted to discover a mutual passion for golf. They talked broadly about Don's areas of interest, identifying some learning gaps he had as a new law associate, and sharing their mutual hopes about a mentoring relationship. Together, they identified two broad goals to work on. Don's first mentoring goal focused on how to better use his billable time and manage his ongoing projects more efficiently. His second goal focused on developing an expertise in real estate transactions. Initially, all went well.

Saul and Don set up their third meeting to begin to tackle the goals. Don opened the meeting by describing the weekend's golf round. The hour they had set aside quickly flew, and although Saul enjoyed the conversation, they hadn't made much progress on Don's billing issues. The next meeting started off in a similar vein and it was hard for Saul to get Don refocused. Saul was getting frustrated. Don seemed incapable or unwilling to stay focused on his professional development.

Effective mentoring relationships strive to balance the relationship and the learning and work on both simultaneously. The learning needs to be centered on achieving goals that mentor and mentee set collaboratively. Without a focus on concrete, important, developmental issues for the mentee and without the discipline to use time wisely, mentoring meetings can become social interactions that don't lead to progress or results.

GETTING THE MOST OUT OF YOUR MENTORING TIME

Time is a challenge for mentors, mentees, and their relationships. Whether related to work, personal demands, or life in general, it seems that these days we just can't get enough time. We end up carving up time for everything and in the process the quality of our time becomes hard to maintain.

Lack of time is one of the most frequently cited reasons for lack of mentoring success. "We couldn't find the time to meet regularly." "We are both busy people and we have a difficult time getting our schedules to mesh." "We set aside the time and then something always comes up and we end up rescheduling more than meeting." These comments or similar ones may resonate for you. Time is an issue that isn't going to go away. As a mentee, you need to be able to manage and take advantage of the time that you do have with your mentoring partner. You *and* your partner need to make a commitment to honor the time, use it well, and monitor it.

Early on, before your relationship began, you considered whether or not you would have the time for mentoring. You and your mentor discussed how you would spend your time and how much of it would be required as part of establishing agreements. Now you are in the mentoring phase when time issues become most pervasive. You may find that with all the other day-to-day challenges, taking time for mentoring becomes less of a priority. But sometimes lack of time is a perception rather than a reality. We often assume we don't have enough time when, in fact, we really do but simply make poor use of it.

How You Spend Your Time

Dealing with time concerns requires an ongoing awareness of how time is spent. It is up to you to manage your mentoring time and take responsibility for monitoring it. Here's a tool that can help you evaluate your mentoring time.

Draw a circle on a piece of paper. This circle represents your mentoring time pie, the time you spend with your mentor. Divide the circle into sections (much like slices of a pie) according to how you spend your time. For example, you might spend a "portion" of your time shadowing your mentor. Another portion of your time pie might be spent reflecting on practice. Perhaps another section would be on day-to-day problem solving. Another section might be on feedback, or catching up with one another. After you've completed your mentoring time pie, share it with your mentoring partner and get some feedback as to whether your perception matches his or her reality. Then with your mentor discuss the following questions: (1) What do we need to do more of? (2) What do we need to do less of?

Some Strategies for Spending Time Well

First, make mentoring prime time. Focus on mentoring totally and completely when you are with your mentoring partner. Be fully present. Your mentor is giving you the gift of his time and you need to do the same. Turn off the cell phone, the e-mail, and bring your full attention to your conversations (face-to-face or virtual). Avoid the temptation to multitask and eliminate interruptions.

Second, come to meetings prepared. Ultimately, you will spend less time if you effectively manage the time you do have. This means that you will need to find strategies for using your mentor's time constructively and maximizing your time together. Follow through, and keep a record or a journal of what you are learning. Partner with your mentor to prepare meeting agendas when you can. At the very least, have a clear idea about what you want to accomplish.

Third, stop if you are wasting time. Time becomes an issue when you can't find enough of it. Acknowledge the need to occasionally call a time-out when life becomes hectic or when you aren't using the time you have wisely. For example, you may find that your role at work is changing or that you are facing a deadline and you are too overloaded to focus on mentoring. Or perhaps the meetings aren't as productive as they could be because you need to take a time-out to process what you are learning.

Monitoring Your Meetings

In the establish agreements stage outlined in the previous chapter, you and your mentoring partner developed some accountability assurances. Exercise 5.1 presents an accountability tool that you can use again and again.

You and your mentor may agree to use this tool periodically to ensure that you are staying on track. But even if you haven't agreed to do so initially, you should feel free to introduce this tool to your mentor at any time during your mentoring relationship. This may prove especially helpful if you suspect that your meeting time could be better utilized and you are uncomfortable raising the issue with your mentor. This tool provides a neutral approach for addressing this concern, as well as for monitoring the relationship.

KEEPING THE FOCUS ON LEARNING

Your learning is the heart of your mentoring relationship. This is the reason you are working together. It needs to be kept front and center. Although a strong mentor can help you, the responsibility for keeping the focus on your learning lies with you. You need to (1) search for and making the most of learning opportunities, (2) help your mentor provide the right kind of challenge, vision, and support, and (3) along with your mentor, monitor your progress toward achieving your SMART goals.

Searching for Learning Opportunities

Earlier we touched on the importance of discussing learning style in your initial mentoring conversation and then again as part of developing your work plan. You may be someone who values discussion (diverging learner). Or perhaps your preferred style is getting facts, information, and data (assimilating learner). Or maybe your modus operandi may be to get the work done yourself as quickly as possible (converging learner). Or perhaps you need to figure things out for yourself (accommodating

EXERCISE 5.1

Mentoring Partnership Accountability Checklist

Rate Your Meetings Against the Criteria Below:	Never	Sometimes	Most of the Time	Always
We meet regularly.				
We do a good job of communicating schedule changes that may affect mentoring meetings.				
We notify one another if we cannot follow up or honor our commitments to each other.				
We eliminate outside influences and distractions when we meet.				
We check out our assumptions.				
Our communication is clear and misunderstandings are infrequent.				
We check in with each other to make sure that we stay on track with the learning goals.				
We provide feedback regularly and make sure it is two-way.				
Our meetings are relevant, focused, and meaningful.				
We acknowledge and address conflict when it occurs.				
We are conscientious about safeguarding confidentiality.				
TOTALS				

learner). Although your learning style is a useful starting point, there is an old saying that is particularly apt here: "If you do what you always do, then you get what you always get." One thing you don't want to get in a mentoring relationship is the learning doldrums, that is, becoming a victim of "the same old same old." Mentoring is an opportunity to experiment with new and different modes of learning. Exercise 5.2 is tool that you can use whether you are in a formal or informal mentoring relationship to expand upon your initial list of learning opportunities. New opportunities are particularly useful to consider in this phase of the relationship because you and your mentoring partner presumably now know each other better, and that knowledge allows you to be creative and innovative.

Another approach to expanding your learning opportunities is the cascade approach. First brainstorm as many ideas as you can as fast as you can. Draw a line under the last opportunity. Ask yourself, what opportunities might Bill Gates suggest if he were your mentor? What would Walt Disney film if he were making a movie of your learning opportunity? Think about your favorite color—what activities does that suggest? The goal here is to challenge yourself to think outside the box and expand your horizons.

Journaling: A Learning Opportunity

Don't overlook the idea of journaling as a learning opportunity. Although the thought of keeping a learning journal might make you uncomfortable initially, it is one of the most powerful ways to promote learning. It forces systematic reflection, helps clarify thinking, stimulates new insights, assists you in remembering specific details and information, captures the richness of your learning as you go along, and becomes a record of your experience that you can refer to time and time again.

Some Journaling Tips

Keeping a journal is a practiced discipline and requires a commitment to action. Commitment requires that you accept journaling as a discipline that works.

1. As you write, keep in mind three words: head, heart, and action. Include factual material, reactions, feelings, goals, and tasks.

2. Write regularly, after each meeting and in between. Even if you are not a journal person by nature, write something down.

3. Schedule journal writing time. If you don't schedule it, it will get lost on the back burner.

4. Review your entries regularly. Doing so will help you monitor your progress.

EXERCISE 5.2

New Learning Opportunities

Instructions: In the spaces provided below, jot down ideas that come to mind as you think about the topic "possible learning opportunities."

Learning Opportunities	Within the Organization	Outside the Organization
Where can I get exposure to new learning?		
What can I do to reinforce what I am learning?		
How can I accelerate my learning?		

The Mentee's Guide by Lois J. Zachary. Copyright © 2009 by John Wiley & Sons, Inc.

Use the approach that works best for you. You may have been a diary writer at one time. Or you may have kept a learning log at one point in your career. Some people find sentence stems helpful in getting them started.

Ira Progoff (1975) offers three sentence stems to stimulate reflection: At first . . . and then . . . and now. . . . *At first* I didn't know where to begin. *And then,* once I got into it I couldn't stop writing. *And now* I couldn't imagine a day without writing in my journal. A response to "what stands out for me" or "questions in my mind" is often enough to trigger some good reflective journal activity.

To help me focus mentoring reflections I've developed a set of questions that I use as a journal template. See the box for these questions and sample mentee responses to those questions. You may want to use these or develop a set of questions that is comfortable and works for you.

Journal Entry

1. The most important work we did today.

Today, it was all important and I mean all! I was amazed at how much we (my mentor and I) accomplished. We spent some significant time debriefing on the school walk-through that we did last week. We talked about a methodology for getting feedback on my performance as a principal from my staff and teachers. We addressed those challenging work and family issues that have been plaguing me all year.

2. The most valuable lesson.

I realized that I saw and heard things in the classrooms I'd never seen before, even though I've done my own walk-throughs many times before. I don't know if it was her (my mentor's) probing questions or the fact that I was walking someone else through the school or a combination of both but I see that I need to work at becoming a more astute observer and listener.

3. How will I apply what I've learned?

I am going to check my assumptions at the door and be more open . . . whether in staff meetings or in future observations, and I am going to raise probing questions in my debrief with them.

4. What are the biggest challenges ahead for me?

I've got to create a new curriculum task force and the teachers are . . . well let's say, ... Less than enthusiastic. We've got a deadline and I truly don't know if we can meet it.

5. What questions still remain for me?

Time. How am I ever going to find enough to do a thorough job at this? With my son moving back home after college and my elderly mom needing more and more of my attention. . . . I don't know but I do know I am going to have to figure it out.

Monitoring Your SMART Goals

Setting SMART goals is critical to achieving learning outcomes. At some point during this phase you may discover that your situation or needs change and the learning goals you agreed on earlier in the relationship are no longer relevant or timely. Going through the motions of working on goals that are no longer important or opportune is a waste of your time and your mentor's time.

You may have achieved your learning goals in a shorter time frame than anticipated. If this is the case, it is time to reexamine where you are and reformulate some new goals or bring the relationship to closure. You may have identified what you thought were SMART goals but found them to be daunting or unreachable when you began to work on them. In this instance, you will want to redefine or reframe them with your mentor. Achievement of a goal often raises new challenges and learning needs. It may mean reprioritizing or abandoning some of your original goals. Exercise 5.3 provides a worksheet and some guidelines for reviewing your goals.

GETTING THE SUPPORT, VISION, AND CHALLENGE YOU NEED

Your mentor provides support, challenges you to stretch, and offers a vision of the possibilities. It is in this way that a mentor facilitates your growth and development. One of the things that you can do to stir the pot is to let your mentor know what you need. Here I describe ways that a mentor can fulfill needs in these three areas. As you read through these examples, think about the *support* you need and that would be most helpful to you, the types of *challenges* that would be most meaningful to you, and what you need from your mentor to *envision* a path for your own development.

Support

There are numerous ways that mentors can provide support. By listening they can get to know and understand your interests, professional and educational background, and point of view (in other words, your context). A mentor can offer support simply by checking in with you between meetings to give you friendly reminders and help you stay on track. Perhaps you need help balancing your personal and professional responsibilities. Mentors also offer support by sharing their stories and making the relationship really special. These are just some forms of support that mentees we have worked with have found helpful.

EXERCISE 5.3

Goal Audit

Review Your Learning Goals

What specifically are you and your mentoring partner working on right now?
Are you making good progress toward achieving your SMART goals?
If no, are the goals still relevant?
If yes, what specific things do you need to do more of to achieve your goal?
What are your next steps?

Vision

Mentors are in a unique position to help you open your eyes to new possibilities by offering a vision of what is available to you now and in the future. In general, a good mentor can help you see the big picture without getting lost in day-to-day concerns and details that can blind you to the possibilities. She can familiarize you with what to expect in certain situations, help you see how you can work differently with various people or form new working relationships, and serve as a model for you to observe in action. You may find it useful, for example, to shadow your mentor for a day or in certain situations to see how she handles the challenges of her job.

Challenge

To get the most out of your mentoring it is important that you challenge yourself and that your mentor challenge you to stretch, do things you haven't done before, take risks, and explore new ways of working. Mentors also guide you through these challenges. For example, a mentor might set a task for you or create some alternative scenarios that might enhance your ability to advocate for yourself with your boss or with others, present your ideas more forcibly, confront colleagues when necessary, or navigate difficult conversations.

Being thoughtful about your needs and stating them with clarity will help accelerate your learning and allow you to play an active role in making sure that your needs are being met. Asking for what you need is as easy as saying, "What I am really looking for is some advice about how to approach my boss." "What I really need is a new way of thinking about this situation. I am in a rut." "What will happen if I follow this path?" It is essential that you learn to understand what you need and ask for it.

MAINTAINING A GOOD RELATIONSHIP WITH YOUR MENTOR

The mentoring relationship must be built on a foundation of trust. As I discuss in Chapter Four, issues of confidentiality must be addressed and revisited often, especially in environments where there can be perceived repercussions. Mentees can only truly benefit from the power of mentoring when they are willing to be vulnerable and open. They need to talk about their weaknesses and areas where they need help, not only about their strengths.

SMART Communication

Developing and maintaining a good relationship with your mentor requires effective communication. The frequency, content, and manner in which you and your mentor communicate will determine your success. Mentoring partners who allow large gaps of time to occur between meetings threaten the continuity of conversation and the momentum toward goal achievement. Make sure that appointments are kept and meetings are rescheduled instead of cancelled. Mentees sometimes feel uncomfortable when their mentor's calendar is strained or crises develop that preclude mentoring meetings. Be persistent in pushing for regular communication.

The manner in which you and your mentoring partner communicate is also a factor. SMART communication (Shared Meaning, Authenticity, Respect, and Trust), like SMART goals (Specific, Measurable, Action-oriented, Realistic, and Timely; see Chapter Four), will contribute to your effectiveness. By modeling SMART communication your behavior will help influence the positive nature of your relationship. Let's look at the building blocks to successful communication with your mentor.

Shared meaning Shared meaning suggests that the two partners truly understand what the other is saying and meaning. Words communicate only a small portion of true meaning. Voice intonation and body language are far more likely to influence deeper meaning. It is too easy to just listen to words and draw conclusions. Therefore, it is up to both mentor and mentee to clarify their understandings and clarify their assumptions to make sure they are valid.

What can you do? Paraphrase and ask for clarification when important issues are being discussed. Summarize your understanding at the end of a mentoring meeting. When you begin to assume your mentor is expressing a particular attitude or you interpret body language in a certain way, stop and verbalize your understanding. For example, "John, when I suggested that I wanted to work on conflict management as a goal instead of strategic planning, the look on your face made me think that you disagreed. Were you thinking that was a mistake?"

Authenticity Communication can become muddled, masked, stilted, half-said, or even insincere for many reasons. Especially mentees who are assigned senior management mentors often feel uncomfortable speaking their minds at the initial stages. For instance, it is difficult to have an authentic conversation about your relationship with your supervisor with a mentor who has a personal friendship or relationship with that supervisor. If you are considering a career move outside the company you may feel awkward revealing your dissatisfaction with the organization or talking about your interest in leaving. You may have experienced a confidentiality breach in a previous relationship and be wary about revealing additional personal information for fear that the same thing may reoccur.

What happens when the communication isn't authentic in a mentoring relationship? Distance grows between mentoring partners. Conversation becomes stilted. As a mentee, you can easily forget what you have said and haven't said in previous conversations. You communicate cautiously and the other party usually detects your lack of candor. Other statements, authentic or not, may be questioned as well.

What can you do? Share your concerns about the safety in the relationship. For example: "I know you are good friends with my boss, so I feel a bit uncomfortable bringing issues to you about my relationship with him. How should we deal with that?" If you are concerned about the safety of discussing a career move: "One of the issues I have been grappling with is whether this organization is the right place for me in five years. I know for the next year or two I have a future here. Is it going to be acceptable to talk about life after this company, or is that not something that fits into the mentoring program?" If confidentiality is or has been an issue and you are uncomfortable addressing it: "I know that one of the things I value in this mentoring relationship is the confidence that I can say something here and it won't come back to bite me or be shared elsewhere. And I hope you have the same feeling and that that is important to you as well."

Respect No matter what issues you and your mentor are working out, it is critical that each of you feels respected. Even if you are being mentored by a senior manager, there needs to be an inherent respect for each other's point of view and value as a person. Respect can easily be undermined when either party speaks or acts disrespectfully, even if in jest. For example, a mentor can easily and unintentionally "put down" a mentee's idea with sarcastic humor. Although the mentor intends it to be funny, it can be painful and leave you wondering about the undercurrent message when something such as "Well, that's a typical statement made by you Gen-Xers." is said or "Just don't say that to anyone who matters in this organization." or "Are you nuts?" Respect is a two-way street. As a mentee you must also maintain respect in your mentoring interactions. This is essential if you are to establish a trusting relationship.

What can you do? If you sense disrespect, even if expressed humorously, and it is getting in the way of the relationship, you need to address it. For example, "Last week, when we were talking about my time management issues, you said I was 'just a slacker.' I know you meant it to be funny, but

I have been thinking about that comment all week, and I wondered if that is what you really think I have been doing."

Trust The bedrock of communication in a mentoring relationship is mutual trust between mentoring partners. When trust is present, an assumption of good intention exists in whatever is communicated. Until trust is established, that intention may be assumed but can easily be undermined. Trust is something that takes time to develop and is tested regularly.

What can you do? Be authentic. Don't break confidences. Follow through with what you say you will do. And if you can't follow through, say so.

Feedback

Success in meeting your goals and getting the most out of your mentoring relationships depends on your ability to draw on the feedback you get from your mentor (and others) and to act on it effectively. It is also essential that you learn how to give feedback to your mentor. Honest, respectful, and straightforward exchange of feedback is the foundation of a good mentoring relationship. The following story reveals just how important feedback can be:

Feedback Story

"I am here today," said a senior account executive at a recent seminar, "because I got hard feedback from a mentor who was willing to give it to me, and I was finally willing to hear it." Avi shared these words with a group of mentors who were talking about providing feedback to their mentees. Many in the group shared how difficult it is to balance maintaining a good relationship with their mentee and at the same time holdup a mirror to the mentee to show them behaviors that are getting in their way.

Avi stood up to remind the mentors how important it is to be frank and candid. He reflected on his own experience as a mentee some ten years earlier. Avi described himself at the time. "I was young, cocky, talented, and I knew it. I knew I was going to get ahead and I knew I was in line for promotion. . . . In retrospect I think people were trying to tell me that my style was getting in the way. I just wasn't willing to hear it. I thought I was doing pretty damn good on my own. I can only imagine what it must have been like to work with me."

Avi laughed at himself, and the group joined in. Everyone in the room knew someone like Avi, a young upstart who didn't take direction, input, or feedback. Every opportunity for performance review was filled with defensiveness. It is difficult to manage the Avis of the world who, if they didn't have the talent to deliver great work, would have been fired long ago. It was too hard on other staff to have them around. Some of the Avis ended up working on projects alone, too talented to dismiss but too problematic to mix with other employees.

Avi made a plea to the mentors. "Don't give up on giving feedback. Sometimes you have to be really direct and frank, even if it isn't your style. I would not be the success I am today if my mentor hadn't sat me down, looked me in the eye, and told me what I was doing was not working. He said it, and I listened. And in retrospect, it made me realize that a lot of other people were trying to tell me it wasn't working, but I wasn't hearing it. Thank God I finally got it."

Your Comfort with Feedback

Giving and receiving feedback are skills that can be developed. We outline below ways to improve your skills in this area; however, it is important as you work to develop your skills that you be aware of your comfort level. In our workshops we do an exercise in which we ask people to line up according to their level of comfort in giving and receiving feedback. What we usually find is that people are more comfortable giving feedback than receiving it. That finding is understandable. Although in many areas of life it is better to give than to receive, in a mentoring relationship it is important to be able to do both. Each aspect is challenging in its own right. There is an art to giving feedback effectively. Receiving it requires openness and receptivity.

How comfortable are you in seeking, receiving, accepting, acting on, and giving feedback? Is your personal reaction to getting feedback affecting your attitude? Use the tips and strategies in Exhibit 5.1 to help you increase your confidence and competence in asking for, receiving, accepting, acting on, and giving feedback effectively.

Seek Feedback

Mentees accelerate their development and advance their mentoring relationship by being proactive and seeking feedback. Mentors welcome it when their mentees come to them and ask for feedback. Don't wait for feedback to come to you. Take the initiative. Make it a habit to ask for feedback regularly. The more specific and descriptive the request, the more specific and helpful the feedback you receive will be. You might say, for example, "I am struggling with how to get more balance in my life. It seems like my

EXHIBIT 5.1

Feedback Tips and Strategies

What You Can Do	Tips	Strategies
Seek feedback	Be proactive about getting feedback from your mentor.	Be specific and descriptive in asking for feedback. Make sure that what you are asking for is clear and understandable. Be sensitive to others' time.
Receive feedback	See feedback as a gift and an opportunity for improvement. Be receptive and keep an open mind. Avoid being defensive.	Be focused. Listen and really hear. Ask questions for clarification. Acknowledge the other person's point of view. Thank your mentor for the input.
Accept feedback	Think about the positive messages you heard. Reflect on the information that surprised you. Challenge your own thinking.	Take time to digest the feedback. Catch yourself being defensive. Look for ways in which the feedback will help with your self-development. Discuss your insights with your mentor.
Act on feedback	Focus on your goals and priorities. Check in with yourself periodically to determine how you are doing. Move forward.	Develop an action plan. Communicate your plan to your mentor. Continuously look for ways to integrate what you've learned from the feedback you received.
Give feedback	Direct feedback toward something that is changeable. Offer feedback when it is most timely and relevant.	Set a context. Be specific and descriptive. Be nonjudgmental. Be authentic. Be respectful of differences.

work has taken over my life. I budget my time carefully every day but it runs away from me as I get into my work. I get home exhausted and seem to have no time to chill out. How do you make it work so well? What suggestions do you have for me?" Or, "I just received some feedback from my supervisor and it just doesn't make any sense to me. I think she doesn't get me, who I am, and how I work. I am wondering what your take is on this and if I am totally off base. I'd appreciate your honest assessment of my leadership strengths and weaknesses." Make sure that what you are asking for is clear and understandable.

Receive Feedback

Receiving feedback is a challenge for many people. It requires not only listening but really hearing the message. It is risky because the perceptions others have of your behavior may not match your perception (witness Avi's feedback story above). The important thing to remember is that you don't have to agree with it. You need to be curious about the impact of your behavior and not defensive. Keep in mind that others often judge us on our behavior, not our intent. Even if you disagree, look for the kernel of truth. Verify what you've heard and then put the message into perspective. Don't take it personally. Feedback is not about your worth, but about your behavior.

Accept Feedback

Getting feedback from someone else affects people differently. Some people have strong reactions. When that happens it is difficult to accept. You may need to vent either with your mentor or a friend, or just let the information percolate before you react to it. Some people react with surprise and even when the feedback is positive go into denial or dismiss it. You may be energized by the feedback and can't wait to use and apply it. In any case, the goal is to learn from the information and use it to expand your thinking and improve. Be open and ready to listen. It's OK to respond honestly to what you've heard, but it is important to do so without becoming defensive. If you are surprised, say so. Ask questions so that you fully understand the feedback. Share your insights with your mentor. "Andy, I am taken aback. I never realized that I came across that way. I am glad you pointed that out. Can you tell me what else you've observed since we started down this path?"

Act on Feedback

Through the feedback process you've gained some insights about yourself. The next step is to take that knowledge and use it to take your development to the next level. Acting on feedback creates momentum. You start by focusing on your goals and priorities, setting some milestones, and targeting check-in dates. Keep your mentor apprised of your progress. "It took me a week or two but the feedback finally sank in and it does make some sense. I went to my peers and asked them for feedback and they completely agreed with what you said. I guess I knew that about myself down deep; now I am going to make addressing it my number one priority. I would be open to your suggestion as to next steps."

Give Feedback

Giving feedback to someone is an act of caring. It is not simply a matter of offering advice or constructive criticism. To be meaningful, it must be relevant, practical, timely, and specific. The way it is delivered affects how it is received, so it needs to be well framed. This means setting a context for the feedback and directing the feedback toward something that can be changed. "Marie, I really appreciated all the links and resources that you sent my way after our last mentoring meeting. I know you worked hard to put it together for me and I really appreciate it. I need to tell you that I have always been a slow reader, and it just takes me more time to go through resources that require lots of reading. I usually keep that info to myself but I felt I needed to tell you. I do much better with the crib notes and more succinct information."

We've addressed the importance of feedback and what you need to consider as a mentee when engaging in feedback conversations. Exhibit 5.2 presents some conversation tips and starters for your reference.

Creating the balance between working effectively and growing a solid relationship with your mentor is the real work of this phase. Both require your focus and attention. The emphasis is on the "you" because you need to be able to step up to the plate and ask for what you need in the relationship while at the same time be open to receiving the wisdom your mentor has to offer. An effective relationship takes work and steadfastness. It requires using time well, ensuring you get the most out of your meeting time, and being smart about your communication and monitoring progress on your goals. None of this can happen without a respect for and openness to the feedback process.

Chapter Six takes you to the natural end of this phase of your mentoring relationship: coming to closure. When you attend to closure in a good way, you enhance the impact of the mentoring relationship.

EXHIBIT 5.2

Tips for Mentees in Engaging in Feedback

What to Do	How to Do It	Examples
Early on provide feedback about what works for you.	Cite what helps you and what you don't respond well to. Offer concrete examples.	"Here's the kind of feedback I am looking for …" "What works for me is …"
Be aware of your communication style and how it meshes with that of your mentoring partner.	Share information about each other's learning style and discuss the implications for feedback.	"I am someone who needs to think about what is said before I respond." "I am more receptive when I receive a balance of positive and negative feedback."
Identify incidents and areas in which you are seeking help and ask for feedback on situations that you did/can do something about.	Tell your mentor what you did, how you did it. Describe your thinking process.	"How do you think I handled it?" "What would you have said if that had happened to you?"
When you talk from your perspective, remember that there might be another reality.	When seeking feedback, set a context and be descriptive, but not defensive, so that your mentor can understand the situation fully.	"Here's where I was coming from." "The way I saw it was …" "What I was trying to do was …"
Check out your understanding of what is being said.	Listen actively. Clarify and summarize.	"If I understand what you are saying …" "Do you mean …"
Use a tone of respect, especially if you see things differently.	Take care not to be defensive or attack your mentor's feedback or point of view.	"I appreciate that you are trying to give me another point of view …" "I am wondering why you think that approach wouldn't work …" "Can I ask you a question about that feedback?"
Avoid responding to feedback when you are angry, defensive, or need more time to process it.	Ask for time to get the information you need. Faking acceptance doesn't work.	"To be honest with you, I need to think about that a little more." "I think I was hoping for a bit more support from you."
Think about feedback as movement forward rather than interruption from the journey.	Continuously link progress and learning to the big picture and the journey and learning goals.	"I have been focusing on the goal of…and your feedback helps me see a pattern I have developed that is getting in the way."

Adapted from Lois J. Zachary, *The Mentor's Guide: Facilitating Effective Learning Relationships*. San Francisco: Jossey-Bass, 2000, p. 153.

COMING TO CLOSURE WITH YOUR MENTOR

CLOSURE OFFERS ONE of the most profound learning experiences of a mentoring relationship. This is the mentoring phase in which you reflect on what you have learned during your mentoring relationship and position yourself to continue the momentum of your own developmental journey long after the relationship is over. It prepares you to leverage the knowledge you have gained and move forward.

Coming to closure also allows you to redefine the relationship and comfortably move on. It doesn't necessarily mean that the relationship ends, but it does signify that it is the end to this phase of the mentoring relationship. You may choose to move on by renegotiating your current mentoring relationship and working on additional goals or completing some of the goals that you hadn't achieved. You may decide to work with a different mentor or to pursue your further goals without a mentor. You may opt out of mentoring or, if you are in a formal mentoring program, the prescribed time for the mentoring to end is reached.

The important thing to keep in mind is that coming to closure does not simply signify an end. Fully embraced, it is a process that leads to further action. Good closure catapults you forward. Although an individual's need for and comfort with closure varies, closure is essential for growth. Whether closure is unanticipated or planned, its importance cannot be overemphasized. It is during this conversation, or series of conversations, that deep learning takes place, appreciation is articulated, and celebration occurs.

WHY CLOSURE IS OFTEN A CHALLENGE

The closure phase of the mentoring relationship is often overlooked or ignored. By the time you reach this phase you may be meeting less frequently, so the temptation is not to engage in closure but let the relationship fade out naturally rather than formally.

Some people avoid closure in any relationship, and this carries over into their mentoring relationships as well. Mentees often avoid closure if they have relied heavily on their mentor and are not sure what the next step might be without them. They have been supported and sustained and now are uneasy about moving forward without their mentor. Some are simply uncomfortable showing gratitude or expressing the emotion they feel. Some don't wish to appear too soft, particularly if their mentor is not the "warm, fuzzy" kind.

As a mentee, you may be expecting your mentor to take the lead and let you know when the time for closure arrives. You may worry that you will be perceived as presumptuous if you take the initiative and say that you are ready to move on. You may be worrying about offending your mentor or be concerned that your mentor may feel hurt. You may have become friends with your mentor and imperceptibly have drifted into a more informal personal relationship as you've gotten to know one another.

It is easy to become complacent about not having closure, but complacency has a cost: missed opportunity. Coming to closure is an integral part of the mentoring cycle. Without it you miss an opportunity to experience mentoring to its fullest and to make the most of your mentoring relationship.

WHAT YOU MISS WITHOUT CLOSURE

What are the opportunities that mentees and mentors forgo when they don't go through the process of closure? Here is an illustration:

Martha was a senior manager in sales, and Mia, two levels below in the quality department, had her eye on advancement in the company. Initially, when the two had been matched, Mia was intimidated by Martha's out-there personality and fast-paced style. Mia, quiet and more reflective, was surprised that the mentoring committee had put them together. It was hard for Mia not to feel overwhelmed by Martha's pace, energy, and quick action.

They had decided to meet monthly, face-to-face, with a mid-month check-in via e-mail, and Martha had invited Mia to drop in if she needed something more from her. Mia was reluctant to take up too much of Martha's time. She used the two prescribed occasions to work on her goals and move them forward.

Despite making some progress, Mia could feel Martha's impatience with her. Martha always seemed to want more from Mia. Even though Martha would acknowledge her progress and complement her on her achievement or results, somehow Mia could feel that something wasn't right. Maybe she wasn't fast enough, dynamic enough, bold enough for someone like Martha.

As the year progressed, Martha became involved in a big sales initiative, and Mia could see it was difficult for Martha to give Mia any of her time. She sensed they were both relieved that the year was coming to a close and the prescribed time for their mentoring relationship to end was approaching.

Mia wasn't sure how to handle the last meeting. Because it had been a difficult relationship she was tempted to simply thank Martha for her help and move on without any discussion or reflection. However, giving in to that temptation would have robbed both Mia and Martha of a chance to learn and grow from the relationship.

Instead of taking the easy way out, Mia summoned up her courage and sat down and faced Martha. "I want to thank you for the time you gave me this year," she started. "I appreciate that the company was willing to invest in me. But there were some things I regret and I wanted to talk about those for a moment. I feel kind of awkward about this conversation. I wasn't sure whether or not I wanted to have to bring these issues up. Then I went over my notes from the training, and it made me realized how important it is."

Mia was uncomfortable, and found it more reassuring to look at her notes. Martha was calm and listened. "You know," said Mia, "when we started, you invited me to call on you whenever I needed time, and I didn't, thinking I was already taking up your time. Then, it became hard to schedule even our monthly time. Well, I just gave up and waited for you to contact me."

Martha replied, "I am pretty sure that six months ago you wouldn't have been brave enough to have this conversation with me. I've seen you really step up to the plate and become much more assertive these last few months. And I am especially glad we are having the conversation we are now."

Mia laughed. "You're right. But you don't know how anxious I was coming here today. But, still, I did it." She continued, "I am wondering what you think about where I am and what part of my goals I should still stick with. Our mentoring is over, but I have a few things that I really need to work on. I was thinking of talking to the mentoring committee to help me find another mentor. What do you think?"

"I can understand where you are coming from and it sounds like a good plan," agreed Martha.

This conversation was clearly pivotal for Mia. Not only did she receive Martha's affirmation that she was indeed becoming more assertive, she was able to use the conversation to enlist Martha's help in identifying goals and finding a new mentor.

HOW TO PLAN FOR CLOSURE

How do you go about planning a meaningful closure experience? Ideally, planning for closure should take place while you are "doing the work," if not before. Ask your mentor what he would like to take away from the closure experience and talk about your hopes and expectations for closure. Discuss the following questions: What would we ideally like to see happen when our mentoring relationship comes to an end? How do we want to celebrate our success? What would make it meaningful? What might get in our way of coming to a positive closure experience? Once you've determined the outcomes you both want, talk about the process and planning.

When planning for closure with your mentor, it helps to revisit the ground rules you set when you were establishing your agreements. Hopefully one of your ground rules was an agreement to end on good terms. Many mentoring partners adopt the no-fault rule, meaning that there is no blaming if the partnership is not working or one person is uncomfortable. If you haven't talked about it before, talk with your mentoring partner as you approach the time to bring the relationship to closure. The bottom line is that if closure is to be a mutually satisfying and meaningful learning experience, mentoring partners must prepare and plan for it.

Right about now you might be thinking, "All this is well and good but what do I do if my mentoring partner isn't interested in meeting again to have closure or doesn't think we need closure?" In that instance, if a closure conversation is not to be had, don't give up. You've played an active role in this relationship from the beginning by asking for what you need, and you may find that *you* need at least some closure for yourself.

CLOSURE CONVERSATIONS

Each mentoring relationship is different, so closure conversations will vary depending on the needs and personalities of the mentor and mentee. However, to reap the full benefits, your closure conversations should contain four elements: what you've learned (coming to a learning conclusion), how you will apply what you've learned (integrating learning), celebration and appreciation, and redefining of the relationship. Your closure conversation can take place over the course of a number of meetings or in a single meeting.

Coming to a Learning Conclusion

A learning conclusion is a highly focused and reflective discussion centering on the specific learning you have taken away from the mentoring experience. Even if the relationship did not live up to your expectation the focus is still on the process, progress, and content of the learning. You will want to make the most of this opportunity and thoughtfully prepare for this discussion. I've listed a number of questions for you to answer as you reflect on your learning. Even if you do no more than answer these questions you will have brought some closure to the relationship for yourself and learned from the experience. Other ways to prepare include creating a time line of your work with your mentor, identifying milestones, and marking events to stimulate your thinking. Or if you've kept a journal, now would be a good time to go back and review it. Here are the questions (see also Exhibit 6.1):

1. Did I achieve my learning goals? If yes, what did I learn as a result?

   If no, what got in the way? In what ways might I have contributed to the lack of progress?

2. What was the most valuable thing my mentor taught me?

3. What specific insight, approach, or perspective did I gain?

4. What else do I still need to learn?

5. What did I learn about mentoring? About being a mentee?

6. What did I learn about myself as a person?

7. What has being in this relationship taught me about myself as a learner?

8. What would I do differently in my next mentoring relationship?

Let's look at how Maggie and Ernie handle their conversation about learning conclusions.

The stage is set. The time is right, and Maggie and Ernie are ready to discuss their learning. Maggie begins by saying how much she has learned this past year and how far she has come in her development. "I've gained so much from this relationship. I'm so much more self-aware and confident. My competence has grown in at least three areas and I'm much happier at work." Ernie agrees and lets her know that he has also observed her progress, specifically her interpersonal skills, her confidence, and her ability to balance short-term objectives with long-term goals.

Maggie reflects on their different styles: "I now realize that I should have seen our different learning styles as an opportunity for me to figure out how to work with others who are different rather than resist it." Ernie stops and thinks about his own learning and then says to Maggie, "Let me chime in here. I've been thinking about my own style since we had that long discussion about learning style back in January, and it has given me pause to think about things that I might have done differently. I was so involved in my project six months ago that I think I didn't give you enough time when you needed it and I really apologize for that." (It was interesting, she mused, that Ernie brought that up because the only time in the relationship when Maggie felt short-changed was when she was feeling very vulnerable six months ago.)

She thinks for a moment and then tells him, "Initially I think I really took it personally, but it also taught me that I need to fight for the time I need. Those insights made me see that I tend to take things too personally generally and that I ought to think about developing a thicker skin." Ernie notes that he was glad that she was aware of that and acknowledges that he used to take things personally too and had to work really hard to become more resilient.

Maggie talked more about things she had learned and what she is going to do differently in the future and asked Ernie what he thought her next steps should be. He turned the question back to her. After she responded he added some other areas for her to consider, such as developing strategic thinking skills and becoming more effective at strategy building and implementation. Maggie was puzzled at first by his response and then realized that her failure to see the big picture in their relationship was very much aligned with strategy. "It's the strategic stuff that trips me up. The day-to-day stuff piles up and often paralyzes my thinking. I remember something you said to me last January. It was about taking the long-view and letting go of some of my perfectionist tendencies. You've taught me that there is a difference between managing and leading and that includes thinking of myself as a leader."

Ernie commented, "That is a hard one but once you make strategy a habit and learn to execute on it, it will become part of you."

Their discussion was a rich and candid one. It left both of them feeling good about the relationship and proud of the work they had accomplished together. More than that, it helped reinforce Maggie's learning, giving her an opportunity to identify and reflect on what she had learned and providing a foundation for the next element of closure—integrating learning.

Integrating Learning

Discussion of the learning conclusion is an important part of the closure conversation, but good closure doesn't stop there. The lessons learned from mentoring beg to be used again and again. The closure conversation expands on the discussion by pushing you to consider how you are going to leverage your learning. That is, now that you've completed your learning goals, how are you going to integrate it into what you do every day?

We turn to Adam and Bert to illustrate the point. Bert, a small business entrepreneur, was completing his MBA at a state university on the East Coast. Adam was his faculty mentor and had been working with him for a couple of years. To Adam, it seemed as though Bert was always in a hurry, moving from one project to the next very quickly. At first Adam had been put off by Bert's brusque and impersonal manner, but as he got to know him, he grew to like him and appreciate his intelligence and insight.

Still, the relationship hit some stumbling blocks along the way because of Bert's lack of openness. The good news was that Bert became more aware of how his personal failings affected his dealings with people. He commented on this to Adam when they had their wrap-up session. "I learned it is not as much what you do, but who you are. When I interact with people now, I am not just thinking about what they can do for me. I have always been a driven, organized person, running ahead on my own path. I have learned to slow down and seek out others and find out where they are. I now draw more from the learning of others and not just try to impress them with what I know. I also seek feedback and realize that it is a constructive way to grow. So much of my awareness is a direct result of working with you, I have become more introspective and open to feedback. Before, I would hear the positive feedback, but never the negative. I forgot that there were things I really did need to work on."

The focus is on how you intend to apply what you've learned. What will you do as a result of what you've learned? Bert talked about how he would take his learning the next step, "I intend to use what I've learned to heal a difficult relationship with one of my team members and to improve my relationship with my customers. I will continue to work on becoming more objective, less judgmental, and more open. The 360 degree feedback process was an eye-opener for me, something I intend to continue to do myself and encourage my employees to do as well."

To realize the full impact of closure, the conversation needs to be expanded to include discussion of the action steps you need to take next. Your mentor can help you identify opportunities to apply the tools you've learned and take your learning to the next level.

Celebrating Success

Celebration is a fundamental part of concluding a mentoring relationship. It reinforces learning and signals the transition process that redefines the relationship. I invite you to look for meaningful ways to celebrate what you've accomplished.

I recall a conversation with someone I was mentoring. We were approaching the end of the relationship and were well aware that our year together was almost up. We said that we wanted to do something that would involve learning for both of us and that would relate to mentoring in some way. We wanted an opportunity to sit down in a comfortable setting and discuss our relationship in terms of milestones, insights, and development. My mentee also was very clear that she wanted to identify her next level development goals and discuss possible mentor candidates to help her achieve them. We talked about several things that we could do to make it celebratory, but we couldn't come up with anything. Of course, there was always "lunch," but we agreed to wait until we could find something that felt special enough. As luck would have it, a few weeks after this conversation she discovered that Marian Wright Edelman, founder of the Washington Research Project and Children's Defense Fund and author of *Lanterns: A Memoir of Mentors* (2000), was speaking in Phoenix about her mentors and the influence they had in shaping her life. The focus of our mentorship had been around developing strategies to mentor young adolescent girls. Prior to this particular mentoring relationship the mentoring needs of adolescent girls was unfamiliar to me. My mentee's passion had piqued my interest and as a result I began to read more about the nuances and challenges involved in those relationships. When she me called to suggest that we attend Ms. Edelman's presentation, I was just as enthusiastic as she was. We agreed that it would be a fitting celebration and that afterward we would go somewhere to talk about what we had heard and how that related to the work we had been doing in the relationship.

It took us a while to come up with a satisfying and fitting way to celebrate, but we did. We didn't celebrate just to celebrate but tied it into what we were learning. It was a perfect conclusion for my learning as a mentor. We listened to the speaker and then held our conversation over lunch. We talked about Edelman's message and how her message fit with my mentee's work and with mine. And then we talked about what she had learned, how she was going to use it in her work as she moved forward, and our plan for staying in touch.

Saying thank you and celebrating in a meaningful way is often a challenge for even the most creative or articulate people. It isn't necessary, of course, to find a major event to attend together. What is important is to find a way to acknowledge the work you have done together that honors your relationship. Doing so doesn't have to take a lot of words, and the words need not be elaborate. What matters is that they are your words and they are authentic.

An excellent example is a letter that I received as a member of an advisory panel that was mentoring the owner of a small business. The mentoring relationship had been challenging and ended abruptly. As individual panel members we had hoped we had touched the business owner in some way but really weren't sure until we received her letter. Here's an excerpt of what she had to say:

> *From the start, your guidance and suggestions were enormously helpful and I took each one as an honor and did my best to follow them. When things came to a crisis point with my business, it was no different. Every time I spoke with any of you, I took away a valuable gem in the form of guidance and perspective. You also shared your network, introducing me to even more wise ones and exposing me to further skill and opportunity. I have been so blessed to receive your mentorship and continue to be amazed by the amount of time, the depth and quality of information and advice, and your commitment to my business and my personal development. I am so respectful and appreciative of each of you. I also learned so much just by witnessing how you all carried yourselves. I will seek opportunities to support others in ways similar to that which you have shown me. It has been a precious experience to be mentored by each of you. You believed in me. And that has been what has mattered most. (Reproduced with permission.)*

Her words touched each of us and made us feel that, when all was said and done, we had indeed made some impact in her life. I know it brought closure for me and the other mentors. It made us feel that all the time and effort was worthwhile. I imagine most mentors would feel the same way.

Sincere expression of your appreciation is one of the greatest gifts you can give a mentor. The expression of appreciation and gratitude benefits you as well. It helps you bring closure to a mentoring relationship and move on. Even if your mentor says to you, "you don't need to thank me," push back and insist on taking the time to celebrate. Don't get talked out of it.

Redefining the Relationship

Your relationship with your mentoring partner will be different once your mentoring relationship ends. You may decide to continue the relationship on an ad hoc basis. Be proactive and talk about these changes before they take place and then move on. Discuss how the relationship will change and whether it moves from professional to colleague, friend, or ceases to exist.

You may have become friends with your mentor as a result of your experience. What would that friendship look like without a formal mentoring relationship attached to it? Are there expectations that the mentoring would continue informally? Often mentoring partners become colleagues. What would that look like? Decide how or if you will maintain contact with your mentor. Will you stay connected to one another and, if so, what will that look like? If you decide to continue your relationship what will be different? What will be the same?

Shelley had a wonderful relationship with her mentor, Amanda. When the twelve-month program came to an end, Shelley knew that she was going to be re-assigned a new mentor in the second year of her master's program. Shelly and Amanda began to talk about closure and had several conversations about what their new relationship would look like. Amanda expressed concern about how their relationship might interfere with Shelley's bonding to a new mentor. On the other hand, they both acknowledged that they wanted to stay connected. Amanda invited Shelley to call occasionally and send e-mail updates on her progress in the program. But she did suggest that Shelley refrain from using her as a mentor as she moved forward. Shelley understood the necessity to cut formal mentoring ties but was relieved that they would be able to maintain the relationship she so highly valued.

Exhibit 6.1 summarizes the four core elements of the closure conversation and the questions to keep in mind as you hold your closure conversations with your mentor.

WHEN IT'S TIME FOR CLOSURE

If you are in a mentoring program, your organization may have predetermined the length of the relationship. Typically the length is defined in terms of a specified number of months or years. In an informal relationship, the length of your relationship *may* be dependent on the completion of a specific goal or a specific number of goals. If either is the case you have a milestone in place to signal closure.

Ideally you have been checking in with your mentoring partner all along and the time to come to closure is clear for you. If that is not true in your situation, be on the lookout for signals that the relationship may be ending. Check out your perceptions and assumptions when the first indications appear. What you think you see may be a reflection of your own

EXHIBIT 6.1

The Closure Conversation: Core Elements

Core Elements	Questions to Address
Coming to a learning conclusion: the specific learning derived from the mentoring experience	Did I achieve my learning goals?
	If yes, what did I learn as a result?
	If no, what got in the way?
	What was the most valuable thing my mentor taught me?
	What specific insight, approach, or perspective did I gain?
	What else do I need to learn?
	What did I learn about mentoring? About being a mentee?
	What did I learn about myself as a person?
	What has being in this relationship taught me about myself as a learner?
	What would I do differently in my next mentoring relationship?
Integrating learning: applying and integrating what you learned and taking it to the next level	How will you apply what you've learned?
	What will you do as a result of what you've learned?
	What specific action steps you will take?
Celebrating success: reinforcing learning and expressing appreciation	What are meaningful ways to celebrate what you've accomplished?
	How will you express your appreciation to your mentor?
Redefining the relationship: spelling out how your relationship will be different once this phase of the relationship ends	What happens after the mentoring relationship?
	Do you want to continue to be in contact? If so, on what basis?

anxiety, fear, or hope. Even if your mentor wants to end the relationship and you don't, you must honor her wishes. Gauge where you and your partner are in the accomplishment of goals and objectives. If you've met all the goals and objectives, it is time to celebrate and move on.

Ending a Relationship Prematurely

Even if the life cycle of the mentoring relationship has been established in advance, there are situations in which it may make sense to end the relationship prematurely. Some examples include relocation or redeployment, promotion to the same position as your mentor, pregnancy or illness that leads to a long absence, a new project or workload that precludes time for mentoring, or a promotion or new responsibility that prompts a change in goals for which the mentor lacks experience. It is easier to identify events like these than it is to sense that something isn't working in the relationship that suggests it may be time to come to closure. It is uncomfortable to end a relationship with a more senior person because of the fear of reprisal or career suicide. These relationships go through the motions of mentoring, but the energy and enthusiasm are missing. The following story illustrates this point:

For Guy, the tell-tale signs were there. He was dragging himself to mentoring meetings with his mentor James because he felt he had to. They kept talking about the same old things and Guy was finding his advice irrelevant. Clearly, the relationship was lacking and Guy even wondered how valuable it could possibly be for James. Guy was also getting increasingly impatient. The longer he stayed in the relationship the more time and opportunity he was losing in furthering his career.

Truth be told, he never really felt the kind of personal connection to James that his colleagues described in their mentoring relationships. Initially, he agreed to participate in mentoring because he knew that top talent were being recruited for the program and he wanted to be counted among them. James, a senior executive in his organization, had been assigned as his mentor. Even as early as their first mentoring meeting, Guy suspected that it might be a bad fit. James was two years away from retirement and in the process of turning over responsibilities. A lot of their meetings were taken up with James sharing war stories from his thirty years with the company.

Guy had been hopeful that the relationship would change over time, but after six months was beginning to consider trying to terminate it before the year was up. However, he was concerned that doing so might be a poor career move. But maintaining the charade of a relationship was becoming a chore and he wondered if it was worth it. How long could he afford to wait if he was to make the career move that would get him on the fast track? On the other hand, was it worth making waves in the organization by closing it out with James? Guy finally decided that the wise move for him was to end the relationship, given that it really wasn't adding value for him personally or professionally. He figured that now was a good time to step up and act like a leader and not become a victim of circumstance. Guy knew that if he wanted to be a rising star in the company, he had to take the risk.

At their next meeting, Guy broached the subject. "I realize during our time together that your experience and the areas that you are most passionate about are really not where I am headed right now. Listening to your stories has been extremely helpful to me. I now have a much better understanding of the company and its culture, but I have also come to realize that the area of the organization that I want to focus on and where I really need some guidance is not an area of expertise of yours. I think that puts both of us at a disadvantage. Given the limited time that has been allocated for mentoring, I believe I now need a mentor who is actively leading the part of the organization I want to move into. I am hoping that maybe you can help me find someone appropriate for the role. Is that something you would be comfortable doing?"

Guy was relieved to hear James express enthusiasm for assisting him. James told him he was only too glad to help him find the right mentor. Had Guy continued the pretense of engagement in this mentoring relationship, he would have lost valuable time and the opportunity to get the learning he needed at a critical time in his career.

Moving On

However you bring your current mentoring relationship to a close—whether you are moving to a new phase of continued work with your mentor, saying goodbye, or entering into a new mode as friends or colleagues—once the work of closure has been completed, it is time to move on. Sometimes it is easier said than done. If you had learned to rely on your mentor, you may feel like Linus without his blanket with nothing to hold onto. If your mentoring relationship continues it is not going to be the same going forward. Whether the relationship morphs into a different form or you continue with your current mentor, you are in a place different from where you began and moving on to new challenges and, you hope, new goals. You will be likely to find, however, that in many ways your mentor is with you. Long after the relationship is over, you may find yourself thinking, what would my mentor have said about this situation? What approach or advice would he have given me?

Even though you expressed your appreciation to your mentor, once you've moved on, you may be prompted to express it again as you hear your mentor's sage advice reverberate in your head. I've often thought that timing for saying thank you was a little bit off. We thank people politely when they give us a gift because it is social protocol. Maybe thanks should be given when we actually use and reap the benefit of that gift.

A friend and I were discussing how difficult it can sometimes feel when mentoring relationships come to an end. For mentors and mentees alike there can often be a huge void. It is tempting to fill this void quickly, but it is there to teach us a lesson. The separation caused by the relationship's absence is a gift, an opening for growth and regeneration. It is an invitation to wisdom.

We know that the best mentors are mentees themselves and continuously commit to their own growth and development in the role. Consider paying it forward and becoming a mentor as well as a mentee. In the final chapter we delve into how you can best transition into that role.

CHAPTER 7

MAKING THE TRANSITION FROM MENTEE TO MENTOR

YOU NOW KNOW from first-hand experience the value of having a mentor in your life. But did you know that there are payoffs equally big for those who mentor? Mentors consistently report that they gain exposure to new and diverse perspectives from mentees that enlarge their thinking. They learn about operations, practices, issues, and people in other parts of the organization to which perhaps they would not otherwise have been exposed. When mentors have the opportunity to share their experience and wisdom and then see a mentee grow and develop into their potential, it is not only personally and professionally satisfying but also often a career highlight. Now it is time to think about building on the skills you learned as a mentee and applying them as you grow into and develop in your new role, the role of mentor. And as you do, you will find that skills you use will transcend the mentoring relationship and add to your competence in other areas of your life.

So let's get started. In this chapter I invite you to shift your focus and prepare to transition into the role of mentor. We'll look at the role of mentor, discuss how you can prepare for that role, and offer some advice for new mentors.

THE ROLE OF MENTOR

Even though the role of mentor is different from that of mentee, there are similarities. Being a mentor requires use of many of the same skills that you had to develop as a mentee. I'll identify four of the most important skills mentors must cultivate. The first one, reflection, is the platform on which the other three—facilitation, listening, and giving and receiving feedback—rest.

113

Reflection

Although people "do" mentoring all the time, effective mentors are not just doers, they are also be-ers. This powerful combination makes them reflective practitioners. *Reflective* practitioners are aware of and consistently test their own their frames of meaning, assumptions, feelings, perceptions, and world-views as a prelude to action. Being reflective is a state of mind and is necessary to promote optimal learning in a mentoring relationship. As reflective practitioners, mentors raise mentees' levels of awareness about their frames of thought and how they make meaning translate into action. To promote higher-level thinking and practice for yourself and your mentee, you need to be critically reflective about what you think and do. To that end, reflection begins in the preparation for the mentor role. It is an essential component of the preparation.

You can begin by reflecting on your personal motivation to be a mentor with Exercise 7.1. This is an important exercise in that your motivation can negatively or positively affect the quality of the mentoring interaction. When you hold a deep understanding of why you are doing something, you end up being more committed to it and better able to use your time and energy.

Assuming that you are now on board, it is time to reflect on your previous mentoring relationships and see what you can learn from them. Mentees who are transitioning to the role of mentor find Exercise 7.2 useful in several ways. Completing it takes you back in time and encourages you to recall what it actually felt like being a mentee in a mentoring relationship. The process of reflecting on your performance is a reminder of the centrality of the role of mentee and how important it will be for you to create a climate that will help your mentee make the most of the relationship.

Facilitation

Artful facilitation is the key to promoting shared learning, reflective practice, and deeper insight for your mentee. Most mentors are eager to share what they've learned, and the temptation would probably be to teach it all and all at once. The challenge for you is to help your mentee grow and develop not so much by inviting them to adopt your newly found or accumulated wisdom as by the way you ask questions. It is these questions that will move your mentees to deeper places of insight and perspective.

Mastery of facilitation skills will help you engage your mentee by encouraging self-reflection and ownership. Skilled facilitators know that specific kinds of questions draw upon the unique thinking and learning style of different mentees. (See Chapter Two for information on learning styles.) When the right kind of question is asked, deeper learning occurs. Effective facilitators maintain flexibility and openness to learning. You may find that

EXERCISE 7.1

Mentoring Motivation Checklist

Instructions: Check all the reasons that becoming a mentor appeals to you. Seven or more checkmarks in the "yes" column indicates that you are probably ready to begin the work.

Reasons Mentoring Appeals to Me	Yes	No
1. I have specific knowledge that I want to pass on to others.		
2. I find that helping others learn is personally rewarding to me.		
3. I enjoy collaborative learning.		
4. I find that working with others who are different from me is energizing.		
5. I am always looking for new opportunities to further my own growth and development.		
6. I want to see this person succeed.		
7. I am seeking an opportunity to enhance my visibility, reputation, and contribution to my organization or community.		
8. I am committed to leadership succession.		
9. I need to meet a performance requirement at work or in my profession.		
10. I want to do the right thing.		
11. I want to pay it forward.		
12. I am interested in mentoring a particular person.		

EXERCISE 7.2

Reflection on Your Experience as a Mentee

Think about your journey as a mentee and your relationship with your mentor(s) to answer these questions.

How did you do? Give yourself a grade.
What could *you* have done differently or better?
Is there anything you wish you had said to your mentor that you didn't say?
What kept you from saying it?
What lesson or lessons are you taking forward with you as you transition to the role of mentor?

you do not agree with your mentee's point of view, but your willingness to respect a different perspective is critical to creating a safe and trusting learning relationship.

Listening

The one attribute that mentees say they value most in a mentor is that they are good listeners. Mentors who are good listeners listen for the noise and for the silence and use what they "hear" as teachable moments to encourage reflective thinking. For example, "I noticed that whenever we start talking about your finance manager you get quiet. I am wondering what that's about and if that is something we need to address."

Listening is hard work. Often we hear the words but not the melody. That is, we hear the words being said but do not always "get" what is really being communicated. How well we hear what is communicated may have to do with our intention to listen, our inability to concentrate, or our failure to listen actively for understanding. As a mentor you need to be able to listen reflectively so that you can hear the silences and observe nonverbal behaviors, as well as the content and context of what is being said. When you listen reflectively your mentee knows that you care.

Effective listeners balance talking and listening. They are aware of how much they talk and how much they listen. One way for you to monitor your balance is to try this exercise. Draw a line down a piece of paper; on the left make a header that says "talking" and on the right a header that says "listening." You can use this paper as a visual reminder during mentoring to maintain a good balance between talking and listening. Or, use it to keep track of how much talking and listening you do by discreetly making hash marks on each side to indicate when you begin to talk and when you begin to listen. After your mentoring meetings you can estimate the percentage of time you talked and percentage you listened. This will enable you to track over time the balance of listening and talking. The balance should improve once you increase your awareness.

Balancing talking and listening is a first and important step. The next step is to assess your effectiveness at listening. To that end, I invite you to complete the Listening Dynamics Profile in Exercise 7.3. Once you've rated yourself look at your total profile score and compare it with the Interpretation of Scores section of the exercise. Then go back and look at each of the four areas: intend to listen, concentrate, check for understanding, use memory aids. Identify the area in which you scored the lowest and pick and commit to one strategy within that area that you will work on over the next ninety days. Identify a date ninety days from now, mark your calendar, and on that date retake the Listening Dynamics Profile. Your score

EXERCISE 7.3

Listening Dynamics Profile

Please rate yourself on the following listening characteristics, which apply to interpersonal listening and to listening to a speaker. Check the number that best reflects your position on each scale below. The higher the number, the more the description on the left applies to you. The lower the number, the more the description on the right applies to you. Add your points for your total profile score when you have completed the profile.

INTEND TO LISTEN	5	4	3	2	1	
1. I usually intend to listen carefully when another person is speaking.						1. I rarely intend to listen carefully when another person is speaking.
2. I continue to intend to listen even if I am "turned off" by the speaker's delivery.						2. I lose my interest and intent quickly if I am "turned off" by the speaker's delivery.
3. I maintain direct eye contact when listening to a person.						3. I look away or avoid direct eye contact when listening to a person.
4. I do not interrupt when listening.						4. I tend to interrupt people.
CONCENTRATE						
5. I concentrate fully when listening.						5. I find it hard to concentrate, my mind wanders, and I am easily distracted.
6. I mentally summarize the main points of what I hear.						6. I do not mentally summarize or review the main points when listening.
7. I focus my attention on what a person is saying during interpersonal communication.						7. I think primarily of what I am going to say next when listening during interpersonal communication.
8. I listen for evidence in a speaker's comments.						8. I do not listen for evidence when listening to a speaker.
9. I anticipate what a speaker will say next.						9. I find it difficult to keep up with a speaker and rarely anticipate what a speaker will say next.
10. I control my emotions when listening.						10. I react or argue before I fully listen and understand.
11. I keep an open mind when listening.						11. I make immediate judgments and jump to conclusions when listening.
12. I do not allow certain words to immediately trigger my emotions.						12. I strongly and immediately react when I hear certain words.

CHECK FOR UNDERSTANDING	5	4	3	2	1	
13. I do not make assumptions after listening without checking them out with the speaker.						13. I frequently make assumptions after listening without checking them out with the speaker.
14. I communicate my understanding of what I heard a person express by putting it into my own words and checking that it is what the person meant.						14. I do not convey my understanding of what I heard a person say, to that person.
15. I communicate my understanding of the feelings I heard a person express, to the person.						15. I do not convey my understanding of the person's expressed feelings, to that person.
16. I listen in order to understand another person's perspective.						16. I do not listen to understand the other person's perspective.
17. I ask open-ended questions when listening.						17. I tend to remain silent if I have questions after listening.
USE MEMORY AIDS						
18. I use memory aids when listening.						18. I typically leave everything to memory when listening.
19. I listen primarily for main ideas rather than every fact.						19. I listen for every fact rather than main ideas.
20. I use note-taking skills when listening.						20. I rarely take notes when listening.
TOTALS						PROFILE SCORE =

Total Number of Points	Interpretation of Scores
90–100	Effective listener
80–90	Good listener
70–80	Average listener
60–70	Poor listener
60	Highly challenged listener
62–70	Where most people actually score the first time they take this assessment

Adapted with permission from the Listening Dynamics Profile © 1987 Frank DiSilvestro.

should have improved. When you take it the second time, repeat the process, but pick a different strategy this time. Mark your calendar, work on the strategy for ninety days, and retake the profile. Your new score should be even better.

Feedback

Mentees count on their mentors for honest and constructive feedback. They want feedback in order to know how they are doing, if they are moving in the right direction, if they are meeting your expectations, and if you are getting anything from of the relationship. It is essential that you create an expectation of regular feedback in your relationship so that you can deepen and enrich your mentoring conversations.

Feedback needs to be candid to be effective. Often in a mentor's desire to protect the relationship or the mentee's ego, the mentor filters feedback. This "shielded" feedback is inauthentic and not as helpful as it might otherwise be. Remember that shielded feedback doesn't raise the bar; it lowers it.

Think about the feedback you received as a mentee. I am sure that there were times you were hungry for it, and you didn't want it or were even afraid to hear it. By habitually building feedback into your mentoring conversations you reinforce its importance.

Asking for Feedback

As a mentor you can model asking for feedback by asking a general question such as, "How are we doing?" You can also model it by asking your mentee more specific questions, such as, "How is the relationship going for you? Is the learning process working for you? Are we moving too fast? Is it too slow? " Be sure to ask for feedback on your feedback.

Giving Feedback

You will want to give feedback to your mentee when it matters most: at the point of need. When you do, focus on learning and behavior change, not personality. Strive to maintain a two-way dialogue and engage your mentee in the feedback process. One approach is to continuously check for understanding. Above all, balance candor and compassion. Be honest, authentic, and genuinely sincere.

Receiving Feedback

Your mentee needs to acknowledge the validity of the feedback you are providing if meaningful change is to occur. Encourage your mentee to keep an open mind. This is easier said then done. As a mentor you'll need to do the same. Your mentee may tell you that the advice you gave her is wrong or that you don't understand her situation or what she is trying to convey to you. You will need to model how to receive feedback by keeping an open mind yourself and not being defensive when feedback is negative. You can do this by acknowledging her point of view and summarizing what it was that she said.

Accepting Feedback

Although feedback is important to help the mentee get to the next level, it can sometimes be difficult to hear. Some mentees (particularly diverging and assimilating learners; see Chapter Two) will need time to consider and process feedback before they are able to move forward with an action plan. You can facilitate your mentee's acceptance of feedback in the following ways:

- Suggest the mentee take some time to think about what she heard.
- Ask the mentee to tell you what she heard as a way of helping her process the feedback.
- Set a time for the two of you to reconvene to talk about the feedback.
- Ask the mentee to develop an action plan based on the feedback.

Acting on Feedback

Helping your mentee formulate an action plan based on your feedback creates momentum. Ask for her ideas of what she might do differently. Pose challenging questions to help her develop new ways of thinking or acting. Suggest ideas based on what has worked for others in overcoming similar problems. Identify a plan together and use it to track progress.

Exercise 7.4 is a tool to help you monitor your own effectiveness as a feedback provider.

Drawing on these four skills—reflection, facilitation, listening, and giving and receiving feedback—ensures that mentors can adequately fulfill two additional important aspects of the mentoring role: accountability and communication.

Accountability

Accountability drives successful delivery of performance expectations and results. Feedback encourages accountability in subtle and not-so-subtle ways. It fosters goal ownership and nurtures commitment. Without shared accountability it is nearly impossible for a mentee to create the positive energy necessary to attain learning and development goals. Feedback helps promote accountability by aligning expectations and giving input to ensure quality and timely results.

EXERCISE 7.4

Feedback Checklist for Mentors

Use the List Below to Give Yourself Feedback on Your Feedback Effectiveness	Yes	Strategies for Improvement
1. I pay attention to and build on my mentee's unique experiences.		
2. I encourage my mentee to reflect on past experience and use it as a learning opportunity.		
3. I allow enough time for my mentee to integrate and reflect on the feedback I give.		
4. I regularly check in with my mentee to confirm that the learning process is effective.		
5. My feedback focuses on behavior that the mentee can actually act on.		
6. I regularly check my understanding about what is said.		
7. I use a tone of respect in providing feedback.		
8. I am sensitive to my mentee's learning style when giving feedback.		
9. I avoid giving feedback when I lack adequate information or the timing is inappropriate.		
10. I encourage my mentee to welcome feedback and see its value in making progress.		

Communication

Lack of communication stalls mentoring dead in its tracks. When trust exists, communication is likely to be open and frequent, and mentoring partners can confront issues, thus quickly resolving conflict and deepening their relationship. When lines of communication are closed, mentees become hungry for connection. They make assumptions about why their mentors haven't been in touch with them and often end up feeling slighted, disaffected, suspicious, and distrustful. Second-guessing, stalling, questioning, and frequent false starts occur without good communication. Feedback becomes impossible and accountability an illusion. The dynamic interaction of reflection, facilitation, listening, and feedback with accountability and communication contributes to and sustains trust in a mentoring relationship.

ARE YOU READY TO MENTOR?

The process of mentoring effectively can be learned and, as with most skills, the more frequently the use the more the improvement. Still, before you make the decision to become a mentor it is useful to consider which of the attributes of a good mentor you currently have and what it might take to develop others. Without at least a number of these attributes to ground you in your development as a mentor, you may find that it is too difficult to fulfill the varied and challenging responsibilities that will be asked of you. These responsibilities include everything from managing time and problem solving to skillfully brokering relationships, coaching, and conflict management.

As a springboard for thinking about how ready you are to start mentoring, I would encourage you to take a look at Exercise 7.5 and review each of the attributes listed. Which ones do you possess? Which ones do you need to work on developing? Do an honest and clear-eyed appraisal of yourself. If most of these are a challenge for you, you might want to wait before diving into a role as a mentor. If, however, you find that many of these are strengths and, more important, that you are excited about taking up the challenge of developing other attributes, then exploring work as a mentor is probably right for you.

Becoming a Mentor

There are many different paths to becoming a mentor. There may be a formal program in your organization through which you can volunteer. Perhaps you may be approached by someone new to your organization for informal mentoring, or you may have observed individuals who seem to need

EXERCISE 7.5

Mentor Attributes

What are your strengths? What are your challenges?

Mentor Attributes	Strength	Challenge
1. Approachable		
2. Capable of honest self-examination		
3. Care about and respect others		
4. Committed to being an active mentoring partner		
5. Committed to self-development and self-improvement		
6. Emotionally intelligent		
7. Empathetic		
8. Feel secure about myself		
9. Follow up on ideas, suggestions		
10. Goal-oriented		
11. Innovative problem solver		
12. Not threatened by others' success		
13. Open to new ideas		
14. Positive role model		
15. Reflective		
16. Resourceful		
17. Strong interpersonal skills		
18. Trustworthy and willing to trust others		
19. Value difference		
20. Willing and able to spend the time		

help whom you can approach. Remember Kendra in Chapter One? She was approached by Sandra, who volunteered to mentor her when Sandra observed that she was floundering.

Let's look at each of these scenarios from the vantage point of your new role as a mentor.

A Prospective Mentee Approaches You

Say that someone approaches you and asks you to mentor her. How would you go about deciding if you should accept the invitation? There are many considerations. First and foremost, you need to consider your own readiness, availability, and willingness to mentor. Second, consider what this prospective mentee brings to the relationship. Does she have the "stuff" that makes a good mentee? Is she competent, committed, conscientious, and both open and ready to learn? Third, consider whether you have the particular skills and experience to help this person on her developmental journey. Is there a *learning fit* between what she wants and needs to learn and what you have to offer? Fourth, would you be comfortable working with her? Finally, determine whether you are sincerely interested and committed to helping this person at this time.

You Approach a Prospective Mentee

You may have your eye on someone who you thought could use a mentor—a superstar, a future leader in the organization, someone who clearly has huge but unrealized potential. If you are not in an organization, you may know someone you think you can help succeed. Don't be afraid to approach him and offer to mentor. You might say something like, "John, I've been watching you and I think I can help you become a better leader in this organization. I admire your energy and your laser focus. In fact, I've been down that path myself and if you are interested I'd be willing to make myself available to mentor you." Several caveats apply here. Make it comfortable for the person you approach to say no without guilt. If you are this person's supervisor, be aware that mentoring a direct report is a slippery slope fraught with challenges. For instance, although you may be mentoring this individual informally on a daily basis as a result of your position, these are usually just moments and conversations—very different from developing a true mentoring relationship. Another challenge is that if you choose to mentor a direct report, consider the ramifications of that choice. For example, almost always those who are not approached will feel slighted or jealous.

Your Mentee Has Been Selected for You

In a formal mentoring program there is usually a protocol for making mentoring matches. It may be that mentees have a free rein and can choose whomever they like, or that they are given some names of possible matches and asked to talk with those individuals and prioritize their choices. In some programs, all of this is done electronically; the prospective mentee goes shopping online for a mentor. Sometimes the match is made using an algorithm or by committee, and the mentee or the mentor is assigned a mentoring partner to contact. Even though you may not have selected your mentee, stay with and trust the process. Don't get distracted by overanalyzing the selection. Put your assumptions aside and approach the relationship as a learner yourself. Be as open with your mentee as you would want the mentee to be open with you. Be aware that your mentee may resent the match if you were not his or her choice. One approach is to acknowledge this and move forward, building the relationship one step at a time.

Revisiting the Mentoring Cycle

And so the mentoring cycle continues. As part of your personal preparation you will want to review to the various phases of the mentoring cycle as laid out in the preceding chapters of this book. Exhibit 7.1 presents a quick summary of those phases, along with some of the essential questions that those phases must address.

Advice to New Mentors

No matter how much you prepare on your own for the new role of mentor, some mistakes are inevitable. Indeed, making and correcting mistakes is the best way to learn. Still, some common traps can be avoided.

Look Before You Leap

Don't agree to participate in a formal mentoring program without really understanding the time and resources required. Be sure you understand the precise purposes of the program, what is expected from you, and the intended outcomes of the program before you say yes.

Make Sure You Are in the Loop

Stay tuned to what is going on in the organization and in your profession so that you are current and can help your mentee avoid missteps. The advice and resources you provide need to be relevant and timely in order to be meaningful.

EXHIBIT 7.1

Mentoring Cycle: Questions for Mentors

Mentoring Phase	Can You Answer the Following Questions?
Getting ready	Am I clear about my role?
	Am I the best person for the job?
	Is this particular relationship right for me?
	Do I have the time to do justice to this relationship?
Establishing agreements: Negotiating	What are the mentee's goals?
	What are our criteria for success?
	Is there mutual understanding of roles and responsibilities?
	What are the norms of the relationship?
	How often should we meet? How often should we connect?
	What are our operating assumptions about confidentiality?
	What are the boundaries and limits of this relationship?
	What is our work plan?
	How and when will the relationship be brought to closure?
Implementing and doing the work: Enabling	Have we established a regular pattern of conduct?
	How well are we communicating with one another?
	What kinds of development opportunities am I providing to support fulfillment of my mentee's goals?
	How can I improve the quality of the mentoring interaction?
	Are we continuing to work at maintaining the trust in this relationship?
	Am I providing thoughtful, candid, and constructive feedback?
	Is my mentee using the feedback to take action?
	Are there some lurking dangers or "undiscussables" in the mentoring relationship?
	What additional learning opportunities, resources, and venues should we add to enhance the learning experience?
	Are we taking time to reflect on our partnership regularly?
	Is the quality of our mentoring interaction satisfactory?
Integrating and moving forward: Coming to closure	Have we proactively established closure protocols?
	What are the signals that indicate now is time for closure?
	How are we going to acknowledge and celebrate accomplishments?
	What are the learning outcomes of this relationship? For me? For my mentee?
	How am I going to apply what I have learned from this relationship?
	In what way(s) can I help my mentee think about taking her learning to the next level?
	Where does the relationship go from here?

Be Patient

It can take a number of meetings to get the relationship moving in an authentic way. Building a trusting relationship takes time and attention. Trust begins with communication and respect. Remember that you and your mentee may be operating on different timetables because of different learning styles, cultural differences, or even a learning disability. As you may remember from your experience as a mentee, it can take time to work out the kinks in a relationship.

Plug In

Know how and when to use technology appropriately. If your mentee is online and "plugged in," you need to be. This may be an opportunity for reverse mentoring, and your mentee can help you learn the tricks of plugging in.

Don't Make Your Goals Your Mentee's Goals

Your mentee's goals are his, not yours. Because they were right for you doesn't mean they will be right for him. And he may have a different view of what that goal fully implemented means for him than you do at this point in your career. Your responsibility is to make sure his goals are on target, are SMART, and provide the right amount of challenge.

Keep Your Biases in Check

Listen for understanding about what your mentee's needs are. The biggest challenge is to keep your own experience and biases out of the picture. But when your bias is showing, acknowledge it.

Don't Be Judgmental

Being judgmental sidetracks you. Your mentee's problems are unique to her, even if her problem is one you have heard before from others. The danger is to think, "This is just so and so whining again." Your approach should be, "What is the issue today? How does it affect her goals, short or long term?"

MAKING THE TRANSITION

As you've worked your way through this chapter and prepared for your role as a mentor you've created a picture about the kind of mentor you want to become. I invite you now to actually envision it and picture yourself in the role. What is the vision you want to grow into? What is your personal development goal as a mentor? What do you need to get there? What is your action plan? These are questions you need to think about in order to propel your own growth and development in the role of mentor.

As you engage in mentoring, you bring our own cycle, your own time-table, your own history, your own individuality, and your own ways of doing things to each relationship. For learning to occur, you must understand who you are, what you bring, and what your mentoring partner(s) brings to the relationship. You must also understand the complexity of the mentoring relationship and the ebb and flow of the learning process. In sum, you must prepare yourself to meet the challenge so that your efforts can have profound, deep, and enduring impact. A mentoring partnership involves conscious choice and challenges each of us to think about what we might become and to remember Ralph Waldo Emerson's sage words, "What lies behind us and what lies before us are tiny matters compared to what lies within us."

DIGGING DEEPER: AN ANNOTATED LIST OF HELPFUL RESOURCES

LORY FISCHLER and I put our heads together to come up with a list of resources organized by the chapter titles in this book to help you increase your competency, confidence, and comfort level. We hope that you will continue to dig deeper and learn all you can about yourself and the practices that will help you make mentoring work for you.

Chapter 1: The Power and Process of Mentoring

Tuesdays with Morrie by Mitch Albom. (New York: Doubleday, 1997)

> Albom reconnects with his former mentor (a college professor) after many years. This time his mentoring relationship is qualitatively different from the earlier one. He is not the same person he was in college and is open to a different kind of learning. His mentor, too, is in a different time and place in his life. Whether you are a mentor or mentee, this heart-warming story has many lessons to teach about life and the dynamics of a mentoring relationship.

The Secret of the Seven Seeds by David Fischman. (San Francisco: Jossey-Bass, 2006)

> The story of Fischman's personal struggle as a stressed-out successful entrepreneur is told through the fictional character of Ignacio Rodriquez, who suffers a heart attack. A spiritual guide helps Ignacio heal and find his path in the secret of the seven seeds: self-knowledge, meditation, egolessness, service to others, goodness, balance, and freedom. Mentors, too, are guides that help us discover our path. This book contains many lessons about balance and the search for happiness.

Mentor: The Kid and the CEO by T. Pace and W. Jenkins. (Edmond, OK: MentorHope Publishing, 2007)

> This inspirational parable focuses on the significance of having a mentor in your life and the importance of being ready to be in the relationship. It will speak to you on many levels—from your own personal development to paying it forward. The words of wisdom at the bottom of each page are an added bonus and are representative of those a mentor might impart.

Chapter 2: Preparing Yourself to Make the Most of Mentoring

Now, Discover Your Strengths by M. Buckingham and D. O. Clifton. (New York: The Free Press, 2001)

> Self-awareness is an essential part of your preparation as a mentee. Instead of focusing just on your gaps and weaknesses, this book shows you how to identify your strengths so that you can improve them even more to become a better contributor to excellence and performance in your organization. You will find a code embedded in the cover of the book that you can use to go online and complete an instrument that will identify your "signature themes." Once you've completed the assessment you will want to dive back into the book and get the interpretations and strategies you can apply and work through with your mentor.

Communicating Your Vision by T. Cartwright and D. Baldwin. (Greensboro, N.C.: Center for Creative Leadership, 2006)

> Having a clear vision will help you decide what it is you really need to learn. This resource is a guide on how to take your vision to the next level. It provides the ABCs of visioning and addresses why a vision is essential. It also offers straightforward tools and examples that you can use to communicate your vision to your mentor.

Awakening the Leader Within by K. Cashman. (Hoboken, N.J.: John Wiley & Sons, 2003)

> The story of Bensen Quinn, a CEO, serves as a catalyst to begin to explore your own development, inside and outside your workplace. There are many valuable lessons that come to life as you read through the case studies, stories, and details of Bensen's journey. Each chapter concludes with a "Wake-Up Call" of reflective questions that will move your thinking to the next level.

Becoming a More Versatile Learner by M. Dalton. (Greensboro, N.C.: Center for Creative Leadership, 1998)

> Dalton's monograph is another practical and action-oriented guidebook from the Center for Creative Leadership. It will aid you in aligning your learning strategy and your learning goals. It suggests ways to go beyond your own traditional learning tactics and explore new options for learning and thinking outside the box.

Finding Your True North—A Personal Guide by B. George, A. McLean, and N. Craig. (San Francisco: Jossey-Bass, 2008)

> Based on the best selling book *True North*, this field guide/workbook offers a road map for helping leaders do the important work of defining their leadership, their passion and their authenticity. The exercises in this book are useful even if you are not in a leadership position. You can use them to take your conversations with your mentor about your life passions to a deeper level.

Self-Directed Learning: A Guide for Learners and Teachers by M. Knowles. (Chicago: Follet Publishing Company, 1975)

> We would be remiss if we didn't include this short classic reference for two reasons. First, learning is the purpose and process of mentoring. Second, self-directed learning (SDL) is the means by which learning takes place in a mentoring relationship. SDL involves identifying learning needs, formulating learning goals, using human and material resources (i.e., mentors), and evaluating your own learning. This book will guide you in developing your own competency as a self-directed learner so that you can make the most of your mentoring relationship.

The Kolb Learning Style Inventory (version 3.1) by D. A. Kolb. (Boston: Hay Group, Inc, 2005)

> This booklet contains the learning style instrument, an interpretation guide, background and application information for strengthening and developing learning style skills, working in teams, resolving conflict, communicating at home and at work, and considering a career. It also includes exercises for further exploration based on learning style.

Type Talk, The 16 Personality Types That Determine How We Live, Love, and Work by O. Kroeger and J. M. Thuesen. (New York: Tilden Press, 1988)

> Myers-Briggs Type Indicator (the MBTI) is a scientifically validated instrument, based on the work of Jung, for understanding ourselves, our

preferences, and how we perform and interact in a variety of settings. It is used in many ways by organizations to strengthen relationships and increase employee productivity. If both you and your mentor each have an understanding of your Myers-Briggs, you already have a tool for speaking the same language and building the relationship.

Let Your Life Speak: Listening for the Voice of Vocation by P. J. Palmer. (San Francisco: Jossey-Bass, 2000)

This little book speaks volumes about self discovery as a prerequisite for vocation. Palmer takes you along on his life's journey and describes his struggles to recognize and use his own voice. His story is the search for authenticity and learning to be who you are and can become. In a thought-provoking and a very profound way, Palmer raises powerful questions to challenge your thinking as you do the "inner work" that is so important in preparing yourself for mentoring.

Emotional Intelligence at Work by H. Weisinger. (San Francisco: Jossey-Bass, 1998)

The author's pragmatic and personal approach to emotional intelligence provides an easy explanation about how to make your emotions work for you by using them most productively. Three particular topics are noteworthy in light of mentoring: communication, interpersonal relationships, and the concept of an emotional mentor.

The Art of Possibility: Transforming Professional and Personal Life by B. Zander and R. S. Zander. (New York: Penguin Books, 2000)

This is one of my favorite books. I give it as a gift frequently because I believe possibility is a precious gift. The Zanders present a dozen practices that will not only help you achieve your dreams but balance your life in the process—no easy feat.

Chapter 3: Finding and Getting to Know Your Mentor

Social Intelligence: The New Science of Success by K. Albrecht. (San Francisco: Jossey-Bass, 2006)

In order to create a meaningful mentoring relationship you must work on and in the relationship. It takes social intelligence to do this successfully. As you read about Albrecht's model of social intelligence, the SPACE model, it will make you more acutely self-aware of what it is you need to do to make sure that you grow your mentoring relationship with your mentoring partner.

Make Your Connections Count! The Six-Step System to Build Your MegaNetwork by M. Giovagnoli. (Chicago: Dearborn Financial Publishing, 1994)

> Using your network to make your "net" work expands the pool of possibilities in selecting a mentor that is right for you. Giovagnoli makes building your connections a step-by-step process starting with discovering the contacts behind your contacts. Whether you are looking for a mentor or growing a business, the skill sets Giovagnoli lays out in this easy-to-read paperback are simple to follow.

The Career Navigation Handbook by C. Hunt and S. Scanlon. (San Francisco: John Wiley & Sons, 2004)

> If you are an executive considering choosing or changing careers you might use this resource to get started and position yourself. This book offers insights by executive recruiters who talk candidly about issues and trends in ten industries. If you are thinking about changing careers or choosing one, you will need a mentor to guide you. It is best to know about some of the issues and trends before you select one.

The Lost Art of Listening by M. P. Nichols. (New York: Guilford Press, 1995)

> Communication is a basic building block for establishing and maintaining a mentoring relationship. Listening is the bedrock for strengthening your communication skill. Nichols offers insights such as the difference between real dialogue and simply taking turns at talking; hearing what people mean, rather than simply what they say; dealing with defensiveness and differences of opinion; and understanding how the nature of a relationship affects listening.

Chapter 4: Establishing Agreements with Your Mentor

Relevance: Hitting Your Goals by Knowing What Matters by David Apgar. (Jossey-Bass, San Francisco, 2008)

> Apgar's book is a technical resource on how to strengthen your strategies for hitting your development targets. Apgar, an experienced business consultant, argues that failure to develop testable strategies and the difficulty of identifying relevant experience often lead to disappointing results. Apgar's four rules for how to develop workable strategies with relevant experience offer intriguing possibilities for dynamic mentor conversations.

The 4 Disciplines of Execution: The Secret to Getting Things Done, on Time, with Excellence by S. Covey and C. McChesney. [CD ROM] (New York: Franklin Covey Company, 2004)

Stephen Covey's four disciplines align well with the work of the negotiating phase of mentoring. Focusing on the wildly important (#1) is a pre-step in formulating initial or starter goals. It is from these that you identify the two or three SMART goals that would be most relevant to you mentoring relationship. The next discipline (#2) is to translate the lofty (starter) goals into specific actions. This is part of your work plan. The third discipline (#3) is to create a compelling scorecard (real-time measures of success). And finally, it is imperative is to build an accountability plan (#4). These imperatives are the four disciplines of execution and are as important to mentoring as they are to performance on the job.

The 3 Big Questions for a Frantic Family by P. Lencioni. (San Francisco: Jossey-Bass, 2008)

One of the most frequent goals that mentees struggle with is the challenge of balancing work and family life. Through the lens of a simple fable, Lencioni provides a set of basic tools for "restoring sanity to the most important organization in your life," your family. Chances are you already know what good business practices look like, but have you ever thought about applying those same business practices to your life at home? Lencioni demonstrates how to take tried and true organizational tools and apply them to balancing work and family.

The First 90 Days: Critical Success Strategies for New Leaders at All Levels by M. Watkins. (Boston: Harvard Business School Press, 2003)

The first ninety days in a new role are crucial to success. During those ninety days you need to get started, establish agreements, and execute on deliverables. As you've learned, the same is true in a mentoring relationship. Watkins offers ten strategies that are as applicable to your mentoring relationship and as to a new job.

Chapter 5: Doing the Work

The Power of Feedback by J. Folkman. (Hoboken, N.J.: John Wiley & Sons, 2006)

Most people don't know how to use feedback to really improve performance. Folkman has studied highly effective leaders and professionals and suggests that they treat and use feedback differently from most of us—they see feedback as a gift rather than a criticism, and they use it to focus and uncover strengths and work on doing a few things well. This book offers thirty-five concrete principles to help you turn feedback into real, effective, and long-term change.

Ongoing Feedback: How to Get It, How to Use It by K. Kirkland and S. Manoogian. (Greensboro, N.C.: Center for Creative Leadership, 1998)

> As a mentee, you need to be able to get the feedback you need and use it well. This little monograph drills down on feedback and provides additional tools and strategies to help you make feedback a personal habit and an ongoing part of your mentoring conversation.

Reaching Your Development Goals by C. D. McCauley and J. W. Martineau. (Greensboro, N.C.: Center for Creative Leadership, 1998)

> What I like about this learning resource is that it suggests various learning opportunities that you might use to further your mentoring goals. These suggestions can be used as a catalyst to brainstorm other learning opportunities that would be pertinent to you. It also has a list of questions you can use to think about other people who may be able to provide a support role in helping you reach your development goals.

Personal Styles and Effective Performance: Make Your Style Work for You by D. W. Merrill and R. H. Reid. (Boca Raton: CRC Press, 1999)

> The effectiveness of mentoring relationships is dependent on the ability to establish meaningful relationships. Merrill and Reid demonstrate how social behaviors—what an individual says and does—form exhibited and predictable patterns that can be identified and responded to. When these behaviors (driver, analytical, expressive, and amiable) are mutually understood, people are more likely to create productive and significant relationships as well as increase the quality of interaction and learning.

Crucial Conversations—Tools for Talking When Stakes Are High by K. Patterson, J. Grenny, R. McMillan, and A. Switzer. (New York: McGraw Hill, 2002)

> This is one of Lory's favorite resources to help mentors and mentees provide honest, straightforward, effective feedback and have conversations that seem difficult or are full of tension. It is easy to avoid dealing with difficult issues as a mentee, especially if you fear you might jeopardize an otherwise helpful relationship. The steps offered help mentees find an effective approach that avoids assumptions, defensiveness, and derailing. Stories from personal and professional life help you understand how to apply the principles.

Work a 4-Hour Day—Achieving Business Efficiency on Your Own Terms by A. K. Robertson and W. Proctor. (New York: William Morrow Company, 1994)

Motivational and business-time expert Robertson suggests that the priorities in our lives are often imposed by others. This book is more about how to rearrange your life to focus on personal and professional goals rather than focus on efficiency and working faster. This is a useful guide for recognizing and managing priorities and how to increase your persuasion and commitment to essential tasks and goals.

Chapter 6: Coming to Closure with Your Mentor

Words to Say Thank You by S. Hoggett and D. Fordham. (London: Cico Books, 2007)

I picked this book up at a conference and have since recommended it to many mentees. Although it is a little book, it is big on sayings, mottos, and phrases that anyone who wants to show appreciation can use. It is one of those inspirational little gifts that help you find the right words to express appreciation and gratitude to your mentoring partner.

Chapter 7: Making the Transition from Mentee to Mentor

Understanding and Facilitating Adult Learning: A Comprehensive Analysis of Principles and Effective Practices by S. D. Brookfield. (San Francisco: Jossey-Bass Publishers, 1986)

Effective facilitation is a basic process skill in the mentor's toolkit. Brookfield's in-depth description of the facilitation process and the six principles of effective practice he presents can help you make sure that the learning relationship stays on track. He offers examples and exercises that will stimulate your own reflection and assist you in helping mentees reflect on their learning processes.

Active Listening: Improve Your Ability to Listen and Lead by M. Hoppe. (Greensboro, N.C.: Center for Creative Leadership, 2006)

Most of us could improve our ability to listen. Since listening is so essential to mentoring, use as many resources as you can to improve your listening competency. This book includes quick and easy strategies for improving your listening skills along with tactical suggestions to raise your level of success.

Facilitator's Guide to Learning by D. Kolb. (Boston: Hay/McBer Training Resources Group, 2000)

One of the roles of a mentor is to be a facilitator of learning. This facilitator's guide is a companion to the Kolb Learning Style Inventory and an introduction to experiential learning theory and the instrument. It is chock-full of exercises that can inform your work with your mentee and includes technical specifications for the instrument itself.

Developing Adult Learners: Strategies for Teachers and Trainers by K. Taylor, C. Marienau, and M. Fiddler. (San Francisco: Jossey-Bass, 2000)

This volume melds theory and practice by presenting an array of field-tested learner-centric strategies for promoting adult learning and development. It includes seventy instructional activities from multiple practitioners in diverse practice contexts that focus on specific learning strategies such as collaborating, inquiring, visioning, and reflecting. These "how-to" strategies are useful as you work with your mentee.

The Mentor's Guide: Facilitating Effective Learning Relationships by L. J. Zachary. (San Francisco: Jossey-Bass, 2000)

After you've digested the topics in Chapter Seven, you may be ready to take a more in-depth look at the dynamics of the mentoring relationship. In *The Mentor's Guide,* I explore the four predictable phases of a mentoring relationship that make up the mentoring cycle and the key components of each phase. Like this book, *The Mentor's Guide* offers pages of templates, exercises, and tips to help you grow as a mentor and learn to steer the relationship in the most effective way to facilitate learning and growth.

REFERENCES

Albom, M. *Tuesdays with Morrie.* New York: Doubleday, 1997.

Albrecht, K. *Social Intelligence: The New Science of Success.* San Francisco: Jossey-Bass, 2006.

Apgar, D. *Relevance: Hitting Your Goals By Knowing What Matters.* San Francisco: Jossey-Bass, 2008.

Barnett, B. G., O'Mahony, F. R., and Matthews, R. J. *Reflective Practice: The Cornerstone for School Improvement.* Hawker Brownlow Education HB 3046, 2004.

Baugh, S. F., and Fagenson-Eland, E. A. *"Formal Mentoring Programs."* In B. R. Ragins and K. E. Kram (eds.), *The Handbook of Mentoring at Work: Theory, Research and Practice.* Thousand Oaks, CA: Sage, 2007.

Block, P. *The Empowered Manager: Positive Political Skills at Work.* San Francisco: Jossey-Bass, 1987.

Brookfield, S. D. *Understanding and Facilitating Adult Learning: A Comprehensive Analysis of Principles and Effective Practices.* San Francisco: Jossey-Bass, 1986.

Buckingham, M., and Clifton, D. O. *Now, Discover Your Strengths.* New York: The Free Press, 2001.

Cartwright, T., and Baldwin, D. *Communicating Your Vision.* Greensboro, NC: Center for Creative Leadership, 2006.

Cashman, K. *Awakening the Leader Within.* Hoboken, NJ: Wiley, 2003.

Collins, J. *Good to Great: Why Some Companies Make the Leap . . . and Others Don't.* New York: HarperCollins, 2001.

Covey, S., and McChesney, C. *The 4 Disciplines of Execution: The Secret to Getting Things Done, on Time, with Excellence.* [CD ROM.] New York: Franklin Covey Company, 2004.

Dalton, M. *Becoming a More Versatile Learner.* Greensboro, NC: Center for Creative Leadership, 1998.

DeLong, T. J., Gabarro, J. J., and Lees, R. J. "Why Mentoring Matters in a Hypercompetitive World." *Harvard Business Review* 2008, *8*(1), 115–121.

DiSilvestro, F. R. *Listening Dynamics Profile.* Bloomington, IN: Communication Dynamics Inc., 1996.

Edelman, M. W. *Lanterns: A Memoir of Mentors.* New York: HarperCollins, 2000.

Fischman, D. *The Secret of the Seven Seeds.* San Francisco: Jossey-Bass, 2006.

Folkman, J. *The Power of Feedback.* Hoboken, NJ: Wiley, 2006.

George, B., McLean, A., and Craig, N. *Finding Your True North—A Personal Guide.* San Francisco: Jossey-Bass, 2008.

Giovagnoli, M. *Make Your Connections Count! The Six-Step System to Build Your MegaNetwork.* Chicago: Dearborn Financial Publishing, 1994.

Hoggett, S., and Fordham, D. *Words to Say Thank You.* London: Cico Books, 2007.

Hoppe, M. *Active Listening: Improve Your Ability to Listen and Lead.* Greensboro, NC: Center for Creative Leadership, 2006.

Hunt C., and Scanlon, S. *The Career Navigation Handbook.* San Francisco: Wiley, 2004.

Kirkland, K., and Manoogian, S. *Ongoing Feedback: How to Get It, How to Use It.* Greensboro, NC: Center for Creative Leadership, 1998.

Klein, K. MentorNet 2008–Reprinted in MentorNet News [http://mentornet.net/documents/about/news/newsart.aspx?nid=35&sid=2]

Kolb, D. A. *Kolb Learning Style Inventory,* Version 3.1, 2008. [http://www.haygroup.com/tl/Questionnaires_Workbooks/Kolb_Learning_Style_Inventory.aspx]

Kolb, D. A. *The Kolb Learning Style Inventory* (version 3.1). Boston: Hay Group, 2005.

Kolb, D. *Facilitator's Guide to Learning.* Boston: Hay/McBer Training Resources Group, 2000.

Kroeger, O., and Thuesen, J. M. *Type Talk: The 16 Personality Types That Determine How We Live, Love, and Work.* New York: Tilden Press, 1988.

Knowles, M. *Self-Directed Learning: A Guide for Learners and Teachers.* Chicago: Follet, 1975.

Lencioni, P. *The 3 Big Questions for a Frantic Family.* San Francisco: Jossey-Bass, 2008.

McCauley, C. D., and Martineau, J. W. *Reaching Your Development Goals.* Greensboro, NC: Center for Creative Leadership, 1998.

McCullough, C. "Developing You!" *Training and Development,* 2007, *16*(12), 64–67.

Merrill, D. W., and Reid, R. H. *Personal Styles and Effective Performance: Make Your Style Work for You.* Boca Raton: CRC Press, 1999.

Nichols, M. P. *The Lost Art of Listening.* New York: Guilford Press. 1995.

Pace, T., with Jenkins, W. *Mentor: The Kid and the CEO.* Edmond, OK: MentorHope Publishing, 2007.

Palmer, P. J. *Let Your Life Speak: Listening for the Voice of Vocation.* San Francisco: Jossey-Bass, 2000.

Patterson, K., Grenny, J., McMillan, R., and Switzer, A. *Crucial Conversations—Tools for Talking When Stakes Are High.* New York: McGraw Hill, 2002.

Progoff, I. *At a Journal Workshop.* New York: Dialogue House, 1975.

Robertson, A. K., and Proctor, W. *Work a 4-Hour Day—Achieving Business Efficiency On Your Own Terms.* New York: William Morrow Company, 1994.

Taylor, K., Marienau, C., Fiddler, M. *Developing Adult Learners: Strategies for Teachers and Trainers.* San Francisco: Jossey-Bass, 2000.

Watkins, M. *The First 90 Days: Critical Success Strategies for New Leaders at All Levels.* Boston: Harvard Business School Press, 2003.

Weisinger, H. *Emotional Intelligence at Work.* San Francisco: Jossey-Bass, 1998.

Zachary, L. J. *The Mentor's Guide: Facilitating Effective Learning Relationships.* San Francisco: Jossey-Bass, 2000.

Index

FOR
STUDENTS

Over the past four years we have spent time in classrooms across Canada, speaking to students just like you.

We've asked what you want to see in a textbook, how you learn, how many hours a week you spend online, and what you find most valuable when preparing for a test. Based on your feedback, we've developed a new hybrid learning solution—**SOC+**. Your textbook, the Chapter in Review cards, and our online resources present a new, exciting, and fresh approach to learning. Check out the website at **www.icansocplus.com** for an unrivalled set of learning tools.

- Flashcards
- Interactive E-book
- Videos
- Games
- Interactive Quizzing
- **And more!**

NELSON EDUCATION

SOC+
by Robert J. Brym and John Lie

**Vice President,
Editorial Director:**
Evelyn Veitch

**Editor-in-Chief,
Higher Education:**
Anne Williams

Acquisitions Editor:
Maya B. Castle

Marketing Manager:
Terry Fedorkiw

Senior Developmental Editor:
Mark Grzeskowiak

**Photo Researcher and Permissions
Coordinator:**
Julie Pratt

**Senior Content Production
Manager:**
Natalia Denesiuk Harris

Production Service:
Bill Smith Group

Copy Editor:
Lisa Berland

Proofreader:
Dawn Hunter

Indexer:
Nancy Bell

Senior Production Coordinator:
Ferial Suleman

Design Director:
Ken Phipps

Managing Designer:
Franca Amore

Interior Design:
Greg Devitt

All design photos:
iStockphoto.com

Cover Design:
Martyn Schmoll

Cover Image:
Purestock/Getty Images

Compositor:
Bill Smith Group

Printer:
RR Donnelley

**Library and Archives Canada
Cataloguing in Publication Data**

Main entry under title:

Brym, Robert J., 1951–
    SOC+ / Robert J. Brym,
John Lie.

Previously published under the
    title : Sociology: the points of
    the compass.

Includes bibliographical references
and indexes.
ISBN 978-0-17-650355-0

    1. Sociology—Textbooks.
2. Sociology—Canada—Textbooks.
I. Lie, John II. Title.

HM586.B792 2011   301
C2010-908083-1

ISBN-13: 978-0-17-650355-0
ISBN-10: 0-17-650355-2

The Student Chapter in Review Cards for SOC+ were prepared and written by Maureen Murphy-Fricker.

BRIEF CONTENTS

Phanie/First Light

CONTENTS

© Images.com/Corbis

elfipics/Shutterstock

© Radius Images/Jupiterimages

3 Socialization 54

4 From Social Interaction to Social Organizations 76

Ieva Geneviciene/Shutterstock

5 Deviance and Crime 98

© Images.com/Corbis

6 Social Stratification: Canadian and Global Perspectives 118

Photos.com

Cre8tive Images/Shutterstock

Jaimie Duplass/Shutterstock

11 Health and Medicine 242

12 Technology, the Environment, and Social Movements 262

Alistair Cotton/Shutterstock

NEL

1 A Sociological Compass

Introduction

WHY YOU NEED A COMPASS FOR A NEW WORLD

"When I was a child, a cleaning lady came to our house twice a month," Robert Brym recalls. "Her name was Lena White, and she was what we then called an 'Indian.' I was fond of Lena because she possessed two apparently magical powers. First, she could let the ash at the end of her cigarette grow five centimetres before it fell off. I sometimes used to play where Lena was working just to see how long she could scrub, vacuum, climb the stepladder, and chatter before the ash made its inevitable descent to the floor. Second, Lena could tell stories. My mother would serve us lunch at the kitchen table. During dessert, as we sipped tea with milk, Lena would spin tales about Gluskap, the creator of the world.

"Like the tale of the Wind Eagle, many of the Gluskap stories Lena told me were about the need for harmony among humans and between humans and nature. You can imagine my surprise, therefore, when I got to school and learned about the European exploration of what was called the New World. My teachers taught me all about the glories of the *conquest* of nature—and of other people. I learned that in the New World a Native population perhaps a hundredth as large as Europe's occupied a territory more than four times larger. I was taught that the New World was unimaginably rich in resources. European rulers saw that by controlling it they could increase their power and importance. Christians recognized new possibilities for spreading their religion. Explorers discerned fresh opportunities for rewarding adventures. A wave of excitement swelled as word spread of the New World's vast potential and challenges. I, too, became excited as I heard stories of conquest quite unlike the tales of Gluskap. Of course, I learned little about the violence required to conquer the New World.

"Back then, I was caught between thrilling stories of conquest and reflective stories that questioned the wisdom of conquest. Today, I think many people are in a similar position. On the one hand, we feel like the European explorers because we, too, have reached the frontiers of a New World. Like them, we are full of anticipation. Our New World

LEARNING OBJECTIVES:

LO¹ Sociology is the systematic study of human behaviour in social context.

LO² The causes of human behaviour lie partly in the patterns of social relations that surround us and permeate our lives.

LO³ Sociologists are often motivated to do research by the desire to improve people's lives, and they adopt scientific methods to test their ideas.

LO⁴ Sociologists have developed a variety of theories to explain human behaviour.

LO⁵ To test their theories, sociologists use experiments, surveys, field work, and analyses of existing documents.

LO⁶ The founders of sociology examined the massive social transformations caused by the Industrial Revolution and suggested ways of overcoming the social problems those transformations created. The Post-industrial Revolution and the process of globalization similarly challenge sociologists today.

sociology The systematic study of human behaviour in social context.

is one of virtually instant long-distance communication, global economies and cultures, weakening nation-states, and technological advances that often make the daily news seem like reports from a distant planet. In a fundamental way, the world is not the same place it was just 50 years ago. Orbiting telescopes now peer to the fringes of the universe; the human genetic code has been laid bare, like a road map; fibre optic cable carries a trillion bits of information per second; spacecraft transport robots to Mars. They all help make this a New World.

"However, we understand that not all is hope and bright horizons; our anticipation is mixed with dread. Gluskap stories make more sense than ever. Scientific breakthroughs are announced almost daily, but the global environment has never been in worse shape and HIV/AIDS is now the leading cause of death in Africa. Marriages and nations unexpectedly break up and then reconstitute themselves in new and unanticipated forms. We celebrate the advances made by women and racial minorities only to find that some people oppose their progress, sometimes violently. Waves of people migrate between continents, establishing both cooperation and conflict between previously separated groups. New technologies make work more interesting and creative for some, offering unprecedented opportunities to make money, but they also make work more routine for many others. The standard of living goes up for many people but stagnates for many more.

"Amid all this contradictory news, uncertainty about the future prevails. That is why we wrote this book: we set out to show undergraduates that sociology can help them to make sense of their lives, however uncertain they may appear to be. Five hundred years ago, the early European explorers of North and South America set themselves the preliminary task of mapping the contours of the New World. We set ourselves a similar task here. Their frontiers were physical; ours are social. Their maps were geographical; ours are sociological. But in terms of functionality, our maps are much like theirs: all maps allow us to find our place in the world and see ourselves in the context of larger forces. *Sociological* maps, as the famous American sociologist C. Wright Mills (1916–62) wrote, allow us to 'grasp the interplay of [people] and society, of biography and history' (Mills, 1959: 4). This book, then, shows you how to draw sociological maps so that you can figure out how to navigate your world, find your place in it, and perhaps discover how to improve it. It is your sociological compass."

THIS CHAPTER'S GOALS

In this chapter we aim to achieve four goals:

1. Because sociology is the systematic study of human behaviour in social context, we first illustrate the power of sociology to dispel foggy assumptions and to help us see the operation of the social world more clearly. To that end, we examine a phenomenon that at first glance appears to be solely the outcome of breakdowns in individual functioning: suicide. We show that, in fact, social relations powerfully influence suicide rates. This exercise introduces you to what is unique about the sociological perspective.

2. We then show that, from its origins, sociological research has been motivated by a desire to improve the social world. Thus, sociology is not just a dry, academic exercise but also a means of charting a better course for society. We illustrate this by briefly analyzing the work of the discipline's founders.

3. We go on to review the main methods of collecting sociological data and assess their strengths and

Lisa M. Ripperton

weaknesses. Although much of sociology is motivated by the desire to improve the social world, sociologists use scientific methods to test their ideas, thus increasing their validity.

4. Finally, we suggest that sociology can help you come to grips with your century, just as it helped the founders of sociology deal with theirs. Today, we are witnessing massive and disorienting social changes. As was the case in the nineteenth century, sociologists today try to understand social phenomena and suggest useful ways to improve society. By promising to make sociology relevant to you, this chapter is an open invitation to participate in sociology's challenge.

Before showing how sociology can help you to understand and improve your world, we look briefly at the problem of suicide. This examination will help to illustrate how the sociological perspective can clarify and sometimes overturn common-sense beliefs.

⓵ The Sociological Perspective

By analyzing suicide sociologically, you can test the claim that sociology offers a unique, surprising, and enlightening perspective on social events. After all, suicide appears to be the supreme antisocial and non-social act. First, nearly everyone in society condemns it. Second, it is typically committed in private, far from the public's intrusive glare. Third, it is comparatively rare: in recent years, about 11 suicides have occurred annually for every 100 000 Canadians. (Canada's suicide rate is close to the world average; see Figure 1.1.) And, finally, when you think about why people commit such an act, you are likely to focus on their individual states of mind rather than on the state of society. In other words, we are usually interested in the aspects of specific individuals' lives that caused them to become depressed or angry enough to commit suicide. We do not usually think about the patterns of social relations that might encourage or inhibit such actions in general. If sociology can reveal the hidden *social* causes of such an apparently non-social and antisocial phenomenon, there must be something to it!

THE SOCIOLOGICAL EXPLANATION OF SUICIDE

At the end of the nineteenth century, French sociologist Émile Durkheim, one of the pioneers of the discipline, demonstrated that suicide is more than just an individual act of desperation that results from psychological disorder, as was commonly believed. Suicide rates, Durkheim showed, are strongly influenced by social forces (Durkheim, 1951 [1897]).

Durkheim made his case by first examining the association between rates of suicide and rates of psychological disorder for different groups. The idea that psychological disorder causes suicide is supported, he wrote, only if the suicide rate tends to be high where the rate of psychological disorder is high, and low where the rate of psychological disorder is low. But his analysis of European government statistics, hospital records, and other sources revealed nothing of the kind. He discovered that slightly more women than men were in insane asylums but that four male suicides occurred for every female suicide. Jews had the highest rate of psychological disorder among the major religious groups in France, but they also had the lowest suicide rate. Psychological disorders occurred most frequently when a person reached maturity, but suicide rates increased steadily with advancing age.

Clearly, suicide rates and rates of psychological disorder did not vary directly. In fact, they often appeared to vary inversely. Why? Durkheim argued that the suicide

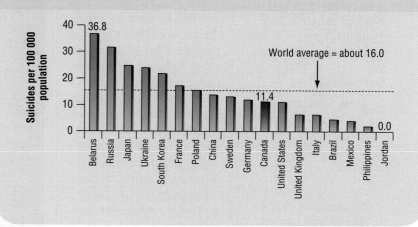

FIGURE 1.1

Suicide Rate, Selected Countries (Most Recent Year Available as of 2009)

Source: World Health Organization. 2010. "Suicide rates per 100 000 by country, year and sex." http://www.who.int/mental_health/prevention/suicide_rates/en/index.html (retrieved 16 February 2010).

rates varied as a result of differences in the degree of social solidarity in different categories of the population. According to Durkheim, the more a group's members share beliefs and values, and the more frequently and intensely they interact, the more social solidarity exists within the group. (Values are ideas about what is good and bad, right and wrong.) In turn, the more social solidarity in a group, the more firmly anchored its individuals are to the social world and the less likely they are to take their own lives. In other words, Durkheim expected high-solidarity groups to have lower suicide rates than low-solidarity groups—at least up to a point (see Figure 1.2).

To support his argument, Durkheim showed that married adults are half as likely as unmarried adults to commit suicide. That is because marriage creates social ties and a sort of moral cement that bind the individual to society. Similarly, women are less likely to commit suicide than men are because women are more involved in the intimate social relations of family life. Jews, Durkheim wrote, are less likely to commit suicide than Christians are because centuries of persecution have turned them into a group that is more defensive and tightly knit. And seniors are more prone than the young and the middle-aged to taking their own lives because they are most likely to live alone, to have lost a spouse, and to lack a job and a wide network of friends. In general, Durkheim wrote, "suicide varies with the degree of integration of the social groups of which the individual forms a part" (Durkheim, 1951 [1897]: 209). Of course, his generalization tells us nothing about why any particular individual may take his or her own life. That issue is

FIGURE 1.2
Durkheim's Theory of Suicide

Suicide rate (vertical axis, Low to High); Social solidarity (horizontal axis, Low to High). U-shaped curve with "Anomic and egoistic suicide" on the upper left and "Altruistic suicide" on the upper right.

Durkheim's **theory** of suicide states that the suicide rate declines and then rises as social solidarity increases. Durkheim called suicides that occur in high-solidarity settings altruistic. **Altruistic suicide** occurs when norms tightly govern behaviour. Soldiers who knowingly give up their lives to protect comrades commit altruistic suicide out of a deep sense of patriotism and comradeship. In contrast, suicide in low-solidarity settings may be egoistic or anomic. **Egoistic suicide** results from the poor integration of people into society because of weak social ties to others. Someone who is unemployed and unmarried is thus more likely to commit suicide than is someone who is employed and married. **Anomic suicide** occurs when vague norms govern behaviour. The rate of anomic suicide is likely to be high among people living in a society that lacks a widely shared code of morality.

Source: From BRYM/LIE. *Sociology: The Points of the Compass.* © 2009 Nelson Education Ltd. Reproduced by permission. www.cengage.com/permissions.

social solidarity Refers to (1) the degree to which group members share beliefs and values, and (2) the intensity and frequency of their interaction.

values Ideas about what is good and bad, right and wrong.

theory A tentative explanation of some aspect of social life that states how and why certain facts are related.

altruistic suicide Occurs in settings that exhibit very high levels of social solidarity, according to Durkheim. In other words, altruistic suicide results from norms very tightly governing behaviour.

egoistic suicide Results from the poor integration of people into society because of weak social ties to others, according to Durkheim.

anomic suicide Occurs in settings that exhibit low levels of social solidarity, according to Durkheim. Anomic suicide results from vaguely defined norms governing behaviour.

Émile Durkheim (1858–1917) was the first professor of sociology in France and is often considered to be the first modern sociologist. In *The Rules of Sociological Method* (1938 [1895]) and *Suicide* (1951 [1897]), he argued that human behaviour is shaped by "social facts," or the social context in which people are embedded. In Durkheim's view, social facts define the constraints and opportunities within which people must act. Durkheim was also keenly interested in the conditions that promote social order in "primitive" and modern societies, and he explored this problem in depth in such works as *The Division of Labor in Society* (1997 [1893]) and *The Elementary Forms of the Religious Life* (1976 [1915/1912]).

© Bettmann/Corbis

the province of psychology. But it does tell us that a person's likelihood of committing suicide decreases as the degree to which he or she is anchored in society increases. It says something surprising and uniquely sociological about how and why the suicide rate varies across groups (see Figure 1.3).

SUICIDE IN CANADA TODAY

The rate of suicide among youth and young adults was low in Durkheim's France. It is higher in Canada today. Durkheim's theory of social solidarity helps us to understand why. In brief, shared moral principles and strong social ties have eroded since the early 1960s for Canada's youth. Consider the following facts:

- Church, synagogue, mosque, and temple attendance is down, particularly among young people. More than 50 percent of Canadians attended religious services weekly in the 1960s. Today, the figure is about 25 percent and is only 15 percent for people born after 1960 (Bibby, 2007).

- Unemployment is up, especially for youth. The unemployment rate remained near 3 percent for most of the 1960s. It rose steadily and stayed near 10 percent for most of the 1990s. As of July 2010, the unemployment rate was 8 percent. However, at 14.1 percent, the unemployment rate was nearly twice as high for Canadians under the age of 24 as it was for older Canadians (Statistics Canada, 2010g).

- The rate of divorce has increased sixfold since the early 1960s. Births outside marriage are also much more common than they used to be. As a result, children are more often brought up in single-parent families than in the past. This fact suggests that they enjoy less frequent and intimate social interaction with parents and less adult supervision.

In sum, the figures cited above suggest that the level of social solidarity is now lower than it was just a few decades ago, especially for young people. Less firmly rooted in society, and less likely to share moral standards, young people in Canada today are more likely than young people

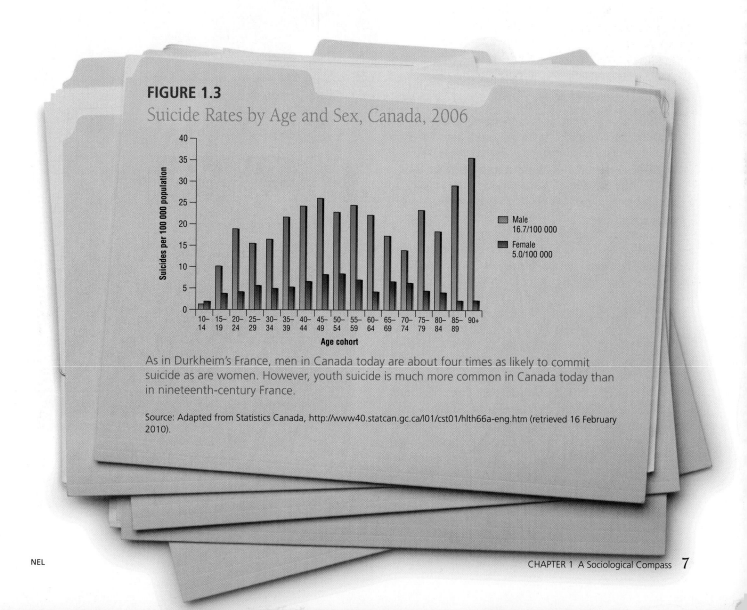

FIGURE 1.3

Suicide Rates by Age and Sex, Canada, 2006

Male 16.7/100 000
Female 5.0/100 000

As in Durkheim's France, men in Canada today are about four times as likely to commit suicide as are women. However, youth suicide is much more common in Canada today than in nineteenth-century France.

Source: Adapted from Statistics Canada, http://www40.statcan.gc.ca/l01/cst01/hlth66a-eng.htm (retrieved 16 February 2010).

were half a century ago to take their own lives if they happen to find themselves in a deep personal crisis.

LO² THE SOCIOLOGICAL IMAGINATION

You have known for a long time that you live in a society. Yet until now, you may not have fully appreciated that society also lives in you. Sociologists call relatively stable patterns of social relations **social structures**. Aspects of social structures, such as the level of social solidarity of the groups you belong to, affect your innermost thoughts and feelings, influence your actions, and thus help to shape who you are.

More than half a century ago, C. Wright Mills (1959) called the ability to see the connection between personal troubles and social structures the **sociological imagination** (see the Sociology at the Movies box). When he wrote about the sociological imagination, he used language that is sexist by today's standards. However, his argument is as true and inspiring today as it was in the 1950s:

> When a society becomes industrialized, a peasant becomes a worker; a feudal lord is liquidated or becomes a businessman. When classes rise or fall, a man is employed or unemployed; when the rate of investment goes up or down, a man takes new heart or goes broke. When war happens, an insurance salesman becomes a rocket launcher; a store clerk, a radar man; a wife lives alone; a child grows up without a father. Neither the life of an individual nor the history of a society can be understood without understanding both.

> Yet men do not usually define the troubles they endure in terms of historical change. . . . The well-being they enjoy, they do not usually impute to the big ups and downs of the society in which they live. Seldom aware of the intricate connection between the patterns of their own lives and the course of world history, ordinary men do not usually know what this connection means for the kind of men they are becoming and for the kind

of history-making in which they might take part. They do not possess the quality of mind essential to grasp the interplay of men and society, of biography and history, of self and world. They cannot cope with their personal troubles in such a way as to control the structural transformations that usually lie behind them.

> What they need . . . is a quality of mind that will help them to [see] . . . what is going on in the world and . . . what may be happening within themselves. It is this quality . . . that . . . may be called the sociological imagination. (Mills, 1959: 3–4)

© David McGlynn/Photographer's Choice/Getty Images

Shake Hands with the Devil

Over a period of 100 days in 1994, the Hutus of Rwanda massacred 800 000 Tutsis—more than a tenth of Rwanda's population—with guns, machetes, hammers, and spears. Bodies were scattered everywhere, and the streets literally flowed with blood. The French trained and armed the Hutus in full knowledge of what would transpire. The Belgians knew too, and their 2000 troops could have done much to prevent it, but they withdrew just before the massacre began. Canadian General Roméo Dallaire, who led a contingent of United Nations troops in Rwanda, reported to his bosses at the UN that he knew where the Hutu arms caches were located and requested permission to destroy them. Permission was denied. Most North Americans were busy watching the O. J. Simpson trial on TV and so barely noticed the genocide.

If Rwanda in 1994 was the site of unspeakable cruelty, it was also a place where compassion and bravery shone through. Dallaire and his small contingent of 450 soldiers from Canada, Ghana, Tunisia, and Bangladesh risked their lives to save an estimated 30 000 Rwandans in one of the twentieth century's great heroic acts. Dallaire courageously swam against the stream of world apathy. *Shake Hands with the Devil*, which won the 2007 Emmy for best documentary, details Dallaire's actions, the heavy toll they took on his mental health, and his recovery from the trauma of 1994.

By highlighting both the cruelty and the bravery surrounding the events in Rwanda, *Shake Hands with the Devil* performs a valuable documentary service. However, it falls short precisely where sociology can contribute most—in uncovering the social context that explains why cruelty and bravery occur in the first place.

Begin with the cruelty. It was not the result of "human nature" but of specific sociological realities. For centuries before 1994, the Hutus were mainly farmers and the Tutsis mainly cattle herders. The Tutsis were the ruling minority yet they spoke the same language as the Hutus, shared the same religious beliefs, live side-by-side, and often intermarried. The two groups never came into serious conflict. Then the Belgians colonized Rwanda in 1916. They made ethnic divisions far more rigid. Now one *had* to be a Tutsi to serve in an official capacity, and the Belgians started distinguishing Tutsis from Hutus by measuring the width of their noses. Tutsi noses, they arbitrarily proclaimed, were thinner. It was a preposterous policy, not least because half the population of Rwanda is of mixed Hutu-Tutsi ancestry, and it served to sharply increase animosity between the two ethnic groups (Organization of African Unity, 2000: 10).

Before the Belgians decolonized Rwanda in 1962, they encouraged power sharing between the Tutsis and the Hutus. However, by then it was too late. The Tutsis objected to any loss of power and civil war broke out. The Hutu majority now took power. In early 1990s, descendants of the Tutsi rebels, backed by the United States and Britain, tried to overthrow the Hutu government, backed by France and Belgium. (Western interest and rivalry in the region is high because it is rich in minerals; see Rose, 2001.) Thus, social contexts marked by intense competition for scarce resources nurtured the genocide.

General Roméo Dallaire

And the heroism? Heroes are typically raised in families and taught in schools that emphasize high moral principle and ethical standards of conduct. These social contexts encourage them to demonstrate independence of character and willingness to defy authority and convention long before they commit any heroic acts. Thus, while heroism sometimes requires a split-second decision, it is usually preceded by years of social learning that predisposes the future hero to act compassionately even if doing so involves refusing to follow the herd (Franco and Zimbardo, 2006–7). We thus see how the sociological perspective helps to illuminate otherwise inexplicable actions, such as cruelty and heroism.

Understanding the social constraints and possibilities for freedom that envelop us requires an active sociological imagination. The sociological imagination urges us to connect our biography with history and social structure—to make sense of our lives against a larger historical and social background and to act in light of our understanding. Although movies are just entertainment to many people, they often achieve by different means what the sociological imagination aims for. Therefore, in each chapter of this book, we review a movie to shed light on topics of sociological importance.

Critical Thinking Questions

Think about a "personal trouble" that you or someone close to you has experienced—perhaps a divorce, a criminal conviction, or a period of unemployment.

- Do you think that people experience such troubles more often in particular historical periods and under certain social conditions?
- If so, can you think of courses of action that might help people deal better with such personal troubles?

Developing answers to these questions will help you start exercising your sociological imagination.

Simon Hayter/GetStock.com

microstructures The patterns of relatively intimate social relations formed during face-to-face interaction. Families, friendship circles, and work associations are all examples of microstructures.

macrostructures Overarching patterns of social relations that lie outside and above a person's circle of intimates and acquaintances. Macrostructures include classes, bureaucracies, and power systems, such as patriarchy.

patriarchy The traditional system of economic and political inequality between women and men.

global structures Patterns of social relations that lie outside and above the national level. They include international organizations, patterns of worldwide travel and communication, and the economic relations among countries.

Mills thus argued that one of the sociologist's main tasks is to identify and explain the connection between people's personal troubles and the social structures in which people are embedded. An important step in broadening our awareness involves recognizing that three levels of social structure surround and permeate us. Think of these structures as concentric circles radiating out from you:

1. **Microstructures** are patterns of intimate social relations formed during face-to-face interaction. Families, friendship circles, and work associations are all examples of microstructures.

2. **Macrostructures** are patterns of social relations that lie outside and above your circle of intimates and acquaintances. Oneimportant macrostructure is **patriarchy**, the traditional system of economic and political inequality between women and men in most societies. Other macrostructures include religious institutions and social classes.

3. **Global structures** are the third level of social structure. International organizations, patterns of worldwide travel and communication, and economic relations among countries are examples of global structures. Global structures are increasingly important because inexpensive travel and communication allow all parts of the world to become interconnected culturally, economically, and politically.[1]

Personal problems are connected to social structures at the micro, macro, and global levels. Whether the personal problem involves finding a job, keeping a marriage intact, or figuring out a way to act justly to end world poverty, social-structural considerations broaden our understanding of the problem and suggest appropriate courses of action.

ORIGINS OF THE SOCIOLOGICAL IMAGINATION

The sociological imagination is only a few hundred years old. Although in ancient times some philosophers wrote about society, their thinking was not sociological. They believed that God and nature controlled society. These philosophers sketched blueprints for the ideal society and urged people to follow the blueprints. They relied on speculation, not evidence, to reach conclusions about how the world worked. The sociological imagination was born when three modern revolutions pushed people to think about society in an entirely new way.

The Scientific Revolution

The Scientific Revolution began about 1550. It encouraged the view that sound conclusions about the workings of society must be based on evidence, not just speculation.

People often link the Scientific Revolution to specific ideas, such as Copernicus's theory that the earth revolves around the sun. However, science is less a collection of ideas than a method of inquiry. For instance, in 1609 Galileo pointed his newly invented telescope at the sky, made some careful observations, and showed that his observations fit Copernicus's theory. This is the core of the scientific method: using evidence to make a case for a particular point of view. By the mid-seventeenth century, some philosophers were calling for a science of society. When sociology emerged as a distinct discipline in the nineteenth century, commitment to the scientific method was one firm pillar of the sociological imagination.

The Democratic Revolution

The Democratic Revolution began about 1750. It suggested that people are responsible for organizing society and that human intervention can therefore solve social problems. Before the Democratic Revolution, most people thought otherwise. They believed that God ordained the social order. The American Revolution (1775–83) and the French Revolution (1789–99) helped undermine that idea. These democratic political upheavals showed that society could experience massive change in a short period. They proved that people could replace unsatisfactory rulers. They suggested that people control society. The implications for social thought were profound, for if it was possible to change society through human action, a science of society could play a big role. It could help people find ways of improving their lives. Much of the justification for sociology as a science arose out of the democratic revolutions that shook Europe and North America.

The Industrial Revolution

The **Industrial Revolution** began about 1775. It created a host of new and serious social problems that attracted the attention of social thinkers. As a result of the growth of industry, masses of people moved from countryside to city, worked agonizingly long hours in crowded and dangerous mines and factories, lost faith in their religions, confronted faceless bureaucracies, and reacted to the filth and poverty of their existence by means of strikes, crime, revolutions, and wars. Scholars had never seen a sociological laboratory like this. The Scientific Revolution suggested that a science of society was possible. The Democratic Revolution suggested that people could intervene to improve society. The Industrial Revolution now presented social thinkers with a host of pressing social problems crying out for solution. They responded by creating the sociological imagination.

LO³ Auguste Comte and the Tension between Science and Values

French social thinker Auguste Comte (1798–1857) coined the term *sociology* in 1838 (Comte, 1975). Comte tried to place the study of society on scientific foundations. He said he wanted to understand the social world as it was, not as he or anyone else imagined it should be. Yet there was a tension in his work: although Comte was eager to adopt the scientific method in the study of society, he was a conservative thinker, motivated by strong opposition to rapid change in French society, as is evident in his writings. When he moved from his small, conservative hometown to Paris, Comte witnessed the democratic forces unleashed by the French Revolution, the early industrialization of society, and the rapid growth of cities. What he saw upset him. Rapid social change was destroying much of what he valued, especially respect for traditional authority. He therefore urged slow change and the preservation of all that was traditional in social life.

To varying degrees, we see the same tension in the work of the three giants in the early history of sociology: Karl Marx (1818–83), Émile Durkheim (1858–1917), and Max Weber (pronounced VAY-ber; 1864–1920). The lives of these three men spanned about a century. They witnessed various phases of Europe's wrenching transition to industrial capitalism. They wanted to explain the great transformation of Europe and suggest ways to improve people's lives. Like Comte, they were committed to the scientific method of research. However, the ideas they developed are not just diagnostic tools from which we can still learn. Like many sociological ideas, they are also prescriptions for combating social ills.

Durkheim, Marx, and Weber stood close to the origins of the major theoretical traditions in sociology: functionalism, conflict theory, and symbolic interactionism. A fourth theoretical tradition, feminism, has arisen in recent decades to correct some deficiencies in the three long-established traditions. It will become clear as you read this

> **Industrial Revolution**
> Often regarded as the most important event in world history since the development of agriculture and cities, the Industrial Revolution refers to the rapid economic transformation that began in Britain around 1775. It involved the large-scale application of science and technology to industrial processes, the creation of factories, and the formation of a working class.

© Musee du Louvre, Paris/Giraudon, Paris/Superstock

Liberty Leading the People. Eugene Delacroix, July 28, 1830. The democratic forces unleashed by the French Revolution suggested that people are responsible for organizing society and that human intervention can therefore solve social problems. As such, democracy was a foundation stone of sociology.

book that many more theories exist in addition to these four. However, because these four traditions have been especially influential in the development of sociology, we present a sketch of each.

LO⁴ Sociological Theory and Theorists

FUNCTIONALISM

Émile Durkheim

Durkheim's theory of suicide is an early example of what sociologists now call **functionalism**. Functionalist theories incorporate four features:

1. Functionalist theories stress that human behaviour is governed by stable patterns of social relations, or social structures. For example, Durkheim emphasized how patterns of social solidarity influence suicide rates. The social structures typically analyzed by functionalists are macrostructures.

2. Functionalist theories show how social structures maintain or undermine social stability. This is why functionalists are sometimes called structural functionalists; they analyze how the parts of society (structures) fit together and how each part contributes to the stability of the whole (its function). For example, Durkheim argued that high social solidarity contributes to the maintenance of social order. However, the growth of industries and cities in nineteenth-century Europe lowered the level of social solidarity and contributed to social instability. Aspects of instability, wrote Durkheim, include higher suicide rates and more frequent strikes by workers.

3. Functionalist theories emphasize that social structures are based mainly on shared values. Thus, when Durkheim wrote about social solidarity, he sometimes meant the frequency and intensity of social interaction, but more often he thought of social solidarity as a kind of moral cement that binds people together.

4. Functionalism suggests that re-establishing equilibrium can best solve most social problems. For instance, Durkheim said that social stability could be restored in late nineteenth-century Europe by creating new associations of employers and workers that would lower workers' expectations about what they should hope for in life. If more people could agree on wanting less, Durkheim wrote, social solidarity would rise, fewer strikes would occur, and suicide rates would drop. Functionalism, then, was a conservative response to widespread social unrest. A more liberal or radical response would have been to argue that if people were expressing discontent because they were getting less out of life than they expected, discontent could be lowered by finding ways for them to get more out of life.

CONFLICT THEORY

The second major theoretical tradition in sociology emphasizes the centrality of conflict in social life. It incorporates the following four features:

1. **Conflict theory** generally focuses on large, macrolevel structures, such as class relations or patterns of domination, submission, and struggle between people of high and low social standing.

2. Conflict theory shows how major patterns of inequality in society produce social stability in some circumstances and social change in others.

3. Conflict theory stresses how members of privileged groups try to maintain their advantages while subordinate groups struggle to acquire advantages. From this point of view, social conditions at a given time are the expression of an ongoing power struggle between privileged and subordinate groups.

4. Conflict theory typically leads to the suggestion that lessening privilege will lower the level of conflict and increase human welfare.

Karl Marx

Conflict theory originated in the work of the German social thinker Karl Marx. A generation before Durkheim, Marx observed the destitution and discontent produced

functionalism Theory that human behaviour is governed by relatively stable social structures. It underlines how social structures maintain or undermine social stability. It emphasizes that social structures are based mainly on shared values or preferences. And it suggests that re-establishing equilibrium can best solve most social problems.

conflict theory Generally focuses on large, macrolevel structures, such as the relations among classes. It shows how major patterns of inequality in society produce social stability in some circumstances and social change in others. It stresses how members of privileged groups try to maintain their advantages while subordinate groups struggle to acquire advantages. And it typically leads to the suggestion that eliminating privilege will lower the level of conflict and increase the sum total of human welfare.

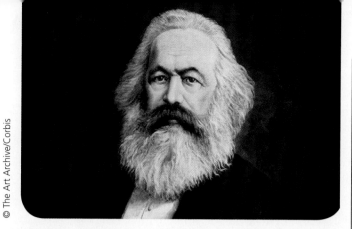

© The Art Archive/Corbis

Karl Marx (1818–83) was a revolutionary thinker whose ideas affected not just the growth of sociology but also the course of world history. He held that major socio-historical changes are the result of conflict between society's main social classes. In his major work, *Capital* (1967 [1867–94]), Marx argued that capitalism would produce such misery and collective strength among workers that they would eventually take state power and create a classless society in which production would be based on human need rather than profit.

by the Industrial Revolution and proposed a sweeping theory about the ways societies develop (Marx, 1904 [1859]; Marx and Engels, 1972 [1848]). Marx's theory differs radically from Durkheim's. **Class conflict**, the struggle between classes to resist and overcome the opposition of other classes, lies at the centre of his ideas.

Marx argued that owners of industry are eager to improve the way work is organized and to adopt new tools, machines, and production methods. These innovations allow them to produce more efficiently, earn higher profits, and drive inefficient competitors out of business. However, the drive for profits also causes capitalists to concentrate workers in larger and larger establishments, keep wages as low as possible, and invest as little as possible in improving working conditions. Thus, wrote Marx, a large and growing class of poor workers opposes a small and shrinking class of wealthy owners.

Marx believed that workers would ultimately become aware of belonging to the same exploited class. He called this awareness **class consciousness**. He believed that working-class consciousness would encourage the growth of trade unions and labour parties. According to Marx, these organizations would eventually try to put an end to private ownership of property and replace it with a communist society, defined as a system in which everyone shares property and wealth according to their needs, and no private property exists.

Max Weber

Although some of Marx's ideas have been usefully adapted to the study of contemporary society, his predictions about the inevitable collapse of capitalism have been questioned. Max Weber, a German sociologist who wrote his major works a generation after Marx, was among the first to point out some of the flaws in Marx's argument

(Weber, 1946). Weber noted the rapid growth of the so-called service sector of the economy, with its many non-manual (or white-collar) workers and professionals. He argued that these occupational groups would stabilize society because they enjoyed more prestige and income than manual (or blue-collar) workers in the manufacturing sector. Weber also showed that class conflict is not the only driving force of history. In his view, politics and religion are also important sources of historical change. Other writers pointed out that Marx did not appreciate how investment in technology would make it possible for

> **class conflict** The struggle between classes to resist and overcome the opposition of other classes.
>
> **class consciousness** Awareness of belonging to the social class of which one is a member.

Brown Brothers

Max Weber (1864–1920), Germany's greatest sociologist, profoundly influenced the development of the discipline worldwide. Engaged in a lifelong "debate with Marx's ghost," Weber held that economic circumstances alone do not explain the rise of capitalism. As he showed in *The Protestant Ethic and the Spirit of Capitalism* (1958 [1904–5]), independent developments in the religious realm had unintended, beneficial consequences for capitalist development in some parts of Europe. He also argued that capitalism would not necessarily give way to socialism. Instead, he regarded the growth of bureaucracy and the overall "rationalization" of life as the defining characteristics of the modern age. These themes were developed in *Economy and Society* (1968 [1914]).

Conflict theory became especially popular in North America in the 1960s and 1970s, decades that were rocked by major labour unrest, peace demonstrations on university campuses, the rise of the black power movement, and the emergence of contemporary feminism. Strikes, demonstrations, and riots were almost daily occurrences in the 1960s and 1970s, and it seemed evident to many sociologists of that generation that conflict among classes, nations, races, and generations was the very essence of social life. For example, John Porter (1921–79) was Canada's premier sociologist in the 1960s and 1970s. Born in Vancouver, he received his Ph.D. from the London School of Economics. He spent his academic career at Carleton University in Ottawa, where he served as chair of the Department of Sociology and Anthropology, dean of Arts and Science, and vice-president. His major work, *The Vertical Mosaic* (1965), is a study of class and power in Canada. Firmly rooted in conflict theory, it influenced a generation of Canadian sociologists in their studies on social inequality, elite groups, French–English relations, and Canadian–American relations.

workers to toil fewer hours under less oppressive conditions. Nor did Marx foresee that higher wages, better working conditions, and welfare-state benefits would pacify manual workers. Thus, many of the particulars of Marx's theory were called into question by Weber and other sociologists. Nevertheless, Marx's insights about the fundamental importance of conflict in social life are still highly influential in modern sociology.

SYMBOLIC INTERACTIONISM

Weber and the Protestant Ethic

Contrary to Marx, Weber argued that favourable economic circumstances alone did not cause early capitalist development. In addition, he said, certain religious beliefs encouraged robust capitalist growth. In particular, sixteenth- and seventeenth-century Protestants believed their religious doubts could be reduced, and a state of grace assured, if they worked diligently and lived modestly. Weber called this belief the **Protestant ethic**. He believed it had an unintended effect: people who adhered to the Protestant ethic saved and invested more than others. Thus, according to Weber, capitalism developed most energetically where the Protestant ethic took hold. He concluded that capitalism did not develop just because of the operation of economic forces. Instead, it depended partly on the religious meaning individuals attached to their work (Weber, 1958 [1904–5]). In much of his research, Weber emphasized the importance of empathically understanding people's motives and the meanings they attach to things to gain a clear sense of the significance of their actions.

The idea that subjective meanings and motives must be analyzed in any complete sociological analysis was only one of Weber's contributions to early sociological theory. Weber was also an important conflict theorist, as you will learn in later chapters. At present, however, it is enough to note that his emphasis on subjective meanings found rich soil among sociologists in North America in the late nineteenth and early twentieth centuries.

The Principles of Symbolic Interactionism

Functionalist and conflict theories assume that people's group memberships—whether they are rich or poor, male or female, black or white—help shape their behaviour. This can sometimes make people seem like balls on a pool table that get knocked around and cannot choose their destinations. We know from our everyday experience, however, that people often make choices, sometimes difficult ones. Sometimes, they change their minds. Moreover, two people with similar group memberships may react differently to similar social circumstances because they interpret those circumstances differently.

Recognizing these issues, some sociologists focus on the subjective side of social life. They work in a school

Protestant ethic The sixteenth- and seventeenth-century Protestant belief that religious doubts can be reduced, and a state of grace assured, if people work diligently and live ascetically. According to Weber, the Protestant work ethic had the unintended effect of increasing savings and investment and thus stimulating capitalist growth.

of thought called **symbolic interactionism**. This tradition incorporates four features:

1. Symbolic interactionism focuses on interpersonal communication in microlevel social settings, distinguishing it from both functionalist and conflict theories.

2. Symbolic interactionism emphasizes that social life is possible only because people attach meanings to things. It follows that an adequate explanation of social behaviour requires understanding the subjective meanings that people associate with their social circumstances.

3. Symbolic interactionism stresses that people help create their social circumstances and do not merely react to them. For example, Canadian-born sociologist Erving Goffman (1922–82), one of the most influential symbolic interactionists of the twentieth century, developed an international reputation for his "dramaturgical" approach to symbolic interactionism. This approach highlights the way people present themselves to others, managing their identities in order to create desired impressions on their "audience," in much the same way as actors do. For Goffman, social interaction is like a play, complete with stage, backstage, defined roles, and props. In this play, a person's age, gender, race, and other characteristics may help shape his or her actions, but there is much room for individual creativity as well (Goffman, 1959).

4. By focusing on the subjective meanings people create in small social settings, symbolic interactionists sometimes validate unpopular and unofficial viewpoints.

Erving Goffman (1922–82) was born in Mannville, Alberta. He studied sociology and anthropology at the University of Toronto. He completed his Ph.D. at the University of Chicago and pursued his academic career at the University of California, Berkeley, and the University of Pennsylvania. Goffman developed an international reputation for his "dramaturgical" approach to symbolic interactionism.

American Sociological Association

This increases our understanding and tolerance of people who may be different from us.

FEMINISM
Women Ignored

Few women figured prominently in the early history of sociology. The strict demands placed on them by the nineteenth-century family and the lack of opportunity for women in the larger society prevented most of them from attaining a higher education and making major contributions to the discipline. The women who did make their mark on the discipline in its early years tended to have unusual biographies. For example, Harriet Martineau (1802–76) is often called the first female sociologist (Martineau, 1985). Born in England in 1802 to a prosperous family, she never married. Martineau translated Comte into English and wrote one of the first books on sociological research methods. She undertook critical studies of slavery, factory laws, and gender inequality. She was also a leading advocate of voting rights and higher education for women, as well as of gender equality in the family. As such, Martineau was one of the first feminists. Exceptional women like Martineau introduced gender issues that were largely ignored by Marx, Durkheim, Weber, and other early sociologists. Appreciation for the sociological contribution of these pioneer women has grown as concern with gender issues has come to form a substantial part of the modern sociological enterprise.

Modern Feminism

Despite its encouraging beginnings, feminist thinking had little impact on sociology until the mid-1960s, when the rise of the modern feminist movement drew attention to the many remaining inequalities between women and men. Because of **feminist theory**'s major influence on

symbolic interactionism
Theory that focuses on face-to-face communication in microlevel social settings. It emphasizes that an adequate explanation of social behaviour requires understanding the subjective meanings people attach to their social circumstances. It stresses that people help to create their social circumstances rather than merely reacting to them. And by underscoring the subjective meanings people create in small social settings, it validates unpopular and unofficial viewpoints, increasing our understanding and tolerance of people who may be different from us.

feminist theory View that patriarchy is at least as important as class inequality in determining a person's opportunities in life. It holds that male domination and female subordination are determined not by biological necessity but by structures of power and social convention. It examines the operation of patriarchy in both micro and macro settings. And it contends that existing patterns of gender inequality can and should be changed for the benefit of all members of society.

Margrit Eichler

Margrit Eichler (1942–) was born in Berlin, Germany. She took her Ph.D. at Duke University in the United States before beginning her academic career in Canada. She served as chair of the Department of Sociology at the Ontario Institute for Studies in Education and was the first director of the Institute for Women's Studies and Gender Studies at the University of Toronto. Eichler is internationally known for her work on feminist methodology (Eichler, 1987). Her work on family policy in Canada has influenced students, professional sociologists, and policy-makers for two decades (Eichler, 1988).

sociology today, it may fairly be regarded as sociology's fourth major theoretical tradition. Modern feminism has several variants (see Chapter 8, Sexuality and Gender). However, the various strands of feminist theory share the following features:

1. Feminist theory focuses on various aspects of patriarchy, the system of male domination in society. Patriarchy, feminists contend, is as important as class inequality, if not more so, in determining a person's opportunities in life.

2. Feminist theory holds that male domination and female subordination are determined not by biological necessity but by structures of social power and social convention. From this point of view, women are subordinate to men only because men enjoy more legal, economic, political, and cultural rights.

3. Feminist theory examines how patriarchy operates in both micro and macro settings.

4. Feminist theory contends that existing patterns of gender inequality can and should be changed for the benefit of all members of society. The main sources of gender inequality include differences in the way boys and girls are brought up; barriers to equal opportunity in education, paid work, and politics; and the unequal division of domestic responsibilities between women and men.

Table 1.1 summarizes feminist theory, symbolic interactionism, conflict theory, and functionalism. As you will see in the following chapters, sociologists have applied these theoretical traditions to all of the discipline's branches and have elaborated and refined each of them. To give you a taste of things to come, we now analyze the problem of fashion to illustrate how sociologists apply all four theoretical traditions.

APPLYING THE FOUR THEORETICAL PERSPECTIVES: THE PROBLEM OF FASHION

"Oh. Two weeks ago I saw Cameron Diaz at Fred Siegel and I talked her out of buying this truly heinous angora sweater. Whoever said orange is the new pink is seriously disturbed."

—Elle Woods (Reese Witherspoon) in *Legally Blonde* (2001)

TABLE 1.1
Four Theoretical Traditions in Society

Theoretical Tradition	Main Levels of Analysis	Main Focus	Main Question
Functionalist	Macro	Values	How do the institutions of society contribute to social stability and instability?
Conflict	Macro	Inequality	How do privileged groups seek to maintain their advantages and subordinate groups seek to increase theirs, often causing social change in the process?
Symbolic interactionist	Micro	Meaning	How do individuals communicate to make their social settings meaningful?
Feminist	Macro and micro	Patriarchy	Which social structures and interaction processes maintain male dominance and female subordination?

Source: From BRYM/LIE. *Sociology: The Points of the Compass.* © 2009 Nelson Education Ltd. Reproduced by permission. www.cengage.com/permissions.

In 2002, the *Wall Street Journal* announced that grunge might be back (Tkacik, 2002). Since 1998, one of the main fashion trends among white, middle-class, pre-teen and young teenage girls had been the Britney Spears look: bare midriffs, highlighted hair, wide belts, glitter purses, big wedge shoes, and Skechers "energy" sneakers. But in 2002 a new star, Avril Lavigne, was rising in the pop charts. Nominated for a 2003 Grammy Award in the "Best New Artist" category, the 17-year-old skater-punk from Napanee in eastern Ontario affected a shaggy, unkempt look. She sported worn-out T-shirts, 1970s-style plaid Western shirts with snaps, low-rise blue jeans, baggy pants, undershirts, ties, backpacks, chain wallets, and, for shoes, Converse Chuck Taylors. The style was similar to the grunge look of the early 1990s, when Nirvana and Pearl Jam were the big stars on MTV and Kurt Cobain was king of the music world.

Why were the glamorous trends of the pop era possibly giving way in one market segment to "neo-grunge"? Why, in general, do fashion shifts take place? Sociological theory has interesting things to say on this subject (Davis, 1992).

Functionalism

Until the 1960s, the standard sociological approach to explaining the ebb and flow of fashion trends was *functionalist*. In the functionalist view, fashion trends worked like this: every season, exclusive fashion houses in Paris, Milan, New York, and London would show new styles. Some of the new styles would catch on among the exclusive clientele of big-name designers. The main appeal of wearing expensive, new fashions was that wealthy clients could distinguish themselves from people who were less well off. Thus, fashion performed an important social function. By allowing people of different rank to distinguish themselves from one another, fashion helped to preserve the ordered layering of society into classes. However, by the twentieth century, thanks to technological advances in clothes manufacturing, it didn't take long for inexpensive knockoffs to reach the market and trickle down to lower classes. New styles then had to be introduced frequently so that fashion could continue to perform its function of helping to maintain an orderly class system. Hence the ebb and flow of fashion.

The functionalist theory was a fairly accurate account of the way fashion trends worked until the 1960s. Then, fashion became more democratic. Paris, Milan, New York, and London are still important fashion centres today. However, new fashion trends are increasingly initiated by lower classes, minority racial and ethnic groups, and people who spurn high fashion altogether. Napanee is, after all, pretty far from Paris, and today big-name designers are more likely to be influenced by the inner-city styles of hip-hop than vice versa. New fashions no longer just trickle down from upper classes and a few high-fashion centres. Upper classes are nearly as likely to adopt lower-class fashion trends that emanate from just about anywhere. As a result, the functionalist theory no longer provides a satisfying explanation of fashion cycles.

Conflict Theory

Some sociologists have turned to *conflict theory* as an alternative view of the fashion world. Conflict theorists typically view fashion cycles as a means by which industry owners make big profits. Owners introduce new styles and render old styles unfashionable because they make more money when many people are encouraged to buy new clothes often. At the same time, conflict theorists think fashion keeps people distracted from the many social, economic, and political problems that might otherwise incite them to express dissatisfaction with the existing social order and even rebel against it. Conflict theorists, like functionalists, thus believe that fashion helps to maintain social stability. Unlike functionalists, however, they argue that social stability bestows advantages on industrial owners at the expense of non-owners.

Conflict theorists have a point. Fashion *is* a big and profitable business. Owners *do* introduce new styles to make more money. They have, for example, created The Color Marketing Group (known to insiders as the "Color Mafia"), a committee that meets regularly to help change the palette of colour preferences for consumer products. According to one committee member, the Color Mafia makes sure that "the mass media, . . . fashion magazines and catalogs, home shopping shows, and big clothing chains all present the same options" (Mundell, 1993).

Reuters NewMedia Inc./Corbis

David Bergman/Corbis

Britney Spears

Avril Lavigne

Yet the Color Mafia and other influential elements of the fashion industry are not all-powerful. Remember what Elle Woods said after she convinced Cameron Diaz not to buy that heinous angora sweater: "Whoever said orange is the new pink is seriously disturbed." Like many consumers, Elle Woods *rejected* the advice of the fashion industry. And, in fact, some of the fashion trends initiated by industry owners flop, one of the biggest being the introduction of the midi-dress (with a hemline midway between knee and ankle) in the mid-1970s. Despite a huge ad campaign, most women would not buy it.

Symbolic Interactionism

This analysis points to one of the main problems with the conflict interpretation: it incorrectly makes it seem as if fashion decisions are dictated from above. Reality is more complicated. Fashion decisions are made partly by consumers. This idea can best be understood by thinking of clothing as a form of *symbolic interaction*, a sort of wordless "language" that allows us to tell others who we are and learn who they are.

If clothes speak, sociologist Fred Davis has perhaps done the most in recent years to help us see how we can decipher what they say (Davis, 1992). According to Davis, a person's identity is always a work in progress. True, we develop a sense of self as we mature. We come to think of ourselves as members of one or more families, occupations, communities, classes, ethnic and racial groups, and countries. We develop patterns of behaviour and belief associated with each of these social categories. Nonetheless, social categories change over time, and so do we as we age and move through them. As a result, our identities are always in flux. We often become anxious or insecure about who we are. Clothes help us express our shifting identities. For example, clothes can convey whether you are sexually available, athletic, conservative, and much else, thus telling others how you want them to see you and the kinds of people with whom you want to associate. At some point you may become less conservative, sexually available, and so on. Your clothing style is likely to change accordingly. (Of course, the messages you try to send are subject to interpretation and may be misunderstood.) For its part, the fashion industry feeds on the ambiguities within us, investing much effort in trying to discern which new styles might capture current needs for self-expression.

Feminism

For example, capitalizing on the need for self-expression among many young girls in the late 1990s, Britney Spears hit a chord. Feminist interpretations of the meaning and significance of Britney Spears are especially interesting in this respect because they focus on the gender aspects of fashion.

Traditionally, feminists thought of fashion as a form of patriarchy, a means by which male dominance was maintained. They argued that fashion was mainly a female preoccupation. It takes a lot of time and money to choose, buy, and clean clothes. Fashionable clothing is often impractical and uncomfortable, and some of it is even unhealthy. Modern fashion's focus on youth, slenderness, and eroticism diminishes women by turning them into sexual objects, say some

Fashion flop: the midi-dress of the mid-70s.

© Trinity Mirror/Mirrorpix/Alamy

feminists. Britney Spears was of interest to traditional feminists because she supposedly helped to lower the age at which girls fell under male domination.

In recent years, this traditional feminist view has given way to a feminist interpretation that is more compatible with symbolic interactionism ("Why Britney Spears Matters," 2001). Some feminists now applaud the "girl power" movement that crystallized in 1996 with the release of the Spice Girls' hit single "Wannabe." They regard Britney Spears as part of that movement. In their judgment, Spears's music, dance routines, and dress style expressed a self-assuredness and assertiveness that resonated with the less submissive and more independent role that girls were carving out for themselves. With her kicks, her shadow boxing, and songs like the 2000 single "Stronger," Spears spoke for the *empowerment* of young women. Quite apart from her musical and dancing talent, then, some feminists think many young girls were wild about Britney Spears because she helped them express their own social and sexual power. Of course, not all girls agreed. Some, like Avril Lavigne, found Spears "phony" and too much of a "showgirl." They wanted "more authentic" ways of asserting their identity through fashion (Pascual, 2002). Still, the symbolic interactionist and feminist interpretations of fashion help us see more clearly the ambiguities of identity that underlie the rise of new fashion trends.

Our analysis of fashion shows that each of the four theoretical perspectives—functionalism, conflict theory, symbolic interactionism, and feminism—can clarify different aspects of a sociological problem. This does not mean that each perspective always has equal validity. Often, the interpretations that derive from different theoretical perspectives are incompatible. They offer *competing* interpretations of the same social reality. It is then necessary to do research to determine which perspective works best for the case at hand.

LO⁵ Conducting Research

Theorizing without research is like trying to paint a picture without paint. You might have a spectacular idea for the picture, but you can never be sure it's going to work out until you get your hands dirty and commit the idea to canvas. Similarly, sociologists conduct research to see how well their theories fit the real world. We devote the second half of this chapter to outlining the research process, given its importance to the sociological enterprise as a whole.

Social conditions and personal values often colour theoretical speculation. Think of the influence of the Industrial Revolution on the founding sociologists and how the wishes of theorists since Comte have helped shape theories. Should we conclude that theories are merely speculative and totally subjective? Not at all. Sociologists have a powerful means of controlling bias and assessing the validity of theories: conducting research.

Before we do research, we rarely see things as they are. We see them as we are. Then, in the research process, a sort of waltz begins. Subjectivity leads, objectivity follows. When the dance is finished, we see things more accurately. As many advances in sociological thinking show, subjective experiences often enhance objective sociological knowledge, leading to the discovery of new problems and new solutions to old problems.

Acknowledging that our experiences inspire us to ask particular questions about the social world is not the same as saying that those questions, or the answers we eventually uncover, are biased. Bias arises only when we remain unaware of our subjectivity. It is the purpose of research to help us become aware of our biases and to test theories against systematic observations of the social world that other researchers can repeat to check up on us. On the basis of research, we reject some theories, modify others, and are forced to invent new ones. Having outlined the main theoretical approaches in sociology, it is now time to discuss the research process.

> **research** The process of systematically observing reality to assess the validity of a theory.

THE RESEARCH CYCLE

Ideally, sociological research is a cyclical process that involves six steps (Figure 1.4 on the next page). The sociologist's first step is to *formulate a research question*. A research question must be stated so that it can be answered by systematically collecting and analyzing sociological data.

Sociological research cannot determine whether God exists or what the best political system is. Answers to such questions require faith more than evidence. However, sociological research can determine why some people are more religious than others and which political system creates most opportunities for higher education. Answers to such questions require evidence more than faith.

The second step involves a *review of the existing research literature*. Researchers must elaborate their research questions in the clear light of what other sociologists have already debated and discovered. Why? Because reading the relevant sociological literature stimulates researchers' sociological imaginations, allows them to refine their initial questions, and prevents duplication of effort.

FIGURE 1.4

The Research Cycle

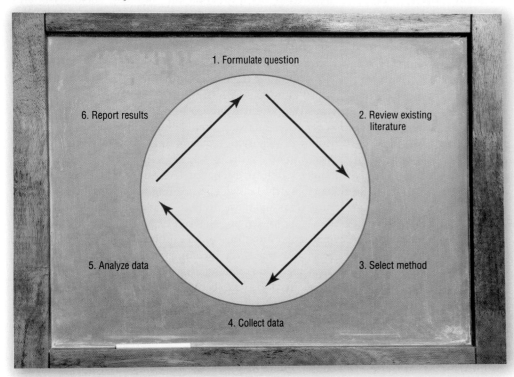

1. Formulate question

6. Report results

2. Review existing literature

5. Analyze data

3. Select method

4. Collect data

Source: From BRYM/LIE. *Sociology: The Points of the Compass.* © 2009 Nelson Education Ltd. Reproduced by permission. www.cengage.com/permissions.

and more sophisticated research questions can be formulated for the next round of research. Science is a social activity governed by rules defined and enforced by the scientific community.

ETHICS IN SOCIOLOGICAL RESEARCH

Researchers must be mindful of the need to respect their subjects' rights throughout the research cycle. This means, first, that researchers must do their subjects no harm. This is the right to *safety*. Second, research subjects must have the right to decide whether their attitudes and behaviours may be revealed to the public and, if so, in what way. This is the right to *privacy*. Third, researchers cannot use data in a way that allows them to be traced to a particular subject. This is the subject's right to *confidentiality*. Fourth, subjects must be told how the information they supply will be used. They must also be allowed to judge the degree of personal risk involved in answering questions so that they can decide whether they will be studied and, if so, in what way. This is the right to *informed consent*.

Ethical issues arise not only in the treatment of subjects but also in the treatment of research results. For example, plagiarism is a concern in academic life, especially among students, who write research papers and submit them to professors for evaluation. One study found that 38 percent of college and university students admitted to committing "cut and paste" plagiarism when writing essays (Edmundson, 2003). Ready-made essays are also widely available for purchase.

Increased plagiarism is a consequence of the spread of the World Wide Web and the growing view that everything on it is public and therefore does not have to be cited. That view is wrong. The Code of Ethics of the American Sociological Association states that we must "explicitly identify, credit, and reference the author" when we make any use of another person's written work, "whether it is published, unpublished, or electronically available" (American Sociological Association, 1999: 16). Making such ethical standards better known can help

Selecting a research method is the third step in the research cycle. As we will see in detail later in this chapter, each data collection method has strengths and weaknesses. Each method is therefore best suited to studying a different kind of problem. When choosing a method, researchers must keep these strengths and weaknesses in mind.

In the fourth stage of the research cycle, researchers *collect data* by observing subjects, interviewing them, reading documents produced by or about them, and so forth. Many researchers think this is the most exciting stage of the research cycle because it brings them face to face with the puzzling sociological reality that so fascinates them.

Other researchers find the fifth step of the research cycle, when they *analyze the data*, the most challenging. During data analysis you can learn things that nobody knew before. At this stage, data confirm some of your expectations and confound others, requiring you to think creatively about familiar issues, reconsider the relevant theoretical and research literature, and abandon pet ideas.

Research is not useful for the sociological community, the subjects of the research, or the wider society if researchers do not complete the sixth step—*publish the results* in a report, a scientific journal, or a book. Publication serves another important function, too: it allows other sociologists to scrutinize and criticize the research. On that basis, errors can be corrected and new

remedy the problem of plagiarism. So can better policing. Powerful Web-based applications are now available that help college and university instructors determine whether essays are plagiarized in whole or in part (visit http://www.turnitin.com). However, the most effective remedy may be for instructors to ensure that what they teach really matters to their students. If they do, students won't be as inclined to plagiarize because they will regard essay writing as a process of personal discovery. You can't cut and paste or buy enlightenment (Edmundson, 2003).

Bearing in mind our sketch of the research cycle, we devote the next part of this chapter to exploring its fourth and fifth stages—gathering and analyzing evidence. We will now describe each of sociology's major research methods: experiments, surveys, field research, and the examination of existing documents and official statistics.

The Main Sociological Research Methods

EXPERIMENTS

In the mid-1960s, the first generation of North American children exposed to high levels of TV violence virtually from birth reached their mid-teens. At the same time, the rate of violent crime began to increase. Some commentators said that TV violence made violence in the real world seem normal and acceptable. As a result, they concluded, North American teenagers in the 1960s and subsequent decades were more likely than pre-1960s teens to commit violent acts. The increasing prevalence of violence in movies, video games, and popular music seemed to add weight to their conclusion.

Social scientists soon started investigating the connection between media and real-world violence by using experimental methods. An **experiment** is a carefully controlled artificial situation that allows researchers to isolate presumed causes and measure their effects precisely by manipulating a **variable**, a concept that can take on more than one value (Campbell and Stanley, 1963).

Experiments use a procedure called **randomization** to create two similar groups. Randomization involves assigning individuals to one of the two groups by chance processes. For example, researchers may ask 50 children to draw a number from 1 to 50 from a covered box. The researchers assign children who draw odd numbers to one group and those who draw even numbers to the other group. By assigning subjects to the two groups by using a chance process, researchers ensure that each group has about the same proportion of boys and girls, members of different races, children highly motivated to participate in the study, and so forth, if the experiment is performed many times.

After randomly assigning subjects to the two groups, the researchers may put the groups in separate rooms and give them toys to play with. They observe the children through one-way mirrors, rating each child in terms of the aggressiveness of his or her play. This is the child's initial score on the dependent variable, which is aggressive behaviour. The **dependent variable** is the effect in a cause-and-effect relationship.

Then the researchers introduce the hypothesized cause to one group—now called the **experimental group**. They may show children in the experimental group an hour-long TV program in which many violent acts take place. They do not show the program to children in the other group, now called the **control group**. In this case, being exposed to the violent TV show or not is the independent variable.

experiment A carefully controlled artificial situation that allows researchers to isolate hypothesized causes and measure their effects precisely.

variable A concept that can take on more than one value.

randomization In an experiment, assigning individuals to groups by chance processes.

dependent variable The presumed effect in a cause-and-effect relationship.

experimental group The group that is exposed to the independent variable in an experiment.

control group The group that is not exposed to the independent variable in an experiment.

Aggressive behaviour among children is common, from siblings fighting to bullying in the schoolyard. Since the inception of home TV in the 1950s, social scientists have sought to find strong research designs capable of examining the causal effects, if any, of viewing violence on television.

© Kuttig, S./plainpicture/Corbis

independent variable The presumed cause in a cause-and-effect relationship.

reliability The degree to which a measurement procedure yields consistent results.

validity The degree to which a measure actually measures what it is intended to measure.

survey Research method in which people are asked questions about their knowledge, attitudes, or behaviour, either in a face-to-face or telephone interview or in a paper-and-pencil format.

sample The part of the population of interest that is selected for analysis.

population The entire group about which the researcher wants to generalize.

respondent A person who answers a researcher's questions.

probability sample Sample in which the units have a known and non-zero chance of being selected.

The **independent variable** is the presumed cause in any cause-and-effect relationship.

Immediately after the children see the TV show, the researchers again observe the children in both groups at play. Each child's play is given a second aggressiveness score. By comparing the aggressiveness scores of the two groups before and after only one of the groups has been exposed to the presumed cause, an experiment can determine whether the presumed cause (watching violent TV) has the predicted effect (increasing violent behaviour).

Many experiments show that exposure to media violence has a short-term effect on violent behaviour in young children, especially boys. However, the results of experiments are mixed when it comes to assessing longer-term effects, especially on older children and teenagers (Anderson and Bushman, 2002; Browne and Hamilton-Giachritsis, 2005; Freedman, 2002).

Experiments allow researchers to isolate the single cause of theoretical interest and measure its effect with high **reliability**, that is, consistently from one experiment to the next. Yet many sociologists argue that experiments are highly artificial situations. They believe that removing people from their natural social settings lowers the **validity** of experimental results, that is, the degree to which they measure what they are actually supposed to measure.

To understand why experiments on the effects of media violence may lack validity, consider that, in the real world, violent behaviour usually means attempting to harm another person physically. Shouting or kicking a toy is not the same thing. In fact, such acts may enable children to relieve frustration, lowering their chance of acting violently in the real world. Moreover, in a laboratory situation, aggressive behaviour may be encouraged because it is legitimized. Simply showing a violent TV program may suggest to subjects how the experimenter expects them to behave. Finally, aggressive behaviour is not punished or controlled in the laboratory setting as it is in the real

world. If a boy watching a violent TV show stands up and delivers a karate kick to his brother, a parent or other caregiver is likely to take action to prevent a recurrence. This usually teaches the boy not to engage in aggressive behaviour. In the lab, lack of discipline may encourage unrealistically high levels of aggression (Felson, 1996).

SURVEYS

Surveys are the most widely used sociological research method, and they have also been used to measure the effects of media violence on behaviour. Overall, the results of surveys show a weaker relationship between exposure to violent mass media and violent behaviour than do experiments, and some surveys show no relationship at all between these two variables (Anderson and Bushman, 2002; Huesmann, Moise-Titus, Podolski, and Eron, 2003; Johnson, Cohen, Smailes, Kasen, and Brook, 2002; see Table 1.2).

In a **survey**, people are asked questions about their knowledge, attitudes, or behaviour. All survey researchers aim to study part of a group—a **sample**—to learn about the whole group of interest—the **population**. To safely generalize about the population on the basis of findings from a sample, researchers must be sure that the characteristics of the people in the sample match those of the population. To draw a sample from which they can safely generalize, researchers must choose **respondents** (people who answer the survey questions) at random, and an individual's chance of being chosen must be known and greater than zero. A sample with these characteristics is known as a **probability sample**.

Researchers collect information through surveys by asking people in a representative sample an identical set of questions. People interviewed on a downtown street corner do not constitute a representative sample of Canadian adults, because the sample does not include people who live outside the urban core, it underestimates the number of older people and people with disabilities, it does not take into account regional diversity, and so on.

Janine Wiedel/Getstock.com

To draw a probability sample you first need a sampling frame, a list of all the people in the population of interest. You also need a randomizing method, a way of ensuring that every person in the sampling frame has a known and non-zero chance of being selected. A frequently used sampling frame is the telephone directory, which is now available for the entire country on CD-ROM. Researchers program computers to dial residential phone numbers at random, thus allowing them to create samples based on all households with phones—roughly 99 percent of Canadian households.

When sociologists conduct a survey, they may mail a form containing questions to respondents. Respondents then mail the completed questionnaire back to the researcher. Alternatively, sociologists may conduct face-to-face interviews in which questions are presented to the respondent by the interviewer during a meeting. Sociologists can also conduct surveys by means of telephone interviews.

Questionnaires can contain two types of questions. A closed-ended question provides the respondent with a list of permitted answers. Each answer is given a numerical code so the data can later be easily input into a computer for statistical analysis. Often, the numerical results of surveys are arranged in tables like Table 1.2.

> **sampling frame** A list of all the people in the population of interest.
>
> **closed-ended question** In a survey, a type of question that provides the respondent with a list of permitted answers. Each answer is given a numerical code so that the data can later be easily input into a computer for statistical analysis.
>
> **association** Relationship between two variables if the value of one variable changes with the value of another.

TABLE 1.2
Watching TV and Approval of Violence (in percentage)

TV Viewing / Punching approval	0–2 Hours/Day	3+ Hours/Day	Total
Yes	69	65	67
No	31	35	33
Total	100	100	100
n	5 188	5 022	10 210

Source: National Opinion Research Center (2006).

This table comes from one of the most respected surveys in the United States, the General Social Survey, conducted most years since 1972. The survey regularly asks people how many hours of TV they watch every day. Until 1994, it also asked respondents if they ever approve of a man punching an adult male. This table shows the results for these two questions, combining responses from 1972 to 1994.

An **association** between two variables exists if the value of one variable changes with the value of the other. For example, if the percentage of people who approve of a man punching an adult male is *higher* among those who watch 3 or more hours of TV a day, a *positive* association exists between the two variables. If the percentage of people who approve of a man punching an adult male is *lower* among those who watch 3 or more hours of TV a day, a *negative* association exists between the two variables. The greater the percentage difference between frequent and infrequent TV viewers, the stronger the association. This table shows that 69 percent of respondents who watched TV 0–2 hours a day approved punching compared with 65 percent of respondents who watched TV 3 or more hours. Is this a positive or a negative association?

To interpret tables, you must pay careful attention to what adds up to 100 percent. The table says that 69 percent *of people who watched TV 0–2 hours a day* approved of a man punching an adult male. It does not say that 69 percent of all people who approved of a man punching an adult male watched TV 0–2 hours a day. We know this because each category of the "TV viewing" variable equals 100 percent.

To test your understanding, calculate the number of respondents represented by the following percentages in the table: 69%, 65%, 31%, and 35%. Answers are given on the right.

> **Answers**
> 69% = (69/100) × 5188 = 3580 respondents
> 65% = (65/100) × 5022 = 3264 respondents
> 31% = (31/100) × 5188 = 1608 respondents
> 35% = (35/100) × 5022 = 1758 respondents

An **open-ended question** allows respondents to answer in their own words. Open-ended questions are particularly useful when researchers don't have enough knowledge to create a meaningful and complete list of possible answers.

To ensure that survey questions elicit valid responses, researchers must guard against four dangers:

1. The exclusion of part of the population from the sampling frame
2. The refusal of some people to participate in the survey
3. The unwillingness of some respondents to answer questions frankly
4. The asking of confusing, leading, or inflammatory questions or questions that refer to several, unimportant or non-current events

Much of the art and science of survey research involves overcoming these threats to validity (Converse and Presser, 1986; Ornstein, 1998). Recall that surveys tend to show a weaker relationship than do experiments between exposure to violent mass media and violent behaviour. That may be because survey researchers have developed more valid measures of violent behaviour.

FIELD RESEARCH

The method that comes closest to people's natural social settings is **field research**. Field research involves systematically observing people wherever they meet, from the ethnic slum to the alternative hard rock scene to the public school classroom (Schippers, 2002; Whyte, 1981).

When they go into the field, researchers go prepared with strategies to ensure their observations are accurate. One such strategy is **detached observation**, which involves classifying and counting the behaviour of interest according to a predetermined scheme. Although useful for some purposes, two main problems confound direct observation. First, the presence of the researcher may

cause **reactivity**; the observed people may conceal certain things or act artificially to impress the researcher (Webb, Campbell, Schwartz, and Sechrest, 1966). Second, the meaning of the observed behaviour may remain obscure to the researcher. A wink may be an involuntary muscle contraction, an indication of a secret being kept, a sexual come-on, and so on. We can't know what a wink means just by observing it.

To avoid reactivity and understand the meaning of behaviour, we must be able to see it in its social context and from the point of view of the people we are observing. To do that, researchers must immerse themselves in their subjects' world by learning their language and their culture in depth. When sociologists observe a social setting systematically and take part in the activities of the people they are studying, they are engaging in **participant observation** research (Lofland and Lofland, 1995).

Participant observation research helps us better understand how media violence may influence youth violence. For example, sociologists have spent time in schools where shooting rampages have taken place. They have developed a deep appreciation of the social and cultural context of school shootings by living in the neighbourhoods where they occur; interviewing students, teachers, neighbourhood residents, and shooters' family members; and studying police and psychological reports, the shooters' own writings, and other relevant materials (Harding, Fox, and Mehta, 2002; Sullivan, 2002). They have tentatively concluded that only a small number of young people—those who are weakly connected to family, school, community, and peers—seem to be susceptible to translating media violence into violent behaviour. A lack of social support allows their personal problems to become greatly magnified, and if guns are readily available, these youth are prone to using violent media messages as models for their own behaviour. In contrast, for the overwhelming majority of young people, violence in the mass media is just a source of entertainment and a fantasy outlet for emotional issues, not a template for action (Anderson, 2003).

Like other research methods, participant observation has strengths and weaknesses. On the plus side, it allows researchers to develop a deep and sympathetic understanding of the way people see the world. It is especially useful in the "exploratory" stage of research, when investigators have only a vague sense of what they are looking for and little sense of what they will discover. On the minus side, because participant observation research usually involves just one researcher in one social setting, it is difficult to know whether other researchers would measure things in the same way (this is the problem of reliability) and it is difficult to know how broadly findings can be generalized to other settings.

ANALYSIS OF EXISTING DOCUMENTS AND OFFICIAL STATISTICS

The fourth important sociological research method involves the **analysis of existing documents and official statistics**. Existing documents and official statistics are created by people other than the researcher for purposes other than sociological research.

Three types of existing documents that sociologists have mined most deeply are diaries, newspapers, and published historical works. Census data, police crime reports, and records of key life events are perhaps the most frequently used sources of official statistics. The modern census tallies the number of Canadian residents and classifies them by place of residence, race, ethnic origin, occupation, age, and hundreds of other variables. Statistics Canada publishes an annual *Uniform Crime Reporting Survey* that reports the number of crimes in Canada and classifies them by the location and type of crime, the age and sex of offenders and victims, and other variables. Statistics Canada also publishes an *Annual Compendium of Vital Statistics* that reports births, deaths, marriages, and divorces by sex, age, and so forth.

Census and crime data put into perspective the limited effect of media violence on violent behaviour. For example, researchers have discovered big differences in violent behaviour when they compare Canada and the United States. The homicide rate (the number of murders per 100 000 people) has historically been about four times as high in the United States. Yet TV programming, movies, and video games are nearly identical in the two countries, so exposure to media violence can't account for the difference. Researchers instead attribute the difference in homicide rates to the higher level of economic and social inequality and the wider availability of handguns in the United States (Government of Canada, 2002; Lenton, 1989; National Rifle Association, 2005; see Figure 1.5).

Existing documents and official statistics have several advantages over other types of data. They can save the researcher time and money because they are usually

> **analysis of existing documents and official statistics** A non-reactive research method that involves the analysis of diaries, newspapers, published historical works, and statistics produced by government agencies, all of which are created by people other than the researcher for purposes other than sociological research.

FIGURE 1.5

Gunshot Death Rate by Percentage of Households with Guns

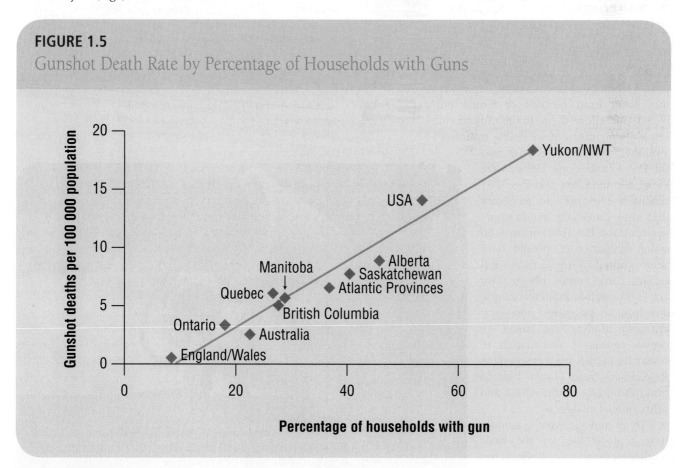

Source: Reprinted from *Accident Analysis and Prevention* vol. 29, Miller, Ted R. and Mark A. Cohen, "Costs of gunshot and cut/stab wounds in the United States, with some Canadian comparisons." p. 339. Copyright 1997, with permission from Elsevier.

available at no cost in libraries or on the World Wide Web. Official statistics usually cover entire populations and are collected by using rigorous and uniform methods, thus yielding highly reliable data. Existing documents and official statistics are especially useful for historical analysis. Finally, since the analysis of existing documents and official statistics does not require live subjects, reactivity is not a problem. The researcher's presence does not influence the subjects' behaviour.

Existing documents and official statistics also share one big disadvantage, however. They are not created with the researcher's needs in mind. In a sense, the researcher starts at stage 4 of the research cycle (data collection; refer back to Figure 1.4) and then works within the limitations imposed by available data, including biases that reflect the interests of the individuals and organizations that created them.

For example, the census under-counts Aboriginal and homeless people. Moreover, it renders certain *characteristics* of individuals invisible and denies the existence of certain groups. For example, until recently the census let people say they were from Jamaica or China but it did not allow them to identify themselves as members of a "visible minority." Similarly, the 1981 census was the first to ask people if they were living common law, and the 2001 census was the first to recognize that some Canadians live in same-sex common-law relationships. So some categories of people have been ignored by the census until recently, and some people still are. This neglect matters because government programs and government funding are based on census counts. It also matters to researchers who use census data. Researchers must always bear in mind the biases of the census and other official statistics.

By now, you should have a good idea of the basic methodological issues that confront any sociological research project. You should also know the

TABLE 1.3

Strengths and Weaknesses of Four Research Methods

Method	Strengths	Weaknesses
Experiment	High reliability; excellent for establishing cause-and-effect relationships	Low validity for many sociological problems because of the unnaturalness of the experimental setting
Survey	Good reliability; useful for establishing cause-and-effect relationships	Validity problems exist unless researchers make strong efforts to deal with them
Participant observation	Allows researchers to develop a deep and sympathetic understanding of the way people see the world; especially useful in exploratory research	Low reliability and generalizability
Analysis of existing documents and official statistics	Often inexpensive and easy to obtain; provides good coverage; useful for historical analysis; non-reactive	Often contains biases reflecting the interests of their creators and not the interests of the researcher

Source: From BRYM/LIE. *Sociology: The Points of the Compass.* © 2009 Nelson Education Ltd. Reproduced by permission. www.cengage.com/permissions.

Homelessness is an increasing focus of public policy. But public support may not be adequate if the homeless are not counted properly in the census. Statistics Canada included a count of the homeless in the 2001 census. However, because the count is based on information about the use of shelters and soup kitchens, combined with an attempt at street counts, these numbers are only rough estimates.

Shutterstock/Oleg Kozlov, Sophy Kozlova

strengths and weaknesses of some of the most widely used data collection techniques (see Table 1.3). In the remainder of this chapter, we outline what you can expect to learn from this book.

LO⁶ Your Sociological Compass

POSTINDUSTRIALISM AND GLOBALIZATION

The founders of sociology developed their ideas to help solve the great sociological puzzle of their time—the causes and consequences of the Industrial Revolution. This raises two questions: What are the great sociological puzzles of *our* time? How are today's sociologists responding to the challenges presented by the social settings in which *we* live? We devote the rest of this book to answering these questions in depth.

It would be wrong to suggest that the research of tens of thousands of sociologists around the world is animated by just a few key issues. Viewed up close, sociology today is a heterogeneous enterprise enlivened by hundreds of theoretical debates, some focused on small issues relevant to particular fields and geographical areas, others focused on big issues that seek to characterize the entire historical era for humanity as a whole. Among the big issues, two stand out. Perhaps the greatest sociological puzzles of our time are the causes and consequences of the Postindustrial Revolution and globalization.

The Postindustrial Revolution is the technology-driven shift from employment in factories to employment in offices, and the consequences of that shift for nearly all human activities (Bell, 1973; Toffler, 1990). As a result of the Postindustrial Revolution, non-manual occupations now outnumber manual occupations, and women have been drawn into the system of higher education and the paid labour force in large numbers. This shift has transformed the way we work and study, our standard of living, the way we form families, and much else.

Globalization is the process by which formerly separate economies, nation-states, and cultures are becoming tied together and people are becoming increasingly aware of their growing interdependence (Giddens, 1990: 64; Guillén, 2001). Especially in recent decades, rapid increases in the volume of international trade, travel, and communication have broken down the isolation and independence of most countries and people. Also contributing to globalization is the growth of many institutions that bind corporations, companies, and cultures together. These processes have caused people to depend more than ever on people in other countries for products, services, ideas, and even a sense of identity.

OPPORTUNITIES AND BARRIERS

Sociologists agree that globalization and postindustrialism promise many exciting opportunities to enhance our quality of life and increase human freedom. However, they also see many social-structural barriers to the realization of that promise.

For example, optimists forecast that postindustrialism will provide more opportunities for people to find creative, interesting, challenging, and rewarding work. In addition, the postindustrial era will generate more equality of opportunity, that is, better chances for *all* people to get an education, influence government policy, and find good jobs.

You will find evidence to support these claims in the following pages. We show that the average standard of living and the number of good jobs are increasing in postindustrial societies, such as Canada. Women are making rapid strides in the economy, the education system, and other institutions. Postindustrial societies, such as Canada, are characterized by a decline in discrimination against members of ethnic and racial minorities, while democracy is spreading throughout the world. The desperately poor form a declining percentage of the world's population.

Yet, as you read this book, it will also become clear that all of these seemingly happy stories have a dark underside. For example, it turns out that the number of routine jobs with low pay and few benefits is growing faster than the number of creative, high-paying jobs. By some measures, inequality between the wealthiest and poorest Canadians has grown in recent decades. An enormous opportunity gulf still separates women from men. Racism and discrimination are still a big part of our world. The absolute number of desperately poor people in the world continues to grow, as does the gap between rich and poor nations. Many people attribute the world's most serious problems to globalization. They have formed organizations and movements—some of them violent—to oppose it. In short, equality of opportunity is an undeniably attractive ideal, but it is unclear whether it is the inevitable outcome of a globalized, postindustrial society.

Optimists also say that postindustrialism and globalization increase our freedom. They have a point. In an earlier era, most people retained

Postindustrial Revolution The technology-driven shift from manufacturing to service industries and the consequences of that shift for virtually all human activities.

globalization The process by which formerly separate economies, nation-states, and cultures are becoming tied together and people are becoming increasingly aware of their growing interdependence.

their religious, ethnic, racial, and sexual identities for a lifetime, even if they were not particularly comfortable with them. They often remained in social relationships that made them unhappy. One of the major themes of this book is that many people are now freer to construct their identities and form social relationships in ways that suit them. To a greater degree than ever before, it is possible to *choose* who you want to be, with whom you want to associate, and how you want to associate with them. The postindustrial/global era frees people from traditional constraints by encouraging virtually instant global communication, international migration, greater acceptance of sexual diversity and a variety of family forms, the growth of ethnically and racially diverse cities, and so forth. For instance, in the past people often stayed in marriages even if they were dissatisfied with them. Families often involved a father working in the paid labour force and a mother keeping house and raising children without pay. Today, people are freer to end unhappy marriages and create family structures that are more suited to their individual needs.

Again, however, we must face the less rosy aspects of postindustrialism and globalization. In the following chapters, we point out how increased freedom is experienced only within certain limits and how social diversity is limited by a strong push to conformity in some spheres of life. For example, we can choose from a far wider variety of consumer products than ever before, but consumerism (that is, seeing yourself as the sum of the products you consume) seems compulsory. Moreover, consumerism threatens the natural environment. Large, impersonal bureaucracies and standardized products and services dehumanize both staff and customers. The tastes and the profit motive of giant mass media companies, most of them U.S.-owned, govern our cultural consumption and threaten the survival of some distinctive national cultures. Powerful interests are trying to shore up the traditional nuclear family even though it does not suit some people. As these examples show, the push to uniformity counters the trend toward growing social diversity. Postindustrialism and globalization may make us freer in some ways, but they also place new constraints on us.

WHERE DO YOU FIT IN?

Our overview of themes in this book drives home the fact that we live in an era "suspended between extraordinary opportunity . . . and global catastrophe" (Giddens, 1987: 166). Giving in to despair and apathy is one possible response to these complex issues, but it is not a response that humans often favour. If it were our nature to give up hope, we would still be sitting around half-naked in the mud outside a cave. People are more inclined to look for ways of improving their lives, and this period of human history is full of opportunities to do so. We have, for example, advanced to the point at which for the first time we have the means to feed and educate everyone in the world. Similarly, it now seems possible to erode some of the inequalities that have always been the major source of human conflict.

Sociology offers useful advice on how to achieve these goals—for sociology is more than just an intellectual exercise. It is also an applied science with practical, everyday uses. Sociologists teach at all levels, from high school to graduate school. They conduct research for governments, colleges and universities, corporations, the criminal justice system, public opinion firms, management consulting firms, trade unions, social service agencies, international non-governmental organizations, and private research and testing firms. They are often involved in the formulation of public policy, the creation of laws and regulations by organizations and governments. This is because sociologists are trained to see not just what is but also what is possible.

One way to see the benefits of a sociological education is to compile a list of some of the famous practical idealists who studied sociology in university. That list includes several former heads of state, among them President Fernando Cardoso of Brazil, President Tomas Masaryk of Czechoslovakia, Prime Minister Edward Seaga of Jamaica, and President Ronald Reagan of the United States. At least four Nobel Prize winners earned sociology degrees: Canadian-born novelist Saul Bellow, American civil rights leader Martin Luther King, Jr., American social reformer Jane Addams, and American peace activist Emily Balch. Michelle Obama graduated with a sociology degree. Former Canadian senator, vice-president of the Liberal Party of Canada, and president of Toronto's York University Lorna Marsden is a sociologist. Anthony Giddens, former director and now emeritus professor of the prestigious London School of Economics and adviser to former British Prime Minister Tony Blair, also holds a doctorate in sociology. So do Martin Goldfarb, CEO of Goldfarb Consultants International, and Donna Dasko, senior vice-president of Environics; they head two of Canada's leading public opinion firms with offices and affiliates around the world. Alex Himelfarb, former clerk of the Privy Council (Canada's top civil servant), former Canadian ambassador to Italy, and now director of the Glendon School of Public and International Affairs at York University, holds a sociology Ph.D. too. British Columbia native Steve Nash of the Phoenix Suns is widely considered the best team player in professional basketball today. His agent claims he is "the most color-blind person I've ever known" (Robbins, 2005). Arguably, Nash's sociology degree contributes to his team-building ability and his performance on the court by helping him to better understand the importance of groups and diverse social conditions in shaping human behaviour.

In sum, we encourage you to consider this book an invitation to explore your society's, and your own, possibilities. We don't provide easy answers. However, we are sure that if you engage with the questions we raise, you will find that sociology can help you figure out where you fit into society and how you can make society fit you.

Note

1. Some sociologists also distinguish "mesostructures," social relations that link microstructures and macrostructures.

2 Culture

Culture as Problem Solving

If you follow sports or participate in them, you probably know that many athletes perform little rituals before each game. For instance, Canadian hockey legend Wayne Gretzky never got his hair cut while playing on the road because the last time he did, his team lost. He always put his equipment on in the same order: left shin pad, left stocking, right shin pad, right stocking, pants, left skate, right skate, shoulder pads, left elbow pad, right elbow pad, and, finally, jersey—with the right side tucked into his pants. During warm-up, he would always shoot his first puck far to the right of the goal. When he went back to the dressing room, he would drink a Diet Coke, a glass of ice water, a Gatorade, and another Diet Coke—in that order (Arace, 2000; "Mad about Hockey," 2002).

Like soldiers going off to battle, undergraduate students about to write final exams, and other people in high-stress situations, athletes invent practices to help them stop worrying and focus on the job at hand. Some wear a lucky piece of jewellery or item of clothing. Others say special words or a quick prayer. Still others cross themselves. And then there are those who engage in more elaborate rituals. For example, two sociologists interviewed 300 university students about their superstitious practices before final exams. One student felt she would do well only if she ate a sausage and two eggs sunny-side up on the morning of each exam. She had to place the sausage vertically on the left side of her plate and the eggs to the right of the sausage so they formed the "100" percent she was aiming for (Albas and Albas, 1989). Of course, the ritual had a more direct influence on her cholesterol level than on her grades. Yet indirectly it may have had the desired effect: if it helped to relieve her anxiety and relax her, she may have done better on her exams.

Sociologists define **culture** broadly as all the ideas, practices, and material objects that people create to deal with real-life problems. For example, when the university student invented the ritual of preparing for exams by eating sausage and eggs arranged just so, she was beginning to create

> **culture** The sum of practices, languages, symbols, beliefs, values, ideologies, and material objects that people create to deal with real-life problems.

LEARNING OBJECTIVES:

LO¹ Culture is the sum of shared ideas, practices, and material objects that people create to adapt to, and thrive in, their environments.

LO² Humans have thrived in their environments because of their unique ability to think abstractly, cooperate with one another, and make tools.

LO³ In some respects, the development of culture makes people freer. For example, culture has become more diversified and consensus has declined in many areas of life, allowing people more choice in how they live.

LO⁴ In other respects, the development of culture puts limits on who we can become. For example, the culture of buying consumer goods has become a virtually compulsory pastime. Increasingly, therefore, people define themselves by the goods they purchase.

culture in the sociological sense. Her practice helped her deal with the real-life problem of anxiety. Similarly, tools help people solve the problem of how to plant crops and build houses. Religion helps people give meaning to life and come to terms with death. Tools and religion are also elements of culture because they, too, help people solve real-life problems.

Sociologists call opera, ballet, art, and similar activities high culture. They distinguish high culture from popular culture or mass culture. While popular or mass culture is consumed by all classes, high culture tends to be consumed mainly by upper classes.

Note that religion, technology, and many other elements of culture differ from the superstitions of athletes in an important way: superstitions may be unique to the individuals who create them. Religion and technology are widely shared. They are even passed on from one generation to the next. How does cultural sharing take place? By means of communication and learning. Thus, culture is socially transmitted and it requires a society to persist. (A society is a number of people who interact, usually in a defined territory, and share a culture.) We conclude that culture is composed of the socially transmitted ideas, practices, and material objects that enable people to adapt to, and thrive in, their environments.

high culture Culture consumed mainly by upper classes.

popular culture (or mass culture) Culture consumed by all classes.

society A number of people who interact, usually in a defined territory, and share a culture.

Culture can solve practical problems. Although some sports rituals are undoubtedly stranger than others, athletes (like Wayne Gretzky, shown here) often develop superstitions to help them manage stress.

The Canadian Press (AP Photo/Ron Frehm)

LO² The Origins and Components of Culture

You can appreciate the importance of culture for human survival by considering the predicament of early humans about 100 000 years ago. They lived in harsh natural environments. They had poor physical endowments, being slower runners and weaker fighters than many other animals. Yet, despite these disadvantages,

Nicholas Moore/Shutterstock

Symbols are things that carry particular meanings. Alphabets, mathematical notations, and signs are all symbols. Symbols allow us to classify experience and generalize from it. For example, we recognize that we can sit on many objects but that only some of those objects have four legs, a back, and space for one person. We distinguish the latter from other objects by giving them a name: chairs. By the time babies reach the end of their first year, they have heard that word repeatedly and understand that it refers to a certain class of objects.

NORMS AND VALUES

Cooperation is the second main tool in the human cultural survival kit. It is the capacity to create a complex social life by sharing resources and working together. This feat is accomplished by establishing norms, or generally accepted ways of doing things, and *values*, or ideas about what is right and wrong, good and bad, beautiful and ugly. For example, family members cooperate to raise children, and in the process, they develop and apply norms and values about which child-rearing practices are appropriate and desirable. Note, however, that different times and places give rise to different norms and values. In Canada today, parents might ground children for swearing, but in pioneer days, parents would typically "beat the devil out of them." As this example suggests, by analyzing how people cooperate and produce norms and values, we can learn much about what distinguishes one culture from another.

they survived. More than that, they prospered and came to dominate nature. Domination was possible largely because humans were the smartest creatures around. Their sophisticated brains enabled them to create cultural survival kits of enormous complexity and flexibility. These cultural survival kits contained three main tools. Each tool was a uniquely human talent, and each gave rise to a different element of culture.

SYMBOLS

The first tool in the human cultural survival kit was abstraction, the capacity to create general ideas or ways of thinking that are not linked to particular instances. Symbols, for example, are one important type of idea.

elfipics/Shutterstock

abstraction The human capacity to create general ideas or ways of thinking that are not linked to particular instances.

symbol Anything that carries a particular meaning, including the components of language, mathematical notations, and signs. Symbols allow us to classify experience and generalize from it.

cooperation The human capacity to create a complex social life by sharing resources and working together.

norms Generally accepted ways of doing things.

By acquiring specialized skills, people are able to accomplish things that no person could possibly do alone.

PRODUCTION, MATERIAL CULTURE, AND NON-MATERIAL CULTURE

production The human capacity to make and use tools. It improves our ability to take what we want from nature.

material culture The tools and techniques that enable people to accomplish tasks.

non-material culture Symbols, norms, and other non-tangible elements of culture.

folkway The least important norms—the norms that evoke the least severe punishment when violated.

mores Core norms that most people believe are essential for the survival of their group or their society.

taboos The strongest norms. When someone violates a taboo, it causes revulsion in the community and punishment is severe.

Production is the third main tool in the human cultural survival kit. It involves making and using tools and techniques that improve our ability to take what we want from nature. Such tools and techniques are known as **material culture** because they are tangible, whereas the symbols, norms, values, and other elements of **non-material culture** are intangible. All animals take from nature to subsist, and an ape may sometimes use a rock to break another object. But only humans are sufficiently intelligent and dexterous to make tools and use them to produce everything from food to computers. Understood in this sense, production is a uniquely human activity.

Table 2.1 illustrates each of the basic human capacities and their cultural offshoots in the field of medicine. As in medicine, so in all fields of human activity: abstraction, cooperation, and production give rise to specific kinds of ideas, norms, and elements of material culture.

THREE TYPES OF NORMS: FOLKWAYS, MORES, AND TABOOS

If a man walks down a busy street wearing nothing on the top half of his body, he is violating a **folkway**. If he walks down the street wearing nothing on the bottom half of his body, he is violating a **more** (the Latin word for "custom," pronounced MORE-ay). Folkways are norms that specify social *preferences*. Mores are norms that specify social *requirements*. People are usually punished when they violate norms, but the punishment is usually minor if the norm is a folkway. Some onlookers will raise their eyebrows at the shirtless man. Others will shake their head in disapproval. In contrast, the punishment for walking down the street without pants is bound to be moderately harsh. Someone is bound to call the police, probably sooner than later (Sumner, 1940 [1907]). The strongest and most central norms, however, are **taboos**. When someone violates a taboo, it causes revulsion in the community, and punishment is severe. Incest is one of the most widespread taboos.

TABLE 2.1

The Building Blocks of Culture

The human capacity for . . .	Abstraction	Cooperation	Production
Gives rise to these elements of culture . . .	Ideas	Norms and values	Material culture
In medicine, for example . . .	Theories are developed about how a certain drug might cure a disease	Experiments are conducted to test whether the drug works as expected	Treatments are developed on the basis of the experimental results

Source: Adapted from Bierstedt (1963). Photos, left to right: Zoran Vukmanov Simokov/Shutterstock; Alexander Raths/Shutterstock; Yuri Arcurs/Shutterstock

LANGUAGE AND THE SAPIR-WHORF THESIS

Language is one of the most important parts of any culture—some would say *the* most important part. A language is a system of symbols strung together to communicate thought. Equipped with language, we can share understandings, pass experience and knowledge from one generation to the next, and make plans for the future. In short, language allows culture to develop. Consequently, sociologists commonly think of language as a cultural invention that distinguishes humans from other animals.

In the 1930s, Edward Sapir and Benjamin Lee Whorf proposed an influential argument about the connection between experience, thought, and language. It came to be known as the Sapir-Whorf thesis (see Figure 2.1). According to the Sapir-Whorf thesis, we form concepts about things that we experience (path 1 to 2) and develop language to express our concepts (path 2 to 3). Controversially, however, the Sapir-Whorf thesis holds that language itself then influences how we see the world (path 3 to 1).

language A system of symbols strung together to communicate thought.

Sapir-Whorf thesis Holds that we experience certain things in our environment and form concepts about those things. We then develop language to express our concepts. Finally, language itself influences how we see the world.

Whorf saw speech patterns as "interpretations of experience" (Whorf, 1956: 137), and this view seems uncontroversial. The Garo of Burma, a rice-growing people, distinguish many types of rice. Nomadic Arabs have more than 20 different words for *camel* (Sternberg, 1998: 305). Verbal distinctions among types of rice and camels are necessary for different groups of people because these objects are important in their environment. As a matter of necessity, they distinguish among many different types of what we may regard as "the same" object. Similarly, terms that apparently refer to the same things or people may change to reflect a changing reality. For example, a committee used to be headed by a "chairman." When women entered the paid labour force in large numbers in the 1960s and some of them became committee heads, the term changed to "chairperson" or simply "chair." In such cases, we see clearly how the environment or our experience influences language.

The controversial part of the Sapir-Whorf thesis is path 3 to 1. In what sense does language *in and of itself* influence the way we experience the world? In the first wave of studies based on the Sapir-Whorf thesis, researchers focused on whether speakers of different languages perceive colour in different ways. By the 1970s, researchers had concluded that they do not. People who speak different languages may have a different number of basic colour terms, but everyone with normal vision is able to see the full visible spectrum. The Russian language has two words for *blue*, whereas the English language has only one. This does not mean that English speakers are handicapped in their ability to distinguish shades of blue.

Source: From BRYM/LIE. *Sociology: The Points of the Compass.* © 2009 Nelson Education Ltd. Reproduced by permission. www.cengage.com/permissions.

FIGURE 2.1
The Sapir-Whorf Thesis

Experience

1

2

3

Verbalization (language)

Conceptualization (thought)

Do Germans and Spaniards see keys differently? *Key* is a masculine noun in German and feminine in Spanish.

Alex Staroseltsev/Shutterstock

In the 1980s and 1990s, researchers found that language itself can affect perception. For example, the German word for *key* is masculine, whereas the Spanish word for *key* is feminine. When German and Spanish speakers are asked to describe keys, German speakers tend to use words like *hard*, *heavy*, and *jagged*, whereas Spanish speakers use words such as *lovely*, *shiny*, and *shaped*. Apparently, the gender of the noun in and of itself influences how people see the thing to which the noun refers (Minkel, 2002). Still, the degree to which language itself influences thought is a matter of controversy. Some men use terms like *fox*, *babe*, *bitch*, *ho*, and *doll* to refer to women. These terms are deeply offensive to many people. They certainly reflect underlying inequalities between women and men. Some people assert that these terms *in and of themselves* influence people to think of women simply as sexual objects, but social scientists have yet to demonstrate the degree to which words influence people.

Culture as Freedom and Constraint

A FUNCTIONALIST ANALYSIS OF CULTURE: CULTURE AND ETHNOCENTRISM

Despite its central importance in human life, culture is often invisible. That is, people tend to take their own culture for granted. It usually seems so sensible and natural they rarely think about it. In contrast, people are often startled when confronted by cultures other than their own. The ideas, norms, values, and techniques of other cultures frequently seem odd, irrational, and even inferior.

Judging another culture exclusively by the standards of our own is known as ethnocentrism (see the Sociology at the Movies box on the next page). Ethnocentrism impairs sociological analysis. This can be illustrated by Marvin Harris's (1974) functionalist analysis of a practice that seems bizarre to many Westerners: cow worship among Hindu peasants in India.

Hindu peasants refuse to slaughter cattle and eat beef because, for them, the cow is a religious symbol of life. Pinup calendars throughout rural India portray beautiful women with the bodies of fat, white cows, milk jetting out of each teat. Cows are permitted to wander the streets, defecate on the sidewalks, and stop to chew their cud in busy intersections or on railroad tracks, forcing traffic to a complete halt. In Madras, police stations maintain fields where stray cows that have fallen ill can graze and be nursed back to health. The government even runs old-age homes for cows, where dry and decrepit cattle are kept free of charge. All this special care seems mysterious to most Westerners, for it takes place amid poverty and hunger that could presumably be alleviated if only the peasants would slaughter their "useless" cattle for food instead of squandering scarce resources to feed and protect these animals.

According to Harris (1974: 3–32), however, ethnocentrism misleads many Western observers. Cow worship, it turns out, is an economically rational practice in rural India. For one thing, Indian peasants can't afford tractors, so cows are needed to give birth to oxen, which are in high demand for plowing. For another, the cows produce hundreds of millions of kilograms of recoverable manure, about half of which is used as fertilizer and half as a cooking fuel. With oil, coal, and wood in short supply, and with the peasants unable to afford chemical fertilizers, cow dung is, well, a godsend. What is more, cows in India don't cost much to maintain because they eat mostly food that is not fit for human consumption. And they represent an important source of protein as well as a livelihood for members of low-ranking castes, who have the right to dispose of the bodies of dead cattle. These "untouchables" eat beef and form the workforce of India's large leather craft industry. The protection of cows by means of cow worship is thus a perfectly sensible and highly efficient economic practice. It seems irrational only when judged by the standards of Western agribusiness.

Harris's (1974) analysis of cow worship in rural India is interesting for two reasons. First, it illustrates how functionalist theory can illuminate otherwise mysterious social practices. You will recall from Chapter 1 the functionalist claim that social structures have consequences that make social order possible. We may now add that some of those consequences are manifest (intended and easily observed), while others are latent (unintended and less obvious; Merton, 1968 [1949]). Harris discovers that cow worship performs a range of latent functions, thus showing how a particular social practice has unintended consequences that make social order possible.

We can also draw an important lesson about ethnocentrism from Harris's analysis. If you refrain from judging other societies by the standards of your own, you will have taken an important first step toward developing a sociological understanding of culture.

ethnocentrism The tendency to judge other cultures exclusively by the standards of your own.

manifest functions Visible and intended effects of social structures.

latent functions The invisible and unintended effects of social structures.

Borat: Cultural Learnings of America for Make Benefit Glorious Nation of Kazakhstan

Borat Sagdiyev (Sacha Baron Cohen) in Borat

The Canadian Press/TM & © 20th Century Fox/The Everett Collection

Borat is a journalist from Kazakhstan who visits the United States so he can learn about American culture and return home with useful lessons. The movie's humour turns on the apparent differences between Borat's culture and that of his audience and the people he meets. His values, beliefs, and norms seem deeply offensive to the Americans he encounters. Since Borat is capable of seeing the world only from his own cultural viewpoint, the movie at one level is a story of ethnocentrism gone mad.

We quickly discover that Kazakhs are anti-Semites, racists, homophobes, and sexists. However, Borat directs many of our biggest laughs against Americans. At one point he secures the agreement of a rodeo organizer in Salem, Virginia, to let him sing the national anthem before the show begins. Borat first makes a little speech: "My name Borat, I come from Kazakhstan. Can I say first, we support your war of terror. [applause and cheers] May we show our support to our boys in Iraq. [*applause and cheers*] May U.S. and A. kill every single terrorist! [*applause and cheers*] May George Bush drink the blood of every single man, woman, and child of Iraq! [*applause and cheers*] May you destroy their country so that for the next 1000 years not even a single lizard will survive in their desert! [*applause and cheers*]" After thus highlighting the inhumanity of his audience, Borat sings the Kazakh national anthem in English to the tune of the United States national anthem:

Kazakhstan is the greatest country in the world.

All other countries are run by little girls.

Kazakhstan is number one exporter of potassium.

Other Central Asian countries have inferior potassium.

Kazakhstan is the greatest country in the world.

All other countries is the home of the gays.

To the suggestion that another country exceeds the United States in glory, the audience responds with jeers and boos that grow so loud, one fears for Borat's life. In this and other scenes, the movie forces us to conclude that American culture is as biased in its own way as Kazakh culture allegedly is.

Is Borat just one long prejudiced rant against Americans, Jews, Kazakhs, blacks, gays, women, and so on? Some people think so. But that opinion is not credible for two reasons. First, it is inconsistent with who Sacha Baron Cohen is. He is a well-educated liberal who completed a degree in history at Cambridge and wrote his thesis on the civil rights movement in the United States. And he is a Jew who strongly identifies with his ethnic heritage. (One of the movie's biggest and largely unappreciated jokes is that Borat speaks mostly Hebrew to his sidekick, Azamat Bagatov [Ken Davitian].)

Borat certainly is one long and very funny rant, but the real objects of its satire are the world's racists, sexists, anti-Semites, and homophobes, regardless of their race, creed, or national origin. The deeper message of Borat is anything but ethnocentric: respect for human dignity is a value that rises above all cultures, and people who think otherwise deserve to be laughed at.

Critical Thinking Questions

- Does Borat help you see the prejudices of other people more clearly?
- Does Borat help you see your own prejudices more clearly?
- Borat talks and acts like a bigot from the opening title to the closing credits. Do you think that the expression of bigotry is inherently offensive and should always be avoided? Or do you believe that the satirical expression of bigotry can usefully reveal hidden prejudices?

Many Westerners find the Indian practice of cow worship bizarre, but it performs several useful economic functions and is, in that sense, entirely rational. By viewing cow worship exclusively as an outsider (or, for that matter, exclusively as an insider), we fail to see its rational core.

LO³ Culture as Freedom

Culture has two faces. First, culture provides us with an opportunity to exercise our *freedom*. We create elements of culture in our everyday life to solve practical problems and express our needs, hopes, joys, and fears.

However, creating culture is just like any other act of construction in that we need raw materials to get the job done. The raw materials for the culture we create consist of cultural elements that either existed before we were born or that other people have created since our birth. We may put these elements together in ways that produce something genuinely new. But we have no other well to drink from, so existing culture puts limits on what we can think and do. In that sense, culture *constrains* us. This is culture's second face. In the rest of this chapter, we take a close look at both faces of culture.

SYMBOLIC INTERACTIONISM AND CULTURAL PRODUCTION

Until the 1960s, many sociologists argued that culture is a "reflection" of society. Using the language introduced in Chapter 1, we can say that they regarded culture as a dependent variable. Harris's (1974) analysis of people in rural India certainly fits that mould. In Harris's view, the social necessity of protecting cows caused the cultural belief that cows are holy.

In recent decades, the symbolic interactionist tradition we discussed in Chapter 1 has influenced many sociologists of culture. Symbolic interactionists regard culture as an *independent* variable. In their view, people do not just accept culture passively; we are not empty vessels into which society pours a defined assortment of beliefs, symbols, and values. Instead, we produce and interpret culture, creatively fashioning it to suit our diverse and changing needs.

The symbolic interactionist idea that people creatively produce and interpret culture implies that, to a degree, we are at liberty to choose how culture influences us. Let us linger a moment on the question of why we enjoy more cultural freedom than ever before.

CULTURAL DIVERSITY

One reason we are increasingly able to choose how culture influences us is that Canadian society has diversified. Historically, Europe provided the great bulk of Canadian immigrants, but that started to change in the 1960s. Today, Europe and the United States supply only about 20 percent of Canadian immigrants while Asia and Africa supply nearly 70 percent. The four top source countries for immigrants are China, India, the Philippines, and Pakistan (Citizenship and Immigration Canada, 2005: 24). As a result, Canada is now a more heterogeneous society, racially and ethnically, than it has ever been. Members of visible minorities composed 4 percent of Canada's population in 1981 and 13 percent in 2001, and are projected to compose 19 percent in 2016 (Statistics Canada, 1998a: 75, 2003a).

The cultural diversification of Canadian society is evident in all aspects of life, from the growing popularity of Latino music, through the increasing influence of Asian design in clothing and architecture, to the ever-broadening international assortment of foods consumed

Grosse Île on the St. Lawrence River was Quebec's quarantine station and the main point of entry for immigrants coming to Canada from 1832 to 1937. In 1909, the Celtic Cross memorial was erected to honour the memory of Irish immigrants who perished from typhus between 1847 and 1848, during the Great Irish Potato Famine.

by most Canadians. Marriage between people of different ethnic groups is widespread, and interracial marriage is increasingly accepted. At the political level, however, cultural diversity has become a source of conflict. This is nowhere more evident than in the debates that have surfaced recently concerning curricula in the Canadian educational system.

MULTICULTURALISM

Although each province and territory in Canada holds jurisdiction over education, it was common until recent decades for schools across Canada to stress the common elements of our culture, history, and society. Students learned the historical importance of the "charter groups"—the English and the French—in Canada's history. School curricula typically neglected the contributions of non-white, non-French, and non-English people to Canada's historical, literary, artistic, and scientific development. Moreover, students learned little about the less savoury aspects of Canadian history, including Canada's racist immigration policies that sought to preserve Canada's "English stock" by restricting or denying entry to certain groups (see Chapter 7, Race and Ethnicity). In general, history books were written from the perspective of the victors, not the vanquished.

For the past few decades, advocates of multiculturalism have argued that school, college, and university curricula should present a more balanced picture of Canadian history, culture, and society—one that better reflects the country's ethnic and racial diversity in the past and its growing ethnic and racial diversity today (Henry, Tator, Mattis, and Rees, 2001; James, 2003). In the words of

one group of experts, "The purpose of schooling must be to 'empower' [minority groups] . . . , to give them the ability to participate fully in struggles, large and small, to gain respect, dignity, and power" (Gaskell, McLaren, and Novogrodsky, 1995: 105). Advocates of multiculturalism suggest that we must bring our educational system in line with Canada's status as the world's first officially multicultural society. They point out that, in launching its multiculturalism policy in 1971, the government declared that Canada, although officially bilingual, has no "official" culture—that is, none of the distinguishable cultures in Canada take precedence over the others. Moreover, with the passage of the Canadian Multiculturalism Act in 1988, the government confirmed its commitment to recognizing all Canadians "as full and equal participants in Canadian society." Multiculturalists conclude that to the extent that school curricula are culturally biased, they fail to provide students with the type of education a country devoted to multiculturalism must demand.

Most critics of multiculturalism do not argue against teaching cultural diversity. What they fear is that multicultural education is being taken too far (Fekete, 1994). Specifically, they say multiculturalism has three negative consequences:

1. Critics believe that multicultural education hurts minority students by forcing them to spend too much time on non-core subjects. To get ahead in the world, they say, students need to be skilled in English, French, science, and math. By taking time away from these subjects, multicultural education impedes the success of minority group members in the work world. (Multiculturalists counter that minority students develop pride and self-esteem from a curriculum that stresses cultural diversity. They argue that this helps minority students get ahead in the work world.)

2. Critics also believe that multicultural education causes political disunity and results in more interethnic and interracial conflict. Therefore, they want school and postsecondary curricula to stress the common elements of the national experience and highlight Europe's contribution to our culture. (Multiculturalists reply that political unity and interethnic and interracial harmony simply maintain inequality in Canadian society. Conflict, they

multiculturalism Policy that reflects Canada's ethnic and racial diversity in the past and enhances its ethnic and racial diversity today.

The Canadian Press (Steve White)

Canada continues to diversify culturally.

say, although unfortunate, is often necessary to achieve equality between majority and minority groups.)

3. Finally, critics of multiculturalism complain that it encourages the growth of cultural relativism. **Cultural relativism** is the opposite of ethnocentrism. It is the belief that all cultures and all cultural practices have equal value. The trouble with this view is that some cultures oppose the most deeply held values of most Canadians. Other cultures promote practices that most Canadians consider inhumane. Critics argue that to the degree it promotes cultural relativism, a truly multicultural system of education might encourage respect for practices that are abhorrent to most Canadians. (Multiculturalists reply that cultural relativism need not be taken to such an extreme. *Moderate* cultural relativism encourages tolerance, and it should be promoted.)

cultural relativism The belief that all cultures have equal value.

rights revolution The process by which socially excluded groups have struggled to win equal rights under the law and in practice.

A CONFLICT ANALYSIS OF CULTURE: THE RIGHTS REVOLUTION

What are the social roots of cultural diversity and multiculturalism? Conflict theory suggests where we can look for an answer. Recall from Chapter 1 the central argument of conflict theory: social life is an ongoing struggle between more and less advantaged groups. Privileged groups try to maintain their advantages while subordinate groups struggle to increase theirs. And sure enough, if we probe beneath cultural diversification and multiculturalism, we find what has been called the **rights revolution**, the process by which socially excluded groups have struggled to win equal rights under the law and in practice.

After the outburst of nationalism, racism, and genocidal behaviour among the combatants in World War II, the United Nations proclaimed the Universal Declaration of Human Rights in 1948. It recognized the "inherent dignity" and "equal and inalienable rights of all members of the human family" and held that "every organ of society" should "strive by teaching and education to promote respect for these rights and freedoms and by progressive measures, national and international, to secure their universal and

effective recognition and observance" (United Nations, 1998). Fanned by such sentiment, the rights revolution was in full swing by the 1960s. Today, women's rights, minority rights, gay and lesbian rights, the rights of people with special needs, constitutional rights, and language rights are all part of our political discourse. Because of the rights revolution, democracy has been widened and deepened. The rights revolution is by no means finished. Many categories of people are still discriminated against socially, politically, and economically. However, in much of the world, all categories of people now participate more fully than ever before in the life of their societies (Ignatieff, 2000).

The rights revolution raises some difficult issues. For example, some members of groups that have suffered extraordinarily high levels of discrimination historically, such as Aboriginal Canadians, Chinese Canadians, and others, have demanded reparations in the form of money, symbolic gestures, land, and political autonomy (see Chapter 7, Race and Ethnicity). Much controversy surrounds the extent to which today's citizens are obligated to compensate past injustices.

Such problems notwithstanding, the rights revolution is here to stay and it affects our culture profoundly. Specifically, the rights revolution fragments Canadian culture by (1) legitimizing the grievances of groups that were formerly excluded from full social participation, and (2) renewing their pride in their identity and heritage. Our history books, our literature, our music, our use of languages, and our very sense of what it means to be Canadian have diversified culturally. White, male, heterosexual property owners of northern European origin are still disproportionately influential in Canada, but our culture is no longer dominated by them in the way that it was just half a century ago.

FROM DIVERSITY TO GLOBALIZATION

The cultural diversification we witness today is not evident in preliterate or tribal societies. In such societies, cultural beliefs and practices are virtually the same for all group members. For example, many tribal societies organize **rites of passage**. These cultural ceremonies mark the transition from one stage of life to another (e.g., from childhood to adulthood) or from life to death (e.g., funerals). They involve elaborate procedures, such as body painting and carefully orchestrated chants and movements. They are conducted in public, and no variation from prescribed practice is allowed. Culture is homogeneous (Durkheim, 1976 [1915/1912]).

In contrast, pre-industrial Western Europe and North America were rocked by artistic, religious, scientific, and political forces that fragmented culture. The Renaissance, the Protestant Reformation, the Scientific Revolution,

the French and American revolutions—between the fourteenth and eighteenth centuries, all these movements involved people questioning old ways of seeing and doing things. Science placed skepticism about established authority at the very heart of its method. Political revolution proved nothing was ordained about who should rule and how they should do so. Religious dissent ensured that the Catholic Church would no longer be the supreme interpreter of God's will in the eyes of all Christians. Authority and truth became divided as never before.

Cultural fragmentation picked up steam during industrialization, as the variety of occupational roles grew and new political and intellectual movements crystallized. Its pace is quickening again today as a result of globalization. *Globalization*, as defined in Chapter 1, is the process by which formerly separate economies, nation-states, and cultures are becoming tied together and people are becoming increasingly aware of their growing interdependence.

One of the most important roots of globalization is the expansion of international trade and investment. Even the most patriotic of Canadians has probably dined at McDonald's—and even a business as "American" as McDonald's now reaps most of its profits from outside the United States. At the same time, members of different ethnic and racial groups are migrating and coming into sustained contact with one another. Influential transnational organizations, such as the International Monetary

> **rites of passage** Cultural ceremonies that mark the transition from one stage of life to another (e.g., baptisms, confirmations, weddings) or from life to death (funerals).

McDonald's ensures that globalization has a local taste. Pictured here—the rice burger, served in Taiwan.

Used with permission from McDonald's Corporation

NEL

CHAPTER 2 Culture **43**

Fund, the World Bank, the European Union, Greenpeace, and Amnesty International, are increasing in number. Relatively inexpensive international travel and communication make contact among people from diverse cultures routine. The mass media make *Who Wants to Be a Millionaire* as well known in Mumbai as in Montreal. MTV brings music to the world via MTV Canada, MTV Latino, MTV Brazil, MTV Europe, MTV Asia, MTV Japan, MTV Mandarin, and MTV India (Hanke, 1998). In short, globalization destroys political, economic, and cultural isolation, bringing people together in what Canadian media analyst Marshall McLuhan (1964) first called a "global village." Because of globalization, people are less obliged to accept the culture into which they are born and freer to combine elements of culture from a wide variety of historical periods and geographical settings. Globalization is a schoolboy in New Delhi listening to Usher on his MP3 player as he rushes to pull on his Levis, wolf down a bowl of Kellogg's Basmati Flakes, and say goodbye to his parents in Hindi because he's late for his English-language school.

ASPECTS OF POSTMODERNISM

Some sociologists think that so much cultural fragmentation and reconfiguration has taken place in the last few decades that a new term is needed to characterize the culture of our times: postmodernism. Scholars often characterize the last half of the nineteenth century and the first half of the twentieth century as the era of modernity. During this hundred-year period, belief in the inevitability of progress, respect for authority, and consensus around core values characterized much of Western culture. In contrast, postmodern culture involves an eclectic mix of elements from different times and places, the erosion of authority, and the decline of consensus around core values. Let us consider each of these aspects of postmodernism in turn.

postmodernism Culture characterized by an eclectic mix of cultural elements from different times and places, the erosion of authority, and the decline of consensus around core values.

Blending Culture

An eclectic mix of elements from different times and places is the first aspect of postmodernism. In the postmodern era, it is easier to create individualized belief systems and practices by blending facets of different cultures and historical periods. Consider religion. Although the vast majority of Canadians say they believe in God and continue to identify themselves as Christians, increasing numbers now identify themselves as adherents of Eastern non-Christian religions or as having "no religion" (see Chapter 10, Religion and Education). In addition, Canadians are increasingly showing a willingness to feast from a religious buffet that combines a conventional menu with a wide assortment of other supernatural beliefs and practices, including astrology, tarot, New Age mysticism, psychic phenomena, and communication with the dead (Bibby, 1987: 233, 2001: 195; see Table 2.2). Simply put, we have many more ways to worship than we used to. For example, a person can easily construct a personalized religion involving, say, belief in the divinity of Jesus *and* yoga (Melton, 1996). In the words of one journalist, "In an age when we trust ourselves to assemble our own investment portfolios and cancer therapies, why not our religious beliefs?" (Creedon, 1998). Individuals thus draw on religions much like consumers shop in a mall. Meanwhile, churches, synagogues, and other religious institutions have diversified their menus to appeal to the spiritual, leisure, and social needs of religious consumers and retain their loyalties in the competitive market for congregants and parishioners (Finke and Stark, 1992).

Erosion of Authority

The erosion of authority is the second aspect of postmodernism. Half a century ago, Canadians were more likely than they are today to defer to authority in the family, schools, politics, medicine, and so forth. As the social bases of authority and truth have multiplied, however,

we have become more likely to challenge authority. Authorities once widely respected, including parents, physicians, and politicians, are now held in lower regard by many people. In the 1950s, Robert Young played the firm, wise, and always-present father in the TV hit *Father Knows Best*. Fifty years later, Homer Simpson plays a fool in *The Simpsons*. Compared with Canadian teenagers in the first decade of the twenty-first century, Canadian teenagers in the 1980s—merely two decades ago—were more likely to express confidence in our police, our politicians, our court systems, and the leaders of religious organizations (Bibby, 2001: 193). Today, both young and old Canadians are likely to be critical of social institutions, such as religious organizations, that previously enjoyed special veneration. The rise of Homer Simpson

TABLE 2.2
Beliefs across Generations, Canada, 2005

"I believe . . ."	Grandparents (%)	Parents (%)	Younger Adults (%)
Conventional			
God exists	83	81	81
God or a higher power cares about you	68	62	67
Jesus was the Divine Son of God	70	66	63
In life after death	63	65	75
Have felt the presence God/higher power	50	47	50
Less Conventional			
In near-death experiences	60	75	74
In ESP	53	64	52
Personally have experienced precognition	45	57	54
Can have contact with the spirit world	33	48	56
In astrology	28	35	36

Source: Reginald W. Bibby, Project Canada 2005 National Survey.

A hallmark of postmodernism is the combining of cultural elements from different times and places. Architect I. M. Pei unleashed a storm of protest when his 22-metre glass pyramid became an entrance to the Louvre in Paris. It created a postmodern nightmare in the eyes of some critics.

and the decline of confidence in government both reflect the society-wide erosion of traditional authority (Nevitte, 1996).

Instability of Core Values

The decline of consensus around core values is the third aspect of postmodernism. Half a century ago, people's values remained quite stable during their adult lives and many values were widely accepted. Today, value shifts are more rapid and consensus has broken down on many issues. For example, in the middle of the twentieth century, most adults remained loyal to one political party from one election to the next. However, specific issues and personalities have increasingly eclipsed party loyalty as the driving forces of Canadian politics (Clarke, Jenson, LeDuc, and Pammett, 1996). Today, people are more likely to vote for different political parties in succeeding elections than they were in 1950.

The decline of consensus can also be illustrated by considering the fate of "big

The father figure of postmodernism?

historical projects." For most of the past 200 years, consensus throughout the world was built around big historical projects. Various political and social movements convinced people they could take history into their own hands and create a glorious future just by signing up. German Nazism was a big historical project. Its followers expected the Reich to enjoy 1000 years of power. Communism was an even bigger big historical project, mobilizing hundreds of millions of people for a future that promised to end inequality and injustice for all time. However, the biggest and most successful big historical project was not so much a social movement as a powerful idea—the belief that progress is inevitable and that life will always improve, mainly because of the spread of democracy and scientific innovation.

The twentieth century was unkind to big historical projects. Russian communism lasted 74 years.

German Nazism endured a mere 12. The idea of progress fell on hard times as 100 million soldiers and civilians died in wars; the forward march of democracy took wrong turns into fascism, communism, and regimes based on religious fanaticism; and pollution from urbanization and industrialization threatened the planet. In the postmodern era, people increasingly recognize that apparent progress, including scientific advances, often have negative consequences (Scott, 1998; see Figure 2.2). As the poet E. E. Cummings once wrote, "nothing recedes like progress."

IS CANADA THE FIRST POSTMODERN COUNTRY?

Until the mid-1960s, the image of Canadians among most sociologists was that of a stodgy people: peaceful, conservative, respectful of authority, and therefore quite unlike our American cousins.

According to conventional wisdom, the United States was born in open rebellion against the British motherland. Its Western frontier was lawless. Vast opportunities for striking it rich bred a spirit of individualism.

Thus, American culture became an anti-authoritarian culture.

Canada developed differently according to this conventional view. It became an independent country not through a revolutionary upheaval but in a gradual, evolutionary manner. The North-West Mounted Police and two hierarchical churches (Roman Catholic and Anglican) established themselves on the Western frontier *before* the era of mass settlement, allowing for the creation of an orderly society rather than a "Wild West." Beginning with the Hudson's Bay Company, large corporations quickly came to dominate the Canadian economy, hampering individualism and the entrepreneurial spirit. Thus, Canadian culture became a culture of deference to authority. That, at least, was the common view until the 1960s (Lipset, 1963).

Although the contrast between deferential Canadian culture and anti-authoritarian American culture had validity 40 years ago, it is inaccurate today (Adams, 1997: 62–95). As we have seen, the questioning of authority spread throughout the Western world beginning in the 1960s. Nowhere, however, did it spread as quickly and thoroughly as in Canada. Canadians used to express more confidence in big business than Americans did, but

FIGURE 2.2

Percentage Who Agree That Science and Technology Make Our Life Change Too Fast

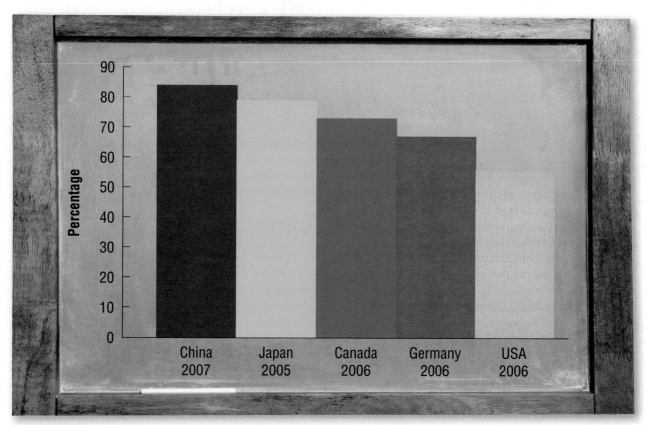

Source: World Values Survey. 2010. http://www.wvsevsdb.com/wvs/WVSAnalizeSample.jsp (accessed 20 October 2010).

surveys now show the opposite. Canadians used to be more religious than Americans were, but that is no longer the case. Fewer Canadians (in percentage terms) say they believe in God and fewer attend weekly religious services. Confidence in government has eroded more quickly in Canada than in the United States. Americans are more patriotic than Canadians, according more respect to the state. Finally, Americans are more likely than Canadians to regard the traditional nuclear family as the ideal family form and to think of deviations from tradition—same-sex couples, single-parent families, cohabitation without marriage—as the source of a whole range of social problems. Thus, whether sociologists examine attitudes toward the family, the state, the government, religion, or big business, they now find that Americans are more deferential to traditional institutional authority than Canadians are.

Because Canadians are less deferential to traditional institutional authority than Americans are, some commentators say that Canadians lack a distinct culture. For example, American patriotism sparks awareness of great national accomplishments in art, war, sports, science, and, indeed, all fields of human endeavour. Anthems, rituals, myths, and festivities celebrate these accomplishments and give Americans a keen sense of who they are and how they differ from non-Americans. Not surprisingly, therefore, a larger percentage of Americans than of Canadians think of themselves in unhyphenated terms—as "Americans" plain and simple rather than, say, Italian Americans. In Canada, a larger percentage of the population thinks of itself in hyphenated terms; compared with the Americans, our identity is qualified, even tentative.

Does this mean that Canadians lack a distinct national culture? Hardly. It means that although American culture is characterized by a relatively high degree of deference to dominant institutions, Canadian culture is characterized by a relatively high degree of tolerance and respect for diversity. We are more likely than Americans are to favour gender equality, accept gay and lesbian relationships, encourage bilingualism and multiculturalism, and accept the right of Aboriginals to political autonomy. Characteristically, a large international survey by a condom manufacturer found that Americans have sex more often than Canadians do, but Canadians are more likely to say that the pleasure of their partner is very important. As public opinion pollster Michael Adams writes,

> Twenty-five years of public-opinion polling in Canada has taught me a seemingly paradoxical truth. Canadians feel *strongly* about their *weak* attachments to Canada, its political institutions and their fellow citizens. In other words, they feel strongly about the right to live in a society that allows its citizens to be detached from ideology and critical of organizations, and not to feel obliged to be jingoistic or sentimentally patriotic. Canadians *lack* of nationalism is, in many ways, a distinguishing feature of the country. (1997: 171)

In short, Canadian culture *is* distinctive, and its chief distinction may be that it qualifies us as the first thoroughly postmodern society.

LO⁴ Culture as Constraint

We noted above that culture has two faces. One we labelled *freedom*, the other *constraint*. Diversity, globalization, and postmodernism are all aspects of the new freedoms that culture allows us today. We now turn to an examination of two contemporary aspects of culture that act as constraining forces on our lives: rationalization and consumerism.

RATIONALIZATION

In fourteenth-century Europe, an upsurge in demand for textiles caused loom owners to look for ways of increasing productivity. To that end, they imposed longer hours on loom workers. They also turned to a new technology for assistance: the mechanical clock. They installed public clocks in town squares. The clocks signalled the beginning of the workday, the timing of meals, and quitting time.

Workers were accustomed to enjoying many holidays and a flexible and vague work schedule regulated only approximately by the seasons and the rising and setting of

NORMA JOSEPH/GetStock.com

the sun. The regimentation imposed by the work clocks made life more difficult. So the workers staged uprisings to silence the clocks—but to no avail. City officials sided with the employers and imposed fines for ignoring the work clocks. Harsher penalties, including death, were imposed on anyone trying to use the clocks' bells to signal a revolt (Thompson, 1967).

Today, 700 years later, many people are, in effect, slaves of the work clock. This is especially true of big-city North American couples who are employed full-time in the paid labour force and have preteen children. For them, life often seems an endless round of waking up at 6:30 a.m., getting everyone washed and dressed, preparing the kids' lunches, getting them out the door in time for the school bus or the car pool, driving to work through rush-hour traffic, facing the increased pace of work that resulted from the recent downsizing, driving back home through rush-hour traffic, preparing dinner, taking the kids to their soccer game, returning home to clean up the dishes and help with homework, getting the kids washed, brushed, and into bed, and (if you haven't brought some office work home) grabbing an hour of TV before collapsing, exhausted, for 6.5 hours of sleep before the story repeats itself. Life is less hectic for residents of small towns, unmarried people, couples without small children, retirees, and the unemployed. But the lives of most people are so packed with activities that time must be carefully regulated, each moment precisely parcelled out so that we may tick off item after item from an ever-growing list of tasks that need to be completed on schedule (Schor, 1992).

After centuries of conditioning, it is unusual for people to rebel against the clock in the town square anymore. In fact, we now wear a watch on our wrist without giving it a second thought, signifying that we have accepted and internalized the regime of the work clock. Allowing clocks to precisely regulate our activities seems the most natural thing in the world—which is a pretty good sign that the internalized work clock is, in fact, a product of culture.

The precise regulation of time is a rational means of ensuring efficiency. Minding the clock maximizes how much work you get done in a day. The regulation of time makes it possible for trains to run on schedule and university classes to begin punctually. But is minding the clock rational as an end in itself? For many people, it is

not. They complain that the precise regulation of time has made life too hectic for them to enjoy. How rational is it that a restaurant in Japan has installed a punch-clock for its customers? The restaurant offers all you can eat for 35 yen per minute. As a result, "the diners rush in, punch the clock, load their trays from the buffet table, and concentrate intensely on efficient chewing and swallowing, trying not to waste time talking to their companions before rushing back to punch out" (Gleick, 2000: 244). In New York and Los Angeles some upscale restaurants have gotten in on the act. An increasingly large number of business clients are so pressed for time, they pack in *two* half-hour lunches with successive guests. The restaurants oblige, making the resetting of tables "resemble the pit-stop activity at the Indianapolis 500" (Gleick, 2000: 155). Arguably, as these examples illustrate, a *rational means* (the use of the work clock) has been applied to a *given goal* (maximizing work) but has led to an *irrational end* (a too-hectic life).

This, briefly, is Max Weber's thesis about the rationalization process. **Rationalization**, in Weber's usage, means (1) the application of the most efficient means to achieve given goals, and (2) the unintended, negative consequences of doing so. Weber claimed that rationality of means has crept into all spheres of life, leading to unintended consequences that dehumanize and constrain us (see Figure 2.3 on the next page). As our analysis of the

rationalization The application of the most efficient means to achieve given goals and the unintended, negative consequences of doing so.

Have we come to depend too heavily on the work clock? Harold Lloyd in *Safety Last* (1923).

HAL ROACH/PATHE EXCHANGE/THE KOBAL COLLECTION/KORNMAN, GENE

way we use time shows, rationalization enables us to do just about everything more efficiently, but at a steep cost. In Weber's view, rationalization is one of the most constraining aspects of contemporary culture; it makes life in the modern world akin to living inside an "iron cage," wrote Weber (1958 [1904–5]: 181).

Sociologist George Ritzer develops this theme. He argues that just as the modern bureaucracy epitomized the rationalization process for Weber at the turn of the twentieth century, the McDonald's restaurant is the epitome of rationalization today (Ritzer, 1993, 1996). Instead of adapting institutions to the needs of people, says Ritzer, people must increasingly adapt to the needs of "McDonaldization." We are dehumanized in the process (Leidner, 1993; Reiter, 1991).

As Ritzer shows, McDonald's has lunch down to a science. The meat and vegetables used to prepare your meal must meet minimum standards of quality and freshness. Each food item contains identical ingredients. Each portion is carefully weighed and cooked according to a uniform and precisely timed process. McDonald's executives have carefully thought through every aspect of your lunch. They have turned its preparation into a model of rationality. With the goal of making profits, they have optimized food preparation to make it as fast and as cheap as possible.

Unfortunately, however, the rationalization of lunch dehumanizes both staff and customers. For instance, meals are prepared by non-unionized, uniformed workers who receive minimum wage. They must execute their tasks within specific time limits. To boost sales, they must smile as they recite fixed scripts ("Would you like fries with your burger?"). Nearly half of all McDonald's employees are so dissatisfied with their work they quit within a year. To deal with this problem, McDonald's is now field-testing vending machines that will be used to replace staff and boost sales. Meanwhile, customers are expected to spend as little time as possible eating the food—hence the drive-through window, chairs designed to be comfortable for only about 20 minutes, and small express outlets in subways and department stores where customers eat standing up or on the run.

Nonetheless, powerful forces make the Big Mac popular. On the demand side, fast food fits the rushed lifestyle of many individuals and families in the more affluent countries of the world and the growing middle class in developing countries. On the supply side, big profits can be made by turning meal preparation into a mass production industry. Motivated by these forces, rationality of means (turning lunch into a science) results in irrationality of ends (dehumanizing staff and customers).

As the examples of the work clock, bureaucracy, and McDonald's show, rationalization enables us to do just about everything more efficiently but at a steep cost. Because it is so widespread, rationalization is one of the most constraining aspects of culture today.

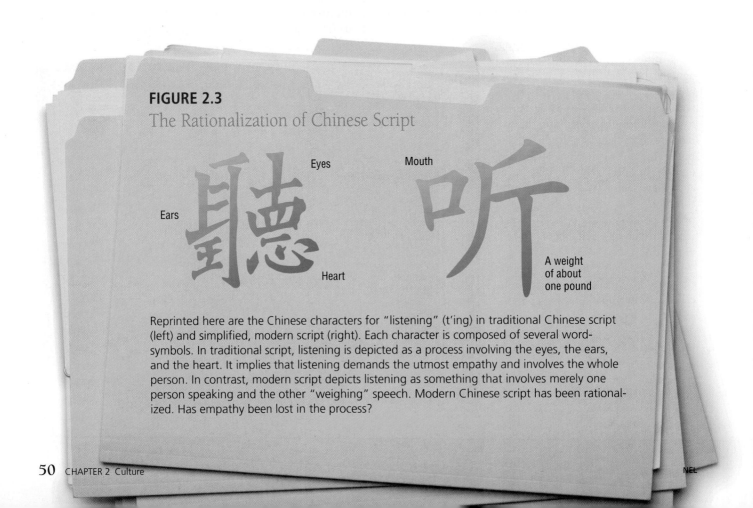

FIGURE 2.3

The Rationalization of Chinese Script

Ears Eyes Heart Mouth

A weight of about one pound

Reprinted here are the Chinese characters for "listening" (t'ing) in traditional Chinese script (left) and simplified, modern script (right). Each character is composed of several word-symbols. In traditional script, listening is depicted as a process involving the eyes, the ears, and the heart. It implies that listening demands the utmost empathy and involves the whole person. In contrast, modern script depicts listening as something that involves merely one person speaking and the other "weighing" speech. Modern Chinese script has been rationalized. Has empathy been lost in the process?

CONSUMERISM

The second constraining aspect of culture we will examine is consumerism, the tendency to define ourselves in terms of the goods and services we purchase.

The rationalization process, when applied to the production of goods and services, enables us to produce more efficiently and to have more of just about everything than our parents did. But it is consumerism that ensures all the goods we produce will be bought. Of course, we have many choices. We can select from dozens of styles of running shoes, cars, toothpaste, and all the rest. We can also choose to buy items that help define us as members of a particular subculture, adherents of a set of distinctive values, norms, and practices within a larger culture.

Recent innovations in advertising take advantage of our tendency to define ourselves in terms of the goods we purchase. For example, when channel surfing and the use of personal video recorders became widespread, advertisers realized they had a problem. Viewers started skipping TV ads that cost millions of dollars to produce. As a result, advertisers had to think up new ways of drawing products to the attention of consumers. One idea they hit on was paying to place their products in TV shows and movies. They realized that when Brad Pitt or some other big star drinks a can of Coke or lights up a Marlboro, members of the audience tend to associate the product with the star. Wanting to be like the star, they are more likely to buy the product. Thus, the 2009 hit movie *Up in the Air* features several travel scenes that focus on George Clooney's luggage. The movie's producers reached a product placement deal with Travelpro, manufacturers of the original "Rollaboard" suitcase. As expected, sales of Travelpro luggage skyrocketed soon after the film was released. The product became part of what many viewers wanted to be.

Regardless of individual tastes and inclinations, nearly all of us have one thing in common: we tend to be good consumers. We are motivated by advertising, which is based on the accurate insight that people will tend to be considered cultural outcasts if they fail to conform to stylish trends. By creating those trends, advertisers push us to buy, even if doing so requires that we work more and incur large debts (Schor, 1999). That is why the "shop-till-you-drop" lifestyle of many North Americans prompted French sociologist Jean Baudrillard to remark pointedly that even what is best in America is compulsory (Baudrillard, 1988 [1986]). And it is why we say that consumerism, like rationalization, acts as a powerful constraint on our lives.

> **consumerism** The tendency to define ourselves in terms of the goods and services we purchase.
>
> **subculture** A set of distinctive values, norms, and practices within a larger culture.

"McDonaldization" is a global phenomenon, as this busy McDonald's restaurant in Beijing, China, suggests.

Rob Crandall/GetStock.com

FROM COUNTERCULTURE TO SUBCULTURE

In concluding our discussion of culture as a constraining force, we note that consumerism is remarkably effective in taming countercultures. Countercultures are subversive subcultures. They oppose dominant values and seek to replace them. The hippies of the 1960s formed a counterculture and so do environmentalists today.

Countercultures rarely pose a serious threat to social stability. Most often, the system of social control, of rewards and punishments, keeps countercultures at bay. In our society, consumerism acts as a social control mechanism that normally prevents countercultures from disrupting the social order. It does that by transforming deviations from mainstream culture into means of making money and by enticing rebels to become entrepreneurs (Frank and Weiland, 1997). Two examples from popular music help illustrate the point:

> **countercultures** Subversive subcultures that oppose dominant values and seek to replace them.

1. Ozzy Osbourne was an important figure in the counterculture that grew around heavy metal music beginning in the late 1960s. He and his band, Black Sabbath, inspired Metallica, Marilyn Manson, and others to play loud, nihilistic music; reject conventional morality; embrace death and violence; and spark youthful rebellion and parental panic. In the early 1980s, Tipper Gore, wife of future presidential candidate Al Gore, formed the Parents Music Resource Center to fight violence and sex in the lyrics of popular music. Osbourne was one of the committee's principal targets. The "Prince of Darkness," as he was often called, was about as rebellious a figure as one could imagine in 1982.

Flash forward 20 years. In 2002, Osbourne, at 55, had one of the most popular shows on American television among 18- to 34-year-olds. MTV placed a dozen cameras throughout his Beverly Hills mansion, and every Tuesday night viewers saw everything going on in the Osbourne household for half an hour. According to *USA Today*, Osbourne is "a lot like anyone's adorable dad. Shuffles a bit. Forgets things. Worries about the garbage. Snores on the couch while the TV blares. Walks the dog" (Gundersen, Keveney, and Oldenburg, 2002: 1A). Rosie O'Donnell says to Ozzy's wife, Sharon, "What I love most about [your show] is not only the relationship you have with Ozzy—and you obviously adore each other—but the honesty with which you relate to your children. The love is so evident between all of you. It's heartwarming" (Gundersen et al., 2002: 2A). Sharon and Ozzy were invited to dinner at the White House in 2002. *The Osbournes*, it turns out, was a comfort to many people. The show seemed to prove that heavy metal's frightening rejection of mainstream culture in the 1970s and 1980s was just a passing phase and that the nuclear family remains intact. Ozzy Osbourne was thus transformed from the embodiment of rebellion against society to a family man, a small industry, and a conservative media icon.

2. The development of hip-hop also illustrates the commercialization and taming of rebellion (Brym, 2007a). Originating in the squalor of inner-city American ghettos in the 1970s, hip-hop gave rise to a highly politicized counterculture. Early hip-hop artists glorified the mean streets of the inner city and blamed the police for arbitrary arrests, the mass media for spreading lies about blacks, and the government for the political suppression of black activists. However, by the late 1980s, MTV had aired its first regular program devoted to the genre, and much of hip-hop's audience was composed of white, middle-class youth. Hip-hop artists were quick to see the potential of commercialization. Soon Wu-Tang

Clan had its own line of clothes, while Gianni Versace was marketing clothing influenced by ghetto styles. Puff Daddy (Sean Combs, now known as Diddy) reminded his audience in his 1999 CD *Forever,* "N—— get money, that's simply the plan." By 2002 he was, according to *Forbes* magazine, one of the 40 richest men under 40; by 2005, he had his own line of clothing: Sean John. Like heavy metal, hip-hop's radicalism gave way to the lures of commerce.

The fate of heavy metal and hip-hop is testimony to the capacity of consumerism to change countercultures into mere subcultures, thus constraining dissent and rebellion.

Ozzy Osbourne (holding plaque) *en famille*

Sean "Diddy" Combs in his Sunday best

3
Socialization

LO¹ Social Isolation and Socialization

One day in 1800, a 10- or 11-year-old boy walked out of the woods in southern France. He was filthy, naked, and unable to speak, and he had not been toilet trained. After being taken by the police to a local orphanage, he repeatedly tried to escape and refused to wear clothes. No parent ever claimed him. He became known as "the wild boy of Aveyron." A thorough medical examination found no major abnormalities of either a physical or a mental nature. Why, then, did the boy seem more animal than human? Because, until he walked out of the woods, he had been raised in isolation from other human beings for years (Shattuck, 1980).

Similar horrifying reports lead to the same conclusion. Occasionally a child is found locked in an attic or a cellar, where he or she saw another person for only short periods each day to receive food. Like the wild boy of Aveyron, such children rarely develop normally. Typically, they remain uninterested in games. They cannot form intimate social relationships with other people. They develop only the most basic language skills.

Some of these children may suffer from congenitally low intelligence. The amount and type of social contact they had before they were discovered is unknown. Some may have been abused. Therefore, their condition may not be due to social isolation alone. However, these examples do at least suggest that the ability to learn culture and become human is only a potential. To be actualized, socialization must unleash this potential. Socialization is the process by which people learn their culture. They do so by (1) entering into and disengaging from a succession of roles and (2) becoming aware of themselves as they interact with others. A role is the behaviour expected of a person occupying a particular position in society.

Convincing evidence of the importance of socialization in unleashing human potential comes from a study conducted by René Spitz (1945, 1962).

> **socialization** The process by which people learn their culture. They do so by (1) entering into and disengaging from a succession of roles and (2) becoming aware of themselves as they interact with others.

> **role** A set of expected behaviours, or the behaviour expected of a person occupying a particular position in society.

LEARNING OBJECTIVES:

LO¹ The view that social interaction unleashes human abilities is supported by studies showing that children raised in isolation do not develop normal social skills.

LO² Although the socializing influence of the family decreased in the twentieth century, the influence of schools, peer groups, and the mass media increased.

LO³ People's identities change faster, more often, and more completely than they did just a couple of decades ago; the self has become more plastic.

LO⁴ Declining parental supervision and guidance, increasing assumption of adult responsibilities by youth, and declining participation in extracurricular activities are transforming the character of childhood and adolescence today.

Spitz compared children who were being raised in an orphanage with children who were being raised in a nursing home attached to a women's prison. Both institutions were hygienic and provided good food and medical care. However, the children's mothers cared for the babies in the nursing home, whereas just six nurses cared for the 45 babies in the orphanage. The orphans therefore had much less contact with other people. Moreover, from their cribs, the nursing home infants could see a slice of society. They saw other babies playing and receiving care. They saw mothers, doctors, and nurses talking, cleaning, serving food, and providing medical treatment. In contrast, the caregivers in the orphanage would hang sheets from the cribs to prevent the infants from seeing the activities of the institution. Depriving the infants of social stimuli for most of the day apparently made them less demanding.

Social deprivation had other effects too. Because of the different patterns of child care just described, by the age of 9 to 12 months the orphans were more susceptible to infections and had a higher death rate than the babies in the nursing home. By the time they were two to three years old, all the children from the nursing home were walking and talking, compared with fewer than 8 percent of the orphans. Normal children begin to play with their own genitals by the end of their first year. Spitz found that the orphans began this sort of play only in their fourth year. He took this as a sign that they might have an impaired sexual life when they reached maturity. This outcome has been observed in rhesus monkeys raised in isolation. Spitz's natural experiment thus amounts to quite compelling evidence for the importance of childhood socialization in making us fully human. Without childhood socialization, most of our human potential remains undeveloped.

THE CRYSTALLIZATION OF SELF-IDENTITY

The formation of a sense of self continues in adolescence. Adolescence is a particularly turbulent period of rapid self-development. Consequently, many people can remember experiences from their youth that helped crystallize their self-identity. Do you? Robert Brym clearly recalls one such defining moment (Brym, 2006).

"I can date precisely the pivot of my adolescence," says Robert. "I was in grade 10. It was December 16. At 4 p.m. I was a nobody, and I knew it. Half an hour later, I was walking home from school, delighting in the slight sting of snowflakes melting on my upturned face, knowing I had been swept up in a sea of change.

"About 200 students had sat impatiently in the auditorium that last day of school before the winter vacation. We were waiting for Mr. Garrod, the English teacher who headed the school's drama program, to announce the cast of *West Side Story*. I was hoping for a small speaking part and was not surprised when Mr. Garrod failed to read my name as a chorus member. However, as the list of remaining characters grew shorter, I became despondent. Soon only the leads remained. I knew that an unknown kid in grade 10 couldn't possibly be asked to play Tony, the male lead. Leads were usually reserved for more experienced grade 12 students.

"Then came the thunderclap. 'Tony,' said Mr. Garrod, 'will be played by Robert Brym.'

"'Who's Robert Brym?' whispered a girl sitting two rows ahead of me. Her friend merely shrugged in reply. If she had asked *me* that question, I

In the 1960s, researchers Harry and Margaret Harlow placed baby rhesus monkeys in various conditions of isolation to study the animals' reactions. Among other things, they discovered that baby monkeys raised with an artificial mother made of wire mesh, a wooden head, and the nipple of a feeding tube for a breast were later unable to interact normally with other monkeys. However, when the artificial mother was covered with a soft terry cloth, the infant monkeys clung to it in comfort and later exhibited less emotional distress. Infant monkeys preferred the cloth mother even when it had less milk than the wire mother. The Harlows concluded that emotional development requires affectionate cradling.

© Hulton-Deutsch Collection/CORBIS

might have responded similarly. Like nearly all 15-year-olds, I was deeply involved in the process of figuring out exactly who I was. I had little idea of what I was good at. I was insecure about my social status. I wasn't sure what I believed in. In short, I was a typical teenager. I had only a vaguely defined sense of self.

"A sociologist once wrote that 'the central growth process in adolescence is to define the self through the clarification of experience and to establish self-esteem' (Friedenberg, 1959: 190). From this point of view, playing Tony in *West Side Story* turned out to be the first section of a bridge that led me from adolescence to adulthood. Playing Tony raised my social status in the eyes of my classmates, made me more self-confident, taught me I could be good at something, helped me to begin discovering parts of myself I hadn't known before, and showed me that I could act rather than merely be acted upon. In short, it was through my involvement in the play (and, subsequently, in many other plays throughout high school) that I began to develop a clear sense of who I am."

The crystallization of self-identity during adolescence is just one episode in a lifelong process of socialization. To paint a picture of the socialization process in its entirety, we first review the main theories of how a sense of self develops during early childhood. We then discuss the operation and relative influence of society's main socializing institutions or "agents of socialization": families, schools, peer groups, and the mass media. In these settings, we learn, among other things, how to control our impulses, think of ourselves as members of different groups, value certain ideals, and perform various roles. You will see that these institutions do not always work hand in hand to produce happy, well-adjusted adults. They often give mixed messages and are often at odds with one another. That is, they teach children and adolescents different and even contradictory lessons. You will also see that although recent developments give us more freedom to decide who we are, they can make socialization more disorienting than ever before. Finally, in the concluding section of this chapter, we examine how decreasing supervision and guidance by adult family members, increasing assumption of adult responsibilities by youths, and declining participation in extracurricular activities are changing the nature of childhood and adolescence today. Some analysts even say that childhood and adolescence are vanishing before our eyes. Thus, the main theme of this chapter is that the development of self-identity is often a difficult and stressful process—and it is becoming more so.

It is during childhood that the contours of the self are first formed. We therefore begin by discussing the most important social-scientific theories of how the self originates in the first years of life.

THE SYMBOLIC INTERACTIONIST FOUNDATIONS OF CHILDHOOD SOCIALIZATION

Socialization begins soon after birth. Infants cry, driven by elemental needs, and are gratified by food, comfort, and

Sigmund Freud (1856–1939).

affection. Because their needs are usually satisfied immediately, they do not at first seem able to distinguish themselves from their main caregivers, usually their mothers. However, social interaction soon enables infants to begin developing a self-image or sense of *self*—a set of ideas and attitudes about who they are as independent beings.

FREUD

Austrian psychoanalyst Sigmund Freud proposed the first social-scientific interpretation of the process by which the self emerges (Freud, 1962 [1930], 1973 [1915–17]). He noted that infants demand immediate gratification but begin to form a self-image when their demands are denied—when, for example, parents decide not to feed and comfort them every time they wake up in the middle of the night. The parents' refusal at first incites howls of protest. However, infants soon learn to eat more before going to bed, sleep for longer periods, and go back to sleep if they wake up. Equally important, the infant begins to sense that its needs differ from those of its parents, it has an existence independent of others, and it must somehow balance its needs with the realities of life. Because of many such lessons in self-control the child eventually develops a sense of what constitutes appropriate behaviour and a moral sense of right and wrong. Soon a personal conscience crystallizes. It is a storehouse of cultural standards. In addition, a psychological mechanism develops that normally balances the pleasure-seeking and restraining components of the self. Earlier thinkers believed that the self emerges naturally, the way a seed germinates. In a revolutionary departure from previous thinking on the subject, Freud argued that only social interaction can allow the self to emerge.

COOLEY

American scholars took ideas about the emergence of the self in a still more sociological direction. Notably, sociologist Charles Horton Cooley introduced the idea of the **looking-glass self**, making him a founder of the symbolic interactionist tradition and an early contributor to the sociological study of socialization.

Cooley observed that when we interact with others, they gesture and react to us. This allows us to imagine how we appear to them. We then judge how others evaluate us. Finally, from these judgments we develop a self-concept or a set of feelings and ideas about who we are. In other words, our feelings about who we are depend largely on how we see ourselves evaluated by others. Just as we see our physical body reflected in a mirror, so we see our social selves reflected in people's gestures and reactions to us (Cooley, 1902). When teachers evaluate students negatively, for example, students may develop a negative self-image that causes them to do poorly in school. Poor performance may have as much to do with teachers' negative evaluations as with students' innate abilities (Hamachek, 1995; see Chapter 10, Religion and Education). Here, succinctly put, we have the hallmarks of what came to be known as symbolic interactionism—the idea that in the course of face-to-face communication, people engage in a creative process of attaching meaning to things.

MEAD

George Herbert Mead (1934) took up and developed Cooley's idea of the looking-glass self. Like Freud, Mead noted that a subjective and impulsive aspect of the self is present from birth. Mead called it the **I**. Again like Freud, Mead argued that a storehouse of culturally approved standards emerges as part of the self during social interaction. Mead called this objective, social component of the self the **me**. However, whereas Freud focused on the denial of impulses as the mechanism that generates the

katielittle/Shutterstock

self's objective side, Mead drew attention to the unique human capacity to "take the role of the other" as the source of the me.

Mead understood that human communication involves seeing yourself from other people's points of view. How, for example, do you interpret your mother's smile? Does it mean "I love you," "I find you humorous," or something else entirely? According to Mead, you can find the answer by using your imagination to take your mother's point of view for a moment and see yourself as she sees you. In other words, you must see yourself objectively as a me to understand your mother's communicative act. All human communication depends on being able to take the role of the other, wrote Mead. The self thus emerges from people using symbols, such as words and gestures, to communicate. It follows that the me is not present from birth. It emerges only gradually during social interaction.

Mead's Four Stages of Development

Mead saw the self as developing in four stages of role-taking.

1. At first, children learn to use language and other symbols by *imitating* important people in their lives, such as their mother and father. Mead called such people **significant others**.

2. Second, children pretend to *be* other people. That is, they use their imaginations to role-play in games, such as "house," "school," and "doctor."

3. Third, about the time they reach the age of seven, children learn to play complex games that require them to simultaneously take the role of *several* other people. In baseball, for example, the infielders have to be aware of the expectations of everyone in the infield. A shortstop may catch a line drive. If she wants to make a double play, she must almost instantly be aware that a runner is trying to reach second base and that the person playing second base expects her to throw there. If she hesitates, she probably cannot execute the double play.

4. Once a child can think in this complex way, he or she can begin the fourth stage in the development of the self, which involves taking the role of what Mead called the **generalized other**. Years of experience may teach an individual that other people, employing the cultural standards of their society, usually regard him or her as funny or temperamental or intelligent. A person's image of these cultural standards and how they are applied to him or her is what Mead meant by the generalized other.

Since Mead, some psychologists interested in the problem of childhood socialization have analyzed how the style, complexity, and abstractness of thinking (or "cognitive skills") develop in distinct stages from infancy to the late teenage years (Piaget and Inhelder, 1969). Others have analyzed how the ability to think morally develops in stages (Kohlberg, 1981). However, from a sociological point of view it is important to emphasize that the development of cognitive and moral skills is more than just the unfolding of a person's innate characteristics. As we will now see, the structure of a person's society and his or her position in it also influences socialization.

significant others The people who play important roles in the early socialization experiences of children.

generalized other According to Mead, a person's image of cultural standards and how they apply to him or her.

GENDER DIFFERENCES

One of the best-known examples of how social position affects socialization comes from the research of Carol Gilligan. Gilligan showed that sociological factors help explain differences in the sense of self that boys and girls usually develop. That is because parents and teachers tend to pass on different cultural standards to each gender. Such adult authorities usually define the ideal woman as eager to please and therefore not assertive. Most girls learn this lesson as they mature. The fact that girls usually encounter more male and fewer female teachers and other authority figures as they grow up reinforces the lesson. Consequently, much research shows that girls tend to develop lower self-esteem than boys do, although it seems doubtful that teenage girls in general experience the decline in self-esteem that Gilligan detected in her early work (Brown and Gilligan, 1992; Kling, Hyde, Showers, and Buswell, 1999).

CIVILIZATION DIFFERENCES

In a like manner, sociological factors help explain the development of different ways of thinking or cognitive styles of different civilizations (Cole, 1995; Vygotsky, 1987).

Consider, for example, the contrast between ancient China and ancient Greece. In part because of complex irrigation needs, the rice agriculture of ancient southern China required substantial cooperation among neighbours. It had to be centrally organized in an elaborate hierarchy within a large state. Harmony and social order were therefore central to ancient Chinese life. Ancient Chinese thinking, in turn, tended to stress the importance of mutual social obligation and consensus rather than debate. Ancient Chinese philosophy focused on the way in which whole systems, not analytical categories, cause processes and events.

Danita Delimont/Gallo Images/Getty Images

Freud and the early symbolic interactionists discovered the fundamental process by which the self develops, and later researchers emphasized the gender, civilization, and other social bases of diverse socialization patterns.

LO² Function, Conflict, Symbolic Interaction, and Gender: How Agents of Socialization Work

Early work on childhood socialization leaves two key questions unanswered. First, does socialization help to maintain social order or does it give rise to conflict that has the potential to change society? Second, if society socializes people, how much freedom do individuals have to choose, modify, or even reject these influences? Functionalists, conflict theorists, symbolic interactionists, and feminists answer these key questions differently:

- Functionalists emphasize how socialization helps to maintain orderly social relations. They also play down the freedom of choice individuals enjoy in the socialization process.

- Conflict and feminist theorists typically stress the discord based on class, gender, and other divisions that is inherent in socialization and that sometimes causes social change.

- Symbolic interactionists highlight the creativity of individuals in attaching meaning to their social surroundings. They focus on the many ways in which we often step outside of, and modify, the values and roles that authorities try to teach us.

Whether it maintains order or engenders conflict, shapes us or allows us to shape it, socialization operates through a variety of social institutions, including families, schools, peer groups, and, in modern times, the mass media. We now consider how these various "agents of socialization" work. As we do so, please take careful note of the functionalist, conflict, symbolic interactionist, and feminist interpretations embedded in our discussion.

In contrast, the hills and seashores of ancient Greece were suited to small-scale herding and fishing. Ancient Greece was less socially complex than ancient China. It was more politically decentralized. It gave its citizens more personal freedom. As a result, philosophies tended to be analytical, which means, among other things, that processes and events were viewed as the result of discrete categories rather than whole systems. Markedly different civilizations grew up on these different cognitive foundations. Ways of thinking depended less on people's innate characteristics than on the structure of society (Nisbett, Peng, Choi, and Norenzayan, 2001).

We thus see that society plays a major role in shaping the way we think and the way we think of ourselves.

The Art Archive/Freer Gallery of Art

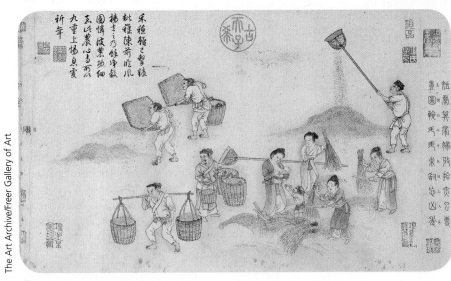

FAMILY FUNCTIONS

Few sociologists would disagree with the functionalist claim that the family is the most important agent of **primary socialization**, the process of mastering the basic skills required to operate in society during childhood. After all, the family is well suited to providing the kind of careful, intimate attention required for primary socialization. It is a small group, its members are in frequent face-to-face contact, and most parents love their children and are therefore highly motivated to care for them. These characteristics make most families ideal for teaching small children everything from language to their place in the world.

Note, however, that the socialization function of the family was more pronounced a century ago, partly because adult family members were more readily available for child care than they are today. As industry grew across Canada, families left farming for city work in factories and offices. Especially after the 1950s, many women had to work outside the home for a wage to maintain an adequate standard of living for their families. Fathers partly compensated by spending somewhat more time caring for their children. However, because divorce rates have increased and many fathers have less contact with their children after divorce, children probably see less of their fathers on average now than they did a century ago. In some countries, such as Sweden and France, the creation of state-funded child-care facilities compensated for these developments by helping teach, supervise, and discipline children (see Chapter 9, Families). In Canada, however, child care—and therefore childhood socialization—became a big social problem, leading in some cases to child neglect and abuse. Families are still the most important agent of primary socialization, but they are less important than they once were, and they sometimes function poorly.

SCHOOLS: FUNCTIONS AND CONFLICTS

For children over the age of five, the child-care problem was partly resolved by the growth of the public school system, which became increasingly responsible for **secondary socialization**, or socialization outside the family after childhood. Industry needed better trained and educated employees. Therefore, by the early twentieth century, every province had passed laws prescribing the minimum and maximum ages between which a child had to attend school. By the time the 2006 census was conducted, nearly 85 percent of Canadian between the ages of 25 and 65 had completed high school and more than 54 percent had postsecondary qualifications (Statistics Canada, 2009f). This made Canadians among the most highly educated people in the world.

Instructing students in academic and vocational subjects is the school's *manifest* function. One of its latent functions is to teach what sociologists call the **hidden curriculum**. The

forestpath/Shutterstock

The family is still an important agent of socialization, although its importance has declined since the nineteenth century.

primary socialization The process of acquiring the basic skills needed to function in society during childhood. Primary socialization usually takes place in the family.

secondary socialization Socialization outside the family after childhood.

hidden curriculum Teaches students what will be expected of them as conventionally good citizens once they leave school.

hidden curriculum instructs students in what will be expected of them in the larger society once they graduate—it teaches them how to be conventionally "good citizens." Most parents approve. According to one survey conducted in several highly industrialized countries, the capacity of schools to socialize students is more important to the public than all academic subjects except math (Galper, 1998).

What is the content of the hidden curriculum? In the family, children tend to be evaluated on the basis of personal and emotional criteria. As students, however, they are led to believe that they are evaluated solely on the basis of their performance on impersonal, standardized tests. They are told that similar criteria will be used to evaluate them in the work world. The lesson is, of course, only partly true. As you will see in Chapter 7 (Race and Ethnicity), Chapter 8 (Sexuality and Gender), and Chapter 10 (Religion and Education), it is not just performance but also class, gender, sexual orientation, and racial criteria that help to determine success in school and in the work world. But the accuracy of the lesson is

not the issue here. The important point is that the hidden curriculum does its job if it convinces students that they are judged on the basis of performance alone. Similarly, a successful hidden curriculum teaches students punctuality, respect for authority, the importance of competition in leading to excellent performance, and other conformist behaviours and beliefs that are expected of good citizens, conventionally defined.

The idea of the hidden curriculum was first proposed by conflict theorists, who, you will recall from Chapter 1, see an ongoing struggle between privileged and disadvantaged groups whenever they probe beneath the surface of social life (Willis, 1984). Their research on socialization in schools highlights the way many students—especially those from working-class and racial-minority families—struggle against the hidden curriculum. Conflict theorists acknowledge that schools teach many working-class and racial-minority students to act like conventional good citizens. However, they also note that a disproportionately large number of such students reject the hidden curriculum because their experience and that of their friends, peers, and family members make them skeptical about the ability of school to open good job opportunities for them. As a result, they rebel against the authority of the school. Expected to be polite and studious, they openly violate rules and neglect their work. Consequently, they do poorly in school and eventually enter the work world near the bottom of the socioeconomic hierarchy. Paradoxically, the rebellion of working-class and racial-minority students against the hidden curriculum typically helps to sustain the overall structure of society, with all its privileges and disadvantages.

SYMBOLIC INTERACTIONISM AND THE SELF-FULFILLING PROPHECY

Early in the twentieth century, symbolic interactionists proposed the **Thomas theorem**, which holds that "situations we define as real become real in their consequences" (Thomas, 1966 [1931]: 301). They also developed the closely related idea of the **self-fulfilling prophecy**, an expectation that helps to cause what it predicts. Our analysis of the hidden curriculum suggests that the expectations of working-class and racial-minority students often act as self-fulfilling prophecies. Expecting to achieve little if they play by the rules, they reject the rules and so achieve little.

The self-fulfilling prophecy does not operate only among students. Teachers, too, develop expectations that help to cause what they predict. In one famous study, two researchers informed the teachers in a primary school that they were going to administer a special test to the pupils to predict intellectual "blooming." In fact, the test was just a standard IQ test. After the test, they told teachers which students they could expect to become high achievers and

Brand X Pictures/Jupiter Images

which students they could expect to become low achievers. In fact, the researchers assigned pupils to the two groups at random. At the end of the year, the researchers repeated the IQ test. They found that the students singled out as high achievers scored significantly higher than those singled out as low achievers. Because the only difference between the two groups of students was that teachers expected one group to do well and the other to do poorly, the researchers concluded that teachers' expectations alone influenced students' performance (Rosenthal and Jacobson, 1968). The clear implication of this research is that if a teacher believes that poor or minority group children are likely to do poorly in school, chances are they will. That is because students who are members of groups that are widely expected to perform poorly *internalize* social expectations. They feel anxiety about their performance and the anxiety lowers their performance level (Steele, 1997).

PEER GROUPS

Like schools, **peer groups** are agents of socialization whose importance grew in the twentieth century. Peer groups consist of individuals who are not necessarily friends but who are about the same age and of similar status. (**Status** refers to a recognized social position an individual can occupy.) Peer groups help children and adolescents to separate from their families and to develop independent sources of identity. They particularly influence such lifestyle issues as appearance, social activities, and dating. In fact, from middle childhood through adolescence, the peer group is often the dominant socializing agent.

As you probably learned from your own experience, conflict often exists between the values promoted by the family and those promoted by the adolescent peer group. Families are controlled by parents. They represent the values of childhood. Under these circumstances, such issues as tobacco, drug, and alcohol use; hair and dress styles; political views; music; and curfew times are likely to become points of conflict between the generations. In contrast, adolescent peer groups are controlled by youth, and through them young people begin to develop their own identities. They do this by rejecting some parental values, experimenting with new elements of culture, and engaging in various forms of rebellious behaviour. For example, according to one Canadian survey, 12- and 13-year-old Canadians who identified themselves as belonging to a group that did "risky" things were up to seven times as likely as others to report smoking, disorderly conduct, skipping school at least once, and attaching low importance to marks. They were also much more likely to report at least three instances of stealing and fighting (Figure 3.1 on the next page). Peer influence also appears to play a significant role in the smoking habits of young adolescents. Eighty-four percent of 12- and 13-year-olds who smoked reported having three or more friends who also smoked, while only 26 percent of their nonsmoking counterparts claimed that three or more of their friends smoked (Figure 3.2 on page 65). Although parents' smoking behaviour—especially that of mothers—was linked to a youth's decision to smoke, the influence of peers was far greater (Statistics Canada, 1999b).

However, we should not overstate the significance of adolescent–parent conflict. For one thing, the conflict is usually temporary. Once adolescents mature, the family exerts a more enduring influence on many important issues. Research shows that families have more influence than peer groups do over the educational aspirations and the

> **peer groups** A person's peer group comprises people who are about the same age and of similar status as that person. The peer group acts as an agent of socialization.
>
> **status** A recognized social position that an individual can occupy.

charles knox/Shutterstock

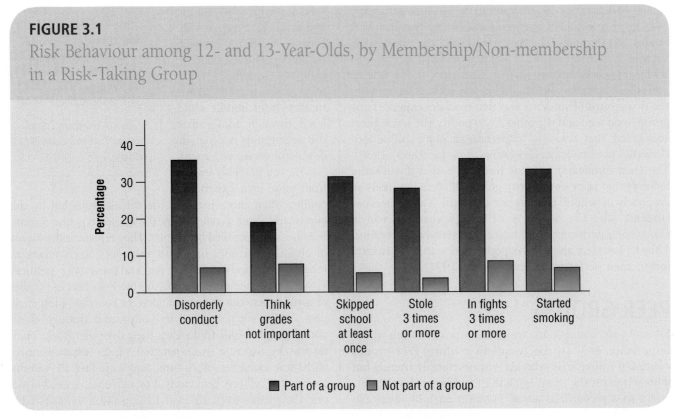

Respondents were asked 29 questions to assess their involvement in several generally unacceptable activities (e.g., staying out all night without permission, running away from home, being questioned by the police, stealing, fighting, vandalizing property, carrying a knife, using drugs, and committing arson). Respondents were then asked whether they had been part of a group that had done "bad" or risky things within the past year.

Source: Adapted from Statistics Canada, "National Longitudinal Survey of Children and Youth: Transition into adolescence," *The Daily*, Tuesday, July 6, 1999. http://www.statcan.gc.ca/daily-quotidien/990706/dq990706a-eng.htm.

political, social, and religious preferences of adolescents and university students (Davies and Kandel, 1981; Milem, 1998). One survey found that 91 percent of Canadian high school students believe that the way they were brought up influences the way they live their lives (Bibby, 2001: 55).

A second reason that we should not exaggerate the extent of adolescent–parent discord is that peer groups are not just sources of conflict. They also help integrate young people into the larger society. A study of pre-adolescent children in a small North American city illustrates the point. Over eight years, two sociologists conducted in-depth interviews at schools with children between the ages of 8 and 11 (Adler and Adler, 1998). They lived in a well-to-do community comprising about 80 000 whites and 10 000 racial minority group members. In each school they visited, they found a system of cliques arranged in a strict hierarchy, much like the arrangement of classes and racial groups in adult society. In schools with a substantial number of visible minority students, cliques were divided by race. Visible minority cliques were usually less popular than white cliques. In all schools, the most popular boys were highly successful in competitive and aggressive achievement-oriented activities, especially athletics. The most popular girls came from

well-to-do and permissive families. One important basis of the students' popularity was that they had the means and the opportunity to participate in the most interesting social activities, ranging from skiing to late-night parties. Physical attractiveness was also an important basis of girls' popularity. Thus, elementary-school peer groups prepared these youngsters for the class and racial inequalities of the adult world and the gender-specific criteria that would often be used to evaluate them as adults, such as competitiveness in the case of boys and attractiveness in the case of girls. (For more on gender socialization, see the discussion of the mass media below and Chapter 8, Sexuality and Gender.) What we learn from this research is that peer groups function not only to help adolescents form an independent identity by separating them from their families but also to teach them how to adapt to the ways of the larger society.

THE MASS MEDIA

Like the school and the peer group, the mass media have also become increasingly important socializing agents in the twenty-first century. The mass media include television,

FIGURE 3.2

Current Smoking Status of Youths, Aged 12 and 13, by Number of Their Friends Who Smoke

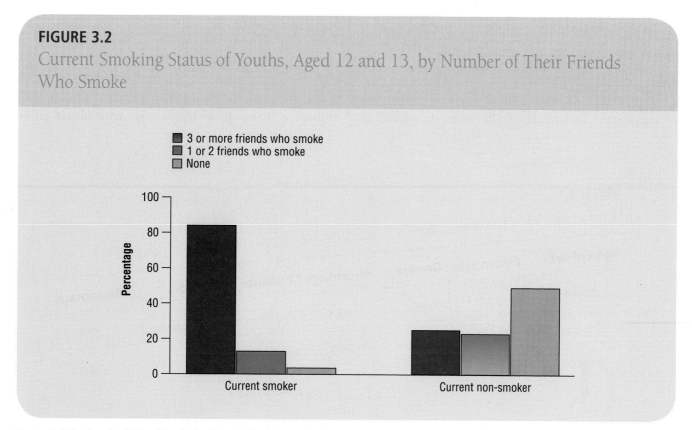

- 3 or more friends who smoke
- 1 or 2 friends who smoke
- None

Source: Statistics Canada, "National Longitudinal Survey of Children and Youth: Transition into adolescence," *The Daily*, Tuesday, July 6, 1999. http://www.statcan.gc.ca/daily-quotidien/990706/dq990706a-eng.htm

FIGURE 3.3

Number of Internet Users Worldwide, 1996–2010

1996
40 million

2000
381 million

2010
1.73 billion

Sources: Internet World Stats. 2010. "World Internet Users and Population Stats." http://www.internetworldstats.com/stats.htm (retrieved 22 February 2010). Copyright © 2001–2010, Miniwatts Marketing Group. All rights reserved worldwide.

radio, movies, videos, CDs, audiotapes, the Internet, newspapers, magazines, and books.

The fastest-growing mass medium is the Internet. Worldwide, the number of Internet users jumped from 40 million in 1996 to more than 1.7 billion in 2010 (see Figure 3.3). However, TV viewing still consumes more of the average Canadian's free time than any other mass medium. Ninety-nine percent of Canadians own at least one colour television set (Statistics Canada, 2001). In 2007, 29.2 percent of Canadians watched television 15 or more hours per week (see Table 3.1 on the next page). Low-income Canadians watch more TV than high-income Canadians, men watch more than women, people over the age of 54 watch more than younger Canadians, and Canadians living in the far north watch more than people in any other province or territory.

SELF-SOCIALIZATION

Young people use the mass media for entertainment and stimulation, to cope with anger, anxiety, and unhappiness, and to help construct their identities—for example, by emulating the appearance and behaviour of appealing movie stars, music idols, and sports heroes. In performing these functions, the mass media offer youth much choice: many Canadians have access to scores of radio stations and TV channels, hundreds of magazines, thousands of CD titles, hundreds of thousands of books, and millions of websites. Most of us can gain access to hip-hop, heavy metal, or Haydn with equal ease. Thus, although adolescents have little choice over how they are socialized by their family and their school, the proliferation of the mass media gives them more say over which media messages will influence them. To a degree, the mass media allow

TABLE 3.1

Percentage Viewing Television 15 or More Hours per Week, Canada, 2007

Age Cohort	Percentage	Gender	Percentage	Province or Territory	Percentage
20–24	20.0	Male	29.5	Newfoundland and Labrador	31.6
25–34	22.4	Female	28.9	Prince Edward Island	29.0
35–44	21.5			Nova Scotia	31.3
45–54	26.1			New Brunswick	32.4
55–64	36.1			Quebec	31.1
65–74	46.9			Ontario	29.1
75+	52.1			Manitoba	30.7
				Saskatchewan	29.8
				Alberta	25.7
				British Columbia	26.7
				Yukon	35.4
				Northwest Territories	33.2
				Nunavut	43.8
				Canada	29.2

Source: Adapted from Statistics Canada, "Screen time among Canadian adults: A profile," Health Reports 82-003-XIE 2008002 vol. 19 no. 2 Released June 18, 2008.

adolescents to engage in self-socialization, the ability to choose socialization influences from the wide variety of mass media offerings (Arnett, 1995).

THE MASS MEDIA AND THE FEMINIST APPROACH TO SOCIALIZATION

Although people are to some extent free to choose socialization influences from the mass media, they choose some influences more often than others. Specifically, they tend to choose influences that are more pervasive, fit existing cultural standards, and are made especially appealing by those who control the mass media. We can illustrate this point by considering what feminist research has found about how the mass media teach us gender roles. Gender roles are widely shared expectations about how males and females are supposed to act.

The teaching of gender roles by the mass media begins when small children learn that only a kiss from Snow White's Prince Charming will save her from eternal sleep. It continues in magazines, in romance novels, on television, in advertisements, in recorded music, and on the Internet. It is big business. For example, Toronto's Harlequin Enterprises, the world's largest publisher of romance fiction, publishes 110 titles a month and sells more than 130 million books a year in 28 languages and 114 countries. Over 60 years of operation, it has sold about 5.8 billion books (Harlequin, 2010).

A central theme in Harlequin romances is the transformation of women's bodies into objects for men's pleasure. In the typical Harlequin romance, the men are expected to be the sexual aggressors. They are typically more experienced and promiscuous than the women. These themes are well reflected in some of the titles on Harlequin's bestseller list for the third week of February, 2010: *In Bed with the Wrangler; Greek Tycoon, Inexperienced Mistress; Seduction and the CEO;* and *Executive's Pregnancy Ultimatum.* The women portrayed in the novels are expected to desire love before sexual intimacy. They are assumed to be sexually passive, giving only subtle cues to indicate their interest in male overtures. Supposedly lacking the urgent sex drive that preoccupies men, women are often held accountable for moral standards and contraception. Readers are assured that adopting this submissive posture ensures that things turn out for the best. As the eHarlequin website says, "Happily ever after is always guaranteed with our books."

People do not passively accept messages about appropriate gender roles. They often interpret them in unique ways and sometimes resist them. For the most part, however, people try to develop skills that will help them to perform gender roles in a conventional way (Eagley and Wood, 1999: 412–13). Of course, conventions change. It is important to note in this regard that what children learn about femininity and masculinity today is less sexist than what they learned just a few generations ago. For example, comparing *Cinderella* and *Snow White* with *Mulan,* we see immediately that children going to Disney movies today are sometimes presented with more assertive and heroic female role models than the passive heroines of the 1930s and 1940s. However, the amount of change in gender socialization should not be exaggerated. *Cinderella* and *Snow White* are still popular movies. Moreover, for every *Mulan* there is a *Little Mermaid,* a movie that simply modernizes old themes about female passivity and male conquest.

As the learning of gender roles through the mass media suggests, then, not all media influences are created equal. We may be free to choose which media messages influence us, but most people are inclined to choose the messages that are most widespread, most closely aligned with existing cultural standards, and made most enticing by the mass media. In the case of gender roles, these messages are those that support conventional expectations about how males and females are supposed to act.

RESOCIALIZATION AND TOTAL INSTITUTIONS

In concluding our discussion of socialization agents, we must underline the importance of resocialization in the lifelong process of social learning. Resocialization takes place when powerful socializing agents deliberately cause rapid change in people's values, roles, and self-conception, sometimes against their will.

You can see resocialization at work in the ceremonies staged when someone joins a fraternity, a sorority, the Canadian Armed Forces, or a religious order. Such a ceremony, or initiation rite, signifies the transition of the individual from one group to another and ensures his or her loyalty to the new group. Initiation rites require new recruits to abandon old self-perceptions and assume new identities. Often the rites comprise three stages: (1) separation from the person's old status and identity (ritual rejection); (2) degradation, disorientation, and stress (ritual death); and (3) acceptance of the new group culture and status (ritual rebirth).

self-socialization Choosing socialization influences from the wide variety of mass media offerings.

gender roles The set of behaviours associated with widely shared expectations about how males or females are supposed to act.

resocialization What occurs when powerful socializing agents deliberately cause rapid change in a person's values, roles, and self-conception, sometimes against that person's will.

initiation rite A ritual that signifies the transition of the individual from one group to another and helps to ensure his or her loyalty to the new group.

Not all initiation rites or rites of passage involve resocialization; some rites of passage are normal parts of primary and secondary socialization and merely signify the transition from one status to another. Here, an Italian family celebrates the first communion of a young girl.

Much resocialization takes place in what Erving Goffman (1961) called **total institutions**. Total institutions are settings in which people are isolated from the larger society and under the strict control and constant supervision of a specialized staff. Asylums and prisons are examples of total institutions. Because of the pressure-cooker atmosphere in such institutions, resocialization in total institutions is often rapid and thorough, even in the absence of initiation rites.

A famous failed experiment illustrates the immense resocializing capacity of total institutions (Haney, Banks, and Zimbardo, 1973; Zimbardo, 1972). In the early 1970s, a group of researchers created their own mock prison. They paid about 24 male volunteers to act as guards and inmates. The volunteers were mature, emotionally stable, intelligent, university students from middle-class American and Canadian homes. None had

total institutions Settings in which people are isolated from the larger society and under the strict control and constant supervision of a specialized staff.

a criminal record. By the flip of a coin, half the volunteers were designated prisoners, the other half guards. The guards made up their own rules for maintaining law and order in the mock prison. The prisoners were picked up by city police officers in a squad car, searched, handcuffed, fingerprinted, booked at the police station, and taken blindfolded to the mock prison. At the mock prison, each prisoner was stripped, deloused, put into a uniform, given a number, and placed in a cell with two other inmates.

To better understand what it means to be a prisoner or a prison guard, the researchers wanted to observe and record social interaction in the mock prison for two weeks. However, they were forced to end the experiment abruptly after only six days because what they witnessed frightened them. In less than a week, the prisoners and prison guards could no longer tell the difference between the roles they were playing and their "real" selves. Much of the socialization these young men had undergone over a period of about 20 years was quickly suspended.

About a third of the guards began to treat the prisoners like despicable animals, taking pleasure in cruelty. Even the guards who were regarded by the prisoners as tough but fair stopped short of interfering in the tyrannical and arbitrary use of power by the most sadistic guards.

All the prisoners became servile and dehumanized, thinking only about survival, escape, and their growing hatred of the guards. Had they been thinking as university students, they could have walked out of the experiment at any time. Some of the prisoners did, in fact, beg for parole. However, by the fifth day of the experiment they were so programmed to think of themselves as prisoners that they returned docilely to their cells when their request for parole was denied.

The Palo Alto experiment suggests that your sense of self and the roles you play are not as fixed as you may think. Radically alter your social setting and, like the university students in the experiment, your self-concept and patterned behaviour are also likely to change. Such change is most evident among people undergoing resocialization in total institutions. However, the sociological eye is able to observe the flexibility of the self in all social settings—a task made easier by the fact that the self has become more flexible over time. We now turn to an examination of the growing flexibility of the self.

Socialization across the Life Course

LO³ ADULT SOCIALIZATION AND THE FLEXIBLE SELF

The development of the self is a lifelong process (Mortimer and Simmons, 1978). When young adults enter a profession or get married, they must learn new occupational and family roles. Retirement and old age present an entirely new set of challenges. Giving up a job, seeing children leave home and start their own families, losing a spouse and close friends—all these changes later in life require people to think of themselves in new ways and to redefine who they are. Many new roles are predictable. To help us learn them we often engage in anticipatory socialization, which involves beginning to take on the norms and behaviours of the roles to which we aspire. (Think of 15-year-old fans of the TV show *Friends* learning from the show what it might mean to be a young adult.) Other new roles are unpredictable. You might unexpectedly fall in love and marry someone from a different ethnic, racial, or religious group. You might experience a sudden and difficult transition from peace to war. If so, you will have to learn new roles and adopt new cultural values or at least modify old ones. Even in adulthood, then, the self remains flexible.

Today, people's identities change faster, more often, and more completely than they did just a few decades ago. One important factor contributing to the growing flexibility of the self is globalization. As we saw in Chapter 2, Culture, people are now less obliged to accept the culture into which they are born. Because of globalization, they are freer to combine elements of culture from a wide variety of historical periods and geographical settings.

A second factor increasing our freedom to design our selves is our growing ability to fashion new bodies from old. People have always defined themselves partly in terms of their bodies; your self-conception is influenced by whether you're a man or a woman, tall or short, healthy or ill, conventionally attractive or plain. However, our bodies used to be fixed by nature. People could do nothing to change the fact that they were born with certain features and grew older at a certain rate.

> **anticipatory socialization**
> Beginning to take on the norms and behaviours of the roles to which one aspires.

American Private Lynndie England became infamous when photographs were made public showing her and other American soldiers abusing Iraqi prisoners in obvious contravention of international law. "She's never been in trouble. She's not the person that the photographs point her out to be," said her childhood friend Destiny Gloin (quoted in "Woman Soldier," 2004). Ms. Gloin was undoubtedly right. Private England at Abu Ghraib prison was not the Lynndie England from high school. As in the Palo Alto prison experiment, she was transformed by a structure of power and a culture of intimidation that made the prisoners seem subhuman.

The Canadian Press (Tony Gutierrez)

a replacement organ. Brisk, illegal international trade in human hearts, lungs, kidneys, livers, and eyes enables well-to-do people to enhance and extend their lives (Rothman, 1998).

As these examples illustrate, many new opportunities for changing our self-conception have been introduced in recent decades.

SELF-IDENTITY AND THE INTERNET

Further complicating the process of identity formation today is the growth of the Internet. In the 1980s and early 1990s, most observers believed that social interaction by means of computer would involve only the exchange of information between individuals. They were wrong. Computer-assisted social interaction profoundly affects how people think of themselves (Brym and Lenton, 2001; Haythornwaite and Wellman, 2002).

Internet users interact socially by exchanging text, images, and sound via e-mail, instant messaging (such as MSN Messenger), Facebook, Twitter, Internet phone, video conferences, computer-assisted work groups, online dating services, and so on. In the process, they often form virtual communities. Virtual communities are associations of people, scattered across the city or around the world, who communicate via computer about subjects of common interest.

Some virtual communities are short-lived and loosely structured in the sense that they have few formal rules and people quickly drift in and out of them. Chat groups are

Now, however, you can change your body, and therefore your self-conception, radically and virtually at will—if, that is, you can afford it. Examples of such changes include the following:

- Bodybuilding, aerobic exercise, and weight-reduction regimens are more popular than ever.

- Sex-change operations, although infrequent, are no longer a rarity.

- Plastic surgery and other cosmetic procedures allow people to buy new breasts, noses, lips, eyelids, and hair—and to remove unwanted fat, skin, and hair from various parts of their body. In North America, plastic surgery procedures rose more than tenfold—from 1.5 million to 17.0 million—between 1992 and 2008. More than 70 percent of plastic surgery procedures are cosmetic, and about 90 percent of them are performed on women. The top five surgical procedures for women in order of frequency are breast augmentation, liposuction, nose reshaping, eyelid surgery, and tummy tuck (American Society of Plastic Surgeons, 2007, 2009).

- Organ transplants are routine. At any given time, about 55 000 North Americans are waiting for

virtual communities An association of people, scattered across the city or around the world, who communicate via computer about a subject of common interest.

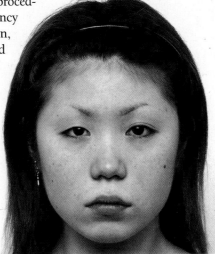
Before plastic surgery

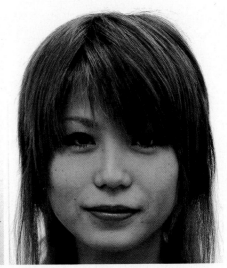
After plastic surgery

© Radius Images/Jupiterimages

AP Photo/The Otsuka Academy of Cosmetic and Plastic Surgery, left, and Katsumi Kasahara

typical of this genre. Other virtual communities are more enduring and structured. For example, discussion groups cater to people's interest in specialized subjects, such as French culture or white-water canoeing. Still other virtual communities are highly structured, with many formal rules and relatively stable membership. For example, MUDs (multiple-user dimensions), such as Second Life, are computer programs that allow people to role-play and engage in a collective fantasy. These programs define the aims and rules of the virtual community and the objects and spaces it contains. Users around the world log on to the MUD from their computers and define their character—their identity—any way they want. They interact with other users by exchanging text messages or by having their avatars (graphical representations) act and speak for them.

Because virtual communities allow interaction by using concealed identities, people are free to assume new identities and are encouraged to discover parts of themselves they were formerly unaware of. In virtual communities, shy people can become bold, normally assertive people can become voyeurs, old people can become young, straight people can become gay, and women can become men (Turkle, 1995). Experience on the Internet thus reinforces our main point: in recent decades, the self has become increasingly flexible, and people are freer than ever to shape their selves as they choose.

However, this freedom comes at a cost, particularly for young people. In concluding this chapter, we con-sider some of the socialization challenges Canadian youth faces today.

DILEMMAS OF CHILDHOOD AND ADOLESCENT SOCIALIZATION

In pre-industrial societies, children are considered small adults. From a young age, they are expected to conform as much as possible to the norms of the adult world. That is largely because children are put to work as soon as they can contribute to the welfare of their families. Often, this contribution means doing chores by the age of 5 and working full-time by the age of 10 or 12. Marriage, and thus the achievement of full adulthood, is common by the age of 15 or 16.

Children in Europe and North America fit this pattern until the late seventeenth century, when the idea of childhood as a distinct stage of life emerged. At that time, the feeling grew among well-to-do Europeans and North Americans that boys should be permitted to play games and receive an education that would allow them to develop the emotional, physical, and intellectual skills they would need as adults. Girls continued to be treated as "little women" (the title of Louisa May Alcott's 1869 novel) until the nineteenth century. Most working-class boys did not enjoy much of a childhood until the twentieth century. Thus, it is only in the past century that the idea of childhood as a distinct and prolonged period of life became universal in the West (Ariès, 1962).

THE EMERGENCE OF CHILDHOOD AND ADOLESCENCE

The idea of childhood emerged when and where it did because of social necessity and social possibility. Prolonged childhood was *necessary* in societies that required better-educated adults to do increasingly complex work, because childhood gave young people a chance to prepare for adult life. Prolonged childhood was *possible* in societies where improved hygiene and nutrition allowed most people to live more than 35 years, the average lifespan in Europe in the early seventeenth century. In other words, before the late seventeenth century, most people did not live long enough to permit the luxury of childhood. Moreover, there existed no social need for a period of extended training and development before the comparatively simple demands of adulthood were thrust on young people.

In general, wealthier and more complex societies whose populations enjoy a long average life expectancy stretch out the pre-adult period of life. For example, we saw that in Europe in the seventeenth century, most people reached mature adulthood by the age of about 16. In contrast, in such countries as Canada today, most people are considered to reach mature adulthood only around the age of 30, by which time they have completed their formal education, possibly gotten married, and "settled down." Once teenagers were relieved of adult responsibilities, a new term had to be coined to describe the teenage years: adolescence. Subsequently, the term young adulthood entered popular usage as an increasingly large number of people in their late teens, 20s, and early 30s delayed marriage to attend university (see

Wedding Crashers

Owen Wilson and Vince Vaughn in a scene from *Wedding Crashers*

John Beckwith (Owen Wilson) and Jeremy Grey (Vince Vaughn) are 30-something partners in a divorce mediation firm. Neither is married because of their belief that, as Jeremy says during one particularly heated mediation, "the real enemy here is the institution of marriage. It's not realistic. It's crazy."

So what do these handsome, single, professional men do for excitement come spring? They crash weddings, party till dawn, and bed the unsuspecting beauties who fall for their fast talk and scripted charm.

Early in the movie, John expresses misgivings:

John: You ever think we're being a little—I don't want to say sleazy, because that's not the right word—but a little irresponsible? I mean . . .

Jeremy: No. One day you'll look back on all this and laugh, and say we were young and stupid. Coupla dumb kids, runnin' around . . .

John: We're not *that* young.

Indeed they're not, which is why John's reflective moment raises an important sociological issue posed by a host of recent movies. *Wedding Crashers, The 40-Year-Old Virgin, Failure to Launch,* and *Clerks II* all raise the question of how it came about that people old enough to be con-

sidered adults just a couple of generations ago now seem stuck between adolescence and adulthood. They aren't married. Some of them live with their parents. They may still be in school. And some of them lack steady, well-paying, full-time jobs. They represent a growing category of young adults who are often a big worry to their elders.

Between 1981 and 2001, the percentage of Canadians between the ages of 25 and 34 living with their parents doubled—rising from 12 percent to 24 percent for the 25–29 age cohort and from 5 percent to 11 percent for the 30–34 age cohort (Beaupré, Turcotte, and Milan, 2007). One reason for this phenomenon is economic. In the first few decades after World War II, housing and education costs were low, and the number of years a person had to spend in school to get a steady, well-paying job was modest. Today, housing and education costs are high, and young people must typically spend more years in school before starting their careers. As a result, many young people continue to live in their parents' home into their 20s and 30s as a matter of economic necessity.

In *Wedding Crashers*, John and Jeremy finally seem able to break the mould when Jeremy marries Gloria (Isla Fisher) and John commits to her sister, Claire (Rachel McAdams). But as the happy foursome drive away, they get the bright idea of posing as a folk-singing quartet from Utah and crashing a wedding for the great Japanese food that is bound to be served. It seems that their parents' worries are far from over.

Critical Thinking Questions

- What are the criteria for "adulthood" in Canadian society?
- How and why do the criteria for adulthood change as societies develop?

the Sociology at the Movies box). Although these new terms describing the stages of life were firmly entrenched in North America by the middle of the twentieth century, some of the categories of the population they were meant to describe began to change dramatically. Somewhat excitedly, some analysts began to write about the "disappearance" of childhood and adolescence (Friedenberg, 1959; Postman, 1982). Although undoubtedly overstating their case, these social scientists did identify some of the social forces responsible for the changing character of childhood and adolescence in recent decades. We examine these social forces in the concluding section of this chapter.

LO⁴ PROBLEMS OF CHILDHOOD AND ADOLESCENT SOCIALIZATION TODAY

Declining adult supervision and guidance, increasing mass media and peer group influence, and increasing assumption of substantial adult responsibilities to the neglect of extracurricular activities have done much to change the socialization patterns of North American youth over the past 40 or 50 years. Let us consider each of these developments in turn.

Declining Adult Supervision and Guidance

In a six-year, in-depth study of adolescence, Patricia Hersch wrote that "in all societies since the beginning of time, adolescents have learned to become adults by observing, imitating and interacting with grown-ups around them" (1998: 20). However, in contemporary North America, adults are increasingly absent from the lives of adolescents. Why? According to Hersch, "society has left its children behind as the cost of progress in the workplace" (1998: 19). What she means is that more adults are working longer hours than ever before. In Canada in 2005, adults in the paid labour force living with a spouse or a child spent nearly 20 percent less time in activities with family members during a typical workday than they did in 1986. The main reason? They are required to spend more time at work (Turcotte, 2007). Because adults have less time to spend with their children than they used to, young people are increasingly left alone to socialize themselves and build their own community.

This community sometimes revolves around high-risk behaviour (see Figure 3.4). It is therefore not coincidental that the peak hours for juvenile crime are between 3 p.m. and 6 p.m. on weekdays—that is, after school and before most parents return home from work (Hersch, 1998: 362). Girls are less likely to engage in juvenile crime than boys, partly because parents tend to supervise and socialize their sons and daughters differently (Hagan,

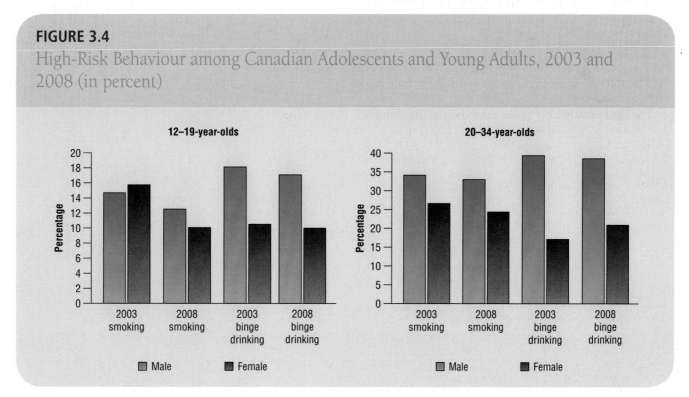

FIGURE 3.4

High-Risk Behaviour among Canadian Adolescents and Young Adults, 2003 and 2008 (in percent)

Note: "Smoking" = smoked daily or occasionally. "Binge drinking" = consumed at least five drinks per occasion at least twelve times in the past year.
Source: Adapted from Statistics Canada, *Health Indicators*, vol. 1 no. 1 82-221-XWE 2007001 Released May 30, 2007.

Simpson, and Gillis, 1987). These research findings suggest that many of the teenage behaviours commonly regarded as problematic result from declining adult guidance and supervision.

Increasing Media Influence

Declining adult supervision and guidance also leave North American youth more susceptible to the influence of the mass media and peer groups. As one parent put it, "When they hit the teen years, it is as if they can't be children anymore. The outside world has invaded the school environment" (quoted in Hersch, 1998: 111). In an earlier era, family, school, church, and community usually taught young people more or less consistent beliefs and values. Now, however, the mass media and peer groups often pull young people in different directions from the school and the family, leaving them uncertain about what constitutes appropriate behaviour and making the job of growing up more stressful than it used to be (Arnett, 1995).

Declining Extracurricular Activities and Increasing Adult Responsibilities

As the chapter's opening anecdote about Robert Brym's involvement in high school drama illustrates, extracurricular activities are important for adolescent personality development. These activities provide opportunities for students to develop concrete skills and thereby make sense of the world and their place in it. In schools today, academic subjects are too often presented as disconnected bits of knowledge that lack relevance to the student's life. Drama, music, and athletics programs are often better at giving students a framework within which they can develop a strong sense of self, because they are concrete activities with clearly defined rules. By training and playing hard on a hockey team, mastering an instrument,

or acting in plays, students can learn something about their physical, emotional, and social capabilities and limitations, about what they are made of, and about what they can and cannot do. These are just the sorts of activities adolescents require for healthy self-development.

If you're like most young Canadians today, you spent fewer hours per week on extracurricular activities associated with school than your parents did when they went to school. Educators estimate that only about a quarter of today's high school students take part in sports, drama, music, and so forth (Hersch, 1998). Many of them are simply too busy with homework, household chores, child-care responsibilities, and part-time jobs to enjoy the benefits of school activities outside the classroom. Half of Canadian teenagers work at jobs averaging 15 hours a week (Bibby, 2001: 35).

"The Vanishing Adolescent"

Some analysts wonder whether the assumption of so many adult responsibilities, the lack of extracurricular activities, declining adult supervision and guidance, and increasing mass media and peer group influence are causing childhood and adolescence to disappear. As early as 1959, one sociologist spoke of "the vanishing adolescent" in North American society (Friedenberg, 1959). More recently, another commentator remarked, "I think that we who were small in the early sixties were perhaps the last generation who actually had a childhood, in the . . . sense of . . . a space distinct in roles and customs from the world of adults, oriented around children's own needs and culture rather than around the needs and culture of adults" (Wolf, 1997: 13). Childhood and adolescence became universal categories of social thought and experience in the twentieth century. Under the impact of the social forces discussed above, however, the experience and meaning of childhood and adolescence now seem to be changing radically.

TEST COMING UP? NOW WHAT?

With **SOC+** you have a multitude of study aids at your fingertips. After reading the chapters, check out these ideas for further help:

Chapter in Review cards include learning outcomes, definitions, and visual summaries for each chapter.

Printable flashcards give you three additional ways to check your comprehension of key **sociology** concepts.

Other great ways to help you study include **interactive games, tutorial quizzes with feedback, note-taking outlines,** and **expanded materials on sociology in the media.**

"I like the flashcards, the videos, and the quizzes. Great format! I love the cards in the back of the book!"

—Asha Thtodort, Algonquin College

Visit **www.icansocplus.com** to find the resources you need today!

4 From Social Interaction to Social Organizations

Eremin Sergey/Shutterstock

NEL

Feminist Theory, Emotion, and the Building Blocks of Social Interaction

A few years ago, a researcher and his assistants eavesdropped on 1200 conversations of people laughing in public places, such as shopping malls (Provine, 2000). When they heard someone laughing, they recorded who laughed (the speaker, the listener, or both) and the gender of the speaker and the listener. To simplify things, they eavesdropped only on two-person groups.

They found that women laugh more than men do in everyday conversations. The biggest discrepancy in laughing occurs when the speaker is a woman and the listener is a man. In such cases, women laugh more than twice as often as men do. However, even when a man speaks and a woman listens, the woman is more likely to laugh than the man is.

Research also shows that men are more likely than women are to engage in long monologues and interrupt when others are talking (Tannen, 1994a, 1994b). They are also less likely to ask for help or directions because doing so would imply a reduction in their authority. Much male–female conflict results from these differences. A stereotypical case is the lost male driver and the helpful female passenger. The female passenger, seeing that the male driver is lost, suggests that they stop and ask for directions. The male driver does not want to ask for directions because he thinks that would make him look incompetent. If both parties remain firm in their positions, an argument is bound to result.

Social interaction involves communication among people acting and reacting to one another, either face to face or via computer. Feminist sociologists are especially sensitive to gender differences in social interaction like those just described. They see that gender often structures interaction patterns. Consider laughter. If we define status as a recognized social position, it is

> **social interaction** Involves people communicating face to face or via computer, acting and reacting in relation to other people. It is structured around norms, roles, and statuses.

LEARNING OBJECTIVES:

LO¹ Social interaction involves people communicating. The character of social interaction depends on people's positions in the interaction, their standards of conduct, and their expected behaviours.

LO² Sometimes people act against their interests and suppress their emotions because groups, networks, and social organizations influence what people do.

LO³ Nonverbal means of communication are as important as language in social interaction.

LO⁴ The patterns of social ties through which emotional and material resources flow form social networks.

LO⁵ People who are bound together by interaction and a common identity form social groups.

emotion management
The act of obeying "feeling rules" and responding appropriately to situations.

generally true that people with higher status (in this case, men) get more laughs, while people with lower status (in this case, women) laugh more. That is perhaps why class clowns are nearly always boys. Laughter in everyday life, it turns out, is not as spontaneous as you may think. It is often a signal of who has higher or lower status. Social structure influences who laughs more.

Social statuses are just one of the three building blocks that structure all social interactions. The others are roles and norms. A *role* is a set of expected behaviours. Whereas people *occupy* a status, they *perform* a role. Students may learn to expect that when things get dull, the class clown will brighten their day. The class clown will rise to the occasion, knowing that his fellow students expect him to do so. A *norm* is a generally accepted way of doing things. Classroom norms are imposed by instructors, who routinely punish class clowns for distracting their classmates from the task at hand (see Figure 4.1).

grizzly bear attacks you in the woods, you can run as fast as possible or calm yourself, lie down, play dead, and silently pray for the best. You are more likely to survive the grizzly bear attack if you control your emotions and follow the second strategy. You will also temper your fear with a new emotion: hope (see Figure 4.2).

When people manage their emotions, they usually follow certain cultural "scripts," like the culturally transmitted knowledge that lying down and playing dead gives you a better chance of surviving a bear attack. That is, individuals usually know the culturally designated emotional response to a particular external stimulus and try to respond appropriately. If they don't succeed in achieving the culturally appropriate emotional response, they are likely to feel guilt, disappointment, or (as in the case of the bear attack) something much worse.

Sociologist Arlie Russell Hochschild is a leading figure in the study of **emotion management**. In fact, she coined the term. She argues that emotion management involves people obeying "feeling rules" and responding appropriately to the situations in which they find themselves (Hochschild, 1979, 1983). So, for example, people

EMOTION MANAGEMENT

Some scholars think that emotions are like the common cold. In both cases, an external disturbance causes a reaction that people presumably experience involuntarily. The external disturbance, for example, could be a grizzly bear attack that causes us to experience fear or exposure to a virus that causes us to catch cold. In either case, we can't control our body's patterned response. Emotions, like colds, just happen to us (Thoits, 1989: 319).

It is not surprising that feminists were among the first sociologists to note the flaw in the view that emotional responses are typically involuntary (Hochschild, 1979, 1983). Seeing how often women, as status subordinates, must *control* their emotions, they generalized the idea. Emotions don't just happen to us, they argued. We manage them. If a

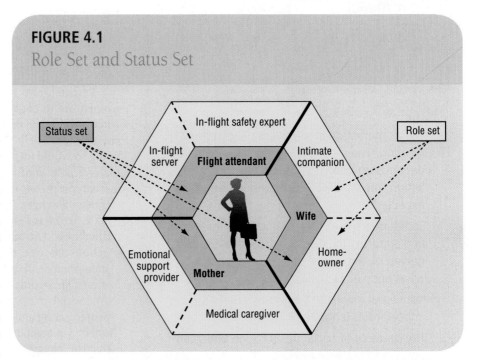

FIGURE 4.1
Role Set and Status Set

A person occupies several recognized positions or statuses at the same time—for example, mother, wife, and flight attendant. All of these statuses together form a status set. Each status is composed of several sets of expected behaviours or roles—for example, a wife is expected to act as an intimate companion to her husband and to assume certain legal responsibilities as co-owner of a house. In Figure 4.1, dashed lines separate roles and dark solid lines separate statuses.

FIGURE 4.2
How People Get Emotional

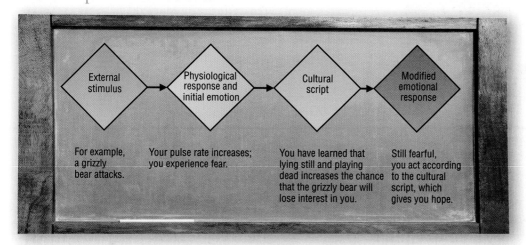

talk about the "right" to feel angry and they acknowledge that they "should" have mourned a relative's death more deeply. People have conventional expectations not only about what they should feel but also about how much they should feel, how long they should feel it, and with whom they should share those feelings. For example, we are expected to mourn the end of a love relationship. Shedding tears is regarded as completely natural today among Canadians, though if you shot yourself—as was the fad among some European Romantics in the early nineteenth century—then you would be regarded as deranged. If you go on a date minutes after you break up with your long-time love, then most people will regard you as callous. Norms and rules govern our emotional life.

EMOTION LABOUR

Hochschild distinguishes emotion management (which everyone does in everyday life) from emotion labour (which many people do as part of their job and for which they are paid). We've all seen teachers deal with students who routinely hand in assignments late, pass notes, chatter during class, talk back, and act as class clowns. Those teachers do emotion labour. Similarly, sales clerks, nurses, and flight attendants must be experts in emotion labour. They spend a considerable part of their workday dealing with other people's misbehaviour, anger, rudeness, and unreasonable demands. They spend another part of their workday in what is essentially promotional and public relations work on behalf of the organizations that employ them. ("We hope you enjoyed your flight on Air Canada and that we can serve you again the next time your travel.") In all these tasks, they carefully manage their own emotions while trying to render their clientele happy and orderly.

Hochschild estimates that in the United States, nearly half the jobs women do and one-fifth of the jobs men do involve substantial amounts of emotion labour. More women than men do emotion labour because they are typically better socialized to undertake caring and nurturing roles.

Note too that as the focus of the economy shifts from the production of goods to the production of services, the market for emotion labour grows. More and more people are selected, trained, and paid for their skill in emotion labour. As a result, business organizations increasingly govern the expression of feelings at work, which becomes less spontaneous and authentic over time. This process affects women more than it does men because women do more emotion labour than men do.

These observations fly in the face of common sense. We typically think of our interactions as outcomes of our emotional states. We interact differently with people depending on whether they love us, make us angry, or make us laugh. We usually think our emotions are evoked involuntarily and result in uncontrollable action. But emotions are not as unique, involuntary, and uncontrollable as people often believe. Underlying the turbulence of emotional life is a measure of order and predictability governed by sociological principles.

Just as building blocks need cement to hold them together, so norms, roles, and statuses require a sort of "social cement" to prevent them from falling apart and to turn them into a durable social structure. What is the nature of the cement that holds the building blocks of social life together? Asked differently, exactly how is social interaction maintained? This is the most fundamental sociological question we can ask, for it is really a question about how social structures, and society as a whole, are possible. It is the subject of the next two sections of this chapter.

Ieva Geneviciene/Shutterstock

competition for attention. Consider the following snippet of dinner conversation:

John: "I'm feeling really starved."
Mary: "Oh, I just ate."
John: "Well, I'm feeling really starved."
Mary: "When was the last time you ate?"

Sociologist Charles Derber recorded this conversation (Derber, 1979: 24). John starts by saying how hungry he is. The attention is on him. Mary replies that she's not hungry, and the attention shifts to her. John insists he's hungry, shifting attention back to him. Mary finally allows the conversation to focus on John by asking him when he last ate. John thus "wins" the competition for attention.

Derber (1979) recorded 1500 conversations in family homes, workplaces, restaurants, classrooms, dormitories, and therapy groups. He concluded that North Americans usually try to turn conversations toward themselves. They usually do so in ways that go unnoticed. Nonetheless, says Derber, the typical conversation is a covert competition for attention. Derber is careful to point out that conversations are not winner-take-all competitions. Unless both people in a two-person conversation receive some attention, the interaction is likely to cease. Therefore, conversation typically involves the exchange of attention.

LO² Conflict Theories of Interaction

COMPETING FOR ATTENTION

Have you ever been in a conversation where you can't get a word in edgewise? If you are like most people, this situation is bound to happen from time to time. The longer a one-sided conversation persists, the more neglected you feel. You may make increasingly less subtle attempts to turn the conversation your way. But if you fail, you may decide to end the interaction altogether. If this experience repeats itself—if the person you're talking to consistently monopolizes conversations—you're likely to want to avoid getting into conversations with him or her in the future. Maintaining interaction (and maintaining a relationship) requires that both parties' need for attention is met.

Most people don't consistently try to monopolize conversations. If they did, there wouldn't be much talk in the world. In fact, taking turns is one of the basic norms that govern conversations; people literally take turns talking to make conversation possible. Nonetheless, a remarkably large part of all conversations involves a subtle

INTERACTION AS COMPETITION AND EXCHANGE

Derber's analysis is influenced by conflict theory, which holds that social interaction involves competition over valued resources. Such resources include attention, approval, prestige, information, money, and so on (Blau, 1964; Coleman, 1990; Hechter, 1987; Homans, 1961). According to conflict theorists, competitive interaction involves people seeking to gain the most—socially, emotionally, and economically—while paying the least.

From this point of view, the chance of a relationship enduring increases if it provides the interacting parties with payoffs. Ultimately, then, payoffs make social order possible. On the other hand, unequal payoffs mean trouble. The greater the inequality of payoffs to interacting parties, the greater the chance that conflict will erupt and lead to a breakdown in the interaction. Thus, conflict never lies far below the surface of competitive social interactions marked by substantial inequality (Bourdieu, 1977 [1972]; Collins, 1982).

Symbolic Interaction

Is social interaction *always* a competitive and conflict-prone struggle over valued resources, as conflict theorists suggest? A moment's reflection suggests otherwise. People frequently act in ways they consider fair or just, even if that does not maximize their personal gain (Gamson, Fireman, and Rytina, 1982). Some people even engage in altruistic or heroic acts from which they gain nothing and risk much. The plain fact is that social life is richer than conflict theorists would have us believe. Selfishness and conflict are not the only bases of social interaction.

When people behave fairly or altruistically, they are interacting with others based on *norms* they have learned. These norms say they should act justly and help people in need, even if it costs a lot to do so. How then do people learn norms (as well as roles and statuses)? The first step involves what George Herbert Mead called "taking the role of the other," that is, seeing yourself from the point of view of the people with whom you interact (see Chapter 3, Socialization, and the Sociology at the Movies box on the next page). According to Mead, we interpret other people's words and nonverbal signals to understand how they see us, and we adjust our behaviour to fit their expectations about how we ought to behave. During such symbolic interaction, we learn norms and adopt roles and statuses.

Such social learning is different from studying a user manual or a textbook. It involves constantly negotiating and modifying the norms, roles, and statuses that we meet as we interact with others, shaping them to suit our preferences. People learn norms, roles and statuses actively and creatively, not passively and mechanically (Blumer, 1969; Berger and Luckmann, 1966; Strauss, 1993). Let us explore this theme by considering the ingenious ways in which people manage the impressions they give to others during social interaction.

GOFFMAN'S DRAMATURGICAL ANALYSIS

One of the most popular variants of symbolic interactionism is **dramaturgical analysis**. As first developed by Erving Goffman (1959), and briefly discussed in Chapter 1, A Sociological Compass, dramaturgical analysis takes literally Shakespeare's line from *As You Like It*: "All the world's a stage and all the men and women merely players."

> **dramaturgical analysis**
> Views social interaction as a sort of play in which people present themselves so that they appear in the best possible light.

From Goffman's point of view, people are constantly engaging in role-playing. This fact is most evident when we are "front stage" in public settings. Just as being front stage in a play requires the use of props, set gestures, and memorized lines, so does acting in public space. A server in a restaurant, for example, must dress in a uniform, smile, and recite fixed lines ("How are you? My name is Sam and I'm your server today. May I get you a drink before you order your meal?"). When the server goes "backstage," he or she can relax from the front-stage performance and discuss it with fellow actors ("Those kids at table six are driving me nuts!"). Thus, we often distinguish between our public roles and our "true" selves. Note, however, that even backstage we engage in role-playing and impression management; it's just that we are less likely to be aware of it. For instance, in the kitchen, a server may try to present herself in the best possible light to impress another server so that she can eventually ask him out for a date. Thus, the implication of dramaturgical analysis is that there is no single self, just the ensemble of roles we play in various social contexts. Servers in restaurants play many roles off the job. They play on basketball

Photos.com

Avatar

TWENTIETH CENTURY-FOX FILM CORPORATION / THE KOBAL COLLECTION

Avatar can be interpreted as a riff on George Herbert Mead in which Canadian filmmaker James Cameron teaches us that we can know ourselves and our world only by taking the role of—and thus truly seeing—the other.

The movie strikes the keynote with its opening frame: the eyes of ex-marine Jake (Sam Worthington) shoot open as he awakes from a deep sleep. He has been in suspended animation aboard a spacecraft for a year but now he is about to land on Pandora, a moon rich in "unobtainium," the most precious mineral known to humans. His job is to help a giant, greedy Earth corporation mine it, even if that means destroying the moon's ecology and its inhabitants.

Because of a war accident, Jake is a paraplegic, but on Pandora he will inhabit an avatar—the body of a Na'vi, the intelligent, three-metre-tall humanoid creatures that inhabit the moon. The Na'vi enjoy the grace (and the directional ears) of a cat and the strength of a lion. Fabulously, they are able to communicate directly with other creatures and with Pandora itself by connecting the tendrils at the end of their tails to matching tendrils on the animals and vegetation of the planet. When Jake inhabits the body of a Na'vi, he is thus freed from a life of immobility. He is also able to see in an entirely new way, understanding and living in complete harmony with his natural environment, just as the Na'vi do.

Events do not unfold as the corporation planned. Jake is assigned to learn the language and the beliefs of the Na'vi but he soon falls in love with Neytiri, a Na'vi princess (Zoe Saldana). They express their devotion to one another not by saying "I love you," as humans do, but in the Na'vi fashion, by proclaiming "I see you." What Jake sees is the world from Neytiri's point of view. He takes the role of the other and soon begins to empathize fully with the Na'vi's harmonious relationship to Pandora—and to understand the poverty of the mining company's plan to destroy the Na'vi and their way of life by exploiting the moon's unobtainium. And so in the movie's climax, Jake goes native. He helps to organize the Na'vi in an effort to save Pandora and its inhabitants from the humans.

The medium is part of *Avatar*'s message. Shot in spectacular 3-D, *Avatar* uses the latest animation technology to help the audience see in a new way. The message is as captivating as the shimmering jellyfish-like animals that float out to entrance the audience: Only if you see the world from the point of view of other people and understand how *they* see things can you learn who you truly are. Such empathy can even save a world.

Critical Thinking Questions

Are group affiliations always social straitjackets? Jake's shifting loyalties suggest otherwise. Answer these questions in the context of religious conversions, changes in citizenship, and alterations in sexual identity:

- Under what social circumstances can group loyalties shift?
- Under what circumstances do group loyalties tend to remain rigid?

White Packert/Photonica/Getty Images

> **role distancing** Involves giving the impression that we are just going through the motions and that we lack serious commitment to a role.

patients. They try to model their behaviour after the doctors who have authority over them. When dealing with patients, they may hide their ignorance under medical jargon to maintain their authority. They may ask questions they know the answer to so that they can impress their teachers. According to one third-year student: "The best way of impressing [advisers] with your competence is asking questions you know the answer to. Because if they ever put it back on you, 'Well what do you think?' then you can tell them what you think and you'd give a very intelligent answer because you knew it. You didn't ask it to find out information. You ask it to impress people." Medical students don't take a course in how to act like a doctor, but they learn their new role in the course of impression management (Haas and Shaffir, 1987).

Let us now inquire briefly into the way people use words and nonverbal signals to communicate in face to face interaction. Having a conversation is actually a wonder of intricate complexity; even today's most advanced super-computer cannot conduct a natural-sounding conversation with a person (Kurzweil, 1999: 61, 91).

teams, sing in church choirs, and hang out with friends at shopping malls. Each role is governed by norms about what kinds of clothes to wear, what kind of conversation to engage in, and so on. Everyone plays on many front stages in everyday life.

They do not always do so enthusiastically. If a role is stressful, people may engage in role distancing. **Role distancing** involves giving the impression of just "going through the motions" but lacking serious commitment to a role. Thus, when people think a role they are playing is embarrassing or beneath them, they typically want to give their peers the impression that the role is not their "true" self. My parents force me to sing in the church choir; I'm working at McDonald's just to earn a few extra dollars, but I'm going back to college next semester; this old car I'm driving is just a loaner. These are the kinds of rationalizations individuals offer when distancing themselves from a role.

Onstage, people typically try to place themselves in the best possible light; they engage in "impression management." For example, when students enter medical school they quickly adopt a new medical vocabulary and wear a white lab coat to set themselves apart from

VERBAL AND NONVERBAL COMMUNICATION

Fifty years ago an article appeared in a British newspaper trumpeting the invention of an electronic translating device at the University of London. According to the article, "As fast as [a user] could type the words in, say, French, the equivalent in Hungarian or Russian would issue forth on the tape" (quoted in Silberman, 2000: 225). The report was an exaggeration, to put it mildly. It soon became a standing joke that if you asked a computer to translate "The spirit is willing, but the flesh is weak" into Russian, the output would read, "The vodka is good, but the steak is lousy." Today we are closer to high-quality machine translation than we were in the 1950s. However, a practical universal translator exists only on *Star Trek*.

The Social Context of Language

Why are human beings better translators than computers are? Because computer programs find it difficult to make sense of the *social and cultural context* in which language is used. The same words can mean different things in different settings, so computers, lacking contextual cues, routinely botch translations. That is why machine translation works best when applications are restricted to a single social context—say, weather forecasting or oil exploration. In such cases, specialized vocabularies and meanings specific to the context of interest are built into the program. Ambiguity is reduced and computers can "understand" the meaning of words well enough to translate them with reasonable accuracy. Similarly, humans must be able to reduce ambiguity and make sense of words to become good translators. They do so by learning the nuances of meaning in different cultural and social contexts over an extended time. *Nonverbal* cues assist them in that task.

Facial Expressions, Gestures, and Body Language

A few years ago, *Cosmopolitan* magazine featured an article advising female readers on "how to reduce otherwise

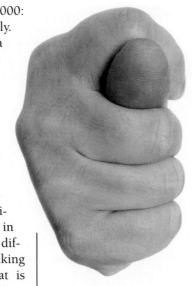

Like many hand gestures, the "fig" means different things in different times and places. You probably know it as a sign that adults make when they play with children and pretend "I've got your nose." But in ancient Rome, the fig was meant to convey good luck; in India it represents a threat; and in Russia, Turkey, and South Korea it means "screw you." It signifies the letter "t" in the American Sign Language alphabet, but it had to be modified in the International Sign Language alphabet to avoid giving offence.

evolved men to drooling, panting fools." Basing his analysis on the work of several psychologists, the author of the article first urges readers to "delete the old-school seductress image (smoky eyes, red lips, brazen stare) from your consciousness." Then, he writes, you must "upload a new inner temptress who's equal parts good girl and wild child." The article recommends invading a man's personal space and entering his "intimate zone" by finding an excuse to touch him. Picking a piece of lint off his jacket ought to do the trick. Then you can tell him how much you like his cologne (Willardt, 2000). If things progress, another article in the same issue of *Cosmopolitan* explains how you can read his body language to tell whether he's lying (Dutton, 2000).

Whatever we may think of the soundness of *Cosmopolitan*'s advice or the images of women and men

Among other things, body language communicates the degree to which people conform to gender roles, or widely shared expectations about how males and females are supposed to act. In these photos, which postures suggest power and aggressiveness? Which suggest pleasant compliance? Which are "appropriate" to the sex of the person?

it tries to reinforce, this example drives home the point that social interaction typically involves a complex mix of verbal and nonverbal messages. The face alone is capable of more than 1000 distinct expressions, reflecting the whole range of human emotion. Arm movements, hand gestures, posture, and other aspects of body language send many more messages to a person's audience (Wood, 1999).

Despite the wide variety of facial expressions in the human repertoire, most researchers believed until recently that the facial expressions of six emotions are similar across cultures. These six emotions are happiness, sadness, anger, disgust, fear, and surprise (Ekman, 1978). However, since the mid-1990s, some researchers have questioned whether a universally recognized set of facial expressions reflects basic human emotions. Among other things, critics have argued that "facial expressions are not the readout of emotions but displays that serve social motives and are mostly determined by the presence of an audience" (Fernandez-Dols, Sanchez, Carrera, and Ruiz-Belda, 1997: 163). From this point of view, a smile will reflect pleasure if it serves a person's interest to present a smiling face to his or her audience. Conversely, a person may be motivated to conceal anxiety by smiling or to conceal pleasure by suppressing a smile.

At times, different cultural expectations can lead to colossal misunderstanding. Until recently, it was considered rude among educated Japanese to say "no." Disagreement was instead conveyed by discreetly changing the subject and smiling politely. Consequently, it was common for visiting North Americans to think that their Japanese hosts were saying "yes" because of the politeness, the smile, and the absence of a "no" when in fact they were saying "no."

Similarly, no gestures or body postures mean the same thing in all societies and all cultures. In our society, people point with an outstretched hand and an extended finger. However, people raised in other cultures tip their head or use their chin or eyes to point out something. We nod our heads "yes" and shake "no," but others nod "no" and shake "yes."

Finally, we must note that in all societies people communicate by manipulating the space that separates them from others (Hall, 1959, 1966). This point is well illustrated in our *Cosmopolitan* example. Sociologists commonly distinguish four zones that surround us. The size of these zones varies from one society to the next. In North America, an intimate zone extends about 0.5 metre from the body. It is restricted to people with whom we want sustained, intimate physical contact. A personal zone extends from about 0.5 metre to 1.5 metres away. It is reserved for friends and acquaintances. We tolerate only a little physical intimacy from such people. The social zone is situated in the area roughly 1.5 metres to 3.5 metres away from us. Apart from a handshake, no physical contact is permitted from people we restrict to that zone. The public zone starts around 3.5 metres from our bodies. It is used to distinguish a performer or a speaker from an audience.

Status Cues

Aside from facial expressions, gestures, and body language, nonverbal communication takes place by means of **status cues**, or visual indicators of other people's social position. Goffman (1959) observed that when individuals come into contact, they typically try to acquire information that

stereotypes Rigid views of how members of various groups act, regardless of whether individual group members really behave that way.

will help them define the situation and make interaction easier. That goal is accomplished in part by attending to status cues.

Although status cues can be useful in helping people define the situation and thus greasing the wheels of social interaction, they also pose a social danger; status cues can quickly degenerate into **stereotypes**, or rigid views of how members of various groups act, regardless of whether individual group members really behave that way. Stereotypes create social barriers that impair interaction or prevent it altogether. For instance, police officers in some places routinely stop young black male drivers without cause to check for proper licensing, possession of illegal goods, and other similar violations (see Figure 4.3). In this case, a social cue has become a stereotype that guides police policy. Young black males, the great majority of whom never commit an illegal act, view this police practice as harassment. Racial stereotyping therefore helps perpetuate the sometimes poor relations between young black men and law enforcement officials.

As these examples show, face to face interaction may at first glance appear to be straightforward and unproblematic. Most of the time, it is. However, underlying the surface of human communication is a wide range of cultural assumptions, unconscious understandings, and nonverbal cues that make interaction possible.

Networks, Groups, and Organizations
THE HOLOCAUST

In 1941, the large stone and glass train station was one of the proudest structures in Smolensk, a provincial capital of about 100 000 people on Russia's western border. Always bustling, it was especially busy on the morning of June 28. Besides the usual passengers and well-wishers, hundreds of Soviet Red Army soldiers were nervously talking, smoking, writing hurried letters to their loved ones, and sleeping fitfully on the station floor while waiting for their train. Nazi troops had invaded the nearby city of Minsk in Belarus a couple of days before. The Soviet soldiers were being positioned to defend Russia against the inevitable German onslaught.

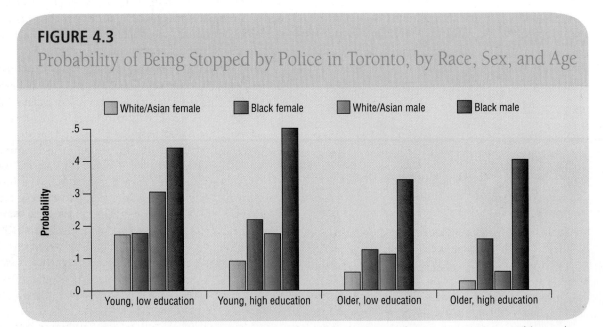

FIGURE 4.3
Probability of Being Stopped by Police in Toronto, by Race, Sex, and Age

Black male drivers are more likely to be stopped by the police than any other race–sex group. White and Asian female drivers are least likely to be stopped. Black males with higher education are more likely to be stopped than black males with lower education. How does stereotyping influence the chance of being stopped by the police?

Source: Wortley, Scot, David Brownfield, and John Hagan. 1996. *The Usual Suspects: Race, Age and Gender Differences in Police Contact*. Paper Presented at the 48th Annual Conference of the American Society of Criminology, Chicago: November.

Robert Brym's father, then in his 20s, had been standing in line for nearly two hours to buy food when he noticed flares arching over the station. Within seconds, *Stuka* bombers, the pride of the German air force, swept down, releasing their bombs just before pulling out of their dive. Inside the station, shards of glass, blocks of stone, and mounds of earth fell indiscriminately on sleeping soldiers and nursing mothers alike. Everyone panicked. People trampled over one another to get out. In minutes, the train station was rubble.

Nearly two years earlier, Robert's father had managed to escape Poland when the Nazis invaded his hometown near Warsaw. Now he was on the run again. By the time the Nazis occupied Smolensk a few weeks after their dive-bombers destroyed its train station, Robert's father was deep in the Russian interior serving in a workers' battalion attached to the Soviet Red Army.

"My father was one of 300 000 Polish Jews who fled eastward into Russia before the Nazi genocide machine could reach them," says Robert. "The remaining 3 million Polish Jews were killed in various ways. Some died in battle. Many more, like my father's mother and younger siblings, were rounded up like diseased cattle and shot. However, most of Poland's Jews wound up in the concentration camps. Those deemed unfit were shipped to the gas chambers. Those declared able to work were turned into slaves until they could work no more. Then they, too, met their fate. A mere 9 percent of Poland's 3.3 million Jews survived World War II. The Nazi regime was responsible for the death of 6 million Jews in Europe.

"One question that always perplexed my father about the war was this: How was it possible for many thousands of ordinary Germans—products of what he regarded as the most advanced civilization on earth—to systematically murder millions of defenceless and innocent Jews, Roma, gays and lesbians, and people with mental disabilities in the death camps?" To answer this question adequately, we must borrow ideas from the sociological study of networks, groups, and bureaucracies.

HOW SOCIAL GROUPS SHAPE OUR ACTIONS

How could ordinary German citizens commit the crime of the twentieth century? The conventional, non-sociological answer is that many Nazis were evil, sadistic, or deluded enough to think that Jews and other undesirables threatened the existence of the German people. Therefore, in the Nazi mind, the innocents had to be killed. This answer is given in the 1993 movie *Schindler's List* and in many other accounts. Yet it is far from the whole story. Sociologists emphasize three other factors:

1. *Norms of solidarity demand conformity.* When we form relationships with friends, lovers, spouses,

teammates, and comrades-in-arms, we develop shared ideas, or *norms of solidarity*, about how we should behave toward them to sustain the relationships. Because these relationships are emotionally important to us, we sometimes pay more attention to norms of solidarity than to the morality of our actions. For example, a study of the Nazis who roamed the Polish countryside to shoot and kill Jews and other "enemies" of Nazi Germany found that the soldiers often did not hate the people they systematically slaughtered, but they did not have many qualms about their actions (Browning, 1992). They simply developed deep loyalty to one another. They felt they had to get their assigned job done or face letting down their comrades. Thus, they committed atrocities partly because they just wanted to maintain group morale, solidarity, and loyalty. They committed evil deeds not because they were extraordinarily bad but because they were quite ordinary— ordinary in the sense that they acted to sustain their friendship ties and to serve their group, just like most people would.

The case of the Nazi regime may seem extreme, but other instances of going along with criminal behaviour uncover a similar dynamic at work. Why do people rarely report crimes committed by corporations? Employees may worry about being reprimanded or fired if they become whistleblowers, but they also worry about letting down their co-workers. Why do gang members engage in criminal acts? They may seek financial gain, but they also regard crime as a way of maintaining a close social bond with their fellow gang members.

A study of the small number of Polish Christians who helped save Jews during World War II helps clarify why some people violate group norms (Tec, 1986). The heroism of these Polish Christians was not correlated with their educational attainment, political orientation, religious background, or even attitudes toward Jews. In fact, some Polish Christians who helped save Jews were quite anti-Semitic. Instead, these Christian heroes were for one reason or another estranged or cut off from mainstream norms. Because they were poorly socialized into the norms of their society, they were freer not to conform and instead to act in ways they believed were right. We could tell a roughly similar story about corporate whistleblowers or people who turn in their fellow gang members. They are disloyal from an insider's point of view but heroic from an outsider's point of view, often because they have been poorly socialized into the group's norms.

2. *Structures of authority tend to render people obedient.* Most people find it difficult to disobey authorities

bureaucracy A large, impersonal organization composed of many clearly defined positions arranged in a hierarchy.

because they fear ridicule, ostracism, and punishment. This was strikingly demonstrated in an experiment conducted by social psychologist Stanley Milgram (1974). Milgram informed his experimental subjects that they were taking part in a study on punishment and learning. He brought each subject to a room where a man was strapped to a chair. An electrode was attached to the man's wrist. The experimental subject sat in front of a console. It contained 30 switches with labels ranging from "15 volts" to "450 volts" in 15-volt increments. Labels ranging from "slight shock" to "danger: severe shock" were pasted below the switches. The experimental subjects were told to administer a 15-volt shock for the man's first wrong answer and then increase the voltage each time he made an error. The man strapped in the chair was, in fact, an actor. He did not actually receive a shock. As the experimental subject increased the current, however, the actor began to writhe, shouting for mercy and begging to be released. If the experimental subjects grew reluctant to administer more current, Milgram assured them the man strapped in the chair would be fine and insisted that the success of the experiment depended on the subject's obedience. The subjects were, however, free to abort the experiment at any time.

Remarkably, 71 percent of experimental subjects were prepared to administer shocks of 285 volts or more, even though the switches at that level were labelled "intense shock," "extreme intensity shock," and "danger: severe shock" and despite the fact that the actor appeared to be in great distress at this level of current (see Figure 4.4).

Milgram's experiment teaches us that as soon as we are introduced to a structure of authority, we are inclined to obey those in power. This is the case even if the authority structure is new and highly artificial, even if we are free to walk away from it with no penalty, and even if we think that by remaining in its grip we are inflicting terrible pain on another human being. In this context, the actions and inactions of German citizens in World War II become more understandable if no more forgivable.

3. *Bureaucracies are highly effective structures of authority.* The Nazi genocide machine was also so effective because it was bureaucratically organized. As Max Weber (1968 [1914]) defined the term, a bureaucracy is a large, impersonal organization comprising many clearly defined positions arranged in a hierarchy. A bureaucracy has a permanent, salaried staff of qualified experts and written goals, rules, and procedures. Staff members always try to find ways of running their organization more efficiently. *Efficiency* means achieving the bureaucracy's

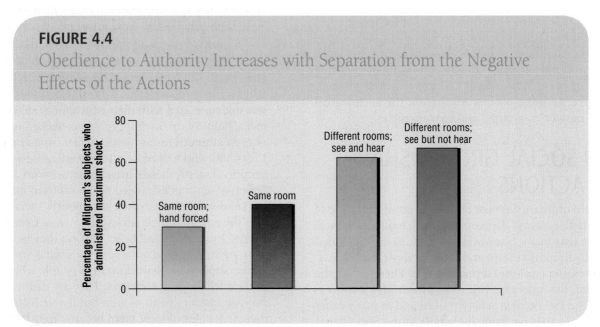

FIGURE 4.4

Obedience to Authority Increases with Separation from the Negative Effects of the Actions

Milgram's experiment supports the view that separating people from the negative effects of their actions increases the likelihood of compliance.

Source: Adapted from "Closeness of the Victim" from *Obedience to Authority*. Chapter 4. Stanley Milgram. Copyright © 1994 by Stanley Milgram.

goals at the least cost. The goal of the Nazi genocide machine was to kill Jews and other undesirables. To achieve that goal with maximum efficiency, the job was broken into many small tasks. Most officials performed only one function, such as checking train schedules, organizing entertainment for camp guards, maintaining supplies of Zyklon B gas, and removing ashes from the crematoria. The full horror of what was happening eluded many officials or at least could be conveniently ignored as they concentrated on their jobs, most of them far removed from the gas chambers and death camps in occupied Poland. Many factors account for variations in Jewish victimization rates across Europe during World War II. One factor was bureaucratic organization. Not coincidentally, the proportion of Jews killed was highest not in the Nazi-controlled countries where the hatred of Jews was most intense (e.g., Romania), but in countries where the Nazi bureaucracy was best organized (e.g., Holland; Bauman, 1989; Sofsky, 1997 [1993]).

In short, the sociological reply to the question posed by Robert's father is that it was not just blind hatred but also the nature of groups and bureaucracies that made it possible for the Nazis to kill innocent people so ruthlessly.

People commonly think that *individual* motives prompt their actions. And for good reason: as you saw in the first half of this chapter, people often make rational calculations to maximize gains and minimize losses. In addition, deeply held emotions partly govern behaviour. However, the second half of this chapter asks you to make a conceptual leap beyond the individual motives that prompt people to act in certain ways. It asks you to consider the way three kinds of social *collectivities* shape people's actions: networks, groups, and organizations. The limitations of an analysis based exclusively on individual motives should be clear from the discussion of the social roots of evil. The advantages of considering how social collectivities affect us will become clear below. We begin by considering the nature and effects of social networks.

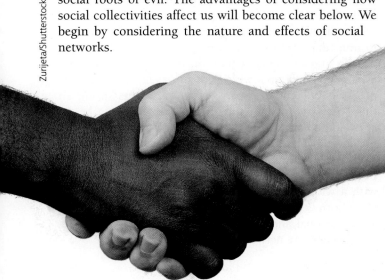

Zurijeta/Shutterstock

LO⁴ Social Networks

Suppose someone asked you to deliver a letter to a complete stranger on the other side of the country by using only acquaintances to pass the letter along. You give the letter to an acquaintance, who can give the letter to one of his or her acquaintances, and so on. Research shows that, on average, it would take no more than about six acquaintances to get the letter to the stranger. This fact suggests that in a fundamental sociological sense, we live in a small world: just a few social ties separate us from everyone else.

Our world is small because we are enmeshed in overlapping sets of social relations, or social networks. Although any particular individual may know a small number of people, his or her family members, friends, co-workers, and others know many more people who extend far beyond that individual's personal network. So, for example, the authors of this textbook are likely to be complete strangers to you. Yet your professor may know one of us or at least know someone who knows one of us. Probably no more than two links separate us from you. Put differently, although our personal networks are small, they lead quickly to much larger networks. We live in a small world because our social networks connect us to the larger world.

Sociologists define a social network as a bounded set of units (individuals, organizations, countries, etc.) linked by the exchange of material or emotional resources, everything from money to friendship. The patterns of exchange determine the boundaries of the network. Network members exchange resources more frequently with each other than with non-members. Individuals in a network think of themselves as network members. Social networks may be formal (i.e., defined in writing) or informal (i.e., defined only in practice). The people you know personally form the boundaries of your personal network. However, each of your network members is linked to other people. This is what connects you to people you have never met, creating a "small world" that extends far beyond your personal network.

> **social network** A bounded set of individuals who are linked by the exchange of material or emotional resources.

THE VALUE OF NETWORK ANALYSIS

The study of social networks is not restricted to ties among individuals (Wasserman and Faust, 1994; Wellman and Berkowitz, 1997). The units of analysis (or *nodes*) in a network can be individuals, groups, organizations, and even countries. Thus, social network analysts have examined everything from intimate relationships between lovers to diplomatic relations among nations.

Unlike organizations, most networks lack names and offices. There is a Boy Scouts of Canada but no North American Trading Bloc. In a sense, networks lie beneath the more visible collectivities of social life, but that makes them no less real or important. Some analysts claim that we can gain only a partial sense of why certain things happen in the social world by focusing on highly visible collectivities. From their point of view, the whole story requires probing below the surface and examining the network level. The study of social networks clarifies a wide range of social phenomena, including how people find jobs and form communities.

Finding a Job

Many people learn about important events, ideas, and opportunities from their social networks. Friends and acquaintances often introduce you to everything from an interesting college course or a great restaurant to a satisfying occupation or a future spouse. Social networks aren't the only source of information, but they are highly significant.

Consider how people find jobs. Do you look in the Help Wanted section of your local newspaper, scan the Internet, or walk around certain areas of town looking for "Employee Wanted" signs? Although these strategies are common, people often learn about employment opportunities from other people.

What kind of people? According to sociologist Mark Granovetter (1973), you may have strong or weak ties to another person. You have strong ties to people who are close to you, such as family members and friends. You have weak ties to mere acquaintances, such as people you meet at parties and friends of friends. In his research, Granovetter found that weak ties are more important than strong ties in finding a job, which is contrary to common sense. You might reasonably assume that a mere acquaintance wouldn't do much to help you find a job, whereas a close friend or relative would make a lot more effort in this regard. However, by focusing on the flow of information in personal networks, Granovetter found something different. Mere acquaintances are more likely to provide useful information about employment opportunities than friends or family members because people who are close to you typically share overlapping networks. Therefore, the information they can provide about job opportunities is often redundant.

In contrast, mere acquaintances are likely to be connected to *diverse* networks. They can therefore provide information about many different job openings and make introductions to many different potential employers. Moreover, because people typically have more weak ties than strong ties, the sum of weak ties holds more information about job opportunities than the sum of strong ties. These features of personal networks allowed Granovetter to conclude that the "strength of weak ties" lies in their diversity and abundance.

Urban Networks

We rely on social networks for a lot more than job information. Consider everyday life in the big city. We often think of big cities as cold and alienating places where few people know one another. In this view, urban acquaintanceships tend to be few and functionally specific; we know someone fleetingly as a bank teller or a server in a restaurant but not as a whole person. Even dating can involve a series of brief encounters. In contrast, people often think of small towns as friendly, comfortable places where everyone knows everyone else (and everyone else's business). Indeed, some of the founders of sociology emphasized just this distinction. Notably, German sociologist Ferdinand Tönnies (1988 [1887]) contrasted *community* with *society*. According to Tönnies, a community is marked by intimate and emotionally intense social ties, whereas a society is marked by impersonal relationships held together largely by self-interest. A big city is a prime example of a society in Tönnies's judgment.

Tönnies's view prevailed until network analysts started studying big-city life in the 1970s. Where Tönnies saw only sparse, functionally specific ties, network analysts found elaborate social networks, some functionally specific and some not. For example, Barry Wellman and his colleagues studied personal networks in Toronto (Wellman, Carrington, and Hall, 1997). They found that each Torontonian had an average of about 400 social ties, including immediate and extended kin, neighbours, friends, and co-workers. These ties provided everything from emotional aid (e.g., visits after a personal tragedy) and financial support (e.g., small loans) to minor services (e.g., fixing a car) and information of the kind Granovetter studied.

Strong ties that last a long time are typically restricted to immediate family members, a few close relatives and friends, and a close co-worker or two. Beyond that, however, people rely on a wide array of ties for different purposes at different times. Downtown residents sitting on their front stoops on a summer evening, sipping beverages, and chatting with neighbours as the kids play road hockey may be less common than they were 50 years ago. However, the automobile, public transportation, the telephone, and the Internet help people stay in close touch with a wide range of contacts for a variety of purposes (Haythornwaite and Wellman, 2002). Far from living in an impersonal and alienating world, the lives of today's city dwellers are network rich.

The Toronto Star/GetStock.com

Nicholas/iStockphoto.com

StockLite/Shutterstock

Comstock/Jupiterimages/Getty Images

lawrence atienza/iStockphoto.com

LO⁵ Groups

Intensity and intimacy characterize many two-person relationships. However, outside forces can often destroy them. For instance, the star-crossed lovers in Romeo and Juliet are torn between their love for each other and their loyalty to the feuding Montague and Capulet families. In the end, Romeo and Juliet die, victims of the feud.

Love thwarted by conflicting group loyalty is the stuff of many tragic plays, novels, and movies. Most audiences have no problem grasping the fact that group loyalty is often more powerful than romantic love. However, why group loyalty holds such power over us is unclear. The sociological study of groups provides some useful answers.

Social groups are composed of one or more networks of people who identify with one another, routinely interact, and adhere to defined norms, roles, and statuses. We usually distinguish social groups from social categories, people who share similar status but do not routinely interact or identify with one another. Coffee drinkers form a social category. They do not normally share norms, routinely interact, and identify with one another. In contrast, members of a family, sports team, or college are aware of shared membership. They think of themselves as members of a collectivity and routinely interact. They form groups.

PRIMARY AND SECONDARY GROUPS

Many kinds of social groups exist. However, sociologists make a basic distinction between primary and secondary groups. In primary groups, norms, roles, and statuses are agreed on but statuses are agreed on but

social group A group composed of one or more networks of people who identify with one another and adhere to defined norms, roles, and statuses.

social category A group composed of people who share similar status but do not identify with one another.

primary group Social groups in which norms, roles, and statuses are agreed upon but are not put in writing. Social interaction leads to strong emotional ties. It extends over a long period and involves a wide range of activities. It results in group members knowing one another well.

are not put in writing. Social interaction creates strong emotional ties, extends over a long period, and involves a wide range of activities. It results in group members knowing one another well. The family is the most important primary group.

Secondary groups are larger and more impersonal than primary groups. Compared with primary groups, social interaction in secondary groups creates weaker emotional ties. It extends over a shorter period and involves a narrow range of activities. It results in most group members having at most a passing acquaintance with one another. Your sociology class is an example of a secondary group. Bearing these distinctions in mind, we can begin to explore the power of groups to ensure conformity.

GROUP CONFORMITY

Television's first reality TV show was *Candid Camera*. In an early episode, an unsuspecting man waits for an elevator. When the elevator door opens, he finds four people, all confederates of the show, facing the elevator's back wall. Seeing the four people with their backs to him, the man at first hesitates. He then tentatively enters the elevator. However, rather than turning around so he faces the door, he remains facing the back wall, just like the others. The scene is repeated several times. Men and women, black and white, all behave the same. Confronting unanimously bizarre behaviour, they all chose conformity over common sense.

Conformity is an integral part of group life, and primary groups generate more pressure to conform than secondary groups do. Strong social ties create emotional intimacy. They also ensure that primary group members

FIGURE 4.5

The Asch Experiment

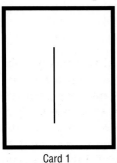

Card 1

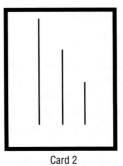

Card 2

share similar attitudes, beliefs, and information. Beyond the family, friendship groups (or cliques) and gangs demonstrate these features. Group members tend to dress and act alike, speak the same lingo, share the same likes and dislikes, and demand loyalty, especially in the face of external threat. Conformity ensures group cohesion.

The Asch Experiment

A famous experiment conducted by social psychologist Solomon Asch more than half a century ago demonstrates how group pressure creates conformity (Asch, 1955). Asch gathered seven men, one of whom was the experimental subject. The other six were Asch's confederates. Asch showed the seven men a card with a line drawn on it. He then showed them a second card with three lines of varying length drawn on it (see Figure 4.5). One by one, he asked the confederates to judge which line on card 2 was the same length as the line on card 1. The answer was obvious. One line on card 2 was much shorter than the line on card 1. One line was much longer. One was exactly the same length. Yet, as instructed by Asch, all six confederates said that either the shorter or the longer line was the same length as the line on card 1. When it came time for the experimental subject to make his judgment, he typically overruled his own perception and agreed with the majority. Only 25 percent of Asch's experimental subjects consistently gave the right answer. Asch thus demonstrated how easily group pressure can overturn individual conviction and result in conformity.

Groupthink

The power of groups to ensure conformity is often a valuable asset. Sports teams could not excel without the willingness of players to undergo personal sacrifice for the good of the group, and armies could not function. In fact, as sociologists have demonstrated and as high-ranking military officers have observed, group cohesion—not patriotism or bravery—is the main factor motivating soldiers to engage in combat (Marshall, 1947: 160–61; Stouffer et al., 1949). As one soldier says in the 2001 movie *Black Hawk Down*, "When I go home people will ask me, 'Hey, Hoot, why do you do it, man? Why? Are

Natural or artificial boundaries—rivers, mountains, highways, railway tracks—typically separate groups or communities.

groupthink Group pressure to conform despite individual misgivings.

in-group Comprises people who belong to a group.

out-group Comprises people who are excluded from the in-group.

you some kinda war junkie?' I won't say a goddamn word. Why? They won't understand. They won't understand why we do it. They won't understand it's about the men next to you. And that's it. That's all it is."

However, being a "good team player" can have a downside, because the consensus of a group can sometimes be misguided or dangerous. Dissent might save the group from making mistakes, but the pressure to conform despite individual misgivings—sometimes called group-think (Janis, 1972)—can lead to disaster. Groupthink was at work in high-level meetings preceding the space shuttle *Columbia* disaster in 2003. Transcripts of those meetings at the National Aeronautics and Space Administration (NASA) show that the official who ran shuttle management meetings, a non-engineer, believed from the outset that foam insulation debris could not damage the spacecraft. She dismissed the issue and cut off discussion when an engineer expressed his concerns. The others present quickly fell into line with the person running the meeting (Wald and Schwartz, 2003). A few days later, damage caused by foam insulation debris caused *Columbia* to break apart on re-entry into the earth's atmosphere. Seven astronauts died.

INCLUSION AND EXCLUSION: IN-GROUPS AND OUT-GROUPS

If a group exists, it follows that some people must not belong to it. Accordingly, sociologists distinguish in-group members (i.e., those who belong) from out-group members (i.e., those who do not). Members of an in-group typically draw a boundary separating themselves from members of the out-group, and they try to keep out-group members from crossing the line. Anyone who has gone to high school knows all about in-groups and out-groups. They have seen firsthand how race, class, athletic ability, academic talent, and physical attractiveness act as boundaries separating groups.

Group Boundaries: Competition and Self-Esteem

Why do group boundaries crystallize? One theory is that group boundaries emerge when people compete for scarce resources. For example, old immigrants may greet new immigrants with hostility if the latter are seen as competitors for scarce jobs (Levine and Campbell, 1972). Another theory is that group boundaries emerge when people are motivated to protect their self-esteem. From this point of view, drawing group boundaries allows people to increase their self-esteem by believing that out-groups have low status (Tajfel, 1981).

Both theories are supported by a classic experiment on prejudice, the Robber's Cave Study (Sherif, Harvey, White, Hood, and Sherif, 1988). Researchers brought two groups of 11-year-old boys to a summer camp at Robber's Cave State Park in Oklahoma in 1954. The boys were strangers to one another, and for about a week the two groups were kept apart. They swam, camped, and hiked. Each group chose a name for itself, and the boys printed their group's name on their caps and T-shirts. Then the two groups met. A series of athletic competitions were set up between them. Soon, each group became highly antagonistic toward the other. Each group came to hold the other in low esteem. The boys ransacked cabins, started food fights, and stole various items from members of the other group. Thus, under competitive conditions, the boys quickly drew sharp group boundaries.

The investigators next stopped the athletic competitions and created several apparent emergencies whose solution required cooperation between the two groups. One such emergency involved a leak in the pipe supplying water to the camp. The researchers assigned the boys to teams comprising members of *both* groups. Their job was to inspect the pipe and fix the leak. After engaging in several such cooperative ventures, the boys started playing together without fighting. Once cooperation replaced competition and the groups ceased to hold each other in low esteem, group boundaries melted away as quickly as they had formed.

Significantly, the two groups of boys were of equal status—the boys were all white, middle-class, and 11 years old—and their contact involved face to face interaction in a setting where norms established by the investigators promoted a reduction of group prejudice. Social scientists today recognize that all these conditions must be in place before the boundaries between an in-group and an out-group can fade away (Sternberg, 1998: 512).

Dominant Groups

The boundaries separating groups often seem unchangeable and even natural. In general, however, dominant groups construct group boundaries in particular circumstances to further their goals (Barth, 1969; Tajfel, 1981). Consider Germans and Jews. By the early twentieth century, Jews were well integrated into German society. They were economically successful, culturally innovative, and politically influential, and many of them considered themselves more German than Jewish. In 1933, the year Hitler seized power, 44 percent of marriages involving at least one German Jew were to a non-Jew. In addition, some German Jews converted before marrying non-Jewish Germans (Gordon, 1984). Yet, although the boundary separating Germans from Jews was quite weak, the Nazis chose to redraw and reinforce it. Defining a Jew as anyone who had at least one Jewish grandparent, they passed a whole series of anti-Jewish laws and, in the end, systematically slaughtered the Jews of Europe. The division between Germans and Jews was not "natural." It came into existence because of its perceived usefulness to a dominant group.

GROUPS AND SOCIAL IMAGINATION

So far, we have focused almost exclusively on face to face interaction in groups. However, people also interact with other group members in their imagination. Take reference groups, for example. A reference group is composed of people against whom an individual evaluates his or her situation or conduct. Put differently, members of a reference group function as "role models." Reference groups may influence us even though they represent a largely imaginary ideal. For instance, the advertising industry promotes certain body ideals that many people try to emulate, although we know that hardly anyone looks like a runway model or a Barbie doll.

We have to exercise our imaginations vigorously to participate in the group life of a large, complex society like ours because much social life involves belonging to secondary groups without knowing or interacting with most group members. For an individual to interact with any more than a small fraction of the 34 million people living in this country is impossible. Nonetheless, most Canadians feel a strong emotional bond to their fellow citizens. Similarly, think about the employees and students at your college or university. They know they belong to the same secondary group, and many of them are probably loyal to it. Yet, how many people at your school have you met? Probably no more than a small fraction of the total. One way to make sense of the paradox of intimacy despite distance is to think of your school or Canada as an "imagined community." It is imagined because you cannot possibly meet most members of the group and can only speculate about what they must be like. It is nonetheless a community because people believe strongly in its existence and importance (Anderson, 1991).

Many secondary groups are formal organizations, or secondary groups designed to achieve explicit objectives. In complex societies like ours, the most common and influential formal organizations are bureaucracies. We now turn to an examination of these often frustrating but necessary organizational forms.

Bureaucracy

Earlier, we noted that Weber regarded bureaucracies as the most efficient type of secondary group. This runs against the grain of common knowledge. In everyday speech, when someone says "bureaucracy," people commonly think of bored clerks sitting in small cubicles spinning out endless trails of "red tape" that create needless waste and frustrate the goals of clients. The idea that bureaucracies are efficient may seem odd.

How can we square the reality of bureaucratic inefficiencies—even tragedies—with Weber's view that bureaucracies are the most efficient type of secondary group? The answer is twofold. First, we must recognize that when Weber wrote about the efficiency of bureaucracy, he was comparing it with older organizational forms. These had operated on the basis of either traditional practice ("We do it this way because we've always done it this way") or the charisma of their leaders ("We do it this way because our chief inspires us to do it this way"). Compared with such "traditional" and "charismatic" organizations, bureaucracies are generally more efficient. Second, we must recognize that Weber thought bureaucracies could operate efficiently only in the ideal case. He wrote extensively about some of bureaucracy's less admirable aspects in the real world. In other words, he understood that reality is often messier than the ideal case. In reality, bureaucracies vary in efficiency. Therefore, rather than proclaiming bureaucracy efficient or inefficient, we need to find out what makes bureaucracies work well or poorly.

One factor underlying bureaucratic inefficiency is size. The larger the bureaucracy, the more difficult it is for functionaries to communicate. Moreover, bigger bureaucracies make it easier for rivalries and coalitions to form.

A second factor underlying bureaucratic inefficiency is social structure. Figure 4.6 shows a typical bureaucratic structure: a hierarchy. The bureaucracy has a head, below which are three divisions, below which are six departments. As you move up the hierarchy, the power of the staff increases. Note also the red lines of communication that join the various bureaucratic units. Departments report only to their divisions. Divisions report only to the head.

Usually, the more levels in a bureaucratic structure, the more difficult communication becomes, because people have to communicate indirectly, through department and division heads, rather than directly with each other. Information may be lost, blocked, reinterpreted, or distorted as it moves up the hierarchy, or an excess of information may cause top levels to become engulfed in a paperwork blizzard that prevents them from clearly seeing the needs of the organization and its clients. Bureaucratic heads may have only a vague and imprecise idea of what is happening "on the ground" (Wilensky, 1967).

Consider also what happens when the lines of communication directly joining departments or divisions are weak or nonexistent. As the lines joining units in Figure 4.6 suggest, department A1 may have information that could help department B1 do its job better, but A1 may have to communicate that information indirectly through the division level. At the division level, the information may be lost, blocked, reinterpreted, or distorted. Thus, just as people who have authority may lack information, people who have information may lack the authority to act on it directly (Crozier, 1964).

In the business world, large bureaucratic organizations are sometimes unable to compete against smaller, innovative firms, particularly in industries that are changing quickly (Burns and Stalker, 1961). This situation occurs partly because innovative firms tend to have flatter and more democratic organizational structures, such as the network illustrated in Figure 4.7. Compare the flat network structure in Figure 4.7 with the traditional bureaucratic structure in Figure 4.6. Note that the network structure has fewer levels than the traditional bureaucratic structure. Moreover, in the network structure, lines of communication link all units. In the traditional bureaucratic structure, information flows only upward.

Much evidence suggests that flatter bureaucracies with decentralized decision making and multiple lines of communication produce more satisfied workers, happier clients, and bigger profits (Kanter, 1989). Some of

FIGURE 4.6
Bureaucratic Structure

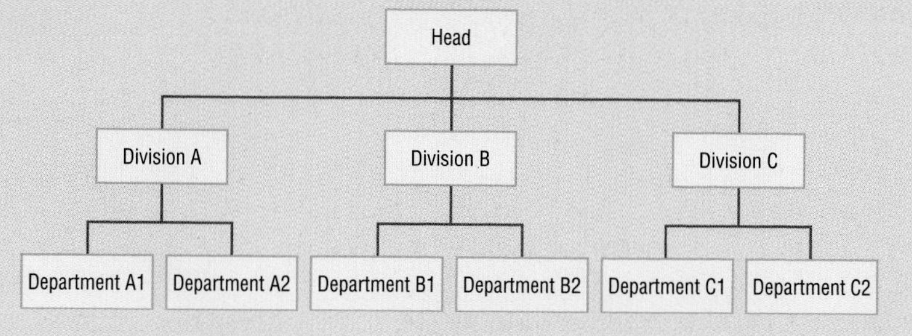

FIGURE 4.7
Network Structure

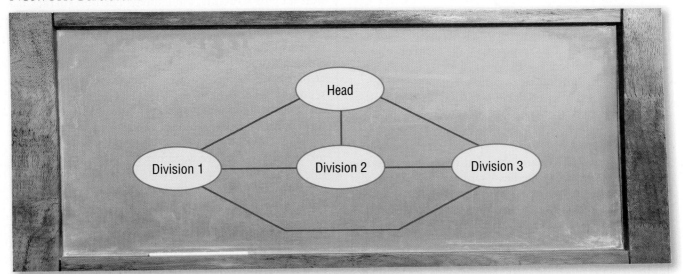

this evidence comes from Sweden and Japan. Beginning in the early 1970s, such corporations as Volvo and Toyota were at the forefront of bureaucratic innovation in those countries. They began eliminating middle-management positions. They allowed worker participation in a variety of tasks related to their main functions. They delegated authority to autonomous teams of a dozen or so workers that were allowed to make many decisions themselves. They formed "quality circles" of workers to monitor and correct defects in products and services. As a result, product quality, worker morale, and profitability improved. Today, these ideas have spread well beyond the Swedish and Japanese automobile industries and are evident in many large North American companies, both in the manufacturing and in the service sectors.

71% The percentage of students who go online to study for a class.

GET ONLINE

The easy-to-navigate website for **SOC+** offers guidance on key topics in **Sociology** in a variety of engaging formats. You have the opportunity to refine and check your understanding via interactive quizzes and flashcards. Videos provide inspiration for your own further exploration. And, in order to make **SOC+** an even better learning tool, we invite you to speak up about your experience with **SOC+** by completing a survey form and sending us your comments.

Get online and discover the following resources:

- Printable and Interactive Flashcards
- Interactive Quizzing
- Crossword Puzzles
- Discipline-specific activities

"I think this book is awesome for students of all ages. It is a much simpler way to study."

—Yasmine Al-Hashimi, Fanshawe College

Visit **www.icansocplus.com** to find the resources you need today!

5 Deviance and Crime

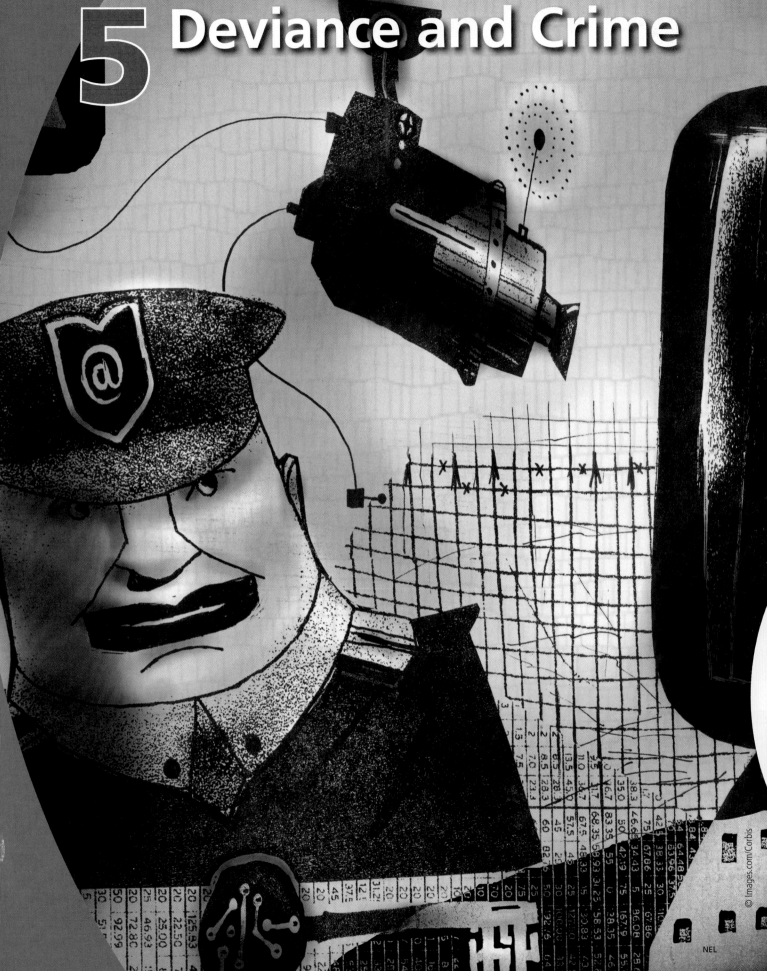

LO¹ The Social Definition of Deviance and Crime

If you happen to come across members of the Tukano tribe in northern Brazil, don't be surprised if they greet you with a cheery "Have you bathed today?" You would probably find the question insulting, but think how you would feel if you were greeted by the Yanomamö people in Brazil's central highlands. A French anthropologist reports that when he first encountered the Yanomamö, they rubbed mucus and tobacco juice into their palms, then inspected him by running their filthy hands over his body (Chagnon, 1992). He must have been relieved to return to urban Brazil and be greeted with a simple kiss on the cheek.

Rules for greeting people vary widely from one country to the next and among different cultural groups within one country. That is why a marketing company created an animated website showing business travellers how to greet their hosts in the 15 countries where the firm does business ("The Business of Touch," 2006). After all, violating local norms can cause great offence and result in the loss of a contract, a fact that one visitor to South Korea found out too late. He beckoned his host with an index finger, after which the host grew quiet. He discovered after he lost the deal that Koreans beckon only cats and dogs with an index finger. If you want to beckon someone politely in South Korea, you should do so with all four fingers facing down, much like Canadians wave goodbye.

Because norms vary widely, deviance is relative. What some people consider normal, others consider deviant, and vice versa. No act is deviant in and of itself. People commit deviant acts only when they break a norm and cause others to react negatively. From a sociological point of view, *everyone* is a deviant in one social context or another.

LEARNING OBJECTIVES:

LO¹ Deviance and crime vary among cultures, across history, and from one social context to another. Rather than being inherent in the characteristics of individuals or actions, deviance and crime are socially defined and constructed. The distribution of power is especially important in the social construction of deviance and crime.

LO² Crime rates vary by age, gender, and race.

LO³ As with deviance and crime, conceptions of appropriate punishment vary culturally and historically.

LO⁴ Imprisonment is one of the main forms of punishment in industrial societies.

LO⁵ Fear of crime may be subject to manipulation by commercial and political groups that benefit from it.

LO⁶ There are cost-effective and workable alternatives to current methods of punishment.

THE DIFFERENCE BETWEEN DEVIANCE AND CRIME

Deviance involves breaking a norm and evoking a negative reaction from others. Societies establish some norms as laws. **Crime** is deviance that breaks a **law**, which is a norm stipulated and enforced by government bodies.

Just as deviance is relative, so is crime. Consider that a list of famous people who have been labelled criminals would include Socrates, Jesus, Martin Luther, Louis Riel, Mahatma Ghandi, Martin Luther King, Jr., and Nelson Mandela. For many people today, these historical figures are heroes. In contrast, those who planned and participated in the extermination of Jews, Romani ("Gypsies"), and gays and lesbians in Nazi Germany were acting in a way that was defined, at the time in Germany, as law-abiding. You would probably consider the actions taken by the Nazis in Germany, rather than the actions of Jesus or Martin Luther, to be deviant or criminal. That is because norms and laws have changed dramatically. Today, anyone who advocates or promotes genocide commits a crime under Canadian law. We conclude that what is considered a crime in some times and places is considered perfectly normal in other times and places (see the Sociology at the Movies box).

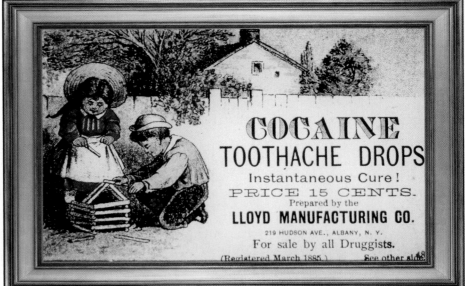

National Library of Medicine, Washington, DC

One of the determinants of the seriousness of a deviant act is its perceived harmfulness. Perceptions vary historically, however. For instance, until the early part of the twentieth century, cocaine was considered a medicine. It was an ingredient in cold formulas and toothache drops, and in these forms it was commonly given to children.

SANCTIONS

Many otherwise deviant acts go unnoticed or are considered too trivial to warrant negative *sanctions*, which are actions indicating disapproval of deviance. People who are observed committing more serious acts of deviance are typically punished, either informally or formally. **Informal punishment** is mild. It may involve raised eyebrows, a harsh stare, an ironic smile, gossip, ostracism, "shaming," or **stigmatization** (Braithwaite, 1989). When people are stigmatized, they are negatively evaluated because of a marker that distinguishes them from others (Goffman, 1963). For example, until recently people with physical or mental disabilities were often treated with scorn or as a source of amusement. Pope Leo X (1475–1521) is said to have retained several mentally retarded dwarves as a form of entertainment. **Formal punishment** results from people breaking laws. For example, criminals can be formally punished by having to serve time in prison or perform community service.

Types of deviance and crime vary in terms of the *severity of the social response*, which ranges from mild disapproval to capital punishment (Hagan, 1994). They vary also in terms of the *perceived harmfulness* of the deviant or criminal act. Note that actual harmfulness is not the only issue here—*perceived* harmfulness is involved too. Coca-Cola got its name because, in the early part of the last century, it contained a derivative of cocaine. Now cocaine is an illegal drug because people's perceptions of its harmfulness changed. Finally, deviance and crime vary in terms of the *degree of public agreement* about whether an act should be considered deviant. Even the social definition of murder varies over time and across cultures and societies. Thus, at the beginning of the twentieth century, Inuit communities sometimes allowed newborns to freeze to death. Life in the far north was precarious. Killing newborns was not considered a punishable offence if community members agreed that investing scarce

deviance Occurs when someone departs from a norm and evokes a negative reaction from others.

crime Deviance that is against the law.

law A norm stipulated and enforced by government bodies.

informal punishment A mild sanction that is imposed during face-to-face interaction, rather than by the judicial system.

stigmatization Process of negatively evaluating people because of a marker that distinguishes them from others.

formal punishment Takes place when the judicial system penalizes someone for breaking a law.

Paradise Now

Of all the social types who populate today's world, perhaps none is more difficult to understand than the suicide attacker. Many people in the West wonder who in their right mind would fly a plane into a building. What kind of person do you have to be to blow yourself up in a bus full of ordinary people or a mosque full of worshippers? Somehow, the terms *deviant* and *criminal* seem inadequate to describe such people; they are widely seen by people in the West as crazy fanatics who lack all conscience and humanity.

Paradise Now, nominated for an Oscar as best foreign-language film, demonstrates that the common Western view is ethnocentric. It sketches the social circumstances that shaped the lives of two suicide bombers, showing that they are a lot like us and that if we found ourselves in similar circumstances, we might turn out to be a lot like them. The film is critical of suicide bombing, but it helps us understand what makes suicide bombers tick, thereby enlightening us sociologically and politically.

Said (Kais Nashif) and Khaled (Ali Suliman) are ordinary 20-something garage mechanics and best friends. They live in the Palestinian city of Nablus, which, like the rest of the West Bank and the Gaza Strip, has been under Israeli military occupation their whole lives. As a result of the occupation, Said and Khaled have never been able to travel outside of the West Bank, they enjoy limited economic opportunities, they are bored stiff, and, most importantly, they have been robbed of their dignity. Like all Palestinians, they want the Israelis out so they can establish an independent country of their own. But their demonstrations, their rock throwing, and their armed attacks have had no effect on the powerful Israeli military. Consequently, some time before the film begins, Said and Khaled volunteered to serve as weapons of last resort: suicide bombers.

A study of all 462 suicide bombers who attacked targets worldwide between 1980 and 2003 found not a single case of depression, psychosis, past suicide attempts, or other such mental health issues among them. The bombers were rarely poor, came most often from working- or middle-class families, and were better educated than the populations from which they were recruited. Many of them were religious, but most of them, like Said and Khaled, were not. What they had in common was an ardent desire to liberate territory from what they regarded as foreign occupation or control (Pape, 2005). Said and Khaled are, then, quite typical suicide bombers: they are convinced by their powerlessness and their experience that they have no weapon other than suicide bombing that might help them achieve their aim of national liberation.

As Paradise Now opens, the two friends are informed that they have been selected for a suicide attack in 48 hours. Their mundane preparations are peppered with humour, errors, and everyday trivia that make Said and Khaled seem like very ordinary people. For example, in the middle of recording his "martyrdom tape" for TV broadcast, Khaled incongruously remembers to tell his mother, whom he knows will watch the tape, that he saw a bargain on water filters at a local merchant's store. But underlying such humanizing events is a tension that gives the movie its force. Said and Khaled are ambivalent about their mission, not just because they have misgivings about dying but also because they feel guilty about its inhumanity to civilians and are unsure of its ultimate political utility.

Ali Suliman and Kais Nashif in Paradise Now

In the end, only Said manages to go through with the attack, but not before we get the full story about his ambivalence. Suha (Lubna Azabal), the woman he loves, is the daughter of a famous martyr for the Palestinian cause, but she strongly opposes suicide bombing. Said listens intently when she argues that suicide bombing is contrary to the spirit of Islam, it kills innocent victims, and it accomplishes nothing because it invites retaliation in a never-ending cycle of violence. But more compelling are the forces pushing Said to carry out the attack. Thousands of Palestinians are paid, threatened, and blackmailed to serve as informants for the Israelis. Said's father was one of them. When he was caught, he was executed by Palestinian militants. Said has been deeply ashamed of his father's actions his whole life and angry with the Israelis for forcing his father to serve as a collaborator. His ultimate motivation for becoming a suicide bomber is retaliation against Israel for turning his father into an informant. Like most suicide bombers in the country, he is driven by the desire for revenge (Brym, 2007b; Brym and Araj, 2006).

Critical Thinking Questions

- From whose point of view are suicide bombers deviant and criminal?
- From whose point of view are suicide bombers normal?
- Must you agree with the actions of suicide bombers to understand them?
- What would you do if you were in Said's position?

resources in keeping the newborn alive could endanger everyone's well-being. Similarly, whether we classify the death of a miner as accidental or a case of manslaughter depends on the kind of worker safety legislation in existence. Some societies have more stringent worker safety rules than others, and deaths considered accidental in some societies are classified as criminal offences in others (McCormick, 1999). So we see that, even when it comes to serious crimes, social definitions are variable.

MEASURING CRIME

Some crimes are more common than others, and rates of crime vary over place and time and among different social groups. We now describe some of these variations. Then we review the main sociological explanations of crime and deviance.

First, a word about crime statistics. Information on crime collected by the police is our main source of crime statistics. Since 1962, Canada has used a system called the Canadian Uniform Crime Reports (UCR). Under this system, information is collected from more than 400 municipal police departments across Canada on 91 detailed categories of crime. Annually, the government publishes data on types of offences and characteristics of offenders.

These statistics have two main shortcomings. First, much crime is not reported to the police. This is particularly true of so-called victimless crimes, which involve violations of the law in which no victim steps forward and is identified. Communicating for the purposes of prostitution, illegal gambling, and the use of illegal drugs are all victimless crimes. In addition, many common or "level 1" assaults go unreported because the assailant is a friend or relative of the victim. Many victims of sexual assault are also reluctant to report the crime because they are afraid they will be humiliated or not believed and stigmatized by making it public. The second main shortcoming of official crime statistics is that

authorities and the wider public decide which criminal acts to report and which to ignore. If, for instance, the authorities decide to crack down on drugs, more drug-related crimes will be counted, not because more drug-related crimes are committed, but because more drug criminals are apprehended. Changes in legislation, which either create new offences or amend existing offences, will also influence the number of recorded offences. Recognizing these difficulties, students of crime often supplement official crime statistics with other sources of information.

Self-report surveys are especially useful. In such surveys, respondents are asked to report their involvement in criminal activities, either as perpetrators or as victims. Self-report data compensate for many of the problems associated with official statistics. In general, self-report surveys report approximately the same rate of serious crime as official statistics but find two or three times the rate of less serious crimes.

Self-report surveys are useful because they tell us that a majority of Canadians have engaged in some type of criminal activity and that about a quarter of the population in any given year believe that they have been the victim of crime. These large proportions remind us that committing an act in violation of the law does not automatically result in being officially labelled a criminal. The process of criminal labelling can be likened to a funnel, wide at one end and narrow at the other. To be officially identified as a criminal, an individual's law-violating behaviour must first be observed and felt to justify action. The behaviour must be reported to the police who, in turn, must respond to the incident, decide that it warrants further investigation, file a report, and make an arrest. Next,

victimless crimes Violations of the law in which no victim has stepped forward and been identified.

self-report surveys Surveys in which respondents are asked to report their involvement in criminal activities, either as perpetrators or as victims.

750581196/Shutterstock

the accused person must appear at a preliminary hearing, an arraignment, and a trial. If the person does not plead guilty, the possibility always exists that he or she will not be convicted because guilt has not been proven "beyond a reasonable doubt."

In victimization surveys, people are asked whether they have been victims of crime. Although these types of surveys date back to the mid-1960s in the United States, no national victimization survey was conducted in Canada until 1988 (Fattah, 1991). The International Crime Victim Survey (ICVS) collected victimization data by using the same questionnaire in many countries, including Canada, in 1989, 1992, 1996–97, and 2000 (Besserer, 2002). It examined householders' experience with crime, policing, crime prevention, and feelings of being unsafe. This survey found that, on average, 55 percent of victimization incidents are reported to police, with property crimes more likely to be reported than crimes against persons. In part, this reflects the general requirement by insurance companies that individuals seeking compensation for property stolen or damaged as the result of a criminal act file a police report. Although victimization surveys provide detailed information about crime victims, they provide less reliable data about offenders.

Bearing these caveats in mind, what does the official record show? Most Canadians would be understandably alarmed to hear that, in 2008, 2.2 million Criminal Code incidents were reported to police agencies (Wallace, 2009). They might assume that each of these incidents mirrored the violent, dramatic, and lurid offences that daily media reports bring to our attention. But that is not the case. In 2008, just 17.6 percent of Criminal Code incidents involved violent crimes (see Figure 5.1). The 2008 Canadian crime rate was almost twice as high as it was 50 years earlier. However, the long crime wave that began its upswing in the early 1960s peaked, fell in the 1990s, and continued to decline in the 2000s. How do we explain the fall?

First, a growing number of well-trained troops are fighting crime (Mohr and Spencer, 1999: 588). Recent declines in Canada's crime rate may reflect the introduction of community policing initiatives, enforcement efforts that target specific types of crime, the refinement of case management methods, improvements in the field of forensics, and crime prevention efforts (Logan, 2001: 3).

> **victimization surveys**
> Surveys in which people are asked whether they have been victims of crime.

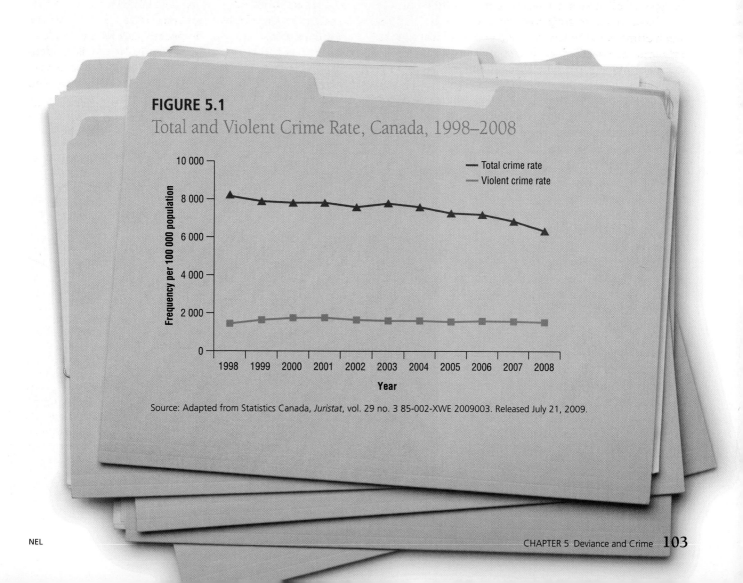

FIGURE 5.1

Total and Violent Crime Rate, Canada, 1998–2008

Source: Adapted from Statistics Canada, *Juristat*, vol. 29 no. 3 85-002-XWE 2009003. Released July 21, 2009.

Second, the people most prone to street crime are young men, but Canada is aging and the number of young people in the population has declined in recent decades.

Third, following a steep recession in 1990–91, the economy grew and unemployment fell every between 1992 and 2007 (except for 2001). Economic conditions likely favoured a decrease in crime because the variable most strongly correlated with the crime rate is the male unemployment rate (John Howard Society, 1999: 3).

Finally, and more controversially, some researchers argue that declining crime rates may be linked to the legalization of abortion (Donahue and Levitt, 2001). Observing that the crime rate started to decline 19 years after abortion was legalized, they suggest that the decline occurred because, with the legalization of abortion, proportionately fewer unwanted children were in the population. They argue that unwanted children are more prone to criminal behaviour than wanted children are, because they tend to receive less parental supervision and guidance.

Note that we have not claimed that putting more people in prison and imposing tougher penalties for crime help to account for lower crime rates. We will explain why these actions generally do not result in lower crime rates when we discuss *social control* (methods of ensuring conformity) and punishment. We will also probe one of the most fascinating questions raised by official statistics: if crime rates fell in the 1990s and 2000s, what accounts for our increased enthusiasm for get-tough policies, our increasing prison population, and our widespread and growing fear of crime?

LO² CRIMINAL PROFILES

Age and Gender

In more than 80 percent of Canadian adult criminal court cases, the accused is a man. Women account for a significant percentage of offenders in only a few types of crimes: nearly half of offences involving prostitution, and nearly three out of ten cases of fraud and theft (including shoplifting; Thomas, 2004: 3). This pattern repeats itself for cases processed in youth courts. However, with every passing year women compose a slightly higher percentage of arrests (Hartnagel, 2000). This change is partly due to the fact that, in the course of

socialization, traditional social controls and definitions of femininity are less often being imposed on women (see Chapter 8, Sexuality and Gender).

Most crime is committed by people who have not reached middle age. The 15- to 24-year-old age cohort is the most prone to criminal behaviour. The percentage of 15- to 24-year-olds who are charged with a *violent* crime is about twice as high as the percentage of 15- to 24-year-olds in the population. For *property* crimes, the percentage is about three times higher (Savoie, 2002: 3).

Race

Analysis of official statistics reveals that race is also a factor in who is arrested. For instance, although Aboriginal people represent about 2 percent of the adult population in Canada, in recent decades they have accounted for 15 to 19 percent of Canadians sentenced to custody (Hendrick and Farmer, 2002: 11). The overrepresentation of Aboriginal people in Canada's prisons is particularly

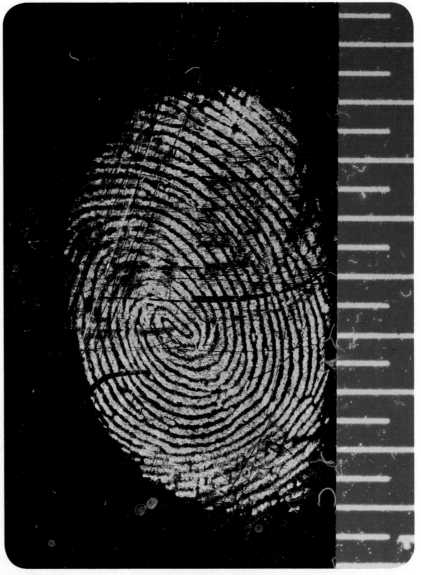

Photos.com

marked in the Prairie provinces and the northern territories, where they form a relatively large part of the population. For example, in Saskatchewan, Aboriginal Canadians account for about 10 percent of the population and 80 percent of people sentenced to custody (Johnson, 2004).

There are several reasons for the overrepresentation of Aboriginal people in Canada's prisons (Hartnagel, 2000). First, a disproportionately large number of Aboriginal people are poor. Although the great majority of poor people are law abiding, poverty and its handicaps are associated with elevated crime rates. Second, Aboriginal people tend to commit so-called street crimes—breaking and entering, robbery, assault, and the like—that are more detectable than white-collar crimes such as embezzlement, fraud, copyright infringement, false advertising, and so on. Third, the police, the courts, and other institutions may discriminate against Aboriginal people. As a result, Aboriginal people may be more likely to be apprehended, prosecuted, and convicted. Fourth, contact with Western culture has disrupted social life in many Aboriginal communities (see Chapter 7, Race and Ethnicity). This disruption has led to a weakening of social control over community members. Some people think that certain "races" are *inherently* more law abiding than others, but they are able to hold such an opinion only by ignoring the powerful *social* forces that cause so many Aboriginal peoples to be incarcerated in Canada (Roberts and Gabor, 1990).

Most of the factors listed above also account for the above-average incarceration rate among black Canadians. Occupying a relatively low class position, engaging mainly in street crime as opposed to white-collar crime, and facing a discriminatory criminal justice system, black people are more likely than are whites to be motivated to commit criminal acts, to be detected and apprehended engaging in criminal acts, and to be prosecuted, convicted, and jailed. The claim that the criminal justice system engages in discriminatory practices based on race may be difficult for some Canadians to accept, but research suggests that the claim is credible. For example, a recent Toronto survey shows that older and better-educated whites and Asians with no criminal record are significantly less likely to be stopped for police searches than are younger and less well-educated whites and Asians with a criminal record. In contrast, age, education, and lack of a criminal record do not insulate blacks from searches. In fact, better-educated and well-to-do blacks are *more* likely to be stopped and searched by police than are less well-educated and poorer blacks. These findings suggest that Toronto police keep a closer eye on blacks than they do on whites and Asians, and are particularly suspicious of blacks with education and money (Wortley and Tanner, 2011).

Explaining Deviance and Crime

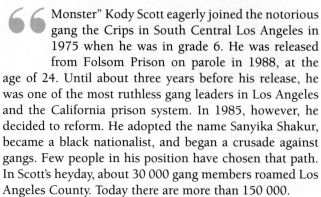

Lep: "I remember your li'l ass used to ride dirt bikes and skateboards, actin' crazy an' shit. Now you want to be a gangster, huh? You wanna hang with real muthaf— and tear shit up, huh? Stand up, get your li'l ass up. How old is you now anyway?"
Kody: "Eleven, but I'll be twelve in November."

—Sanyika Shakur (1993: 8)

Monster" Kody Scott eagerly joined the notorious gang the Crips in South Central Los Angeles in 1975 when he was in grade 6. He was released from Folsom Prison on parole in 1988, at the age of 24. Until about three years before his release, he was one of the most ruthless gang leaders in Los Angeles and the California prison system. In 1985, however, he decided to reform. He adopted the name Sanyika Shakur, became a black nationalist, and began a crusade against gangs. Few people in his position have chosen that path. In Scott's heyday, about 30 000 gang members roamed Los Angeles County. Today there are more than 150 000.

What makes engaging in crime an attractive prospect to so many people? In general, why do deviance and crime occur at all? Sociologists rely on symbolic interactionism, functionalism, conflict theories, and feminist theories for explanations.

SYMBOLIC INTERACTONIST APPROACHES TO DEVIANCE AND CRIME

People may learn deviant and criminal behaviour when they interact with others. Identifying the social circumstances that promote the learning of deviant and criminal roles is a traditional focus of symbolic interactionists.

Learning Deviance

The idea that becoming a habitual deviant or criminal is a learning process that occurs in a social context was firmly established by Howard S. Becker's classic study of marijuana users (Becker, 1963: 41–58). In the 1940s, Becker financed his Ph.D. studies by playing piano in Chicago jazz bands.

> **street crime** Crimes including arson, break and enter, assault, and other illegal acts disproportionately committed by people from lower classes.

> **white-collar crime** Illegal acts committed by respectable, high-status people in the course of work.

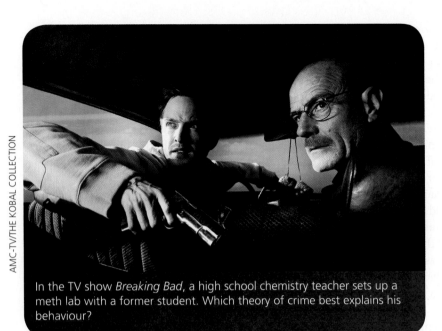

In the TV show *Breaking Bad*, a high school chemistry teacher sets up a meth lab with a former student. Which theory of crime best explains his behaviour?

He used the opportunity to carefully observe 50 fellow musicians, informally interview them in depth, and write up detailed field notes after performances.

Becker found that his fellow musicians had to pass through a three-stage learning process before becoming regular marijuana users. Failure to pass a stage meant failure to learn the deviant role and become a regular user. These are the three stages:

1. *Learning to smoke the drug in a way that produces real effects.* First-time marijuana smokers do not ordinarily get high. To do so, they must learn how to smoke the drug in a way that ensures a sufficient dosage to produce intoxicating effects (taking deep drags and holding their breath for a long time). This process takes practice, and some first-time users give up, typically claiming that marijuana has no effect on them or that people who claim otherwise are just fooling themselves. Others are more strongly encouraged by their peers to keep trying. If they persist, they are ready to go to stage two.

2. *Learning to recognize the effects and connect them with drug use.* Those who learn the proper smoking technique may not recognize that they are high or they may not connect the symptoms of being high with smoking the drug. They may get hungry, laugh uncontrollably, play the same song for hours on end, and yet still fail to realize that these are symptoms of intoxication. If so, they will stop using the drug. Becker found, however, that his fellow musicians typically asked experienced users how they knew whether they were high. Experienced users identified the symptoms of marijuana use and helped novices make the connection between what they were experiencing and smoking the drug. Once they

made that connection, novices were ready to advance to stage three.

3. *Learning to enjoy the perceived sensations.* Smoking marijuana is not inherently pleasurable. Some users experience a frightening loss of self-control (paranoia). Others feel dizzy, uncomfortably thirsty, itchy, forgetful, or dangerously impaired in their ability to judge time and distance. If these negative sensations persist, marijuana use will cease. However, Becker found that experienced users typically helped novices redefine negative sensations as pleasurable. They taught novices to laugh at their impaired judgment, take pleasure in quenching their deep thirst, and find deeper meaning in familiar music. If and only if novices learned to define the effects of smoking as pleasurable did they become habitual marijuana smokers.

Learning *any* deviant or criminal role requires a social context in which experienced deviants or criminals teach novices the "tricks of the trade." It follows that more exposure to experienced deviants and criminals increases the chance that an individual will come to value a deviant or criminal lifestyle and consider it normal (Sutherland, 1939, 1949). Moreover, the type of deviant or criminal that predominates in one's social environment has a bearing on the type of deviant or criminal that a novice will become. For example, depending on the availability of different types of deviants and criminals in their neighbourhoods, delinquent youths will turn to different types of crime. In some areas, delinquent youths are recruited by organized crime, such as the Mafia. In areas that lack organized crime networks, delinquent youths are more likely to create violent gangs. Thus, the relative availability of different types of deviants and criminals influences the type of deviant or criminal role a delinquent youth learns (Cloward and Ohlin, 1960).

Labelling

One night in Saskatchewan, after a night of heavy drinking, two 20-year-old university students, Alex Ternowetsky and Steven Kummerfield, both white and middle class, picked up Pamela George, an Aboriginal single mother who occasionally worked as a prostitute, in downtown Regina. They drove the 28-year-old woman outside the city limits, had her perform oral sex without pay, and then savagely beat her to death. Although originally charged with first-degree murder, a jury later found them guilty of the lesser charge of manslaughter. Justice Ted Malone of the Saskatchewan Court of Queen's Bench instructed the jurors to consider that the two men had been drinking and that George was "indeed a prostitute." Members of the victim's family were appalled, Native leaders outraged. Tone Cote of the Yorkton Tribal Council said the sentence would send the message that "it's all right for little white boys to go out on the streets, get drunk and use that for an excuse to start hunting down our people."

A variant of symbolic interactionism known as labelling theory holds that deviance results not just from the actions of the deviant but also from the responses of others, who define some actions as deviant and other actions as normal. As the above example suggests, terms like *deviant* or *criminal* are not applied automatically when a person engages in rule-violating behaviour. Some individuals escape being labelled as deviants despite having engaged in deviant behaviour. Others, like Ternowetsky and Kummerfield, are labelled deviant but found to be guilty of a lesser charge than would typically be the case. Still others, such as Pamela George, who do not engage in deviant acts at all or are the victims of such acts, may find themselves labelled as deviant (Matsueda, 1988, 1992).

That labelling plays an important part in who is caught and charged with crime was demonstrated more than 40 years ago by Aaron Cicourel (1968). Cicourel examined the tendency to label rule-breaking adolescents as juvenile delinquents if they came from families in which the parents were divorced. He found that police officers tended to use their discretionary powers to arrest adolescents from divorced families more often than adolescents from intact families who committed similar delinquent acts. Judges, in turn, tended to give more severe sentences to adolescents from divorced families than to adolescents from intact families who were charged with similar delinquent acts. Sociologists and criminologists then collected data on the social characteristics of adolescents who were charged as juvenile delinquents, "proving" that children from divorced families were more likely to become juvenile delinquents. Their finding reinforced the beliefs of police officers and judges. Thus, the labelling process acted as a self-fulfilling prophecy.

FUNCTIONALIST EXPLANATIONS

If symbolic interactionists focus on the learning and labelling of deviant and criminal roles, functionalists direct their attention to the social dysfunctions that lead to deviant and criminal behaviour.

Durkheim

Functionalist thinking on deviance and crime originated with Durkheim (1938 [1895]), who made the controversial claim that deviance and crime are beneficial for society. For one thing, he wrote, when someone breaks a rule, it provides others with a chance to condemn and punish the transgression, remind them of their common values, clarify the moral boundaries of the group to which they belong, and thus reinforce social solidarity. For another, deviance and crime help societies adapt to social change. Martin Luther King, Jr., was arrested in Alabama in February 1965 for taking part in a demonstration supporting the idea that blacks should be allowed to vote, but later that year the passage of the Voting Rights Acts made it a crime to *prevent* blacks from voting in the United States. King's crime (and similar crimes by other civil rights activists) brought about positive social change, demonstrating the validity of Durkheim's point about the positive functions of deviance and crime.

Merton

Robert Merton (1938) further developed Durkheim's theory by emphasizing the *dysfunctions* of deviance and crime. Merton argued that cultures often teach people to value material success. Just as often, however, societies do not provide enough legitimate opportunities for everyone to succeed. In Merton's view, such a discrepancy between cultural ideals and structural realities is dysfunctional, producing what he called strain.

Most people who experience strain will force themselves to adhere to social norms despite the strain, Merton wrote. The rest adapt by engaging in one of four types of action: (1) They may drop out of conventional society. (2) They may reject the goals of conventional society but continue to follow its rules. (3) They may protest against convention and support alternative values. (4) They may find alternative and illegitimate means of achieving their society's goals—that is, they may become criminals. The value of material success starkly contradicts the lack of opportunity available to poor youths, Merton argued. As a result, poor youths sometimes engage in illegal means of attaining socially approved goals.

Criminal Subcultures

It is not only individuals who adapt to the strain caused by social dysfunction. In addition, social groups adapt by forming criminal gangs. Gang members feel the legitimate world has rejected them. They return the favour by rejecting the legitimate world. In the process, they develop distinct norms and values—a criminal subculture (Cohen, 1955).

> **labelling theory** Holds that deviance results not so much from the actions of the deviant as from the response of others, who label the rule breaker a deviant.
>
> **strain** What results when a culture teaches people the value of material success and society fails to provide enough legitimate opportunities for everyone to succeed.
>
> **subculture** A set of distinctive values, norms, and practices within a larger culture.

An important part of any gang subculture consists of the justifications its members spin for their criminal activities. These justifications make illegal activities appear morally acceptable and normal, at least to the gang members. Typically, criminals deny personal responsibility for their actions ("It wasn't my fault!") or deny the wrongfulness of the act ("I was just borrowing it."). They condemn those who pass judgment on them ("The cops are bigger crooks than anyone!"). They claim their victims get what they deserve ("She had it coming to her."). And they appeal to higher loyalties, particularly to friends and family ("I had to do it because he dissed my gang."). Such rationalizations enable criminals to clear their consciences and get on with the job (Sykes and Matza, 1957).

Although deviants may depart from mainstream culture in many ways, they are strict conformists when it comes to the norms of their own subculture. They tend to share the same beliefs, dress alike, eat similar food, and adopt the same mannerisms and speech patterns. Although most members of the larger society consider gang subcultures deviant, gang members strongly discourage deviance *within* the subculture.

Functionalism and the Relationship between Crime and Class

One of the main problems with functionalist accounts is that they exaggerate the connection between crime and class. Many self-report surveys find, at most, a weak tendency for criminals to come disproportionately from lower classes. Some self-report surveys report no such tendency at all, especially among young people and for less serious types of crime (Weis, 1987). A stronger correlation exists between *serious street crimes* and class. Armed robbery and assault, for instance, are more common among people from lower classes. A stronger correlation also exists between *white-collar* crime and class. Middle- and upper-class people are most likely to commit fraud and embezzlement, for example. Thus, generalizations about the relationship between class and crime must be qualified by taking into account the severity and type of crime (Braithwaite, 1981). Note also that official statistics usually exaggerate class differences because they are more accurate barometers of street crime than suite crime; more police surveillance occurs in lower-class neighbourhoods than in upper-class boardrooms, and widely cited police statistics do not record some white-collar crimes because they are handled by agencies other than the police. As we will now see, conflict theories help to overcome functionalism's inadequate explanation of the relationship between crime and class.

CONFLICT THEORIES

Conflict theorists maintain that the rich and powerful members of society impose deviant and criminal labels on others, particularly those who challenge the existing social

Former Canadian millionaire Conrad Black was convicted in 2007 of diverting funds from money due his company for his personal benefit. Sentenced to 78 months in prison, he was released on bail after serving two years.

The Canadian Press (AP Photo/Kiichiro Sato, File)

order. Meanwhile, the rich and powerful are usually able to use their money and influence to escape punishment for their own misdeeds.

Steven Spitzer (1980) summarizes this school of thought. He notes that capitalist societies are based on private ownership of property. Moreover, their smooth functioning depends on the availability of productive labour and respect for authority. When thieves steal, they challenge private property. Theft is therefore a crime. When so-called bag ladies and drug addicts drop out of conventional society, they are defined as deviant because their refusal to engage in productive labour undermines a pillar of capitalism. When young, politically volatile students demonstrate and militant trade unionists strike, they, too, represent a threat to the social order. Authorities may therefore define them as deviant or criminal.

Of course, Spitzer notes, the rich and powerful engage in deviant and criminal acts too. However, they are less likely to be reported, convicted, and prosecuted for criminal acts than other people are (Blumberg, 1989; Clinard and Yeager, 1980; Hagan, 1989; Sherrill, 1997; Snider, 1999; Sutherland, 1949). *Reporting* is less frequent because much white-collar crime takes place in private and is therefore difficult to detect. For instance, corporations may collude to fix prices and divide markets—both crimes—but executives may make such decisions in boardrooms, private clubs, and homes that are not generally subject to police surveillance. *Conviction* and *prosecution* are less frequent partly because wealthy white-collar criminals, including corporations, can afford legal experts, public relations firms, and advertising agencies that advise their clients on how to bend laws, build up their corporate image in the public mind, and influence lawmakers to pass laws "without teeth." In addition, the law is more lenient in meting out punishment for white-collar than for street crime. Compare the crime of break and enter with that of fraud. Fraud almost certainly costs society more than break and enter but breaking and entering is a street crime committed mainly by lower-class people, while fraud is a white-collar crime committed mainly by middle- and upper-class people. Not surprisingly, prison sentences are nearly twice as likely in break and enter convictions as they are in fraud convictions (Thomas, 2002: 9).

Social Control

Conflict theorists argue that the rich and powerful exercise disproportionate control over the criminal justice system and are therefore able to engage in deviance and crime with relative impunity. One variant of conflict theory, known as control theory, generalizes this argument. According to control theorists, nearly everyone would like to have the fun, pleasure, excitement, and profit that deviance and crime promise. Moreover, they say, if we could get away with it, most of us would commit deviant and criminal acts to acquire more of these rewards. For control theorists, the reason most of us do not engage in deviance and crime is that we are prevented from doing so. In contrast, deviants and criminals break norms and laws because social controls imposed by various authorities are too weak to ensure conformity.

Travis Hirschi developed the control theory of crime (Hirschi, 1969; Gottfredson and Hirschi, 1990). He argued that adolescents are more prone to deviance and crime than adults are because they are incompletely socialized and therefore lack self-control. Adults and adolescents may both experience the impulse to break norms and laws, but adolescents are less likely to control that impulse. Hirschi went on to show that the adolescents who are most prone to delinquency are likely to lack four types of social control. They tend to have few social *attachments* to parents, teachers, and other respectable role models; few legitimate *opportunities* for education and a good job; few *involvements* in conventional institutions; and weak *beliefs* in traditional values and morality. Because of the lack of control stemming from these sources, these adolescents are relatively free to act on their deviant impulses. For similar reasons, boys are more likely to engage in juvenile delinquency than girls, and people who experience job and marital instability are more likely than others to engage in crime (Hagan et al., 1987; Peters, 1994; Sampson and Laub, 1993). Tighter social control by authorities in all spheres of life decreases the frequency of deviant and criminal acts.

> **control theory** Holds that the rewards of deviance and crime are ample. Therefore, nearly everyone would engage in deviance and crime if they could get away with it. The degree to which people are prevented from violating norms and laws accounts for variations in the level of deviance and crime.

FEMINIST CONTRIBUTIONS

Although conflict theory shows how the distribution of power in society influences the definition, detection, and prosecution of deviance and criminality, it neglects the consequences of something you will learn about in detail

Comstock/Jupiterimages

in Chapter 11, Sexuality and Gender: on average, women are less powerful than men are in all social institutions. Feminist sociologists hold that gender-based power differences influence the framing of laws and therefore the definition and detection of crime and the prosecution of criminals.

To support their claim, feminists note that, until recently, many types of crime against women were largely ignored in Canada and most other parts of the world. This was true even when the crime involved non-consensual sexual intercourse, an act that was defined under Canadian criminal law as *rape* before 1983 and is now considered a form of *sexual assault*. Admittedly, the authorities sometimes severely punished rapes involving strangers. However, so-called date and acquaintance rape were rarely prosecuted, while Canadian law viewed marital rape as a contradiction in terms, as if it were logically impossible for a woman to be raped by her husband. Law professors, judges, police officers, rapists, and even victims did not think date rape was "real rape" (Estrich, 1987). Similarly, judges, lawyers, and social scientists rarely discussed physical violence against women and sexual harassment until the 1970s. Governments did not collect data on the topic, and few social scientists showed any interest in the subject. Relative powerlessness allowed many women to be victimized while the violence against them often went unnoticed by the larger society and their assailants went free.

It follows from the feminist argument that a shift in the distribution of power between women and men would alter this state of affairs. And in fact, that is precisely what happened after about 1970. A series of changes to Canadian criminal law since 1970 have emphasized that non-consensual sexual acts are sexual assaults. The new laws have helped raise people's awareness of date, acquaintance, and marital rape. Sexual assault is more often prosecuted now than it used to be. The same is true for other types of violence against women and for sexual harassment. These changes occurred because women's position in the economy, the family, and other social institutions has improved since 1970. Women now have more autonomy in the family, earn more, and enjoy more political influence. They also created a movement for women's rights that heightened concern about crimes disproportionately affecting them (MacKinnon, 1979). Social definitions of crimes against women changed as women became more powerful in Canadian society.

In the 1970s, some feminists expected that growing gender equality would also change the historical tendency for women to be far less crime-prone than men are. They reasoned that control over the activities of girls and women would weaken, thus allowing them to behave more like men. Widely publicized cases of violent crime by teenage girls add weight to such claims, and official data support them too. As Figure 5.2 shows, the

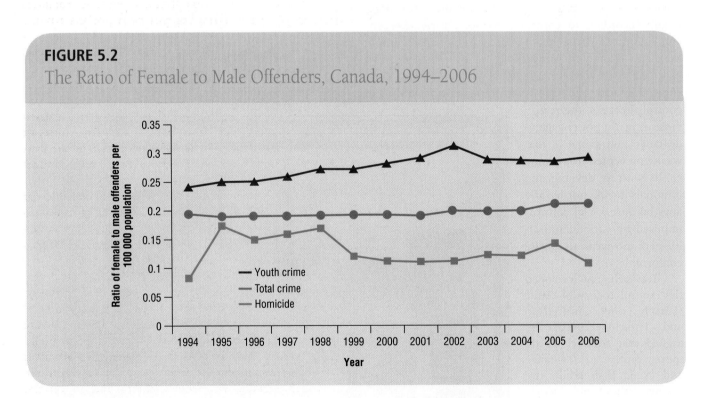

FIGURE 5.2

The Ratio of Female to Male Offenders, Canada, 1994–2006

Sources: Statistics Canada. 2010. "Youth court survey, number of cases, by sex of accused, annually." CANSIM Database. Table 2520048. www.chass.utoronto.ca (retrieved 7 March 2010); Statistics Canada. 2010. "Homicide survey, victims and persons accused of homicide, by age group and sex, Canada, annually (Number)." CANSIM Database. Table 2530003. www.chass.utoronto.ca (retrieved 7 March 2010); Statistics Canada. 2010. "Adult criminal court survey, number of cases, by sex of accused, annually (Number)." CANSIM Database. Table 2520044. www.chass.utoronto.ca (retrieved 7 March 2010).

ratio of women to men convicted of homicide shows no clear trend between 1998 and 2006. However, the ratio of women to men convicted of all crimes rose by 2 percent, and the ratio of women to men convicted of youth crime rose by 6 percent. It seems that, with the exception of the most violent crimes, the ratio of female to male criminals is slowly increasing, and the tendency is most pronounced among youth offenders.

In sum, our overview shows that many theories contribute to understanding the social causes of deviance and crime (see Table 5.1). Each focuses on a different aspect of the phenomena, so familiarity with all of them allows us to develop a fully rounded appreciation of the complex processes surrounding the sociology of deviance and crime.

TABLE 5.1
Major Theoretical Approaches to Deviance and Crime

Theory	Summary
Symbolic interactionism	Deviant and criminal roles must be learned in the course of social interaction if they are to become habitual activities. Moreover, deviance results not just from the actions of the deviant but also from the responses of others, who define some actions as deviant and other actions as normal.
Functionalism	Deviance and crime have positive functions for society insofar as they provide opportunities to clarify societal values, define moral boundaries, increase social solidarity, and allow useful social change. They also have dysfunctions. In particular, if societies do not provide enough legitimate opportunities for everyone to succeed, strain results, one reaction to which is to find alternatives and illegitimate means of achieving one's goals.
Conflict theory	It is the rich and powerful who are most likely to impose deviant and criminal labels on others, particularly those who challenge the existing social order. Meanwhile, the rich and powerful are usually able to use their money and influence to escape punishment for their own misdeeds. Most people do not engage in deviance and crime because they are prevented from doing so by authorities. Deviants and criminals break norms and laws because social controls imposed by various authorities are too weak to ensure their conformity.
Feminist theory	Changes over time in the distribution of power between women and men influence the degree to which crimes against women are identified and prosecuted, and the degree to which women become criminals.

LO³ Punishment

All societies seek to ensure that their members obey norms and laws. All societies impose sanctions on rule breakers. However, the *degree* of social control varies over time and place. *Forms* of punishment also vary.

In many respects people are freer today than ever. We elect leaders, choose consumer products, change religions, and so forth. In other respects, however, social control has intensified over time. Much of the regimentation of modern life is tied to the growth of capitalism and the state. Factories require strict labour regimes, with workers arriving and leaving at a fixed time and, while there, performing fixed tasks at a fixed pace. Institutions regulated by the state's armies, police forces, public schools, health care systems, and various other bureaucracies also demand strict work regimes, curricula, and procedures. These institutions existed on a much smaller scale in pre-industrial times or did not exist at all. Today, they penetrate our lives and sustain strong norms of belief and conduct (Foucault, 1977 [1975]).

Electronic technology makes it possible for authorities to exercise more effective social control than ever. With millions of cameras mounted in public places and workplaces, some sociologists say we now live in a "surveillance society" (Lyon and Zureik, 1996). Spy cameras enable observers to see deviance and crime that would otherwise go undetected and to take quick action to apprehend rule breakers. Moreover, when people are aware of the presence of surveillance cameras, they tend to alter their behaviour. For example, attentive shoplifters migrate to stores that lack electronic surveillance. On factory floors and in offices, workers display more conformity to management-imposed work norms. On campuses, students are inhibited from engaging in organized protests (Boal, 1998).

Among the most important recent developments in social control are the "medicalization of deviance" and the rise of the prison. Let us examine these reactions to deviance and crime in turn.

THE MEDICALIZATION OF DEVIANCE

Increasingly, we deal with deviance by medicalizing it. The **medicalization of deviance** refers to the fact that "medical definitions of deviant behavior are becoming more prevalent in . . . societies like our own" (Conrad and Schneider, 1992: 28–29). In an earlier era, much deviant behaviour was labelled evil. Deviants tended to be chastised, punished, and otherwise socially controlled by members of the clergy, neighbours, family members, and the criminal justice system. Today, however, a person prone to drinking sprees is more likely to be declared an alcoholic and treated in a detoxification centre. A person predisposed to violent rages is more likely to be medicated. A person inclined to overeating is more likely to seek therapy and, in extreme cases, surgery. A heroin addict is more likely to seek the help of a methadone program. As these examples illustrate, what used to be regarded as wilful deviance is now often regarded as involuntary deviance. Increasingly, what used to be defined as "badness" is defined as "sickness." As our definitions of deviance change, deviance is increasingly coming under the sway of the medical and psychiatric establishments (see Figure 5.3).

The Spread of Mental Disorders

Many mental disorders have obvious organic causes, such as chemical imbalances in the brain. Researchers can often identify these problems precisely, treat them with drugs or other therapies, and conduct experiments to verify their existence and establish the effectiveness of one treatment or another. Little debate takes place over whether such ailments should be listed in the psychiatrist's "bible," the *Diagnostic and Statistical Manual of Mental Disorders (DSM)*.

The organic basis for other ailments is unclear. In such cases, social values and political conflict can determine whether they are listed in the *DSM*. For instance, in the 1970s and 1980s, North American psychiatrists fiercely debated whether neurosis, posttraumatic stress disorder (PTSD), homosexuality, and self-defeating personality disorder were real mental disorders. In the end, homosexuality

---

FIGURE 5.3

An Example of the Medicalization of Deviance

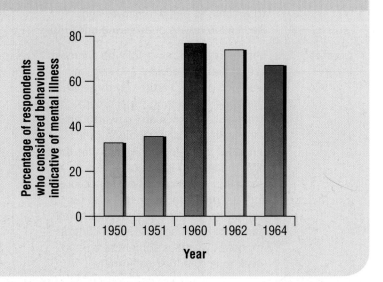

"Now here's a young woman in her twenties, let's call her Betty Smith . . . she has never had a job, and she doesn't seem to want to go out and look for one. She is a very quiet girl, she doesn't talk much to anyone—even her own family, and she acts like she is afraid of people, especially young men her own age. She won't go out with anyone, and whenever someone comes to visit her family, she stays in her own room until they leave. She just stays by herself and daydreams all the time and shows no interest in anything or anybody."

Five North American surveys conducted in the 1950s and 1960s presented respondents with the accompanying anecdote. The graph shows the percentage of respondents who considered the behaviour described in the anecdote evidence of mental illness. Notice the difference between the 1950s and the 1960s. (Nearly 100 percent of psychiatrists who evaluated the anecdote thought it illustrated "simple schizophrenia.")

Source: Material adapted from table "Results of Studies Using Vignettes in Defining Problem Behavior" from *Deviance and Medicalization: From Badness to Sickness, Expanded Edition* by Peter Conrad and Joseph W. Schneider. Used by permission of Temple University Press. © 1992 by Temple University. All Rights Reserved.

was dropped from the *DSM*, largely in response to the efforts of liberal-minded psychiatrists, as was self-defeating personality disorder, thanks to the efforts of feminists. Neurosis was retained at the insistence of Freudians. PTSD was added to the *DSM* after a strenuous lobbying campaign by Vietnam War veterans and their supporters (Scott, 1990). These cases illustrate that the medicalization of deviance is in part a social and political process.

In the mid-nineteenth century there was just one officially recognized mental disorder: idiocy/insanity. The current *DSM* lists 297. As the number of mental disorders has grown, so has the proportion of North Americans presumably affected by them. In the mid-nineteenth century, few people were defined as suffering from mental disorders, but one respected survey conducted in the early 1990s found that 48 percent of people will suffer from a mental disorder—very broadly defined, of course—during their lifetime (Blazer, Kessler, McGonagle, and Swartz, 1994; Shorter, 1997: 294).

The number and scope of mental disorders have grown partly because North Americans are now experiencing more stress than ever before, mainly because of the increased demands of work and a growing time crunch. At the same time, traditional institutions for dealing with mental health problems are less able to cope with them. The weakening authority of the church and the weakening grip of the family over the individual leave the treatment of mental health problems more open to the medical and psychiatric establishments.

The cultural context also stimulates inflation in the number and scope of mental disorders. North Americans are inclined to turn their problems into medical and psychological issues, sometimes without inquiring deeply into the disadvantages of doing so. For example, in 1980 the term "attention deficit disorder" (ADD) was coined to label hyperactive and inattentive schoolchildren, mainly boys. By the mid-1990s, doctors were writing more than 6 million prescriptions a year for Ritalin, an amphetamine-like compound that controls ADD. Evidence shows that some children diagnosed with ADD have certain problems with their brain chemistry. Yet the diagnosis of ADD is typically conducted clinically, that is, by interviewing and observing children to see if they exhibit signs of serious inattention, hyperactivity, and impulsivity. This means that many children diagnosed with ADD may have no organic disorder at all. Some cases of ADD may be due to the school system failing to capture children's imagination. Some may involve children acting out because they are deprived of attention at home. Some may involve plain, old-fashioned youthful enthusiasm. (Doctors at Dalhousie University Medical School in Halifax made a plausible case that Winnie the Pooh suffered from ADD; see Shea, Gordon, Hawkins, Kawchuk, and Smith, 2000.) However, once hyperactivity and inattentiveness in school are defined as a medical and psychiatric condition, officials routinely prescribe drugs to control the problem and tend to ignore possible social causes.

Finally, we have witnessed inflation in the number and scope of mental disorders because various professional organizations have an interest in it. Consider PTSD. There is no doubt that PTSD is a real condition and that many veterans suffer from it. However, once the disorder was officially recognized in the 1970s, some therapists trivialized the term. By the mid-1990s some therapists were talking about PTSD "in children exposed to movies like *Batman*" (Shorter, 1997: 290). Some psychiatric social workers, psychologists, and psychiatrists may magnify the incidence of such mental disorders because doing so increases their stature and their patient load. Others may do so simply because the condition becomes trendy. Whatever the motive, overdiagnosis is the result.

LO⁴ THE PRISON

In October 2001, a 63-year-old man with Parkinson's disease and addicted to cocaine was arrested in Ottawa. A passer-by had noticed that the man had a shotgun in his gym bag and had notified the police. The man, who was charged with possession of a weapon, did not resist arrest. He knew what awaited him. Roger Caron, dubbed Mad Dog Caron by the press, had first

An example of the medicalization of deviance. A lobotomy is performed in Vacaville State Prison in California in 1961 to "cure" the inmate of criminality.

© Ted Streshinsky/Corbis

Roger Caron, who was 16 years old when he was first sentenced to prison for breaking and entering, has spent much of his life behind bars. His acclaimed book *Go-Boy!* provides a chilling account of his life in almost all the major prisons in Eastern Canada.

been sentenced to prison at the age of 16 for breaking and entering. He had spent most of his adult life as an inept robber, going in and out of Eastern Canada's major prisons.

After having already spent almost 20 years in prison, Caron wrote a chilling account of his life behind bars. The book describes in harrowing detail the harshness of the prison experience—the violence, the intense hatreds, the hard labour, the horrors of solitary confinement, the twisted, manipulative friendships, and the brutal use of corporal punishment. (Caron, 1979: 59).

Go-Boy! was honoured with the Governor General's Literary Award and, in the years that followed, Caron wrote other books. However, he was unable to leave his past life behind. Following imprisonment for another botched robbery attempt, Caron was released from prison in 1998 and was still on parole at the time of his 2001 arrest. Regardless of the initial factors that caused Caron to turn to crime, it was his experiences in prison that turned him into a career criminal (CyberPress, 2001). His experience follows a pattern known to sociologists for a long time. Prisons are agents of socialization, and new inmates often become more serious offenders as they adapt to the culture of long-term prisoners (Wheeler, 1961).

Origins of Imprisonment

Because prison often turns criminals into worse criminals, it is worth pondering the institution's development and current dilemmas. As societies industrialized, imprisonment became one of the most important forms of punishment for criminal behaviour (Garland, 1990; Morris and Rothman, 1995). In pre-industrial societies, criminals were publicly humiliated, tortured, or put to death, depending on the severity of their transgressions. In the industrial era, depriving criminals of their freedom by putting them in prison seemed more "civilized" (Durkheim, 1973 [1899–1900]).

Goals of Incarceration

Some people still take a benign view of prisons, even seeing in them opportunities for *rehabilitation*. They believe that prisoners, while serving time, can be taught how to be productive citizens on release. In Canada, this idea predominated from the 1950s to the early 1970s,

In pre-industrial societies, criminals who committed serious crimes were put to death, often in ways that seem cruel by today's standards. One method involved hanging them upside down, bound and alive, so that starving dogs could rip them apart.

when many prisons sought to reform criminals by offering them psychological counselling, drug therapy, skills training, education, and other programs that would help at least the less violent offenders reintegrate into society (McMahon, 1992: xvii).

Today, however, many Canadians scoff at the idea that prisons can rehabilitate criminals. We have adopted a tougher line. Some politicians campaign on promises of a get-tough approach to crime and to criminals. Many people now see prison as a means of *deterrence*. In this view, people will be less inclined to commit crimes if they know they are likely to be caught and serve long and unpleasant prison terms. Others think of prisons as institutions of *revenge*. They believe that depriving criminals of their freedom and forcing them to live in poor conditions is fair retribution for their illegal acts. Still others see prisons as institutions of *incapacitation*. From this viewpoint, the chief function of the prison is to keep criminals out of society as long as possible to ensure they can do no more harm (Simon, 1993; Zimring and Hawkins, 1995).

In 2008, 116 of every 100 000 Canadians were in prison (see Figure 5.4). Canada's incarceration rate is higher than that of some

Conservative Prime Minister Stephen Harper and Minister of Public Safety Vic Toews have championed Canada's recent efforts to "get tough on crime" and build more prisons although crime rates have been falling since the 1990s. Are their actions part of a moral panic?

FIGURE 5.4
World Prison Population, 2008

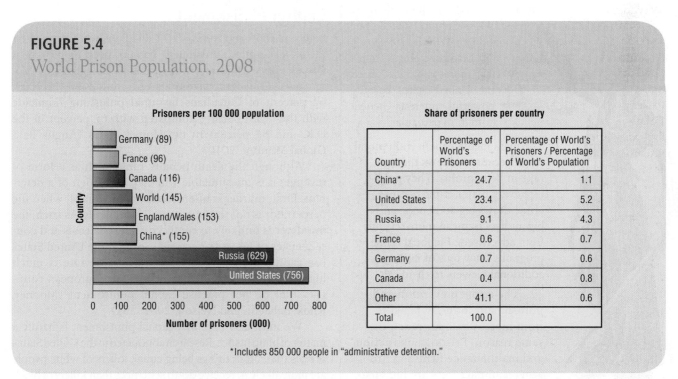

Prisoners per 100 000 population

Germany (89)
France (96)
Canada (116)
World (145)
England/Wales (153)
China* (155)
Russia (629)
United States (756)

Country (vertical axis)

Number of prisoners (000): 0 100 200 300 400 500 600 700 800

Share of prisoners per country

Country	Percentage of World's Prisoners	Percentage of World's Prisoners / Percentage of World's Population
China*	24.7	1.1
United States	23.4	5.2
Russia	9.1	4.3
France	0.6	0.7
Germany	0.7	0.6
Canada	0.4	0.8
Other	41.1	0.6
Total	100.0	

*Includes 850 000 people in "administrative detention."

Source: Walmsley, Roy. 2009. "World Prison Population List (eighth edition)." http://www.kcl.ac.uk/depsta/law/research/icps/downloads/wppl-8th_41.pdf (retrieved 7 March 2010).

European countries, such as France and Germany, but it is only 15 percent of the rate of the United States, which leads the world with 756 inmates per 100 000 people. Some 4.5 percent of the world's population lives in the United States—and 23.4 percent of the world's prisoners.

The size of the U.S. prison population has more than quadrupled since 1980, yet little solid evidence supports the view that throwing more people into jail lowers the crime rate in the United States, or anywhere else for that matter. In fact, many sociologists and criminologists believe that in some cases prison has the opposite effect, turning small-time crooks into hardened criminals (Ore and Birgden, 2003). Why then has the U.S. prison population grown so quickly?

LO⁵ MORAL PANIC

Some analysts say that the United States has been gripped by moral panic, or widespread fear that crime poses a grave threat to society's well-being. Partly in response to lurid news stories and TV dramas that direct attention to the most notorious and atypical crimes, many members of the public incorrectly conclude that most crime is violent and predatory and that the current crime rate endangers just about everyone, even though it has been falling since the early 1990s (Cohen, 1972; Goode and Ben-Yehuda, 1994).

Many sociologists agree that moral panic has seized the United States because powerful interests benefit from it. In particular,

Oleg Golovnev/Shutterstock

1. The mass media benefit from moral panic because it allows them to rake in hefty profits. They publicize every major crime because crime draws big audiences, and big audiences mean more revenue from advertisers. Fictional crime programs draw tens of millions of additional viewers to their TVs.

2. The crime prevention and punishment industry benefits from moral panic for much the same reason. Prison construction and maintenance firms and fire-arms manufacturers are big businesses that flourish in a climate of moral panic. Such industries want people to own more guns and imprison more people, so they lobby hard for relaxed gun laws and invigorated prison construction programs.

3. The criminal justice system is a huge bureaucracy with many employees. They benefit from moral panic because increased spending on crime prevention, control, and punishment secures their jobs and expands their turf.

4. Perhaps most important, the moral panic is useful politically. Since the early 1970s, many politicians have instilled fear of crime in the public, criticized opponents for being "soft on crime," and promised voters that endorsing a "get-tough" policy will bring them more security. Such arguments have formed the basis of entire political careers.

OTHER FORMS OF PUNISHMENT: TWO EXTREMES

Imprisonment is not the only form of punishment for criminal acts. In concluding this chapter, we consider two of the most hotly debated issues concerning other forms of punishment: (1) Should Canada reintroduce the death penalty for the most violent criminals? (2) Should we more often use strategies other than imprisonment for non-violent criminals?

Capital Punishment

Between 1859 and 1962, 710 Canadians were hanged by the state. Capital punishment has not been employed in Canada since 1962 and was formally abolished in 1976, but most Canadians favour its re-introduction. In 2009, 62 percent of Canadians favoured punishing homicide with the death penalty, compared with 67 percent in the U.K. and 84 percent in the United States (Angus Reid Global Monitor, 2010).

Although the death penalty ranks high as a form of revenge, it is questionable whether it is much of a deterrent. First, murder is often committed in a rage, when the perpetrator is not thinking entirely rationally. As such, the murderer is unlikely to coolly consider the costs and consequences of his or her actions. Second, the United States has capital punishment, but its homicide rate is much higher than that of Canada and Western European countries that do not practise capital punishment (Mooney, Knox, Schacht, and Nelson, 2001: 131).

We must also note that capital punishment is hardly a matter of blind justice. Research conducted in the United States reveals that, other things being equal, killers of white people are more likely to receive death sentences than killers of black people, especially if the murderer is black (Culver, 1992).

Social class is also a factor. A study conducted in Texas found that people represented by court-appointed lawyers were 28 percent more likely to be convicted than those who could afford to hire their own lawyers and, once convicted, 44 percent more likely to be sentenced to death (Vago and Nelson, 2003: 205). As such, we cannot view the death penalty as a justly administered punishment.

Sometimes people favour capital punishment because they think it saves money. They argue that killing someone outright costs less than keeping the person alive in prison for the rest of his or her life. However, the experience of the United States suggests otherwise. In that country, where an exhaustive system of judicial review is required before anyone is executed, trials of capital cases cost more than $2.6 million each on average—enough to keep a man in prison in Canada for almost 40 years (Costanzo, 1997).

Finally, in assessing capital punishment, it is important to remember that mistakes are common. Nearly 40 percent of death sentences in the United States since 1977 have been overturned because of new evidence or mistrial (Haines, 1996). In Canada, the wrongful convictions of Donald Marshall, Guy Paul Morin, David Milgaard, and many others for murders they did not commit should be sufficient to remind us that the wheels of justice do not always turn smoothly.

LO⁶ Alternative Strategies

In recent years, some analysts have suggested two main reforms to our prison regime. First, they have argued that we should reconsider rehabilitation. Advocates of rehabilitation suggest that the recidivism rate, or the proportion of convicted offenders who commit another crime, can be reduced through such programs as education and job training, individual and group therapy, substance abuse counselling, and behaviour modification. Second, they argue that, whenever possible, we should attempt to reduce the number of incarcerated offenders. Proponents of this idea say that at least part of the increase in crime in the past four decades is attributable to the introduction of new and broadened definitions of criminal conduct. They believe that charging and imprisoning more Canadians, especially youth, is unlikely to help these individuals develop pro-social behaviour. Accordingly, they advise us to seek alternative methods that divert adults and juveniles from formal criminal justice system processing.

Although alternative procedures vary in each province and territory, their use generally arises after the police or Crown prosecutor recommends that an offender be considered suitable for "diversion." One example of an alternative measure is a victim–offender reconciliation program (VORP)

in which victim and offender meet under controlled circumstances. Victims have the opportunity to describe the impact the crime has had on them, and offenders are usually required to apologize to their victims and compensate them financially. Alternative measures programs handle tens of thousands of youth cases every year. Most cases referred for diversion involve theft under $5000 (e.g., shoplifting), which is not surprising because to be recommended for diversion, the offence must be minor. To be considered candidates for diversion, offenders must first acknowledge that they are guilty of the act they have been accused of committing. Young offenders selected for inclusion in the program are usually more than 15 years old, and they generally complete the provisions of the agreements they make (Tufts, 2000).

Similarly, the Supreme Court of Canada has urged judges to "take into account the primary importance of restorative justice principles within Aboriginal conceptions of sentencing," especially for less serious offences (Hendrick and Farmer, 2002: 11). Restorative justice deals with the harmful effects of crime "by engaging victims, offenders and the community in a process of reparation and healing" (Solicitor General, 2002). This model of justice views crime as behaviour that violates people and relationships rather than the state and its laws. Within a restorative justice framework, each offence is considered in terms of its moral, social, economic, political, religious, and cosmic considerations (Bryant, 1999). Rather than focusing on punishment, restorative justice emphasizes individual and social healing, communication, and joint problem solving through restitution and reconciliation. Although the behaviour of the offender is condemned, the essential value of the individual is affirmed and the offender reassured that, through conformity, the stigma associated with a crime can be removed.

In like fashion, proponents of decarceration recommend that such options as fines (the most commonly used penal sanction in Canada), probation, and community service become more widely used as alternatives to imprisonment.

Not everyone views such strategies as desirable. Some observers argue that the increased use of community programs does not reduce the numbers of people subject to formal social control. Rather, such strategies may simply "widen the net" through the creation of more intensive, intrusive, and prolonged control mechanisms (Lowman, Menzies, and Palys, 1987). Noting such objections, some analysts suggest that we go further still and lobby for legislative reform that would decriminalize certain categories of conduct currently prohibited under Canadian criminal law, such as marijuana possession. This last suggestion serves to remind us, yet again, that crime and deviance are social constructs.

recidivism rate The proportion of convicted offenders who commit another crime.

6 Social Stratification: Canadian and Global Perspectives

Social Stratification: Shipwrecks and Inequality

Writers and filmmakers sometimes tell stories about shipwrecks and their survivors to make a point about social inequality. They use the shipwreck as a literary device. It allows them to sweep away all traces of privilege and social convention. What remains are human beings stripped to their essentials, guinea pigs in an imaginary laboratory for the study of wealth and poverty, power and powerlessness, esteem and disrespect.

The tradition began with Daniel Defoe's *Robinson Crusoe*, first published in 1719. Defoe tells the story of an Englishman marooned on a desert island. His strong will, hard work, and inventiveness turn the poor island into a thriving colony. Defoe was one of the first writers to portray capitalism favourably. He believed that people get rich if they possess the virtues of good businesspeople—and stay poor if they don't.

The 1975 Italian movie *Swept Away* tells almost exactly the opposite story. In the movie, a beautiful woman, one of the idle rich, boards her yacht for a cruise in the Mediterranean. She treats the hardworking deckhands in a condescending and abrupt way. The deckhands do their jobs but seethe with resentment. Then comes the storm. The yacht is shipwrecked. Only the beautiful woman and one handsome deckhand remain alive, marooned on a desert island. Now equals, the two survivors soon have passionate sex and fall in love. All is well until the day of their rescue. As soon as they return to the mainland, the woman resumes her haughty ways. She turns her back on the deckhand, who is reduced again to the role of a common labourer. Thus, the movie sends the audience three harsh messages. First, it is possible to be rich without working hard, because a person can inherit wealth. Second, people can work hard without becoming rich. Third, something about the structure of society causes inequality, for inequality disappears only on the desert island, without society as we know it.

Titanic is a more recent movie on the shipwreck-and-inequality theme. At one level, the movie shows that class differences are important. For example, in first class, living conditions are luxurious, whereas in third class they are cramped. Indeed, on the *Titanic*, class differences spell the difference between life and death. After the *Titanic*

LEARNING OBJECTIVES:

LO¹ Wealth and income are unequally distributed in Canada.

LO² Although talent and hard work influence a person's socioeconomic success, being a member of certain groups limits opportunities.

LO³ Some theories of social inequality regard inequality as inevitable and others regard it as doomed to disappear, but the reality lies between these two extremes.

LO⁴ Global inequality has increased tremendously since industrialization and is still increasing in some respects today.

LO⁵ One theory of global inequality stresses how the deficiencies of some societies contribute to their lack of economic growth. Another theory stresses how the history of social relations among countries enriched some nations at the expense of others.

LO⁶ Some non-Western countries have industrialized.

strikes the iceberg off the coast of Newfoundland and Labrador, the ship's crew prevents second- and third-class passengers from entering the few available lifeboats. They give priority to rescuing first-class passengers. Consequently, 75 percent of third-class passengers perished, compared with 39 percent of first-class passengers (see Table 6.1).

As the tragedy of the *Titanic* unfolds, however, another contradictory theme emerges. Under some circumstances, we learn, class differences can be insignificant. In the movie, the sinking of the *Titanic* is the backdrop to a fictional love story about a wealthy young woman in first class and a working-class youth in the decks below. The sinking of the *Titanic* and the collapse of its elaborate class structure give the young lovers an opportunity to cross class lines and profess their devotion to each other. At one level, then, the movie *Titanic* is an optimistic tale that holds out hope for a society in which class differences matter little.

Robinson Crusoe, Swept Away, and *Titanic* raise many of the issues we address in this chapter. What are the sources of social inequality? Do determination, industry, and ingenuity shape the distribution of advantages and disadvantages in society, as the tale of *Robinson Crusoe* portrays? Or is *Swept Away* more accurate? Do certain patterns of social relations underlie and shape that distribution? Is *Titanic's* first message of social class differences still valid? Does social inequality still have big consequences for the way we live? What about *Titanic's* second message? Can people overcome or reduce inequality in society? If so, how?

To answer these questions, we first sketch patterns of social stratification in Canada and globally. We then critically review major theories of social stratification, the way society is organized in layers or strata. We also analyze the movement of individuals up and down the stratification system over time and their perceptions of the stratification system.

LO¹ Patterns of Social Inequality

WEALTH

Your wealth is what you own. For most adults, it includes a house (minus the mortgage), a car (minus the car loan), and some appliances, furniture, and savings (minus the credit card balance). Wealth is assets minus liabilities. Owning a nice house and a good car and having a substantial sum of money invested securely enhances your sense of well-being. You know you have a cushion to fall back on in difficult times and you know you don't have to worry about paying for your children's postsecondary education or how you will make ends meet during retirement. Wealth can also give you more political influence. Campaign contributions to political parties and donations to favourite political causes increase the chance that policies you favour will become law. Wealth even improves your health. Because you can afford to engage in leisure pursuits, turn off stress, consume high-quality food, and employ superior medical services, you are likely to live a healthier and longer life than someone who lacks these advantages.

TABLE 6.1
Survivors of the 1912 Titanic Disaster by Class (percent)

	First Class	Second Class	Third Class	Crew
Children	100	100	34.2	n.a.
Women	97.2	86.0	46.1	n.a.
Men	32.6	8.3	16.2	21.7
Total	62.5	41.4	25.2	21.7

Source: Adapted from Anesi, Charles 1997. "The Titanic Casualty Figures." Based on British Parliamentary Papers, Shipping Casualties (Loss of the Steamship "Titanic"), 1912, cmd. 6352, Report of a Formal Investigation into the circumstances attending the foundering on the 15th April, 1912, of the British Steamship "Titanic," of Liverpool, after striking ice in or near Latitude 41° 46' N., Longitude 50° 14' W., North Atlantic Ocean, whereby loss of life ensued. (London: His Majesty's Stationery Office, 1912). http://www.anesi.com/titanic.htm (retrieved 11 March 2010).

We list all 23 Canadian billionaires in Table 6.2. Their net worth ranges from US$1.0 billion to US$19.0 billion. These sums are so big that they are hard to imagine. You can begin to grasp them by considering that it would take you three years to spend $1 million at the rate of $1000 a day. How long would it take you to spend $1 billion? If you spent $1000 a day, you couldn't spend the entire sum in a lifetime. It would take nearly 3000 years to spend $1 billion at the rate of $1000 a day—assuming you didn't invest part to earn still more money.

Unfortunately, figures on wealth are sparse. However, one government study gives us some insight into how net worth (defined as assets minus debt) changed between 1984 and 2005 (see Figure 6.1). Dividing Canadian families into the poorest fifth (or "quintile"), the second-poorest fifth, the middle fifth, the second-richest fifth, and the richest fifth, we see that over this 21-year period the big winners were the richest families. The net worth of the richest quintile increased by more than 64 percent, taking inflation into account. Gains in wealth decrease as you move down the scale and turn into losses for the bottom 40 percent of families. The second quintile of families was, on average, more than 11 percent poorer in 2005 than in 1984, and the bottom quintile of families was on average $1000 poorer. This permits us to conclude that, in terms of wealth, the rich are getting richer while the poor are getting poorer.

INCOME

Income is the amount of money earned in a given period. In 1951 the average Canadian family earned about $3500, while in 2007 it earned $71 900. That is a more than 20-fold increase, but it is less impressive than it sounds. More than half the gain is due to inflation. After all, a soft drink that once cost a dime now costs a dollar. Moreover, the number of earners per family increased as more women entered the paid labour force. As a result, more people are now generating the income of the average family than was the case in 1951. Even so, Canadian families earn considerably more now than they did half a century ago because they are more productive. That is, the average worker is more skilled and is using more sophisticated technology to produce more goods and services.

How has the distribution of income changed over time? Is economic inequality growing or shrinking? To answer these questions, we again divide the population into fifths, but this time by income: the top 20 percent of

TABLE 6.2

Canada's 23 Billionaires, 2010

World Rank	Surname	$USbil	Source
20	D. Thomson & family	19.0	Publishing
100	G. Weston & family	7.2	Retail food
212	J., A., & J. Irving	4.0	Oil refining, etc.
212	J. Pattison	4.0	Advertising, etc.
232	P. Desmarais	3.9	Financial services, communications
237	B. Sherman	3.8	Pharmaceuticals
374	D. Azrieli & family	2.5	Real estate
374	R. Miller	2.5	Electronics
374	G. Laliberté	2.5	Entertainment
400	E. Saputo	2.4	Dairy
400	J. Skoll	2.4	Internet
421	W. McCain	2.3	Food processing
421	J. Balsillie	2.3	Electronics
437	M. Lazaridis	2.2	Electronics
488	C. Bronfman	2.0	Liquor
616	D. Cheriton	1.6	Internet
655	S. Jarislowsky	1.5	Finance
721	D. Katz	1.4	Pharmacies
773	C. Ridell	1.3	Natural gas
773	A. Shnaider	1.2	Steel, etc.
828	J. Coutu	1.2	Pharmacies
937	M. Lee-Chin	1.0	Finance
937	D. Freggin	1.0	Electronics

Inherited millions

Enjoyed a middle- or upper-middle class childhood

A "rags to riches" story

Source: Forbes.com. 2010. "The World's Billionaires." http://www.forbes.com/lists/2010/10/billionaires-2010_The-Worlds-Billionaires_Rank.html (retrieved 11 March 2010). Reprinted by Permission of Forbes Media LLC © 2010

Gina Sanders/Shutterstock

FIGURE 6.1

Median Net Worth of Families, Canada, 1984, 1999, 2005 (in 1999 dollars)

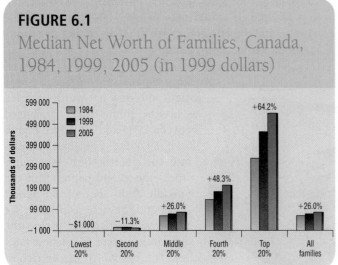

In each 20 percent category, half the cases are wealthier than the median and half are less wealthy. The following assets are not included: employer-sponsored pension plans, contents of the home, collectibles and valuables, annuities, and registered retirement income funds. If these items were included, wealth inequalities would be greater than shown.

Source: Adapted from Statistics Canada, "Median wealth of families (including unattached individuals), by quintile, 1984 to 2005," *The Daily*, Wednesday, December 13, 2006 http://www.statcan.gc.ca/daily-quotidien/061213/t061213c-eng.htm

families and unattached individuals by income, the second 20 percent, the middle 20 percent, and so forth. We can then determine what percentage of all income earned in Canada in a year is earned by each fifth. A completely unequal distribution would exist if the top quintile earned 100 percent of the country's income. A completely equal distribution would exist if each quintile earned 20 percent of the country's income.

Figure 6.2 shows that in 2007, the bottom quintile of families and unattached individuals earned just 4.8 percent of all income, while the top quintile earned 44.2 percent. This means that $4.40 of every $10 earned in Canada in 2007 was earned by the richest 20 percent of families. Moreover, the distribution of income has become more unequal since 1976. All quintiles earned a smaller share of total national income in 2007 than in 1976—except for the top quintile, which earned 3.2 percent more. This pattern mirrors the trend in most rich countries: income gaps have been widening for more than three decades (Förster and Pellizzari, 2000).

The incomes just reported represent the money that Canadians earn after paying income tax and receiving

government benefits. Canada is a welfare state that collects taxes and redistributes them in the form of welfare payments, employment insurance payments, child tax credits, GST credits, and so on. The richest fifth of Canadians lose about a fifth of their income to income tax, while the poorest fifth of Canadians see their incomes increase by nearly two-thirds as a result of government transfers. If Canadians relied only on the market to distribute income, inequality would be much greater.

POVERTY AND ITS FEMINIZATION

LO² Explanations of Income Inequality

Why do some people fall into the highest quintile and others into the lowest? What explains the distribution of income? Obviously, a person's job has a significant influence. Bank managers are paid more than bank tellers, schoolteachers more than daycare workers. As well, people who work more earn more. But these are rather obvious factors that predict earnings. They can't be ignored, but are there more general factors that explain income inequality?

We know that some individuals earn high salaries because of their natural talent. Jarome Iginla (hockey), Steve Nash (basketball), Karen Kain (ballet), Measha Brueggergosman (opera), Jim Carrey (acting), Shania

FIGURE 6.2

The Distribution of Total Income among Families and Unattached Individuals, Canada, 1976 and 2007

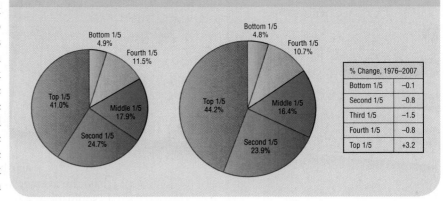

% Change, 1976–2007	
Bottom 1/5	−0.1
Second 1/5	−0.8
Third 1/5	−1.5
Fourth 1/5	−0.8
Top 1/5	+3.2

Note: (1) Percentages may not add to 100 because of rounding. (2) The diameter of the 2007 pie chart is 16.5 percent bigger than that of the 1976 pie chart, reflecting change in average real income.
Source: Statistics Canada. 2010. "Upper income limits and income shares of after-tax income quintiles, by economic family type, 2007 constant dollars, annually." CANSIM Table 202064. www.chass.utoronto.ca (retrieved 10 March 2010); Statistics Canada. 2010. "Adjusted and unadjusted market, total and after-tax income by economic family type and adjusted after-tax income quintiles, 2007 constant dollars, annually." www.chass.utoronto.ca (10 March 2010).

Twain (popular music), and Mike Weir (golf) are Canadians whose success on the world stage has provided them with substantial earnings. The principal reason for their excellence is a natural endowment in dance, music, athletics, and so on. A genetic gift sets them apart. At the other end of the economic spectrum, some people have the genetic misfortune of Down syndrome, schizophrenia, or autism, conditions that prevent them from earning big salaries. Such people, at both ends of the spectrum, are exceptions, however. Sociologists believe that for the vast majority of people, genes play only a minor role in determining income.

Even for people with a natural talent in the performing arts or athletics, effort is essential. Practice and years of dedication to the basics of a profession are common to all who enjoy success. Effort is also significant for many Canadians who spend long hours at work—whether amassing billable hours in a law practice, doing the endless chores in a small business, or working overtime at a construction site. However, although diligence and perseverance might be necessary conditions for rewards, they are not sufficient. Effort alone does not result in high income (see Figure 6.3).

Raw talent needs to be sharpened. Training, coaching, schooling—these are crucial ways in which skills are developed and nurtured. Natural talent and effort are important ingredients in this process, to be sure, but education matters. Indeed, the importance of education as a determinant of occupation and income continues to increase (Baer, 1999; Statistics Canada, 2003c: 9). As the Canadian occupational structure moves further away from its traditional resource-based foundation to a more mature knowledge-driven economy, the importance of education will continue to grow (see Table 6.3 on the next page).

If physical capital is investment in industrial plants and equipment, **human capital** is investment in education and training. Just as productivity increases by upgrading manufacturing plants and introducing new technology, productivity gains can also result from investment in the skills and abilities of people. Jobs requiring advanced skills are increasingly numerous in Canada. Better

educated workers are more skilled and more productive in these jobs because they have made investments in acquiring the skills and knowledge essential to our economy (Betcherman and Lowe, 1997).

Much evidence supports a human capital interpretation of the link between schooling and incomes (Baer, 1999). However, this is not a complete explanation for why people earn what they earn. For example, in the legal profession, almost everyone makes the same human capital investment. Every lawyer acquires a law degree. Yet economic rewards vary even for people with the same experience and type of legal practice (Kay and Hagan, 1998).

Part of the reason that people with the same amount of human capital may receive different economic rewards is that they possess different amounts of social capital. **Social capital** refers to people's networks or connections. Individuals are more likely to succeed if they have strong bonds of trust, cooperation, mutual respect, and obligation with well-positioned individuals or families. Knowing the right people, and having strong links to them, helps in finding opportunities and taking advantage of them (Coleman, 1988).

A related version of this argument is captured in the notion of cultural capital (Bourdieu and Passeron, 1990). **Cultural capital** comprises the set of social skills people have: their ability to impress others, to use tasteful language and images effectively, and thus to influence and persuade people. Although the notion of social capital stresses your networks and connections with others, the idea of cultural capital emphasizes your impression man-

human capital Investment in education and training. Just as productivity increases by upgrading manufacturing plants and introducing new technology, productivity gains can also result from investment in the skills and abilities of people.

social capital The networks or connections that individuals possess.

cultural capital The widely shared, high-status cultural signals (attitudes, preferences, formal knowledge, behaviours, goals, and credentials) used for social and cultural inclusion and exclusion.

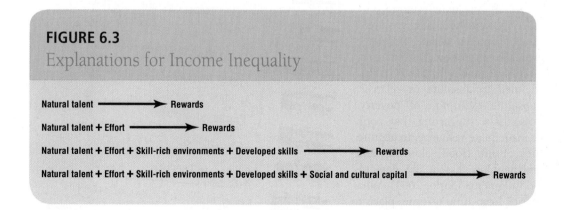

FIGURE 6.3

Explanations for Income Inequality

Natural talent ⟶ Rewards

Natural talent + Effort ⟶ Rewards

Natural talent + Effort + Skill-rich environments + Developed skills ⟶ Rewards

Natural talent + Effort + Skill-rich environments + Developed skills + Social and cultural capital ⟶ Rewards

CHAPTER 6 Social Stratification: Canadian and Global Perspectives **123**

poverty Lacks an agreed-on definition. Analysts disagree whether poverty should be defined in absolute or relative terms and whether it should be based on income or consumption. Canada does not have an official poverty line. Statistics Canada reports a low-income cutoff that marks "the income level at which a family may be in straitened circumstances because it has to spend a greater proportion of its income on necessities than the average family of similar size."

agement skills, your ability to influence others. In different ways, both concepts emphasize being part of the right "social club."

What the concepts of social and cultural capital also have in common is the idea that families higher in the social hierarchy enjoy more capital of all types. Connections and culture help you find a good job. The hiring of new recruits, then, depends on the talent, effort, and skills that people bring to the interview, but it also depends on the connections and culture that people have. Indeed, culture and connections often influence who gets an interview.

In summary, natural talent and effort are important, and for a few occupations very significant. For most Canadians, level of education (or developed skill) is a critical factor in finding continuous, well-paying employment. In addition, social and cultural capital are consequential for many people in achieving economic success. Explaining an individual's position in the income hierarchy depends on several factors, but the factors outlined in Figure 6.3 are crucial.

Defining Poverty

At the bottom of the income distribution are the homeless. In recent decades the number of people with no fixed address has increased considerably. We do not know how many Canadians are homeless, but in cities across the country, people sleep under bridges, in back allies, behind dumpsters, and in thickets in public parks. They do so night after night, month after month.

Homelessness is one manifestation of **poverty**. Exactly how many Canadians are poor is a matter of intense debate. Poverty lacks an agreed-on definition. A first disagreement occurs around whether poverty should be defined in absolute or relative terms. An absolute definition of poverty focuses on essentials, suggesting that poor families have inadequate resources to acquire the necessities of life (food, clothing, and shelter). Agreement on "essentials" depends on values and judgments (Sarlo, 2001). What is essential varies from time to time, place to

place, and group to group. Many of our ancestors lived without indoor plumbing, and some Canadians still do, but most people would define indoor plumbing as essential. A family could survive on a steady diet of cod and potatoes, but most would define such a family as poor.

A relative poverty line also has certain drawbacks. Two issues are central: relative to what, and how relative? Whether poverty ought to be defined narrowly in terms of economic measures (e.g., income) or more broadly with respect to community standards (e.g., safety of working conditions, environmental quality, type of housing) illustrates this second area of disagreement. Most definitions tend to be narrow, focusing primarily on income. But even if a relative poverty line is defined narrowly, how relative ought it to be? One-third of average income? one-half? some other fraction?

Yet another disagreement plagues any definition. Should poverty be defined on the basis of income or consumption? Because "bare essentials" is a core idea in any definition of poverty, it makes good sense to think about, and measure, poverty as the cost of purchasing bare essentials. Deprivation occurs when a family cannot acquire the essentials, not necessarily when income is too low. Income and consumption are correlated, of course, but wealthy people can live off their savings even with low income.

TABLE 6.3
Average Hourly Earnings by Selected Occupational Group, 2009–10

Occupational Group	Average Hourly Earnings ($)
Managerial	34.01
Natural and applied sciences	30.73
Social science, education, government service, and religion	28.10
Health	25.94
Trades, transport, and equipment operators	21.79
Art, culture, recreation, and sport	21.61
Processing, manufacturing, and utilities	18.91
Primary industry	18.68
Clerical	18.25
Sales and service	14.86

Source: The Statistics Canada CANSIM database, http://cansim2.statcan.gc.ca Table 282-0070 (retrieved 11 March 2010).

Answers to the question of why some people are poor vary from individual-level to structural explanations.

In one sense, the definition of poverty means little to a homeless person sleeping on a hot air vent. The immediate experience of poverty by families in remote coastal communities, by single parents in the urban core, and by marginal Prairie farmers is unaffected by whether poverty is defined absolutely or relatively, narrowly or broadly, by income or by consumption. However, the definition of poverty is consequential for these people because social policies are enacted, or not enacted, based on levels and trends in poverty. Definitions matter.

Social policy has a profound impact on the distribution of opportunities and rewards in Canada. Politics can reshape the distribution of income and the system of inequality by changing laws governing people's right to own property. Politicians can also alter patterns of inequality by entitling people to various welfare benefits and by redistributing income through tax policies. When politicians de-emphasize poverty, legislative efforts to maintain or expand welfare benefits and redistribute income are less likely. A definition of poverty showing fewer poor Canadians implies little need for government action. Conversely, for politicians and political parties supporting the poor, a definition of poverty showing a growing proportion of poor people is beneficial to their cause.

Poverty definitions are also important for political reasons. A democratic society depends on the full participation of all citizens—everyone has the right to vote, anyone can run for political office, and everyone's voice should influence political choices. As the National Council of Welfare (1999a: 4) argues, the proportion of Canadians who are poor is "one measure of how well our democracy is working." Can someone without a permanent home or someone in a family with bare cupboards participate fully in our national affairs?

Unlike some other countries, such as the United States, Canada does not have an official definition of poverty. Statistics Canada argues that there is no internationally accepted definition of poverty and that any definition is arbitrary. Therefore, it does not attempt to estimate the number of Canadians who are poor (Fellegi, 2000: 124). Instead, Statistics Canada reports what it calls a "low-income cutoff." This cutoff conveys "the income level at which a family may be in straitened circumstances because it has to spend a greater proportion of its income on necessities than the average family of similar size" (Statistics Canada, 2000c: 122). The threshold is reported for seven different family sizes and for five sizes of community because "straitened circumstances" depend on the number of people in your family and where you live. Most advocates for the poor interpret these thresholds, shown for 2007 in Table 6.4, as poverty lines. For example, in Canada's largest cities, a family of four with an income less than $33 946 after government transfer payments would be considered poor. In 2007, 9.2 percent of Canadians lived in poverty by this definition, down from 13.0 percent 30 years earlier.

Myths about Poverty

The language we use to speak of the poor is often revealing. For example, referring to someone as "poor but honest" or "poor but virtuous" implicitly suggests that we view such

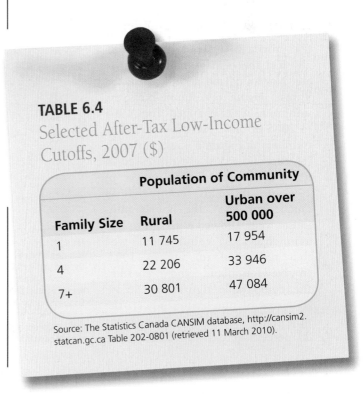

TABLE 6.4
Selected After-Tax Low-Income Cutoffs, 2007 ($)

	Population of Community	
Family Size	Rural	Urban over 500 000
1	11 745	17 954
4	22 206	33 946
7+	30 801	47 084

Source: The Statistics Canada CANSIM database, http://cansim2.statcan.gc.ca Table 202-0801 (retrieved 11 March 2010).

combinations as unlikely and feel it necessary to single out those who possess both characteristics as exceptions to the rule. Popular mythology also depicts the poor—especially those who receive public assistance (i.e., welfare)—as lazy, irresponsible, and lacking in motivation, abilities, and moral values. These images are potent and contribute to stereotypes of the "deserving" and the "undeserving" poor (e.g., war veterans and children versus "welfare bums" and those "looking for a handout"). However, research conducted in the past few decades shows that many of the stereotypes about the poor are myths.

- *Myth 1: People are poor because they don't want to work.* The myth that poor people don't want to work ignores that many poor people cannot work because of a disability or because they must take care of their young children because of inadequate child-care provisions in Canada. Moreover, it ignores that many poor people work full time, and many more work part time. But having a job is no guarantee of escaping poverty because the minimum wage set by provincial and territorial governments is so low. In 2010, the minimum wage varied from $8 (in British Columbia) to $10.25 (in Ontario), with a provincial and territorial average of $8.61. Even if a person living in a large Canadian city worked 50 weeks at 40 hours a week for $8.61 an hour, he or she would earn only $17 220 a year—$734 below the low-income cutoff (see Table 6.4). But it gets worse. Among Canada's ten provinces, Quebec has historically had the highest minimum wage and Newfoundland and Labrador the lowest. Figure 6.4 shows how the minimum wage changed from 1965 to 2006 in these two provinces. The numbers in Figure 6.4 take inflation into account; they are expressed in terms of the purchasing power of 1992 dollars. This means that in Quebec in 2006, the hourly minimum wage allowed a person to buy as much as $5.97 would have allowed that individual to buy in 1992. In Newfoundland and Labrador, the comparable figure was $5.39. In terms of purchasing power, the minimum wage thus *fell* by about 25 percent across Canada from the

mid-1970s to the mid-2000s. The low minimum wage thus ensures widespread low income and poverty.

- *Myth 2: Most poor people are immigrants.* Actually, only recent immigrants experience poverty rates significantly higher than the Canadian-born; and recent immigrants are only a small fraction of all Canadian immigrants. Moreover, once they are established, immigrants have lower poverty rates than do people born in Canada (National Council of Welfare, 2004).

- *Myth 3: Most poor people are trapped in poverty.* In fact, more than 92 percent of people with low income in a given year escape poverty in less than two years; 80 percent escape in less than a year. Fewer than 8 percent are mired in poverty for more than two years (Statistics Canada, 2010n). We conclude that most people try to move out of difficult financial circumstances and most succeed, at least for a time.

The Feminization of Poverty

In the 1970s, feminist sociologists introduced the notion of the feminization of poverty, by which they meant that (1) women were more likely to be low-income earners than men were, and (2) the low-income gap between women and men was growing (Duffy and Mandell, 2011: 130–33). It is

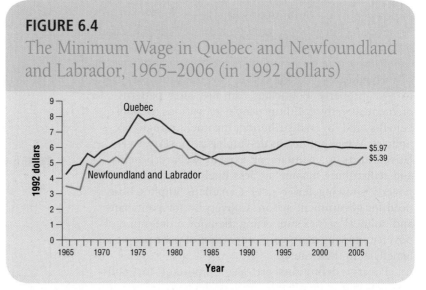

FIGURE 6.4

The Minimum Wage in Quebec and Newfoundland and Labrador, 1965–2006 (in 1992 dollars)

Note: (1) Until the early 1970s, women received a lower minimum wage than men did. The data reported here are for the male minimum wage. (2) The minimum wage declined from about 1973 until the mid- to late 1980s because conflict in the Middle East caused the price of oil to triple and then triple again, leading to rapid inflation, while, for part of this period, the federal government imposed wage controls. Subsequently, the real minimum wage recovered about 20 percent by 2006.
Sources: Human Resources and Social Development Canada. 2006. "Database on Minimum Wages." Found at http://srv116.services.gc.ca/wid-dimt/mwa/menu.aspx (1 April 2007); Statistics Canada. 2007. "Consumer price index, historical summary, by province or territory." Found at http://www40.statcan.ca/l01/cst01/econ46a.htm (1 April 2007).

true that in 1976 there were 33 percent more low-income women than low-income men in Canada. However, by 2006, there were only 4 percent more. This trend contradicts the prediction that the low-income gap between women and men would grow.

Comparing single-parent families headed by a woman with single-parent families headed by a man, we find a similar, if more erratic, tendency (see Figure 6.5). In 1976, there were nearly three times as many low-income families headed by a woman as low-income families headed by a man. By 2006, there were about 2.2 times as many. Although the direction of change is favourable, Canadians can take little pride in the fact that single-parent families headed by a woman are still more than twice as likely to be poor as single-parent families headed by a man are. This pattern exists partly because divorce typically results in decreased income for the wife and increased income for the husband; in about six out of seven divorce cases, children wind up residing mainly with the wife, while child support payments from higher-earning husbands are often inadequate. In addition, with the exception of Quebec, Canada provides little in the way of affordable child care that would make it easier for single mothers to work full-time in the paid labour force. Hence the much higher incidence of poverty in single-parent families headed by a woman.

The feminization of poverty is most evident when we turn to Canadians over the age of 64. Here we find a sharp increase in the incidence of low-income women compared with low-income men between 1976 and 2006. As Figure 6.5 shows, the percentage of poor Canadian women over the age of 64 was about twice the corresponding percentage for men in 1976. By 2006, however, Canadian women over the age of 64 were nearly *five* times as likely to be poor as were Canadian men over the age of 64. This state of affairs exists for three main reasons. First, women typically spend fewer years working in the paid labour force than men do, largely because they assume the bulk of domestic and childrearing responsibilities in most families. As a result, they usually accumulate smaller pensions and more modest savings than men do. Second, women typically earn less than men do when they work in the paid labour force—again minimizing the size of their pensions and their savings. And finally, women live on average five years longer than men do, so their resources have more time to become depleted. None of this is to say that older women are more impoverished now than they were three decades ago; between 1976 and 2006, the low-income rate for older women fell from about 47 percent to about 16 percent. It's just that over this same period the poverty rate among older men fell much faster, and stood at a mere 3.3 percent in 2006. In absolute terms, then, older women are better off, but relative to men they are worse off. As feminist sociologists correctly point out, they will remain so until labour force inequalities based on gender are sharply reduced.

Explaining Poverty

Definitions aside, why are some Canadians poor? Answers to this question vary from individual-level explanations to structural explanations.

Individual-level explanations focus on the attributes of people who are poor, asking

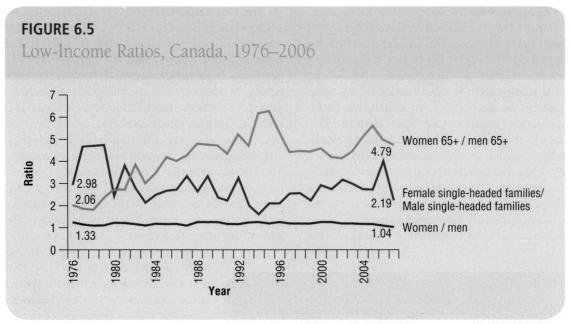

FIGURE 6.5
Low-Income Ratios, Canada, 1976–2006

Source: The Statistics Canada CANSIM database, http://cansim2.statcan.gc.ca Table 202-0802 (retrieved 11 March 2010.)

how these people differ from people who are not poor. This type of explanation focuses on causes that lie "within the person." Someone is poor, according to this logic, because of a personal attribute, such as low intelligence or a behaviour abnormality.

Some evidence suggests that individual attributes do explain a small amount of poverty. For example, we have noted that people with disabilities have a higher risk of living in poverty than do others. Not all people with disabilities live in poverty, however, and the vast majority of people living in poverty do not have a disability. On balance, this reminds us that poverty is, for the most part, not a consequence of individual attributes even though they are important in some cases.

A related explanation focuses more on the attitudes of individuals—not on attributes that are inherited, but on attributes or stigmas that are acquired. A social-psychological type of explanation emphasizes low self-esteem, lack of achievement motivation, and an inability to delay gratification. Poverty is perpetuated, on this logic, because poor families employ inadequate child-rearing practices, practices that enhance bad attitudes. A related version of this argument stresses a "culture of poverty," a way of thinking and acting shared by poor families. This culture reinforces and perpetuates itself through poor upbringing and ill-formed personalities.

Various objections undermine this type of explanation. First, it presents a chicken or egg problem. People who are poor may develop "bad attitudes," but these may result from poverty and not be causes of poverty. The culture of poverty might provide an adequate description for some circumstances, but it is not an adequate explanation

in general. Put differently, descriptions of poverty stressing a culture of depression, lack of hope, and fatalism may be accurate, but these effects of poverty should not be confused with the causes of poverty. Second, many people who are poor do work, are religious, don't smoke or drink, and so on. Therefore, evidence that supports explanations founded on these personal deficits is often lacking.

Another type of explanation, one with greater currency in sociology, stresses the social organization of society, or subsystems in society, as explanations of poverty. The organization of our economy, for example, affects poverty. Capitalist economies feature cyclical booms and busts, periods of low unemployment and high profits, followed by high unemployment and low profits. During recessions, more people lose their jobs and fall into poverty. Moreover, as we have seen, people with minimum-wage jobs don't earn enough to escape poverty. The lack of good jobs is thus a major cause of poverty.

Other analysts stress social policy as a factor affecting poverty levels. For example, as noted above, if you received the minimum hourly wage while working full time, full year, you would still be poor, especially if you had children to support. In this sense, minimum wage legislation is a social policy that creates a group of working poor.

The social world is not quite so simple, of course, and if minimum wages were to rise too much or too quickly, so too might the level of unemployment because some employers might not be able to afford a sudden big jump in wages. Debate over these issues continues, but the point is that our social policies affect people's well-being, and understanding the consequences of policies is critical.

The system of tax collection and tax allocation illustrates another way that social policies affect poverty. A *progressive* tax system is one in which a greater proportion of income is paid in tax as incomes rise. For example, those who earn $100 000 pay a larger percentage of their income as tax than do those who earn $50 000. In Canada, although our income tax system is progressive, the overall tax system is relatively neutral. Most Canadian families pay about the same percentage of their total income in tax. This occurs because two interrelated factors undermine the "Robin Hood" effect of progressive income taxes. First, other taxes, such as the GST and fuel taxes, are regressive. They are not based on the income of the taxpayer. Second, those who earn more are able to shelter much of their income from taxation in registered education saving plans and registered retirement savings plans, through capital gains tax exemptions, and so on. As a result, the tax system does little to erode poverty.

Finally, other sociologists stress ways of thinking, or ideological perspectives, as explanations for poverty. Negative images of various groups lead to an undervaluing of the ways of life of some people, such as Aboriginal people, recent immigrants, and members of visible minorities. Discrimination follows from this undervaluing. Discrimination causes poverty because it leads to less success in finding jobs and, when jobs are found, to more unsteady and low-paying work.

Is poverty an inevitable feature of society? It may be, at least to the extent that inequality is known to exist in all societies. However, the extent of poverty in Canada could be reduced if we chose to follow the example of Western European nations. Many countries in Western Europe have poverty rates well below Canada's, because many European governments have established job training and child-care programs that allow poor people to take jobs with livable wages and benefits. This is, however, clearly a political choice. Many Canadians argue that providing welfare benefits dampens the work ethic and actually perpetuates poverty. Although the Western European evidence does not support that view, the political will does not currently exist in Canada to change our social policies and alleviate poverty.

Is inequality inevitable? That question has concerned sociologists for more than 150 years. We next review some classical answers to shed light on our prospects today.

class According to Marx, a grouping that is determined by a person's relationship to the means of production. In Weber's usage, class position is determined by a person's "market situation," including the possession of goods, opportunities for income, level of education, and level of technical skill.

bourgeoisie Owners of the means of production, including factories, tools, and land, according to Marx. They do not do any physical labour. Their income derives from profits.

proletariat The term Marx gave to the working class. Members of the proletariat perform physical labour but do not own means of production. They are thus in a position to earn wages.

LO³ Is Stratification Inevitable? Three Theories

MARX'S CONFLICT THEORY

Karl Marx can fairly be regarded as the founder of conflict theory in sociology. It is ironic, therefore, that social stratification and the accompanying conflict between classes are *not* inevitable in Marx's view (Marx, 1904 [1859]; Marx and Engels, 1972 [1848]). He believed that capitalist growth would eventually produce a society without classes and therefore without class conflict.

In Marx's sense of the term, **class** is determined by a person's "relationship to the means of production" or the source of that person's income. The source of income is profit if the person owns a factory or a mine. It is a wage if he or she must work in a factory or a mine. Accordingly, Marx argued that capitalist societies have two main classes: the ownership class (or **bourgeoisie**, to use his term) and the working class (or what Marx termed the **proletariat**), distinguished from each other by whether they own productive property.

functional theory of stratification Argues that (1) some jobs are more important than others, (2) people must make sacrifices to train for important jobs, and (3) inequality is required to motivate people to undergo these sacrifices.

According to Marx, during the Industrial Revolution that began in Great Britain in the late eighteenth century, industrial owners were eager to adopt new tools, machines, and production methods so they could produce goods more efficiently and earn higher profits. Such innovations had unforeseen consequences, however. First, some owners were driven out of business by more efficient competitors. They were forced to become members of the working class. Together with former peasants pouring into the cities from the countryside to take factory jobs, this caused the working class to grow. Second, the drive for profits motivated owners to concentrate workers in increasingly larger factories, keep wages as low as possible, and invest as little as possible in improving working conditions. Thus, as the bourgeoisie grew richer and smaller, the proletariat grew larger and more impoverished.

As described in Chapter 1, A Sociological Compass, Marx felt that workers would ultimately become aware of their exploitation. Their sense of *class consciousness* would, he wrote, encourage the growth of unions and workers' political parties. These organizations would eventually try to create a new "communist" society in which there would be no private wealth. Instead, under communism, everyone would share wealth, said Marx.

Critical Evaluation of Marx's Conflict Theory

Things did not work out the way Marx had predicted. First, industrial societies did not polarize into two opposed classes engaged in bitter conflict. Instead, a large and heterogeneous middle class of white-collar workers emerged. Some of them are non-manual employees. Others are professionals. Many of them enjoy higher income and status than manual workers do. With a bigger stake in capitalism than propertyless manual workers, non-manual employees and professionals have generally acted as a stabilizing force in society. Second, although Marx correctly argued that investment in technology makes it possible for capitalists to earn high profits, he did not expect investment in technology also to make it possible for workers to earn higher wages and toil fewer hours under less oppressive conditions. Yet that is just what happened. Their improved living standard tended to pacify workers, as did the availability of various welfare state benefits, such as employment insurance. Third, communism took root not where industry was most highly developed, as Marx predicted, but in semi-industrialized countries, such as Russia in 1917 and China in

1949. Moreover, instead of evolving into classless societies, new forms of privilege emerged under communism. According to a Russian quip from the 1970s, "under capitalism, one class exploits the other, but under communism it's the other way around."

THE FUNCTIONALIST THEORY OF DAVIS AND MOORE

In the mid-twentieth century, American sociologists Kingsley Davis and Wilbert Moore proposed a **functional theory of stratification** that, in contrast to Marx's theory, asserts the inevitability of social stratification (Davis and Moore, 1945). Davis and Moore observed that jobs differ in importance. A judge's work, for example, contributes more to society than does the work of a janitor. This presents a problem: how can people be motivated to undergo the long training they need to serve as physicians,

In 1989, the Berlin Wall separating communist East Germany from capitalist West Germany was torn down. The Soviet Union was dissolved in 1991. A historical era came to an end.

Associated Press

engineers, and so on? Higher education is expensive. You earn little money while training. Long and hard study rather than pleasure seeking is essential. Clearly, an incentive is needed to motivate the most talented people to train for the most important jobs. The incentives, said Davis and Moore, are money and prestige. More precisely, social stratification is necessary (or "functional") because the prospect of high rewards motivates people to undergo the sacrifices needed to get a higher education. Without substantial inequality, they conclude, the most talented people would have no incentive to become judges, physicians, and so forth.

Critical Evaluation of Functionalism

Although the functional theory of stratification may at first seem plausible, we can quickly uncover one of its chief flaws by imagining a society with just two classes of people—physicians and farmers. The farmers grow food. The physicians tend the ill. Then, one day, a rare and deadly virus strikes. The virus has the odd property of attacking only physicians. Within weeks, there are no more doctors in our imaginary society. As a result, the farmers are much worse off. Cures and treatments for their ailments are no long available. Soon the average farmer lives fewer years than his or her predecessors. The society is less well off, though it survives.

Now imagine the reverse. Again we have a society comprising only physicians and farmers. Again a rare and lethal virus strikes. This time, however, the virus has the odd property of attacking only farmers. Within weeks, the physicians' stores of food are depleted. After a few more weeks, the physicians start dying of starvation. The physicians who try to become farmers catch the new virus and expire. Within months, the society has been wiped out. Who, then, does the more important work, physicians or farmers? Our thought experiment suggests that farmers do, for without them society cannot exist.

From a historical point of view, we can say that none of the jobs regarded by Davis and Moore as "important"

would exist without the physical labour done by people in "less important" jobs. To sustain the witch doctor in a tribal society, hunters and gatherers had to produce enough for their own subsistence plus a surplus to feed, clothe, and house the witch doctor. To sustain the royal court in an agrarian society, peasants had to produce enough for their own subsistence plus a surplus to support the royal family. By using taxes, tithes, and force, government and religious authorities have taken surpluses from ordinary working people for thousands of years. Among other things, these surpluses were used to establish the first institutions of higher learning in the thirteenth century. Out of these, modern universities developed.

Thus, the question of which occupations are most important is not clear-cut. To be sure, physicians earn a lot more money than farmers today, and they also enjoy a lot more prestige. But it is not because their work is more important in any objective sense of the word.

Sociologists have noted other problems with the functional theory of stratification (Tumin, 1953). First it stresses how inequality helps society discover talent. But it ignores the pool of talent lying undiscovered because of inequality. Bright and energetic adolescents may be forced to drop out of high school to help support themselves and their families. Capable and industrious high school graduates may be forced to forgo a postsecondary education because they can't afford it. Inequality may encourage the discovery of talent but only among those who can afford to take advantage of the opportunities available to them. For the rest, inequality prevents talent from being discovered.

Second, the functional theory of stratification fails to examine how advantages are passed from generation to generation. Like *Robinson Crusoe,* the functional theory correctly emphasizes that talent and hard work often result in material rewards. However, it is also the case that inheritance allows parents to transfer wealth to children regardless of their talent. For example, glancing back at Table 6.1, we see that more than one-quarter of the largest personal fortunes in Canada were substantially inherited.

Left: Photos.com; right: Sean Prior/Shutterstock

WEBER'S COMPROMISE

Like the functionalists, Max Weber argued that the emergence of a classless society is highly unlikely. Like Marx, however, he recognized that under some circumstances people can act to lower the level of inequality in society.

Writing in the early twentieth century, Weber held that a person's class position is determined by his or her "market situation," including the possession of goods, opportunities for income, level of education, and level of technical skill. Accordingly, in Weber's view four main classes exist in capitalist societies: large property owners, small property owners, propertyless but relatively highly educated and well-paid employees, and propertyless manual workers (Weber, 1946: 180–95).

Weber also recognized that two types of groups other than classes—status groups and parties—have a bearing on the way a society is stratified. Status groups differ from one another in the prestige or social honour they enjoy and in their style of life. Consider members of a minority ethnic community who have recently immigrated. They may earn relatively high income but endure relatively low prestige. The longer-established members of the majority ethnic community may look down on them as vulgar "new rich." If their cultural practices differ from those of the majority ethnic group, their style of life may become a subject of scorn. Thus, the position of the minority ethnic group in the social hierarchy does not derive just from its economic position but also from the esteem in which it is held.

In Weber's usage, parties are not just political groups but, more generally, organizations that seek to impose their will on others through the exercise of power (Weber, 1947: 152). Control over parties, especially large bureaucratic organizations, does not depend just on wealth. A person can head a military, scientific, political, or other bureaucracy without being rich, just as a person can be rich and still have to endure low prestige.

Weber argued that to draw an accurate picture of a society's stratification system we must analyze classes, status groups, and parties as somewhat independent bases of social inequality. Each basis of stratification influences the others. For example, one political party may want to tax the rich and distribute benefits to the poor, thus increasing opportunities for upward mobility. Another political party may want to cut taxes to the rich and decrease benefits to the poor, thus decreasing opportunities for upward mobility. The class system will be affected in different ways depending on which party comes to power. From this point of view, nothing is inevitable about the level of social stratification in society. We are neither headed inexorably toward classlessness nor are we bound to endure high levels of inequality. Instead, the level of social stratification depends on the complex interplay of class, status, and party, and their effect on social mobility, or movement up and down the stratification system. We devote the next section to exploring these themes.

status groups Groups that differ from one another in terms of the prestige or social honour they enjoy and in terms of their style of life.

parties In Weber's usage, organizations that seek to impose their will on others.

social mobility Movement up or down the stratification system.

Social Mobility

Mordecai Richler's *The Apprenticeship of Duddy Kravitz* (1959) is one of the true classics of modern Canadian literature. Made into a 1974 film starring Richard Dreyfuss as Duddy, it is the story of a poor 18-year-old Jewish Montrealer in the mid-1940s who is desperately seeking to establish himself in the world. To that end, he waits on tables, smuggles drugs, drives a taxi, produces wedding and bar mitzvah films, and rents out pinball machines. He is an obnoxious charmer with relentless drive, a young man so fixed on making it that he is even willing to sacrifice his girlfriend and his only co-worker to achieve his goals. We cannot help but admire Duddy for his ambition and his artfulness even while we are shocked by his guile and his single-mindedness.

Part of what makes *The Apprenticeship of Duddy Kravitz* universally appealing is that it could be a story about anyone. It is not just some immigrants and their children who may start out as pushy little people engaged in shady practices and unethical behaviour. As Richler reminds us repeatedly, many of the wealthiest establishment families in Canada and elsewhere started out in just this way. Duddy, then, is a universal symbol of "upward mobility"—and the compromises a person must sometimes make to achieve it.

Much of our discussion to this point has focused on how we describe inequality and how we explain its persistence. Here we take up a different, though related, set of questions. To what extent are we trapped in a disadvantaged social position or assured of maintaining an advantaged position? At birth, do all people have the same freedom to gain wealth and fame? Are the opportunities we enjoy, our "life chances," equally accessible to everyone?

Sociologists use the term *social mobility* to refer to the dynamics of the system of inequality and, in particular, to movement up and down the stratification system. If we think about inequality as either a hierarchy of more or less privileged positions or a set of higher and lower social classes, an important question is how much opportunity people have to change positions. Typically, change has been measured by using one of two benchmarks: your first position in the hierarchy (e.g., your first full-time job) and the position of your parents in the hierarchy. Comparing your first job with your current job

Arne Pastoor/Shutterstock

is an examination of occupational or *intragenerational mobility*. Comparing the occupations of parents with their children's current occupation is an examination of the inheritance of social position or *intergenerational mobility*.

Whichever benchmark is used, social mobility analysts are interested in the openness or fluidity of society. Open or fluid societies have greater equality of access to all positions in the hierarchy of inequality, both the low and the high. Regardless of your social origins, in more open societies you are more likely to rise or fall to a position that reflects your capabilities. In contrast, in closed or rigid societies, your social origins have major consequences for where you are located in the hierarchy of inequality. In such societies, poverty begets poverty, wealth begets wealth. In feudal Europe or in the Indian caste system, your birth determines your fate—you are a peasant or a lord, a member of an upper caste or a lower caste, based on the position of the family to which you are born.

In modern times, societies have become more open. The circumstances of your birth do not completely determine your fate. Think about the changes in Canadian society over the past century. A mainly agrarian, resource-based economy has transformed into a modern, advanced postindustrial nation. We have experienced substantial growth in well-paying occupations in finance, marketing, management, and the professions. To what extent have people from all walks of life, from all economic backgrounds, been able to benefit from this transformation?

This question introduces a second, related theme to discussions of mobility—equality of opportunity.

In the 1950s and 1960s, proponents of the functional theory of stratification and human capital theory imagined that equality of opportunity would predominate. They argued that as more and more skilled jobs are created in the new economy, the best and the brightest must rise to the top to take those jobs and perform them diligently. We would then move from a society based on *ascription* to one based on *achievement*. In a system of inequality based on ascription, your family's station in life determines your own fortunes. In a system based on achievement, your own talents determine your lot in life. If you achieve good grades in school, your chance of acquiring a professional or managerial job rises.

Other sociologists, however, cautioned that this scenario of high individual social mobility might not follow from the transformation of the economy. They emphasized how advantaged families have long attempted to ensure that their offspring inherit their advantages (Collins, 1979).

On the world stage, Blossfeld and Shavit (1993) demonstrated that in 11 of 13 advanced industrial countries, little evidence supports the view that greater equality of opportunity exists in societies with expanding education systems (Sweden and the Netherlands are the two exceptions). In most countries, the openness of the system of inequality did not increase over the last half of the twentieth century. Richard Wanner (1999) tested

intragenerational mobility Social mobility that occurs within a single generation.

intergenerational mobility Social mobility that occurs between generations.

ascription-based stratification system A system in which the allocation of rank depends on the features with which a person is born (ascribed characteristics).

achievement-based stratification system A system in which the allocation of rank depends on a person's accomplishments.

Roy Thomson

Ken Thomson

David Thomson

Left: Reg Innell/GetStock.com; middle: The Canadian Press (BILL BECKER); right: The Canadian Press (Darren Calabrese)

CHAPTER 6 Social Stratification: Canadian and Global Perspectives **133**

these ideas by using Canadian data. He asked whether "Canada's investment in educational expansion reduced the amount of ascription in educational attainment" (Wanner, 1999: 409). In other words, has the growth of education—more high schools, colleges, and universities—benefited people from all social backgrounds equally?

If in earlier decades the chances of children from poorer families going to university were small, then these chances should have increased in more recent decades if ascription were weakening. As measures of socioeconomic background, Wanner (1999) used mother's and father's education and father's occupation. He tested his central question by using detailed information from a sample of 31 500 Canadians. Wanner found that class-based ascription still operates strongly. Despite the fact that more Canadians are acquiring more years of schooling and more degrees than ever, the long arm of family socioeconomic background continues to exert a strong hold on educational attainment. The link between family advantage and children's educational achievement has not weakened.

Explanations for how and why this occurs remain a matter of controversy (Davies, 1999). One explanation focuses on the way the school system has become increasingly differentiated. New high school programs have proliferated. These include storefront schools for at-risk students in poorer neighbourhoods, language-immersion streams, private schools, and enriched learning tracks. These different types of schools tend to enroll students from different socioeconomic backgrounds. Students from lower socioeconomic backgrounds tend to take various routes through high school vocational programs and college diploma programs. Students from higher socioeconomic backgrounds typically continue on to university. That is how it is possible for Canadians to acquire more years of schooling and more degrees while the link between family background and educational achievement persists.

Politics and the Perception of Class Inequality

We expect you have had some strong reactions to our review of sociological theories and research on social stratification. You may therefore find it worthwhile to reflect more systematically on your own attitudes to social inequality. Do you consider the family in which you grew up to have been lower class, working

class, middle class, or upper class? Do you think the gaps between classes in Canadian society are big, moderate, or small? How strongly do you agree or disagree with the view that big gaps between classes are needed to motivate people to work hard and maintain national prosperity? How strongly do you agree or disagree with the view that inequality persists because it benefits the rich and powerful? How strongly do you agree or disagree with the view that inequality persists because ordinary people don't join together to get rid of it? Answering these questions will help you to clarify the way you perceive and evaluate the Canadian class structure and your place in it. If you take note of your answers, you can compare them with the responses of representative samples of Canadians, which we review below.

Surveys show that few Canadians have trouble placing themselves in the class structure when asked to do so. Most Canadians consider themselves to be middle class or working class. They also think that the gaps between classes are relatively large. But do Canadians think that these big gaps between classes are needed to motivate people to work hard, thus increasing their own wealth and the wealth of the nation? Some Canadians think so, but most do not. A survey conducted in 18 countries, including Canada, asked more than 22 000 respondents if large differences in income are necessary for national prosperity. Canadians were among the most likely to disagree with that view (Pammett, 1997: 77).

So Canadians know that they live in a class-divided society. They also tend to think that deep class divisions are not necessary for national prosperity. Why then do Canadians think inequality continues to exist? The 18-nation survey sheds light on that issue. One of the survey questions asked respondents how strongly they agree or disagree with the view that "inequality continues because it benefits the rich and powerful." Most Canadians agreed with that statement. Only about a quarter of them disagreed with it in any way. Another question asked respondents how strongly they agree or disagree with the view that "inequality continues because ordinary people don't join together to get rid of it." Again, most Canadians agreed, with less than a third disagreeing in any way (Pammett, 1997: 77–78).

Despite widespread awareness of inequality and considerable dissatisfaction with it, most Canadians are opposed to the government playing an active role in reducing inequality. Most do not want governments to provide citizens with a basic income. They tend to oppose government job-creation programs. They even resist the idea that government should reduce income differences through taxation (Pammett, 1997: 81). Most Canadians remain individualistic and self-reliant. On the whole, they persist in the belief that opportunities for mobility are abundant and that it is up to the individual to make something of those opportunities by means of talent and effort.

Significantly, however, all the attitudes summarized above vary by class position. For example, discontent with the level of inequality in Canadian society is stronger at the bottom of the stratification system than at the top. The belief that Canadian society is full of opportunities for upward mobility is stronger at the top of the class hierarchy than at the bottom. We find considerably less opposition to the idea that government should reduce inequality as we move down the stratification system. This permits us to conclude that, if Canadians allow inequality to persist, it is because the balance of attitudes—and of the power that supports those attitudes—favours continuity over change.

LO⁴ Global Inequality

LEVELS AND TRENDS IN GLOBAL INEQUALITY

Despite the existence of considerable social stratification in Canada, we live in one of the 20 or so richest counties in the world—an elite club that also includes the United States, Japan, Australia, Germany, France, the U.K., and a dozen or so other Western European countries. In contrast, the world's poor countries cover much of Africa and parts of South America and Asia. Inequality between rich and poor countries is staggering. In a Manhattan restaurant, pet owners can treat their cats to US$100-a-plate birthday parties. In Cairo (Egypt) and Manila (the Philippines), garbage dumps are home to entire families who sustain themselves by picking through the refuse.

The average income of citizens in the highly industrialized countries far outstrips that of citizens in the developing societies. Yet because poor people live in rich countries and rich people live in poor countries, averages fail to capture the extent of inequality between the richest of the rich and the poorest of the poor. Noting that the total worth of the world's 1011 billionaires equalled the gross domestic product (GDP) of 143 *countries* in 2010 is perhaps more revealing (Forbes.com, 2010; Central Intelligence Agency, 2010). The three richest people in the world owned more than the combined GDP of the 54 least developed countries. The richest 1 percent of the world's population earns as much income as the bottom 57 percent (United Nations, 2002). According to the UN, 800 million people in the world are malnourished and two-thirds of the world's population are poor in the sense that they lack the ability to obtain adequate food, clothing, shelter, and other basic needs. The citizens of the 20 or so rich, highly industrialized countries spend more on cosmetics or alcohol or ice cream or pet food than it would take to provide basic education or water and sanitation or basic health and nutrition for everyone in the world (see Table 6.5).

Has global inequality increased or decreased over time? Between 1975 and 2000, the annual income gap between the 20 or so richest countries and the rest of the world grew enormously. The share of world income going to the top 10 percent of individuals has also been increasing, and the share of world income going to the bottom 20 percent of individuals has been falling. On the slightly brighter side, the number of people in the world living on $1 a day or less peaked in 1950 and then started to decline gradually. However, if we consider only the less developed countries, the number of people living on $1 a day or less *increased* by 20 million in the 1990s. Even by the most optimistic interpretation, these figures are little cause for joy. Nearly half of the world's population lives on $2 a day or less (Milanovic, 2005; Figure 6.6).

Statistics never speak for themselves. We need theories to explain them. Let us now outline and critically assess the two main theories that seek to explain the origins and persistence of global inequality.

JORGEN SCHYTTE/Photolibrary

A half-hour's drive from the centre of Manila, the capital of the Philippines, an estimated 70 000 Filipinos live on a 22-hectare mountain of rotting garbage 45 metres high. It is infested with flies, rats, dogs, and disease. On a lucky day, residents can earn up to $5 retrieving scraps of metal and other valuables. On a rainy day, the mountain of garbage is especially treacherous. In July 2000 an avalanche buried 300 people alive. People who live on the mountain of garbage call it "The Promised Land."

TABLE 6.5
Global Priorities: Annual Cost of Various Goods and Services

Good/Service	Annual Cost (US$ billion)
Basic education for everyone in the world	6
Cosmetics in the United States	8
Water and sanitation for everyone in the world	9
Ice cream in Europe	11
Reproductive health for all women in the world	12
Perfumes in Europe and the United States	12
Basic health and nutrition for everyone in the world	13
Pet foods in Europe and the United States	17
Business entertainment in Japan	35
Cigarettes in Europe	50
Alcoholic drinks in Europe	105
Narcotic drugs in the world	400
Military spending in the world	780

Source: Table: "Global Priorities: Annual cost of various goods and services" (p. 37) from *Human Development Report 1998* by United Nations (1998). Reprinted by permission of Oxford University Press, Inc.

FIGURE 6.6
World Poverty

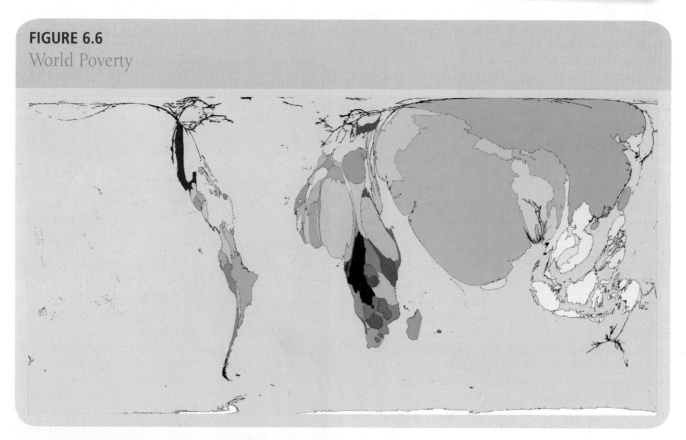

Note: The size of each country is proportional to the percentage of people in that country living on US$2 a day or less in purchasing power.
Source: University of Sheffield. 2006. "Absolute Poverty." http://www.worldmapper.org/posters/worldmapper_map180_ver5.pdf (retrieved 11 March 2010).
© Copyright 2006 SASI Group (University of Sheffield) and Mark Newman (University of Michigan).

LO⁵ MODERNIZATION THEORY: A FUNCTIONALIST APPROACH

Two main sociological theories claim to explain global inequality. The first, modernization theory, is a variant of functionalism. According to modernization theory, global inequality results from various dysfunctional characteristics of poor societies themselves. Specifically, modernization theorists say the citizens of poor societies lack sufficient *capital* to invest in Western-style agriculture and industry. They lack rational, Western-style *business techniques* of marketing, accounting, sales, and finance. As a result, their productivity and profitability remain low. They lack stable, Western-style *governments* that could provide a secure framework for investment. Finally, they lack a Western *mentality*: values that stress the need for savings, investment, innovation, education, high achievement, and self-control in having children (Inkeles and Smith, 1976; Rostow, 1960). Societies characterized by these dysfunctions are poor. It follows that people living in rich countries can best help their poor cousins by transferring Western culture and capital to them and eliminating the dysfunctions. Only then will the poor countries be able to cap population growth, stimulate democracy, and invigorate agricultural and industrial production. Government-to-government foreign aid can accomplish some of this. Much work also needs to be done to encourage Western businesses to invest directly in poor countries and to increase trade between rich and poor countries.

DEPENDENCY THEORY: A CONFLICT APPROACH

Proponents of dependency theory, a variant of conflict theory, have been quick to point out the chief flaw in modernization theory (Baran, 1957; Cardoso and Faletto, 1979; Wallerstein, 1974–89). For the past 500 years, the most powerful countries in the world have deliberately impoverished the less powerful countries. Focusing on internal characteristics blames the victim rather than the perpetrator of the crime. It follows that an adequate theory of global inequality should not focus on the internal characteristics of poor countries themselves. Instead, it should follow the principles of conflict theory and focus on patterns of domination and submission—specifically, in this case, on the relationship between rich and poor countries. That is just what dependency theory does.

According to dependency theorists, less global inequality existed in 1500 and even in 1750 than today. However, beginning around 1500, the armed forces of the world's most powerful countries subdued and then annexed or colonized most of the rest of the world. The Industrial Revolution began around 1775. It enabled the Western European countries, Russia, Japan, and the United States to amass enormous wealth, which they used to extend their global reach. They forced their colonies to become a source of raw materials, cheap labour, investment opportunities, and markets for the conquering nations. The colonizers thereby prevented industrialization and locked the colonies into poverty.

In the decades following World War II, nearly all the colonies in the world became politically independent. However, the dependency theorists say that exploitation by direct political control was soon replaced by new means of achieving the same end: substantial foreign investment, support for authoritarian governments, and mounting debt.

- *Substantial foreign investment.* Multinational corporations invested in the poor countries to siphon off wealth in the form of raw materials and profits. True, they created some low-paying jobs in the process. But they created many more high-paying jobs in the rich countries where the raw materials were used to produce manufactured goods. They also sold part of the manufactured goods back to the poor, unindustrialized countries for additional profit.

- *Support for authoritarian governments.* According to dependency theorists, multinational corporations and rich countries continued their exploitation of the poor countries in the postcolonial period by giving economic and military support to local authoritarian governments. These governments managed to keep their populations subdued most of the time. When that was not possible, Western governments sent in troops and military advisers, engaging in what became known as "gunboat diplomacy." In the postcolonial period, the United States has been particularly active in using gunboat diplomacy in Central America. For example, in 1952 the democratic government of Guatemala began to redistribute land to impoverished peasants.

---

modernization theory
Holds that global inequality results from various dysfunctional characteristics of poor societies: lack of investment capital, Western-style business techniques, stable Western-style governments, and a Western mentality.

dependency theory
Holds that global inequality is the result of patterns of domination and submission between rich and poor countries. From this point of view, rich countries have impoverished poor countries in order to enrich themselves.

Olga Popova/Shutterstock

CHAPTER 6 Social Stratification: Canadian and Global Perspectives **137**

Some of the land was owned by the United Fruit Company, a U.S. multinational corporation and the biggest landowner in Guatemala. Two years later, the CIA backed a right-wing coup in Guatemala, preventing land reform and allowing the United Fruit Company to continue its highly profitable business as usual (LaFeber, 1993).

- *Mounting debt.* The governments of the poor countries struggled to create transportation infrastructures (airports, roads, harbours, etc.), build their education systems, and deliver safe water and at least the most basic health care to their people. To accomplish these tasks, they had to borrow money from Western banks and governments. Some rulers also squandered money on luxuries. So it came about that debt—and the interest payments that inevitably accompany debt—grew every year. Crushing interest payments leave governments of poor countries with too little money for development tasks. Foreign aid helps, but not much. In 2002, foreign aid to the world's developing countries was only one-seventh the amount that the developing countries paid to Western banks in loan interest (United Nations, 2004: 201).

LO⁶ CORE, PERIPHERY, AND SEMIPERIPHERY

Although dependency theory provides a more realistic account of the sources of global inequality than modernization theory does, it leaves a big question unanswered: how have some countries managed to escape poverty and start rapid economic development? After all, the world does not consist just of **core countries** that are major sources of capital and technology (the United States, Japan, and Germany) and **peripheral countries** that are major sources of raw materials and cheap labour (the former colonies). In addition, a middle tier of **semiperipheral countries** consists of former colonies that are making considerable headway in their attempts to become prosperous (South Korea, Taiwan, and Israel, for example; Wallerstein, 1974–89). Comparing the poor peripheral countries with the more successful semiperipheral countries presents us with a useful natural experiment. The comparison suggests the circumstances that help some poor countries overcome the worst effects of colonialism.

core countries Capitalist countries that are the world's major sources of capital and technology (the United States, Japan, and Germany).

peripheral countries that are the world's major sources of raw materials and cheap labour (the former colonies).

semiperipheral countries that are former colonies and that are making considerable headway in their attempt to become prosperous.

In 1893 leaders of the British mission pose before taking over what became Rhodesia and is now Zimbabwe. To raise a volunteer army, every British trooper was offered about 23 square kilometres of native land and 20 gold claims. The Matabele and Mashona peoples were subdued in a three-month war. Nine hundred farms and 10 000 gold claims were granted to the troopers and about 100 000 cattle were looted, leaving the native survivors without a livelihood. Forced labour was subsequently introduced by the British so that the natives could pay a £2 a year tax.

Weidenfeld and Nicolson Archives

The semiperipheral countries differ from the peripheral countries in four main ways, which we outline next (Kennedy, 1993: 193–227; Lie, 1998).

Type of Colonialism

Around the turn of the twentieth century, Taiwan and Korea became colonies of Japan. They remained so until 1945. However, in contrast to the European colonizers of Africa, Latin America, and other parts of Asia, the Japanese built up the economies of their colonies. They established transportation networks and communication systems. They built steel, chemical, and hydroelectric power plants. After Japanese colonialism ended, Taiwan and South Korea were thus at an advantage compared with the former colonies of Britain and France. South Korea and Taiwan could use the Japanese-built infrastructure and Japanese-trained personnel as springboards to development.

Geopolitical Position

Although the United States was the leading economic and military power in the world by the end of World War II, it began to feel its supremacy threatened in the late 1940s by the Soviet Union and China. Fearing that South Korea and Taiwan might fall to the communists, the United States poured unprecedented aid into both countries in the 1960s. It also gave them large, low-interest loans and opened its domestic market to Taiwanese and South Korean products. Because the United States saw Israel as a crucially important ally in the Middle East, it also received special economic assistance. Other countries with less strategic importance to the United States received less help in their drive to industrialize.

State Policy

A third factor that accounts for the relative success of some countries in their efforts to industrialize and become prosperous concerns state policies. As a legacy of colonialism, the Taiwanese and South Korean states were developed on the Japanese model. They kept workers' wages low, restricted trade union growth, and maintained quasi-military discipline in factories. Moreover, by placing high taxes on consumer goods, limiting the import of foreign goods, and preventing their citizens from investing abroad, they encouraged their citizens to put much of their money in the bank. This situation created a large pool of capital for industrial expansion. The South Korean and Taiwanese states also gave subsidies, training grants, and tariff protection to export-based industries from the 1960s onward. (Tariffs are taxes on foreign goods.) These policies did much to stimulate industrial growth. Finally, the Taiwanese and South Korean states invested heavily in basic education, health care, roads, and other public goods. A healthy and well-educated labour force, combined with good transportation and communication systems, laid solid foundations for economic growth.

Social Structure

Taiwan and South Korea are socially cohesive countries, which makes it easy for them to generate consensus around development policies. It also allows them to get their citizens to work hard, save a lot of money, and devote their energies to scientific education.

Social solidarity in Taiwan and South Korea is based partly on the sweeping land reform they conducted in the late 1940s and early 1950s. By redistributing land to small farmers, both countries eliminated the class of large landowners, who usually oppose industrialization. Land redistribution got rid of a major potential source of social conflict. In contrast, many countries in Latin America and Africa have not undergone land reform. The United States often intervened militarily in Latin America to prevent land reform because U.S. commercial interests profited handsomely from the existence of large plantations (LaFeber, 1993).

Another factor underlying social solidarity in Taiwan and South Korea is that neither country suffered from internal conflicts like those that wrack Africa south of the Sahara desert. British, French, and other Western European colonizers often drew the borders of African countries to keep antagonistic tribes in the same jurisdiction and often sought to stir up tribal conflict. Keeping tribal tensions alive made it possible to play one tribe against another. That made it easier for imperial powers to dominate. This policy led to much social and political conflict in postcolonial Africa. Today, the region suffers from frequent civil wars, coups, and uprisings. It is the most conflict-ridden area of the world. This high level of internal conflict acts as a barrier to economic development.

In sum, postcolonial countries that enjoy a solid industrial infrastructure, strategic geopolitical importance, strong states with strong development policies, and socially cohesive populations are in the best position to join the ranks of the rich countries in the coming decades. Countries that have some of these characteristics are likely to experience economic growth and an increase in the well-being of their populations. Such countries include China, India, Chile, Thailand, Indonesia, Mexico, Turkey, Russia, and Brazil (see the Sociology at the Movies box on the next page). We conclude that, as is the case for social stratification within highly developed countries like Canada, the existing level of global inequality is not inevitable and can under some circumstances change for the better. We take up this theme again in the book's final chapter.

Slumdog Millionaire

FILM 4/CELADOR FILMS/PATHE INTERNATIONAL/THE KOBAL COLLECTION

centre of the world now, *bhai* [brother]. And I, I am at the centre of the centre. This is all Javed *bhai's*."

Jamal: "Javed Khan, the gangster from our slum? You work for him? What do you do for him?"

Salim: "Anything he asks."

Slumdog Millionaire grossed more than $250 million including DVD sales, but a scandal erupted when it was learned that the actors who had major roles playing Jamal and Latika as children received a pittance for their efforts (Nelson and Henderson, 2009). According to the children's parents, Rubina Ali and Azaharuddin Ismail, both plucked from a Mumbai slum, received, respectively, £500 and £1700 for a year's work. The exploitation of Ali and Ismail caused widespread outrage, hardly softened by the statement of a spokesperson for Fox Searchlight, the film's American distributor, that (1) these payments equal three times the adult yearly salary in the slum, (2) the children are also receiving £20 a month each for books and food, and (3) a fund has been established which the children will receive when they turn 18 if they remain in school. (The spokesperson declined to disclose the size of the fund when asked.)

This is not an isolated case involving exploitation of child actors from less developed countries. The poor Afghan child stars of *The Kite Runner* embarrassed their Hollywood producers two years earlier when they disclosed that they had been paid just £9000 for their efforts. As noted earlier, "transformed" does not mean "improved beyond recognition."

A shift of world-historic proportions is taking place in the global economy. The rich countries' share of world gross domestic product is slowly shrinking while the share produced by some less developed countries, notably China and India, is rapidly increasing (see Table 6.6). In China and India, most rural residents of non-coastal areas remain poor. However, as peasants move to cities and governments and real estate developers tear down slums and build high-rises in their place, the conditions of existence for hundreds of millions of people are being transformed. "Transformed" does not, of course, mean "improved beyond recognition," despite the theme of *Slumdog Millionaire,* the winner of a best-picture Oscar.

Slumdog Millionaire is the improbable story of Jamal K. Malik (Dev Patel), a young slum dweller who becomes a contestant on the Indian version of *Who Wants to Be a Millionaire.* He answers every question correctly by drawing on his harrowing experiences growing up in a Mumbai slum, and wins not only the grand prize but also the affection of the beautiful Latika (Freida Pinto), the girlfriend of the dangerous criminal kingpin Javed Khan (Mahesh Manjrekar). All this takes place amid boisterous Bollywood dance numbers and India's frenzied economic growth. "That . . . used to be our slum. Can you believe that, huh?" asks Salim, Jamal's brother, pointing to a high-rise development. "We used to live right there, man. Now, it's all business. India is at the

Critical Thinking Questions

As India becomes richer, its standard of living increases and its middle class grows. However, inequality also increases.
- Is increased inequality the *inevitable* result of economic growth? If not, then why not?
- Does growing inequality matter as long as there is more wealth for everyone?

TABLE 6.6

Share of World Gross Domestic Product by Selected Countries, 1980 and 2010 (in percent)

	1980	2010	Percentage Change
United States	22.4	19.6	−12.5
Canada	2.2	1.8	−18.2
Japan	8.3	6.0	−28.8
Germany	6.1	4.0	−34.4
India	2.2	5.1	131.8
China	2.0	12.7	535.0

Note: Figures are based on purchasing power and therefore control for inflation. Data for 2010 are estimated.

Source: International Monetary Fund. 2009. "World Economic and Financial Surveys: World Economic Outlook Database." http://www.imf.org/external/pubs/ft/weo/2009/02/weodata/index.aspx (retrieved 2 January 2010).

LO¹ Defining Race and Ethnicity

WHAT IS RACE?

Race and Intelligence

In the 1920s, Peter Sandiford, a professor in the Department of Education at the University of Toronto, administered some IQ tests and concluded that Canada must adopt a policy of selective immigration to ensure that "misfits" and "defectives" are kept out of the country. He encouraged the immigration of Britons, Germans, and Danes, and discouraged the immigration of Poles, Italians, Greeks, and Asians. The latter groups scored low on his IQ tests, and he believed that their apparent intellectual inferiority was rooted in their biological makeup (McLaren, 1990). Around the same time in the United States, Jewish immigrants were scoring below non-Jews on IQ tests. These results were used by many people as an argument against Jewish immigration. In modern times, blacks have, on average, scored below European Americans on IQ tests. Some people say this justifies slashing budgets for schools in the inner city, where many black people live. Why invest good money in inner-city schooling, such people ask, if low IQ scores are rooted in biology and therefore fixed (Herrnstein and Murray, 1994)?

The people who argued against the immigration of certain groups and better education for inner-city blacks ignored two facts. First, IQ scores are remarkably flexible. The descendants of Sandiford's low-IQ Asians are among the stars of the Canadian system of higher education today. As Jews experienced upward mobility and could afford better education, their IQ scores rose to above-average levels. Enriched educational facilities routinely boost the IQ scores and achievements of inner-city black children (Campbell and Ramey, 1994; Frank Porter Graham Child Development Center, 1999; Gould, 1996; Hancock, 1994). We are obliged to conclude that the social setting in which a person is raised and educated has a big impact on IQ. The average IQ of members of racial and ethnic groups has nothing to do with biology (Cancio, Evans, and Maume, 1996; Fischer et al., 1996).

LEARNING OBJECTIVES:

LO¹ Race and ethnicity are socially constructed labels that change over time. These labels, which have profound consequences for people's lives, distinguish people by perceived physical or cultural differences.

LO² Racial and ethnic identities change over time and place. Relations among racial and ethnic groups help to shape racial and ethnic identities.

LO³ In Canada, racial and ethnic groups are blending over time. However, this tendency is weaker among members of highly disadvantaged groups, especially First Nations peoples, members of some visible minority groups, and recent immigrants.

LO⁴ Identifying with some racial or ethnic group can be economically, politically, and emotionally advantageous or disadvantageous.

LO⁵ Racial and ethnic inequality is likely to persist in Canada.

Race and Sports

prejudice An attitude that judges a person on his or her group's real or imagined characteristics.

discrimination Unfair treatment of people because of their group membership.

The view persists, nonetheless, that races differ biologically. For instance, we commonly hear that, for biological reasons, black people are better than whites at sports. Is there any evidence to support that belief? At first glance, the evidence might seem strong. Aren't 67 percent of NFL players and 65 percent of NBA players black? Don't blacks of West African descent hold the 200 fastest 100-metre-dash times, all under 10 seconds? Don't North and East Africans regularly win 40 percent of the top international distance-running honours yet represent only a fraction of 1 percent of the world's population (Entine, 2000; Lapchick, 2004)? Although these facts are undeniable, the argument for the genetic basis of black athletic superiority begins to falter once we consider two additional points. First, no gene linked to general athletic superiority has ever been identified. Second, black athletes do not perform unusually well in many sports, such as equestrian events, swimming, hockey, cycling, tennis, gymnastics, and soccer. The idea that black people are in general superior athletes is simply untrue.

Sociologists have identified certain *social* conditions that lead to high levels of participation in sports. These operate on all groups of people, whatever their race. Specifically, people who face widespread prejudice and discrimination often enter sports in disproportionately large numbers for lack of other ways to improve their social and economic standing. For such people, other avenues of upward mobility tend to be blocked. (**Prejudice** is an attitude that judges a person on his or her group's real or imagined characteristics. **Discrimination** is unfair treatment of people because of their group membership.) For example, it was not until the 1950s that prejudice and discrimination against North American Jews began to decline appreciably. Until then, Jews played a prominent role in some professional sports, such as boxing, baseball, and basketball. When the New York Knicks played their first game on November 1, 1946, beating the Toronto Huskies 68–66, the starting lineup for New York consisted of Ossie Schechtman, Stan Stutz, Jake Weber, Ralph Kaplowitz, and Leo "Ace" Gottlieb—an all-Jewish squad ("New York Knicks History," 2000). Similarly, Koreans in Japan today are subject to much prejudice and discrimination. They often pursue careers in sports. In contrast, Koreans in Canada face less

prejudice and discrimination. Few of them become professional athletes.

The idea that black people are genetically superior to whites in athletic ability is the complement of the idea that they are genetically inferior to whites in intellectual ability. Both ideas have the effect of reinforcing black–white inequality. For although there are just a few thousand professional athletes in North America, there are millions of pharmacists, graphics designers, lawyers, systems analysts, police officers, nurses, and people in other interesting occupations that offer steady employment and good pay. By promoting only the Chris Boshes of the world as suitable role models for youth, the idea of "natural" black athletic superiority and intellectual inferiority in effect asks blacks to bet on a high-risk proposition—that they will make it in professional sports. At the same time, it deflects attention from a much safer bet—that they can achieve upward mobility through academic excellence (Guppy and Davies, 1998; Hoberman, 1997).

ASSOCIATED PRESS

Racial Mixing

Another problem undermines the argument that genes determine the behaviour of racial groups: it is impossible to neatly distinguish races based on genetic differences. A high level of genetic mixing has taken place among people throughout the world. In North America, for instance, it was not uncommon for white male slave owners to rape black female slaves, who then gave birth to children of mixed race. Many Europeans had children with Aboriginal peoples in the eighteenth and nineteenth centuries. We know from the census that racial intermarriage has been increasing in Canada at least since 1871. Usually, people who report multiple racial identities have parents of different racial origins (Kalbach and Kalbach, 1998). A growing number of North Americans are similar to Tiger Woods. Woods claims he is of "Cablinasian" ancestry—part Caucasian, part black, part Native American Indian, and part Asian. As these examples illustrate, the differences among black, white, Asian, and so forth are often anything but clear-cut.

Some respected scholars believe we all belong to one human race, which originated in Africa (Cavalli-Sforza, Menozzi, and Piazza, 1994). They argue that subsequent migration, geographical separation, and inbreeding led to the formation of more or less distinct races. However, particularly in modern times, humanity has experienced so much intermixing that race as a biological category has lost nearly all meaning. Some biologists and social scientists therefore suggest we drop the term *race* from the vocabulary of science.

A Sociological Definition of Race

Sociologists, however, continue to use the term. They do so because perceptions of race continue to affect the lives of most people profoundly. Everything from your wealth to your health is influenced by whether others see you as black, white, brown, or something else. Race as a sociological concept is thus an invaluable analytical tool. It is valuable, however, only to the degree that people who use the term remember that it refers to socially significant physical differences (e.g., skin colour) rather than to biological differences that shape behaviour patterns.

Said differently, perceptions of racial difference are socially constructed and often arbitrary. The Irish and the Jews were regarded as "blacks" by many people long ago, and today many northern Italians still think of southern Italians from Sicily and Calabria as "blacks" (Gilman, 1991; Ignatiev, 1995; Roediger, 1991). During World War II, some people made arbitrary physical distinctions between Chinese allies and Japanese enemies that helped to justify the Canadian policy of placing Japanese Canadians in internment camps. These examples show that racial distinctions are social constructs, not biological givens.

Finally, then, we can define **race** as a social construct used to distinguish people in terms of one or more physical markers. However, this definition raises an interesting question. If race is merely a social construct and not a useful biological term, why are perceptions of physical difference used to distinguish groups of people in the first place? Why, in other words, does race matter? Most sociologists believe that race matters because it allows social inequality to be created and perpetuated. The English who colonized Ireland, the Americans who went to Africa looking for slaves, and the Germans who used the Jews as a scapegoat to explain their deep economic and political troubles after World War I, all created systems of racial domination. (A **scapegoat** is a disadvantaged person or category of people that others blame for their own problems.) Once colonialism, slavery, and concentration camps were established, behavioural differences developed between subordinates and their masters. For example, North American slaves and Jewish concentration camp inmates, with little motivating them to work hard except the ultimate threat of the master's whip, tended to do only the minimum work necessary to survive. Their masters noticed this and characterized their subordinates as inherently slow and unreliable workers (Collins, 1982, pp. 66–69). In this way, racial stereotypes are born. The stereotypes then embed themselves in literature, popular lore, journalism, and political debate. This reinforces racial inequalities (see Figure 7.1). We thus see that race matters to the degree that it helps create and maintain systems of social inequality.

> **race** A social construct used to distinguish people in terms of one or more physical markers, usually with profound effects on their lives.
>
> **scapegoat** A disadvantaged person or category of people whom others blame for their own problems.

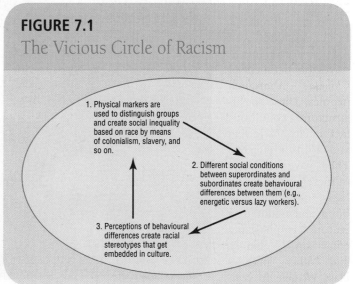

FIGURE 7.1
The Vicious Circle of Racism

1. Physical markers are used to distinguish groups and create social inequality based on race by means of colonialism, slavery, and so on.

2. Different social conditions between superordinates and subordinates create behavioural differences between them (e.g., energetic versus lazy workers).

3. Perceptions of behavioural differences create racial stereotypes that get embedded in culture.

Source: From BRYM/LIE. *Sociology: The Points of the Compass.* © 2009 Nelson Education Ltd. Reproduced by permission. www.cengage.com/permissions.

ETHNICITY, CULTURE, AND SOCIAL STRUCTURE

Race is to biology as ethnicity is to culture. A *race* is a socially defined category of people whose perceived *physical* markers are deemed significant. An **ethnic group** comprises people whose perceived *cultural* markers are deemed significant. Ethnic groups differ from one another in terms of language, religion, customs, values, ancestors, and the like. However, just as physical distinctions don't *cause* differences in the behaviour of various races, so cultural distinctions are often not by themselves the major source of differences in the behaviour of various ethnic groups. In other words, ethnic values and other elements of ethnic culture have less of an effect on the way people behave than we commonly believe. That is because *social structural* differences frequently underlie cultural differences.

An example will help drive home the point. People often praise Jews, Koreans, and other economically successful groups for their cultural values, including an emphasis on education, family, and hard work. People less commonly notice, however, that Canada's immigration policy has been highly selective. For the most part, the Jews and Koreans who arrived in Canada were literate, urbanized, and skilled. Some even came with financial assets (Brym, Shaffir, and Weinfeld, 1993; Li, 1995; Wong and Ng, 1998). They certainly confronted prejudice and discrimination but far less than that reserved for the descendants of slaves or members of Canada's Aboriginal peoples. These social-structural conditions facilitated Jewish and Korean success. They gave members of these groups a firm basis on which to build and maintain a culture emphasizing education, family, and other middle-class virtues. In con-

trast, descendants of slaves and members of Canada's Aboriginal peoples were typically illiterate and unskilled, and they experienced more prejudice and discrimination than other ethnic or racial groups in Canada. These social-structural disadvantages—not their culture—made them less economically successful than Jews and Koreans on average.

In general, much Canadian research supports the argument that culture by itself is unimportant in determining the economic success of nearly all racial or ethnic groups. There *are* substantial differences in average annual income among some racial groups. For example, the average annual income of Aboriginal peoples is substantially below that of white Canadians. So is the average annual income of non-white immigrants. The point, however, is that these differences are due largely to such factors as how many years of education the average Aboriginal Canadian has and how many years the average non-white immigrant has been in the country. Few significant income differences exist between white Canadians and the Canadian-born children of non-white immigrants. (An important exception that we will consider later is black men, who continue to suffer discrimination in the paid labour force beyond the immigrant generation.) A professor who happens to be an Aboriginal Canadian earns as much as a white professor with the same training, years of work experience, research and publication record, and so on. The problem is that there are so few Aboriginal professors because of the centuries-long discriminatory treatment of Aboriginal Canadians by the white majority (again, discussed later in the chapter).

Fuse/Jupiterimages

RESOURCES AND OPPORTUNITIES

As we saw in our brief comparison of Koreans and Jews with Aboriginal peoples, what really matters in determining the economic success of an ethnic or racial group are the *resources* people possess, such as education, literacy, urbanity, and financial assets. We can now add that what also matters in determining economic success are the kinds of *economic opportunities* open to people. The latter point can be seen clearly if we compare Canada in the mid-twentieth century with Canada today.

Half a century ago, Canada was a society sharply stratified along ethnic and racial lines. The people with the most power and privilege were of British origin. WASPs (White Anglo-Saxon Protestants) controlled almost all the big corporations in the country and dominated politics. Immigrants who arrived later enjoyed less power and privilege. Even among them, big economic differences were evident, with European immigrants enjoying higher status than immigrants of Asian ancestry, for example.

John Porter, one of the founders of modern Canadian sociology, called mid-twentieth-century Canada a **vertical mosaic**, a highly ethnically and racially stratified society. He thought that the retention of ethnic and racial culture was a big problem in Canada because it hampered the upward mobility of immigrants. In his view, the "Canadian value system" encouraged the retention of ethnic culture, making Canada a low-mobility society (Porter, 1965, 1979: 91).

> **vertical mosaic** A highly ethnically and racially stratified society.

By the 1970s, however, many Canadian sociologists, including Porter himself, had to reject or at least qualify the view that ethnic and racial culture determines economic success or failure. Events upset their earlier assumptions. The Canadian economy grew quickly in the decades after World War II. Many members of ethnic and racial minority groups were economically successful despite ethnic and racial prejudice and discrimination. Economic differences among ethnic groups and, to a lesser degree, among racial groups, diminished. Among the wealthiest Canadians, and among politicians at all levels of government, ethnic and racial diversity increased. Such diversity became even more evident among professional groups. For the most part, visible minority status had little bearing on educational, occupational, and income attainment in Canada, especially among the Canadian-born (Guppy and Davies, 1998; Lautard and Guppy, 2008; Lian and Matthews, 1998; Pendakur and Pendakur, 1998; see Table 7.1). Aboriginal Canadians and black men (even black men born in Canada) continued to face discrimination that significantly impeded their upward mobility. But for the great majority of Canadians in the decades after World War II, ethnic and racial culture mattered less than the structure of mobility opportunities in determining a person's economic success.

True, in the 1990s, recent immigrants who were members of visible minority groups were significantly less successful economically than we would expect given their educational and other resources. However, their cultural values had little to do with that. Canada experienced an unusually high rate of unemployment in the 1990s, hovering around 10 percent until late in the decade. This situation made it more difficult than in previous decades for recently arrived visible minority immigrants to succeed economically.

It has now become evident that many recent visible minority immigrants face a second problem limiting their upward mobility. Although they may be selected to come to Canada because they are highly educated, their credentials are often not recognized by employers here. The mechanisms for receiving accreditation for foreign credentials are poorly developed in this country and need to be improved (Reitz, 2008). But the relative lack of success of recent visible minority immigrants reinforces our point. In addition to the resources a person possesses, it is the structure of opportunities for economic

TABLE 7.1
Percentage with Below-Average Income by Ethnic Identity and Place of Birth, Canada, 2001

	Born Abroad (%)	Born in Canada (%)
British	53	51
French	51	52
Other European	59	45
African	65	20
Arab	67	35
Other Asian	64	27
Caribbean	67	20
Other Latin, Central, and South American	55	34
Aboriginal	77	54
Canadian	62	50

Note: Data are for a random sample of 31 100 Canadian residents who gave a single ethnic origin in the 2001 census. Average individual annual income was $27 141. The income data were truncated at $200 000.

Source: Adapted from Statistics Canada (2005a).

advancement that determines income and occupational and educational attainment. Ethnic or racial culture by itself plays at best a minor role.

In sum, we see that racial and ethnic inequality is more deeply rooted in social structure than in biology and culture. The biological and cultural aspects of race and ethnicity are secondary to their sociological character when it comes to explaining inequality. The interesting question from a sociological point of view is why social definitions of race and ethnicity change. We now consider that issue.

LO² Symbolic Interactionism, Race, and Ethnic Relations

LABELS AND IDENTITY

John Lie moved with his family from South Korea to Japan when he was a baby. He moved from Japan to Hawaii when he was 10 years old, and again from Hawaii to the American mainland when he started university. The move to Hawaii and the move to the U.S. mainland changed the way John thought of himself in ethnic terms.

In Japan, Koreans form a minority group. Before 1945, when Korea was a colony of Japan, some Koreans were brought to Japan to work as miners and unskilled labourers. The Japanese thought the Koreans who lived there were beneath and outside Japanese society (Lie, 2001). Not surprisingly, Korean children in Japan—including John—were often teased and occasionally beaten by their Japanese schoolmates. "The beatings hurt," says John, "but the psychological trauma resulting from being socially excluded by my classmates hurt more. In fact, although I initially thought I was Japanese like my classmates, my Korean identity was literally beaten into me.

"When my family immigrated to Hawaii, I was sure things would get worse. I expected Americans to be even meaner than the Japanese. (By Americans, I thought only of white European Americans.) Was I surprised when I discovered that most of my schoolmates were not white European Americans, but people of Asian and mixed ancestry! Suddenly I was a member of a numerical majority. I was no longer teased or bullied. In fact, I found that students of Asian and non-European origin often singled out white European Americans (called *haole* in Hawaiian) for abuse. We even had a 'beat up *haole* day' in school. Given my own experiences in Japan, I empathized somewhat with the white Americans. But I have to admit that I also felt a great sense of relief and an easing

of the psychological trauma associated with being Korean in Japan.

"As the years passed, I finished public school in Hawaii. I then went to college in Massachusetts and got a job as a professor in Illinois and then in Michigan. I associated with, and befriended, people from various racial and ethnic groups. My Korean origin became an increasingly less important factor in the way people treated me. There was simply less prejudice and discrimination against Koreans during my adulthood in the United States than in my early years in Japan. I now think of myself less as Japanese or Korean than as American. My ethnic identity has changed over time in response to the significance others have attached to my Korean origin. I now understand what the French philosopher Jean-Paul Sartre meant when he wrote that 'the anti-Semite creates the Jew'" (Sartre, 1965 [1948]: 43).

The details of John Lie's life are unique. But experiencing a shift in racial or ethnic identity is common. Social contexts, and in particular the nature of a person's relations with members of other racial and ethnic groups, shape and continuously reshape a person's racial and ethnic identity. Change your social context and your racial and ethnic self-conception eventually change too (Miles, 1989; Omi and Winant, 1986).

Consider Italian Canadians. Around 1900, Italian immigrants thought of themselves as people who came from a particular town or perhaps a particular province, such as Sicily or Calabria. They did not usually think of themselves as Italians. Italy became a unified country only in 1861. A mere 30 years later, many Italian citizens still did not identify with their new Italian nationality. In both Canada and the United States, however, government officials and other residents identified the newcomers as Italians. The designation at first seemed odd to many of the new immigrants. However, over time it stuck. Immigrants from Italy started thinking of themselves as Italian Canadians because others defined them that way. A new ethnic identity was born (Yancey, Ericksen, and Leon, 1979).

As symbolic interactionists emphasize, the development of racial and ethnic labels, and ethnic and racial identities, is typically a process of negotiation. For example, members of a group may have a racial or an ethnic identity, but outsiders may impose a new label on them. Group members then reject, accept, or modify the label. The negotiation between outsiders and insiders eventually results in the crystallization of a new, more or less stable ethnic identity. If the social context changes again, the negotiation process begins anew.

One such case involves the labelling of the indigenous peoples of North America by European settlers. When Christopher Columbus landed in North America in 1492, he assumed he had reached India. He called the indigenous peoples "Indians" and the misnomer stuck—not only among European settlers but also among many indigenous peoples themselves. Indigenous peoples still identified themselves in tribal terms—as Mi'kmaq or Mohawk or Haida—but they typically thought of themselves collectively and *in opposition to European settlers* as Indians. A new identity was thus grafted onto tribal identities because indigenous peoples confronted a group that had the power to impose a name on them.

In time, however, an increasingly large number of indigenous people began to reject the term *Indian*. White settlers and their governments took land from the indigenous peoples, forced them onto reserves, and thus caused their resentment, anger, and solidarity to grow. Especially since the 1960s, indigenous North Americans have begun to fight back culturally and politically, asserting pride in their languages, art, and customs and making legal claims to the lands that were taken from them. One aspect of their resistance involved questioning use of the term *Indian*. In Canada, many of them preferred instead to be called Native Canadians, indigenous peoples, Aboriginal Canadians, or First Nations. These new terms, especially the last one, were all assertions of newfound pride. Today, many North Americans of European origin accept these new terms out of respect for indigenous North Americans and in recognition of their neglected rights. New, more or less stable ethnic identities have thus been negotiated as the power struggle between indigenous peoples and more recent settlers continues. As the social context changed, the negotiation of ethnic identities proceeded apace.

LO³ IMPOSITION VERSUS CHOICE

The idea that race and ethnicity are socially constructed does not mean that everyone can always choose their racial or ethnic identity freely. Wide variations occur over time, between societies, and within societies in the degree to which people can exercise such freedom of choice.

The Canadians with the most freedom to choose their ethnic identity are whites whose ancestors arrived in Canada more than two generations ago. For example, identifying as an Irish Canadian no longer has negative implications it did in, say, 1900. Then, wherever a substantial number of Irish immigrants were concentrated, the English-Protestant majority typically regarded working-class Irish Catholics as often drunk, inherently lazy, and born superstitious. This strong anti-Irish sentiment, which often erupted into conflict, meant that the Irish found it difficult to escape their ethnic identity even if they wanted to. Since then, however, Irish Canadians have followed the path taken by many other white European groups: they have achieved upward mobility and blended with the majority.

As a result, Irish Canadians no longer find their identity imposed on them. Instead, they can choose whether to march in a St. Patrick's Day parade, enjoy the remarkable contributions of Irish authors to English-language literature and drama, and take pride in the athleticism and artistry of Riverdance. For them, ethnicity is largely a symbolic matter, as it is for the other white European groups that have undergone similar social processes. Herbert Gans defines symbolic ethnicity as "a nostalgic allegiance to the culture of the immigrant generation, or that of the old country; a love for and a pride in a tradition that can be felt without having to be incorporated in everyday behavior" (Gans, 1991: 436).

symbolic ethnicity A nostalgic allegiance to the culture of the immigrant generation, or that of the old country, that is not usually incorporated in everyday behaviour.

Fuse/Jupiterimages

In contrast, most black Canadians lack the freedom to enjoy symbolic ethnicity. They may well take pride in their cultural heritage. However, their identity as black people is not optional because a considerable number of non-blacks are racists and impose it on them daily. **Racism** is the belief that a visible characteristic of a group, such as skin colour, indicates group inferiority and justifies discrimination. **Institutional racism** is bias that is inherent in social institutions and is often not noticed by members of the majority group. Recent surveys show that between 30 percent and 55 percent of Canadians (depending on the wording of the question) hold racist views (Henry et al., 2001: 147–51).

In his autobiography, the black militant Malcolm X poignantly noted how racial identity can be imposed on people. He described one of his black Ph.D. professors as "one of these ultra-proper-talking Negroes" who spoke and acted snobbishly. "Do you know what white racists call black Ph.D.s?" asked Malcolm X. "He said something like, 'I believe that I happen not to be aware of that . . .' And I laid the word down on him, loud: 'Nigger!'" (X, 1965: 284). Malcolm X's point is that it doesn't matter to a racist whether a black person is a professor or a panhandler, a genius or a fool, a saint or a criminal. Where racism is common, racial identities are compulsory and at the forefront of a person's self-identity.

As the contrast between Irish Canadians and black Canadians suggests, then, relations among racial and ethnic groups can take different forms. We next examine how various forms of inequality promote conflict between racial and ethnic groups and thus help to sustain racial and ethnic distinctiveness.

The St. Patrick's Day parade in Toronto.

The Canadian Press (The Toronto Star/Charla Jones)

Conflict Theories of Race and Ethnic Relations

COLONIALISM AND INTERNAL COLONIALISM

Conflict theorists argue that one of the most important mechanisms promoting inequality and conflict between racial and ethnic groups is colonialism. Colonialism involves people from one country invading another. In the process, the invaders gain control over the native population and change or destroy their culture. The invaders develop the belief that the natives are inherently inferior and they confine them to unskilled jobs. All this serves to create and reinforce ideas about "inherent" racial and ethnic differences.

Once they are entrenched, colonizers may engage in internal colonialism, preventing the assimilation of subordinate racial or ethnic groups by segregating them residentially, occupationally, and in social contacts ranging from friendship to marriage (Blauner, 1972; Hechter, 1974). In Canada, the main victims of colonialism and internal colonialism are Aboriginal peoples, the Québécois, and black people.

CANADA'S ABORIGINAL PEOPLES

The single word that best describes the treatment of Canada's Aboriginal peoples by European immigrants is *expulsion*. Expulsion is the forcible removal of a population from a territory claimed by another population.

Expulsion is dramatically illustrated by the plight of the Beothuk, the Aboriginal inhabitants of what is today Newfoundland and Labrador. The Beothuk were Algonkian-speaking hunter-gatherers who probably numbered fewer than a thousand people at the time of European contact. In the sixteenth century, European fishers used Newfoundland and Labrador as a fishing port, returning to Europe each year after the fishing season. In the seventeenth century, year-round European settlement began. This caused a revolution in the life of the Beothuk because the Europeans viewed them as a nuisance. They offered incentives to Mi'kmaq Indians from Nova Scotia to kill off the Beothuk. The Beothuk population declined and gradually withdrew from European contact.

As European settlement grew in the eighteenth century, the Beothuk were squeezed into the interior. There they competed for scarce resources with fur traders. Eventually the Beothuk were reduced to a small refugee population living off the meagre resources of the Newfoundland and Labrador interior. The expulsion of the Beothuk from their traditional territories because of European colonization led to their eventual extinction. Today, all that remains of the Beothuk aside from their tragic history and a few artifacts is a statue outside the Newfoundland and Labrador provincial legislature in St. John's.

The story of the Beothuk is an extreme case. However, *all* First Nations had broadly similar experiences. In the eighteenth and nineteenth centuries, as the European settlers' fur trade gave way to the harvesting of timber, minerals, oil, and gas, Aboriginal peoples were shunted aside so that the Canadian economy could grow. At the time, Europeans thought they were "assimilating" the Aboriginal peoples. The 1876 Indian Act underlined the importance of transforming a hunting-gathering people into an agricultural labour force (Menzies, 1999). Sir John A. Macdonald, Canada's first prime minister, spoke of the need "to do away with the tribal system and assimilate the Indian people in all respects with the inhabitants of the Dominion, as speedily as they are fit to change" (quoted in Montgomery, 1965: 13).

Many Aboriginal peoples understood the settlers' actions as an attempt to obliterate their heritage. No other conclusion seems warranted when one considers the collaboration between government and various churches in establishing Canada's 130 "residential schools." Aboriginal children were removed from their families and forced to study in boarding schools. They were prevented from speaking their languages and practising their religions, and were compelled to adopt the dominant, white European culture, often by means of physical abuse. Sexual abuse of children attending residential schools was also common. Little wonder that the government of Canada has been accused by some Aboriginal peoples of perpetuating cultural genocide (Cardinal, 1977). Genocide is the intentional extermination of an entire population defined as a race or a people.

Adding insult to injury, early historical writing about Canada depicted the First

---

colonialism Involves people from one country invading and taking political, cultural, and economic control over people from another country.

internal colonialism Involves one race or ethnic group subjugating another in the same country. It prevents assimilation by segregating the subordinate group in terms of jobs, housing, and social contacts.

expulsion The forcible removal of a population from a territory claimed by another population.

genocide The intentional extermination of an entire population defined as a race or a people.

The Canadian policy of assimilation. In its annual report of 1904, the Department of Indian Affairs published the photographs of Thomas Moore of the Regina Industrial School, "before and after tuition." These images are "a cogent expression of what federal policy had been since Confederation and what it would remain for many decades. It was a policy of assimilation, a policy designed to move Aboriginal communities from their 'savage' state to that of 'civilization' and thus to make in Canada but one community—a non-Aboriginal one" (Milloy, 1999).

Nations as either irrelevant or evil. Typically, in *The History of the Dominion of Canada*, a book widely used in Canadian schools at the turn of the twentieth century, only five pages were devoted to Aboriginal peoples (Clement, 1897). They are described as "cruel," "rude," "false," "crafty," "savages," and "ferocious villains" who plotted against the Europeans with "fiendish ingenuity." Canadian schoolbooks continued to portray Aboriginal peoples in this way until the mid-twentieth century.

Throughout North America, the confrontation with European culture undermined the way of life of the Aboriginal peoples. Because of internal colonialism and, in particular, expulsion from their traditional lands, Canada's Aboriginal peoples were prevented from practising their traditional ways and from assimilating into the larger society. Most of them languished on reserves and, in more recent times, in urban slums. There they experienced high rates of unemployment, poverty, ill health, and violence. The history of Canada's Aboriginal peoples raises in the most distressing way possible the issue of whether and in what form white society should take responsibility for past injustices.

THE QUÉBÉCOIS

In Canada, colonialism and internal colonialism involved not just expulsion but also conquest, the forcible capture of land and the economic and political domination of its inhabitants. For example, as part of their centuries-long struggle to control North America, the English conquered New France and its 60 000 Canadien settlers in 1759. They thereby created a system of ethnic stratification that remained in place for more than 200 years and became a major source of political conflict (McRoberts, 1988).

The British recognized that any attempt to impose their language, religion, laws, and institutions on the former French colony could result in unacceptably high levels of resistance and conflict. Therefore, they tried to

conquest The forcible capture of land and the economic and political domination of its inhabitants.

accommodate farmers and the Catholic clergy by reinforcing their rights and privileges. The British believed this would win the allegiance of these two Canadien groups, who would in turn help to build loyalty to Britain among the population as a whole. In contrast, the British undermined the rights and privileges of Canadien merchants engaged mainly in the fur trade. They took over virtually all large-scale commerce. In this manner, big business became a British domain. Agriculture, religion, and politics remained the province of the French. This pattern of ethnic stratification remained intact for two centuries.

True, by 1950 most farmers had been transformed into urban, industrial workers. Some Québécois had become physicians, lawyers, and members of the "new middle class" of administrators, technicians, scientists, and intellectuals. However, the upper reaches of the stratification system remained overwhelmingly populated by people of British origin. Social separation reinforced economic segregation. The French and the British tended to speak different languages, live in different towns and neighbourhoods, interact occasionally, befriend one another infrequently, and intermarry rarely. The novel that became emblematic of the social relations between French and English in Quebec is entitled *Two Solitudes* (MacLennan, 1945).

Apart from its rigid system of ethnic stratification, Quebec in the middle of the twentieth century was remarkable because of its undeveloped government services. Health, education, and welfare were largely controlled by the Catholic Church. Intervention of the government in economic matters was almost unknown. Because of this political backwardness, members of Quebec's new middle class, together with blue-collar workers, began campaigning to modernize the provincial political system in the late 1940s. They pressed for more liberal labour laws that would recognize the right of all workers to form unions and to strike. They wanted state control over education and a new curriculum that stressed the natural and social sciences rather than the classical languages and catechism. They desired a government that would supply a wide range of social services to the population. They demanded that the state provide better infrastructure for economic development and assist francophone entrepreneurs in expanding their businesses. The partial realization of these aims in the 1960s came to be known as the Quiet Revolution.

However, the modernization of the Quebec state failed to resolve four issues:

1. *The potential demographic decline of the Québécois.*
   By 1981, Québécois women were giving birth to fewer children on average than women in any other province. In fact, they were having fewer than the 2.1 children women must bear on average to ensure that the size of the population does not decline (Romaniuc, 1984: 14–18). Noticing this trend in the 1970s, many Québécois felt they were becoming an endangered species.

2. *The assimilation of immigrants into English culture.*
   Fears of demographic decline were reinforced by the preference of most new immigrants to have their children educated in English-language schools. Together with the falling birth rate, this development threatened to diminish the size—and therefore, potentially, the power—of Quebec's francophone population.

3. *Persistent ethnic stratification.* The Quiet Revolution helped create many thousands of jobs for highly educated francophones—but almost exclusively in the government bureaucracy, the educational system, and new Crown corporations, such as Hydro-Québec. It became apparent in the 1970s that management positions in the private sector remained the preserve of English-origin Canadians.

4. *The continued use of English as the language of private industry.* English remained the language of choice in the private sector because the largest and technologically most advanced businesses were controlled by English Canadians and Americans. This situation was felt particularly keenly when the expansion of the state sector, and therefore the upward mobility of the francophone new middle class, slowed in the 1970s.

Because of the issues just listed, many Québécois felt that the survival and prosperity of their community required active state intervention in non-francophone institutions. For example, many Québécois came to believe that most shares of banks, trust companies, and insurance firms should be held in Quebec and that these financial institutions should be obliged to reinvest their profits in the province. They argued that the state should increase its role as economic planner and initiator of development and should forbid foreign ownership of cultural enterprises. Finally, the Québécois increasingly demanded compulsory French-language education for the children of most immigrants, obligatory use of French among private-sector managers, and French-only signs in public places. Most Québécois regarded these proposals as the only means by which their community could survive and attain equality with other groups. Moreover, because the Quebec state did not have the legal authority to enact some of the proposed changes, they felt that the province ought to negotiate broader constitutional powers with the federal government. A large minority of Québécois went a step further. They became convinced that Quebec ought to become a politically sovereign nation, albeit a nation economically associated with Canada.

Réné Levesque (1922–87), the founder of the Parti Québécois and the 23rd premier of Quebec.

The pro-independence Parti Québécois won the provincial election in 1976. In 1980, it held a referendum to see whether Quebecers favoured "sovereignty-association." Nearly 60 percent voted "no." A second referendum was held in 1995. This time, the forces opposed to sovereignty-association won by the narrowest of margins—about 1 percent. The Parti Québécois promises to hold additional referenda until it gets the result it wants. Thus, in the early twenty-first century, Canada's future is still uncertain because of the economic, social, and cultural segregation of the Québécois from English Canada that is a legacy of the conquest.

BLACK CANADIANS

We have seen that colonialism and internal colonialism, whether accomplished by expulsion or conquest, create big barriers to assimilation than can endure for centuries. A third form of colonial action—slavery—creates similar barriers. **Slavery** is the ownership and control of people.

By about 1800, 24 million Africans had been captured and placed on slave ships headed to North, Central, and South America. Because of violence, disease, and shipwreck, fewer than half survived the passage. Black slaves were bought and sold in Canada at least until the 1820s. Only in 1833, when the British government banned slavery throughout the British Empire, did the practice become illegal in all of what is now Canada. Slavery was abolished in the United States 30 years later.

slavery The ownership and control of people.

It is true that the extent of slavery in Canada paled in comparison with its widespread use in the United States, where tobacco and cotton production depended entirely on the work of dirt-cheap black labour. It is also true that for decades Canada served as the terminus of the "underground railway," a network that smuggled escaped slaves out of the United States to freedom in Canada. As Martin Luther King, leader of the American civil rights movement in the 1950s and 1960s, said in Toronto in 1967:

> Deep in our history of struggle for freedom Canada was the North Star. The Negro slave knew that far to the north a land existed where a fugitive slave, if he survived the horrors of the journey, could find freedom. The legendary underground railroad started in the south and ended in Canada. Our spirituals, now so widely admired around the world, were often codes. We sang of "heaven" that awaited us, and the slave masters listened in innocence, not realizing that we were not speaking of the hereafter. Heaven was the word for Canada and the Negro sang of the hope that his escape on the underground railroad would carry him there. One of our spirituals, "Follow the Drinking Gourd," in its disguised lyrics contained directions for escape. The gourd was the big dipper, and the North Star to which its handle pointed gave the celestial map that directed the flight to the Canadian border. (King, 1967: 1) [King, Martin Luther.

Upper Canada Gazette, February 10, 1806

TO BE SOLD,

A BLACK WOMAN, named PEGGY, aged about forty years ; and a Black boy her son, named JUPITER, aged about fifteen years, both of them the property of the Subscriber.

The Woman is a tolerable Cook and washer woman and perfectly understands making Soap and Candles.

The Boy is tall and strong of his age, and has been employed in Country business, but brought up principally as a House Servant—They are each of them Servants for life. The Price for the Woman is one hundred and fifty Dollars—for the Boy two hundred Dollars, payable in three years with Interest from the day of Sale and to be properly secured by Bond &c.— But one fourth less will be taken in ready Money.

PETER RUSSELL.

York, Feb. 10th 1806.

Black Slave for Sale: Many distinguished persons were slave owners, including Peter Russell, who held positions in the executive and legislative councils and became administrator of Upper Canada.

1967. *Conscience for Change*. Toronto: CBC Learning Systems. Reprinted by arrangement with The Heirs to the Estate of Martin Luther King Jr., c/o Writers House as agent for the proprietor New York, NY. Copyright 1967 Dr. Martin Luther King Jr; copyright renewed 1994 Coretta Scott King.]

What King neglected to mention is that after the American Civil War (1861–65) the practice of encouraging black settlement in Canada was reversed. Government policy required the rejection of most immigration applications by black people. This policy reflected a deeply felt prejudice on the part of the Canadian population that persisted throughout the twentieth century (Sissing, 1996). Moreover, social relations between black Canadians and the white European majority were anything but intimate and based on equality. Until the mid-twentieth century, blacks tended to do unskilled labour and be residentially and socially segregated— for example, in the Halifax community of

TABLE 7.2
Immigrants by Category, Canada, 2008

Category	Number	Percentage
Family class	65 567	26.5
Economic immigrants	149 072	60.3
Refugees	21 860	8.8
Other	10 742	4.3
Not stated	2	0
Total	247 243	100.00

Source: Citizenship and Immigration Canada. 2008. "Facts and Figures: Immigration Overview Permanent and Temporary Residents 2008" p. 12. http://www.cic.gc.ca/english/pdf/research-stats/facts2008.pdf (retrieved 14 March 2010). Adapted and reproduced with the permission of the Minister of Public Works and Government Services Canada, 2010.

Jacob Lawrence. *The Migration of the Negro*, Panel No. 57. 1940–1941. The Phillips Collection, Washington DC. © Jacob Lawrence Estate / SODRAC (2010).

The Migration of the Negro, Panel No. 57. Jacob Lawrence, 1940–1941. Jacob Lawrence's *The Great Migration* series of paintings illustrates the mass exodus of black Americans from the South to the North in search of a better life. Many former slaves came to Canada by using the "underground railway," a network of blacks and whites who opposed slavery, and settled mainly in southern Ontario after Lieutenant Governor John Graves Simcoe signed the Upper Canadian Act Against Slavery in 1793.

Africville, established around 1850 by runaway American slaves (Clairmont and Magill, 1999).

Canadian immigration policy was liberalized in the 1960s. Racial and ethnic restrictions were removed. Immigrants were now admitted on the basis of their potential economic contribution to Canada, their close family ties with Canadians, or their refugee status (see Table 7.2). As a result, Canada became a much more racially and ethnically diverse society (see Figure 7.2 on the next page). Today, about three-quarters of Canadian immigrants are members of visible minority groups, most of them from Africa, Asia, and South and Central America. Among them, according to the 2006 census, are 815 000 blacks. They form Canada's third largest visible minority (after Chinese and East Indians), representing 2.5 percent of the population and 15.4 percent of the visible minority population (see Table 7.3 on the next page).

With the influx of new immigrants in recent decades, the social standing of Canada's black community has improved significantly. Many new immigrants had completed postsecondary education before their arrival. Others attended colleges and universities in Canada. Nonetheless, black Canadians still tend to interact little with white Canadians of European descent, especially in their intimate relations, and they still tend to live in different neighbourhoods. Like the aftermath of expulsion and conquest, the aftermath of slavery—prejudice, discrimination, disadvantage, and segregation— continues to act as a barrier to assimilation (see the Sociology at the Movies box on page 157).

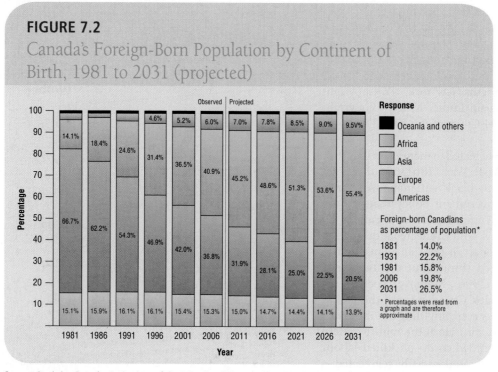

FIGURE 7.2

Canada's Foreign-Born Population by Continent of Birth, 1981 to 2031 (projected)

Source: Statistics Canada, *Projections of the Diversity of the Canadian Population, 2006 to 2031*, 91-551-XIE 2010001 2006 to 2031. Released March 9, 2010.

TABLE 7.3

Population by Visible Minority Group, Canada, 2006 and 2031 (projected)

Group	2006		2031	
	Thousands	Percentage	Thousands	Percentage
South Asian	1 320	4.1	3 640	8.7
Chinese	1 269	3.9	2 714	6.4
Black	815	2.5	1 809	4.3
Filipino	427	1.3	1 020	2.4
Latin American	317	1.0	733	1.7
Arab	276	0.8	930	2.2
Southeast Asian	250	0.8	449	1.1
West Asian	164	0.5	523	1.2
Korean	148	0.5	407	1.0
Japanese	85	0.3	142	0.3
Other	213	0.7	489	1.2
Subtotal	5 285	16.3	12 855	30.6
Rest of population	27 237	83.7	29 222	69.4
Total	32 522	100.0	42 078	100.0

Source: Statistics Canada, *Projections of the Diversity of the Canadian Population, 2006 to 2031*, 91-551-XIE 2010001 2006 to 2031. Released March 9, 2010.

Crash

Written and directed by London, Ontario's Paul Haggis, and winner of a best picture Oscar, *Crash* is a story about residents of Los Angeles colliding into one another because of their racist assumptions and then, in some cases, learning that people who differ from them are as human as they are.

The movie mirrors the ethnic and racial complexities of Los Angeles by presenting many intersecting plot lines. Neighbours think an Iranian-American shopkeeper (Shaun Toub) is an Arab so they apparently feel little remorse when they loot his store. The shopkeeper thinks a Chicano locksmith (Michael Peña) is a gang member who will bring his homies in to rob him blind once he finishes the repair job. The locksmith is in fact a hardworking family man and an exemplary father. A black police officer (Don Cheadle) has an affair with his Latina partner (Jennifer Esposito) but keeps on insulting her by not remembering what country she was born in and stopping just one step short of saying "you people all look the same to me." Ryan, a white police officer (played by Matt Dillon, who was nominated for an Oscar for best supporting actor), arbitrarily stops what he at first thinks is a white woman and a black man in an expensive car. He conducts a humiliating, overly thorough body search of the woman (who, he discovers, is actually a light-skinned African American) while her enraged husband looks on, unable to do anything because the police officer makes it clear what would happen if he tried. Later, we learn that Ryan is a compassionate man who is angry about his inability to help his dying father. Perversely, he expresses anger over his impotence by insulting blacks and making them feel powerless. Yet he partly redeems himself when he risks his life to rescue a woman from a horrible car accident—realizing partway through the rescue that the victim is the same black woman he had earlier body-searched.

White police officers harass a black couple in *Crash*.

Some critics have complained that *Crash* exaggerates the extent of racism in the United States. After all, we don't often hear explicit racist comments in public. It seems to us, however, that these critics miss the point of the movie. The apparent intention of *Crash*—and in this it succeeds admirably—is to strip away all political correctness and tell us what people are thinking to themselves or saying to members of their own ethnic or racial group about members of other groups. In that sense it may be more realistic than what we hear in public. At the same time, *Crash* offers a measure of hope that things can be better. Ryan risks his life to save the woman after realizing that she is black. He helps us appreciate that underlying our prejudices lies a deeper humanity.

Critical Thinking Questions

- Are Americans as racist as *Crash* makes them out to be? Are Canadians? Does racism lie beneath the surface of our civility and political correctness?
- Do you sometimes rely on ethnic or racial stereotypes to account for someone's behaviour?
- Do you sometimes discover that your prejudices are misconceptions? If so, under what circumstances do you make such discoveries?
- Do you believe that beneath racist sentiments lies a deeper humanity?

SPLIT LABOUR MARKETS AND ASIAN CANADIANS

We have seen how the theory of colonialism and internal colonialism explains the persistence of inequality and segregation among racial and ethnic groups. A second theory that focuses on the social-structural barriers to assimilation is the theory of the split labour market, first proposed by sociologist Edna Bonacich (1972). Bonacich's theory explains why racial identities are reinforced by certain labour market conditions. In brief, she argues that where low-wage workers of one race and high-wage workers of another race compete for the same jobs, high-wage workers are likely to resent the presence of low-wage competitors and conflict is bound to result. Consequently, racist attitudes develop or are reinforced.

Resentment certainly crystallized during the early years of Asian immigration in Canada. Chinese, then Japanese, and later Sikhs were allowed into Canada from about the 1850s to the early 1920s for one reason: to provide scarce services and cheap labour in the booming West. Chinese-owned restaurants, grocery stores, laundries, and import businesses dotted the West and especially British Columbia by the early twentieth century (Li, 1998; Whitaker, 1987). Numerically more important, however, were the Asian labourers who worked in lumbering, mining, and railway construction. For example, 15 000 Chinese men were allowed into Canada to complete construction of the final and most difficult section of the Canadian Pacific Railway (CPR), which involved blasting tunnels and laying rail along dangerous Rocky Mountain passes. The Chinese were paid half the wages of white workers. It is said that they "worked like horses." It is also said that they "dropped like flies" because of exposure, disease, malnutrition, and explosions. Three Chinese workers died for every kilometre of track laid.

Asian immigration in general was widely viewed as a threat to cherished British values and institutions, an evil to be endured only as long as absolutely necessary. Therefore, once the CPR was completed in 1885, the Chinese were no longer welcome in British Columbia. A prohibitively expensive "head tax" equal to two months' wages was placed on each Chinese immigrant. The tax was increased tenfold in 1903. In 1923, Chinese immigration was banned altogether. During the Great Depression, more than 28 000 Chinese were deported because of high unemployment. Asian immigration did not resume on a large scale until the 1960s, when racial criteria were finally removed from Canadian immigration regulations.

Underlying European-Canadian animosity against Asian immigration was a split labour market. The fact that Asian immigrants were willing to work for much lower wages than European Canadians fuelled deep resentment among European Canadians, especially when the labour market was flooded with far too many job seekers. European Canadians formed "exclusion leagues" to pressure the government to restrict Asian immigration, and on occasion they even staged anti-Asian riots. Such actions solidified racial identities among both the rioters and the victims of the riots and made assimilation impossible.

In sum, the theory of split labour markets, like the theory of internal colonialism, emphasizes the social-structural roots of race and ethnicity. The groups that have had most trouble assimilating into the British values and institutions that dominate Canadian society are those that were subjected to expulsion from their native lands, conquest, slavery, and split labour markets. These circumstances have left a legacy of racism that has created social-structural impediments to assimilation—such impediments as forced segregation in low-status jobs and low-income neighbourhoods.

⒧⁴ Some Advantages of Ethnicity

Conflict theories emphasize how social forces outside a racial or an ethnic group create inequality and bind group members together, preventing their assimilation into the dominant values and institutions of society. They focus on the disadvantages of race and ethnicity. Moreover, they deal only with the most disadvantaged minorities. The theories have less to say about the internal conditions that promote group cohesion and in particular about the value of group membership. They do not help us understand why some European Canadians of Greek or German or Irish origin continue to participate in the life of their ethnic communities, even if their families have been in the country for more than two or three generations.

High levels of immigration renew racial and ethnic communities by providing them with new members who are familiar with ancestral languages, customs, and so forth. Part of the reason that ethnic communities remain vibrant in Canada is that immigration continues at a rapid pace; only Australia and Israel have a larger percentage of immigrants than Canada does (see Figure 7.2). However, as we have seen, little of Canada's current immigration is composed of white Europeans. Immigration levels do not explain the persistence of ethnic identity among members of some white ethnic groups of European origin.

Among white European groups, three main factors enhance the value of continued ethnic group membership:

split labour market Exists where low-wage workers of one race and high-wage workers of another race compete for the same jobs. In that situation, high-wage workers are likely to resent the presence of low-wage competitors. Conflict is bound to result and racist attitudes to develop or become reinforced.

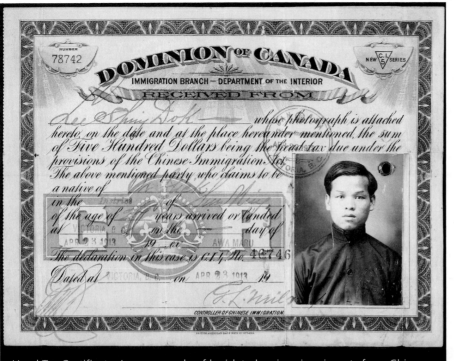

Head Tax Certificate: In an example of legislated racism, immigrants from China were required by law to pay a "head tax" to enter Canada between 1885 and 1923. The tax began at $50 and rose as high as $500.

Liberals promoted a policy of bilingualism. French and English were made official languages. This policy meant that federal government services would be made available in both languages and instruction in French would be encouraged in English schools. Members of some ethnic groups, such as people of Ukrainian origin in Western Canada, felt neglected by this turn of events. They saw no reason that the French should be accorded special status and wanted a share of the resources available for promoting ethnic languages and cultures. As a result, the Trudeau government proclaimed a new policy of multiculturalism in 1971. Federal funds became available for the promotion of Ukrainian and all other ethnic cultures in Canada. This entire episode of Canadian ethnic history bolstered Western support for the Liberal Party and softened Western opposition to bilingualism. Moreover, it helped to stimulate ethnic culture and ethnic identification throughout the country. We thus see that ethnicity can be a political tool for achieving increased access to resources.

1. *Ethnic group membership can have economic advantages.* The economic advantages of ethnicity are most apparent for immigrants, who often lack extensive social contacts and fluency in English or French. They commonly rely on members of their ethnic group to help them find jobs and housing. In this way, immigrant communities become tightly knit. However, some economic advantages extend into the third generation and beyond. For example, community solidarity is an important resource for "ethnic entrepreneurs." These are businesspeople who operate largely within their ethnic community. They draw on their community for customers, suppliers, employees, and credit, and they may be linked economically to the homeland as importers and exporters. They often pass on their businesses to their children, who in turn can pass the businesses on to the next generation. In this way, strong economic incentives encourage some people to remain ethnic group members, even beyond the immigrant generation (Light, 1991; Portes and Manning, 1991).

2. *Ethnic group membership can be politically useful.* Consider, for instance, the way some Canadians reacted to the rise of separatism in Quebec in the 1960s. To bridge the growing divide between francophone Quebec and the rest of the country, the federal government under Pierre Trudeau's

3. *Ethnic group membership tends to persist because of the emotional support it provides.* Like economic benefits, the emotional advantages of ethnicity are most apparent in immigrant communities. Speaking the ethnic language and sharing other elements of our own native culture are valuable sources of comfort in an alien environment. Even beyond the second generation, however, ethnic group membership can perform significant emotional functions. For example, some ethnic groups have experienced unusually high levels of prejudice and discrimination involving expulsion or attempted genocide. For people who belong to such groups, the resulting trauma is so severe it can be transmitted for several generations. In such cases, ethnic group membership offers security in a world still seen as hostile long after the threat of territorial loss or annihilation has disappeared (Bar-On, 1999). Ethnic group membership also offers emotional support beyond the second generation by providing a sense of rootedness. Especially in a highly mobile, urbanized, technological, and bureaucratic society such as ours, ties to an ethnic community can be an important source

transnational communities
Communities whose boundaries extend between or among countries.

pluralism The retention of racial and ethnic culture combined with equal access to basic social resources.

of stability and security (Isajiw, 1978).

Retaining ethnic ties beyond the second generation has never been easier. Inexpensive international communication and travel allow ethnic group members to maintain strong ties to their ancestral homeland in a way that was never possible in earlier times. Immigration used to involve cutting all or most ties to a country of origin because of the high costs of travel and long-distance telephone rates. This lack of communication encouraged assimilation in people's newly adopted countries. Today, however, ties to the ancestral communities are often maintained in ways that sustain ethnic culture. For example, about 50 000 Jews have immigrated from the former Soviet Union to Canada since the early 1970s, settling mainly in Toronto. They frequently visit relatives in the former Soviet Union and Israel, speak with them on the phone, and use the Internet to exchange e-mail with them. They also receive Russian-language radio and TV broadcasts, act as conduits for foreign investment, and send money to relatives abroad (Brym, 2001; Brym with Ryvkina, 1994; Markowitz, 1993). This sort of intimate and ongoing connection with the motherland is typical of most recent immigrant communities in North America. Thanks to inexpensive international travel and communication, some ethnic groups have become transnational communities whose boundaries extend among countries.

In sum, ethnicity remains a vibrant force in Canadian society for a variety of reasons. Even some white Canadians whose families settled in this country more than two generations ago have reason to identify with their ethnic group. Bearing this in mind, what is the likely future of race and ethnic relations in Canada? We conclude by offering some tentative answers to that question.

LO⁵ The Future of Race and Ethnicity in Canada

The world comprises more than 200 countries and more than 5000 ethnic and racial groups. As a result, no country is ethnically and racially homogeneous and in many countries, including Canada, the largest ethnic group forms less than half the population (see Figure 7.3 and Table 7.4). Canada's British roots remain important. Our parliamentary democracy is based on the British model; the Queen's representative, the governor general, is our head of state; we still celebrate May 24, Queen Victoria's birthday; and English is the country's predominant language, with more than 56 percent of Canadians over the age of 14 claiming it as their mother tongue. Our French patrimony is also strong, especially of course in Quebec. Nationwide, 22 percent of Canadians claim French as their mother tongue (Statistics Canada, 2010p). Nonetheless, Canada is one of the most racially and ethnically heterogeneous societies in the world, and it will become still more diverse in coming decades (Pendakur, 2000).

As racial and ethnic diversity has increased, Canadian ethnic and race relations have changed. Two hundred years ago, Canada was a society based on expulsion, conquest, slavery, and segregation. Today, we are a society based on segregation, pluralism, and assimilation—pluralism being understood as the retention of racial and ethnic culture combined with equal access to basic social resources. On a scale of tolerance, Canada has come a long way in the past 200 years (see Figure 7.4).

Courtesy of the Pier 21 Society/Library and Archives Canada/PA-111579

Pier 21 is located at 1055 Marginal Road, Halifax, Nova Scotia. Many immigrants to Canada were processed there. It opened its doors in 1928. As the era of ocean travel was coming to an end in March 1971, the Immigration Service left Pier 21.

TABLE 7.4
Canada's 25 Biggest Ethnic Groups, 2006

	Total Responses	Single Responses	Multiple Responses
Canadian	10 066 290	5 748 725	4 317 570
English	6 570 015	1 367 125	5 202 890
French	4 941 210	1 230 535	3 710 675
Scottish	4 719 850	568 515	4 151 340
Irish	4 354 155	491 030	3 863 125
German	3 179 425	670 640	2 508 785
Italian	1 445 335	741 045	704 285
Chinese	1 346 510	1 135 365	211 145
North American Indian	1 253 615	512 150	741 470
Ukrainian	1 209 085	300 590	908 495
Dutch (Netherlands)	1 035 965	303 400	732 560
Polish	984 565	269 375	715 190
East Indian	962 665	780 175	182 495
Russian	500 600	98 245	402 355
Welsh	440 965	27 115	413 855
Filipino	436 190	321 390	114 800
Norwegian	432 515	44 790	387 725
Portuguese	410 850	262 230	148 625
Métis	409 065	77 295	331 770
Other British Isles	403 915	94 145	309 770
Swedish	334 765	28 445	306 325
Spanish	325 730	67 475	258 255
American	316 350	28 785	287 565
Hungarian (Magyar)	315 510	088 685	226 820
Jewish	315 120	134 045	181 070

Source: Statistics Canada, *Ethnic origins, 2006 counts, for Canada, provinces and territories—20% Sample Data*, Ethnocultural Portrait of Canada Highlight Tables, 2006 Census 97-562-XWE2006002 Census year 2006, Released April 2, 2008.

FIGURE 7.3
Percentage of Population Accounted for by Largest Ethnic Group

Major ethnic group as percentage of population (number of cases in parentheses)

- 94.0%–99.7% (40)
- 81.0%–93.0% (27)
- 61.0%–80.0% (37)
- 46.0%–60.0% (36)
- 17.0%–45.0% (35)
- Not available

Sources: "Ethnic Groups in the World," *Scientific American*. Found at http://www.sciam.com/1998/0998issue/0998numbers.html (December 4, 2001). *CIA World Factbook 2001*. Found at http://www.cia.gov/cia/publications/factbook/(January 10, 2002).

FIGURE 7.4

Six Degrees of Separation: Types of Ethnic and Racial Group Relations

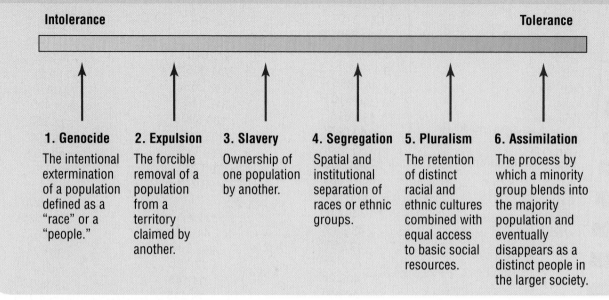

Source: From KORNBLUM. *Sociology in a Changing World*, 4E. © 1997 Wadsworth, a part of Cengage Learning, Inc. Reproduced by permission. www.cengage.com/permissions

Canada is a tolerant land compared with other countries too. In the late twentieth and early twenty-first centuries, racial and ethnic tensions in some parts of the world erupted into wars of secession and attempted genocide. In the 1990s, conflict among Croats, Serbs, and other ethnic groups tore Yugoslavia apart. Russia fought two bloody wars against its Chechen ethnic minority. In Rwanda, Hutu militia and soldiers massacred many thousands of Tutsi civilians. A few years later, Tutsi soldiers massacred many thousands of Hutu civilians. Comparing Canada with countries that are not rich, stable, and postindustrial may seem to stack the deck in favour of concluding that Canada is a relatively tolerant society. However, even when we compare Canada with other rich, stable, postindustrial countries, it seems relatively tolerant by most measures. For example, a survey of 44 countries found that "only in Canada does a strong majority of the population (77 percent) have a positive view of immigrants." Far behind in second place came the United States, at 49 percent (Pew Research Center, 2002: 43; see also Figure 7.5).

Growing tolerance does not imply the absence of ethnic and racial stratification. Although Canada is becoming less ethnically and racially stratified from one census to the next, serious problems remain (Lautard and Guppy, 2011). For one thing, the upward mobility of immigrants has slowed since the early 1990s, partly because many highly educated immigrants are finding it difficult to gain academic and professional recognition for credentials earned abroad (Reitz, 2011). For another, Aboriginal Canadians are making slow progress in their efforts to raise their educational and economic standing. They remain clustered at the bottom of Canada's socioeconomic hierarchy. And finally, while the Canadian-born children of most immigrants are not disadvantaged because of their ethnicity or race, that is simply not true for black men. Even black men who are Canadian-born face persistent discrimination and below-average earnings. Thus, if present trends continue, Canada's mosaic will continue to be stratified, mainly along racial lines. Unless dramatic changes occur, a few groups will continue to enjoy less wealth, income, education, good housing, health care, and other social rewards than other Canadians do.

Political initiatives could decrease racial stratification, speeding up the movement from segregation to pluralism and assimilation for the country's most disadvantaged groups. Such political initiatives include more compensation for historical injustices committed against Aboriginal peoples. The historic 2008 apology by Prime Minister Harper for the havoc wrought on Aboriginal communities by Canada's residential schools, the $1.9 billion compensation package for victims of those schools, and the recent settlement of some Native land disputes gives hope in that regard. In addition, affirmative action or **employment equity** programs that encourage the hiring of qualified members of disadvantaged minorities, government-subsidized job training and child care, and the creation of a system for efficiently upgrading credentials earned abroad to meet Canadian standards would benefit disadvantaged Canadians and increase ethnic and racial equality.

employment equity
A policy that gives preference to minority group members if equally qualified people are available for a position.

FIGURE 7.5
Influence of Immigrants

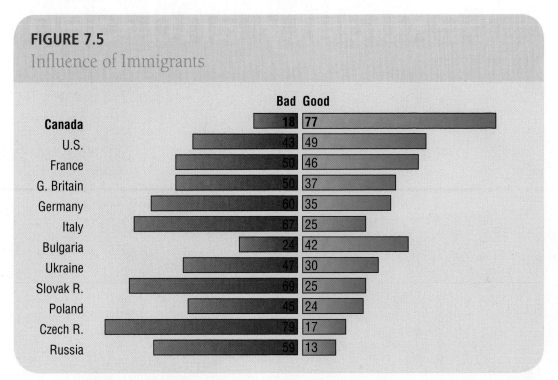

	Bad	**Good**
Canada	18	77
U.S.	43	49
France	50	46
G. Britain	50	37
Germany	60	35
Italy	67	25
Bulgaria	24	42
Ukraine	47	30
Slovak R.	69	25
Poland	45	24
Czech R.	79	17
Russia	59	13

Source: What the world thinks in 2002: How global publics view their lives, their countries, the world, America. December 4, 2002. Reprinted by permission of The Pew Global Attitudes Project.

8 Sexuality and Gender

LEARNING
OBJECTIVES:

LO¹ Although biology determines sex, social structure and culture largely determine gender, or the expression of culturally appropriate masculine and feminine roles.

LO² The social construction of gender is evident in the way parents treat babies, teachers treat pupils, and the mass media portray ideal body images.

LO³ The social forces pushing people to assume conventionally masculine or feminine roles, including heterosexuality, are usually compelling.

LO⁴ The social forces pushing people toward heterosexuality operate with even greater force.

LO⁵ The social distinction between men and women serves as an important basis of inequality in the family and in the workplace.

LO⁶ Male aggression against women is rooted in gender inequality.

LO¹ Sex versus Gender

IS IT A BOY OR A GIRL?

On 27 April 1966, what was supposed to be a routine circumcision of an eight-month-old twin at the St. Boniface Hospital in Winnipeg, Manitoba, went horribly wrong. Either because of mechanical malfunction or physician error, the infant's penis was burned off by the electric cauterizing machine.

A parade of specialists informed the boy's distraught parents that their son's prognosis was grim. Medical technology of the time did not permit the reconstruction of a penis that would resemble a normal organ in appearance or sexual function. A psychiatric report prepared on the boy's projected future concluded that "he will be unable to live a normal sexual life from the time of adolescence . . . he will be unable to consummate marriage or have normal heterosexual relations, . . . he will have to recognize that he is incomplete, physically defective and . . . must live apart" (Colapinto, 2001: 16).

About 10 months after the accident, the child's parents experienced a glimmer of hope when they saw a TV interview of John Money, a psychologist at the renowned Johns Hopkins Hospital in Baltimore. Money was the driving force behind the creation of the world's first "sex change" clinic at Johns Hopkins Hospital in Baltimore (Bullough, 2000). He was well known for his research on **intersexed** infants, babies born with ambiguous genitals because of a hormone imbalance in the womb or some other cause. It was Money's opinion that infants with "unfinished genitals" should be assigned a sex by surgery and hormone treatments, and reared in accordance with their newly assigned sex (Money and Ehrhardt, 1972). According to Money, these strategies would lead to the child's eventual possession of a self-identity that was consistent with the assigned sex.

The Winnipeg couple wrote to Dr. Money, who urged them to bring their child to Baltimore immediately. After consultation with various physicians and with Money, the parents agreed to have their son's sex reassigned. In anticipation of what would follow, the boy's parents stopped

> **intersexed** Babies born with ambiguous genitals because of a hormone imbalance in the womb or some other cause.

cutting his hair, began dressing him in feminine clothes, and changed his name from Bruce to Brenda. Surgical castration was performed when the twin was 22 months old.

Early reports of the child's progress indicated success (Money and Ehrhardt, 1972). In contrast to her biologically identical brother, Brenda was said to disdain cars, gas pumps, and tools. She was supposedly fascinated by dolls, a dollhouse, and a doll carriage. Brenda's mother reported that, at the age of four and a half, Brenda preferred and took pleasure in her feminine clothing: "She is so feminine. I've never seen a little girl so neat and tidy . . . and yet my son is quite different. I can't wash his face for anything . . . She is very proud of herself, when she puts on a new dress, or I set her hair" (quoted in Money and Ehrhardt, 1972: 11).

The "twins case" generated worldwide attention. Textbooks in medicine and the social sciences were rewritten to incorporate Money's reports of the child's progress (Robertson, 1977: 316; Mackie, 1991: 69). However, later reports on the reassigned twin cast doubt on the accuracy of Dr. Money's report and on the apparent success of the transformation (Diamond and Sigmundson, 1999). Brenda insisted on urinating standing up, refused to undergo the

further "feminizing" surgeries that had been planned for her, and, from age seven, daydreamed of her ideal future self "as a twenty-one-year-old male with a moustache, a sports car, and surrounded by admiring friends" (Colapinto, 2001: 93). She experienced academic failure and rejection and ridicule from her classmates, who dubbed her "Cavewoman" (Diamond, 1982). At age nine, Brenda had a nervous breakdown. At age 14, in a state of acute despair, she attempted suicide (Colapinto, 2001: 96, 262).

In 1980, Brenda learned the details of her sex reassignment from her father. At age 16, she decided to be reassigned once more and to live as a man rather than a woman. Advancements in medical technology made it possible for Brenda, who then adopted the name David, to have an artificial penis constructed. At age 25, David married a woman and adopted her three children, but that did not end his ordeal (Gorman, 1997). In May 2004, at the age of 38, David committed suicide.

LO² GENDER IDENTITY AND GENDER ROLE

The story of Bruce/Brenda/David introduces the first big question of this chapter. What makes us male or female? Of course, part of the answer is biological. Your **sex** depends on whether you are born with distinct male or female genitals and a genetic program that releases male or female hormones to stimulate the development of your reproductive system. However, the case of Bruce/Brenda/David also shows that more is involved in becoming male or female than biological sex differences.

Redferns/Getty Images

Recalling his life as Brenda, David said: "Everyone is telling you that you're a girl. But you say to yourself, 'I don't *feel* like a girl.' You think girls are supposed to be delicate and *like* girl things—tea parties, things like that. But I like to *do* guy stuff. It doesn't match" (quoted in Colapinto, 1997: 66; our emphasis). As this quotation suggests, being male or female involves not just biology but also certain "masculine" and "feminine" feelings, attitudes, and behaviours. Accordingly, sociologists distinguish biological sex from sociological **gender**. Your gender comprises the feelings, attitudes, and behaviours typically associated with being male or female. **Gender identity** is your identification with, or sense of belonging to, a particular sex—biologically, psychologically, and socially. When you behave according to widely shared expectations about how males or females are supposed to act, you adopt a *gender role*.

The Social Learning of Gender

Contrary to first impressions, the case of Bruce/Brenda/David suggests that, unlike sex, gender is not determined solely by biology. Research suggests that babies first develop a vague sense of being a boy or a girl at about the age of one. They develop a full-blown sense of gender identity between the ages of two and three (Blum, 1997). We can therefore be confident that baby Bruce already had a good idea he was a boy when he was assigned a female gender identity at the age of 22 months. He had seen boys behaving differently from girls on TV and in storybooks, and he lived with the role model of masculinity provided by his twin brother. Despite his parents' efforts to reinforce his identity as a girl, these early childhood lessons in masculinity were likely influential. Many researchers still believe that if gender reassignment occurs before the age of 18 months, it can be successful (Creighton and Mihto, 2001; Lightfoot-Klein, Chase, Hammond, and Goldman, 2000).

However, once the social learning of gender takes hold, as with baby Bruce, it is apparently very difficult to undo, even by means of reconstructive surgery, hormones, and parental and professional pressure. The main lesson we draw from this story is not that biology is destiny but that the social learning of gender begins very early in life.

The first half of this chapter helps you better understand what makes us male or female. We first outline two competing perspectives on gender differences. The first perspective argues that gender is inherent in our biological makeup and that society must reinforce those tendencies if it is to function smoothly. Functionalist theory is compatible with this argument. The second perspective argues that gender is constructed mainly by social influences and can be altered to benefit society's members. The second perspective is compatible with conflict, feminist, and symbolic interactionist theories.

In the course of our discussion we examine how people learn gender roles during socialization in the family and at school. We show how everyday social interactions and advertising reinforce gender roles. We also discuss how members of society enforce **heterosexuality**—the preference for members of the opposite sex as sexual partners. For reasons that are still poorly understood, some people resist and even reject the gender roles that are assigned to them based on their biological sex. When this occurs, negative sanctions are often applied to get them to conform or to punish them for their deviance. Members of society are often eager to use emotional and physical violence to enforce conventional gender roles.

The second half of the chapter examines one of the chief consequences of people learning conventional gender roles. Gender, as currently constructed, creates and maintains social inequality. We illustrate this in two ways. We investigate why gender is associated with the earnings gap between women and men in the paid labour force. We also show how gender inequality encourages sexual harassment and rape. In concluding our discussion of sexuality and gender, we discuss some social policies that sociologists have recommended to decrease gender inequality and improve women's safety.

heterosexuality The preference for members of the opposite sex as sexual partners.

essentialism A school of thought that views gender differences as a reflection of biological differences between women and men.

social constructionism A school of thought that views gender differences as a reflection of the different social positions occupied by women and men.

Theories of Gender

Most arguments about the origins of gender differences in human behaviour adopt one of two perspectives. Some analysts see gender differences as a reflection of naturally evolved tendencies and argue that society must reinforce those tendencies if it is to function smoothly. Sociologists call this perspective **essentialism** because it views gender as part of the nature or "essence" of one's biological and social makeup (Weeks, 1986). Functionalists typically view gender in essentialist terms. Other analysts see gender differences mainly as a reflection of the different social positions occupied by women and men. Sociologists call this perspective **social constructionism** because it views gender as "constructed" by social structure and culture. Conflict, feminist, and symbolic interactionist theories focus on various aspects of the social construction of gender.

Cre8tive Images/Shutterstock

ESSENTIALISM

Sociobiologists and evolutionary psychologists have proposed one popular essentialist theory. They argue that humans instinctively try to ensure that their genes are passed on to future generations. However, they say, men and women develop different strategies for achieving that goal. A woman has a bigger investment than a man does in ensuring the survival of their offspring because she produces only a small number of eggs during her reproductive life. At most, she can give birth to about 20 children. It is therefore in a woman's best interest to maintain primary responsibility for her genetic children and to seek out the single mate who can best help support and protect them. In contrast, men can produce as many as a billion sperm per ejaculation and this feat can be replicated every day or two (Saxton, 1990: 94–95). To maximize their chance of passing on their genes to future generations, men must have many sexual partners.

According to sociobiologists and evolutionary psychologists, as men compete with other men for sexual access to many women, competitiveness and aggression emerge (DeSteno and Salovey, 2001). Women, says one evolutionary psychologist, are greedy for money, while men want casual sex with women, treat women's bodies as their property, and react violently to women who incite male sexual jealousy. These are supposedly "universal features of our evolved selves" that contribute to the survival of the human species (Buss, 2000). Thus, from the point of view of sociobiology and evolutionary psychology, gender differences in behaviour are based in biological differences between women and men.

iStockphoto.com/Jaroslaw Wojcik

FUNCTIONALISM AND ESSENTIALISM

Functionalists reinforce the essentialist viewpoint when they claim that traditional gender roles help to integrate society (Parsons, 1942). In the family, wrote Talcott Parsons, women traditionally specialize in raising children and managing the household. Men traditionally work in the paid labour force. Each generation learns to perform these complementary roles by means of *gender role socialization*.

For boys, noted Parsons, the essence of masculinity is a series of "instrumental" traits, such as rationality, self-assuredness, and competitiveness. For girls, the essence of femininity is a series of "expressive" traits, such as nurturance and sensitivity to others. Boys and girls first learn their respective gender traits in the family as they see their parents going about their daily routines. The larger society also promotes *gender role conformity*. It instills in men the fear that they won't be attractive to women if they are too feminine, and it instills in women the fear that they won't be attractive to men if they are too masculine. In the functionalist view, then, learning the essential features of femininity and masculinity integrates society and allows it to function properly.

A CRITIQUE OF ESSENTIALISM FROM THE CONFLICT AND FEMINIST PERSPECTIVES

Criticisms

Conflict and feminist theorists disagree sharply with the essentialist account. They have lodged four main criticisms against it.

1. *Essentialists ignore the historical and cultural variability of gender and sexuality.* Wide variations exist in what constitutes masculinity and femininity. Moreover, the level of gender inequality, the rate of male violence against women, the criteria used for mate selection, and other gender differences that appear universal to the essentialists vary widely too. This variation deflates the idea that there are essential and universal behavioural differences between women and men. Three examples help illustrate the point:
   - In societies with low levels of gender inequality, the tendency decreases for women to stress the good provider role in selecting male partners, as does the tendency for men to stress women's domestic skills (Eagley and Wood, 1999).
   - When women become corporate lawyers or police officers or take other jobs that involve competition or threat, their production of the hormone testosterone is stimulated, causing them to act more aggressively. Aggressiveness is partly role-related (Blum, 1997: 158–88).
   - Hundreds of studies conducted mainly in North America show that women are developing traits that were traditionally considered masculine. Women have become considerably more assertive,

competitive, independent, and analytical in the last 40 years or so (Biegler, 1999; Nowell and Hedges, 1998).

As these examples show, gender differences are not constants, and they are not inherent in men and women. They vary with social conditions.

2. *Essentialism tends to generalize from the average, ignoring variations within gender groups.* On average, women and men do differ in some respects. For example, one of the best-documented gender differences is that men are on average more verbally and physically aggressive than women. However, when sociobiologists and evolutionary psychologists say men are inherently more aggressive than women, they make it seem as if this is true of all men and all women. As Figure 8.1 shows, however, it is not. When trained researchers measure verbal or physical aggressiveness, scores vary widely within gender groups. Aggressiveness is distributed so that considerable overlap exists between women and men. Many women are more aggressive than the average man and many men are less aggressive than the average woman.

3. *Little or no direct evidence directly supports the essentialists' major claims.* Sociobiologists and evolutionary psychologists have not identified any of the genes that, they claim, cause male jealousy, female nurturance, the unequal division of labour between men and women, and so forth.

4. *Essentialists' explanations for gender differences ignore the role of power.* Essentialists assume that existing

behaviour patterns help ensure the survival of the species and the smooth functioning of society. However, as conflict and feminist theorists argue, this assumption overlooks the fact that men are usually in a position of greater power and authority than women.

Conflict Theory

Conflict theorists dating back to Marx's collaborator, Friedrich Engels, have located the root of male domination in class inequality (Engels, 1970 [1884]). According to Engels, men gained substantial power over women when preliterate societies were first able to produce more than their members needed for their own subsistence. At that point, some men gained control over the economic surplus. They soon devised two means of ensuring that their offspring would inherit the surplus. First, they imposed the rule that only men could own property. Second, by means of socialization and force, they ensured that women remained sexually faithful to their husbands. As industrial capitalism developed, Engels wrote, male domination increased because industrial capitalism made men still wealthier and more powerful while it relegated women to subordinate, domestic roles.

Feminist Theory

Feminist theorists doubt that male domination is so closely linked to the development of industrial capitalism. For one thing, they note that gender inequality is greater in agrarian than in industrial capitalist societies. For another, male domination is evident in societies that call themselves socialist or communist. These observations lead many feminists to conclude that male domination is rooted less in industrial capitalism than in the patriarchal authority relations, family structures, and patterns of socialization and culture that exist in most societies (Lapidus, 1978: 7).

Despite this disagreement, conflict and feminist theorists concur that behavioural differences between women and men result less from any essential differences between them than from men being in a position to advance their interests over the interests of women. From the

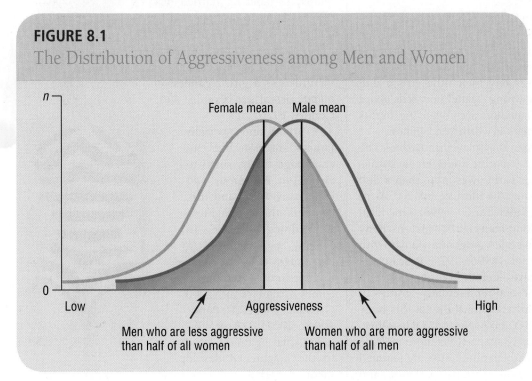

FIGURE 8.1

The Distribution of Aggressiveness among Men and Women

Female mean · Male mean

Low · Aggressiveness · High

Men who are less aggressive than half of all women

Women who are more aggressive than half of all men

conflict and feminist viewpoints, functionalism, socio-biology, and evolutionary psychology can themselves be seen as examples of the exercise of male power, that is, as rationalizations for male domination and sexual aggression.

LO³ SOCIAL CONSTRUCTIONISM AND SYMBOLIC INTERACTIONISM

Essentialism is the view that masculinity and femininity are inherent and universal traits of men and women, whether because of biological or social necessity or some combination of the two. In contrast, social constructionism is the view that *apparently* natural or innate features of life, such as gender, are actually sustained by *social* processes that vary historically and culturally. As such, conflict and feminist theories can be regarded as types of social constructionism. So can symbolic interactionism. Symbolic interactionists, you will recall, focus on the way people attach meaning to things in the course of their everyday communication. One of the things to which people attach meaning is what it means to be a man or a woman. We illustrate the symbolic interactionist approach by first considering how boys and girls learn masculine and feminine roles in the family and at school. We then show how gender roles are maintained in the course of everyday social interaction and through advertising in the mass media.

Gender Socialization

Barbie dolls have been around since 1959. Based on the creation of a German cartoonist, Barbie is the first modern doll modelled after an adult. (Lili, the German original, became a pornographic doll for men.) Some industry experts predicted mothers would never buy their little girls a doll that had breasts. Were *they* wrong. Mattel now sells about 10 million Barbies and 20 million accompanying outfits annually. The Barbie trademark is worth US$1 billion.

What do girls learn when they play with Barbie? The author of a website devoted to Barbie undoubtedly speaks for many when she writes, "Barbie was more than a doll to me. She was a way of living: the Ideal Woman" (Elliott, 1995; see also Nicolaiedis, 1998; Turkel, 1998). One ideal that Barbie stimulates among many girls concerns body image. After all, Barbie is a scale model of a woman with a 40-18-32 figure (Hamilton, 1996: 197). Researchers who compared Barbie's gravity-defying proportions with the actual proportions of several representative groups of adult women concluded that the probability of this body shape was less than 1 in 100 000 (Norton, Olds, Olive, and Dank, 1996). (Ken's body shape is far more realistic at 1 in 50.) The closets of Barbie's pink house are jammed with outfits. Bathrooms, gyms, beauty parlours, and vanity sets feature prominently among the Barbie accessories available. Presumably, this quest for physical perfection is designed to attract Ken, Barbie's boyfriend. The message Barbie conveys to girls is that the ideal woman is defined primarily by her attractiveness to men.

A comparable story, with competition and aggression as its theme, could be told about how boys' toys, such as GI Joe, teach stereotypical male roles. True, a movement to market more gender-neutral toys arose in the 1960s and 1970s; there is now even a Presidential Barbie. However, a strong tendency remains to market toys based on gender. Typically, in the late 1990s, toy manufacturer Mattel produced a pink, flowered Barbie computer for girls with fewer educational programs than its blue Hot Wheels computer for boys (Mooney, Schacht, Knox, and Nelson, 2003: 232).

Toys are only part of the story of gender socialization and hardly its first or final chapter. Research conducted in the early 1970s showed that from birth, infant boys and girls who are matched in length, weight, and general health are treated differently by parents—fathers in particular. Girls tend to be identified as delicate, weak, beautiful, and cute; boys as strong, alert, and well coordinated (Rubin, Provenzano, and Lurra, 1974). Recent research shows that although parents' gender-stereotyped perceptions of newborns have declined, especially among fathers, they have not disappeared (Fagot, Rodgers, and Leinbach, 2000; Gauvain, Fagot, Leve, and Kavanagh, 2002). One experiment found that when viewing a videotape of a nine-month-old infant, subjects tended to label its startled reaction to a stimulus as "anger" if the child had earlier been identified by the experimenters as a boy, and as "fear" if it had earlier been identified as a girl, *regardless of the infant's actual sex* (Condry and Condry, 1976).

Parents, and especially fathers, are more likely to encourage their sons to engage in boisterous and competitive play and discourage their daughters from doing likewise. In general, parents tend to encourage girls to engage in cooperative, role-playing games (Fagot et al., 2000; Gauvain et al., 2002; Parke, 2001, 2002). These different play patterns lead to the heightened development of verbal and emotional

Robin Beckham/BEEPstock/Alamy

skills among girls and to more concern with winning and the establishment of hierarchy among boys (Tannen, 1990). Boys are more likely than girls to be praised for assertiveness. Girls are more likely than boys to be rewarded for compliance (Kerig, Cowan, and Cowan, 1993). Given this early socialization, it seems perfectly "natural" that boys' toys stress aggression, competition, spatial manipulation, and outdoor activities, while girls' toys stress nurturing, physical attractiveness, and indoor activities (Hughes, 1995). Still, what seems natural must be continuously socially reinforced. Presented with a choice between playing with a tool set and a dish set, preschool boys are about as likely to choose one as the other—unless the dish set is presented as a girl's toy and they think their fathers would view playing with it as "bad." Then, they tend to pick the tool set (Raag and Rackliff, 1998).

Our own experience suggests that although traditional patterns of gender socialization weigh heavily on

most men, they are not inescapable. For example, John Lie grew up in a patriarchal household. His father worked outside the home, and his mother stayed home to do nearly all the housework and child care. "I remember my grandfather telling me that a man should never be seen in the kitchen," recalls John, "and it is a lesson I learned well. In fact, everything about my upbringing— the division of labour in my family, the games I played, the TV programs I watched—prepared me for the life of a patriarch. I vaguely remember seeing members of the 'women's liberation movement' staging dem-

onstrations on the TV news in the early 1970s. Although I was only about 11 or 12 years old, I recall dismissing them as slightly crazed, bra-burning man haters. Because of the way I grew up and what I read, heard, and saw, I assumed the existing gender division of labour was natural. Doctors, pilots, and professors should be men, I thought, and people in the 'caring' professions, such as nurses and teachers, should be women.

"But socialization is not destiny," John insists. "Entirely by chance, when I got to college I took some courses taught by female professors. It is embarrassing to say so now, but I was surprised that they seemed brighter, more animated, and more enlightening than my male high school teachers had been. In fact, I soon realized that many of my best professors were women. I think this is one reason why I decided to take the first general course in women's studies offered at my university. It was an eye opener. I soon became convinced that gender inequalities are about as natural and inevitable as racial inequalities. I also came to believe that gender equality could be as enriching for men as for women. Sociological reflection overturned what my socialization had taught me. Sociology promised—and delivered. I think many college-educated men have similar experiences today, and I hope I now contribute to their enlightenment."

Gender Segregation and Interaction

Only someone who has spent very little time in the company of children would think they are passive objects of socialization. They are not. Parents, teachers, and other authority figures typically try to impose their ideas of appropriate gender behaviour on children, but children creatively interpret, negotiate, resist, and self-impose these ideas all the time. Gender, we might say, is something that is done, not just given (Messner, 2000; West and Zimmerman, 1987).

How do children "do" gender? Consider the grade-four and grade-five classroom that sociologist Barrie Thorne (1993) observed. The teacher periodically asked the children to choose their own desks. With the exception of one girl, they always segregated *themselves* by gender. Similarly, when children played chasing games in the schoolyard, groups often *spontaneously* crystallized along gender lines. The teacher often reaffirmed such gender boundaries by pitting the boys against the girls in spelling and math contests. These contests were marked by cross-gender antagonism and expression of within-gender solidarity.

However, Thorne also observed many cases of boys and girls playing together. She also noticed quite a lot of "boundary crossing." Boundary crossing involves boys playing stereotypically girls' games and girls playing stereotypically boys' games. The most common form of boundary crossing involved girls who were skilled at specific sports that were central to the boys' world, such as soccer, baseball, and basketball. Boys and girls also interacted easily and without strong gender identities coming to the fore in activities requiring cooperation, such as a group project. Mixed-gender interaction was also more common in less public and crowded settings. Thus, boys and girls were more likely to play together and in a relaxed way in the relative privacy of their neighbourhoods. In contrast, in the schoolyard, where they were under the scrutiny of their peers, gender segregation and antagonism were more evident.

In sum, Thorne's research makes two important contributions to our understanding of gender socialization. First, children are actively engaged in the process of constructing gender roles. They are not just passive recipients of adult demands. Second, while schoolchildren tend to segregate themselves by gender, boundaries between boys and girls are sometimes fluid and sometimes rigid, depending on social circumstances. In other words, the content of children's gendered activities is by no means fixed.

This is not to suggest that adults have no gender demands and expectations. They do, and their demands and expectations contribute importantly to gender socialization. For instance, many schoolteachers and guidance counsellors still expect boys to do better in sciences and math and girls to achieve higher marks in English (Lips, 1999). Parents often reinforce these stereotypes in their evaluation of different activities (Eccles, Jacobs, and Harold, 1990). Although not all studies comparing mixed- and single-sex schools suggest that girls do much better in the latter (Bornholt, 2001; Jackson and Smith, 2000), most do. In single-sex schools, girls experience faster cognitive development; higher occupational aspirations and attainment; greater self-esteem and self-confidence; and more teacher attention, respect, and encouragement in the classroom. They also develop more egalitarian attitudes toward the role of women in society. Why? Because such schools place more emphasis on academic excellence and less on physical attractiveness and heterosexual popularity; they provide more successful same-sex role models, and they eliminate sex bias in teacher–student and student–student interaction because there are no boys around (Hesse-Biber and Carter, 2000: 99–100).

Adolescents must usually start choosing courses in school by the age of 14 or 15. By then, their gender ideologies are well formed. Gender ideologies are sets of interrelated ideas about what constitutes appropriate masculine and feminine roles and behaviour. One aspect of gender ideology becomes especially important around grades 9 and 10: adolescents' ideas about whether, as adults, they will focus mainly on the home, paid work outside the home, or a combination of the two. Adolescents usually make course choices with gender ideologies in mind. Boys are strongly inclined to consider only their careers in making course choices. Most girls are inclined to consider both home responsibilities and careers, although a minority considers only home responsibilities and another minority considers only careers. Consequently, boys tend to choose career-oriented courses, particularly in math and science, more often than girls do. In college and university, the pattern is accentuated. Young women tend to choose easier courses that lead to lower-paying jobs because they expect to devote a large part of their lives to child rearing and housework (Hochschild with Machung, 1989: 15–18). The top 10 fields of study for university and college graduates clearly indicate the continuing impact of gender ideologies on Canadian men and women (Table 8.1). We examine the wage gap between women and men in the second half of this chapter.

THE MASS MEDIA AND BODY IMAGE

If you systematically observe the roles played by women and men on TV programs and in ads one evening, you will probably discover a pattern noted by sociologists since the 1970s. Women will more frequently be seen cleaning house, taking care of children, modelling clothes, and acting as objects of male desire. Men will more frequently

TABLE 8.1
University and College Graduates by Subject of Study and Gender, Canada, 2006 (in percent)

Bachelor's Degree

Men		Women	
Architecture, engineering, and related technologies	22.1	Social and behavioural sciences and law	20.4
Business, management and public administration	19.9	Education	18.9
Social and behavioural sciences and law	17.5	Business, management and public administration	16.5
Humanities	8.5	Health, parks, recreation and fitness	12.8
Physical and life sciences and technologies	7.7	Humanities	12.7
Education	7.5	Physical and life sciences and technologies	6.4
Mathematics, computer and information sciences	7.1	Visual and performing arts, and communications technologies	4.1
Health, parks, recreation and fitness	4.2	Architecture, engineering, and related technologies	3.9
Visual and performing arts, and communications technologies	2.7	Mathematics, computer and information sciences	2.9
Agriculture, natural resources and conservation	2.4	Agriculture, natural resources and conservation	1.3
Personal, protective and transportation services	0.4	Personal, protective and transportation services	0.1
Other fields of study	0.0	Other fields of study	0.1
Total	100.0	Total	100.0

College/CEGEP Certificate or Diploma

Men		Women	
Architecture, engineering, and related technologies	42.6	Business, management and public administration	36.3
Business, management and public administration	18.5	Health, parks, recreation and fitness	26.3
Personal, protective and transportation services	8.1	Social and behavioural sciences and law	10.3
Mathematics, computer and information sciences	7.5	Education	5.0
Visual and performing arts, and communications technologies	5.6	Visual and performing arts, and communications technologies	4.7
Health, parks, recreation and fitness	4.6	Personal, protective and transportation services	4.4
Agriculture, natural resources and conservation	4.2	Mathematics, computer and information sciences	4.0
Humanities	3.1	Humanities	3.8
Social and behavioural sciences and law	2.9	Architecture, engineering, and related technologies	2.6
Physical and life sciences and technologies	2.1	Physical and life sciences and technologies	1.4
Education	0.9	Agriculture, natural resources and conservation	1.2
Other fields of study	0.0	Other fields of study	0.0
Total	100.0	Total	100.0

Source: Statistics Canada, *Major Field of Study – Classification of Instructional Programs, 2000 (13), Highest Postsecondary Certificate, Diploma or Degree (12), Age Groups (10A) and Sex (3) for the Population 15 Years and Over with Postsecondary Studies of Canada, Provinces, Territories, Census Metropolitan Areas and Census Agglomerations, 2006 Census—20% Sample Data, Education, 2006 Census 97-560-XCB2006005 Census year 2006, Released October 28, 2008.*

The "White Rock Girl" in 1894 (left) and 1947 (right).

Both images courtesy of the White Rock Beverage Company

be seen in aggressive, action-oriented, and authoritative roles (Signorielli, 1998). The effect of these messages on viewers is much the same as that of the Disney movies and Harlequin romances we discussed in Chapter 3 (Socialization). They reinforce the normality of traditional gender roles. Many people even try to shape their bodies after the body images portrayed in the mass media.

Survey data show just how widespread dissatisfaction with our bodies is and how important a role the mass media play in generating our discomfort. One survey of North American university graduates showed that 56 percent of women and 43 percent of men were dissatisfied with their overall appearance (Garner, 1997). Only 3 percent of the dissatisfied women, but 22 percent of the dissatisfied men, wanted to "bulk up." This difference reflects the greater desire of men for muscular, stereotypically male physiques. Most of the dissatisfied men, and even more of the dissatisfied women (89 percent), wanted to lose weight. This fact reflects the general societal push toward slimness and its greater effect on women. Another survey shows that Canadian women are far more likely than men to attempt losing weight, even if they fall within the range of healthy weights (Health Canada, 1999b: 118).

Figure 8.2 reveals gender differences in body ideals in a different way. It compares North American women's and men's attitudes toward their stomachs. It also compares women's attitudes toward their breasts with men's attitudes toward their own chests. It shows, first, that women are more concerned about their stomachs than men are about their own. Second, it shows that men are more concerned about their chests than women are about their breasts. Clearly, then, people's body ideals are influenced by their gender. Note also that Figure 8.2 shows trends over time. North Americans' anxiety about their bodies increased substantially over the 25-year period covered by the survey.

Table 8.2 suggests that advertising is highly influential in creating anxiety and insecurity about appearance and particularly about body weight. We see that nearly 30 percent of North American women compared themselves with the fashion models they saw in advertisements, felt insecure about their own appearance, and wanted to lose weight as a result. Among women who were dissatisfied with their appearance, the percentages were much larger, with about 45 percent making comparisons with fashion models and two-thirds feeling insecure and wanting to lose weight.

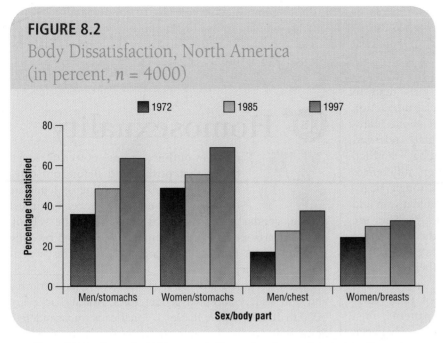

FIGURE 8.2

Body Dissatisfaction, North America
(in percent, *n* = 4000)

Note: The *n* of 4000 refers to the 1997 survey only. The number of respondents in the earlier surveys was not given.
Source: "The 1997 Body Image Results". David M. Garner. *Psychology Today*, Vol. 30, No. 1, pp. 30–44. REPRINTED WITH PERMISSION FROM PSYCHOLOGY TODAY MAGAZINE, Copyright © 1997 Sussex Publishers, LLC.

Body dissatisfaction, in turn, motivates dieting. For many people, achieving their weight goals is a life or death issue: about a quarter of women and a sixth of men say they would willingly trade more than three years of their lives to achieve their weight goals (Garner, 1997).

Body dissatisfaction prompts some people to take dangerous and even life-threatening measures to reduce their weight. Smoking is often employed as a strategy to control and lose weight, especially among adolescent and young adult women (Boles and Johnson, 2001). In addition,

between 1 percent and 5 percent of North American women suffer from anorexia nervosa (characterized by drastic weight loss, excessive exercise, food aversion, distorted body image, and an intense and irrational fear of body fat and weight gain). About the same percentage of North American female university students suffer from bulimia, characterized by cycles of binge eating and purging (through self-induced vomiting and the use of laxatives, purgatives, or diuretics). For university men, the prevalence of bulimia is between 0.2 percent and 1.5 percent (Averett and Korenman, 1996: 305–06).

MALE–FEMALE INTERACTION

The gender roles children learn in their families, at school, and through the mass media form the basis of their social interaction as adults. For instance, by playing team sports, boys tend to learn that social interaction is most often about competition, conflict, self-sufficiency, and hierarchical relationships (leaders versus the led). They understand the importance of taking centre stage and boasting about their talents (Messner, 1995). Because many of the most popular video games for boys exclude female characters, use women as sex objects, or involve violence against women, they reinforce some of the most unsavoury lessons of traditional gender socialization (Dietz, 1998). To cite just one example, in

TABLE 8.2

The Influence of Fashion Models on Feelings about Appearance, North America (*n* = 4000)

	Men (%)	Women (%)	Extremely Dissatisfied (%)
I always or often			
Compare myself with models in magazines	12	27	43
Carefully study the shape of models	19	28	47
Very thin or muscular models make me			
Feel insecure about my weight	15	29	67
Want to lose weight	18	30	67

Source: Adapted from Garner, David M. 1997. "The 1997 Body Image Survey Results." *Psychology Today* 30, 1: 30–44.

glass ceiling A social barrier that makes it difficult for women to rise to the top level of management.

transgendered People who break society's gender norms by defying the rigid distinction between male and female. They may be hetero sexual or homosexual.

transsexuals People who want to alter their gender by changing their appearance or resorting to medical intervention. Transsexuals believe they were born with the "wrong" body. They identify with, and want to live fully as, members of the opposite sex.

heterosexuals People who prefer members of the opposite sex as sexual partners.

homosexuals People who prefer sexual partners of the same sex. People usually call homosexual men *gay* and homosexual women *lesbians*.

bisexuals People who enjoy sexual partners of either sex.

Grand Theft Auto 3 a player can have sex with a prostitute, beat her up, and steal his money back. Conversely, by playing with dolls and baking sets, girls tend to learn that social interaction is most often about maintaining cordial relationships, avoiding conflict, and resolving differences of opinion through negotiation (Subrahmanyam and Greenfield, 1998). They are informed of the importance of giving advice and of not promoting themselves or being bossy.

Because of these early socialization patterns, misunderstandings between men and women are common. A stereotypical example: Harold is driving around lost. However, he refuses to ask for directions because doing so would amount to an admission of inadequacy and therefore a loss of status. Meanwhile, it seems perfectly "natural" to Sybil to want to share information, so she urges Harold to ask for directions. The result: conflict between Harold and Sybil (Tannen, 1990: 62).

Gender-specific interaction styles have serious implications for who is heard and who gets credit at work. For instance, Deborah Tannen's research discovered the typical case of the female office manager who doesn't want to seem bossy or arrogant. Eager to preserve consensus among her co-workers, she spends much time soliciting their opinions before making an important decision. However, her boss perceives her approach as indecisive and incompetent. He wants to recruit leaders for upper-management positions, so he overlooks the woman and selects an assertive man for a senior job that just opened up (Tannen, 1994a: 132).

The contrasting interaction style between male and female managers can lead to women not getting credit for competent performance. That is why they sometimes complain about a **glass ceiling**, a social barrier that makes it difficult for them to rise to the top level of management. As we will see soon, factors other than interaction styles—such as outright discrimination and women's generally

greater commitment to family responsibilities—also restrict women's upward mobility. But gender differences in interaction styles also play a role in constraining women's career progress.

LO⁴ Homosexuality

We have outlined some powerful social forces that push us to define ourselves as conventionally masculine or feminine in behaviour and appearance. For most people, gender socialization by the family, the school, and the mass media is compelling and sustained by daily interactions. A minority of people, however, resist conventional gender roles.

Transgendered people defy society's gender norms and blur widely accepted gender roles. About 1 in every 5000 to 10 000 people in North America is transgendered. Some transgendered people are **transsexuals.** Transsexuals are people who want to alter their gender by changing their appearance or resorting to medical intervention. Transsexuals believe they were born with the "wrong" body. They identify with, and want to live fully as, members of the opposite sex. They often take the lengthy and painful path to a sex-change operation. About 1 in every 30 000 people in North America is a transsexual (Nolen, 1999).

While **heterosexuals** are people who desire sexual partners of the other sex, **homosexuals** are people who prefer sexual partners of the same sex, and **bisexuals** are people

On April 1, 2001, the Netherlands became the first country to recognize full and equal marriage rights for homosexual couples. Within hours, Dutch citizens were taking advantage of the new law. The Dutch law is part of a worldwide trend to legally recognize long-term same-sex unions. On July 20, 2005, Canada became the fourth country to legalize homosexual marriage.

REUTERS/Michael Kooren

who enjoy sexual partners of either sex. People usually call homosexual men gays and homosexual women lesbians.

Based on a sample of nearly 8000 university students in Canada and the United States, researchers found that different measures of sexual orientation produced widely different results (see Table 8.3). Only 3.4 percent of men and 2.4 percent of women did not define themselves as heterosexual, but 12 percent of men and 13.4 percent of women expressed at least occasional attraction to members of their own sex, 21 percent of men and 25.8 percent of women said they had sexual fantasies about members of their own sex at least sometimes, and 12.5 percent of men and 8 percent of women said they had at least one intimate sexual experience with a member of the same sex.

Homosexuals were not identified as a distinct category of people until the 1860s, when the term *homosexuality* was coined. The term *lesbian* is of even more recent vintage. Nevertheless, homosexual behaviour has existed in every society. Some societies, such as ancient Greece, have encouraged it. More frequently, homosexual acts have been forbidden.

TABLE 8.3
The Sexual Orientation of Canadian and American University Students

	Men	Women
Self-reported sexual orientation		
Heterosexual	96.6	97.6
Homosexual, bisexual, other	3.4	2.4
Total	100.0	100.0
Attraction		
Only to one's own sex	88.0	86.6
At least partly to other sex	12.0	13.4
Total	100.0	100.0
Sexual fantasies		
Always involving only the other sex	79.0	74.2
Sometimes involving the same sex	21.0	25.8
Total	100.0	100.0
Same-sex intimate sexual experiences		
Only with other sex	87.5	92.0
At least once with same sex	12.5	8.0
Total	**100.0**	**100.0**

Sources: "Homosexuality and Bisexuality," 2000; Michael, Gagnon, Laumann, and Kolata (1994, pg. 40); Statistics Canada. 2004. "Canadian Community Health Survey." Found at http://www.statcan.ca/Daily/English/040615/d040615b. htm (April 21, 2007).

We do not yet understand well why some individuals develop homosexual orientations. Some scientists believe that the cause of homosexuality is mainly genetic, others think it is chiefly hormonal, while still others point to life experiences during early childhood as the most important factor. According to the American Psychological Association (1998), it "emerges for most people in early adolescence without any prior sexual experience . . . . [It] is not changeable."

In general, sociologists are less interested in the origins of homosexuality than in the way it is socially constructed, that is, in the wide variety of ways it is expressed and repressed (Foucault, 1990 [1978]; Plummer, 1995). Homosexuality has become less of a stigma over the past century. Two factors are chiefly responsible for this, one scientific, the other political. In the twentieth century, sexologists—psychologists and physicians who study sexual practices scientifically—first recognized and stressed the wide diversity of existing sexual practices. Alfred Kinsey was among the pioneers in this field. He and his colleagues interviewed thousands of men and women. In the 1940s, they concluded that homosexual practices were so widespread that homosexuality could hardly be considered an illness affecting a tiny minority (Kinsey, Pomeroy, and Martin, 1948; Kinsey, Pomeroy, Martin, and Gebhard, 1953).

If sexologists provided a scientific rationale for belief in the normality of sexual diversity, sexual minorities themselves provided the social and political energy needed to legitimize sexual diversity among a large section of the public. Especially since the middle of the twentieth century, gays and lesbians have built large communities and subcultures, particularly in major urban areas (Greenhill, 2001; Ingram, 2001). They have gone public with their lifestyles (Owen, 2001). They have organized demonstrations, parades, and political pressure groups to express their self-confidence and demand equal rights with the heterosexual majority (Goldie, 2001). These actions have done much to legitimize homosexuality and sexual diversity in general.

Nonetheless, opposition to people who don't conform to conventional gender roles remains strong at all stages of the life cycle (see the Sociology at the Movies box on the next page). When you were a child, did you ever poke fun at a sturdily built girl who was good at sports by calling her a "dike"? As an adolescent or young adult, have you ever attempted to insult a man by calling him a "fag"? If so, your behaviour was not unusual. Many children and young adults continue to express the belief that heterosexuality is superior to homosexuality

Brokeback Mountain

Heath Ledger (left) and Jake Gyllenhaal in *Brokeback Mountain*

Brokeback Mountain, nominated for a best picture Oscar, traces the romantic love between two cowboys. They fall in love in the early 1960s, when both are 19 years old, long before they had heard of gay culture or even the notion of homosexual identity. They lead seemingly conventional married lives. Yet they continue to love each other and carry on their affair for two decades, periodically telling their wives that they are going on fishing trips together but raising suspicions when they fail to bring any fish home. More than the passion, however, what the movie depicts is the high emotional cost of keeping sexual orientation and love a secret. Eventually, their marriages crumble, their social relationships suffer, and happiness and fulfilment prove elusive.

It would not be an exaggeration to say that Westerns—often called "Cowboy and Indian" movies—shaped a generation of North Americans' expectations about gender and sexuality. John Wayne, Gary Cooper, Jimmy Stewart, and many others became role models for North American men and their idea of masculinity: silent but strong, gentle toward the weak (women and children) but ferocious toward the evil (often Aboriginals), community-minded but ultimately lone, rugged individualists. Even today, it's hard not to be stirred and engrossed by such classic Westerns as *The Man Who Shot Liberty Valence* and *High Noon*.

Westerns, however, have not been a popular genre since the 1970s. The civil rights movement questioned the racial ideology of many Westerns, which presumed the superiority of the white race against the native populations. The movement against the Vietnam War challenged the vision of the world as a place that should be pacified and ruled by white Americans. The feminist movement criticized the patriarchal masculine viewpoint of Westerns. The few Westerns since the 1970s have therefore deviated from classical Westerns, often parodying them.

One of the reasons that Ennis (Heath Ledger, nominated for a best actor Oscar) cannot imagine the possibility of settling down with Jack (Jake Gyllenhaal, nominated for a best supporting actor Oscar) is a childhood experience. His father took him to see two men who were beaten to death, two "tough old birds" who happened to be "shacked up together." Fear of expressing his homosexuality was thus instilled early on. In fact, both men deny their homosexuality. After their first night together, Ennis says to Jack, "You know I ain't queer." To which Jack replies, "Me neither." Jack and Ennis's affair ends when Jack is beaten to death by homophobic men. Three grisly murders of gay men, then, provide the tragic backdrop to *Brokeback Mountain*.

Critical Thinking Questions
- How much have things changed since the 1960s, 1970s, and 1980s?
- Could Brokeback Mountain be set in 2011? Why or why not?

(Bibby, 2001). "That's gay!" is a common expression of disapproval among teenagers.

Among adults, such opposition is also strong. What is your attitude today toward transgendered people, transsexuals, and homosexuals? Do you, for example, think relations between adults of the same sex are always, or almost always, wrong? If so, you are not that unusual. In Canada, about 4 out of 10 adults hold that opinion. Rejection of homosexuality is correlated with age, gender, and region. Older adults, men, and residents of provinces other than Quebec and British Columbia are most rejecting of homosexuality (Bibby, 2006: 21–22).

Antipathy to homosexuals is so strong among some people that they are prepared to back up their beliefs with force. A study of about 500 young adults in the San Francisco Bay area (probably the most sexually tolerant area in North America) found that 1 in 10 admitted physically attacking or threatening people they believed were homosexuals. Twenty-four percent reported engaging in anti-gay name-calling. Among male respondents, 18 percent reported acting in a violent or threatening way and 32 percent reported name-calling. In addition, a third of those who had *not* engaged in anti-gay aggression said they would do so if a homosexual flirted with or propositioned them (Franklin, 2000).

The consequences of homophobia, or fear of homosexuals, can be devastating. For example, when 14-year-old Christian Hernandez told his best friend that he was gay, the consequences proved disastrous. "He told me he couldn't accept it," recalls Hernandez. "And he began to spread it around." For two years, the Niagara Falls student was teased and harassed almost daily. After school one day, a group of boys waited for him. Their leader told Hernandez that "he didn't accept faggots, that we brought AIDS into the world" and stabbed him in the neck with a knife. Hernandez required a week's hospitalization. When he told his parents what had happened, his father replied that he'd "rather have a dead son than a queer son" (Fisher, 1999).

Research suggests that some anti-gay crimes may result from repressed homosexual urges on the part of the aggressor (Adams, Wright, and Lohr, 1998). From this point of view, aggressors are homophobic because they cannot cope with their own, possibly subconscious, homosexual impulses. Their aggression is a way of acting out a denial of these impulses. Although this psychological explanation may account for some anti-gay violence, it seems inadequate when set alongside the finding that fully half of all young male adults admitted to some form of anti-gay aggression in the San Francisco study cited above. An analysis of the motivations of these San Franciscans showed that some of them did commit assaults to prove their toughness and heterosexuality. Others committed assaults just to alleviate boredom and have fun. Still others believed they were defending themselves from aggressive sexual propositions. A fourth group acted violently because they wanted

to punish homosexuals for what they perceived as moral transgressions (Franklin, 1998). It seems clear, then, that anti-gay violence is not just a question of abnormal psychology but a broad cultural problem with several sources. Still, anecdotal evidence suggests that opposition to anti-gay violence is also growing.

homophobia The fear of homosexuals.

In sum, strong social and cultural forces lead us to distinguish men from women and heterosexuals from homosexuals. We learn these distinctions throughout the socialization process, and we continuously construct them anew in our daily interactions. Most people use positive and negative sanctions to ensure that others conform to conventional heterosexual gender roles. Some people resort to violence to enforce conformity and punish deviance.

Our presentation also suggests that the social construction of conventional gender roles helps create and maintain social inequality between women and men. In the remainder of this chapter, we examine some of the present-day consequences of gender inequality.

LO⁵ Gender Inequality

THE EARNINGS GAP

You might think that gender inequality is a thing of the past. If so, you would be wrong. That fact is evident if we focus on the earnings gap between men and women, one of the most important expressions of gender inequality today.

When Canadian data on female and male earnings were first collected in 1967, the ratio of female to male earnings for full-year, full-time workers stood at about 58 percent. This means that women were earning 58 cents for every dollar men earned. By 1980, the ratio was 64 percent and it rose fairly steadily to about 73 percent in 1993 (Statistics Canada, 2003f). Since then, however, the ratio has fluctuated between about 68 percent and 72 percent. In 2007, the most recent year for which data are available as of this writing, women earned 71 cents for every dollar men earned. At the 1967–2007 rate of improvement, women will achieve earnings equality with men in 2095 (see Figure 8.3 on the next page).

Table 8.4 shows the gender wage gap in the average earnings of people in the 10 highest-paying and 10 lowest-paying occupations in Canada. If the wage gap were due to universal gender differences, it would not vary across occupations. But it does vary considerably, suggesting that social conditions specific to given occupations account in part for the magnitude of the gender wage gap.

Four main factors contribute to the gender gap in earnings (Bianchi and Spain, 1996; England, 1992):

gender discrimination
Rewarding men and women differently for the same work.

occupational sex segregation The concentration of women in certain occupations and men in others

1. Gender discrimination. In February 1985, when Microsoft already employed about 1000 people, it hired its first two female executives. According to a well-placed source involved in the hiring, both women got their jobs because Microsoft was trying to win a U.S. Air Force contract. Under the government's guidelines, Microsoft didn't have enough women in top management positions to qualify. The source quotes then 29-year-old Bill Gates, president of Microsoft, as saying, "Well, let's hire two women because we can pay them half as much as we will have to pay a man, and we can give them all this other 'crap' work to do because they are women" (quoted in Wallace and Erickson, 1992: 291).

This incident is a clear illustration of gender discrimination, rewarding women and men differently for the same work. Discrimination on the basis of sex is against the law in Canada. Yet progress is slow; as noted earlier, the female-to-male earnings ratio has actually deteriorated since 1993.

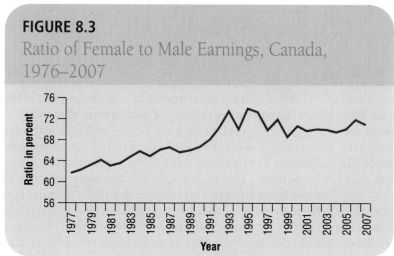

FIGURE 8.3

Ratio of Female to Male Earnings, Canada, 1976–2007

Note: Data are for full-time workers and are expressed in constant (2007) dollars.
Source: Adapted from Statistics Canada 2010. "Average female and male earnings, and female-to-male earnings ratio, by work activity, 2007 constant dollars, annual (720 series)." CANSIM database. Found at http://cansim2.statcan.ca, Table 202-0102.

2. *Women tend to be concentrated in low-wage occupations and industries.* The second factor leading to lower earnings for women is that the programs they select in high school and afterward tend to limit them to jobs in low-wage occupations and industries. The concentration of women in certain occupations and men in others is referred to as occupational sex segregation. Although women have made big strides since the 1970s in several fields, including management, business and financial professions, medicine, and law, they are still concentrated in lower-paying clerical and service occupations and the teaching profession, and underrepresented in higher-paying manual occupations (see Table 8.5 on page 182). This pattern is particularly strong for women of colour, Aboriginal women, and women with disabilities (Chard, 2000: 229; Shain, 1995).

3. *Heavy domestic responsibilities reduce women's earnings.* In 2003, single women who had never been married earned 93 cents for every dollar earned by men. The comparable figure for all women was 70.5 cents. A substantial part of this 22.5-cent gap represents the economic cost to women of getting married and assuming disproportionately heavy domestic responsibilities. Of course, raising children can be one of the most emotionally satisfying experiences. That should not, however, blind us to the fact it is also work that decreases the time available for education, training, and paid work. Because women are disproportionately involved in child rearing, they suffer the brunt of this economic reality. They devote fewer hours to paid work than men do, experience more labour-force interruptions, and are more likely than men to take part-time jobs, which pay less per hour and offer fewer benefits than full-time work does (Waldfogel, 1997). Women also do considerably more housework and eldercare than men do (Sauve, 2002). Globally, women do between two-thirds and three-quarters of all unpaid child care, housework, and care for aging parents (Boyd, 1997: 55). Even when they work full time in the paid labour force, women continue to shoulder a disproportionate share of domestic responsibilities (Chapter 9, Families).

4. *Work done by women is commonly considered less valuable than work done by men, because it is viewed as involving fewer skills.* Women tend to earn less than men because the skills involved in their work are often undervalued (Figart and Lapidus, 1996; Sorenson, 1994). For example, kindergarten teachers (nearly all of whom are women) earn less than office machine repair technicians (nearly all of whom are men). It is, however, questionable whether it takes less training and skill to teach a young child the basics of counting and cooperation than it takes to get a photocopier to collate paper properly. As this example suggests, we apply somewhat arbitrary standards to reward different occupational roles. In our society, these standards systematically

TABLE 8.4
Earnings of Men and of Women and Gender Composition in the Ten Best and Ten Worst Paid Occupations, Canada, 2000

Occupation	Average Annual Earnings	Percentage Women	Female-to-Male Earnings Ratio
Ten highest-earning occupations			
Judges	$142 518	24.4	90.2
Specialist physicians	141 597	30.8	61.2
Senior managers: financial, communications carriers, and other business services	130 802	21.5	63.9
General practitioners and family physicians	122 463	30.8	72.5
Dentists	118 350	22.9	63.7
Senior managers: goods production, utilities, transportation, and construction	115 623	11.6	62.2
Lawyers and Quebec notaries	103 287	31.0	67.4
Senior managers: trade, broadcasting and other services, N.E.C	101 176	17.8	61.8
Securities agents, investment dealers, and traders	98 919	36.8	44.5
Petroleum engineers	96 703	10.0	60.7
Ten lowest-earning occupations			
Babysitters, nannies, and parents' helpers	15 846	97.1	104.3
Food and beverage servers	18 319	77.1	75.1
Service station attendants	18 470	9.2	80.9
Food counter attendants, kitchen helpers, and related occupations	19 338	71.8	94.1
Bartenders	19 877	58.2	83.4
Cashiers	19 922	85.0	84.5
Harvesting labourers	20 158	48.8	83.0
Tailors, dressmakers, furriers, and milliners	20 499	81.6	68.2
Sewing machine operators	20 575	91.5	74.7
Ironing, pressing, and finishing occupations	20 663	63.9	83.8

Note: Only full-time, full-year workers are included.
Source: Department of Justice Canada, 2004: adapted from the Canada Census of 2001.

undervalue the kinds of skills needed for jobs in which women are concentrated.

We thus see that the gender gap in earnings is based on several *social* circumstances rather than on any inherent difference between women and men. This means that people can reduce the gender gap if they want to. Later in the chapter, we discuss social policies that could create more equality between women and men. But first, to stress the urgency of such policies, we explain how the persistence of gender inequality encourages sexual harassment and rape.

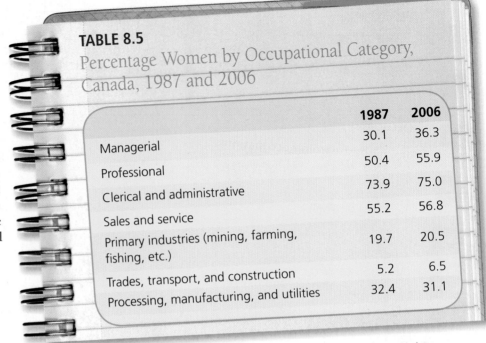

TABLE 8.5

Percentage Women by Occupational Category, Canada, 1987 and 2006

	1987	2006
Managerial	30.1	36.3
Professional	50.4	55.9
Clerical and administrative	73.9	75.0
Sales and service	55.2	56.8
Primary industries (mining, farming, fishing, etc.)	19.7	20.5
Trades, transport, and construction	5.2	6.5
Processing, manufacturing, and utilities	32.4	31.1

Source: Adapted from Statistics Canada, *Women in Canada: Work Chapter Updates*, 89F0133XWE 2006000. Released April 20, 2007.

LO⁶ MALE AGGRESSION AGAINST WOMEN

Serious acts of aggression between men and women are common. The great majority are committed by men against women. For example, in recent years, about 25 000 sexual assaults have been reported to Canadian police annually. More than 8 out of 10 victims are women and nearly all of the accused perpetrators are men. Among young singles, the rate of sexual assault is higher than in the population as a whole (Statistics Canada, 2008e; see Figure 8.4).

Consider research on **acquaintance rape**—sexual assaults involving intercourse committed by someone the victim knows (Meyer, 1984; Senn, Desmarais, Veryberg, and Wood, 2000). One Canadian study found that more than a fifth of female postsecondary students said they had given in to unwanted sexual intercourse because they had been overwhelmed by a man's continued arguments and pressure. Nearly 7 percent reported they had unwanted sexual intercourse because a man threatened or used some degree of physical force, and almost 14 percent claimed that a man had attempted unwanted sexual intercourse while they were either intoxicated or under the influence of drugs (DeKeseredy and Kelly, 1993). Although Canadian law requires that people take "reasonable steps to ascertain consent" before engaging another in any sexual act, interpretations of what is "reasonable" vary. Moreover, the courts have failed to provide explicit norms for what "reasonable steps" should be. Indeed, the biggest category of cases in which men accused of

acquaintance rape A sexual assault involving intercourse committed by someone the victim knows.

sexual assault successfully argue "reasonable steps" and win acquittals are cases in which women have been deliberately drugged or are unconscious because of excessive alcohol use at the time of the assault (Sheehy, 2003: 579).

Why do men commit more frequent (and more harmful) acts of aggression against women than women commit against men? It is *not* because men on average are physically more powerful than women. Greater physical power is more likely to be used to commit acts of aggression only when norms justify male domination and men have much more *social* power than women. When women and men are more equal socially, and norms justify gender equality, the rate of male aggression against women is lower. This point is evident if we consider sexual assault and sexual harassment (see also the discussion of wife abuse in Chapter 9, Families).

Sexual Assault

Some people think rapists are men who suffer a psychological disorder that compels them to achieve immediate sexual gratification even if violence is required. Others think rape occurs because of flawed communication. They believe some victims give mixed signals to their assailants by, for example, wearing revealing clothes or flirting.

Such explanations are not completely invalid. Interviews with victims and perpetrators show that some offenders do suffer from psychological disorders. Others misinterpret signals in what they regard as sexually ambiguous situations (Hannon, Hall, Kuntz, Laar, and

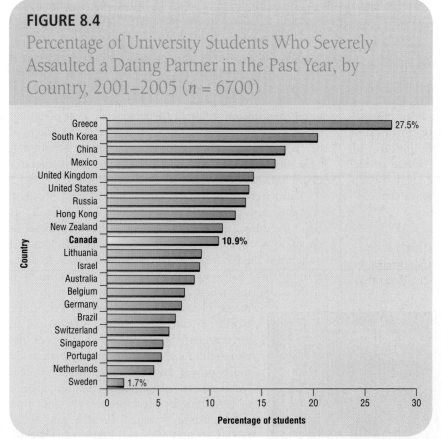

FIGURE 8.4

Percentage of University Students Who Severely Assaulted a Dating Partner in the Past Year, by Country, 2001–2005 (*n* = 6700)

Note: Some of the American data were collected in 1998. "Severely assaulted" was defined as students who, in the year preceding the survey, used a knife or a gun on a partner, punched or hit a partner with something that could hurt, choked a partner, slammed a partner against a wall, beat up a partner, burned or scalded a partner, or kicked a partner.

Source: International Dating Violence Study. Tabulation courtesy of Murray A. Straus based on Douglas, Emily M. and Murray A. Straus, (2006) "Assault and injury of dating partners by university students in 19 nations and its relation to corporal punishment experienced as a child," *European Journal of Criminology* 3:293–318. Reprinted with permission by the authors.

Williams, 1995). But such cases account for only a small proportion of the total. Men who commit sexual assault rarely have a mental illness, and it is abundantly clear to most assailants that they are doing something their victims strongly oppose.

What then accounts for sexual assault being as common as it is? A sociological answer is suggested by the fact that sexual assault is sometimes not about sexual gratification at all. Some offenders cannot ejaculate or even achieve an erection. Significantly, however, all forms of sexual assault involve domination and humiliation as principal motives. It is not surprising, therefore, that some offenders were physically or sexually abused in their youth. They develop a deep need to feel powerful as psychological compensation for their early powerlessness. Others are men who, as children, saw their mothers as potentially hostile figures who needed to be controlled or as mere objects available for male gratification. They saw their fathers as emotionally cold and distant. Raised in such an atmosphere, rapists learn not to empathize with women. Instead, they learn to want to dominate them (Lisak, 1992).

Psychological factors aside, certain social situations also increase the rate of sexual aggression. One such situation is war. In war, conquering male soldiers often feel justified humiliating the vanquished, who are powerless to stop them. Rape is often used for this purpose, as was especially well documented in the ethnic wars that accompanied the breakup of Yugoslavia in the 1990s (Human Rights Watch, 1995).

The relationship between male dominance and sexual aggression is also evident in research on American fraternities. Many college and university fraternities tend to emphasize male dominance and aggression as a central part of their culture. Sociologists who have interviewed fraternity members have shown that most fraternities try to recruit members who can reinforce a macho image and avoid any suggestion of effeminacy and homosexuality. Research also shows that fraternity houses that are especially prone to sexual assault tend to sponsor parties that treat women in a particularly degrading way. By emphasizing a very narrow and aggressive form of masculinity, some fraternities tend to facilitate sexual assault on campuses (Boswell and Spade, 1996).

Another social circumstance that increases the likelihood of sexual assault is participation in athletics. Of course, the overwhelming majority of athletes are not rapists. However, there are proportionately more rapists among men who participate in athletics than among non-athletes (Welch, 1997). That is because many sports embody a particular vision of masculinity in North American culture: competitive, aggressive, and domineering. By recruiting men who display these characteristics and by encouraging the development of these characteristics in athletes, sports can contribute to off-field aggression, including sexual aggression. Furthermore, among male athletes, there is a distinct hierarchy of sexual aggression. Male athletes who engage in contact sports are more prone to be rapists than other athletes. There are proportionately even more rapists among athletes involved in collision and combative sports, notably football (Welch, 1997).

Sexual assault, we conclude, involves the use of sex to establish dominance. Its incidence is highest in situations in which early socialization experiences predispose men to want to control women, where norms justify the domination of women, and where a big power imbalance between men and women exists.

Sexual Harassment

Sexual harassment comes in two forms. Quid pro quo sexual harassment takes place when sexual threats or bribery are made a condition of employment decisions.

(The Latin phrase *quid pro quo* means "something for something.") Hostile environment sexual harassment involves sexual jokes, touching, and comments that interfere with work or create a hostile work environment. Research suggests that relatively powerless women are the most likely to be sexually harassed. Specifically, women who are young, unmarried, and employed in nonprofessional jobs are most likely to become objects of sexual harassment, particularly if they are temporary workers, if the ratio of women to men in the workplace is low, and if the organizational culture of the workplace tolerates sexual harassment (Sev'er, 1999; Welsh, 1999).

Ultimately then, male aggression against women, including sexual harassment and sexual assault, is encouraged by a lesson most of us still learn at home, in school, at work, through much of organized religion, and in the mass media: it is natural and right for men to dominate women. To be sure, recent decades have witnessed important changes in the way women's and men's roles are defined. Nevertheless, in the world of paid work, in the household, in government, and in all other spheres of life, men still tend to command substantially more power and authority than women. Daily patterns of gender domination, viewed as legitimate by most people, are built into our courtship, sexual, family, and work norms. From this point of view, male aggression against women is simply an expression of male authority by other means.

These facts do not mean that all men endorse the principle of male dominance, much less that all men are inclined to engage in sexual assault or other acts of aggression against women. Indeed, scholars increasingly speak of *masculinities* in the plural, rather than the singular, to acknowledge differences among men and to emphasize that "masculinity" is neither innate nor a fixed entity (Messerschmidt, 1993). Many men favour gender equality, and most men never abuse a woman. Nevertheless, the fact remains that many aspects of our culture legitimize male dominance, making it seem valid or proper. For example, pornography, jokes about "dumb blondes," and leering might seem examples of harmless play. At a subtler, sociological level, however, they are assertions of the appropriateness of women's submission to men. Such frequent and routine reinforcements of male authority increase the likelihood that some men will consider it their right to assault women physically or sexually if the opportunity to do so exists or can be created. "Just kidding" has a cost. For instance, researchers

No means no. Not now means no. I have a boy/girlfriend means no. Maybe later means no. No thanks means no. You're not my type means no. $#@!!! off means no. I'd rather be alone right now means no. Don't touch me means no. I really like you but ... means no. Let's just go to sleep means no. I'm not sure means no. You've/I've been drinking means no. Silence means no. ▬▬▬ means no.

DATE RAPE \dāt_\'rāp\n: Not understanding no

Men still need to be reminded that no means no.

have found that university men who enjoy sexist jokes are most likely to report engaging in acts of sexual aggression against women (Ryan and Kanjorski, 1998).

We thus see that male aggression against women and gender inequality are not separate issues. Gender inequality is the foundation of aggression against women. In concluding this chapter, we consider how gender equality can be increased in the coming decades. As we proceed, you should bear in mind that gender equality is not just a matter of justice; it is also a matter of safety.

TOWARD 2095

The twentieth century witnessed growing equality between women and men in many countries. In Canada, the decline of the family farm made children less economically useful and more costly to raise. As a result, women started having fewer children. The industrialization of Canada, and then the growth of the economy's service sector, increased demand for women in the paid labour force (see Figure 8.5). This demand gave women substantially more economic power and also encouraged them to have fewer children. The legalization and availability of contraception made it possible for women to exercise unprecedented control over their own bodies. The women's movement fought for, and won, increased rights for women on a number of economic, political, and legal fronts. All these forces brought about a massive cultural shift, a fundamental reorientation of thinking on the part of many Canadians about what women could and should do in society.

One indicator of the progress of women is the Gender Empowerment Measure (GEM). The GEM is computed by the United Nations. It takes into account women's share of seats in Parliament; women's share of administrative, managerial, professional, and technical jobs; and women's earning power. A score of 1.0 indicates equality with men on these three dimensions.

As Figure 8.6 on the next page shows, Sweden, Norway, Finland, and Denmark were the four most

FIGURE 8.5

Percentage of Men and Women in the Paid Labour Force, Canada, 1946–2008

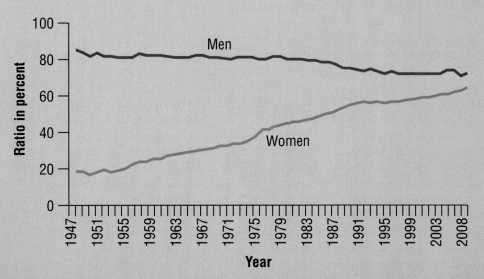

Sources: Statistics Canada. 1999. *Historical Statistics of Canada, 1983,* Catalogue 11-516, July 29, 1999, Series D160-174. http://www.statcan.ca/english/freepub/11-516-XIE/sectiond/sectiond.htm (retrieved 2 May 2008); Statistics Canada. 2008b. CANSIM Database, Table 282-0002, Using E-STAT (distributor), available at http://estat.statcan.ca/cgi-win/CNSMCGI.EXE? CANSIMFILE=Estat\English\CII_1_E.htm (retrieved 2 May 2008); Statistics Canada. 2008a. "Labour force indicators by age groups for males, participation rate (2006), for Canada, provinces and territories—20% sample data." http://www12.statcan. ca/english/census06/data/highlights/Labour/Table601.cfm?SR=1 (retrieved 2 May 2008); Statistics Canada. 2008c. "Labour markets." http://www45.statcan.gc.ca/2009/cgco_2009_008-eng.htm (retrieved 21 March 2010).

FIGURE 8.6

Gender Empowerment Measure, Top 12 and Bottom 12 Countries, 2006

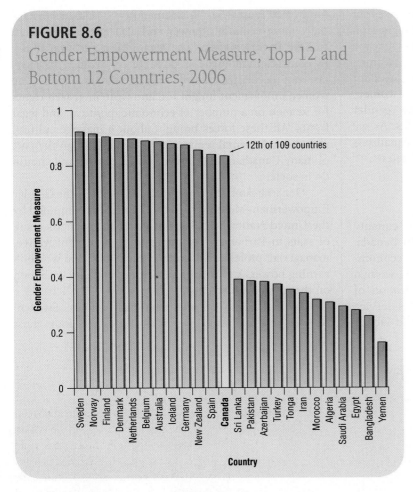

Source: United Nations. 2009. "Gender Empowerment Measure and its Components." *Human Development Report 2009.* http://hdrstats.undp.org/en/indicators/126.html (19 March 2010).

equality a matter of public policy while many Islamic countries do just the opposite (Brym et al., 2005).

The GEM figures suggest that Canadian women still have a considerable way to go before they achieve equality with men. We have also seen that the gender gap in earnings is shrinking but will disappear only in 2095— and then only if it continues to diminish at the same rate as it did from 1967 to 2007. That is a big "if," because progress is never automatic.

Socializing children at home and in school to understand that women and men are equally adept at all jobs is important in motivating them to excel in non-traditional fields. Hiring more women to compensate for past discrimination in hiring, firing, promotion, and training is also important. However, without in any way minimizing the need for such initiatives, we should recognize that their impact will be muted if women continue to undertake disproportionate domestic responsibilities and if occupations with a high concentration of women continue to be undervalued in monetary terms.

Two main policy initiatives will probably be required in the coming decades to bridge the gender gap in earnings. One is the development of a better child-care system. The other is the development of a policy of pay equity. Let us briefly consider these issues.

gender-egalitarian countries among the 109 countries on which data were available in 2009. They had GEM scores ranging from 0.909 to 0.896. This means that women in these countries were between 90 percent and 91 percent of the way to equality with men on these three dimensions. Canada ranked 12th, with a GEM score of 0.83.

In general, more gender equality exists in rich than in poor countries. The top-ranked countries are all rich, suggesting that gender equality is a function of economic development. However, our analysis of the GEM data suggests that there are some exceptions to the general pattern. For example, Barbados and Costa Rica rank considerably higher on the GEM than the richer country of Japan. This fact suggests that gender equality may also be a function of government policy. This impression is reinforced by the fact that, in some of the former communist countries of Eastern Europe—such as the Czech Republic, Slovakia, and Latvia— gender equality is *higher* than we would expect given their level of economic development. Meanwhile, in some of the Islamic countries, gender inequality is *lower* than we would expect given their level of economic development (e.g., the United Arab Emirates, Saudi Arabia). These anomalies exist because the former communist countries made gender

Child Care

High-quality, government-subsidized, affordable child care is widely available in most Western European countries. Sixty percent of children in the United Kingdom are in regulated child care, as are 69 percent of children in France and 78 percent in Denmark. In contrast, a team from the Organisation for Economic Co-operation and Development (OECD) strongly faulted Canada's efforts as a patchwork that has been chronically underfunded. Only 20 percent of Canadian children under the age of seven are in regulated child care (OECD, 2004: 7). As a result, many Canadian women with small children are either unable to work outside the home or able to work outside the home only on a part-time basis.

A universal system of daycare was proposed in Canada as early as 1970 but little was done at the federal level or in most provinces and territories. Quebec is an exception. In 1997 that province introduced a comprehensive family policy that attempts to integrate family benefits, paid parental leave, child care, and kindergarten. Its child-care component heralded universally available, affordable child care. A rapid expansion in the number of spaces occurred, although waiting lists grew as well. By

2004, 40 percent of the regulated daycare spaces available in Canada were in Quebec. Unfortunately, that was in part because no new spaces had been added outside Quebec in the preceding decade.

The need exists. In 2001, 52 percent of Canadian preschoolers received some kind of care outside of the home, up from 42 percent just seven years earlier. But only 25 percent of these children were enrolled in daycare programs; a growing number were cared for by relatives: 14 percent, up from 8 percent in 1994 (Statistics Canada, 2005b.)

In 2004, affordable, high-quality, regulated daycare was a central electoral promise of the victorious Liberal Party. By mid-2005, the beginnings of a national system began to take shape when the federal government reached child-care agreements with Saskatchewan, Manitoba, Ontario, and Newfoundland and Labrador. The system, had it taken root across the country, would have paid for itself. One study estimated that a high-quality, affordable, universal system of child care and early child-care education would cost $7.9 billion annually, while the increased employment of mothers would be worth $6.2 billion and the improvement in child development would be worth $4.3 billion (Cleveland and Krashinsky, 1998). However, after his election in 2006, Prime Minister Stephen Harper scrapped the agreements in favour of taxable benefits of $1200 for every child under six. The amount and the targeting were widely criticized as failing to address the burdens of women who work for pay needed to support their families. In 2007–8, government child care funding ranged from $195 per child in Alberta to $1694 per child in Quebec, with 7 of Canada's 10 provinces contributing less than $400 per child. Nationwide, there were enough regulated daycare spaces for just under 20 percent of children up to age 12 (Beach, Friendly, Ferns, Prabhu, and Forer, 2009: 183, 186; see Figure 8.7).

> **pay equity** Equal pay for work of equal value, or the equal dollar value of different jobs. It is established in gender-neutral terms by comparing jobs in terms of the education and experience needed to do them and the stress, responsibility, and working conditions associated with them.

Equal Pay for Work of Equal Value

On paper, Canadian women have had the right to equal pay for the same jobs done by men since the 1950s. Unfortunately, although early laws proclaimed lofty goals, they failed to result in fair wages.

In the 1980s, researchers found that women earn less than men partly because jobs in which women are concentrated are valued less than jobs in which men are concentrated. They therefore tried to establish gender-neutral standards by which they could judge the dollar value of work. These standards include such factors as the education and experience required to do a particular job and the level of responsibility, amount of stress, and working conditions associated with it. Researchers felt that, by using these criteria to compare jobs in which women and men are concentrated, they could identify pay inequities. The underpaid could then be compensated accordingly. In other words, women and men would receive equal pay for work of equal value, even if they did different jobs. During the mid-1980s, some governments amended the law to state that women should be paid equally for work of equal value. This amendment required employers to compare the rates of pay for women and men in dissimilar jobs that nevertheless involved the same level of skill, effort, and responsibility, and the same working conditions. In 1985, Manitoba became the first Canadian province to demand that its public sector be proactive and implement plans for equal pay for work of equal value—or **pay equity**, as it came to be called. Pay equity is now official policy in 10 of 13 Canadian jurisdictions (Alberta, Saskatchewan, and

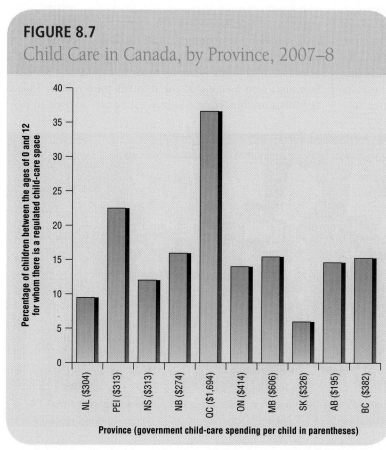

FIGURE 8.7

Child Care in Canada, by Province, 2007–8

Y-axis: Percentage of children between the ages of 0 and 12 for whom there is a regulated child-care space

X-axis: Province (government child-care spending per child in parentheses)

NL ($304), PEI ($313), NS ($313), NB ($274), QC ($1,694), ON ($414), MB ($606), SK ($326), AB ($195), BC ($382)

Source: Beach, Jane, Martha Friendly, Carolyn Ferns, Nina Prabhu, and Barry Forer. 2009. *Early Childhood Education and Care in Canada 2008,* 8th ed. http://www.childcarecanada.org/ECEC2008/#toc (retrieved 21 March 2010).

the Northwest Territories are the exceptions). However, provisions vary widely. Enforcement mechanisms are meagre and employers have found various ways to argue that unequal wages do not signify discrimination based on sex. Thus, although pay equity is undoubtedly a significant step toward achieving gender equality, inequity remains, as evidenced by the persistence of the wage gap between working men and women.

The Women's Movement

Improved daycare and pay equity would do much to bridge the gender gap in earnings between women and men. However, improvements in the social standing of women do not depend just on the sympathy of government and business leaders. Progress on this front has always depended in part on the strength of the organized women's movement. That is likely to be true in the future, too. In concluding this chapter, it is therefore fitting to consider the state of the women's movement and its prospects.

The "first wave" of the women's movement emerged during the late nineteenth century and lasted into the early 1920s. The most important public achievements of this movement in Canada were the right to vote and the right to be considered *persons* under Canadian law (Nelson and Robinson, 2002). In 1916, women in Alberta, Manitoba, and Saskatchewan won the right to vote in provincial elections. Other provinces and territories followed: British Columbia (1917), Ontario (1917), Nova Scotia (1918), New Brunswick (1919), Yukon (1919), Prince Edward Island (1922), Newfoundland and Labrador (1925), Quebec (1940), and, finally, the Northwest Territories (1951). These rights were first granted to white women. Women from certain ethnic and racial groups did not receive the franchise until later (Nelson and Robinson, 2002).

In the mid-1960s, the "second wave" of the women's movement emerged. Second-wave feminists were inspired in part by the successes of the civil rights movement in the United States. They felt that women's concerns were largely ignored despite persistent and pervasive gender inequality. Like their counterparts more than a century earlier, they held demonstrations, lobbied politicians,

and formed women's organizations to further their cause. They demanded equal rights with men in education and employment, the elimination of sexual violence, and women's control over reproduction.

Currently, considerable intellectual diversity exists in the feminist movement concerning ultimate goals. Three main streams may be distinguished (Tong, 1989).

Liberal feminism is the most popular current in the women's movement today. Its advocates believe that the main sources of women's subordination are learned gender roles and the denial of opportunities to women. Liberal feminists advocate non-sexist methods of socialization and education, more sharing of domestic tasks between women and men, and extending to women all the educational, employment, and political rights and privileges that men enjoy.

Socialist feminists regard women's relationship to the economy as the main source of women's disadvantages. They believe that the traditional nuclear family emerged along with inequalities of wealth. In their opinion, once men possessed wealth, they wanted to ensure that their property would be transmitted to their children, particularly their sons. They accomplished this in two ways. First, men exercised complete economic control over their property, thus ensuring it would not be squandered and would remain theirs and theirs alone. Second, they enforced female monogamy, thus ensuring that their property would be transmitted only to *their* offspring. Thus, according to socialist feminists, the economic and sexual oppression of women has its roots in capitalism. Socialist feminists also assert that the reforms proposed by liberal feminists are inadequate because they can do little to help

© SuperStock

The "first wave" of the women's movement achieved its main goal—the right of women to vote—as a result of much demonstrating, lobbying, organizing, and persistent educational work.

The "second wave" of the women's movement started to grow in the mid-1960s. Members of the movement advocated equal rights with men in education and employment, the elimination of sexual violence, and women's control over reproduction.

working-class women, who are too poor to take advantage of equal educational and work opportunities. Socialist feminists conclude that only the elimination of private property and the creation of economic equality can bring about an end to the oppression of all women.

Radical feminists find the reforms proposed by liberals and the revolution proposed by socialists inadequate. Patriarchy—male domination and norms justifying that domination—is more deeply rooted than capitalism, say the radical feminists. After all, patriarchy predates capitalism. Moreover, it is just as evident in self-proclaimed communist societies as it is in capitalist societies. Radical feminists conclude that the very idea of gender must be changed to bring an end to male domination. Some radical feminists argue that new reproductive technologies, such as in vitro fertilization, are bound to be helpful in this regard because they can break the link between women's bodies and child-bearing (see Chapter 9, Families). However, the revolution envisaged by radical feminists goes beyond the realm of reproduction to include all aspects of male sexual dominance. From their point of view, pornography, sexual harassment, restrictive contraception, sexual assault, incest, sterilization, and physical assault must be eliminated so that women can reconstruct their sexuality on their own terms.

This thumbnail sketch by no means exhausts the variety of streams of the contemporary women's movement. Indeed, some observers say the movement entered its "third wave" in the mid-1980s, characterized by *anti-racist* and *postmodernist* feminists criticizing liberal, socialist, and radical feminists for generalizing from the experience of white women and for failing to understand how women's lives are rooted in particular historical and racial experiences (Cassidy, Lord, and Mandell, 1998: 26; hooks, 1984). These new currents have done much to extend the relevance of feminism to previously marginalized groups.

Partly because of the political and intellectual vigour of the women's movement, some feminist ideas have gained widespread acceptance in Canadian society over the past three decades. For example, opposition to women in the paid labour force has declined and most Canadians now believe that both spouses should contribute to household income when possible (Ghalam, 1997). However, these values appear to conflict with other attitudes and beliefs. For example, one national survey reports that 46 percent of women and 44 percent of men agree or strongly agree with the statement that a "job is alright, but what most women really want is a home and children" (Ghalam, 1997: 16). It appears that the tapestry of our social lives is interwoven with threads of the new and the old.

CHAPTER 8 Sexuality and Gender **189**

9 Families

Introduction

WINNIPEG (March 21, 2010)—A 61-year-old man is in police custody facing second-degree murder charges in connection with the death of his 59-year-old wife.

Winnipeg police were called to an apartment block just after midnight Sunday . . . and found the female victim suffering from serious head trauma.

Police said she died a short time later in the first-floor suite . . .

Police spokesman Const. Jason Michalyshen . . . said the couple had been married for decades and said no previous incidents of domestic violence between the man and woman were reported to city police.

The victim was allegedly assaulted with what police would only say was a piece of "typical hardware" . . .

Second-floor resident Stewart Shaw said he heard noises coming from the suite below him before police arrived.

"There was loud banging that went on for about 30 seconds or so," he said. "It was really loud. Something was going on. It could have been like something really heavy hitting against something else. . ."

Main-floor resident Brian Kahan said he was stunned to hear of the incident.

"They were a quiet couple but would always smile at me and return my greetings," he said. "It's a shock that something like this could happen between them."

Kahan said the couple emigrated from eastern Europe and had lived in the block for almost a decade. He said they always seemed to get along well with one another.

[Jason Halstead, Sun Media. "Husband faces charges in wife's death." EdmontonSun. com. http://www.edmontonsun.com/news/canada/2010/03/21/13311596.html (retrieved 22 March 2010)]

LEARNING OBJECTIVES:

LO¹ The traditional nuclear family is less common than it used to be. Several new family forms are becoming more popular.

LO² The entry of women into the paid labour force and the legalization of contraception have changed family forms.

LO³ Marital satisfaction varies with identifiable social circumstances.

LO⁴ The worst effects of divorce on children can be eliminated.

LO⁵ A more equal division of power between spouses leads to men contributing more to domestic labour and to a decline in domestic violence.

LO⁶ The decline of the traditional nuclear family is sometimes associated with a host of social problems, such as poverty, welfare dependency, and crime. However, policies have been adopted in some countries that reduce these problems.

For better or for worse, our most intense emotional experiences are bound up with our families. We love, hate, protect, hurt, express generosity toward, and envy nobody as much as our parents, siblings, children, and mates. Some families are islands of domestic bliss. A few, like the family described in the news story above, are sites of the most violent acts imaginable; between 1974 and 2008, about 43 percent of homicides in Canada occurred within family or intimate relationships (see Figure 9.1). Given the intensity of our emotional involvement with our families, should we be surprised that most people are passionately concerned with the rights and wrongs, the dos and don'ts, of family life? Should we be surprised that family issues lie close to the centre of political debate in this country?

nuclear family Consists of a cohabiting man and woman who maintain a socially approved sexual relationship and have at least one child.

traditional nuclear family A nuclear family in which the husband works outside the home for money and the wife works without pay in the home.

LO¹ Is "The Family" in Decline?

Because families are emotional minefields, few subjects of sociological inquiry generate as much controversy. Much of the debate centres on a single question: Is the family in decline and, if so, what should be done about it? These questions are hardly new. John Laing, a Protestant minister in Ontario, wrote in 1878, "We may expect to see further disintegration until the family shall disappear. . . . In all things civil and sacred the tendency of the age is towards individualism . . . its plausible aphorisms and popular usages silently undermining the divine institution of the family" (quoted in Sager, 2000: vii). This alarm, or one much like it, is sounded whenever the family undergoes rapid change, and particularly when the divorce rate increases.

Today, when some people speak about the decline of the family, they are referring to the nuclear family. The nuclear family comprises a cohabiting man and woman who maintain a socially approved sexual relationship and have at least one child. Others are referring more narrowly to what we call the traditional nuclear family. The traditional nuclear family is a nuclear family in which the wife works in the home without pay while the husband works outside the home for money. This makes him the "primary provider and ultimate authority" (Popenoe, 1988: 1; see the Sociology at the Movies box).

In the 1940s and 1950s, many sociologists and much of the Canadian public considered the traditional nuclear family to be the most widespread

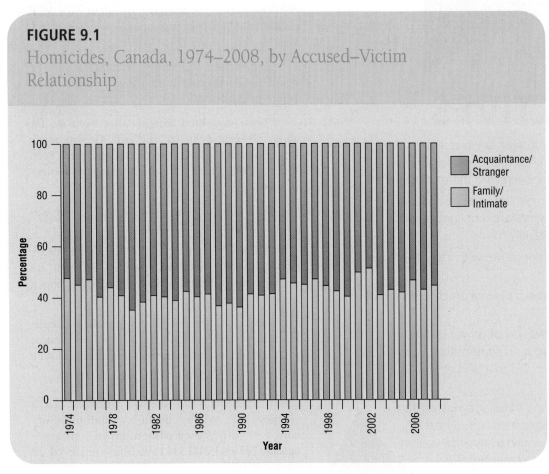

FIGURE 9.1

Homicides, Canada, 1974–2008, by Accused–Victim Relationship

Acquaintance/Stranger

Family/Intimate

Walk the Line

When legendary country singer Johnny Cash was 12, his older brother was killed in an accident and his father screamed that "God took the wrong son," assuming, unjustly and without evidence, that Johnny was to blame for the boy's death. Burdened by the loss of his beloved brother and his father's constant rejection, Johnny Cash became a deeply troubled adult. Fame didn't help. He drank too much, popped amphetamine pills like they were Tic Tacs, neglected his children, ruined his marriage, and did time for trying to smuggle narcotics across the border from Mexico.

Joaquin Phoenix and Reese Witherspoon in *Walk the Line*

Redemption arrived in the form of fellow performer June Carter (Reese Witherspoon, who won the best actress Oscar). Cash (played by Joaquin Phoenix, nominated for a best actor Oscar) pursues her relentlessly for years, eventually resorting to a proposal onstage in the middle of a performance, which she accepted. From that moment, Cash's life changed. But it was not just June who rescued him with her love and support. It was the entire Carter family. The Carters displayed all the grace and generosity one would expect of a royal family, which is just about what they were in the country music scene. At a Thanksgiving dinner attended by the Carters and the Cashes at Johnny's new house, Johnny's father starts in on him with the usual putdowns. "So how do you like it?" Johnny asks his father, referring to the house. "Jack Benny's is bigger," snaps the father. But Mr. Carter springs to Johnny's defence, mildly rebuking Mr. Cash by asking rhetorically, "Oh, have you been to Jack Benny's house?" Johnny is upset enough to leave the meal but Mrs. Carter encourages June to go after him and ease his pain. Later, Johnny's supplier arrives with a fresh bag of pills, but June's parents chase him away with shotguns. They integrate Johnny into their family as the beloved son he always wanted and needed to be, and Johnny lives with June and their four girls from previous marriages happily ever after.

What is a family? A cohabiting man and woman who maintain a socially approved sexual relationship and perhaps have at least one child? By that standard definition, Mr. and Mrs. Cash and their children formed a family—but a pretty sorry one by any reasonable standard because their family failed to provide the emotional support that could have allowed Johnny to thrive and become a happy adult. The Carters were not part of Johnny's family according to the standard definition, but their generosity of spirit led them to treat him like a son anyway. Johnny eventually became part of their extended family, but only because they cared deeply for his welfare. The story of Johnny Cash suggests that the definition of a family as a cohabiting man and woman who maintain a socially approved sexual relationship and perhaps have at least one child may be too narrow. Perhaps it is appropriate to think of a family more broadly as a set of intimate social relationships that adults create to share resources so as to ensure the welfare of themselves and their dependents.

Critical Thinking Questions

- What values are implicit in the two definitions of the family offered above?
- Which definition of family do you prefer? Why?

and ideal family form. However, for reasons we will examine below, fewer than 39 percent of Canadian families in 2006 were nuclear families, compared with 55 percent in 1981 and 69 percent in 1901 (see Figure 9.2). Moreover, because about 80 percent of mothers with school-aged children are in the paid labour force, only a small minority of Canadian adults live in traditional nuclear families today (Canadian Council on Social Development, 2001). New family forms, including single-parent families, common-law families, and gay and lesbian families, have become increasingly prevalent in recent decades (see Table 9.1).

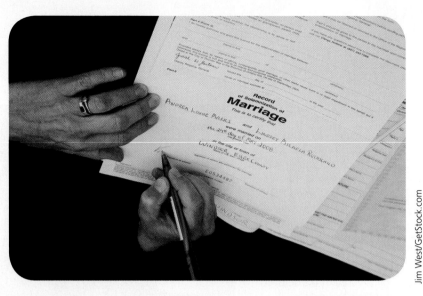
Jim West/GetStock.com

Some sociologists, many of them functionalists, view the decreasing prevalence of the married-couple family and the rise of the "working mother" as an unmitigated disaster (Popenoe, 1996, 1998). In their view, rising rates of crime, illegal drug use, poverty, and welfare dependency (among other social ills) can be traced to the fact that so many children are not living in two-parent households with stay-at-home mothers. They call for various legal and cultural reforms to shore up the traditional nuclear family. For instance, they want to make it harder to get a divorce, and they want people to place less emphasis on individual happiness at the expense of family responsibility.

Other sociologists, influenced by conflict and feminist theories, disagree with the functionalist assessment (Coontz, 1992; Stacey, 1996). In the first place, they argue that it is inaccurate to talk about *the* family, as if this important social institution assumes or should assume only a single form. They emphasize that families have been structured in many ways and that the diversity of family forms is increasing as people accommodate the demands of new social pressures. Second, they argue that changing family forms do not necessarily represent

FIGURE 9.2

The Growing Diversity of Families, Canada, 1981–2006 (in percent)

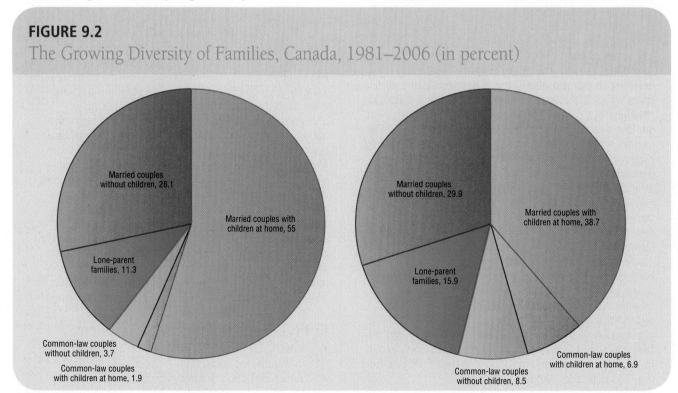

Sources: Statistics Canada. n.d. "Census families – time series." Online at http://www12.statcan.ca/english/census01/products/analytic/companion/fam/family.cfm (22 April 2007); Statistics Canada. 2010. "Number of Children at Home (8) and Census Family Structure (7) for the Census Families in Private Households of Canada, Provinces, Territories, Census Metropolitan Areas and Census Agglomerations, 2001 and 2006 Censuses—20% Sample Data." http://www12.statcan.gc.ca/census-recensement/2006/dp-pd/tbt/Rp eng.cfm?LANG=E&APATH=3&DETAIL=0&DIM=0&FL=A&FREE=0&GC=0&GID=0&GK=0&GRP=1&PID=89016&PRID=0&PTYPE=88971,97154&S=0&SHOWALL=0&SUB=689&Temporal=2006&THEME=68&VID=0&VNAMEE=&VNAMEF= (retrieved 22 March 2010).

TABLE 9.1
The Traditional Nuclear Family and New Alternatives

Traditional Nuclear Family	New Alternatives
Legally married	Never-married singlehood, non-marital cohabitation
With children	Voluntary childlessness
Two-parent	Single-parent (never married or previously married)
Permanent	Divorce, remarriage (including binuclear family involving joint custody, stepfamily, or "blended" family)
Male primary provider, ultimate authority	Egalitarian marriage (including dual-career and commuter marriage)
Sexually exclusive	Extramarital relationships (including sexually open marriage, swinging, and intimate friendships)
Heterosexual	Same-sex intimate relationships or households
Two-adult household	Multi-adult households (including multiple spouses, communal living, affiliated families, and multigenerational families)

Source: Adapted from Macklin (1980: 906).

deterioration in the quality of people's lives. In fact, such changes often represent *improvement* in the way people live. These sociologists believe that the decreasing prevalence of the traditional nuclear family and the proliferation of diverse family forms have benefited many men, women, and children and have not harmed other children as much as the functionalists think. They also believe that various economic and political reforms, such as the creation of an affordable nationwide daycare system, could eliminate most of the negative effects of single-parent households.

We first outline the functional theory of the family because the issues raised by functionalism are still a focus of sociological controversy (Mann, Grimes, Kemp, and Jenkins, 1997). Borrowing from the work of conflict theorists and feminists, we next show that the nuclear family has been in decline since the nineteenth century and is less prevalent than is often assumed. We then explain how change in the distribution of power between husbands and wives has affected mate selection, marital satisfaction, divorce, reproductive choice, domestic labour, and wife abuse. The discussion then turns to alternative family forms—how they are structured and how their frequency varies by class and sexual orientation. Finally, you will learn that although postindustrial families solve some problems, they are hardly an unqualified blessing. The chapter's concluding section considers the kinds of policies that might help alleviate some of the most serious concerns faced by families today.

Functionalism and the Nuclear Ideal
FUNCTIONAL THEORY

For any society to survive, its members must cooperate economically. They must have babies. And they must raise offspring in an emotionally supportive environment so the offspring can learn the ways of the group and eventually operate as productive adults. Since the 1940s, functionalists have argued that the nuclear family is ideally suited to meet these challenges. In their view, the nuclear family provides a basis for five main functions: regulated sexual activity, economic cooperation, reproduction, socialization, and emotional support (Murdock, 1949: 1–22; Parsons, 1955).

Functionalists cite the pervasiveness of the nuclear family as evidence of its ability to perform these functions.

Tim Bieber/The Image Bank/Getty Images

The idealized North American family of the 1950s.

To be sure, other family forms exist. **Polygamy** expands the nuclear unit "horizontally" by adding one or more spouses (almost always wives) to the household. Polygamy is still legally permitted in many less industrialized countries in Africa and Asia. However, the overwhelming majority of families are monogamous because they cannot afford to support several wives and many children. The **extended family** expands the nuclear family "vertically" by adding another generation—one or more of the spouses' parents—to the household. Extended families used to be common throughout the world. They still are in some places. However, according to the functionalists, the basic building block of the extended family (and of the polygamous family) is the nuclear unit.

George Murdock was a functionalist who conducted a famous study of 250 mainly preliterate societies in the 1940s. Murdock wrote, "Either as the sole prevailing form of the family or as the basic unit from which more complex familial forms are compounded, [the nuclear family] exists as a distinct and strongly functional group in every known society" (Murdock, 1949: 2). Moreover, the nuclear family, Murdock continued, is everywhere based on **marriage**. He defined marriage as a socially approved, presumably long-term, sexual and economic union between a man and a woman. It involves rights and obligations between spouses and between spouses and their children.

FUNCTIONS OF THE NUCLEAR FAMILY

Let us consider the five main functions of marriage and the nuclear family in more detail.

polygamy Expands the nuclear family "horizontally" by adding one or more spouses (usually women) to the household.

extended family Expands the nuclear family "vertically" by adding another generation— one or more of the spouses' parents—to the household.

marriage Traditionally defined, is a socially approved, presumably long-term sexual and economic union between a man and a woman. It involves reciprocal rights and obligations between spouses and between parents and children.

1. *Sexual regulation*. The nuclear family defines the boundaries within which legitimate sexual activity is permitted, thus making an orderly social life possible. Of course, sex is readily available outside marriage. Murdock found that only 22 percent of 250 mainly preliterate societies forbade or disapproved of premarital sex between non-relatives, and in more than half the societies, a married man could legitimately have an extramarital affair with one or more female relatives (Murdock, 1949: 5–6). It is hardly news that premarital and extramarital sex are common in postindustrial societies (especially if you believe half of what you see in *Desperate Housewives* or *Mad Men*). So sex is not the primary motivation for marrying.

2. *Economic cooperation*. People marry also because "a man and a woman make an exceptionally efficient cooperating unit" (Murdock, 1949: 7). Historically, pregnancy and nursing have restricted women in their activities, whereas men possess superior strength. Therefore, women have traditionally performed lighter tasks close to home while men have specialized in lumbering, mining, quarrying, land clearing, house building, hunting, fishing, herding, and trade (Murdock, 1937). Thus, "marriage exists only when the economic and the sexual are united into one relationship, and this combination occurs only in marriage" (Murdock, 1949: 8).

3. *Reproduction*. Before the invention of modern contraception, sex often resulted in the birth of a baby. In pre-modern societies, children are an investment in the future. By the age of six or seven, children in such societies do some chores. Their economic value to the family increases as they mature. When children become adults, they often help support their aging parents. Thus, there is a big economic incentive to having children.

4. *Socialization*. The investment in children can be realized only if adults rear the young to maturity. This involves not only caring for them physically but also teaching them language, values, beliefs, skills, religion, and much else. Some functionalists regarded socialization as the "basic and irreducible" function of the family (Parsons, 1955: 16).

5. *Emotional support*. Functionalists note that the nuclear family universally gives its members love, affection, and companionship. In the nuclear family, it is mainly the mother who is responsible for ensuring the family's emotional well-being. It falls on the father to take on the role of earning a living outside the family (Parsons, 1955: 23). The fact that he is the "primary provider" makes him the ultimate authority.

Does this functionalist account provide an accurate picture of family relations across history? To assess the adequacy of the theory, let us discuss the families in which the early functionalists themselves lived: families in urban and suburban middle-class North America in the 1950s.

THE CANADIAN MIDDLE-CLASS FAMILY IN THE 1950S

As a description of family patterns in the 15 years after World War II, functionalism has its merits. During the Great Depression (1929–39) and World War II (1939–45), Canadians were forced to postpone marriage because of widespread poverty, government-imposed austerity, and physical separation. After this long and dreadful ordeal, many Canadians just wanted to settle down, have children, and enjoy the peace, pleasure, and security that family life seemed to offer. Conditions could not have been better for doing just that. The immediate postwar era was one of unparalleled optimism and prosperity. Real per capita income rose, as did the percentage of Canadians who owned their own homes. Laws passed during World War II to encourage women to join the paid labour force were cancelled. Things were now supposed to return to "normal," meaning that women were supposed to go back to being housewives and men to being breadwinners (Kingsbury and Scanzoni, 1993).

As a result of these conditions, Canadians experienced a marriage boom (see Figure 9.3). Increasingly, Canadians lived in married-couple families. The proportion of "never married" Canadians decreased and the average age

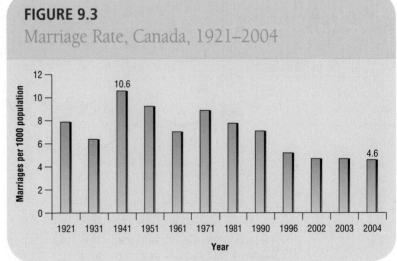

FIGURE 9.3

Marriage Rate, Canada, 1921–2004

Sources: Adapted from the Statistics Canada products "Selected Marriage Statistics, 1921–1990—Diskette," Catalogue 82-552, October 1, 1992, and *The Daily*, Catalogue 11-001, Thursday, January 29, 1998. Found at http://www.statcan.ca/Daily/English/980129/d980129.htm#ART1, and Tuesday, December 21, 2004, available at http://www.statcan.ca/Daily/English/041221/d04122d.htm; Statistics Canada. 2007. "Table 101-1002, Mean age and median age of males and females, by type of marriage and marital status, Canada, provinces and territories, annual." Found at http://cansim2.statcan.ca/cgi-win/cnsmcgi.exe?Lang=E&RootDir=CII/&ResultTemplate=CII/CII___&Array_Pick=1&ArrayId=1011002 (22 April 2007).

at first marriage dropped for both women and men (McVey and Kalbach, 1995: 225; see Figure 9.4). As we might expect, the marriage boom soon gave way to a baby boom. The average Canadian family had four children; nearly all married women stayed home to raise their children (Nikiforuk, 1999). In 1951, 90 percent of married men but only 11.2 percent of married women worked in the paid labour force. Most women engaged in what has been called an "orgy of domesticity" in the postwar years, devoting increasing attention to child rearing and housework. They also became increasingly concerned with the emotional quality of family life as love and companionship became firmly established as the main motivation for marriage (Coontz, 1992: 23–41; Skolnick, 1991: 49–74).

The 1950s: A Historical Anomaly

What many functionalists fail to appreciate is that the immediate postwar period was in many respects a historical anomaly (Cherlin, 1992: 6–30). Trends in divorce, marriage, and child-bearing show a gradual *weakening* of the nuclear family from the second half of the nineteenth century until the mid-1940s, and continued weakening after the 1950s. Specifically, throughout the nineteenth century, the divorce rate rose slowly. The **divorce rate** is the number of divorces that occur in a year for every 1000 people in the population. Meanwhile, the marriage rate fell. The **marriage rate** is the number of marriages that occur in a year for every 1000 people in the population. The total fertility rate also fell (see Figure 9.5). The **total fertility rate** is the average number of children that would be born to a woman over her lifetime if she had the same number of children as do women in each age cohort in a given year.

Canada's marriage rate started falling after 1946. The divorce rate started rising in the 1960s when the law was changed to make it easier to divorce. The total fertility started falling after 1961. Thus, by the early 1960s, the earlier trends had reasserted themselves. Only the

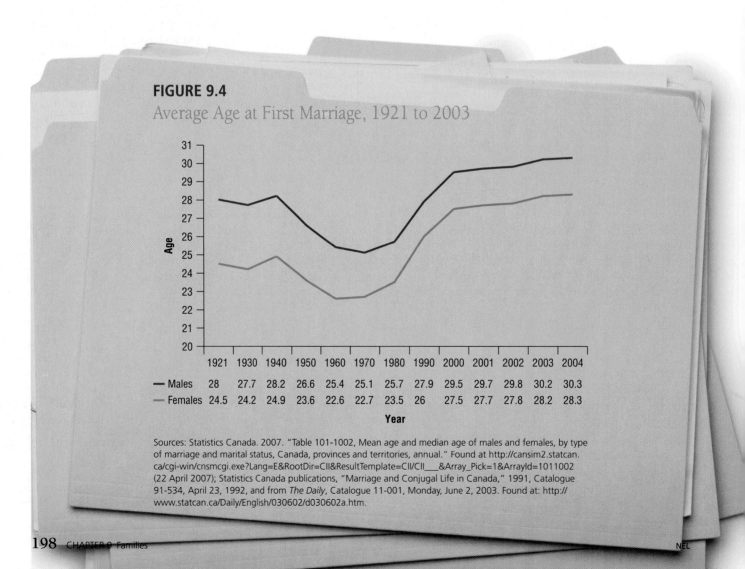

FIGURE 9.4

Average Age at First Marriage, 1921 to 2003

	1921	1930	1940	1950	1960	1970	1980	1990	2000	2001	2002	2003	2004
— Males	28	27.7	28.2	26.6	25.4	25.1	25.7	27.9	29.5	29.7	29.8	30.2	30.3
— Females	24.5	24.2	24.9	23.6	22.6	22.7	23.5	26	27.5	27.7	27.8	28.2	28.3

Year

Sources: Statistics Canada. 2007. "Table 101-1002, Mean age and median age of males and females, by type of marriage and marital status, Canada, provinces and territories, annual." Found at http://cansim2.statcan.ca/cgi-win/cnsmcgi.exe?Lang=E&RootDir=CII&ResultTemplate=CII/CII___&Array_Pick=1&ArrayId=1011002 (22 April 2007); Statistics Canada publications, "Marriage and Conjugal Life in Canada," 1991, Catalogue 91-534, April 23, 1992, and from *The Daily*, Catalogue 11-001, Monday, June 2, 2003. Found at: http://www.statcan.ca/Daily/English/030602/d030602a.htm.

FIGURE 9.5

Total Fertility Rate, 1950–2007

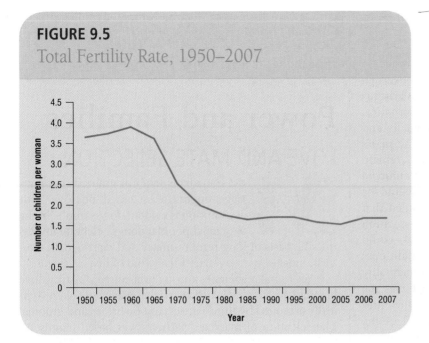

Source: United Nations Statistical Division Common Database.

LO² Conflict and Feminist Theories

Other sociologists, influenced less by functionalism than by the conflict and feminist traditions, see the proliferation of non-nuclear families as a response to changes in power relations between women and men.

The idea that power relations between women and men explain the prevalence of different family forms was first suggested by Marx's close friend and co-author, Friedrich Engels. Engels argued that the traditional nuclear family emerged along with private property and inequalities of wealth.

According to Engels, little inequality existed in nomadic, hunting-and-gathering societies. Even in pastoral societies (which domesticated cattle and other animals) and horticultural societies (which used small hand tools for planting and harvesting), families did not own land. They considered land common property. A family might work a particular plot of land for some time, even generations, but if the plot fell into disuse then another family had the right to use it. Substantial inequalities in wealth emerged only in early agricultural societies, when people attached large animals, such as oxen, to plows and it became possible to farm large tracts of land. That was when private property was legally recognized. That was when some families

peculiar historical circumstances of the postwar years, noted above, temporarily reversed them. The big picture from the nineteenth century until the present is that of a gradually weakening nuclear family. The early functionalists, it seems, generalized too hastily from the families they knew best—their own.

The Displacement of Family Functions

According to many modern-day functionalists, the nuclear family has become less prevalent since the nineteenth century because many of the traditional functions of the nuclear family have been eroded or partly taken over by other institutions. For example, the traditional division of labour, based on the physical capabilities and limitations of husband and wife, has weakened. That is because contraception and child-care services are now available, while demand for women to enter the paid labour force and pursue a higher education has increased. Women are no longer tied to the home in the way they once were. Children are not the economic asset they were in agricultural societies that lacked a social welfare system. Quite the opposite: it is now very expensive to raise children. Meanwhile, part of the task of socialization has been taken over by schools, the mass media, and peer groups, while reproduction outside the nuclear family is possible because of the introduction of in vitro fertilization and other reproductive technologies. Thus, contemporary functionalists argue that the traditional nuclear family has been in decline for more than a century because other institutions perform many of the economic, reproductive, and socialization functions that were formerly reserved for the nuclear family.

began to amass wealth. And that was when men came to enjoy legal control of property and the wealth it generated.

Once legal control of property was concentrated in the hands of a man, wrote Engels, he became concerned about how to transmit it to his children, particularly his sons. How could a man safely pass on an inheritance, asked Engels? Only by controlling his wife sexually and economically. Economic control ensured that the man's property would not be squandered and would remain his and his alone. Sexual control, in the form of enforced female monogamy, ensured that his property would be transmitted only to *his* offspring. Engels concluded that only the elimination of private property and the creation of economic equality—in a word, communism—could bring an end to gender inequality and the traditional nuclear family (Engels, 1970 [1884]: 138–39). Inequality deriving from men's control of private property was the basis of the nuclear family in Engels's view, and the elimination of private property would spell the end of the nuclear family.

Engels was of course right to note the long history of male economic and sexual domination in the traditional nuclear family. A century ago, any money a wife earned typically belonged to her husband. As recently as the 1950s, a Canadian wife could not rent a car, take a loan, or sign a contract without her husband's permission. It was only in the 1980s that it became illegal in Canada for a husband to rape his wife.

However, Engels was wrong to think that communism would eliminate gender inequality in the family. Gender inequality has been as common in societies that call themselves communist as in those that call themselves capitalist. For example, the Soviet Union left "intact the fundamental family structures, authority relations, and socialization patterns crucial to personality formation and sex-role differentiation. Only a genuine sexual revolution [or, as we prefer to call it, a *gender revolution*] could have shattered these patterns and made possible the real emancipation of women" (Lapidus, 1978: 7).

Because gender inequality exists in non-capitalist societies, most feminists believe something other than, or in addition to, capitalism accounts for gender inequality and the persistence of the traditional nuclear family. In their view, *patriarchy*—male dominance and norms justifying that dominance—is more deeply rooted in the economic, military, and cultural history of humankind than the classical Marxist account allows. For them, only a "genuine gender revolution" can alter this state of affairs.

Just such a revolution in family structures, authority relations, and socialization patterns picked up steam in Canada and other rich industrialized countries about half a century ago, although its roots extend back to the eighteenth century. As you will now see, the revolution is evident in the rise of romantic love and happiness as bases for marriage, the rising divorce rate, and women's increasing control over reproduction through their use of contraceptives, among other factors. We begin by considering the sociology of mate selection.

Power and Families
LOVE AND MATE SELECTION

Most Canadians take for granted that marriage ought to be based on love. Our assumption is evident, for example, in the way most popular songs celebrate love as the sole basis of long-term intimacy and marriage. In contrast, most of us view marriage devoid of love as tragic.

Yet in most societies throughout human history, love has had little to do with marriage. Marriages were typically arranged by third parties, not by brides and grooms. The selection of marriage partners was based mainly on calculations intended to increase their families' prestige, economic benefits, and political advantages.

The idea that love should be important in the choice of a marriage partner first gained currency in eighteenth-century England with the rise of liberalism and individualism, philosophies that stressed the freedom of the individual over community welfare (Stone, 1977). The intimate linkage between love and marriage that we know today emerged only in the early twentieth century, when Hollywood and the advertising industry began to promote self-gratification on a grand scale. For these new spinners of fantasy and desire, an important aspect of self-gratification was heterosexual romance leading to marriage (Rapp and Ross, 1986). Today, wherever individualism is highly prized, love has come to be defined as the essential basis for marriage. A survey of college undergraduates in 11 countries asked, "If a man (woman) had all the qualities you desired, would you marry this person if you were not in love with him (her)?" In the five rich countries plus Brazil, between 3 percent and 8 percent of students said they would marry someone they were not in love with if that person possessed all the qualities they were looking for in a partner. In the five developing countries, the comparable percentage ranged from 10 percent to 50 percent (Levine et al., 1995; see Figure 9.6).

Still, it would be a mistake to think that love alone determines mate selection in our society—far from it. Three sets of social forces influence whom you are likely to fall in love with and marry (Kalmijn, 1998: 398–404):

1. *Marriage resources*. Potential spouses bring certain resources with them to the "marriage market." They use these resources to attract mates and compete against rivals. These resources include financial assets, status, values, tastes, and knowledge. Most

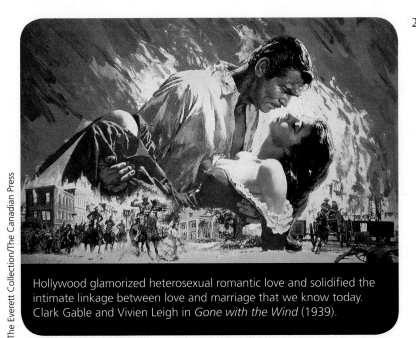

Hollywood glamorized heterosexual romantic love and solidified the intimate linkage between love and marriage that we know today. Clark Gable and Vivien Leigh in *Gone with the Wind* (1939).

2. *Third parties.* A marriage between people from two different groups can threaten the internal cohesion of one or both groups. Therefore, to varying degrees, families, neighbourhoods, communities, and religious institutions raise young people to identify with the groups they are members of and think of themselves as different from members of other groups. They may also apply sanctions to young people who threaten to marry outside the group. For example, although ethnic intermarriage has become increasingly common in Canada, parents often encourage their children to marry within their own ethnic group to preserve their unique culture (Kalbach, 2000; Kitano and Daniels, 1995). This is especially true among immigrants who come to Canada from cultures in which arranged marriage has been the tradition (Dugger, 1996). As a result, whom you fall in love with and choose to marry is determined partly by the influence of third parties.

3. *Demographic and compositional factors.* The probability of marrying inside your group increases with the group's size and geographical concentration. If you are a member of a small group or a group that is dispersed geographically, you stand a greater chance of having to choose an appropriate mate from outside your group. There may simply be too few prospects in your group from which to choose (Brym, Gillespie, and Gillis, 1985). In addition, the ratio of men to women in a group influences the degree to which members of each sex marry inside or outside the group. For instance, war and imprisonment can eliminate many male group members as potential marriage partners and encourage female group members to marry outside the group or forgo marriage altogether. Finally, because people usually meet potential spouses in "local marriage markets"— schools, universities and colleges, places of work, neighbourhoods, bars, and clubs—the degree to which these settings are socially segregated influences mate selection. You are more likely to marry

people want to maximize the financial assets and status they gain from marriage, and they want a mate who has similar values, tastes, and knowledge. As a result, whom you fall in love with and choose to marry is determined partly by the assets you bring to the marriage market.

FIGURE 9.6

Responses to Question: "If a man (woman) had all the other qualities you desired, would you marry this person if you were not in love with him (her)?"

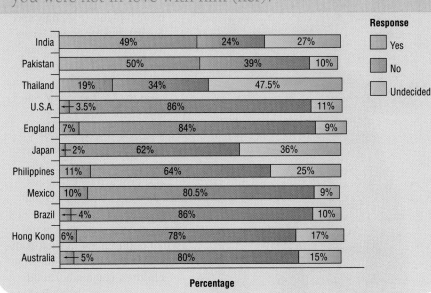

	Response
	Yes
	No
	Undecided

Country	Yes	No	Undecided
India	49%	24%	27%
Pakistan	50%	39%	10%
Thailand	19%	34%	47.5%
U.S.A.	3.5%	86%	11%
England	7%	84%	9%
Japan	2%	62%	36%
Philippines	11%	64%	25%
Mexico	10%	80.5%	9%
Brazil	4%	86%	10%
Hong Kong	6%	78%	17%
Australia	5%	80%	15%

Percentage

Note: Percentages may not add up to 100 because of rounding.
Source: *Journal of cross-cultural psychology* by Levine, Sata, Hashimoto, Verma. Copyright 1995 by SAGE PUBLICATIONS INC. JOURNALS. Reproduced with permission of SAGE PUBLICATIONS INC. JOURNALS in the format Textbook via Copyright Clearance Center.

outside your group if local marriage markets are socially heterogeneous. As a result, whom you fall in love with and choose to marry is determined partly by the size, geographical dispersion, and sex ratio of the groups you belong to and the social composition of the local marriage markets you frequent.

As a result of the operation of these three sets of social forces, the process of falling in love and choosing a mate is far from random. Most of us have selected or will select a partner of similar racial or ethnic background, age, and social class.

LO³ MARITAL SATISFACTION

Just as mate selection came to depend more on romantic love over the years, so marital stability came to depend more on having a happy rather than merely a useful marriage. This change occurred because women in Canada and many other societies have become more autonomous, especially over the past half century; one aspect of the gender revolution women are experiencing is that they are freer than ever to leave marriages in which they are unhappy.

One factor that contributed to women's autonomy was the legalization of birth control measures in Canada in 1969. The birth control pill made it easier for women to delay childbirth and have fewer children. A second factor that contributed to women's autonomy was their increased participation in the paid labour force. Once women enjoyed a source of income independent of their husbands, they gained the means to decide the course of their own lives to a greater extent than ever before. A married woman with a job outside the home is less tied to her marriage by economic necessity than is a woman who works only at home. If the woman who works outside the home is deeply dissatisfied with her marriage, she can more easily leave. In addition, beginning in the late 1960s, laws governing divorce were changed to make divorce easier.

The Social Roots of Marital Satisfaction

If marital stability now depends largely on marital satisfaction, what are the main factors underlying marital satisfaction? The sociological literature emphasizes five sets of forces (Collins and Coltrane, 1991: 394–406, 454–64):

1. *Economic forces.* Money issues are the most frequent subjects of family quarrels, and money issues loom larger when there isn't enough money to satisfy a family's needs and desires. Accordingly, marital satisfaction tends to fall and the divorce rate tends to rise as you move down the socioeconomic hierarchy. The lower the social class and the lower the educational level of the spouses, the more likely it is that financial pressures will make them unhappy and the marriage unstable. Marital dissatisfaction and divorce are also more common among groups with high poverty rates. In contrast, the marital satisfaction of wives and, even more, of husbands, generally increases when wives enter the paid labour force (Hughes, Galinsky, and Morris, 1992; Lupri and Frideres, 1988). This increase is due mainly to the beneficial financial effects. However, if *either* spouse spends so much time on the job that he or she neglects the family, marital satisfaction falls.

2. *Divorce laws.* Many surveys show that, on average, married people are happier than unmarried people are. Moreover, when people are free to end unhappy marriages and remarry, the average level of happiness increases among married people. Thus, the level of marital happiness has increased in Canada over the past few decades, especially for wives, partly because it has become easier to get a divorce. For the same reason, in countries where getting a divorce is more difficult (e.g., Italy and Spain), husbands and wives tend to be less happy than in countries where getting a divorce is easier (e.g., Canada and the United States; Stack and Eshleman, 1998).

3. *The family life cycle.* In Canada, the rate of divorce per 1000 population reaches a peak in the fifth year of marriage and then falls (Ambert, 1998: 5). For marriages that last, marital satisfaction generally starts high, falls when children are born (especially for wives), reaches a low point when children are in their teenage years, and rises again when children reach adulthood (Glenn, 1990; Rollins and Cannon, 1974). Couples without children

and parents whose children have left home (so-called empty nesters) enjoy the highest level of marital satisfaction. Parents who are just starting families or who have adult children living at home enjoy intermediate levels of marital satisfaction. Marital satisfaction is lowest during the "establishment" years, when children are attending school. Although most people get married at least partly to have children, it turns out that children, and especially teenagers, usually put big emotional and financial strains on families. These strains result in relatively low marital satisfaction.

4. *Housework and child care*. Marital happiness is higher among couples who perceive an equitable distribution of housework and child care (Rosenbluth, Steil, and Whitcomb, 1998). The further couples are from an equitable sharing of domestic responsibilities, the more tension there is among all family members (Risman and Johnson-Sumerford, 1998). Research finds that equitable sharing tends to increase with education (Berk, 1985).

5. *Sex*. Having a good sex life is associated with marital satisfaction. Contrary to popular belief, surveys show that sex generally improves during a marriage. From these findings, some experts conclude that general marital happiness leads to sexual compatibility (Collins and Coltrane, 1991: 344). However, the reverse can also be true. Good sex can lead to a good marriage. After all, sexual preferences are deeply rooted in our psyches and our earliest experiences. We cannot easily alter them to suit our partners. If spouses are sexually incompatible, they may find it hard to change, even if they communicate well, argue little, and are generally happy on other grounds. However, if a husband and wife are sexually compatible, they may work hard to resolve other problems in the marriage for the sake of preserving their good sex life. Thus, the relationship between marital satisfaction and sexual compatibility is probably reciprocal. Each factor influences the other.

Let us now see what happens when low marital satisfaction leads to divorce.

DIVORCE

Before 1968, adultery was the only grounds for divorce in Canada, except in Nova Scotia, where cruelty was sufficient grounds even before Confederation (Morrison, 1987).

The Divorce Act of 1968, the first federal divorce statute, expanded the grounds under which a divorce could be granted. The amendment of Canada's Divorce Act in 1985 allowed only one ground for divorce—marital breakdown, defined in three ways: (1) the spouses have lived apart for one year, (2) one of the spouses has committed an act of adultery, (3) one spouse has treated the other with mental or physical cruelty. Today, a spouse seeking divorce no longer has to prove grounds. Instead, a marriage is legally "dissolved" because the relationship is "irretrievably broken." Following these amendments, the divorce rate reached a historic high in 1987 but has since declined (Statistics Canada, 2000d). About 38 percent of Canadian marriages now end in divorce.

Economic Effects

Women's income usually falls after divorce, while men's generally rises (Finnie, 1993). That is because husbands tend to earn more than wives, children typically live with their mothers after divorce, and child-support payments are often inadequate.

In the past, Canadian laws regarding the division of marital assets on divorce and the awarding of alimony contributed to women's declining living standards after divorce. For example, in the early 1970s, Irene Murdock, a farm wife, claimed that her labours over 15 years had earned her a share in the family farm. However, the Supreme Court of Canada ruled that her work was simply that of an "ordinary farm wife" and did not entitle her to share in the property that she and her husband had accumulated during their marriage (Steel, 1987: 159).

Although all Canadian provinces and territories now have laws requiring spouses to share assets in the event of marital breakdown, the precise definition of what constitutes a family asset varies and creates inconsistencies

across jurisdictions (Dranoff, 2001: 257). In addition, although the monetary value of tangible family assets (e.g., money in the bank, a house) can be calculated and shared, the valuable "new property" today is the earning power of a professional degree, highly paid employment, work experience, a skilled trade, or other "human capital" (Glendon, 1981). On divorce, the wife may receive an equal share of tangible property, but that does not usually result in her beginning post-divorce life on an equal footing with her former husband, especially if she retains physical custody of the couple's children and if she sacrificed her education and career so that he could earn a college or university degree.

Child support is money paid by the non-custodial parent to the custodial parent to support the children of a separated marital, cohabiting, or sexual relationship. Under the Divorce Act, either parent can be ordered to pay child support. However, because mothers retain custody in the great majority of cases—and because women are more likely to be economically disadvantaged in employment—those ordered to pay child support are usually fathers.

Every jurisdiction in Canada requires parents to support their children following separation or divorce. However, court orders do not guarantee that child support will be paid. In practice, orders for child and spousal support have often been difficult to enforce, and default rates have been high. All Canadian provinces and territories now have their own programs to protect against non-payment of child support. Nonetheless, the problem of "deadbeat parents" remains serious (Families Against Deadbeats, 2000).

Some analysts argue that the main reason for non-payment of child support is the unemployment or underemployment of the non-custodial parent (Meyer and Bartfield, 1996). If that is correct, "coercive child-support collection policies, such as automatic wage withholding, will have only limited success" and solving the problem "will be the old and unglamorous one, of solving un- and underemployment, both for the fathers and the mothers" (Braver, Fitzpatrick, and Bay, 1991: 184–85).

Emotional Effects

Although divorce enables spouses to leave unhappy marriages, questions have been raised about the emotional consequences of divorce for children, particularly in the long term. Some scholars claim that divorcing parents are simply trading the well-being of their children for their own happiness. What does research say about this issue?

child support Money paid by the non-custodial parent to the custodial parent for the purpose of supporting the children of a separated marital, cohabiting, or sexual relationship.

Research shows that children of divorced parents tend to develop behavioural problems and do less well in school than do children in intact families (Demo, Fine, and Ganong, 2000). They are more likely to engage in delinquent acts and to abuse drugs and alcohol. They often experience an emotional crisis, particularly in the first two years after divorce. What is more, when children of divorced parents become adults, they are less likely than children of non-divorced parents to be happy. They are more likely to suffer health problems, depend on welfare, earn low incomes, and experience divorce themselves. In one study, almost half the children of divorced parents entered adulthood as worried, underachieving, self-deprecating, and sometimes angry young men and women (Wallerstein, Lewis, and Blakeslee, 2000). Clearly, divorce can have serious, long-term, negative consequences for children.

However, much of the research that seems to establish a link between divorce and long-term negative consequences for children is based on families who seek psychological counselling. Such families are a small and unrepresentative minority of the population. By definition, they have more serious emotional problems than the large majority, who do not need psychological counselling after divorce. We must be careful not to generalize from such studies. Another problem with much of this research is that some analysts fail to ask whether factors other than divorce might be responsible for the long-term distress experienced by many children of divorced parents.

LO⁴ Factors Affecting the Well-Being of Children

Researchers who rely on representative samples and examine the separate effects of many factors on children's well-being provide the best evidence on the consequences of divorce for children. For example, a re-analysis of 92 relevant studies showed that, on average, the overall effect of divorce on children's well-being is not strong and is declining over time (Amato and Keith,

1991). This research also found that three factors account for much of the distress among children of divorce:

1. *A high level of parental conflict.* A high level of parental conflict creates long-term distress among children (Jekielek, 1998). Divorce without parental conflict does children much less harm. In fact, children in divorced families have a higher level of well-being on average than children in high-conflict *intact* families. The effect of parental conflict on the long-term well-being of children is substantially greater than the effect of any other factor.

2. *A decline in living standards.* By itself, the economic disadvantage experienced by most children in divorced families exerts a small impact on their well-being. Nonetheless, it is clear that children of divorce who do not experience a decline in living standards suffer less harm.

3. *The absence of a parent.* Children of divorce usually lose a parent as a role model and a source of emotional support, practical help, and supervision. By itself, this factor also has a small effect on children's well-being, even if the child has continued contact with the non-custodial parent (Resnick et al., 1997).

Subsequent studies confirm these generalizations and add an important observation. Many of the behavioural and adjustment problems experienced by children of divorce existed before the divorce took place. We cannot therefore attribute them to the divorce itself (Nielsen, 1999; Pasley and Minton, 2001; Stewart, Copeland, Chester, Malley, and Barenbaum, 1997; Thompson and Amato, 1999).

In sum, claiming that divorcing parents selfishly trade the well-being of their children for their own happiness is an exaggeration. Although the heightened risk of poverty is real, high levels of parental conflict can also have serious negative consequences for children, even when they enter adulthood. In such high-conflict situations, divorce can benefit children. By itself, the absence of a parent has a small negative effect on children's well-being. But this effect is becoming smaller over time, perhaps in part because divorce is so common it is no longer a stigma.

REPRODUCTIVE CHOICE

We have seen that the power women gained from working in the paid labour force put them in a position to leave a marriage if it made them deeply unhappy. Another aspect of the gender revolution women are experiencing is that they are increasingly able to decide what happens in the marriage if they stay. For example, women now have more say over whether they will have children and, if so, when they will have them and how many they will have.

Children are increasingly expensive to raise. They no longer give the family economic benefits, as they did, say, on the family farm. Most women want to work in the paid labour force, many of them to pursue a career. As a result, most women decide to have fewer children, to have them farther apart, and to have them at an older age. Some decide to have none at all (Dalphonse, 1997).

Women's reproductive decisions are carried out by means of contraception and abortion. Abortion was declared a criminal offence in Canada in 1892. In the 1960s, an abortion reform movement spearheaded by Dr. Henry Morgentaler urged the repeal of abortion laws that, in his words, "compelled the unwilling to bear the unwanted" (quoted in Dranoff, 2001: 16). In 1969 the law was changed to permit "therapeutic abortion" if performed by a physician in an accredited hospital and if a three-member committee certified that the continuation of the pregnancy would likely endanger the health of the mother. In 1988, the Supreme Court of Canada struck down the law on abortion on the grounds that it contravened a woman's right to control her own reproductive life and, as such, contravened her constitutionally protected guarantees to security of her person. In 1989, the Supreme Court also unanimously determined that the civil law in Quebec, the Quebec Charter, and the common law do not protect fetal life or interests. In 1993, the Supreme Court of Canada struck down legislation that banned abortion clinics. By 1995, abortion clinics outside hospitals operated throughout Canada with the exception of Prince Edward Island, Saskatchewan, and the territories.

In 2006, 91 377 Canadian women obtained abortions (Statistics Canada, 2010f). On a global scale, the abortion rate in Canada is low at about 15 per 1000 women between the ages of 15 and 44. The comparable rate is 21 in the United States, 45 in Russia, and 57 in Cuba (Sedgh et al., 2007: 219).

Attitudes toward abortion are mixed. A 2006 survey showed that 31 percent of Canadians believe that the life of a fetus should be protected at conception, 33 percent believe that it should be protected at some point during pregnancy, and 30 percent believe that legal protection should start at birth. Since 2002, the proportion of Canadians believing that legal protection of the fetus should start at conception fell by 6 percent ("Two Canadian," 2006). Attitudes toward abortion vary by age, with teens more likely than adults to approve of the availability of legal abortion for any reason (55 percent versus 43 percent, respectively; Bibby, 2001: 250–51). Ninety percent of adults and 84 percent of teens support the availability of legal abortion when rape is involved.

Right-to-life versus pro-choice activists have been clashing since the 1970s. Right-to-life activists object to the decriminalization of abortion; pro-choice activists want the current situation preserved. Both groups have tried to influence public opinion and lawmakers to achieve their aims. A few extreme right-to-life activists (almost all men) have resorted to violence (Gegax and Clemetson, 1998).

As sociologists Randall Collins and Scott Coltrane (1995) note, it seems likely that the criminalization of abortion would likely return us to the situation that existed in the 1960s. Many abortions took place then, but because they were illegal, they were expensive, hard to obtain, and posed dangers to women's health. If abortion laws were repealed, they predict that poor women and their unwanted children would suffer most. Taxpayers would wind up paying bigger bills for social assistance and medical care.

LO⁵ HOUSEWORK AND CHILD CARE

As we have seen, women's increased participation in the paid labour force, their increased participation in the system of higher education, and their increased control over reproduction transformed several areas of family life. Despite this far-ranging gender revolution, however, one domain remains more resistant to change: housework, child care, and senior care. This fact was first documented in detail by sociologist Arlie Hochschild in the 1980s. She showed that even women who worked full time in the paid labour force usually began a "second shift" when they returned home. There, they prepared meals, helped with homework, did laundry, and so on (Hochschild with Machung, 1989).

Today, men take a more active role in the day-to-day running of the household. Still, a 2000 study of household labour in 10 rich countries found that "women continue to be responsible for the majority of hours of unpaid labour" ranging from a low of 70 percent in Sweden to a high of 88 percent in Italy (Bittman and Wajcman, 2000: 173). In Canada, 20 percent of women—but only 8 percent of men—devoted 30 hours or more to unpaid household work according to the 2006 census. Men were almost twice as likely as women were to claim that they did not devote any time to such work (see Table 9.2).

Even these figures do not reveal the whole picture, however. Men tend to do low-stress chores that can often wait a day or a week. These jobs include mowing the lawn, repairing the car, and painting the fence. Although fathers of young children under the age of five are often

TABLE 9.2

Unpaid Housework in Canada for Women and Men over the Age of 14, 2006 (in percent)

	Women	Men
No hours	7	12
Fewer than 5 hours	18	30
5 to 14 hours	31	34
15 to 29 hours	24	16
30 or more hours	20	8
Total	100	100

Source: Statistics Canada. 2010. "Unpaid Work (20), Age Groups (9) and Sex (3) for the Population 15 Years and Over of Canada, Provinces, Territories, Census Divisions and Census Sub-divisions, 2006 Census—20% Sample Data." http://www12.statcan.gc.ca/census-recensement/2006/dp-pd/tbt/Rp-eng.cfm?LANG=E&APATH=3&DETAIL=0&DIM=0&FL=A&FREE=0&GC=0&GID=0&GK=0&GRP=1&PID=92108&PRID=0&PTYPE=88971,97154&S=0&SHOWALL=0&SUB=745&Temporal=2006&THEME=74&VID=0&VNAMEE=&VNAMEF=0 (retrieved 22 March 2010).

happy to play with their children, they spend less time than mothers do providing the more time-intensive forms of child care, such as feeding, washing, dressing, and medical care. In general, women tend to do the repetitive, higher stress chores that cannot wait. In short, the picture falls short of a revolution (Harvey, Marshall, and Frederick, 1991).

Two main factors shrink the gender gap in housework, child care, and senior care. First, the smaller the difference between the husband's and the wife's earnings, the more equal the division of household labour. Women who earn relatively high incomes use some of their money to pay outsiders to do domestic work. In addition, such women are able to translate earning power into domestic influence. Their increased financial status enables them to get their husbands to do more around the house.

Attitude is the second factor that shrinks the gender gap in domestic labour. The more the husband and wife agree that there *should* be equality in the household division of labour, the more equality there is. Seeing eye to eye on this issue is often linked to both spouses having a postsecondary education (Greenstein, 1996). Thus, if greater equality is going to exist between men and women in doing household chores, two things have to happen: (1) there must be greater equality between men and women in the paid labour force and (2) broader cultural acceptance of the need for gender equality must be achieved.

SPOUSAL VIOLENCE

About 12 percent of police-reported violent crime in Canada involves spousal violence, and 83 percent of victims of spousal violence are women. Women were three times as likely as men to suffer an injury, five times as likely to require medical attention, and five times as likely to report that the violence they experienced caused them to fear for their lives. Compared with men, women are more likely to report being beaten, choked, or threatened with a gun or knife, or having these weapons used against them. Compared with women, men are more likely to report being slapped, having something thrown at them, or being kicked, bitten, or hit (Bunge, 2000; Statistics Canada, 2009d).

Three main types of spousal violence exist (Johnson and Ferraro, 2000):

- *Common couple violence* occurs when partners have an argument and one partner lashes out physically at the other. For a couple that engages in this type of violence, violent acts are unlikely to occur often, escalate over time, or be severe. Both partners are about equally likely to engage in common couple violence, regardless of their gender.

- *Intimate terrorism* is part of a general desire of one partner to control the other. Where one partner engages in intimate terrorism, violent acts are likely to occur often, escalate over time, and be severe. Among heterosexual couples, the aggressor is usually the man.

- *Violent resistance* is the third main type of domestic violence. Among heterosexual couples, it typically involves a woman violently defending herself against a man who has engaged in intimate terrorism.

Gender Inequality and Spousal Violence

For heterosexual couples, spousal violence is associated with the level of gender equality in the family and in the larger society. The higher the level of gender inequality, the greater the frequency of spousal violence. Thus, severe wife assault is more common in lower-class, less highly educated families in which gender inequality tends to be high and men are likely to believe that male domination is justified. Severe wife abuse is also more common among couples who witnessed their mothers being abused and who were themselves abused when they were children, although research suggests that these socialization factors are considerably less influential than was once believed (Gelles, 1997; Simons, Wu, Johnson, and Conger, 1995; Smith, 1990). Still, male domination in both childhood socialization and current family organization increases the likelihood of severe wife assault. In addition, Straus (1994) has shown that wife assault is associated with gender inequality in the larger society. Comparing measures of wife assault and gender inequality in each U.S. state, he found that as gender equality increases—as women and men become more equal in the larger society—wife assault declines. We conclude that for heterosexual couples, the incidence of domestic violence is highest where a big power imbalance between men and women exists, where norms justify the male domination of women, and, to a lesser extent, where early socialization experiences predispose men to behave aggressively toward women.

Summing up, we can say that conflict theorists and feminists have performed a valuable sociological service by emphasizing the importance of power relations in structuring family life. A substantial body of research shows that the gender revolution that has been taking place for nearly half a century has influenced the way we select mates, our reasons for being satisfied or dissatisfied with marriage, our propensity to divorce, the reproductive choices women make, the distribution of housework and child care, variations in the rate of spousal violence—in short, all aspects of family life. As you will now learn, the gender revolution has also created a much greater diversity of family forms.

Family Diversity

HETEROSEXUAL COHABITATION

About 90 percent of Canadians marry at least once, but marriage is becoming less important for some Canadians. Even in 1995, when asked, "In order for you to be happy in life, is it very important, important, not very important, or not at all important to be married?" just two-thirds of Canadian women rated marriage as important or very important. Younger Canadians were less likely than older Canadians to consider marriage important or very important. Those living in Quebec were markedly less likely to do so: 53 percent of women and 59 percent of men in Quebec considered marriage important or very important (Wu, 2000: 65–66). Although living in a common-law relationship may be a prelude to marriage for some people, for others it has become an alternative to legal marriage.

Since the Canadian census first started collecting information on cohabitation in 1981, the number of cohabiting people 15 years of age and older has increased dramatically. The proportion of common-law families in Canada nearly tripled between 1981 and 2006—from 5.6 percent to 15.4 percent of all families. In Quebec, the 2006 figure was fully 35 percent (Statistics Canada, 2009b). Most Canadian women aged 18 to 49 approve of premarital sex and non-marital cohabitation when couples intend to marry at some point in the future. Some 55 percent of women outside Quebec and 73 percent of women in Quebec believe it is acceptable for couples to live together when they have no intention of making a long-term commitment and are simply sexually attracted to each other. In both cases, younger women and women in Quebec are particularly likely to voice such approval (Wu, 2000: 59).

SAME-SEX MARRIAGE AND CIVIL UNIONS

In 2001, the Netherlands became the first country to legalize same-sex marriage. Belgium and Spain soon followed suit. Canada did so in July 2005. Within 10 months, 7465 Canadian same-sex couples got married, 54 percent of them male, 46 percent of them female (see Figure 9.7). South Africa, Norway, and Sweden also now allow same-sex marriage.

Many Western European countries allow homosexuals to register their partnerships under the law in so-called civil unions. Civil unions recognize the partnerships as having some or all of the legal rights of marriage. In the United States, more opposition to registered partnerships and same-sex marriages exists than in Europe and Canada. Dozens of American states have passed laws opposing such unions. A 2008 *Newsweek* poll showed that 31 percent of Americans support same-sex marriage, 32 percent favour civil unions, and 30 percent prefer no legal recognition at all for same-sex couples ("Longitudinal," 2010). Yet, despite continuing opposition to same-sex marriage, the ultimate direction of change in many parts of the world is clear. Amid sharp controversy, the legal and social definition of "family" is being broadened to include cohabiting,

same-sex partners in long-term relationships. This change reflects the fact that most homosexuals, like most heterosexuals, want a long-term, intimate relationship with one other adult (Chauncey, 2005). In fact, in Denmark, where homosexual couples can register partnerships under the law, the divorce rate for registered homosexual couples is lower than for heterosexual married couples (Ontario Consultants on Religious Tolerance, 2000).

Raising Children in Homosexual Families

Some same-sex couples are raising children who (1) were the offspring of previous, heterosexual marriages, (2) were adopted, or (3) resulted from artificial insemination. Many people believe that children brought up in homosexual families will develop a confused sexual identity, exhibit a tendency to become homosexuals themselves, and suffer discrimination from children and adults in the "straight" community. Unfortunately, there is little research in this area and much of it is based on small, unrepresentative samples. Nevertheless, the research findings are consistent. They suggest that children who grow up in homosexual families are much like children who grow up in heterosexual families. For example, a 14-year study assessed 25 young adults who were the offspring of lesbian families and 21 young adults who were the offspring of heterosexual families (Tasker and Golombok, 1997). The researchers found that the two groups were equally well adjusted and displayed little difference in sexual orientation. Two respondents from the lesbian families considered themselves lesbians, whereas all of the respondents from the heterosexual families considered themselves heterosexual. Even violence between same-sex partners occurs at approximately the same rate as it does in heterosexual relationships (Chesley, MacAulay, and Ristock, 1991).

Homosexual and heterosexual families do differ in some respects. Lesbian couples with children record higher satisfaction with their partnerships than do lesbian couples without children. In contrast, among heterosexual couples, it is the childless who record higher marital satisfaction (Koepke, Hare, and Moran, 1992). On average, the partners of lesbian mothers spend more time caring for children than do the husbands of heterosexual mothers. Because children usually benefit from adult attention, this must be considered a plus. Homosexual couples also tend to be more egalitarian than heterosexual couples, sharing most decision making and household duties equally (Rosenbluth, 1997). That is because they tend to reject traditional marriage patterns. The fact that they tend to have similar gender socialization and earn about the same income also encourages equality (Kurdek, 1996; Reimann, 1997). In sum, available research suggests that raising children in lesbian families has no apparent negative consequences for the children. Indeed, there may be some benefits for all family members above the benefits offered by families in which the spouses are heterosexual.

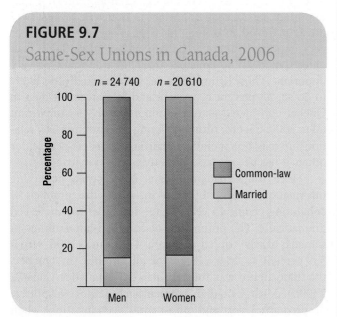

FIGURE 9.7

Same-Sex Unions in Canada, 2006

Source: Statistics Canada. 2009. "Same-sex couples by type of union (married, common-law) and sex, 2006 Census—20% sample data." http://www12.statcan.ca/census-recensement/2006/dp-pd/hlt/97-553/tables/Table4.cfm?Lang=E (retrieved 22 March 2010).

The Canadian Press (Clement Allard)

In 2002, in a precedent-setting move hailed by gay-right activists as the first of its kind in the world, full parental rights were extended to same-sex couples in Quebec. In addition, same-sex couples were granted the same status and obligations as heterosexual married couples when they entered into a civil union. Here, lesbians react as the Quebec legislature passes the law.

LONE-PARENT FAMILIES

During the first half of the twentieth century, lone-parent families were generally the result of the death of one parent (Oderkirk and Lochhead, 1992). Today, solo parenting is usually the product of separation or divorce, after which child custody is typically granted to mothers. In 2006, 16 percent of Canadian families were headed by a lone parent and 81 percent of those families were headed by women.

Sean Bolt/Shutterstock

Poverty is far more prevalent among female-headed single-parent families than among any other type of family. The poverty rate in female-headed single-parent families is more than double the rate in male-headed single parent families (refer back to Figure 6.5).

Low levels of social support, family dysfunction, and parental depression all have significant negative effects on children and are more common in low-income households (National Council of Welfare, 1999b). Child poverty is related to school failure, negative involvement with parents, stunted growth, reduced cognitive abilities, limited emotional development, and a high likelihood of dropping out of school (Duncan, Yeung, Brooks-Gunn, and Smith, 1998; Fields and Smith, 1998).

ZERO-CHILD FAMILIES

In Canada, what we prefer to call "zero-child families" are increasingly common. Our admittedly clumsy term seems necessary because the alternatives are so value laden: a "childless family" implies that a family without children lacks something it should have, while the more recent "child-free family" suggests that a family without a child is unencumbered and that a child is therefore a burden. To maintain neutrality, we resort to clumsiness.

Roughly a fifth of women between the ages of 40 and 44 have never given birth (Lamanna and Riedmann, 2003: 369). To explain this fact we must first recognize that not having a child may be the result of circumstances beyond a couple's control. For example, one or both partners may be infertile, and some evidence suggests that infertility is a growing issue, perhaps because of chemical pollutants in the air and water. It seems that not having a child is more often a matter of choice, however, and the main reasons for the increasing prevalence of zero-child families are the rising cost of raising a child and the growth of attractive alternatives.

Just how expensive are children? In 2004, the cost of raising a child in Manitoba to the age of 18 was about $167 000 (Canadian Council on Social Development, 2007). Add the cost of college or university and that is a lot of money that could be spent on investments, the couple's own education, and other desirable things. Mothers bear most of the cost of lost economic opportunities. Usually, they are the ones whose careers are disrupted when they decide to stay home to raise children and who lose income, benefits, and pension payments in the process. Couples also incur non-economic costs when they have a child, the most important of which is stress. The birth of

a child requires that couples do more work in the home, give up free time and time alone together, develop an efficient daily routine, and divide responsibilities. All this adds sources of disagreement and tension to daily life, so it is little wonder that marital satisfaction declines with a child in the house, as noted earlier.

Alternative attractions decrease the desire of some couples to have a child. People with high income, high education, and professional and managerial occupations are most likely to have zero-child families. Such people tend to place an especially high value on mobility, careers, and leisure-time pursuits. Usually, they are neither frustrated nor unhappy that they do not have a child. Despite their tendency to feel negatively stereotyped as "selfish," they tend to be more satisfied with their marriage than are couples with a child (Lamanna and Riedmann, 2003: 380).

LO⁶ Family Policy

Having discussed several aspects of the decline of the traditional nuclear family and the proliferation of diverse family forms, we can now return to the big question posed at the beginning of this chapter: Is the decline of the nuclear family a bad thing for society? Said differently, do two-parent families—particularly those with stay-at-home moms—provide the kind of discipline, role models, help, and middle-class lifestyle that children need to stay out of trouble with the law and grow up to become well-adjusted, productive members of society? Conversely, are family forms other than the traditional nuclear family the main source of teenage crime, poverty, welfare dependency, and other social ills?

The answer suggested by research is clear: yes and no (Houseknecht and Sastry, 1996; Popenoe, 1996; Sandqvist and Andersson, 1992). Yes, the decline of the traditional nuclear family can be a source of many social problems. No, it doesn't have to be that way.

The United States is a good example of how social problems can emerge from nuclear family decline. Sweden

210 CHAPTER 9 Families

NEL

TABLE 9.3

The "Decline" of the Nuclear Family and the Well-Being of Children: The United States and Sweden Compared

Indicators of Nuclear Family "Decline"	United States	Sweden	#1 "Decline"
Median age at first marriage			
Men	26.5	29.4	Sweden
Women	24.4	27.1	Sweden
Percentage of 45–49 population never married			
Men	5.7	15.4	Sweden
Women	5.1	9.1	Sweden
Non-marital birth rate	25.7	50.9	Sweden
One-parent households with children < 15 as % of all households with children < 15	25.0	18.0	U.S.A.
% of mothers in labour force with children < 3	51.0	84.0	Sweden
Total fertility rate	2.0	2.0	Tie
Average household size	2.7	2.2	Sweden

Indicators of Child Well-Being	United States	Sweden	#1 Well-Being
Mean reading performance score at 14	5.14	5.29	Sweden
% of children in poverty			
Single-mother households	59.5	5.2	Sweden
Two-parent households	11.1	2.2	Sweden
Death rate of infants from abuse	9.8	0.9	Sweden
Suicide rate for children 15–19 (per 100 000)	11.1	6.2	Sweden
Juvenile delinquency rate (per 100 000)	11.6	12.0	U.S.A.
Juvenile drug offence rate (per 100 000)	558.0	241.0	Sweden

Source: Adapted from Houseknecht and Sastry (1996).; Houseknecht, Sharon K., and Jaya Sastry. 1996. "Family 'Decline' and Child Well-Being: A Comparative Assessment." *Journal of Marriage and the Family* 58: 726–39.

is a good example of how such problems can be averted. Table 9.3 illustrates this. On almost all indicators of nuclear family decline, Sweden leads the United States. In Sweden, a smaller percentage of people get married. People usually get married at a later age than in the United States. The proportion of births outside of marriage is twice as high as in the United States. A much larger proportion of Swedish than American women with children under the age of three work in the paid labour force. Significantly, however, on almost all measures of children's well-being, Sweden also leads the United States. Thus, in Sweden, children enjoy higher average reading test scores than children in the United States do. The poverty rate in two-parent families is only one-tenth the U.S. rate, while the poverty rate in single-parent families is only one-twelfth as high. The rate of infant abuse is one-eleventh the U.S. rate. Overall,

then, the decline of the traditional nuclear family has gone further in Sweden than in the United States, but children are much better off on average (Houseknecht and Sastry, 1996). How is this possible?

One explanation is that Sweden has something the United States lacks: a substantial family support policy. When a child is born in Sweden, a parent is entitled to a year of parental leave at 80 percent of his or her salary and an additional 90 days at a flat rate. Fathers can take 10 days of leave with pay when the baby is born. Parents are entitled to free consultations at "well baby clinics." Like all citizens of Sweden, they receive free health care from the state-run system. Temporary parental benefits are available for parents with a sick child under the age of 12. One parent can take up to 60 days off per sick child per year at 80 percent of salary. All parents can send their children to heavily government-subsidized, high-quality daycare. Finally, Sweden offers its citizens generous direct cash payments based on the number of children in each family.[1]

Among industrialized countries, the United States stands at the other extreme. Since 1993, a parent has been entitled to 12 weeks of *unpaid* parental leave. Until recently 15 percent of Americans had no health care coverage; this figure will fall in the next few years because of new laws. Health care is at a low standard for many millions more. There is no system of state daycare and no direct cash payments to families based on the number of children they have. The value of the dependent deduction on income tax has fallen nearly 50 percent in current dollars since the 1940s. Thus, when an unwed Swedish woman has a baby, she knows she can rely on state institutions to maintain her standard of living and help give her child an enriching social and educational environment. When an unwed American woman has a baby, she is pretty much on her own. She stands a good chance of sinking into poverty, with all the negative consequences that has for her and her child.

In a study of 33 countries, Canada tied for fifth place on the number of weeks it allows new parents to take off work, but stood in fifteenth place in terms of the generosity of its maternity leave payments (Smyth, 2003). There are enough regulated daycare spaces for only a fifth of Canadian children up to age 12, and on average governments allocate $468 per year per child for child care. These averages are far below compar-

able figures for Western European countries. Moreover, they are boosted by Quebec, where regulated daycare spaces are twice as plentiful as in the rest of the country, and government support for regulated daycare is more than three times as generous (look back at Figure 8.7). Overall, Canada stands between the United States and Sweden. Much of the debate surrounding family policy in Canada concerns whether we should move in the direction of the American or the Swedish model.

In Canada, three criticisms are commonly raised against generous family support policies. First, some people say these policies encourage long-term dependence on welfare, illegitimate births, and the breakup of two-parent families. However, research shows that the divorce rate and the rate of births to unmarried mothers are not higher when welfare payments are more generous (Albelda and Tilly, 1997). Moreover, not all people who prefer to work are able to find full-time, secure employment, and part-time jobs offer little in the way of job security, decent wages, or benefits. Some provinces, such as Ontario, have incorporated "workfare" in their welfare systems. Workfare requires able-bodied people to do specific jobs as a condition of receiving welfare. However, most workfare jobs are menial dead-end jobs that are unlikely to lead to permanent employment. Finally, it is surely absurd to believe that living on welfare represents a preferred lifestyle. For the overwhelming majority of welfare recipients, it indicates the loss of a job, spouse, or health—personal tragedies to which none of us is immune (National Council of Welfare, 1999b: 68).

A second criticism of generous family support policies focuses on child care. Some critics say that non-family child care is bad for children under the age of three. In their view, only parents can provide the love, interaction, and intellectual stimulation infants and toddlers need for proper social, cognitive, and moral development. However, when studies compare family care and daycare involving a strong curriculum, a stimulating environment, plenty of caregiver warmth, low turnover of well-trained staff, and a low ratio of caregivers to children, they find that

Painting class in a state-subsidized daycare facility in Stockholm, Sweden.

© Jonathan Blair/Corbis

daycare has no negative consequences for children over the age of one (Clarke-Stewart, Gruber, and Fitzgerald, 1994; Harvey, 1999). Research also shows that daycare has some benefits, notably enhancing a child's ability to make friends. The benefits of high-quality daycare are even more evident in low-income families, which often cannot provide the kind of stimulating environment offered by high-quality daycare.

The third criticism lodged against generous family support policies is that they are expensive and have to be paid for by high taxes. That is true. Swedes are more highly taxed than the citizens of any other country. They have made the political decision to pay high taxes, partly to avoid the social problems and associated costs that sometimes emerge when the traditional nuclear family is replaced with other family forms and no institutions are available to help family members in need. The Swedish experience teaches us, then, that there is a clear trade-off between expensive family support policies and low taxes. It is impossible to have both, and the degree to which any country favours one or the other is a political choice.

Note

1. We are grateful to Gregg Olsen, Department of Sociology, University of Manitoba, for some of this information.

10
Religion and Education

LEARNING OBJECTIVES:

LO¹ The structure of society and one's place in it influence one's religious beliefs and practices.

LO² Under different circumstances religion can create societal cohesion, social conflict, and social inequality.

LO³ Religion governs fewer aspects of most people's lives than in the past, but recently, a religious revival has taken place in many parts of the world.

LO⁴ A religious upbringing and advancing years increase religious observance.

LO⁵ Secular schools have substantially replaced the church and religious schools as educational institutions.

LO⁶ The educational system often creates social cohesion. In the process, it also reinforces existing class, racial, and ethnic inequalities.

LO¹ Religion

In 1902, psychologist William James observed that religion is the common human response to the fact that we all stand at the edge of an abyss. It helps us to cope with the terrifying fact that we must die (James, 1976 [1902]: 116). It offers us immortality, the promise of better times to come, and the security of benevolent spirits who watch over us. It provides meaning and purpose in a world that might otherwise seem cruel and senseless.

The motivation for religion may be psychological, as James argued. However, the content and intensity of our religious beliefs, and the form and frequency of our religious practices, are influenced by the structure of society and our place in it. Why does one religion predominate here, another there? Why is religious belief stronger at one time than at another? Under what circumstances does religion act as a source of social stability, and under what circumstances does it act as a force for social change? Are we becoming more or less religious? These are all questions that have occupied sociologists of religion, and we will touch on all of them here. Note that we will not have anything to say about the truth of religion in general or the value of any religious belief or practice in particular. These are questions of faith, not science. They lie outside the province of sociology. As the New Testament says, "faith is the substance of things hoped for, the evidence of things not seen" (Hebrews 11:1).

The cover of *Time* magazine once asked "Is God dead?" As a sociological observation, the idea that God is dead is preposterous. In Canada, more than 80 percent of adults and 70 percent of teenagers agree with the statement "God or a higher power cares about you" (Bibby, 2001: 252). By this measure (and by other measures we will examine below), God is still very much alive in Canada. Nonetheless, as we will show, the scope of religious authority has declined in Canada and many other parts of the world. That is, religion governs fewer aspects of life than it used to. Some Canadians still look to religion to deal with all of life's problems. But increasingly more Canadians expect that religion can help them deal with only a restricted range of spiritual issues. Other institutions—medicine, psychiatry, criminal justice, education, and so forth—have grown in importance as the scope of religious authority has declined.

Foremost among these other institutions is the system of education. Organized religion used to be the main purveyor of formal knowledge and the most important agent of socialization apart from the family. Today, the education system is the main purveyor of formal knowledge and the most important agent of socialization apart from the family. It is the partial displacement of religion by the educational system that justifies our analyzing religion and education side by side in a single chapter.

Although Canadians hold a strong belief in the importance of education, we have only a moderate level of confidence in our public education system. Just 44 percent of Canadians are satisfied with the educational system and most Canadians think it is in worse shape now than it was 25 years ago. Our chief concerns are low academic performance, lack of discipline and respect, the future employability of students, and equality of opportunity (Bricker and Greenspon, 2001: 162–5). We will address these issues below, paying particular attention to the way they are related to the larger problem of social inequality.

By taking this approach, we follow tradition. Sociologists of education have long been interested in the relationship between education and inequality. Some say that education promotes upward mobility. Others argue that education reproduces inequality generation after generation. As you will see, the evidence offers stronger support for the second argument. Before tackling these issues, however, we first examine the influence of society on religion and the influence of religion on society.

Classical Approaches in the Sociology of Religion

LO² DURKHEIM'S FUNCTIONALIST APPROACH

More than one person has said that hockey is Canada's "national religion." Do you agree with that opinion? Before making up your mind, consider that 80 percent of Canadians tuned in to at least part of the gold medal men's hockey game between Canada and the United States at the 2010 Vancouver Winter Olympics, making them the largest TV audience in Canadian history ("Gold Medal," 2010). As when Canada's men's hockey team came from behind to defeat the Soviets in 1972, the nation virtually came to a standstill.

Few events attract the attention and enthusiasm of Canadians as much as the annual Stanley Cup finals. Apart from drawing a huge audience, the Stanley Cup playoffs generate a sense of what Durkheim would have called "collective effervescence." That is, the Stanley Cup finals excite us by making us feel part of something larger than us: the Montreal Canadiens, the Edmonton Oilers, the Toronto Maple Leafs, the Vancouver Canucks, the Calgary Flames, the Ottawa Senators, the institution of Canadian hockey, the spirit of Canada itself. As celebrated Canadian writer Roch Carrier (1979: 77) wrote in his famous short story, "The Hockey Sweater," "School was . . . a quiet place where we could prepare for the next hockey game, lay out our next strategies. As for church . . . there we forgot school and dreamed about the next hockey game. Through our daydreams it might happen that we would recite a prayer: we would ask God to help us play as well as Maurice Richard." For many hours each year, hockey enthusiasts transcend their everyday lives and experience intense enjoyment by sharing the sentiments and values of a larger collective. In their fervour, they banish thoughts of their own mortality. They gain a glimpse of eternity as they immerse themselves in institutions that will outlast them and athletic feats that people will remember for generations to come.

So, do you think the Stanley Cup playoffs are a religious event? There is no god of the Stanley Cup (although the nickname of Canadian hockey legend Wayne Gretzky—The Great One—certainly suggests that he transcended the status of a mere mortal). Nonetheless, the Stanley Cup playoffs may meet Durkheim's definition of a religious experience. Durkheim said that when people live together, they come to share common sentiments and values. These common sentiments and values form a collective conscience that is larger than any individual. On occasion, we experience the collective conscience directly. This causes us to distinguish the secular everyday world of the profane from the religious, transcendent world of the sacred. We designate certain objects as symbolizing the sacred. Durkheim called these objects totems. We invent set practices to connect us with the sacred. Durkheim referred to these practices as rituals.

The effect (or function) of rituals and of religion as a whole is to reinforce social solidarity, said Durkheim. The ritual heightens our experience of belonging to certain groups, increases our respect for certain institutions, and strengthens our belief in certain ideas. Thus,

Religious rituals are set practices that help unite people into a moral community.

the game is a sacred event, in Durkheim's terms. It cements society in the way Durkheim said all religions do (Durkheim, 1976 [1915/1912]). Durkheim would have found support for his theory in research showing that, in the United States, the suicide rate dips during the two days preceding Super Bowl Sunday and on Super Bowl Sunday itself, just as it does for the last day of the World Series, Christmas Day, and other collective celebrations (Curtis, Loy, and Karnilowicz, 1986). He would have found additional support in the finding that in Quebec, the suicide rate among young men is higher when the Montreal Canadiens are not in the Stanley Cup playoffs than when they are (Trovato, 1998). These patterns are consistent with Durkheim's theory of suicide, which predicts a lower suicide rate when social solidarity increases (see Chapter 1, A Sociological Compass).

RELIGION, FEMINIST THEORY, AND CONFLICT THEORY

Durkheim's theory of religion is a functionalist account. It offers useful insights into the role of religion in society. Yet conflict and feminist theorists lodge two main criticisms against it. First, it overemphasizes religion's role in maintaining social cohesion. In reality, religion often incites social conflict. Second, it ignores the fact that when religion does increase social cohesion, it often reinforces social inequality.

Religion and Social Inequality

Consider first the role of major world religions and social inequality (see Figure 10.1 on page 222 and Table 10.1 on

pages 218–21). Little historical evidence helps us understand the social conditions that gave rise to the first world religions, Judaism and Hinduism, 3800 to 4000 years ago. But we know enough about the rise of Buddhism, Christianity, and Islam between 2700 and 1500 years ago to say that the impulse to find a better world is often encouraged by adversity in this one. We also know that Moses, Jesus, Muhammad, and Buddha all promoted a message of equality and freedom. Finally, we know that over generations, the charismatic leadership of the world religions became "routinized." The **routinization of charisma** is Weber's term for the transformation of divine enlightenment into a permanent feature of everyday life. It involves turning religious inspiration into a stable social institution—a church—with defined roles, such as interpreters of the divine message, teachers, dues-paying laypeople, and so forth. The routinization of charisma typically makes religion less responsive to the needs of ordinary people, and it often supports social inequalities and injustices, as you will now see.

Religion and the Subordination of Women

It was Marx who first stressed how religion often tranquillizes the underprivileged into accepting their lot in life. He called religion "the opium of the people" (Marx, 1970 [1843]: 131). We can draw evidence for Marx's interpretation from many times, places, and institutions. For example, the major world religions have traditionally placed women in a subordinate position. Catholic priests and Muslim mullahs must be men, as must Jewish rabbis in the Conservative and Orthodox denominations. Women have been allowed to serve as Protestant ministers only since the mid-nineteenth century and as rabbis in the more liberal branches of Judaism since the 1970s. There are also many scriptural examples of the subordination of women, including the following:

> **routinization of charisma** Weber's term for the transformation of the unique gift of divine enlightenment into a permanent feature of everyday life. It involves turning religious inspiration into a stable social institution with defined roles (interpreters of the divine message, teachers, dues-paying laypeople, and so on).

TABLE 10.1
The Five World Religions: Origins, Beliefs, and Divisions

	Origins
Judaism	Judaism originated about 4000 years ago in what is now Iraq, when Abraham first asserted the existence of just one God. About 800 years later, Moses led the Jews out of Egyptian bondage. The emancipation of the Jews from slavery was a defining moment in the history of Judaism.
Christianity	Christianity originated about 35 C.E. in what is now Israel. Jesus, a poor Jew, criticized the Judaism of his time for its external conformity to tradition and ritual at the expense of developing a true relationship to God as demanded by the prophets.
Islam	Islam originated about 600 C.E. in what is now Saudi Arabia. The powerful merchants of Mecca had become greedy and corrupt, impoverishing and enslaving many people. Also, fear grew that the Persian and Roman Empires might soon fall, bringing the end of the world. Into this crisis stepped Muhammad, who claimed to have visions from God.

Beliefs

The central teachings rest on belief in one God (*Yahweh*) and on the idea that God sanctions freedom and equality. The 613 divine commandments (*mitzvot*) mentioned in the Five Books of Moses (Torah) form the core of orthodox Jewish practice. The *mitzvot* include prescriptions for justice, righteousness, and observance: rest and pray on the Sabbath, honour the old and the wise, do not wrong a stranger in buying or selling, do not seek revenge or hold a grudge, and so on. The Torah forms part of the Old Testament.

Believe in God and love him; love your neighbour—these are the two main lessons of Jesus. These teachings were novel because they demanded that people match outward performance with inner conviction. It was not enough not to murder; people should not even hate. Nor was it enough not to commit adultery; no one should even lust after a neighbour's wife (Matthew V, 21–30). These teachings made Jesus anti-authoritarian and even revolutionary. Admonishing people to love their neighbours impressed on them the need to emancipate slaves and women. Christians retained the Jewish Bible as the Old Testament, adding the gospels and letters of the apostles as the New Testament.

People who profess Islam have five duties. At least once in their life they must recite the Muslim creed aloud, correctly, with full understanding, and with heartfelt belief. (The creed is: "There is no god but Allah and Muhammad is his prophet.") Five times a day they must worship in a religious service. They must fast from sunrise to sunset every day during the ninth month of the lunar calendar (Ramadan). They must give charity to the poor. And at least once in their life they must make a pilgrimage to the holy city of Mecca. Muhammad's teachings were written down in the Koran.

Divisions

In seventeenth-century Eastern Europe, ecstatic *Chasidic* sects broke away from the bookish Judaism of the time. In nineteenth-century Germany, the Reform movement allowed prayer in German, the integration of women in worship, and so on. Orthodox Judaism was a reaction against the liberalizing tendencies of Reform and involved a return to traditional observance. Conservative Judaism crystallized in Britain and the United States in the nineteenth century to reconcile what its practitioners regarded as the positive elements in Orthodoxy with the dynamism of Reform. Reconstructionism is a liberal twentieth-century movement known for its social activism and gender egalitarianism.

In 312 C.E., the Roman Emperor converted to Christianity and turned Christianity into a state religion, after which the Church became the dominant institution in Europe. In the sixteenth century, Martin Luther, a German priest, challenged the Christian establishment by seeking to establish a more personal relationship between the faithful and God. His ideas quickly captured the imagination of half of Europe and led to the split of Christianity into Catholicism and Protestantism. In the Middle Ages, Christianity had split into Western and Eastern halves, the former centred in Rome, the latter in Constantinople (now Istanbul, Turkey). Various Orthodox churches today derive from the Eastern tradition. Protestantism has been especially prone to splintering because it emphasizes the individual's relationship to God rather than a central authority. Today, there are hundreds of different Protestant churches.

A dispute broke out over how the followers of Muhammad could identify his successor. The Sunni argued that the successor should be an elected member of a certain Meccan tribe. The Shia claimed that the successor should be Muhammad's direct descendant. Today, most Muslims are Sunni. The Shia, concentrated in Iran and southern Iraq, are generally more conservative and fundamentalist. Islam spread rapidly in the Middle East, Africa, and parts of Europe. It began a great cultural flowering and considerable religious tolerance. Wahabbism, a Sunni fundamentalist movement, originated in the eighteenth century and became the state religion of what is now Saudi Arabia. Shia subgroups include the "Twelvers" (about 80 percent of the Shia) and the Ismailis. Sufism is a mystical sect within Islam.

(continued)

TABLE 10.1 (continued)
The Five World Religions: Origins, Beliefs, and Divisions

	Origins
Hinduism	Hinduism originated about 2000 B.C.E. in India in unknown circumstances. It had no single founder.
Buddhism	About 600 B.C.E., Gautama Buddha objected to the stale ritualism of Hinduism and sought to achieve a direct relationship with God. He rejected Hindu ideas of caste and reincarnation, and offered a new way for everyone to achieve spiritual enlightenment, promising salvation to everyone.

Sources: Brown (1996); Flood (1996); Gombrich (1996); Gottwald (1979); Hodgson (1974); Lapidus (2002); Lopez (2001); McManners (1990); Robinson and Johnson (1997); Rodinson (1996); Roth (1961); Schwartz (2003).

Beliefs

Hinduism has many gods, all of them thought to be aspects of the one true God. The major texts are epic poems, such as the *Bhagavad Gita*. Only the body dies in Hindu belief. The soul returns in a new form after death. The form in which it returns depends on how the person lived his or her life. Hindus believe that people who live in a way that is appropriate to their position in society will live better future lives. People can reach a state of spiritual perfection (*nirvana*) that allows the soul to escape the cycle of birth and rebirth, and reunite with God. However, people who do not live in a way that is appropriate to their position in society supposedly live an inferior life when they are reincarnated. These ideas made vertical social mobility nearly impossible because, according to Hindu belief, striving to move out of your station in life ensures reincarnation in a lower form.

Buddha promoted the "Four Noble Truths": (1) Life is suffering. Moments of joy are overshadowed by sorrow. (2) All suffering derives from desire. We suffer when we fail to achieve what we want. (3) Suffering ceases by training ourselves to eliminate desire. (4) We can eliminate desire by behaving morally, focusing intently on our feelings and thoughts, meditating, and achieving wisdom. Buddhism does not presume the existence of one true God. Rather, it holds out the possibility of everyone becoming a god of sorts. Similarly, it does not have a central church or text, such as the Bible.

Divisions

Unlike the Western religions, Hinduism assimilates rather than excludes other religious beliefs and practices. Traditionally, Western religions rejected non-believers unless they converted. God tells Moses on Mount Sinai: "You shall have no other gods before me." In contrast, in the *Bhagavad Gita*, Krishna says that "whatever god a man worships, it is I who answers the prayer." This attitude of acceptance helped Hinduism absorb many of the ancient religions of the peoples of the Indian subcontinent. It also explains why there are such wide regional and class variations in Hindu beliefs and practices. Hinduism as it is practised bears the stamp of many other religions.

Buddhism is notable for the diversity of its beliefs and practices. Buddhism spread rapidly across Asia after India's ruler adopted it as his own religion in the third century B.C.E. He sent missionaries to convert people in Tibet, Cambodia (Kampuchea), Nepal, Sri Lanka (formerly Ceylon), Myanmar (formerly Burma), China, Korea, and Japan. The influence of Buddhism in the land of its birth started to die out after the fifth century C.E. and is negligible in India today. One of the reasons for the popularity of Buddhism in East and Southeast Asia is that Buddhism is able to coexist with local religious practices. Unlike Western religions, Buddhism does not insist on holding a monopoly on religious truth.

FIGURE 10.1
The World's Predominant Religions

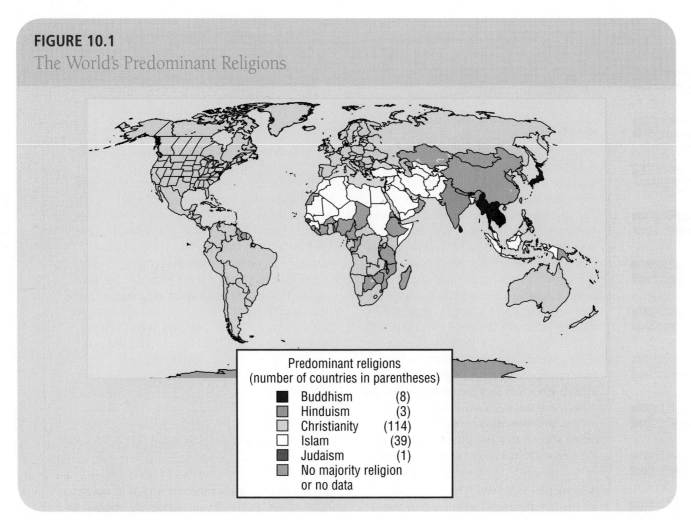

Predominant religions
(number of countries in parentheses)

■	Buddhism	(8)
▨	Hinduism	(3)
▢	Christianity	(114)
□	Islam	(39)
▨	Judaism	(1)
▨	No majority religion or no data	

This map shows the predominant religion in each of the world's countries, defined as the religion to which more than 50 percent of a country's population adheres.

Source: Adherents.com (2001).

• Corinthians in the *New Testament* emphasizes that "women should keep silence in the churches. For they are not permitted to speak, but should be subordinate, as even the law says. If there is anything they desire to know, let them ask their husbands at home. For it is shameful for a woman to speak in church."

• The *Sidur*, the Jewish prayer book, includes this morning prayer, which is recited by Orthodox and ultra-Orthodox men: "Blessed are you, Lord our God, King of the Universe, who did not make me a woman."

• The *Koran*, the holy book of Islam, contains a Book of Women in which it is written that "righteous women are devoutly obedient. . . . As to those women on whose part you fear disloyalty and ill-conduct, admonish them, refuse to share their beds, beat them."

church A bureaucratic religious organization that has accommodated itself to mainstream society and culture.

Religion and Class Inequality

If, after becoming routinized, religion has often supported gender inequality, it has also often supported class inequality. In medieval and early modern Europe, Christianity promoted the view that the Almighty ordains class inequality, promising rewards to the lowly in the afterlife ("the meek shall inherit the earth"). The Hindu scriptures say that the highest caste sprang from the lips of the supreme creator, the next highest caste from his shoulders, the next highest from his thighs, and the lowest, "polluted" caste from his feet. They warn that if people attempt to achieve upward mobility, they will be reincarnated as animals. And the Koran says that social inequality is due to the will of Allah (Ossowski, 1963: 19–20).

Religion and Social Conflict

In the sociological sense of the term, a **church** is any bureaucratic religious organization that has accommodated itself

to mainstream society and culture. As we have seen, church authorities often support gender and class inequality. However, religiously inspired protest against inequality often erupts from below.

A famous example of such protest involves the role of black churches in spearheading the American civil rights movement during the 1950s and 1960s (Morris, 1984). Their impact was both organizational and inspirational. Organizationally, black churches supplied the ministers who formed the civil rights movement's leadership and the congregations whose members marched, boycotted, and engaged in other forms of protest. Additionally, Christian doctrine inspired the protesters. Perhaps their most powerful religious idea was that blacks, like the Jews in Egypt, were slaves who would be freed. (It was, after all, Michael—regarded by Christians as the patron saint of the Jews—who rowed the boat ashore.) Some white segregationists reacted strongly against efforts at integration, often meeting the peaceful protesters with deadly violence. But the American South was never the same again. Religion had helped promote the conflict needed to make the South a more egalitarian and racially integrated place.

Closer to home, it is worth remembering the important role played in the creation of our medicare system and our social welfare network by the radical Christianity of the early twentieth-century Social Gospel movement. The Social Gospel movement took on force in the depths of the Great Depression (1929–39). It emphasized that Christians should be as concerned with improving the here and now as with life in the hereafter. The efforts of Tommy Douglas, a Baptist minister, the leader of the Co-operative Commonwealth Federation (precursor of the New Democratic Party), and the father of socialized medicine in Canada, exemplify the Social Gospel concern with social justice. In Canada too, then, religion has sometimes promoted conflict and change.

In sum, religion can maintain social order under some circumstances, as Durkheim said. When it does so, however, it often reinforces social inequality. Moreover, under other circumstances religion can promote social conflict.

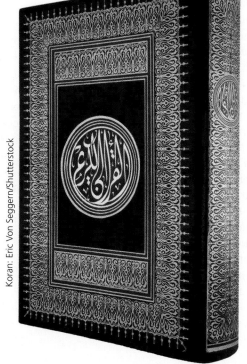

WEBER AND THE PROBLEM OF SOCIAL CHANGE: A SYMBOLIC INTERACTIONIST INTERPRETATION

If Durkheim highlighted the way religion contributes to social order, Max Weber stressed the way religion can contribute to social change. Weber captured the core of his argument in a memorable image: if history is like a train, pushed along its tracks by economic and political interests, then religious ideas are like railroad switches, determining exactly which tracks the train will follow (Weber, 1946: 280).

Weber's most famous illustration of his thesis is his short book, *The Protestant Ethic and Spirit of Capitalism.* Like Marx, Weber was interested in explaining the rise of modern capitalism. Again like Marx, he was prepared to recognize the "fundamental importance of the economic factor" in his explanation (Weber, 1958 [1904–5]: 26). But Weber was also bent on proving the one-sidedness of any exclusively economic interpretation. He did so by offering what we would today call a symbolic interactionist interpretation of religion. True, the term *symbolic interactionism* was not introduced into sociology until more than half a century after Weber wrote *The Protestant Ethic.*

Bruce Rolff/Shutterstock

Yet Weber's focus on the worldly significance of the *meanings* people attach to religious ideas makes him a forerunner of the symbolic interactionist tradition.

For specifically religious reasons, wrote Weber, followers of the Protestant theologian John Calvin stressed the need to engage in intense worldly activity and to display industry, punctuality, and frugality in their everyday life. In the view of such men as John Wesley and Benjamin Franklin, people could reduce their religious doubts and ensure a state of grace by working diligently and living simply. Many Protestants took up this idea. Weber called it the Protestant ethic (Weber, 1958 [1904–5]: 183). According to Weber, the Protestant ethic had wholly unexpected economic consequences. Where it took root, and where economic conditions were favourable, early capitalist enterprise grew most robustly.

Subsequent research showed that the correlation between the Protestant ethic and the strength of capitalist development is weaker than Weber thought. In some places, Catholicism has coexisted with vigorous capitalist growth and Protestantism with relative economic stagnation (Samuelsson, 1961 [1957]). Nonetheless, Weber's treatment of the religious factor underlying social change is a useful corrective to Durkheim's emphasis on religion as a source of social stability. Along with Durkheim's work, Weber's contribution stands as one of the most important insights into the influence of religion on society.

> **secularization thesis** Theory that religious institutions, actions, and consciousness are on the decline worldwide.

LO³ The Rise, Decline, and Partial Revival of Religion

SECULARIZATION

In 1651, British political philosopher Thomas Hobbes described life as "poore, nasty, brutish, and short" (Hobbes, 1968 [1651]: 150). The standard of living in medieval and early modern Europe was abysmally low. On average, a person lived only about 35 years. The forces of nature and human affairs seemed entirely unpredictable. In this context, magic was popular. It offered easy answers to mysterious, painful, and capricious events.

As material conditions improved, popular belief in magic, astrology, and witchcraft gradually lost ground (Thomas, 1971). Christianity substantially replaced them. The better and more predictable times made Europeans more open to the teachings of organized religion. In addition, the Church campaigned vigorously to stamp out opposing belief systems and practices. The persecution of witches in this era was partly an effort to eliminate competition and establish a Christian monopoly over spiritual life.

The Church succeeded in its efforts. In medieval and early modern Europe, Christianity became a powerful presence in religious affairs, music, art, architecture, literature, and philosophy. Popes and saints were the rock musicians and movie stars of their day. The Church was the centre of life in both its spiritual and its worldly dimensions. Church authority was supreme in marriage, education, morality, economic affairs, politics, and so forth. European countries proclaimed official state religions. They persecuted members of religious minorities.

In contrast, a few hundred years later, Max Weber remarked on how the world had become thoroughly "disenchanted." By the turn of the twentieth century, he said, scientific and other forms of rationalism were replacing religious authority. His observations formed the basis of what came to be known as the secularization thesis, undoubtedly the most widely accepted argument in the sociology of religion until the 1990s. According to the secularization thesis, religious institutions, actions, and consciousness are unlikely to disappear, but they are certainly on the decline worldwide (Tschannen, 1991).

RELIGIOUS REVIVAL AND RELIGIOUS FUNDAMENTALISM

Despite the consensus about secularization that was evident in the 1980s, many sociologists modified their judgments in the 1990s. One reason for the change was that accumulated survey evidence showed that religion was not in an advanced state of decay. Actually, in many places, it was in robust health (see Figure 10.2). In Canada, 45 percent of Canadians said they attended religious services about once a week or more often in 2005. True, that figure was down by more than 20 percent from the 1940s, yet in 2005, 82 percent of Canadians still said they believed in God—49 percent definitely, and 33 percent with occasional doubt (Clark, 2003: 2; Bibby, 2011: 316).

The second reason many sociologists have modified their views about secularization is that an intensification of religious belief and practice has taken place among some people in recent decades. For example, since the 1960s, fundamentalist religious organizations have increased their membership. In North America, this tendency has been especially pronounced among Protestants (Finke and Starke, 1992). **Fundamentalists** interpret their scriptures literally,

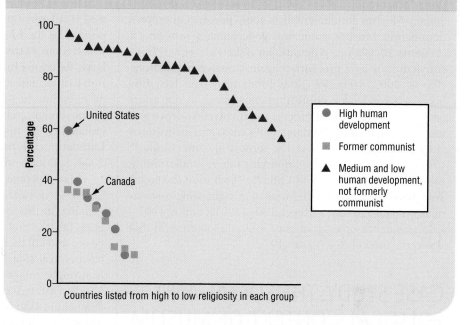

FIGURE 10.2
Percentage of People Who Think Religion Is Very Important, 44 Countries, 2002

Countries listed from high to low religiosity in each group

Legend:
- High human development
- Former communist
- Medium and low human development, not formerly communist

This figure is derived from a survey of 38 000 people in 44 countries. (Poland is a former communist country and the UN ranks it 37th in its list of 53 countries in the "high human development" group. It is classified here as a former communist country.)

Sources: Pew Research Center (2002); United Nations (2002).

seek to establish a direct, personal relationship with the higher being(s) they worship, and are relatively intolerant of non-fundamentalists (Hunter, 1991). Fundamentalists often support conservative social and political issues (Bruce, 1988).

During the same period, religious movements became dominant forces in many other countries. Hindu nationalists formed the government in India from 1998 to 2004. Jewish fundamentalists were always important players in Israeli political life, often holding the balance of power in Israeli

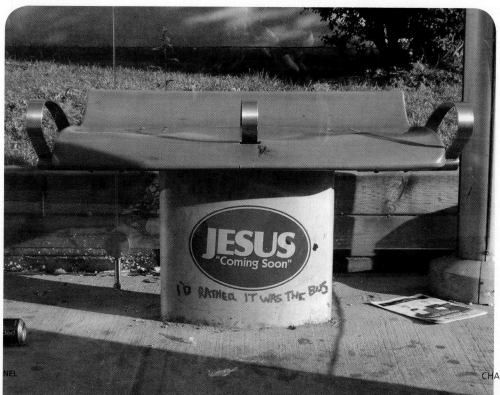

fundamentalists People who interpret their scriptures literally, seek to establish a direct, personal relationship with the higher being(s) they worship, and are relatively intolerant of non-fundamentalists.

governments, but they have become even more influential in recent years (Kimmerling, 2001: 173–207). A revival of Muslim fundamentalism began in Iran in the 1970s. Muslim fundamentalism then swept much of the Middle East, Africa, and parts of Asia. In Iran, Afghanistan, and Sudan, Muslim fundamentalists took power. Other predominantly Muslim countries' governments introduced elements of Islamic religious law (*shari'a*), either from conviction or as a precaution against restive populations (Lewis, 2002: 106). Religious fundamentalism has thus become a worldwide political phenomenon. In not a few cases it has taken extreme forms and involved violence as a means of establishing fundamentalist ideas and institutions (Juergensmeyer, 2000). At the same time, the Catholic Church played a critically important role in undermining communism in Poland, and Catholic "liberation theology" animated the successful fight against right-wing governments in Latin America (Kepel, 1994 [1991]; Smith, 1991). All these developments amount to a religious revival that was quite unexpected in, say, 1970.

CASE STUDY: THE SOCIAL AND POLITICAL CONTEXT OF MUSLIM FUNDAMENTALISM

In 1972, Robert Brym was finishing his B.A. at the Hebrew University of Jerusalem. One May morning he switched on the radio to discover that a massacre had taken place at Lod (now Ben Gurion) International Airport, just 42 kilometres from his apartment. Three Japanese men dressed in business suits had arrived on Air France flight 132 from Paris. They were members of the Japanese Red Army, a small, shadowy terrorist group with links to the General Command of the Popular Front for the Liberation of Palestine. Both groups wanted to help wrest Israel from Jewish rule.

After they picked up their bags, the three men pulled out automatic rifles and started firing indiscriminately. Before pausing to slip in fresh clips, they lobbed hand grenades into the crowd at the ticket counters. One man ran onto the tarmac, shot some disembarking passengers, and then blew himself up. This was the first suicide attack in modern Middle East history. Security guards shot a second terrorist and arrested the third, Kozo Okamoto. When the firing stopped, 26 people lay dead. Half were non-Jews. In addition to the two terrorists, 11 Catholics were murdered. They were Puerto Rican tourists who had just arrived on a pilgrimage to the Holy Land.

Both the Japanese Red Army and the General Command of the Popular Front for the Liberation of Palestine were strictly non-religious organizations. Yet something unexpected happened to Kozo Okamoto, the sole surviving terrorist of the Lod massacre. Israel sentenced him to life in prison but freed him in 1985 in a prisoner exchange with Palestinian forces. Okamoto wound up living in Lebanon's Beka'a Valley, the main base of the Iranian-backed Hezbollah fundamentalist organization. A revival of Islamic fundamentalism was sweeping the Middle East, and in 2000, he converted to Islam.

Kozo Okamoto's life tells us something important and not at all obvious about religious fundamentalism and politics in the Middle East and elsewhere. Okamoto was involved in extremist politics first and came to religion later. Religious fundamentalism became a useful way for him to articulate and implement his political views. This is quite common. Religious fundamentalism often provides a convenient vehicle for framing political extremism, enhancing its appeal, legitimizing it, and providing a foundation for the solidarity of political groups (Pape, 2003; Sherkat and Ellison, 1999: 370).

Many people regard Islamic fundamentalism as an independent variable and extremist politics as a dependent variable. In this view, some people happen to become religious fanatics and then their fanaticism commands them to go out and kill their opponents. But Islamic fundamentalism has political sources (Brym, 2008). For example, Al-Qaeda is strongly antagonistic to American foreign policy in the Middle East. It despises U.S. support for repressive and nondemocratic Arab governments like those of Kuwait and Saudi Arabia, which fail to distribute the benefits of oil wealth to the largely impoverished Arab people. It is also strongly opposed to the American position on the Israeli–Palestinian conflict, which it regards as too pro-Israeli and insufficiently supportive of Palestinian interests (to put it mildly). These political complaints are the breeding ground of support for Al-Qaeda in the Arab world. Thus, recent public opinion polls show that Arabs in the Middle East hold largely favourable attitudes toward American culture, democracy, and the American people, but extremely negative attitudes toward precisely those elements of American Middle East policy that Al-Qaeda opposes (Zogby International, 2001). Al-Qaeda and other extremist organizations in the Middle East gain in strength to the degree that these political issues are not addressed in a meaningful way. As Zbigniew Brzezinski, national security adviser to former President Jimmy Carter, wrote, "To win the war on terrorism, one must . . . set two goals: first, to destroy the terrorists and, second, to begin a political effort that focuses on the conditions that brought about their emergence" (Brzezinski, 2002; Hunter, 1998). These are wise words. They are based on the sociological understanding that fundamentalism, like other forms of religion, is powerfully influenced by the social and political context in which it emerges.

THE REVISED SECULARIZATION THESIS

The spread of fundamentalist religion and the resilience and relative importance of religion in some highly developed countries led some sociologists to revise the secularization thesis in the 1990s. The revisionists acknowledge that religion has become increasingly influential in the lives of some individuals and groups over the past 30 years. They insist, however, that the scope of religious authority has continued to decline in most people's lives. That is, for most people, religion has less and less to say about education, family issues, politics, and economic affairs even though it may continue to be an important source of spiritual belief and practice. In this sense, secularization continues (Chaves, 1994; Yamane, 1997).

According to the **revised secularization thesis**, in most countries, worldly institutions have broken off (or "differentiated") from the institution of religion over time. One such worldly institution is the education system. Religious bodies used to run schools and institutions of higher learning that are now run almost exclusively by non-religious authorities. Moreover, like other specialized institutions that separated from the institution of religion, the education system is generally concerned with worldly affairs rather than spiritual matters. The overall effect of the differentiation of secular institutions has been to make religion applicable only to the spiritual part of most people's lives. Because the scope of religious authority has been restricted, people look to religion for moral guidance in everyday life less often than they used to. Moreover, most people have turned religion into a personal and private matter rather than one imposed by a powerful, authoritative institution. Said differently, people feel increasingly free to combine beliefs and practices from various sources and traditions to suit their own tastes. As supermodel Cindy Crawford said in a *Redbook* interview in 1992, "I'm religious but in my own personal way. I always say that I have a Cindy Crawford religion—it's my own" (quoted in Yamane, 1997: 116). No statement could more adequately capture the decline of religion as an authoritative institution suffusing all aspects of life.

THE MARKET MODEL

Another way to understand how a religious revival can take place in the midst of an overall decline in religious participation is to think of religion as a market. In this view, religious organizations are suppliers of services such as counselling, pastoral care, youth activities, men's and women's groups, performance groups, lectures, and discussions. These services are demanded by people who desire religious activities. Religious denominations are similar to product brands offering different "flavours" of religious experience (Barna, 2002; Bibby, 2002, 2004).

The market model raises the question of what motivates people to participate in religion. Some sociologists highlight the role of otherworldly or supernatural rewards (Stark and Bainbridge, 1987, 1997). They argue

that religion promises such rewards in exchange for particular types of behaviour. It follows that religion is particularly appealing to poor people because the wealthy enjoy material benefits and therefore have less need and desire for supernatural promises.

W. Scott/Shutterstock

> **revised secularization thesis** Theory that worldly institutions break off from the institution of religion over time. As a result, religion governs an ever-smaller part of most people's lives and has become largely a matter of personal choice.

However, some sociologists question whether supernatural rewards interest only the poor, noting the many historical examples of people who gave up their wealth to live a simple, spiritual life. They also argue that religions offer worldly benefits that attract the well-to-do (Collins, 1993). For instance, religious organizations regularly bestow public recognition on the wealthiest and most powerful people in society, as Toronto's Timothy Eaton Memorial Church, among others, testifies. For such reasons, religion may appeal to the rich just as much as it appeals to the poor.

The market model usefully clarifies the social bases of heterogeneity and change in religious life by emphasizing that religious observance in North America is a highly decentralized, largely unregulated "industry" in which innovation and competition flourish. The market model also draws attention to the potential advantages of diversification. People often assume that an official or a state religion, such as Christianity in the Roman Empire or Islam in contemporary Iran, is the best guarantee of religiosity. However, the market model emphasizes that religious diversity can also be a source of strength because it allows individuals to shop around for a religious organization that corresponds to their particular tastes. This may help explain why the United States, which has long

ecclesia State-supported churches.

denominations The various streams of belief and practice that some churches allow to coexist under their overarching authority.

sects Groups that usually form by breaking away from churches because of disagreement about church doctrine. Sects are less integrated into society and less bureaucratized than churches. They are often led by charismatic leaders, who tend to be relatively intolerant of religious opinions other than their own.

charismatic leaders Religious leaders who claim to be inspired by supernatural powers and whose followers believe them to be so inspired.

banned state support for religion, has an exceptionally high rate of religious participation for a highly industrialized country (refer back to Figure 10.2). In contrast, some regions in which state and religion remained entwined until quite recently, such as Quebec, have experienced some of the sharpest drop-offs in participation in religious organizations.

Religion in Canada

CHURCH, SECT, AND CULT

Sociologists generally divide religious groups into just three types: churches, sects, and cults (Troeltsch, 1931 [1923]; Stark and Bainbridge, 1979; see Table 10.2). As noted earlier, a *church* is a bureaucratic religious organization that has accommodated itself to mainstream society and culture. Because of this accommodation, it may endure for many hundreds if not thousands of years. The bureaucratic nature of a church is evident in the formal training of its leaders, its strict hierarchy of roles, and its clearly drawn rules and regulations. Its integration into mainstream society is evident in its teachings, which are generally abstract and do not challenge worldly authority. In addition, churches integrate themselves into the mainstream by recruiting members from all classes of society.

Churches take two main forms. First are **ecclesia**, or state-supported churches. For example, Christianity became the state religion in the Roman

Empire in the fourth century, and Islam is the state religion in Iran and Sudan today. State religions impose advantages on members and disadvantages on non-members. Tolerance of other religions is low in societies with ecclesia.

Churches can also be pluralistic, allowing diversity within the church and expressing tolerance of non-members. Pluralism allows churches to increase their appeal by allowing various streams of belief and practice to coexist under their overarching authority. These sub-groups are called **denominations**. For example, United Church, Anglican, Baptist, Lutheran, and Presbyterian are the major Protestant denominations in Canada today.

Sects typically form by breaking away from churches because of disagreement about church doctrine. Sometimes, sect members choose to separate themselves geographically, as the Hutterites do in their some 200 colonies, mostly in the Western provinces. However, even in urban settings, strictly enforced rules concerning dress, diet, prayer, and intimate contact with outsiders can separate sect members from the larger society. Chasidic Jews in Toronto and Montreal prove the viability of this isolation strategy. Sects are less integrated into society and less bureaucratized than churches are. They are often led by **charismatic leaders**, men and women who claim to be inspired by supernatural powers and whose followers believe them to be so inspired. These leaders tend to be relatively intolerant of religious opinions other than their own. They tend to recruit like-minded members mainly from lower classes and marginal groups. Worship in sects tends to be highly emotional and based less on abstract principles than immediate personal experience (Stark, 1985: 314). Usually, sect-like groups appeal to the less

TABLE 10.2
Church, Sect, and Cult Compared

	Church	Sect	Cult
Integration into society	High	Medium	Low
Bureaucratization	High	Low	Low
Longevity	High	Low	Low
Leaders	Formally trained	Charismatic	Charismatic
Class base	Mixed	Low	Various but segregated

Source: From BRYM/LIE. *Sociology: The Points of the Compass.* © 2009 Nelson Education Ltd. Reproduced by permission. www.cengage.com/permissions.

Even in urban settings, strictly enforced rules concerning dress, diet, prayer, and intimate contact with outsiders can separate sect members from the larger society.

Canada's changing immigration patterns have resulted in large gains for some religious groups. Notably, the number of Muslims more than doubled between 1991 and 2001 and reached an estimated 884 000 or 2.7 percent of the population in 2006. Hindus, Sikhs, Buddhists, and Jews each represent just over 1 percent of the population. Yet Catholics and Protestants still compose 75 percent of Canada's population, and about two-thirds of recent immigrants are Christian, while an estimated 16.2 percent

affluent and churchlike groups to the more affluent. Many sects are short-lived, but those that do persist tend to bureaucratize and turn into churches. If religious organizations are to enjoy a long life, they require rules, regulations, and a clearly defined hierarchy of roles.

Although major Muslim subgroups are sometimes called denominations by non-Muslims, they are in some respects more appropriately seen as sects. That is because they often do not recognize one another as Muslim and sometimes come into violent conflict with one another, like the Sunni and Shi'a in Iraq today.

Cults are small groups of people deeply committed to a religious vision that rejects mainstream culture and society. Cults are generally led by charismatic individuals. They tend to be class-segregated groups, recruiting members from only one segment of the stratification system: high, middle, or low. For example, many North American cults today recruit nearly all their members from among the university educated. Some of these cults seek converts almost exclusively on university and college campuses (Kosmin, 1991). Because they propose a radically new way of life, cults tend to recruit few members and soon disappear. There are, however, exceptions—and some extremely important ones at that. Jesus and Muhammad were both charismatic leaders of cults. They were so compelling that they and their teachings were able to inspire a large number of followers, including rulers of states. Their cults were thus transformed into churches.

of Canadians had no religious affiliation in 2001 (see Table 10.3 and Figure 10.3; Statistics Canada, 2003e: 8, 2010q: 25).

> **cults** Small groups of people deeply committed to a religious vision that rejects mainstream culture and society.

TABLE 10.3
Religious Groups, Canada, 2001

Group	Percentage
Roman Catholic	43.2
Protestant	29.2
United Church	9.6
Anglican	6.9
Baptist	2.5
Lutheran	2.0
Presbyterian	1.4
Other Protestant	6.8
Christian Orthodox	1.6
Other Christian	2.6
Muslim	2.0
Jewish	1.1
Buddhist	1.0
Hindu	1.0
Sikh	0.9
Other	1.2
No religion	16.2
Total	100.0

Source: Adapted from Statistics Canada, *Top 10 religious denominations*, Religions in Canada, 2001 Census, 96F0030XIE2001015, Census year 2001. Released May 13, 2003.

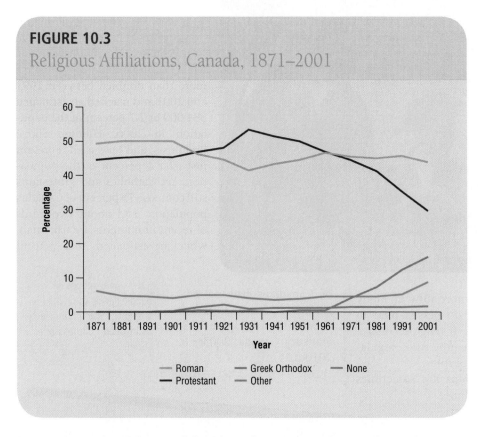

FIGURE 10.3

Religious Affiliations, Canada, 1871–2001

Percentage (y-axis) ranges from 0 to 60.

Year (x-axis): 1871 1881 1891 1901 1911 1921 1931 1941 1951 1961 1971 1981 1991 2001

Legend: Roman — Greek Orthodox — None — Protestant — Other

Sources: 1871–1971 from Statistics Canada (1999a); 1981 from Ontario Consultants on Religious Tolerance (2005); 1991 and 2001 from Statistics Canada (2003e).

LO⁴ Religiosity

It is now time to consider some social factors that determine how important religion is to people, that is, their religiosity. We can measure religiosity in various ways. Strength of belief, emotional attachment to a religion, knowledge about a religion, frequency of performing rituals, and frequency of applying religious principles in daily life all indicate how religious a person is (Glock, 1962). Ideally, we ought to examine many measures to get a fully rounded and reliable picture of the social distribution of religiosity. For simplicity's sake, however, we focus on just one measure here. In a Canada-wide survey, respondents were asked to indicate whether their level of involvement in religious activities at various points in their lives was "high," "moderate," "low," or "none." Figure 10.4 summarizes the results.

Some fascinating patterns emerge from the data. First, the people most heavily involved in religious activities are preteens and seniors. As a result, involvement forms a U-shaped curve, falling among teenagers and young adults and then beginning to rise steadily after the age of about 24.

religiosity The degree to which religion is important to people.

How can we explain this pattern? Preteens have little say over whether they attend Sunday school, Hebrew school, confirmation classes, and the like. For many preteens, religious involvement is high because it is required of them, even if their parents do not always follow suit. Seniors have more time and more need for religion. Because they are not usually in school, employed in the paid labour force, or busy raising a family, they have more opportunity than young people do to attend religious services. Moreover, because seniors are generally closer to illness and death than are young people, they are more likely to require the solace of religion. To a degree, then, involvement in religious activities is a life-cycle issue. That is, children are relatively actively involved in religious activities because they are required to be and seniors are relatively actively involved because they feel greater need for religious involvement and are in a position to act on that need.

Another issue is at stake here, too. Different age groups live through different times, and today's seniors reached maturity when religion was a more authoritative force in society. A person's current religious involvement depends partly on whether he or she grew up in more religious times. Thus, although young people are likely to become more religiously involved as they age, they are unlikely ever to become as involved as seniors are today.

Second, the region of the country in which you live also correlates with the likelihood that you will attend religious services weekly. Newfoundland and Labrador, Prince Edward Island, and New Brunswick have the highest rates of monthly attendance; Quebec, Alberta, and British Columbia have the lowest. However, Figure 10.5 shows pockets of high attendance in Cape Breton, Gaspé, and parts of southwestern Ontario, southern Manitoba, Saskatchewan, and Alberta (Clark, 2003: 3).

Third, respondents whose parents attended religious services frequently are more likely to do so themselves (Jones, 2000). Religiosity is partly a learned behaviour. Whether parents give a child a religious upbringing is likely to have a lasting impact on the child.

This is by no means an exhaustive list of the factors that determine the frequency of attending religious services. For example, research also indicates that social inequality can promote religiosity. Thus, rich countries with the lowest levels of social inequality, such as Denmark, tend to have the lowest levels of church attendance. Rich countries with the highest levels of social inequality, such as the United States, tend to have the highest levels of church attendance. However, even this brief overview suggests that religiosity depends partly on obligation, opportunity, need, and learning. The people who attend religious services most frequently are those who must, those who were taught to be religious as children, those who need organized religion most because of their advanced age, and those who have the most time to go to services.

THE FUTURE OF RELIGION

Secularization and religious revival are two of the dominant influences on religion worldwide. We can detect secularization in survey data that track religious attitudes and practices over time and also in the growing percentage of people who indicate in succeeding censuses that they have no religious affiliation (see Figure 10.3). We also know that various secular institutions are taking over some of the functions formerly performed by religion, thus robbing it of its once pervasive authority over all aspects of life. It is an exaggeration to claim, as Max Weber did, that the whole world is gradually becoming "disenchanted." However, part of it certainly is.

At the same time, we know that even as secularization grips many people, many others have been caught up in a religious revival of vast proportions. Religious belief and practice are intensifying for these people, partly because religion serves as a useful vehicle for political expression. The fact that this revival was quite unexpected

FIGURE 10.4
Religious Involvement over the Life Cycle by Group

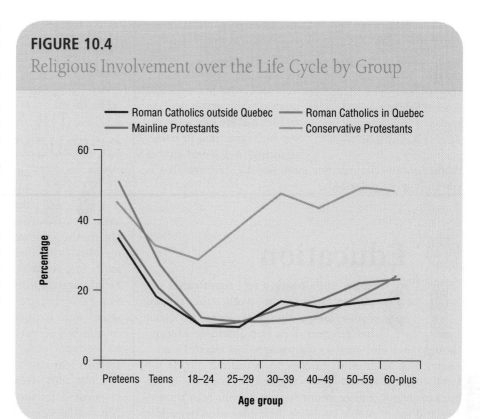

Source: Bibby (2001: 275).

FIGURE 10.5
Canada, Monthly Religious Attendance 1999–2001

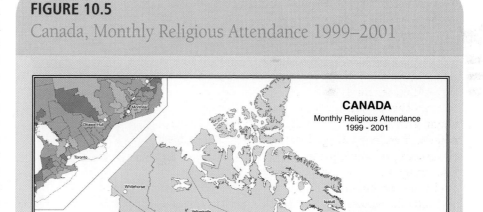

Source: Statistics Canada, *Canadian Social Trends*, 11-008-XIE 2002004 Spring 2003, no. 68. Released March 18, 2003. http://www.statcan.gc.ca/pub/11-008-x/2002004/article/6493-eng.pdf.

CHAPTER 10 Religion and Education **231**

educational attainment
The number of years of school that students complete.

educational achievement
How much students actually learn.

just a few decades ago should warn us not to be overly bold in our forecasts. It seems to us, however, that the two contradictory social processes of secularization and revival are likely to persist for some time to come, resulting in a world that is neither more religious nor more secular, but one that is certainly more polarized.

LO⁵ Education

Despite the continuing significance of religion around the world, the revised secularization thesis is right to claim that religion does not dominate life and thought as it did even a century ago. For example, education, not religion, dominates socialization outside the family in most rich countries. Almost everyone in Canada goes to school, a large minority goes to college or university, and many people continue their education in middle age. Beyond its importance as an agent of socialization, education is also a central determinant of opportunities for upward mobility. We care deeply about education not just because it shapes us but also because it influences how well we do.

LO⁶ THE FUNCTIONS OF EDUCATION

Many Canadians believe that we enjoy equal access to basic schooling. They think schools identify and sort students based on merit and effort. They regard the education system as an avenue of upward mobility. From their point of view, the brightest students are bound to succeed, whatever their economic, ethnic, racial, or religious background. In their view, educational attainment is largely an outcome of individual talent and hard work. Educational attainment refers to number of years of school completed. (In contrast, educational achievement refers to how much students actually learn.)

The view that the Canadian education system is responsible for *sorting* students based on talent and effort is a central component of the functional theory of education. The functional theory also stresses the *training* role of schools. That is, in schools, most people learn how to read, write, count, calculate, and perform other tasks essential to the workings of postmodern society. A third function of the education system involves the *socialization* of the young (Durkheim, 1956, 1961 [1925]). Schools teach the young to view Canada with pride, respect the law, think of democracy as the best form of government, and value capitalism. Finally, schools *transmit culture* from generation to generation, fostering a common identity and social cohesion in the process. Schools have played a particularly important role in assimilating the disadvantaged, minorities, and immigrants into Canadian society, although in recent decades our common identity has been based increasingly on respect for cultural diversity.

Durkheim emphasized the role of schools in socializing the young and promoting social integration. People, he said, are torn between egoistic needs and moral impulses. Like religion in an earlier era, educational institutions must ensure that the moral side predominates. By instilling a sense

© Omni Photo Communications/Index Stock Imagery

Religiosity is partly a learned behaviour. Whether parents give a child a religious upbringing is likely to have a lasting impact on the child.

Jamie Duplass/Shutterstock

ensure that the most talented students eventually get the most rewarding jobs. Conflict theorists argue that, in fact, schools distribute the benefits of education *unequally*, allocating most of the benefits to children from upper classes and higher-status racial and ethnic groups. Because amount and type of formal education are strongly correlated with earning power (see Figure 10.6), schools tend to reproduce the stratification system generation after generation (Jencks et al., 1972; Lucas, 1999).

Much evidence supports the conflict perspective. For instance, the green columns in Figure 10.7 on the next page show that Canadians from high-income families are 61 percent more likely than are those from low-income families to be enrolled in university at the age of 19. (Here, "high-income" families are those in the top 25 percent of family income and "low-income" families are those in the bottom 25 percent.) Research also shows that about 60 percent of 25- to 34-year-old Canadians whose fathers are professionals or managers attend university. The figure falls to 35 percent for those whose fathers are supervisory workers and to less than 30 percent for those whose fathers are skilled workers. Among those whose fathers are unskilled workers, fewer than 20 percent attend university, and for those whose fathers are farmers, the

of authority, discipline, and morality in children, schools make society cohesive (Durkheim, 1956, 1961 [1925]).

Sorting, training, socializing, and transmitting culture are *manifest* functions, or positive goals that schools accomplish intentionally. However, schools also perform certain *latent*, or unintended, functions. For example, schools encourage the development of a separate youth culture that often conflicts with parents' values (Coleman, Campbell, and Hobson, 1966). Especially at the college and university levels, educational institutions bring potential mates together, thus serving as a "marriage market." Schools perform a useful custodial service by keeping children under surveillance for much of the day and freeing parents to work in the paid labour force. By keeping millions of young people temporarily out of the full-time paid labour force, colleges and universities restrict job competition and support wage levels (Bowles and Gintis, 1976). Finally, because they can encourage critical, independent thinking, educational institutions sometimes become "schools of dissent" that challenge authoritarian regimes and promote social change (Brower, 1975; Freire, 1972).

THE EFFECT OF ECONOMIC INEQUALITY FROM THE CONFLICT PERSPECTIVE

From the conflict perspective, the chief problem with the functionalist view is that it exaggerates the degree to which schools sort students by ability and thereby

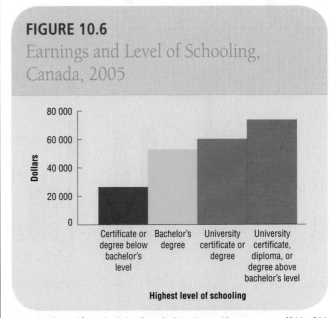

FIGURE 10.6

Earnings and Level of Schooling, Canada, 2005

Source: Adapted from Statistics Canada, http://www40.statcan.gc.ca/l01/cst01/labor50a-eng.htm (retrieved 26 March 2010).

figure is around 10 percent (Guppy and Davies, 1998). Clearly, class strongly influences whether a person gets to university.

But exactly how does class exert this influence? The sociological literature emphasizes four mechanisms that operate in conjunction with the school system to reproduce inequality:

1. *Financial constraint.* Some people do not attend university because they feel they can't afford it, even if they work part time and take advantage of student loans. More than twice as many 19-year-olds from low-income families feel this way compared with 19-year-olds from high-income families (see the yellow columns in Figure 10.7).

2. *One-parent households.* Low-income parents are more likely than are high-income parents to experience the kinds of financial problems that can make marriage difficult and contribute to divorce. In turn, children from one-parent households are usually unable to rely on adults for tutoring, emotional support and encouragement, supervision, and role modelling to the same degree as children from two-parent households can. This puts children from one-parent households at a big disadvantage. Significantly, the red columns in Figure 10.7 show that 19-year-olds from low-income families are six times as likely as 19-year-olds from high-income families to have been raised in a one-parent household.

3. *Lack of cultural capital.* High-income parents are two-and-a-half times as likely as low-income parents to have earned undergraduate degrees (see the blue columns in Figure 10.7). This fact is important because university education gives people cultural capital that they can transmit to their children, thus improving their chance of financial success. Cultural capital refers to "widely shared, high status cultural signals (attitudes, preferences, formal knowledge, behaviours, goals, and credentials) used for social and cultural exclusion" (Lamont and Lareau, 1988: 156).

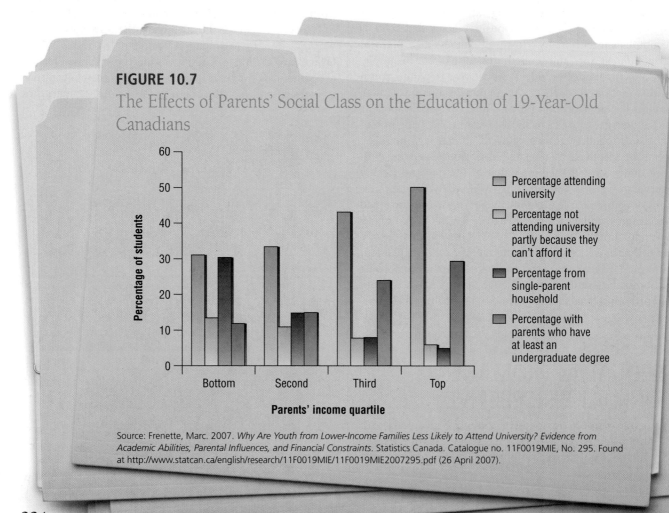

FIGURE 10.7

The Effects of Parents' Social Class on the Education of 19-Year-Old Canadians

Source: Frenette, Marc. 2007. *Why Are Youth from Lower-Income Families Less Likely to Attend University? Evidence from Academic Abilities, Parental Influences, and Financial Constraints.* Statistics Canada. Catalogue no. 11F0019MIE, No. 295. Found at http://www.statcan.ca/english/research/11F0019MIE/11F0019MIE2007295.pdf (26 April 2007).

For example, if you own a lot of cultural capital, you are more likely to have "highbrow" tastes in literature, music, art, dance, and sports, and behave according to established rules of etiquette. You are likely to create a household environment that promotes refined taste, provides formal lessons to help instill such taste in your children, and thus increases their chance of success in school and, eventually, in the paid labour force (Bourdieu and Passeron, 1990; DiMaggio, 1982; Kingston, 2001).

4. *Streaming.* The more intelligent you are, the more likely you are to do well in school and to achieve economic success later in life. IQ and other standardized tests are employed to sort students by intelligence; test scores are used to channel them into high-ability ("enriched"), middle-ability, and low-ability ("basic" or "special education") classrooms. The trouble is that IQ and other standardized tests can only measure acquired proficiency in a given cultural system. The quantity and quality of a person's exposure to whatever is counted as proper or correct plays a large role here. Even the most able Anglo-Canadian children would perform abysmally if tested in Mongolian. The results of IQ and other standardized tests thus depend on two factors: (1) how effectively an individual absorbs what his or her environment offers and (2) how closely his or her environment reflects what the test includes. As a result, members of underprivileged groups tend to score low on IQ and other standardized tests—not because they are on average less intelligent than members of privileged groups but because they do not have the training and the cultural background needed to score high (Fischer et al., 1996). Still, educators persist in using IQ and other standardized tests to sort students into different types of classes (Samuda, Crawford, Philip, and Tinglen, 1980). The result: streaming reproduces class differences, determines who goes to university and who doesn't, and influences who enters which social class in the larger society).

CASE STUDY: FUNCTIONALIST VERSUS CONFLICT THEORIES OF THE COMMUNITY COLLEGE

We can more fully illustrate how sociologists of education use functionalist and conflict theories by applying them to the case of the community college system, with its more than 400 000 full-time students in Canada. Aside from Canada's general population increase, two social forces contributed most heavily to the rise of the community college system. First, the country needed skilled workers in industry and services. Second, the belief grew that higher education would contribute to upward mobility and greater equality. The accuracy of that belief has become a point of contention among sociologists.

Functionalists examine the social composition of the student body in community colleges and find a somewhat disproportionate number of students from lower socioeconomic strata and minority ethnic groups. Many community colleges are located close to the neighbour-hoods of disadvantaged students, allowing them to live at home while studying. Community college tuition fees are generally lower than in universities. Graduates of community colleges are usually able to find relatively good jobs and steady employment. These facts seem to confirm the functionalist view that the community college system creates new opportunities for disadvantaged youth who might otherwise have less rewarding jobs.

Conflict theorists deny that the growth of community colleges increases upward mobility and equality. In the long run, they argue, it is the entire stratification system that is upwardly mobile. That is, the quality of nearly *all* jobs improves but the *relative* position of community college graduates versus university graduates remains the same. In fact, conflict theorists argue that community colleges reinforce prevailing patterns of social and class inequality by directing students from disadvantaged backgrounds away from universities and thus decreasing the probability that they will earn a four-year degree and a high-status position in society (Karabel, 1986: 18).

Functionalists and conflict theorists both have a point. Community colleges do create opportunities for individual upward mobility that some students would otherwise not have. Community colleges do not, however, change the overall pattern of inequality in Canadian society. In fact, expecting community colleges or, for that matter, any part of the institution of education to change the stratification system as a whole is probably naive. Decreasing the level of inequality in society requires comprehensive preschool programs to help disadvantaged children and laws that change people's entitlements and the rewards they receive for doing different kinds of work, not just increasing educational opportunities.

We conclude that functionalists paint a somewhat idealized picture of the education system. Although usefully identifying the manifest and latent functions of education, they fail to emphasize sufficiently the far-reaching effects of stratified home environments on student achievement and placement. A similar conclusion is warranted if we examine the effects of gender on education.

GENDER AND EDUCATION: THE FEMINIST CONTRIBUTION

In some respects, women are doing better than men are in the Canadian education system. Women in colleges and universities have higher grade point averages than men do and they complete their degrees faster. The number of women enrolled as college and university undergraduates has exceeded the number of men for decades, and more women than men are enrolled in some graduate and professional programs, such as medicine and law. The enrolment gap between women and men is growing—not just in Canada but also in the United States, the U.K., France, Germany, and Australia (Berliner, 2004). Men received fewer than 40 percent of the 241 551 degrees granted by Canadian colleges and universities in 2007 (Statistics Canada, 2010s).

The facts just listed represent considerable improvement over time in the position of women in the education system. Yet feminists who have looked closely at the situation have established that women are still at a disadvantage. Consider level of education and field of study (see Table 10.4 and Figure 10.8). Although women receive more degrees than men do, the gap narrows considerably at the master's level and reverses at the Ph.D. level, where men receive more than 55 percent of degrees. Moreover, a disproportionately large number of men earn Ph.D.s and professional degrees in engineering, computer science, dentistry, and specialized areas of medicine—all relatively high-paying fields, most requiring a strong math and science background. A disproportionately large number of women earn Ph.D.s and professional degrees in education, English, foreign languages, and other relatively low-paying fields

TABLE 10.4

Degrees Granted, Canadian Universities, by Degree and Gender, 2007

	Bachelor's	Master's	Doctorate
Men	38.0	46.1	55.4
Women	62.0	53.9	44.6
Total	100.0	100.0	100.0

Source: Adapted from the Statistics Canada CANSIM database, http://cansim2.statcan.gc.ca Table 477-0014 (April 26, 2007).

FIGURE 10.8

Degrees Granted, Canadian Universities and Colleges, by Program and Gender, 2007

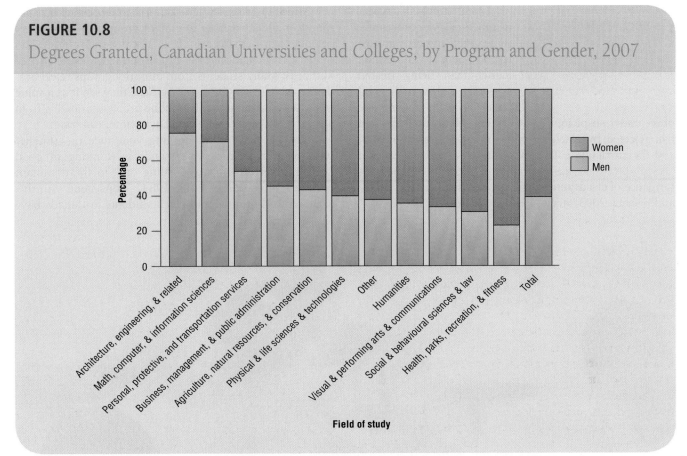

Source: Adapted from the Statistics Canada CANSIM database, http://cansim2.statcan.gc.ca Table 477-0014 (retrieved 26 March 2010).

requiring little background in math and science. Parents and teachers are partly responsible for these choices because they tend to direct boys and girls toward what they regard as masculine and feminine fields of study. Gender segregation in the labour market also influences choice of field of study. University students know women are more likely to get jobs in certain fields than in others and they make career choices accordingly (Spade, 2001). Like class, gender structures the educational experience and its consequences.

Microsociological Processes

THE STEREOTYPE THREAT: A SYMBOLIC INTERACTIONIST VIEW

Macrosociological issues, such as the functions of education and the influence of class and gender on educational achievement, do not exhaust the interests of sociologists of education. They have also contributed much to our understanding of the face-to-face interaction processes that influence the educational process. Consider this finding from American research: When black and white children begin school, their achievement test scores are similar. Yet the longer they stay in school, the more black students fall behind. By grade 6, blacks in many school districts are two full grades behind whites in achievement. Clearly, something happens in school to increase the gap between black and white students. Symbolic interactionists suggest that this something is the self-fulfilling prophecy, an expectation that helps bring about what it predicts.

We encountered examples of self-fulfilling prophecies in educational settings in Chapter 4 (From Social Interaction to Social Organizations). For instance, we discussed one famous experiment in which, at the beginning of a school year, researchers randomly identified students as high or low achievers to their teachers. At the end of the school year, they found that the students arbitrarily singled out as high achievers scored higher on an IQ test than those arbitrarily singled out as low achievers. The researchers concluded that teachers' expectations influenced students' performance (Rosenthal and Jacobson, 1968; Weinstein, 2002).

stereotype threat The impact of negative stereotypes on the school performance of disadvantaged groups.

Many teachers expect members of lower classes and some visible minority groups to do poorly in school. Rather than being treated as young people with good prospects, such students are often under suspicion of intellectual inferiority and often feel rejected by teachers, white middle-class classmates, and the curriculum. This expectation, sometimes called a **stereotype threat**, has a negative impact on the school performance of disadvantaged groups (Massey, Charles, Lundy, and Fischer, 2003; Steele, 1997).

Minority-group students often cluster together because they feel alienated from dominant groups in their school or college or perhaps even from the institution itself. Too often, such alienation turns into resentment and defiance of authority. Many students from minority groups reject academic achievement as a goal because they see it as a value of the dominant culture. Discipline problems, ranging from apathy to disruptive and illegal behaviour, can result.

The corollary of identifying your race or ethnicity with poor academic performance is thinking of good academic performance as "selling out" to the dominant culture (Ogbu, 2003; Willis, 1984). Consistent with this argument, Aboriginal and black students in Canada have

Although the composition of Canada's student population is becoming increasingly multicultural, this is less true of Canada's teachers. An ongoing debate in Canada is whether students at all levels would be better served by a faculty whose composition reflects the diversity of our population and who offer a more inclusive curriculum.

higher-than-average school dropout rates (Livingstone, 1999: 743; Toronto Board of Education, 1993). In contrast, research shows that challenging lower-class and minority students, giving them emotional support and encouragement, giving greater recognition in the curriculum to the accomplishments of the groups from which they originate, creating an environment in which they can relax and achieve—all these strategies explode the self-fulfilling prophecy and improve academic performance (Steele, 1992). Anecdotal evidence supporting this argument can be found in the compelling 1988 movie *Stand and Deliver,* based on the true-life story of high school math teacher Jaime Escalante. Escalante refused to write off his failing East Los Angeles Chicano pupils as "losers" and inspired them to remarkable achievements as they registered the best performance in the Advanced Placement Calculus Exam in the southern California school system (see also the Sociology at the Movies box).

In sum, the stereotype threat at the microsociological level combines with the macrosociological processes described earlier to help reproduce the stratification system. These social mechanisms increase the chance that those who are socially marginal and already disadvantaged will earn low grades and wind up with jobs closer to the bottom than to the top of the occupational structure.

Canadian Education in an International Perspective

In Europe 300 years ago, the nobility and the wealthy usually hired personal tutors to teach their children to read and write; learn basic history, geography, and foreign languages; and study how to dress properly, conduct themselves in public, greet status superiors, and so on. Few people went to college. Only a few professions, such as theology and law, required extensive schooling. The great majority of Europeans were illiterate. As late as the 1860s, more than 80 percent of Spaniards and more than 30 percent of the French could not read (Vincent, 2000). Even as recently as a century ago, most people in the world had never attended even a day of school. As late as 1950 only about 10 percent of the world's countries boasted systems of compulsory mass education (Meyer, Ramirez, and Soysal, 1992).

The Canadian Press (Winnipeg Free Press/Marc Gallant)

Recent surveys suggest that Canadians have only a moderate level of confidence in the job being done by the public education sector.

The Great Debaters

The Civil War (1861–65) outlawed slavery in the United States, but legal and violent resistance against black rights persisted for more than a century. In 1866, for example, an amendment to the Texas Constitution stipulated that all taxes paid by blacks had to be used to maintain black schools, and that it was the duty of the legislature to "encourage colored schools" ("Jim Crow Laws: Texas," 2008). In this segregationist atmosphere, the Methodist Church founded Wiley College in the northeast corner of Texas in 1873 "for the purpose of allowing Negro youth the opportunity to pursue higher learning in the arts, sciences and other professions" (Wiley College, 2007).

Melvin Tolson (Denzel Washington) and his students prepare in *The Great Debaters*.

In 1923, Wiley College hired Melvin B. Tolson as a professor of speech and English. He proceeded to build up the school's debating team to the point where they challenged and beat the mighty University of Southern California for the 1935 national debating championship. The victory shocked and scandalized much of the country's white population even as it instilled pride in African Americans, provided them with a shining model of academic achievement, and motivated black youth to strive to reach new heights. No self-fulfilling prophecy condemning black students to academic mediocrity operated at Wiley. To the contrary, Tolson worked his students hard, demanded excellence, and expected the best from them. Supported by the black community, they rose to his challenge.

The Great Debaters shows why the 1935 victory was anything but easy. Tolson (played by Denzel Washington) is harassed by the local sheriff, who brands him a trouble-maker for trying to unionize local black and white share-croppers. On an out-of-town road trip, Tolson and his debating team come across a white mob that has just lynched a black man and set his body on fire. They barely escape with their lives. The pervasive racism of the times might discourage and immobilize lesser people, but it steels Tolson and his debaters, who feel compelled to show the world what blacks are capable of achieving even in the most inhospitable circumstances.

Historically black colleges have played an important role in educating the black middle class in the United States, but since the 1960s blacks have been able to enroll in integrated colleges and universities, causing many black colleges to fall on hard times. Wiley itself was in deep financial trouble until *The Great Debaters* sparked new enrollments and endowments (Beil, 2007).

The successes of historically black colleges raise an important policy issue that is being debated in Canada's big cities today. Can segregated black public schools benefit black youth and should they be funded out of general tax revenue? Critics of separate black public schools argue that Canadian multiculturalism seeks to teach tolerance and respect for all cultures, and that separate public schools for any minority group would therefore be a step backward. Arguably, however, integrated public schools are still the home of self-fulfilling prophecies that make it difficult for black students to excel. Their curricula do little if anything to instill pride in the achievements of black individuals and the black community. Consequently, some black public school students dangerously identify academic excellence with "acting white," thus helping to condemn themselves to mediocre academic achievement and restricted social mobility. From this point of view, the achievements of historically black colleges like Wiley should be taken as a model of what is possible when black students are academically challenged and nourished in a non-threatening environment.

Critical Thinking Questions

- What are the pros and cons of establishing segregated black public schools in Canada today?
- Do the pros outweigh the cons or vice-versa?
- Does your argument about the pros and cons of establishing black public schools in Canada apply to the establishment of separate schools for members of other visible minority and ethnic groups?

Today the situation is vastly different. Compulsory mass education became a universal feature of European and North American life by the early twentieth century, and nearly universal literacy was achieved by the middle of the twentieth century (Curtis, 1988; Vincent, 2000). Every country in the world now has a system of mass schooling. Still, universal literacy is a remote goal. Eighteen percent of the world's adults are illiterate, nearly two-thirds of them women. In sub-Saharan Africa, 40 percent of primary-school-age children do not attend school (UNESCO, 2008: 58, 2010)

In contrast, more than 48 percent of Canadians between the ages of 25 and 64 had a college or university education in 2006, higher than the comparable percentage for any other country (Statistics Canada, 2003b: 10, 2010d).

Nonetheless, many Canadians believe that our public school system has turned soft if not rotten. They argue that the youth of Japan and South Korea spend long hours concentrating on the basics of math, science, and language, while Canadian students spend fewer hours in school and study more non-basic subjects (e.g., art, music, drama, physical education) that are of little practical value. If students do not spend more school time on subjects that "really" matter, they warn, Canada will suffer declining economic competitiveness in the twenty-first century. Many Canadians—8 in 10 according to one poll—want province-wide standardized tests for students and teachers because they presumably allow school performance to be objectively assessed (Bricker and Greenspon, 2001: 165–66). Because of the perceived decline in school standards, an increasingly large number of parents who can afford to do so—about 5 percent of all Canadian parents—are sending their children to private school and a small number are schooling their children at home.

In reality, international comparisons show that Canadians perform relatively well in standardized math, science, and literacy tests. According to the most comprehensive and widely respected international study of student performance, Canada's school system ranks third in the world, behind Finland's and Hong Kong's, but ahead of South Korea's and Japan's (see Table 10.5). Students from Alberta, British Columbia, and Quebec score above the Canadian national average. Moreover, Canada is among the top six countries in terms of providing good education to students from all socioeconomic classes (the others are Finland, Iceland, Japan, South Korea, and Sweden; Sokoloff, 2001). None of this is cause for complacency. Much still needs to be done to improve the quality of Canadian education, particularly for students from disadvantaged families, but the public's fears about poor and declining educational standards are likely overdrawn.

TABLE 10.5
The World's Top Ten School Systems, 2006

Rank	Science	Reading	Math	Overall
1	Finland	South Korea	Taiwan	Finland
2	Hong Kong	Finland	Finland	Hong Kong
3	**Canada**	Hong Kong	Hong Kong	**Canada**
4	Taiwan	**Canada**	South Korea	South Korea
5	Estonia	New Zealand	Netherlands	Taiwan
6	Japan	Ireland	Switzerland	New Zealand
7	New Zealand	Australia	**Canada**	Netherlands
8	Australia	Liechtenstein	Macao	Liechtenstein
9	Netherlands	Poland	Liechtenstein	Australia
10	Liechtenstein	Sweden	Japan	Japan

Source: OECD. 2007. "PISA 2006 Results." http://www.pisa.oecd.org/document/2/0,3343,en_32252351_32236191_39718850_1_1_1_1,00.html (retrieved 26 March 2010).

NEL

11
Health and Medicine

LEARNING OBJECTIVES:

LO¹ Health risks are unevenly distributed across class, gender, race, and other factors.

LO² Although Canada's health care system ranks among the top in the world, many low-income and moderate-income Canadians have limited access to health services.

LO³ The average health status of Americans is lower than that of Canadians.

LO⁴ The dominance of medical science is due to its successful treatments and the way in which doctors established control over their profession and their clients.

LO⁵ The wide availability of antibiotics has led to the spread of drug-resistant germs.

LO⁶ Patient activism, alternative medicine, and holistic medicine promise to improve the quality of health care.

The Black Death

In 1346, rumours reached Europe of a plague sweeping the East. Originating in Asia, the epidemic spread along trade routes to China and Russia. A year later, 12 galleys sailed from southern Russia to Italy. Diseased sailors were on board. Their lymph nodes were terribly swollen and eventually burst, causing a painful death. Anyone who came in contact with the sailors was soon infected. As a result, their ships were driven out of several Italian and French ports in succession. Yet the disease spread relentlessly, again moving along trade routes to Spain, Portugal, and England. Within two years, the Black Death, as it came to be known, killed a third of Europe's population. Six hundred and fifty years later, the plague still ranks as the most devastating catastrophe in human history (Herlihy, 1998; McNeill, 1976; Zinsser, 1935).

Today we know that the cause of the plague was a bacillus that spread from fleas to rats to people. It spread so efficiently because many people lived close together in unsanitary conditions. In the middle of the fourteenth century, however, nobody knew anything about germs. Therefore, Pope Clement VI sent a delegation to Europe's leading medical school in Paris to discover the cause of the plague. The learned professors studied the problem. They reported that a particularly unfortunate conjunction of Saturn, Jupiter, and Mars in the sign of Aquarius had occurred in 1345. The resulting hot, humid conditions caused the earth to emit poisonous vapours. To prevent the plague, they said, people should refrain from eating poultry, waterfowl, pork, beef, fish, and olive oil. They should not sleep during the daytime or engage in excessive exercise. Nothing should be cooked in rainwater. Bathing should be avoided at all costs.

We do not know whether the pope followed the professors' advice. We do know he made a practice of sitting between two large fires to breathe pure air. Because the plague bacillus is destroyed by heat, this may have saved his life. Other people were less fortunate. Some rang church bells and fired cannons to drive the plague away. Others burned incense, wore charms, and cast spells. But, other than the pope, the only people to have much luck in avoiding the plague were the well-to-do (who could afford to flee the densely populated cities for remote areas in the countryside) and the Jews (whose religion required that they wash their hands before meals, bathe once a week, and conduct burials soon after death).

The Black Death

Some of the main themes of the sociology of health and medicine are embedded in the story of the Black Death, or at least implied by it. First, recall that some groups were more likely to die of the plague than others were. This is a common pattern. Health risks are always unevenly distributed. Women and men, upper and lower classes, rich and poor countries, and privileged and disadvantaged members of racial and ethnic groups are exposed to health risks to varying degrees. This suggests that health is not just a medical issue but also a sociological one. The first task we set ourselves here is to examine the sociological factors that account for the uneven distribution of health in society.

Second, the story of the Black Death suggests that health problems change over time. Epidemics of various types still break out, but there can be no Black Death where sanitation and hygiene prevent the spread of disease. Today we are also able to treat many infectious diseases, such as tuberculosis and pneumonia, with antibiotics. Twentieth-century medical science developed these wonder drugs and many other life-saving therapies. Medical successes allow people to live longer than they used to. **Life expectancy** is the average age at death of the members of a population. Life expectancy in Canada in 1831 was approximately 40 years for men and 42 years for women (Lavoie and Oderkirk, 2000: 3). In contrast, a Canadian girl born in 2006 can hope to live to 83, a boy to 78 (Statistics Canada, 2010j). Yet, because of increased life expectancy, degenerative conditions, such as cancer and heart disease, have an opportunity to develop in a way that was not possible a century ago (see Table 11.1).

The story of the Black Death raises a third issue, too. We cannot help being struck by the superstition and ignorance surrounding the treatment of the ill in medieval times. Remedies were often herbal but also included earthworms, urine, and animal excrement. People believed it was possible to maintain good health by keeping body fluids in balance. Therefore, cures that released body fluids were common. These included hot

life expectancy The average age at death of the members of a population.

TABLE 1.1

Ten Leading Causes of Death, Canada, 1901 and 2005

Percentage of Deaths

1901		2005	
1. Tuberculosis	12.0	1. Cancer	29.3
2. Bronchitis and pneumonia	10.0	2. Major heart disease	22.4
3. Infections of the intestines	9.1	3. Stroke	6.1
4. Senile debility	7.4	4. Chronic lower respiratory diseases	4.6
5. Congenital debility	7.0	5. Accidents	4.1
6. Diseases of the heart	5.6	6. Diabetes	3.4
7. Apoplexy and paralysis	4.4	7. Influenza and pneumonia	2.5
8. Diphtheria and croup	3.9	8. Alzheimer's disease	2.5
9. Accidents	3.4	9. Kidney infection	1.6
10. Cancer	2.8	10. Suicide	1.6
Other	34.4	Other	21.9
Total	100.0	Total	100.0

Sources: Dawson (1906); Statistics Canada (2010i).

baths, laxatives, and diuretics, which increase the flow of urine. If these treatments didn't work, bloodletting was often prescribed. No special qualifications were required to administer medical treatment. Barbers doubled as doctors.

However, the backwardness of medieval medical practice, and the advantages of modern scientific medicine, can easily be exaggerated. For example, medieval doctors stressed the importance of prevention, exercise, a balanced diet, and a congenial environment in maintaining good health. We now know this is sound advice. Conversely, one of the great shortcomings of modern medicine is its emphasis on high-tech cures rather than on preventive and environmental measures. Therefore, in the final section of this chapter, we investigate how the medical professions gained substantial control over health issues and promoted their own approach to well-being, and how those professions have been challenged in recent years.

LO¹ Health and Inequality

DEFINING AND MEASURING HEALTH

According to the World Health Organization (WHO), **health** is

> A state of complete physical, social and mental well-being, and not merely the absence of disease or infirmity. Health is a resource for everyday life, not the object of living. It is a positive concept emphasizing social and personal resources as well as physical capabilities. (World Health Organization, 2010b)

The WHO definition lists in broad terms the main factors that promote good health. However, when it comes to *measuring* the health of a population, sociologists typically examine the negative: rates of illness and death. They reason that healthy populations experience less illness and longer life than unhealthy populations. This is the approach we follow here.

Assuming ideal conditions, how long can a person live? To date, the record is held by Jeanne Louise Calment, a French woman who died in 1997 at the age of 122. (Other people claim to be older, but they lack authenticated birth certificates.)

Calment was an extraordinary individual. She took up fencing at age 85, rode a bicycle until she was 100, gave up smoking at 120, and released a rap CD at 121 (Matalon, 1997). Only 1 in 100 people in the world's rich countries now lives to be 100. Since 1840, life expectancy in the world's rich countries has increased at a fairly steady rate of about 2.5 years per decade. Further increases seem likely, and if there is an upper limit we don't know what it might be. By 2009, the world's highest life expectancy was 83 years in Japan. By 2050, life expectancy in Japan is projected to reach 92 years (Oeppen and Vaupel, 2002).

Unfortunately, life expectancy outside Japan is less than 83 years today. Figure 11.1 shows life expectancy in selected countries. Life expectancy was two years shorter in Canada and in most other rich postindustrial countries than it was in Japan. But in India, life expectancy was only 64 years. People in the impoverished African country of Lesotho have the world's shortest life expectancy at 40 years, only five years more than life expectancy in Europe in 1600. More than half a billion people in 32 countries—most in sub-Saharan Africa—have a life expectancy of less than 50 years (Geohive.com, 2005).

If the maximum observed life expectancy in a population is now 83 years, then Canadians are being deprived of about two years of life because of avoidable social causes (83 − 81 = 2). Avoidable social causes deprive the average citizen of Lesotho of 43 years of life (83 − 40 = 43). Clearly, social causes have a big—and variable—impact on illness and death. We must therefore discuss them in detail.

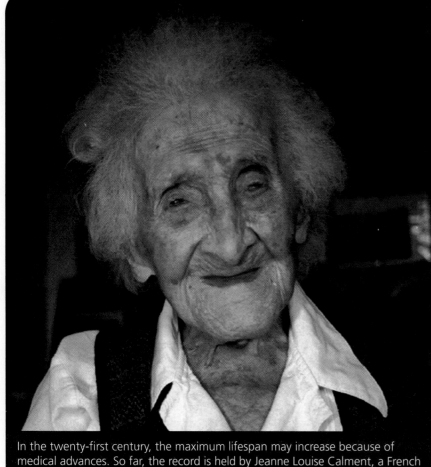

The Canadian Press (Associated Press)

In the twenty-first century, the maximum lifespan may increase because of medical advances. So far, the record is held by Jeanne Louise Calment, a French woman who died in 1997 at the age of 122.

FIGURE 11.1
Life Expectancy, Selected Countries and Years

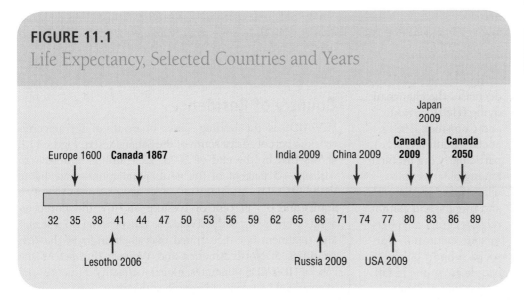

Sources: Population Reference Bureau (2009); Tuljapurkar, Li, and Boe (2000).

THE SOCIAL CAUSES OF ILLNESS AND DEATH

People get sick and die partly because of natural causes. One person may have a genetic predisposition to cancer. Another may come in contact with a deadly Ebola virus in the environment. However, over and above such natural causes of illness and death, we can single out three types of *social* causes:

1. *Human-environmental factors.* Major health risks arise from how environments are shaped by human activity. Divisions such as social class, occupation, and nationality often correspond to sharp differences in the surroundings in which people work and live. Some environments foster good health, while others impose added risks for poor health. For example, the introduction of sour gas wells and logging operations around the reserves of the Lubicon First Nation in Alberta has resulted in a dramatic increase in illness. More than one in three members of the Lubicon population suffers from such health problems as tuberculosis, respiratory difficulties, and cancer at rates far above the national average (Barlow and May, 2000: 183). **Environmental racism**, or the tendency for hazardous waste sites and polluting industries to be located near First Nations communities or areas populated by the poor, the politically marginalized, or certain visible minority groups, also contributes to lower levels of health. For example, in the 1980s, the pulp-and-paper industry's mercury poisoning of the English-Wabigoon river system in western Ontario near the Manitoba border led to the virtual destruction of the Grassy Narrows Indians' way of life and means of livelihood (Shkilnyk, 1985). More recently, "patterns of atmospheric cycling have made the North a dumping ground for industrial chemicals that . . . [are] never used there. The chemicals bioaccumulate, delivering a higher level of toxic concentration to each level up the food chain. As a result, the breast milk of Inuit mothers is 10 times as contaminated as that of southern Canadian women" (Barlow and May, 2000: 184). This situation provides a striking illustration of how human–environmental conditions can cause illness and death (see Chapter 12, Technology, the Environment, and Social Movements).

2. *Lifestyle factors.* Smoking, excessive use of alcohol and drugs, poor diet, lack of exercise, and social isolation are among the chief lifestyle factors associated with poor health and premature death. For example, smoking is associated with lung cancer, cardiovascular disease, strokes, emphysema, spontaneous abortion, premature birth, and neonatal death. In Canada, about 50 000 deaths a year are caused by smoking and other use of tobacco products. About a fifth of all deaths can be attributed to tobacco use (Makomaski Illing and Kaiserman, 2004). Social isolation, too, affects a person's chance of becoming ill and dying prematurely. Thus, unmarried people have a greater chance of dying prematurely than do

Photos.com

married people. At any age, the death of a spouse increases a person's chance of dying, while remarrying decreases the chance of dying (Helsing, Szklo, and Comstock, 1981). Social isolation is a particularly big problem among older people who retire, lose a spouse and friends, and cannot rely on family members or state institutions for social support. Such people are prone to fall into a state of depression, which contributes to ill health.

3. *Factors related to the public health and health care systems*. The state of a nation's health depends partly on public and private efforts to improve people's well-being and treat their illnesses. The public health system comprises government-run programs that ensure access to clean drinking water, basic sewage and sanitation services, and inoculation against infectious diseases. The absence of a public health system is associated with high rates of disease and low life expectancy. The health care system comprises a nation's clinics, hospitals, and other facilities for ensuring health and treating illness. The absence of a system that ensures its citizens access to a minimum standard of health care is also associated with high rates of disease and shorter life expectancy.

A health worker at Nazareth House in Cape Town, South Africa, lavishes care and attention on some of the 41 infected children in her care. Nearly 11 percent of South Africa's adult population is infected with HIV/AIDS.

© Mike Hutchings/Reuters/Corbis

Exposure to all three sets of social causes of illness and death listed above is strongly related to country of residence, class, race, and gender. We now consider the impact of these factors, beginning with country of residence.

Country of Residence

HIV/AIDS is the leading cause of death in the poverty-stricken part of Africa south of the Sahara desert. Figure 11.2 shows that by the end of 2008, 22.4 million sub-Saharan Africans—5 percent of the adult population—were living with HIV/AIDS. In contrast, 0.6 percent of North American adults and 0.3 percent of Western and Central European adults were living with HIV/AIDS. Yet spending on research and treatment is concentrated overwhelmingly in the rich countries of North America and Western Europe. As the case of HIV/AIDS illustrates, global inequality influences the exposure of people to different health risks.

You might think that prosperity increases health through biomedical advances, such as new medicines and diagnostic tools. If so, you are only partly correct. Biomedical advances do increase life expectancy. In particular, vaccines against infectious diseases have done much to improve health and ensure longer life. However, the creation of a sound public health system is even more important in this regard. If a country can provide its citizens with clean water and a sewage system, epidemics decline in frequency and severity while life expectancy soars.

The industrialized countries started developing their public health systems in the mid-nineteenth century. Social reformers, concerned citizens, scientists, and doctors joined industrialists and politicians in urging governments to develop health policies that would help create a healthier labour force and citizenry (Bricker and Greenspon, 2001: 178–83; Goubert, 1989 [1986]; McNeill, 1976). But what was possible in North America and Western Europe 150 years ago is not possible in many developing countries today. Most of us take clean water for granted, but more than a sixth of the world's people do not have access to a sanitary water supply (de Villiers, 1999).

Other indicators of health inequality for selected countries are given in Table 11.2 on page 250. We see that, in general, there is a positive association between national wealth and good health. Canada, the United States, and Japan are rich countries. They spend a substantial part of their wealth on health care. Many physicians and nurses service the populations. As a result, infant mortality (the annual number of deaths before the age of one for every 1000 live births) is low. India, which is poorer than Canada, the United States, and Japan, spends a smaller proportion of its wealth on health care. Accordingly, its population is less healthy in a number of respects. The sub-Saharan country of Lesotho is one of the poorest

FIGURE 11.2

People with HIV/AIDS, 2008 (adult prevalence in parentheses)

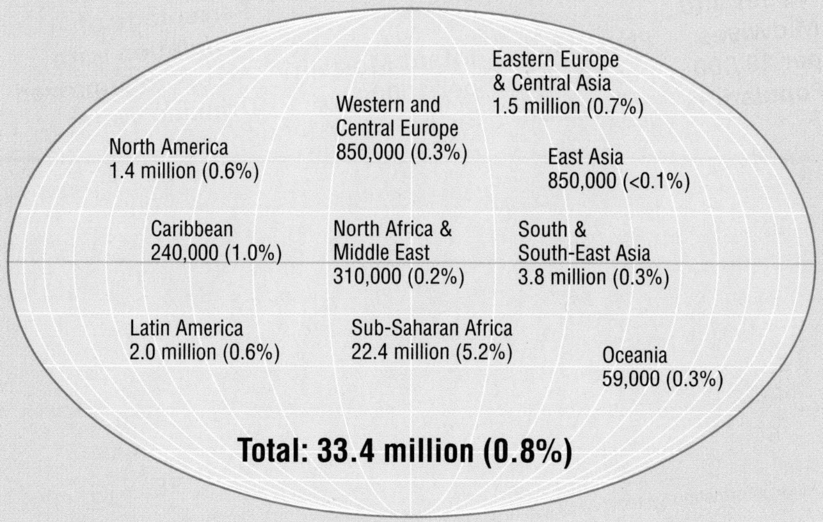

North America
1.4 million (0.6%)

Western and
Central Europe
850,000 (0.3%)

Eastern Europe
& Central Asia
1.5 million (0.7%)

East Asia
850,000 (<0.1%)

Caribbean
240,000 (1.0%)

North Africa &
Middle East
310,000 (0.2%)

South &
South-East Asia
3.8 million (0.3%)

Latin America
2.0 million (0.6%)

Sub-Saharan Africa
22.4 million (5.2%)

Oceania
59,000 (0.3%)

Total: 33.4 million (0.8%)

Sources: UNAIDS. 2009. 09 AIDS Epidemic Update. Geneva. http://data.unaids.org/pub/Report/2009/JC1700_Epi_Update_2009_en.pdf (retrieved 1 April 2010).

Biomedical advances increase life expectancy, but the creation of a sound public health system has even more dramatic benefits.

Mark Richards/PhotoEdit

countries in the world. It spends little on health care, has few medical personnel, and suffers from high rates of infant mortality.

LO² Class Inequalities and Health Care

In Canada, despite our system of universal health care, socioeconomic status is related to numerous aspects of health and illness (Raphael, 2004). On average, people with low income die at a younger age than do people with high income. Canadians enjoy a lower rate of illness and longer life expectancy at each step up the income ladder (Health Canada, 1999a, 1999b). Poverty is associated with high rates of tobacco and alcohol consumption, obesity, physical inactivity, and violence (Health Canada, 1999b).

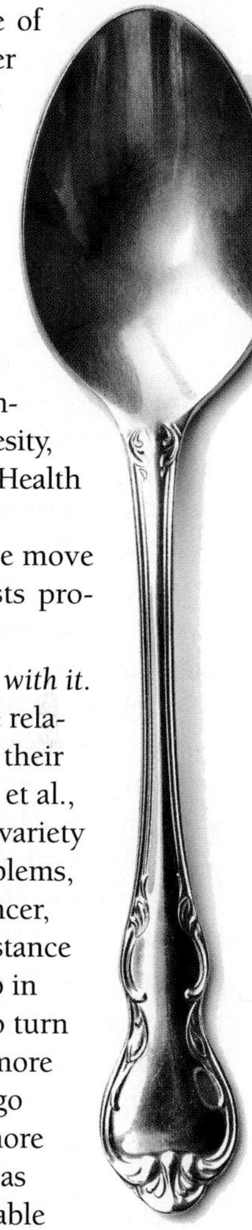

Why does health deteriorate as we move down the class hierarchy? Sociologists propose several explanations:

1. *High stress and the inability to cope with it.* People in lower classes experience relatively high stress levels because of their difficult living conditions (Kessler et al., 1994). Stress has been linked to a variety of physical and mental health problems, including high blood pressure, cancer, chronic fatigue, violence, and substance abuse. Moreover, people higher up in the class structure are often able to turn stress off. They can, for instance, more easily take a few days off work or go on vacation. Many problems are more burdensome when such resources as money and influence are not available to address them. Upper-class people can pay others to fix their cars or their offspring's legal mishaps. Lower-class families may have to go into debt or simply accept some bad outcomes as unavoidable (Cockerham, 1998; Epstein, 1998; Evans, 1999; Wilkinson and Marmot, 2003). Mishaps aside, lower-class families must endure greater crowding; poorer dwelling quality; working conditions that

Aaron Amat/Shutterstock

TABLE 11.2
Health Indicators, Selected Countries, 2009

Country	Expenditure on Health as Percentage of GDP (2006)	Nurses and Midwives per 10 000 Population	Physicians per 10 000 Population	Infant Mortality per 1000 Live Births	Percentage of Population with Access to Improved Drinking Water Source
Japan	7.7	95	21	1	100
Canada	8.8	101	19	3	100
United States	13.2	94	26	4	99
India	4.3	13	6	39	89
Lesotho	6.2	6	1	52	78

Source: World Health Organization. 2010. WHO Statistical Information System (WHOSIS). http://www.who.int/whosis/en/index.html (retrieved 1 April 2010).

are more noxious, dangerous, and unpleasant; and longer hours of work to make ends meet.

2. *Differences in the earliest stages of development that have lifelong consequences.* Inequalities at the start of life have strong health consequences for a lifetime (Forrest and Riley, 2004). Poor nutrition during pregnancy, stress, maternal smoking and misuse of drugs and alcohol, insufficient exercise and inadequate prenatal care typically lead to suboptimal fetal development (Wilkinson and Marmot, 2003: 14). Mothers with low incomes are more likely to provide such unfavourable starts to life.

3. *Lack of knowledge.* People who are less educated and who have less exposure to educated advisers tend to have less knowledge about healthy lifestyles. For example, they are less likely to know what constitutes a nutritious diet. This, too, contributes to their propensity to illness. Illness, in turn, makes it more difficult for poor people to escape poverty (Abraham, 1993).

4. *Unequal access to health resources.* A disproportionately large number of poor Canadians live in areas that have inferior medical services. For example, there are fewer hospitals, physicians, and nurses per capita in rural areas than in urban areas. As well, the quality of preventive, diagnostic, and treatment facilities is generally superior in urban areas. Moreover,

many low- and middle-income Canadians have limited or no access to eye care, dentistry, mental health counselling, and prescription drugs (Boychuk, 2002; Health Canada, 1999a).

5. *Environmental exposure.* As we saw earlier, poor people are more likely than rich people to be exposed to environmental risks that have a negative impact on their health. There is a striking lack of incinerators, pulp and paper mills, oil refineries, dumpsites, factories, and mines in Westmount (Montreal), Tuxedo (Winnipeg), Rosedale (Toronto), and other wealthy Canadian neighbourhoods (see Chapter 12, Technology, the Environment, and Social Movements).

Racial Inequalities in Health Care

Racial disparities in health status are also large. For example, the life expectancy of Status Indians is seven to eight years shorter than that of non-Aboriginal Canadians, and illegal drug use is high among Aboriginal peoples (Canadian Aboriginal News, 2001; Canadian Institute for Health Information, 2004; Scott, 1997). Despite the health risks to both the mother and the developing fetus, more than half of Indian women and three-quarters of Inuit women smoke during pregnancy, compared with about 20 percent for all women in Canada (Canadian Centre on Substance Abuse, 1999).

Such health disparities are partly due to economic differences among racial groups. In addition, researchers have begun to emphasize how racially marginalized groups are subject to negative health outcomes because of the cumulative effects of social exclusion based on race. Researchers have observed these effects for African Americans in the United States, Aboriginal Canadians, and other groups (Galabuzi, 2004; Wilkinson and Marmot, 2003).

How does social exclusion influence health apart from the obvious fact that excluded groups experience higher rates of poverty? In brief, labour market segregation, high unemployment, low occupation status, substandard housing, dangerous or distressed neighbourhoods, homelessness, dangerous worksites, extended hours, multiple jobs, and experience with everyday forms of racism lead to unequal health service utilization and differential health status (Galabuzi, 2004: 3). Even when members of socially excluded groups are employed, they are more likely to continue to live in inferior areas because of racial discrimination in housing, and such areas typically suffer from reduced access to medical services. Those who nevertheless seek medical services often encounter racially based misunderstanding or even hostility. The cumulative result of these and other factors is considerable—27 percent of First Nations members living on reserves recently reported fair or poor health, compared with only 12 percent of other Canadians (Canadian Institute for Health Information, 2004: 81).

Gender Inequalities in Health Care: The Feminist Contribution

Feminist scholars have brought health inequalities based on gender to the attention of the sociological community. In a review of the relevant literature, one researcher concluded that such gender inequalities are substantial (Haas, 1998):

- Gender bias exists in medical research. Public health systems have been slower to address and more likely to neglect women's health issues than men's health issues. Thus, more research has focused on "men's diseases," such as cardiac arrest, than on "women's diseases," such as breast cancer. Similarly, women have been excluded from participating in major health research studies that have examined the relationship between Aspirin use and heart disease; and how cholesterol levels, blood pressure, and smoking affect heart disease (Johnson and Fee, 1997). Medical research is only beginning to

explore the fact that women may react differently from men to some illnesses and may require different treatment regimes.
- Gender bias also exists in medical treatment. For example, women undergo fewer kidney transplants, cardiac procedures, and other treatments than men do.
- Because, on average, women live longer than men do, they experience greater lifetime risk of functional disability and chronic illness, and greater need for long-term care. The low status of women in many less-developed countries results in their being nutritionally deprived and having less access to medical care than men do. As a result, women in developing countries suffer high rates of mortality and morbidity (acute and chronic illness) because of high rates of complication associated with pregnancy and childbirth. About one-quarter to one-half of deaths among women in less developed countries are attributed to pregnancy-related complications ("Maternal Mortality," 1998).
- Canadian women face a higher risk than men do of poverty after divorce or widowhood. Because poverty contributes to ill health, we would expect improvements in women's economic standing to be reflected in improved health status for women.

In sum, although on average women live longer than men do, gender inequalities have a negative impact on women's health. Women's health is negatively affected by differences between women and men in access to gender-appropriate medical research and treatment, as well as the economic resources needed to secure adequate health care.

LO³ COMPARATIVE HEALTH CARE FROM A CONFLICT PERSPECTIVE

We noted earlier that rich countries spend more on health care than poor countries do, as a result of which their populations enjoy longer life expectancy. This does not mean that money always buys good health. The United States spends about 50 percent more per person on health care than Japan does and 20 percent more than Canada does. The United States has 37 percent more doctors

morbidity Acute and chronic illness.

per 10 000 people than Canada does and almost 24 percent more than Japan does. Yet the United States has a higher rate of infant mortality and shorter life expectancy than Canada and Japan do. The American case shows that spending more money on health care does not always improve the health of a nation.

What accounts for the American anomaly? Why do Americans spend more on health care than any other country yet wind up with a population that, on average, is less healthy than the population of other rich countries?

One reason for the anomaly is that the gap between rich and poor is greater in the United States than in Canada, Japan, Sweden, France, and other rich countries. In general, the higher the level of inequality in a country, the less healthy its population is (Wilkinson, 1996). Because, as we saw in Chapter 6, Social Stratification: Canadian and Global Perspectives, the United States contains a higher percentage of poor people than other rich countries do, its average level of health is lower. Moreover, because income inequality has widened in the United States since the early 1970s, health disparities among income groups have grown (Williams and Collins, 1995).

A second reason for the American anomaly is that physicians, hospitals, pharmaceutical companies, and other providers of health care are able to charge substantially higher prices in the United States than elsewhere (Anderson, Reinhardt, Hussey, and Petrosyan, 2003: 89). To understand why, we must examine the American health care system from a comparative, conflict perspective.

You will recall that conflict theory is concerned mainly with the question of how privileged groups seek to maintain their advantages and subordinate groups seek to increase theirs. As such, conflict theory is an illuminating approach to analyzing the American health care system. We can usefully see health care in the United States as a system of privilege for some and disadvantage for others. It thus contributes to the poor health of less well-to-do Americans.

Consider, for example, that the United States lacks a public health care system that covers the entire population. In the U.K., Sweden, and Denmark, public spending

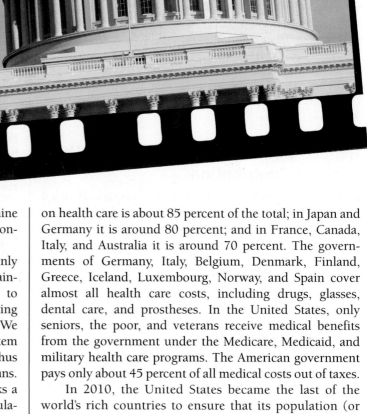

Jonathan Larsen/Shutterstock

on health care is about 85 percent of the total; in Japan and Germany it is around 80 percent; and in France, Canada, Italy, and Australia it is around 70 percent. The governments of Germany, Italy, Belgium, Denmark, Finland, Greece, Iceland, Luxembourg, Norway, and Spain cover almost all health care costs, including drugs, glasses, dental care, and prostheses. In the United States, only seniors, the poor, and veterans receive medical benefits from the government under the Medicare, Medicaid, and military health care programs. The American government pays only about 45 percent of all medical costs out of taxes.

In 2010, the United States became the last of the world's rich countries to ensure that its population (or at least 95 percent of it) would at least be covered by health insurance. Before the new law was passed, about 15 percent of Americans lacked health insurance and another 15 percent lacked adequate coverage (Anderson et al., 2003; "Health Care Systems," 2001; Schoen, Doty, Collins, and Holmgren, 2005; Starr, 1994). But even after the new law is fully implemented in 2016, the distinctive feature of the American health care system—substantial private provision—will persist. It is a very expensive mechanism that leaves many people poorly served. The relatively privileged obtain health services at high prices while the less well-off are effectively priced out (see the Sociology at the Movies box on the next page).

The Canadian Health Care System

In contrast to the United States, Canada has a national health insurance system that is sometimes loosely described as socialized medicine. Despite differences in how socialized medicine works in different countries, common to all such systems

> **socialized medicine** In countries with socialized medicine, the government (1) directly controls the financing and organization of health services, (2) directly pays providers, (3) guarantees equal access to health care, and (4) allows some private care for individuals who are willing to pay for their medical expenses.

Barry Philp/GetStock.com

Tommy Douglas (1904–86), leader of the Co-operative Commonwealth Federation (the precursor of the NDP) and the father of socialized medicine in Canada.

CHAPTER 11 Health and Medicine

Sicko

In *Sicko,* an astonished Michael Moore learns that in Britain, doctors are paid more if their patients become healthier.

The Canadian Press (© Lions Gate/The Everett Collection)

In 2010, about 15 percent of Americans had no access to health care and another 15 percent lacked adequate coverage. It would be too easy to tell horror stories about the former, so Michael Moore's *Sicko* does not dwell on them. Instead, his widely acclaimed documentary tells viewers how ordinary Americans who had health care were routinely shocked to discover just how inadequate their coverage was. Here are three cases in point:

- A woman faints on a sidewalk and is taken to the hospital by ambulance, but her insurer bills her for the trip because she didn't have it pre-authorized. "How could I have it pre-authorized when I was unconscious?" she asks.
- When the World Trade Center was attacked in 2001, some brave souls volunteered to help rescue people. Many of them later developed respiratory and other medical problems but their insurers refused to cover their medical and drug expenses because they voluntarily put themselves at risk.
- A life of hard work enabled Larry and Donna to own their own house and put all six of their children through college. Now retired, and with Larry in poor health, they

must sell their house to pay for medical fees not covered by their insurer. They are forced to move into a small room in the home of one of their adult children.

The lack of a public health care system and relatively little government regulation of the private system have made such occurrences common in the United States. Privately owned health maintenance organizations (HMOs) administer medical treatment in return for a fee paid by individuals, unions, and employers. As profit-seeking companies, HMOs have routinely sought to deny claims and avoid expensive procedures. Some of the worst excesses of HMOs will be curbed by new American laws that started to come into effect in 2010, but they have until now acted in a way that lowers life expectancy in the United States below the level of life expectancy in other rich countries.

Moore visits Canada, France, the U.K., and Cuba, and makes the health care systems of these countries seem perfect. They are not. For example, Canadians know all too well that governments and the medical community are working hard to shorten waiting times for elective surgery and diagnostic procedures, increase the availability of expensive imaging equipment, and so on. But whatever the shortcomings of universal medical care, *Sicko* serves as a cautionary tale for those who sing the praises of privatization. As Moore says, "If you want to stay healthy in America, don't get sick."

Critical Thinking Question

- Some Canadians have proposed a "two-tiered" health system. All Canadians would have access to a certain level of health care in the public tier but it would be possible to buy special services in the private sphere. What do you think the advantages and disadvantages of such a system would be?

is the fact that the government (1) directly controls the financing and organization of health services, (2) directly pays providers, (3) guarantees equal access to health care, and (4) allows some private care for individuals who are willing to pay for their medical expenses (Cockerham, 1998). Canada does not have a true system of socialized medicine, however, because the government does not employ Canadian doctors. Most of Canada's doctors are independent practitioners who are generally paid on a fee-for-service basis and submit claims directly to the provincial or territorial health insurance plan for payment.

Tommy Douglas is widely credited with being Canada's "father of medicare." Douglas led the Co-operative Commonwealth Federation (CCF) to political victory in Saskatchewan in 1944, making it the first socialist party to win a North American election. (Later, Douglas helped turn the CCF into the New Democratic Party.) He served as premier of Saskatchewan from 1944 to 1961, introducing many social reforms including universal medical care. His government's actions stirred up sharp opposition, including a province-wide physicians' strike, but Saskatchewan's medicare ultimately succeeded. In 1968 it became a model for the whole country (CBC, 2004a).

Although Canada's health care system is often lauded as among the best in the world, problems exist. One source of concern is waiting times for non-emergency services. Although our health care system is based on the premise that "all citizens will have access to the care they need within a reasonable time period" (Health Canada, 1999a), most people agree that some waits are too long. In 2007, 46 percent of Canadians who needed to consult a specialist for a new condition received an appointment within a month, but 14 percent had to wait three months or more. Waiting periods were slightly longer for non-emergency surgery and somewhat shorter for diagnostic tests (Health Canada, 2009; see Figure 11.3). Such waits are often unpleasant. Nearly a fifth of people who seek specialist care for a new condition report ill effects from waiting; 1 in 12 complain of pain (Statistics Canada, 2006a).

Still, about two-thirds of Canadians view their health care system positively. In contrast, only about one-third of Americans see their health care system in a positive light (Angus Reid Global Monitor, 2009). Most of the Canadians

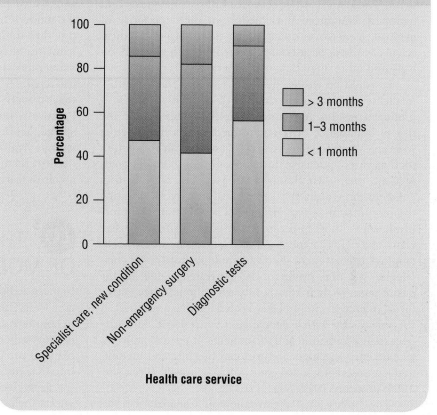

FIGURE 11.3

Waiting Times for Canadians Seeking Non-Emergency Health Care Services, 2007

Source: Health Canada. 2009. "Healthy Canadians: A Federal Report on Comparable Health Indicators 2008." http://www.hc-sc.gc.ca/hcs-sss/pubs/system-regime/2008-fed-comp-indicat/index-eng.php (retrieved 2 April 2010).

who hold negative opinions prefer a more American, two-tiered system that would allow people who can afford superior care to buy it. Most Americans who hold negative opinions prefer a Canadian-type system with greater government regulation. In both countries, therefore, health care remains a subject of political conflict.

LO⁴ THE PROFESSIONALIZATION OF MEDICINE

Earlier, we noted that from the conflict perspective the health system can usefully be viewed as a system of privilege and disadvantage. We now extend that argument by showing how physicians became such a privileged part of the health care system.

In the early nineteenth century, the practice of medicine was in a chaotic state. Herbalists, faith healers, midwives, druggists, and medical doctors vied to meet the health needs of the public. A century later, the dust had settled. Medical science was victorious. Its first series of breakthroughs involved identifying the bacteria and viruses responsible for various diseases and then developing effective procedures and vaccines to combat them. These and subsequent triumphs in diagnosis and treatment convinced most people of the superiority of medical science over other approaches to health. Medical science worked, or at least it seemed to work more effectively and more often than other therapies.

It would be wrong, however, to think that scientific medicine came to dominate health care only because it produced results. A second, sociological reason for the rise to dominance of scientific medicine is that doctors were able to professionalize. A **profession** is an occupation that requires extensive formal education. Professionals regulate their own training and practice. They restrict competition within the profession, mainly by limiting the recruitment of practitioners. They minimize competition with other professions, partly by laying exclusive claim to a field of expertise. Professionals are usually self-employed. They exercise considerable authority over their clients. And they profess to be motivated mainly by the desire to serve their community even though they earn a lot of money in the process. Professionalization, then, is the process by which people gain control and authority over their occupation and their clients. It results in professionals enjoying high occupational prestige and income, and considerable social and political power (Freidson, 1986; Johnson, 1972; Starr, 1982).

The professional organization of Canadian doctors is the Canadian Medical Association (CMA), founded in 1867 by 167 doctors in Quebec City. It quickly set about broadcasting the successes of medical science and criticizing alternative approaches to health as quackery and charlatanism. The CMA was able to have laws passed to restrict medical licences to graduates of approved schools and to ensure that only graduates of those schools could train the next generation of doctors. By restricting entry into the profession, and by specifying what "paramedical" practitioners could and could not do, members of the medical establishment ensured their own status, prestige, and high incomes. For example, midwifery was originally included in the work of the Victorian Order of Nurses, founded in 1897 by the National Council of Women to assist rural women who otherwise lacked access to health care. However, "the opposition of the medical establishment in Canada was so great to what it saw as an infringement of its

prerogatives that the idea was allowed to die" (Mitchinson, 1993: 396). When medicine became a profession, it also became a monopoly.

The modern hospital is the institutional manifestation of the medical doctor's professional dominance. Until the twentieth century, most doctors operated small clinics and visited patients in their homes. However, the rise of the modern hospital was guaranteed by medicine's scientific turn in the mid-nineteenth century. Expensive equipment for diagnosis and treatment had to be shared by many physicians. This required the centralization of medical facilities in large, bureaucratically run institutions that strongly resist deviations from professional conduct. Practically nonexistent in 1850, hospitals are now widespread. Yet despite their undoubted benefits, economic as well as health related, hospitals and the medicine practised in them are not an unqualified blessing, as you are about to learn.

LO⁵ THE SOCIAL LIMITS OF MODERN MEDICINE

In early February 2003, a 64-year-old professor of medicine from Guangzhou, the capital of Guangdong Province in southern China, came down with an unidentified respiratory ailment. It did not bother him enough to cancel a planned trip to Hong Kong, so on February 12 he checked into that city's Metropole Hotel. Ironically, as it turned out, the desk clerk assigned him room 911. Other ninth-floor guests included an older couple from Toronto and three young women from Singapore. All these people, along with a local resident who visited the hotel during this period, fell ill between February 15 and 27 with the same medical problem as the professor. The professor died on March 4. The Canadian couple returned to Toronto on February 23 and the woman died at her home on March 5. The eventual diagnosis: severe acute respiratory syndrome, or SARS, a new (and in 9 percent of cases, deadly) pneumonia-like illness for which there is no vaccine and no cure.

SARS originated in Guangdong Province. By June 12, 8445 cases of SARS had been identified in 29 countries, and 790 people had died of the disease. Quickly and efficiently, global travel had spread HIV/AIDS, West Nile virus, and now SARS from remote and isolated locales to the world's capitals. The United Nations has called Toronto the world's most multicultural city. It has a large Chinese population, mainly from Hong Kong. It is therefore not surprising that, outside of China, Hong Kong, and Taiwan, Toronto became the world's number one SARS hot spot (Abraham, 2003; World Health Organization, 2003).

Once identified as a potential SARS case, a person is quarantined at home for 10 days. However, if people exhibit symptoms of the disease, they go to a poorly ventilated

profession An occupation that requires extensive formal education and whose practitioners regulate their own training practice, restrict competition, and exercise considerable authority over their clients.

institution where the air is maintained at a constant warm temperature that is ideal for the multiplication of germs. In this institution, many young and older people with weakened immune systems congregate. A steady stream of germs pours in around the clock. Staff members too often fail to follow elementary principles of good hygiene. That institution is a hospital. There, germs spread. Most of the 238 people in Toronto who had SARS as of June 12, 2003, caught it while in hospital, before stringent isolation and disinfection procedures were imposed.

Our characterization of hospitals as ideal environments for the spread of germs may seem harsh. It is not. Hospitals have become dangerous places in North America. In Canada, about 80 percent of hospitals fall seriously short in preventing patients from getting hospital infections. Some 250 000 patients experience hospital infections every year. If the government classified hospital infections as a cause of death, it would be the fourth-leading cause of death in the country (Zoutman et al., 2003).

The situation has deteriorated largely because we invest disproportionately in expensive, high-tech, cutting-edge diagnostic equipment and treatment while we skimp on simple, labour-intensive, time-consuming hygiene. Cleaning staffs are too small and insufficiently trained. Nurses are too few. According to research by the Harvard School of Public Health, these are the kinds of factors correlated with hospital-acquired infections. As one registered nurse says, "When you have less time to save lives, do you take 30 seconds to wash your hands? When you're speeding up you have to cut corners. We don't always wash our hands. I'm not saying it's right, but you've got to deal with reality" (quoted in Berens, 2002).

It was not always the reality. Until the 1940s, North American hospital workers were obsessed with cleanliness. They had to be. In the era before the widespread use of penicillin and antibiotics, infection often meant death. In the 1950s, however, the prevention of infections in hospitals became less of a priority because penicillin and antibiotics became widely available. It was less expensive to wait until a patient got sick and then respond to symptoms by prescribing drugs than to prevent the sickness in the first place. Doctors and nurses have grown lax about hygiene over the past half-century.

One American report cites a dozen health care studies showing that about half of doctors and nurses do not disinfect their hands between patients (Berens, 2002). Just a few years ago, one small hospital north of Montreal cut serious infections by 80 percent simply by improving hygiene (CBC, 2004b).

Using penicillin and antibiotics indiscriminately has its own costs. When living organisms encounter a deadly threat, only the few mutations that are strong enough to resist the threat survive and go on to reproduce. Accordingly, if you use a lot of penicillin and antibiotics, "super germs" that are resistant to these drugs multiply. This is just what has happened. (It hasn't helped that antibiotics are routinely added to cattle feed to prevent disease and thereby lower beef production costs. This practice builds up resistance to antibiotics in humans.)

Penicillin could kill nearly all staphylococcus germs in the 1940s, but by 1982 it was effective in fewer than 10 percent of cases. In the 1970s, doctors turned to the more powerful methicillin, which in 1974 could kill 98 percent of staphylococcus germs. By the mid-1990s, it could kill only about 50 percent of them. Various strains of drug-resistant germs now cause pneumonia, blood poisoning, tuberculosis, and other infectious diseases. Drug-resistant germs that could formerly survive only in the friendly hospital environment have now adapted to the harsher environment outside the hospital walls. True, some pharmaceutical companies are developing new antibiotics to fight drug-resistant bugs. However, their efforts lack energy because antibiotics are prescribed for only short periods and are therefore not big money makers (Groopman, 2008).

The epidemic of infectious diseases caused by slack hospital hygiene and the overuse of antibiotics suggests that social circumstances constrain the success of modern medicine. It is difficult to see how we can solve these problems without enforcing strict rules regarding hospital disinfection and getting governments to incentivize pharmaceutical companies to invest more in developing new antibiotics.

Meanwhile, many people are growing skeptical of the claims of modern medicine. They are beginning to challenge traditional medicine and explore alternatives that rely less on high technology and drugs and are more sensitive to the need for maintaining balance between humans and their

environment in the pursuit of good health. In concluding this chapter, we explore some of these challenges and alternatives.

LO⁶ CHALLENGES TO TRADITIONAL MEDICAL SCIENCE

Patient Activism

By the mid-twentieth century, the dominance of medical science in Canada was virtually complete. Any departure from the dictates of scientific medicine was considered deviant. Thus, when sociologist Talcott Parsons defined the sick role in 1951, he pointed out that illness suspends routine responsibilities and is not deliberate. He stressed that people playing the sick role must want to be well and must seek competent help, cooperating with health care practitioners at all times (Parsons, 1951: 428 ff.). Must they? According to Parsons's definition, a competent person suffering from a terminal illness cannot reasonably demand that doctors refrain from using heroic measures to prolong his or her life. And by his definition, a patient cannot reasonably question doctors' orders, no matter how well-educated the patient and how debatable the effect of the prescribed treatment. Although Parsons's definition of the sick role may sound plausible to many people born before World War II, it probably sounds authoritarian and utterly foreign to most young people today.

That is because things have changed. The public is more highly educated now than it was 50 years ago. Many people now have the knowledge, vocabulary, self-confidence, and political organization to participate in their own health care rather than passively accepting whatever experts tell them. Research shows that this trend is evident even among older Canadians and lower-income earners. Canadian baby boomers and younger generations are even less likely to follow a doctor's advice uncritically; in fact, only one-third do so (Bricker and Greenspon, 2001: 221). Increasingly, patients are taught to perform simple, routine medical procedures themselves. Many people now use the Internet to seek information about various illnesses and treatments. Increasingly, they are uncomfortable with doctors acting as authoritarian parents and patients acting as dutiful children. Surveys reveal that 90 percent of Canadians now prefer that their doctor offer several treatment options rather than a single course of action, 86 percent say they usually ask their doctor many questions about procedures, 76 percent say they are more likely to question their doctor now than they were in the past, while about 70 percent claim to always ask their doctor about medicines that are prescribed (Bricker and Greenspon, 2001: 119–220). Doctors now routinely seek patients' informed consent for some procedures rather than deciding what to do on their own. Similarly, most hospitals have established ethics committees, which were unheard of in the 1960s (Rothman, 1991). These are responses to patients wanting a more active role in their own care.

Some recent challenges to the authority of medical science are organized and political. For example, when AIDS activists challenged the stereotype of AIDS as a "gay disease" and demanded more research funding to help find a cure, they changed research and treatment priorities in a way that could never have happened in the 1960s (Epstein, 1996). Similarly, when feminists supported the reintroduction of midwifery and argued against medical intervention in routine childbirths, they challenged the wisdom of established medical practice. The previously male-dominated profession of medicine considered the male body the norm and paid relatively little attention to "women's diseases," such as breast cancer, and "women's issues," such as reproduction. This, too, is now changing thanks to feminist intervention (Boston Women's Health Book Collective, 1998; Rothman, 1982, 1989; Schiebinger, 1993). And although doctors and the larger society traditionally treated people with disabilities as incompetent children, various movements now seek to empower them (Charlton, 1998; Zola, 1982). As a result, attitudes toward people with disabilities are changing.

Alternative Medicine

Other challenges to the authority of medical science are less organized and less political than those just mentioned. Consider, for example, alternative medicine. In 2005, about 10 percent of Canadian men and 18 percent of Canadian women over the age of 12 used some form of alternative medicine during the preceding year, with the percentage rising from east to west (see Figure 11.4). The most widely used health alternative is chiropractic services. Those with chronic disorders, including back problems and multiple chemical sensitivities, are more likely to consult an alternative health service provider. Use of alternative medicine increases with income and education (Park, 2005).

Despite its growing popularity, many medical doctors were hostile to alternative medicine until recently. They lumped all alternative therapies together and dismissed them as unscientific (Campion, 1993). By the late 1990s, however, a more tolerant attitude was evident in many quarters. For some kinds of ailments, physicians

> sick role Playing the sick role, according to Talcott Parsons, involves the non-deliberate suspension of routine responsibilities, wanting to be well, seeking competent help, and cooperating with health care practitioners at all times.

began to recognize the benefits of at least the most popular forms of alternative medicine. For example, a 1998 editorial in the respected *New England Journal of Medicine* admitted that the beneficial effect of chiropractic on low back pain is "no longer in dispute" (Shekelle, 1998). This change in attitude was due in part to new scientific evidence from Canadian research showing that spinal manipulation is a relatively effective and inexpensive treatment for low back pain (Manga, Angus, and Swan, 1993). At the same time, however, alternative forms of medicine should not be assumed to be entirely risk-free. For example, to date, the majority of Canadian lawsuits against chiropractors have involved claims of muscular skeletal dysfunction, strains and sprains, and rib fractures. In other cases, however, more serious injury has occurred, including ruptured vertebral arteries and death (Cohen, 1999: 50).

Nevertheless, the medical profession's grudging acceptance of chiropractic in the treatment of low back pain indicates what we can expect in the uneasy relationship between scientific and alternative medicine in coming decades. Although many, if not most, alternative therapies (such as aromatherapy and foot reflexology) are non-invasive and relatively harmless, doctors and the general public will, for the most part, remain skeptical of alternative therapies unless properly conducted experiments demonstrate their beneficial effects.

Holistic Medicine

Medical doctors understand that a positive frame of mind often helps in the treatment of disease. For example, research shows that strong belief in the effectiveness of a cure can by itself improve the condition of about one-third of people suffering from chronic pain or fatigue (Campion, 1993). This is known as the **placebo effect**. Doctors also understand that conditions in the human environment affect people's health. However, despite their appreciation of the effect of mind and environment on the human body, traditional scientific medicine tends to respond to illness by treating disease symptoms as a largely physical and individual problem. Moreover, scientific medicine continues to subdivide into more specialized areas of practice that rely more and more heavily on drugs and high-tech machinery. Most doctors are less concerned with maintaining and improving health by understanding the larger mental and social context within which people become ill.

Traditional Indian and Chinese medicine takes a different approach. India's Ayurvedic medical tradition views individuals in terms of the flow of vital fluids or "humours" and their health in the context of their environment. In this view, maintaining good health requires not only balancing fluids in individuals but also balancing the relationship between individuals and the world around them (Zimmermann, 1987 [1982]). Despite significant differences, the fundamental outlook is similar in traditional Chinese medicine. Chinese medicine and its remedies, ranging from acupuncture to herbs, seek to restore individuals' internal balance, as well as their relationship to the outside world (Unschuld, 1985). Contemporary **holistic medicine**, the third and final challenge to traditional scientific medicine we will consider, takes an approach

FIGURE 11.4

Percentage of Canadians Who Contacted an Alternative Health Care Provider in Past Year, by Sex and Province, 2005

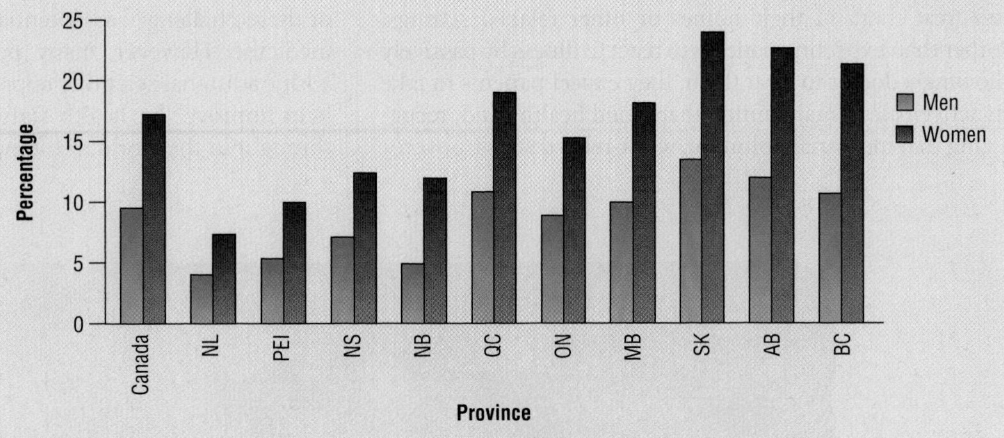

Source: Adapted from the Statistics Canada CANSIM database, http://cansim2.statcan.gc.ca Table 105-0462 (retrieved 2 April 2010).

placebo effect The positive influence on healing of a strong belief in the effectiveness of a cure.

holistic medicine Medical practice that emphasizes disease prevention. Holistic practitioners treat disease by taking into account the relationship between mind and body and between the individual and his or her social and physical environment.

similar to these "ethnomedical" traditions. Practitioners of holistic medicine argue that good health requires maintaining a balance between mind and body, and between the individual and the environment.

Most holistic practitioners do not reject scientific medicine. However, they emphasize disease *prevention*. Holistic practitioners seek to establish close ties with their patients and treat them in their homes or other relaxed settings. Rather than expecting patients to react to illness by passively allowing a doctor to treat them, they expect patients to take an active role in maintaining their good health. And, recognizing that industrial pollution, work-related stress, poverty, racial and gender inequality, and other social factors contribute heavily to disease, holistic practitioners sometimes become political activists (Hastings, Fadiman, and Gordon, 1980).

In sum, patient activism, alternative medicine, and holistic medicine represent the three biggest challenges to traditional scientific medicine today. Few people think of these challenges as potential replacements for scientific medicine. However, many people believe that, together with traditional scientific approaches, these challenges will help improve the health status of people in Canada and throughout the world in the twenty-first century.

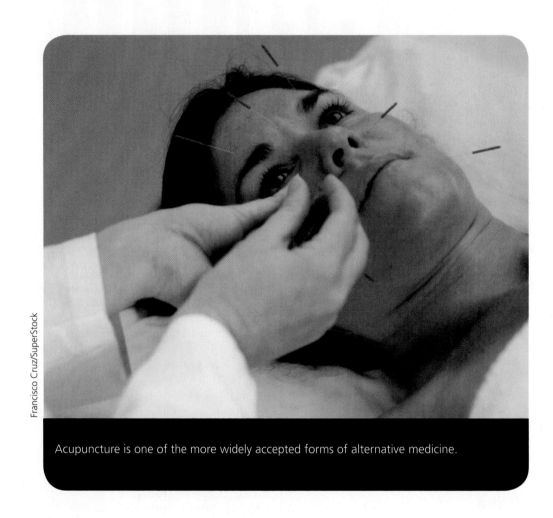

Francisco Cruz/SuperStock

Acupuncture is one of the more widely accepted forms of alternative medicine.

NEL

12

Technology, the Environment, and Social Movements

LEARNING OBJECTIVES:

LO¹ Technology transforms society and history, but human need shapes technological growth.

LO² Environmental issues become social problems only under certain social conditions.

LO³ Economically disadvantaged groups experience more environmental risks than others do.

LO⁴ Many people will not act to create a safe environment until repeated environmental catastrophes motivate them.

LO⁵ People are more inclined to form a social movement when strong social ties, resources, and opportunities allow them to express discontent.

LO⁶ Social movements grow when members make the activities, goals, and ideology of the movement consistent with the interests, beliefs, and values of potential recruits.

Technology: Saviour or Frankenstein?

On 6 August 1945, the United States Air Force dropped an atomic bomb on Hiroshima. The bomb killed about 200 000 Japanese, almost all of them civilians. It hastened the end of the World War II, thus making it unnecessary for American troops to suffer heavy losses in a land invasion of Japan.

Scholars interested in the relationship between technology and society recognize that Hiroshima divided the twentieth century into two distinct periods. We can call the period before Hiroshima the era of naive optimism. During that time, technology could do no wrong, or so it seemed to nearly all observers. **Technology** was widely defined as the application of scientific principles to the *improvement* of human life. It seemed to be driving humanity down a one-way street named progress, picking up speed with every passing year thanks to successively more powerful engines: steam, turbine, internal combustion, electric, jet, rocket, and nuclear. Technology produced tangible benefits. Its detailed workings rested on scientific principles that were mysterious to all but those with advanced science degrees. Therefore, most people regarded technologists with reverence and awe. They were viewed as a sort of priesthood whose objectivity allowed them to stand outside the everyday world and perform near-magical acts.

With Hiroshima, the blush was off the rose. Growing pessimism was, in fact, evident three weeks earlier, when the world's first nuclear bomb exploded at the Alamogordo Bombing Range in New Mexico. The bomb was the child of J. Robert Oppenheimer, appointed head of the top-secret Manhattan Project just 28 months earlier. After recruiting what General Leslie Groves called "the greatest collection of eggheads ever," including three past and seven future Nobel Prize winners, Oppenheimer organized the largest and most sophisticated technological project in human history up to that time. As an undergraduate at Harvard, Oppenheimer had studied Indian philosophy, among other subjects. On the morning of 16 July 1945, as the flash of intense white light faded and the purplish fireball rose, sucking desert sand and debris into a mushroom cloud more than 12 kilometres high, Oppenheimer quoted from Hindu scripture: "I am become Death, the shatterer of worlds" (quoted in Parshall, 1998).

> **technology** The practical application of scientific principles.

J. Robert Oppenheimer, the "father" of the atomic bomb.

activity as the blast at Hiroshima. It resulted in mass evacuations, more than 10 000 deaths, countless human and animal mutations, and hundreds of square kilometres of unusable cropland. In 1989, the *Exxon Valdez* ran aground in Prince William Sound, Alaska, spilling 42 million litres of crude oil, producing a dangerous slick more than 1600 kilometres long, causing billions of dollars of damage, and killing hundreds of thousands of animals.

By the mid-1980s, sociologist Charles Perrow was referring to such events as "normal accidents." The term normal accident recognizes that the very complexity of modern technologies ensures they will *inevitably* fail, though in unpredictable ways (Perrow, 1984). For example, a large computer program contains many thousands of conditional statements. They take the form if $x = y$, do z; if $a = b$, do c. When in use, the program activates many billions of *combinations* of conditional statements. As a result, complex programs cannot be tested for all possible eventualities. Therefore, when rare combinations of conditions occur, they have unforeseen consequences that are usually minor, occasionally amusing, sometimes expensive, and too often dangerous. You experience normal accidents when your home computer crashes or hangs.

German sociologist Ulrich Beck also coined a term that stuck when he said we live in a risk society. A risk society is a society in which technology distributes danger among all categories of the population. Some categories, however, are more exposed to technological danger than others. Moreover, in a risk society, danger does not result from technological accidents alone. In addition, increased risk is due to mounting *environmental* threats that are more widespread, chronic, and ambiguous than technological accidents—and therefore more stressful (Beck, 1992 [1986]; Freudenburg, 1997). New and frightening terms—greenhouse effect, global warming, acid rain, ozone depletion, endangered species—have entered our vocabulary. To many people, technology seems to be spinning out of control. From their point of view, it enables the production of ever

Overall, North Americans value science and technology highly. Still, in the postwar years a growing number of people have come to share Oppenheimer's doubts about the bomb. Indeed, they have extended those doubts not just to the peaceful use of nuclear energy but also to technology in general. Increasingly, people are beginning to think of technology as a monster run amok, a Frankenstein rather than a saviour.

In the 1970s and 1980s, a series of horrific disasters alerted many people (including some sociologists) to the fact that technological advance is not always beneficial, not even always benign. A gas leak at a poorly maintained Union Carbide pesticide plant in Bhopal, India, killed about 4000 people in 1984 and injured 30 000, a third of whom died excruciating deaths in the following years. In 1986, the No. 4 reactor at Chernobyl, Ukraine, exploded, releasing 30 to 40 times as much radio-

normal accidents Accidents that occur inevitably though unpredictably because of the very complexity of modern technologies.

risk society A society in which technology distributes environmental dangers among all categories of the population, albeit to varying degrees.

more goods and services, but at the cost of breathable air, drinkable water, safe sunlight, plant and animal diversity, and normal weather patterns.

These considerations raise four tough questions. We tackle each of them below. First, is technology *the* great driving force of historical and social change? This is the opinion of both cheerleaders and naysayers, those who view technology as our saviour and those who fear it as a Frankenstein. In contrast, we argue that technology is able to transform society only when it is coupled with a powerful social need. People control technology as much as technology transforms people. Second, if some people do control technology, then exactly who are they? We argue against the view that scientific and engineering wizards are in control. The military and big corporations now decide the direction of most technological research and its application. Third, what are the most dangerous spinoffs of technology and how is risk distributed among various social groups? We focus on global warming and "genetic pollution." We show

that although these dangers put all of humanity at risk, the degree of danger varies by class, race, and country. In brief, the socially and economically disadvantaged are most at risk. Fourth, how can we overcome the dangers of environmental degradation? We argue that market and technological solutions are insufficient by themselves. In addition, much self-sacrifice, cooperation, and political activism will be required.

LO¹ TECHNOLOGY *AND* PEOPLE MAKE HISTORY

Russian economist Nikolai Kondratiev was the first social scientist to notice that technologies are invented in clusters. As Table 12.1 shows, a new group of major inventions has cropped up every 40 to 60 years since the Industrial Revolution. Kondratiev argued that these flurries of creativity cause major economic growth spurts beginning

TABLE 12.1
"Kondratiev Waves" of Modern Technological Innovation and Economic Growth

Wave	Invention Dates	New Technologies	Base	Economic Growth Spurt
1	1760s–70s	Steam engine, textile manufacturing, chemistry, civil engineering	Britain	1780–1815
2	1820s	Railways, mechanical engineering	Britain, Continental Western Europe	1840–70
3	1870s–80s	Chemistry, electricity, internal combustion engine	Germany, United States	1890–1914
4	1930s–40s	Electronics, aerospace, chemistry	United States	1945–70
5	1970s	Microelectronics, biotechnology	United States, Japan	1985–?

Source: Adapted from Pacey (1983:32).; Pacey, Arnold. 1983. *The Culture of Technology.* Cambridge, MA: MIT Press.

technological determinism The belief that technology is the main factor shaping human history.

10 to 20 years later and lasting 25 to 35 years each. Thus, Kondratiev subscribed to a form of **technological determinism**, the belief that technology is the major force shaping human society and history (Ellul, 1964 [1954]).

Is it true that technology helps shape society and history? Of course it is. James Watt invented the steam engine in Britain in 1766. It was the main driving force in the mines, mills, factories, and railways of the Industrial Revolution. Gottlieb Daimler invented the internal com-

bustion engine in Germany in 1883. It was the foundation stone of two of the world's biggest industries: automobiles and petroleum. John Atanasoff was among the first people to invent the computer in 1939 at Iowa State College (now University). It utterly transformed the way we work, study, and entertain ourselves. It also put the spurs to one of the most sustained economic booms ever. We could easily cite many more examples of how technology shapes history and transforms society.

However, if we probe a little deeper into almost any technology, we notice a pattern: they did not become engines of economic growth until *social* conditions allowed them to do so. The original steam engine, for

U.S. Army Photos

ORDVAC, an early computer developed at the University of Illinois, was delivered to the Ballistic Research Laboratory at the Aberdeen Proving Ground of the United States Army. Technology typically advances when it is coupled with an urgent social need.

instance, was invented by Hero of Alexandria in the first century C.E. He used it as an amusing way of opening a door. People then promptly forgot the steam engine. Some 1700 years later, when the Industrial Revolution began, factories were first set up near rivers and streams, where water power was available. That was several years before Watt patented his steam engine. Watt's invention was all the rage once its potential became evident. But it did not cause the Industrial Revolution and it was adopted on a wide scale only after the social need for it emerged (Pool, 1997: 126–27).

Similarly, Atanasoff stopped work on the computer soon after the outbreak of World War II. But once the military potential of the computer became evident, its development resumed. The British computer Colossus helped decipher secret German codes in the last two years of the war and played an important role in the Allied victory. The University of Illinois delivered one of the earliest computers, the ORDVAC, to the Ballistic Research Laboratory at the Aberdeen Proving Ground of the U.S. Army. Again we see how a new technology becomes a major force in society and history only after it is coupled with an urgent social need. We conclude that technology and society influence each other. Scientific discoveries, once adopted on a wide scale, often transform societies. But scientific discoveries are turned into useful technologies only when social need demands it.

HOW HIGH TECH BECAME BIG TECH

Enjoying a technological advantage usually translates into big profits for businesses and military superiority for countries. In the nineteenth century, gaining technological advantage was still inexpensive. It took only modest capital investment, a little knowledge about the best way to organize work, and a handful of highly trained workers to build a shop to manufacture stirrups or even steam engines. In contrast, mass-producing cars, sending people to outer space, and performing other feats of twentieth- and twenty-first century technology requires enormous capital investment, detailed attention to the way work is organized, and legions of technical experts. Add to this the intensely competitive business and geopolitical environment of the twentieth and twenty-first centuries, and you can readily understand why ever larger sums have been invested in research and development over the past hundred years.

It was, in fact, already clear in the last quarter of the nineteenth century that turning scientific principles into technological innovations was going to require not just genius but also substantial resources, especially money and organization. Thus, Thomas Edison established the first "invention factory" at Menlo Park, New Jersey, in the late 1870s. Historian of science Robert Pool notes,

The most important factor in Edison's success—outside of his genius for invention—was the organization he had set up to assist him. By 1878, Edison had assembled at Menlo Park a staff of thirty scientists, metalworkers, glassblowers, draftsmen, and others working under his close direction and supervision. With such support, Edison boasted that he could turn out "a minor invention every ten days and a big thing every six months or so." (Pool, 1997: 22)

The phonograph and the electric light bulb were two such "big things." Edison inspired both. Both, however, were also expensive team efforts, motivated by vast commercial possibilities. (Edison founded General Electric, one of the biggest companies in the world.)

At the beginning of the twentieth century, the scientific or engineering genius operating in isolation was only rarely able to contribute much to technological innovation. By mid-century, most technological innovation was organized along industrial lines. Entire armies of experts and vast sums of capital were required to run the new invention factories. The prototype of today's invention factory was the Manhattan Project, which built the nuclear bomb in the last years of World War II. By the time of Hiroshima, the manufacturing complex of the U.S. nuclear industry was about the same size as that of the U.S. automobile industry. The era of big science and big technology had arrived. Only governments and, increasingly, giant multinational corporations could afford to sustain the research effort of the second half of the twentieth century.

As the twentieth century ended, there seemed to be no limit to the amount that could be spent on research and development. During the twentieth century, the number of research scientists in North America increased a hundredfold. In the last 40 years of the century, research and development spending tripled, taking inflation into account. In that same period, industry's share of spending rose from one-third to two-thirds of the total while government's share dropped proportionately (Hobsbawm, 1994: 523; U.S. Department of Commerce, 1998: 609; Woodrow Federal Reserve Bank of Minneapolis, 2000; see Figure 12.1).

As a result of these developments, it should come as no surprise that military and profit-making considerations now govern the direction of most research and development. A reporter once asked bank robber Willie Sutton why he robbed banks. Sutton answered, "Because that's where the money is." This is hardly the only motivation prompting scientists and engineers to research particular topics. Personal interests, individual creativity, and the state of a field's intellectual development still influence the direction of inquiry. This is especially true for theoretical work done in universities, as opposed to applied research funded by governments and private industry. It would, however, be naive to think that practicality doesn't also enter the scientist's calculation of what he or she ought to study. Many researchers—even many of those who do theoretically driven research in universities—are pulled in particular directions by large research grants, well-paying jobs, access to expensive state-of-the-art equipment, and the possibility of winning patents and achieving commercial success. For example, many leading molecular biologists in North America have established genetic engineering companies, serve on their boards of directors, or receive research funding from them. In not a few cases,

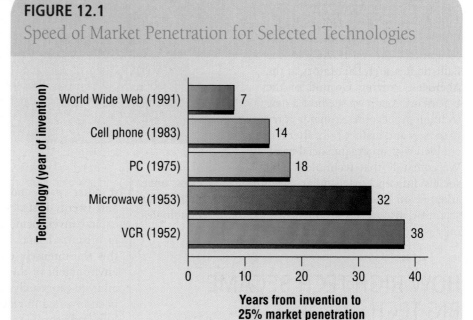

FIGURE 12.1
Speed of Market Penetration for Selected Technologies

Because large multinational corporations now routinely invest astronomical sums in research and development to increase their chance of being the first to bring innovations to market, the time lag between new scientific discoveries and their technological application is continually shrinking.

Source: Based on data from "The Silent Boom," *Forbes*, July 7, 1997. Adapted by permission of ESR Research.

major pharmaceutical and agrochemical corporations have bought out these companies because they see their vast profit potential (Rural Advancement Foundation International, 1999). Close to a majority of leading biotechnology scientists have industry affiliations (Rifkin, 1998: 56).

Economic lures, increasingly provided by the military and big corporations, have generated moral and political qualms among some researchers. Some scientists and engineers wonder whether work on particular topics achieves optimum benefits for humanity. Certain researchers are troubled by the possibility that some scientific inquiries may be harmful to humankind. However, a growing number of scientists and engineers recognize that to do cutting-edge research, they must still any residual misgivings, hop on the bandwagon, and adhere to military and industrial requirements and priorities. That, after all, is where the money is.

GLOBAL WARMING

The side effect of technology that has given people the most serious cause for concern is environmental degradation, two aspects of which we now consider: global warming and genetic pollution.

Since the Industrial Revolution, humans have been burning increasing quantities of fossil fuels (coal, oil, gasoline, natural gas, etc.) to drive their cars, furnaces, and factories. Burning these fuels releases carbon dioxide into the atmosphere. The accumulation of carbon dioxide allows more solar radiation to enter the atmosphere and less heat to escape. This process contributes to global warming, a gradual increase in the world's average surface temperature. Figure 12.2 graphs the world's annual average surface air

> **global warming** The gradual worldwide increase in average surface temperature.

FIGURE 12.2

Annual Mean Global Surface Air Temperature and Atmospheric Carbon Dioxide Concentration, 1880–2009

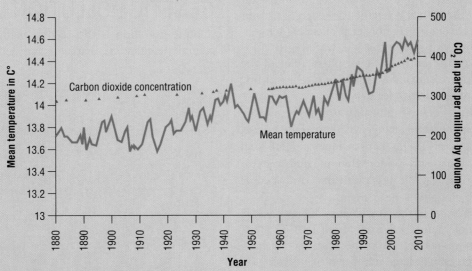

Note: Pre-1959 carbon dioxide concentration estimates come from intermittent Antarctic ice core measurements. Post-1958 carbon dioxide concentration estimates are based on continuous atmospheric measurements from the Mauna Loa Observatory in Hawaii.

Sources: Carbon Dioxide Information Analysis Center. 1998. "Historical CO$_2$ Records from the Law Dome DE08, DE08-2, and DSS Ice Cores." http://cdiac.ornl.gov/trends/co2/lawdome.html (retrieved 29 March 2010); Goddard Institute for Space Studies. 2010. "GLOBAL Land-Ocean Temperature Index in 0.01 degrees Celsius." http://data.giss.nasa.gov/gistemp/tabledata/GLB.Ts+dSST.txt (retrieved 29 March 2010); National Oceanic and Atmospheric Administration. 2010. "Use of NOAA ESRL Data." ftp://ftp.cmdl.noaa.gov/ccg/co2/trends/co2_annmean_mlo.txt (retrieved 29 March 2010).

Because of global warming, glaciers are melting, the sea level is rising, and extreme weather events are becoming more frequent.

temperature and the concentration of carbon dioxide in the atmosphere from 1866 to 2009. The graph shows a warming trend that mirrors the increased concentration of carbon dioxide in the atmosphere. It also shows that the concentration of carbon dioxide increased sharply beginning around 1958 while the warming trend intensified about seven years later. From 1965 to 2004, average surface air temperature rose at a rate of 1.51 degrees Celsius per century. This average may not seem like a big temperature change until you realize that the warming trend is much stronger in the northern hemisphere than in the southern hemisphere, and that, at a certain temperature, even slight warming will turn ice to water.

Most scientists believe global warming is already producing serious climatic change. As temperatures rise, more water evaporates. This causes more rainfall and bigger storms, which leads to more flooding and soil erosion, which in turn leads to less cultivable land. People suffer and die all along the causal chain.

Figure 12.3 graphs the worldwide dollar cost of damage because of "natural" disasters from 1970 to 2009. ("Natural" is in quotation marks because, as we have just seen, an increasingly large number of meteorological events are rendered extreme by human action.) Clearly, the damage caused by extreme meteorological events is on the upswing. This, however, may be only the beginning. It seems that global warming is causing the oceans to rise. That is partly because warmer water expands and partly because the partial melting of the polar ice caps puts more water in the oceans. In the twenty-first

genetic pollution The potential dangers of mixing the genes of one species with those of another.

century, this may result in the flooding of some heavily populated coastal regions throughout the world. For instance, just a one-metre rise in the sea level would flood about 12 percent of the surface area of heavily populated Egypt and Bangladesh (Kennedy, 1993: 110).

GENETIC POLLUTION

Genetic pollution is the second main form of environmental degradation that we consider here. It refers to

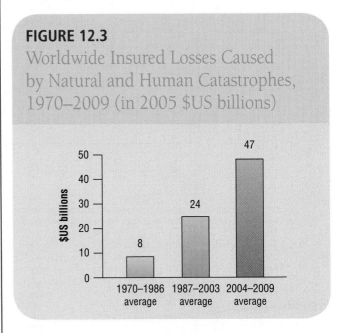

FIGURE 12.3

Worldwide Insured Losses Caused by Natural and Human Catastrophes, 1970–2009 (in 2005 $US billions)

Sources: Swiss Re (2005: 5, 2007: 7, 2008: 18, 2009: 18, 2010: 15); U.S. Department of Labor (2010).

the health and ecological dangers that may result from artificially splicing genes together (Rifkin, 1998).

The genetic information of all living things is coded in a chemical called DNA. When members of a species reproduce, the characteristics of the mates are naturally transmitted to their offspring through DNA. **Recombinant DNA**, in contrast, is a technique developed by molecular biologists in the last few decades. It involves removing a segment of DNA from a gene or splicing together segments of DNA from different living things, thus effectively creating a new life form. For example, scientists inserted the gene that makes fireflies sparkle at night into a tobacco plant. The offspring of the plant had leaves that glowed in the dark. Researchers inserted human growth hormone into a mouse embryo. This created mice that grew twice as big and twice as fast as ordinary mice. Biologists combined embryo cells from a sheep and a goat and placed them in the womb of a surrogate animal. The surrogate animal then gave birth to an entirely new species, half sheep, half goat.

These wonders of molecular biology were performed in the mid-1980s and helped to dramatize and publicize the potential of recombinant DNA. Since 1990, governments and corporations have been engaged in a multibillion-dollar international effort to create a complete genetic map of humans and various plants, micro-organisms, and animal species. With human and other genetic maps in hand, and by using recombinant DNA and related techniques, it is possible to design what some people regard as more useful animals and plants and superior humans. By 2000, scientists had identified the location and chemical structure of every one of the approximately 30 000 human genes. This will presumably enable them to understand the function of each gene. They can then detect and eliminate hereditary propensities to a wide range of diseases. Recombinant DNA will also enable farmers to grow disease- and frost-resistant crops with higher yields. It will allow miners to pour ore-eating microbes into mines, pump the microbes above ground after they have had their fill, and then separate out the ore. This will greatly reduce the cost and danger of mining. Recombinant DNA will allow companies to grow plants that produce cheap biodegradable plastic and micro-organisms that consume oil spills and absorb radioactivity. The potential health and economic benefits to humankind of these and many other applica-

tions of recombinant DNA are truly startling.

But so are the dangers that genetic pollution poses to human health and the stability of ecosystems (Rifkin, 1998: 67–115). For example, when a non-native organism enters a new environment, it usually adapts without a problem. Sometimes it unexpectedly wreaks havoc. Now, the potential for ecological catastrophe has multiplied, because scientists are regularly testing genetically altered plants (effectively, non-native organisms) in the field. Some have gone commercial, and many more will soon be grown on a wide scale. These plants are resistant to insects, disease, and frost. However, once their pollen and seeds escape into the environment, weeds, insects, and micro-organisms will eventually build up resistance to the genes that resist herbicides, pests, and viruses. Thus, superbugs, superweeds, and superviruses will be born. We cannot predict the exact environmental consequences of these developments. That is why the insurance industry refuses to insure genetically engineered crops against the possibility of their causing catastrophic ecological damage.

Global warming and genetic pollution threaten everyone. However, as you will now see, the degree to which they are perceived as threatening depends on certain social conditions being met. Moreover, the threats are not evenly distributed in society.

recombinant DNA

Removing a segment of DNA from a gene or splicing together segments of DNA from different living things, thus effectively creating a new life form.

Alistair Cotton/Shutterstock

LO² The Social Construction of Environmental Problems

Environmental problems do not become social issues spontaneously. Before they can enter the public consciousness, policy-oriented scientists, the environmental movement, the mass media, and respected organizations must discover and promote them. People have to connect real-life events to the information learned from these groups. Because some scientists, industrial interests, and politicians dispute the existence of environmental threats, the public can begin to question whether environmental issues are, in fact, social problems that require human intervention.

We must not, then, think that environmental issues will inevitably be perceived as problematic. Rather, they are contested phenomena. They can be socially constructed by proponents, and they can be socially demolished by opponents (Hannigan, 1995).

The controversy over global warming is a good example of how people create and contest definitions of environmental problems (Gelbspan, 1999; Ungar, 1992, 1999). The theory of global warming was first proposed about a century ago but an elite group of scientists began serious research on the subject only in the late 1950s. They attracted no public attention until the 1970s, when the environmental movement emerged and gave new legitimacy and momentum to the scientific research and helped secure public funds for it. Respected and influential scientists now began to promote the issue of global warming. The mass media, always thirsting for sensational stories, were highly receptive to these efforts. Newspaper and television reports about the problem began to appear in the late 1970s and proliferated in the mid- to late 1980s.

The summer of 1988 brought the worst drought in half a century to North America. Respected organizations outside the scientific community, the mass media, and the environmental movement began expressing concern about the effects of global warming. By the early 1990s, public opinion polls showed that most North Americans with an opinion on the subject thought that using coal, oil, and gas contributes to global warming.

However, some industrialists, politicians, and scientists began to question whether global warming was, in fact, taking place. This group included Western coal and oil companies, the member states of the Organization of the Petroleum Exporting Countries (OPEC), other coal- and oil-exporting nations, and right-wing think-tanks, such as Canada's Fraser Institute in Vancouver, which is subsidized in part by major oil companies operating in Canada. "Bad scientific reporting, bad economics and bad judgement" is how the Fraser Institute summarized the analyses of those who regarded global warming as a serious issue requiring immediate action (Jones, 1997). Largely as a result of this onslaught, public concern about global warming began to falter.

Yet the evidence that global warming was substantial, dangerous, and caused by human activity continued to accumulate. In Canada, for example, ordinary people experienced firsthand ongoing drought on the Prairies, falling water levels in the Great Lakes, the melting of glaciers in the North, and the collapse of fish stocks on the east coast. In 2007, a large blue-ribbon panel of international climate experts, the Intergovernmental Panel on Climate Change (IPCC) issued a definitive report showing that global warming was real, dangerous, but stoppable through human intervention (Intergovernmental Panel on Climate Change, 2007). The public mood again shifted, and all of Canada's political parties adopted "green" platforms that promised swift and effective action. In 2009, the IPCC report was shown to contain a couple of errors, while scientists responsible for one of its data sets stupidly kept the data from public scrutiny. Again a furor erupted, although it was soon shown that the report's conclusions were accurate ("U.K. Panel," 2010). The ongoing debate clearly demonstrates that environmental issues become social problems only when social, political, and scientific circumstances allow them to be defined as such.

As you will now see, in addition to being socially defined, environmental problems are socially distributed. That is, environmental risks are greater for some groups than for others.

LO³ THE SOCIAL DISTRIBUTION OF RISK

You may have noticed that after a minor twister touches down on some unlucky community, TV reporters often rush to interview the surviving residents of trailer parks. The survivors stand amid the rubble that was their lives. They heroically remark on the generosity of their neighbours, their good fortune in still having their family intact, and our inability to fight nature's destructive forces. Why trailer parks? Small twisters aren't particularly attracted to them, but reporters are. That is because trailers are pretty flimsy in the face of a small tornado. They often suffer a lot of damage from twisters and therefore make a more sensational story than the minor damage typically inflicted on upper-middle-class homes with firmly shingled roofs and solid foundations. This is a general pattern. Whenever disaster strikes, economically and politically disadvantaged people almost always suffer most. That is because their circumstances render them most vulnerable. In fact,

Stephen Finn/Shutterstock

the advantaged often consciously put the disadvantaged in harm's way to avoid risk themselves. This is what is known as environmental racism, the tendency to heap environmental dangers on the disadvantaged and especially on disadvantaged racial minorities.

The Canadian Case

Environmental racism is evident in Canada. For example, the uranium used to construct the atom bombs that were dropped on Hiroshima and Nagasaki came from Port Radium in the Northwest Territories, the world's first uranium mine. More than 30 Dene hunters and trappers were recruited from the nearby village of Deline to haul and barge 45-kilogram burlap sacks of the raw ore along a 2100 kilometre route to Fort McMurray, Alberta, for $3 a day. The American and Canadian governments had known about the dangers of exposure to uranium at least since 1931 (McClelland, 1931). Yet they withheld this information from the workers, who were completely unprotected from the ore's deadly radiation. In the surrounding community, the Dene ate fish from contaminated dredging ponds and hunted and camped in contaminated areas. Dene children played with ore dust at docks and landings. Dene women sewed tents from used uranium sacks. Until recent decades, cancer was unknown in the community. Elders often lived into their 90s. By 1998, however, nearly half the uranium workers had died of cancer while still in their 60s and 70s. Cancer and lung disease are alarmingly widespread in the community. Deline is known locally as "The Village of the Widows." Neither the workers nor their families have received any compensation from the government, not even an apology (Nikiforuk, 1998).

Broadly similar stories of environmental racism are legion. There is a disturbing association in Canada between level of contamination and the concentration of Aboriginal populations. Figure 12.4 illustrates this association. Using a broad measure of airborne pollution, it shows that where Aboriginal Canadians form a larger proportion of the population, the per capita weight of particulates in the air is heaviest.

Class also structures exposure to environmental risk in Canada. For example, Sydney, Nova Scotia, is a poor, working-class town with the highest rate of cancer of any city in Canada. The people who lived around Frederick Street, the poorest part of Sydney, had the highest neighbourhood cancer rate in town. Skin ailments, birth defects, respiratory problems, diseases of the nervous system, and other medical conditions were also unusually common around Frederick Street. The main reason? Sydney was home to a large steel mill for a century. Waste from the mill poured into the so-called tar ponds, a 50-hectare site polluted to a depth of 24 metres with cancer-causing chemicals. Frederick Street borders the tar ponds. Sludge oozed into people's basements, seeped into their vegetable gardens, and ran in open streams where children played. Billions of federal and provincial tax dollars were spent subsidizing the steel mill that was the source of the problem. Yet a serious cleanup effort began only in 2010, 30 years after elevated levels of toxins were first detected in the Sydney Harbour and in local lobsters (Barlow and May, 2000: 144; see Figure 12.5 on the next page).

The Less-Developed Countries

What is true for disadvantaged classes and racial groups in North America also holds for the less-developed countries. The underprivileged face more environmental dangers than the privileged (Kennedy, 1993: 95–121 on the next page). Mexico, Brazil, China, India, and other southern countries are industrializing rapidly. That puts tremendous strain on their natural resources. Rising

> **environmental racism**
> The tendency to heap environmental dangers on the disadvantaged, and especially on disadvantaged racial minorities.

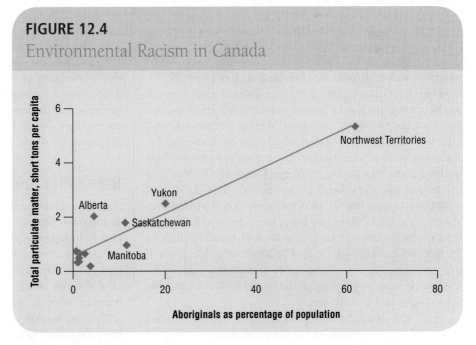

FIGURE 12.4
Environmental Racism in Canada

Note: The data are for 1995.
Sources: Statistics Canada (2000a, 2000b); U.S. Environmental Protection Agency, Office of Air Quality Planning and Standards (2000).

FIGURE 12.5

Class and Exposure to Environmental Risk: Nova Scotia

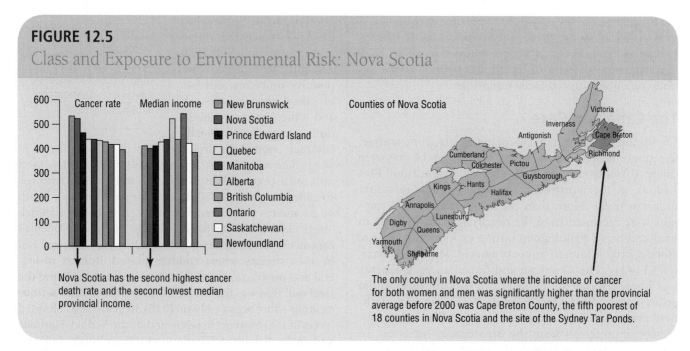

Nova Scotia has the second highest cancer death rate and the second lowest median provincial income.

The only county in Nova Scotia where the incidence of cancer for both women and men was significantly higher than the provincial average before 2000 was Cape Breton County, the fifth poorest of 18 counties in Nova Scotia and the site of the Sydney Tar Ponds.

Sources: Cancer Care Nova Scotia, "Cancer Statistics in Nova Scotia." 2004. http://cancercare.ns.ca/media/documents/CancerinNS_Overview.pdf (retrieved 27 February 2008); Health Canada. "Canadian Cancer Statistics, 2003." http://www.cancer.ca/Canada-wide/About%20cancer/Cancer%20statistics/Canadian%20 Cancer%20Statistics.aspx?sc_lang=en (retrieved 30 March 2010); Province of Nova Scotia. 2010. "Counties of Nova Scotia." http://www.gov.ns.ca/snsmr/muns/info/ mapping/counties.asp (retrieved 30 March 2010); Rural Communities Impact Policy Project. 2003. "Painting the Landscape of Rural Nova Scotia." 2003. http://www. ruralnovascotia.ca/RCIP/PDF/RR_final_full.pdf (retrieved 30 March 2010).

demand for water, electricity, fossil fuels, and consumer products is creating more polluted rivers, dead lakes, and industrial waste sites. At a quickening pace, rain forests, grazing land, cropland, and wetlands are giving way to factories, roads, airports, and housing complexes. Smog-blanketed megacities continue to sprawl. Eighteen of the world's 21 biggest cities are in less-developed countries.

Given the picture sketched above, it should be unsurprising that, on average, people in less-developed countries are more concerned about the environment than people in rich countries are (Brechin and Kempton, 1994). However, the developing countries cannot afford much in the way of pollution control, so anti-pollution regulations are lax by North American, Western European, and Japanese standards. This state of affairs is an incentive for some multinational corporations to situate some of their foulest operations in the Southern Hemisphere. It is also the reason that the industrialization of the less-developed countries is proving so punishing to the environment. When car ownership grows from, say, 5 percent to 20 percent of the population in China, and when 50 million or 75 million Indians with motor scooters upgrade to cars, the result will be a choking mess. China and India have few regulations for phasing in the use of technologies that save energy and pollute less.

For the time being, however, the rich countries do most of the world's environmental damage. That is because their inhabitants earn and consume more than the inhabitants of less-developed countries. How much more? The richest fifth of humanity earns about 80 times as much as the poorest fifth (up from 30 times as much in 1950). In the past half-century, the richest fifth doubled its per capita consumption of energy, meat, timber, steel, and copper, and quadrupled its car ownership. In that same period, the per capita consumption of the poorest fifth hardly changed. The United States has only 4.5 percent of the world's population, but it uses about 25 percent of the earth's resources. And it produces more than 20 percent of global emissions of carbon dioxide, the pollutant responsible for about half of global warming. Thus, the inhabitants of the Northern Hemisphere cause a disproportionately large share of the world's environmental problems, enjoy a disproportionate share of the benefits of technology, and live with fewer environmental risks than do people in the Southern Hemisphere.

Inequality and Biotechnology

Social inequalities are also apparent in the field of biotechnology. For instance, the large multinational companies that dominate the pharmaceutical, seed, and agrochemical industries now routinely send anthropologists, biologists, and agronomists to all corners of the world. There they take samples of wild plants, the crops people grow, and human blood. They hope to find genetic material with commercial value in agriculture and medicine. If they discover genes with commercial value, the company they work for patents the discovery. This gives them the exclusive legal right to manufacture and sell the genetic material without compensating the donors.

Thus, Indian farmers and then scientists worked for a hundred generations discovering, skillfully selecting, cultivating, and developing techniques for processing the neem tree, which has powerful antibacterial and pesticidal properties. However, a giant corporation based in the United States (W. R. Grace) became the sole commercial beneficiary of their labour. Monsanto (U.S.), Novartis (Switzerland), GlaxoSmithKline (U.K.), and other prominent companies in the life sciences call this "protection of intellectual property." Indigenous people and their advocates throughout the world call it "bio-piracy" (Rifkin, 1998: 37–66).[1]

Finally, consider the possible consequences of people having their babies genetically engineered. This should be possible on a wide scale in 10 or 20 years. Free of inherited diseases and physical abnormalities, and perhaps genetically programmed to enjoy superior intellectual and athletic potential, these children would, in effect, speed up and improve the slow and imperfect process of natural evolution. That, at least, is the rosy picture sketched by proponents of the technology. In practice, because only the well-to-do are likely to be able to afford fully genetically engineered babies, the new technology could introduce an era of increased social inequality and low social mobility, effectively dividing humanity into two or more subspecies. Only the economically underprivileged would bear a substantial risk of genetic inferiority.

Monkey Business Images/Shutterstock

What Is to Be Done?

THE MARKET AND HIGH-TECH SOLUTIONS

Some people believe the environmental crisis will resolve itself. More precisely, they think we already have two weapons that will work together to end the crisis: the market and high technology. The case of oil illustrates how these weapons can combine forces. If oil reserves drop or oil is withheld from the market for political reasons, the price of oil goes up. This makes it worthwhile for oil exploration companies to develop new technologies to recover more oil. When they discover more oil and bring it to market, prices fall back to where they were. Generalizing this principal and projecting it into the future, optimists believe global warming, industrial pollution, and other forms of environmental degradation will be dealt with similarly. In their view, human inventiveness and the profit motive will combine to create the new technologies we need to survive and prosper.

Some evidence supports this optimistic scenario. For example, following the oil shocks of 1973 (when prices tripled) and 1978–79 (when prices tripled again), new discoveries were made and new efficiencies were implemented so oil reserves grew and prices fell. In recent years, we have adopted new technologies to combat some of the worst excesses of environmental degradation. For example, we have replaced brain-damaging leaded gas with unleaded gas. We have developed environmentally friendly refrigerants and stopped the production of ozone-destroying CFCs. In a model of international cooperation, rich countries have even subsidized the cost of replacing CFCs in the developing countries. Efficient windmills and solar panels are now common. More factories are equipped with high-tech pollution-control devices, preventing dangerous chemicals from seeping into the air and water. We have introduced cost-effective ways to recycle metal, plastic, paper, and glass. New methods are being developed for eliminating carbon dioxide emissions from the burning of fossil fuels. We can now buy hybrid cars.

Laura Gangi Pond/Shutterstock

However, three factors suggest market forces cannot solve environmental problems on their own:

1. *Imperfect price signals.* The price of many commodities does not reflect their actual cost to society. Gasoline costs about a dollar a litre at the time of this writing. But the social cost, including the cost of repairing the environmental damage caused by burning the gas, is four times that. Because of many such price distortions, the market often fails to send signals that might result in the speedy adoption of technological and policy fixes.

2. *The slow pace of change.* Our efforts so far to deal with the environmental consequences of rapid technological change are just not good enough. For example, global warming continues to accelerate, partly because automobile use is increasing as public transportation ridership declines and standards on automobile emissions remain weak. All of the world's renewable resources are in decline (see Figure 12.6).

3. *The importance of political pressure.* Political pressure exerted by environmental activists, community groups, and public opinion is often necessary to motivate corporate and government action on

environmental issues. For instance, organizations like Greenpeace have successfully challenged the practices of logging companies, whalers, the nuclear industry, and other groups engaged in environmentally dangerous practices. Without the efforts of such organizations, it is doubtful many environmental issues would be defined as social problems by corporations and governments.

LO⁴ THE COOPERATIVE ALTERNATIVE

The alternative to the market and high-tech approach involves people cooperating to reduce greatly their overconsumption of just about everything. This strategy includes investing heavily in energy-saving technologies, environmental cleanup, and subsidized, environmentally friendly industrialization in the developing countries. It would require renewed commitment to voluntary efforts, new laws and enforcement bodies to ensure compliance, increased environmentally related research and development by industry and government, more environmentally directed foreign aid, and new taxes (Livernash and

Rodenburg, 1998). In addition, a cooperative strategy entails careful assessment of all the risks associated with biotechnology projects and consultation with the public before such projects are allowed to go forward. Profits from genetic engineering would also have to be shared equitably with donors of genetic material.

Is the solution realistic? Not in the short term. It would be political suicide for anyone in the rich countries to propose the drastic measures listed above. Not too many Canadian drivers would be happy paying $4 a litre for gas, for example. For the solution to be politically acceptable, the broad public in North America, Western Europe, and Japan must be aware of the gravity of the environmental problem and be willing to make substantial economic sacrifices to get the job done.

Survey data suggest that nearly all Canadians are aware of the environmental problem and are doing something about it. For instance, in 2006, sorting and recycling programs for glass, cans, plastic, and paper were available to about 90 percent of Canadians, 95 percent of whom used them. However, it seems that we are in general prepared to act only when it doesn't inconvenience us much. When asked to indicate their main ways of getting to work, 81 percent of Canadians said they usually go by motor vehicle and 17 percent said they usually take public transit, cycle, or walk (Statistics Canada, 2006b: 52, 62).

Other surveys reveal much the same pattern. Many people know about the environmental crisis, say they want it dealt with, but are unwilling to be inconvenienced or pay much of the cost themselves. They regard environmental problems as too remote and abstract to justify making big personal sacrifices. It follows that more and bigger environmental catastrophes may have to occur before more people are willing to take remedial action. The good news is that we still have time to act.

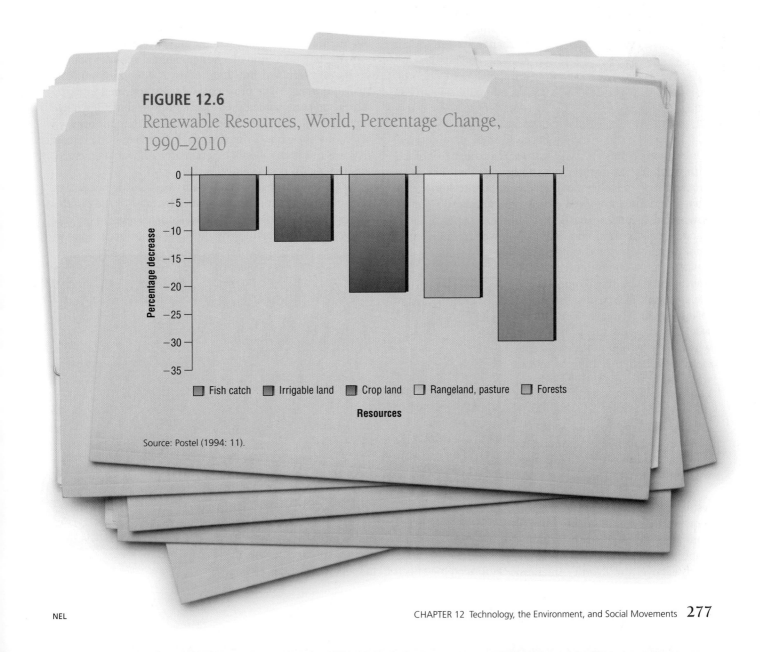

FIGURE 12.6
Renewable Resources, World, Percentage Change, 1990–2010

Source: Postel (1994: 11).

Social Movements

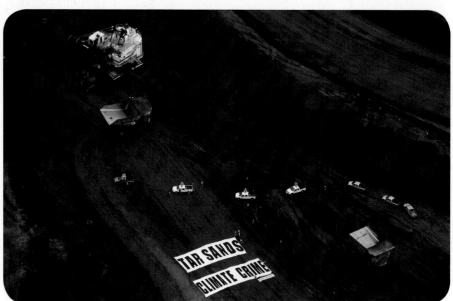

We noted above that governments and corporations are inclined to act on environmental issues only if they are pressured to do so by the public. But under what circumstances do many individuals engage in **collective action**, working in unison to bring about or resist social, political, and economic change by means of demonstrations, strikes, riots, and the like? And under what circumstances is collective action turned into a **social movement**, an enduring collective attempt to change or resist change to part or all of society by establishing organizations, lobbies, unions, and political parties?

Answers to these questions are unclear, as Robert Brym learned in grade 11: "One day in chemistry class I learned that water combined with sulphur dioxide produces sulphurous acid. The news shocked me. To understand why, you have to know that I lived in Saint John, New Brunswick, about 100 metres downwind of one of the largest pulp and paper mills in Canada. Waves of sulphur dioxide billowed from the mill's smokestacks day and night. The town's pervasive rotten-egg smell was a long-standing complaint in the area. But, for me, disgust turned to upset when I realized the fumes were toxic. Suddenly it was clear why many people I knew—especially people living near the mill—woke up in the morning with a kind of 'smoker's cough.' Through the simple act of breathing we were causing the gas to mix with the moisture in our bodies and form an acid that our lungs tried to expunge, with only partial success.

"Twenty years later, I read the results of a medical research report showing that area residents suffered from rates of lung disease, including emphysema and lung cancer, significantly above the North American average. But even in 1968 it was evident my hometown had a serious problem. I therefore hatched a plan. Our high school was about to hold its annual model parliament. The event was notoriously boring, partly because, year in year out, virtually everyone voted for the same party, the Conservatives. But here was an issue, I thought, that could turn things around. A local man, K. C. Irving, owned the pulp and paper mill. *Forbes* magazine ranked him as one of the richest men in the world. I figured that when I told my fellow students what I had discovered, they would quickly demand the closure of the mill until Irving guaranteed a clean operation.

"Was *I* naive. As head of the tiny Liberal Party, I had to address the entire student body during assembly on election day to outline the party platform and rally votes. When I got to the part of my speech that explained why Irving was our enemy, the murmuring in the audience, which had been growing like the sound of a hungry animal about to pounce on its prey, erupted into loud boos. A couple of students rushed the stage. The principal suddenly appeared from the wings and commanded the student body to settle down. He then took me by the arm and informed me that, for my own safety, my speech was finished. So, I discovered on election day, was our high school's Liberal Party. And so, it emerged, was my high-school political career.

"This incident troubled me for years, partly because of the embarrassment it caused, partly because of the puzzles it presented. Why didn't my fellow students rebel in the way I thought they would? Why did they continue to support

> **collective action** Occurs when people act in unison to bring about or resist social, political, and economic change.

> **social movement** Collective attempts to change all or part of the political or social order by means of rioting, petitioning, striking, demonstrating, and establishing pressure groups, unions, and political parties.

Protesting the effects of the Alberta tar sands

an arrangement that was enriching one man at the cost of a community's health? Couldn't they see the injustice? I didn't know it at the time, but to answer such questions, it is necessary to turn to the literature on social movements."

BREAKDOWN THEORY: A FUNCTIONALIST ACCOUNT

Until about 1970, most sociologists believed that two conditions must be met for social movements to form:

1. *Social marginality*. The early leaders of social movements and their first recruits must be poorly integrated in society. Without such socially marginal people, social movements supposedly cannot form.

2. *Strain*. People's norms must be strained or disrupted. For example, one of the most popular variants of breakdown theory is relative deprivation theory. Relative deprivation refers to the growth of an intolerable gap between the social rewards people expect to receive and those they actually receive. (Social rewards are widely valued goods, such as money, education, security, prestige, and so forth.) Supposedly, people are most likely to form social movements when the gap between rising expectations (brought on by, say, rapid economic growth and migration) and the receipt of social rewards (sometimes lowered by economic recession or war) becomes intolerable (Davies, 1969; Gurr, 1970; see Figure 12.7).

Following sociologist Charles Tilly and his associates, we can group these two conditions together as the breakdown theory of collective action. That is because

both conditions assume that social movements result from the disruption or breakdown of previously integrative social structures and norms (Tilly, Tilly, and Tilly, 1975: 4–6). At a more abstract level, breakdown theory can be seen as a variant of functionalism because it regards collective action as a form of social imbalance that results from the improper functioning of social institutions.

Can breakdown theory adequately account for the crystallization of social movements? The short answer is no. Since 1970, sociologists have uncovered two main flaws in the theory. First, research shows that in most cases, leaders and early joiners of social movements are well-integrated members of their community, not socially marginal outsiders (Brym, 1980; Lipset, 1971). Second, researchers have found that high levels of relative deprivation are generally not associated with the crystallization of social movements. That is because certain social conditions can prevent people from translating their discontent into an enduring social movement with a more or less stable membership, hired office personnel, a publicity bureau, a regularly published newsletter, and the like (McPhail, 1994; Tilly et al., 1975; Torrance, 1986: 115–45). We now consider those social conditions.

relative deprivation An intolerable gap between the social rewards people feel they deserve and the social rewards they expect to receive.

breakdown theory Suggests that social movements emerge when traditional norms and patterns of social organization are disrupted.

solidarity theory Holds that social movements are social organizations that emerge when potential members can mobilize resources, take advantage of new political opportunities, and avoid high levels of social control by authorities.

LO⁵ SOLIDARITY THEORY: A CONFLICT APPROACH

Solidarity theory is a type of conflict theory that focuses on the social conditions that allow people to turn their discontent into a unified (or "solidary") political force. It identifies three such social conditions: adequate resource mobilization, sufficient political opportunity, and weak or inconsistent social control.

Resource Mobilization

Most collective action is part of a power struggle. The struggle usually intensifies as groups whose members feel disadvantaged become more powerful relative to other groups. How do disadvantaged groups become more powerful? By gaining new members, becoming better organized, and increasing their access to scarce resources, such as money, jobs, and means of communication

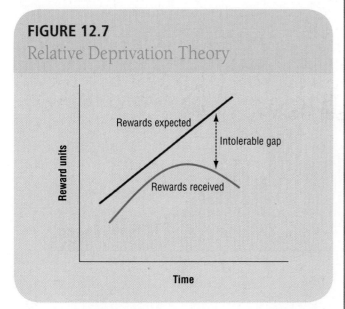

FIGURE 12.7
Relative Deprivation Theory

Source: From BRYM/LIE. *Sociology: The Points of the Compass.* © 2009 Nelson Education Ltd. Reproduced by permission. www.cengage.com/permissions.

(Bierstedt, 1974). **Resource mobilization** is the process by which groups engage in more collective action as their power increases because of their growing size and increasing organizational, material, and other resources (Jenkins, 1983; Zald and McCarthy, 1979).

Consider the effect of resource mobilization on the frequency of strikes in Canada. Research shows that in Canada between the mid-1940s and the mid-1970s, strike frequency was high when (1) unemployment was low, (2) union membership was high, and (3) governments were generous in their provision of social welfare benefits. *Low unemployment* indicates a strong economy. Workers are inclined to strike when business activity is robust because in such conditions they accumulate healthy strike funds, enjoy many alternative job opportunities, and know that employers and governments can afford to make concessions (employers make bigger profits and governments collect more taxes during economic booms). *A high level of unionization* is conducive to more strike activity because unions provide workers with leadership, strike funds, and coordination. Finally, *generous government benefits* give workers an economic buffer and thus increase their readiness to strike. Thus, as resource mobilization theory suggests, strong social ties among workers (as indicated by a high level of unioniza-

> **resource mobilization** The process by which social movements crystallize because of the increasing organizational, material, and other resources of movement members.

tion) and access to jobs and money (as indicated by a booming economy and generous government benefits) increase challenges to authority (as indicated by strikes).

Figure 12.8 shows the pattern of strike activity in Canada between 1946 and 2006. It adds substance to the resource mobilization approach. Until 1974, the trend in strike activity was upward. This was a period of growing prosperity, low unemployment, expanding state benefits, and increasing unionization. With access to increasing organizational and material resources, workers challenged authority increasingly more often in the three decades after World War II. In 1973, however, economic crisis struck. As a result of war and revolution in the Middle East, oil prices tripled, and then tripled again at the end of the decade. Inflation increased and unemployment rose. Soon, the government was strapped for funds and had to borrow heavily to maintain social welfare programs. Eventually, the debt burden was so heavy the government felt obliged to cut various social welfare programs. At the same time, federal and provincial governments introduced laws and regulations limiting the right of some workers to strike and putting a cap on the wage gains that workers could demand.

The percentage of Canadian workers who belonged to unions began to decline. Strike action was made even more difficult when Canada signed free trade deals with the United States in 1988 and Mexico in 1994. It was now possible for employers to threaten to relocate in the United States or Mexico in the face of protracted strikes. Thus, in the post-1973 climate, the organizational and material resources of workers fell. As a result, strike

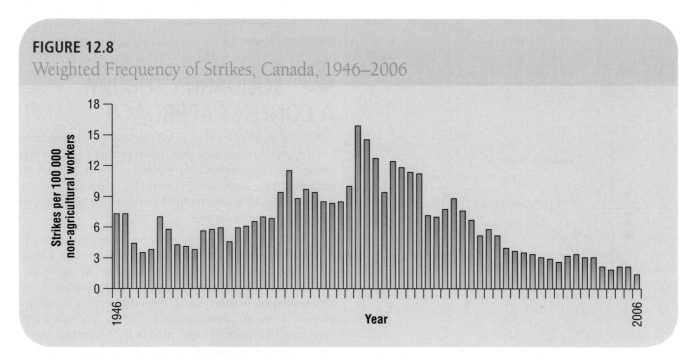

FIGURE 12.8
Weighted Frequency of Strikes, Canada, 1946–2006

Sources: International Labour Organization (2008); *Labour Organizations* (1973: xxii–xxiii); *1994–1995 Directory* (1995: xiii); *1998 Directory* (1998: 15); "Chronological Perspective" (1999, 2001a, 2001b); *Strikes and Lockouts in Canada 1968* (1970: 12–13); *Strikes and Lockouts in Canada 1985* (1985: 9); Workplace Information Directorate (1996).

activity plummeted. In 2000, the frequency of strikes per 100 000 Canadian non-agricultural workers was less than 20 percent that of 1974 (Brym, 2003).

Political Opportunities

A second social condition that allows mass discontent to be translated into social movement formation involves the emergence of new political opportunities (McAdam, 1982; Piven and Cloward, 1977; Tarrow, 1994). Specifically, chances for protest and social movement formation emerge when influential allies offer support, when ruling political alignments become unstable, when elite groups are divided and come into conflict with one another, and when election campaigns provide a focus for discontent and a chance to put new representatives with new policies in positions of authority (Tarrow, 1994: 86–9; Useem, 1998). Said differently, collective action takes place and social movements crystallize not just when disadvantaged groups become more powerful but also when privileged groups and the institutions they control are divided and therefore become weaker. As economist John Kenneth Galbraith once said about the weakness of the Russian ruling class at the time of the 1917 revolution, if someone manages to kick in a rotting door, some credit has to be given to the door.

Social Control

The third main lesson of solidarity theory is that government reactions to protests influence subsequent protests. Specifically, governments can try to lower the frequency and intensity of protest by taking various *social control* measures (Oberschall, 1973: 242–83). These measures include making concessions to protesters, co-opting the most troublesome leaders (for example, by appointing them advisers), and violently repressing collective action. Note, however, that social control measures do not always have the desired effect. If grievances are very deeply felt, and yielding to protesters' demands greatly increases their hopes, resources, and political opportunities, government concessions may encourage protesters to press their claims further. And although the firm and decisive use of force usually stops protest, using force moderately or inconsistently often backfires. That is because unrest typically intensifies when protesters are led to believe that the government is weak or indecisive (Piven and Cloward, 1977: 27–36; Tilly et al., 1975: 244).

LO⁶ FRAMING THEORY: THE CONTRIBUTION OF SYMBOLIC INTERACTIONISM

As we have seen, solidarity theory helps to overcome the flaws in breakdown theory. Still, the rise of a social movement sometimes takes strict solidarity theorists by surprise. So does the failure of an aggrieved group to press its claims by means of collective action. It seems, therefore, that something lies between (1) the capacity of disadvantaged people to mobilize resources for collective action, and (2) the recruitment of a substantial number of movement members. That "something" is frame alignment (Benford, 1997; Goffman, 1974; Snow, Rochford, Jr., Worden, and Benford, 1986). Frame alignment is the process by which social movement leaders make their activities, ideas, and goals congruent with the interests, beliefs, and values of potential new recruits to their movement—or fail to do so. Thanks to the efforts of scholars operating mainly in the symbolic interactionist tradition, frame alignment has recently become the subject of sustained sociological investigation.

Types of Frame Alignment

Frame alignment can be encouraged in several ways:

1. Social movement leaders can reach out to other organizations that, they believe, contain people who may be sympathetic to their movement's cause. Thus, leaders of an anti-nuclear movement may use the mass media, telephone campaigns, and direct mail to appeal to feminist, anti-racist, and environmental organizations. In doing so, they assume these organizations are likely to have members who would agree, at least in general terms, with the anti-nuclear platform.

2. Movement activists can stress popular values that have so far not featured prominently in the thinking of potential recruits. They can also elevate the importance of positive beliefs about the movement and what it stands for. For instance, in trying to win new recruits, movement members might emphasize the seriousness of the social movement's purpose. They might analyze the causes of the problem the movement is trying to solve in a clear and convincing way. Or they might stress the likelihood of the movement's success. By doing so, they can increase the movement's appeal to potential recruits and perhaps win them over to the cause.

3. Social movements can stretch their objectives and activities to win recruits who are not initially sympathetic to the movement's original aims. This may

political opportunities
Chances for collective action and social movement growth that occur during election campaigns, when influential allies offer insurgents support, when ruling political alignments become unstable, and when elite groups become divided and conflict with one another.

frame alignment The process by which individual interests, beliefs, and values become congruent and complementary with the activities, goals, and ideology of a social movement.

The Day after Tomorrow

Scene from *The Day after Tomorrow*

Most summers, Hollywood releases a disaster movie in which a highly implausible catastrophe serves as the backdrop for heroism and hope. Audiences return home momentarily frightened but ultimately safe in the knowledge that the chance of any such cataclysm occurring is vanishingly remote. *The Day after Tomorrow* follows that formula. The movie opens with a sequence of bizarre meteorological events. A section of ice the size of Rhode Island breaks off the Antarctic ice cap. Snow falls in New Delhi. Grapefruit-size hail pounds Tokyo. Enter Jack Hall (Dennis Quaid), a scientist whose research suggests an explanation: sudden climate change. The idea becomes a political football when it is ridiculed by the vice president of the United States, but once torrential rains and a tidal wave flood New York City, Hall's theories are vindicated. In a matter of days, temperatures plummet—at one point, they fall 10 degrees a minute to 150 below the freezing point. The entire Northern Hemisphere is plunged into a new ice age. Almost everyone freezes to death in the northern United States, while millions of desperate southerners flee into Mexico.

Although it seems like standard fare, *The Day after Tomorrow* is a Hollywood disaster movie with a difference: It is based on a three-part idea with considerable scientific support. Part one is agreed on by everyone: Since the Industrial Revolution, humans have released increasing quantities of carbon dioxide into the atmosphere as we burn more and more fossil fuels to operate our cars, furnaces, and factories. Part two is agreed on by the majority of—but not all—scientists: The accumulation of carbon dioxide allows more solar radiation to enter the atmosphere and less heat to escape, contributing to global warming. As temperatures rise, more water evaporates and the polar ice caps begin to melt, causing more rainfall, bigger storms, and more flooding.

Part three is the most recent and controversial part of the argument: The melting of the polar ice caps may be adding enough freshwater to the oceans to disrupt the flow of the Gulf Stream, the ocean current that carries warm water up the east coast of North America and the west coast of Europe. Computer simulations suggest that decreased salinity could push the Gulf Stream southward, causing average winter temperatures to drop by 12 degrees Celsius in the northeastern United States and other parts of the Northern Hemisphere. A recent Pentagon study suggests that such a climate change could cause droughts, storms, flooding, border raids, large-scale illegal migration from poor regions, and even war between nuclear powers over scarce food, drinking water, and energy (Joyce and Keigwin, 2004; Stipp, 2004). *The Day after Tomorrow* greatly exaggerates the suddenness and magnitude of what scientists mean by abrupt climate change. "Abrupt" can mean centuries to climatologists, and temperature drops of 10 degrees a minute are pure fantasy. Still, at the movie's core lies an ominous and real possibility.

The Day after Tomorrow also teaches us an important sociological lesson about the framing of issues by members of social movements and their opponents. Environmental problems do not become social issues spontaneously. They are socially constructed in what might be called a "framing war." Just as Jack Hall and the vice president spar over the credibility of Hall's prediction of sudden climate change, so do groups with different interests dispute all environmental problems, framing them in different ways so as to win over public opinion.

The Day after Tomorrow became involved in the framing war because in the month leading up to the release of the movie, environmentalists started piggybacking their message on it. They bombarded journalists with e-mails explaining global warming and offering interviews with leading scientists on the subject. Newspapers and magazines around the world subsequently carried stories on the issue. Environmentalists then distributed flyers to moviegoers leaving theatres (Houpt, 2004). In this way, The Day after Tomorrow became not just another disaster movie but part of the framing war around a major environmental issue.

Critical Thinking Question

- When a controversial issue such as global warming is framed differently by different sides in the debate, how can you decide which side is right?

The Canadian Press (Andrew Vaughan)

involve a watering down of the movement's ideals. Alternatively, movement leaders may decide to take action calculated to appeal to non-sympathizers on grounds that have little or nothing to do with the movement's purpose. When rock, punk, or reggae bands play at nuclear disarmament rallies or gay liberation festivals, it is not necessarily because the music is relevant to the movement's goals, and bands do not play just because movement members want to be entertained. The purpose is also to attract non-members. Once attracted by the music, however, non-members may make friends and acquaintances in the movement and then be encouraged to attend a more serious-minded meeting.

As we see, then, there are many ways in which social movements can make their ideas more appealing to a larger number of people. However, movements must also confront the fact that their opponents routinely seek to do just the opposite. That is, while movements seek to align their goals, ideas, and activities with the way potential recruits frame issues, their adversaries seek to *disalign* the way issues are framed by movements and potential recruits.

The B.C. Forest Alliance provides a good illustration of this process (Doyle, Elliott, and Tindall, 1997). Launched in British Columbia in 1991, the B.C. Forest Alliance was created and bankrolled by a group of senior forest industry executives and guided by the world's largest public relations firm. Its goal was to counter the province's environmental movement. It did so in two main ways. First, in its TV and print ads, the alliance claimed it represented the "middle ground" in the debate between forest companies and environmentalists. In practice, the alliance rarely criticized forest companies while it routinely characterized environmentalists as dope-smoking hippies with untenable ideas, such as shutting down the entire forest industry. Actually, very few environmentalists hold such

extreme opinions, and research shows that the middle class in British Columbia broadly supports environmental groups.

The second way the alliance sought to counter the environmental movement was by arguing that more environmentalism means fewer jobs. This was a huge oversimplification. Job losses in the forest industry were also caused by the introduction of new technologies in some areas, aging equipment in others, First Nations land claims, and resource depletion because of overharvesting and inadequate reforestation. Muddying the waters in this way is typical of social movement opponents. Frame alignment should therefore be viewed as a conflict-ridden process in which social movement partisans and their opponents use all the resources at their disposal to compete for the way in which potential recruits and sympathizers view movement issues (see the Sociology at the Movies box).

An Application of Frame Alignment Theory: Back to 1968

Frame alignment theory stresses the strategies employed by movement members to recruit non-members who are like-minded, apathetic, or even initially opposed to the movement's goals. Solidarity theory focuses on the broad social-structural conditions that facilitate the emergence of social movements. One theory usefully supplements the other.

The two theories certainly help clarify the 1968 high-school incident described earlier in this chapter. In light of our discussion, it seems evident that two main factors prevented Robert Brym from influencing his classmates when he spoke to them about the dangers of industrial pollution from the local pulp and paper mill.

First, he lived in a poor and relatively unindustrialized region of Canada where people had few resources they could mobilize on their own behalf. Per capita income and the level of unionization were among the lowest of any state or province in North America. The unemployment rate was among the highest. In contrast, K. C. Irving, who owned the pulp and paper mill, was so powerful that most people in the region could not even conceive of the need to rebel against the conditions of life he created for them. He owned most of the industrial establishments in the province. Every daily newspaper, most of the weeklies, all of the TV stations, and most of the radio stations were his, too. Little wonder anyone rarely heard a critical word about his operations. Many people believed that Irving could make or break local governments single-handedly. Should we therefore be surprised that mere high-school students refused to take him on? In their reluctance, Robert's fellow students were only mimicking their parents, who, on the whole, were as powerless as Irving was mighty (Brym, 1979).

Second, many of Robert's classmates did not share his sense of injustice. Most of them regarded Irving as the great provider. They thought his pulp and paper mill, as well as his myriad other industrial establishments, gave many people jobs. They regarded that fact as more important for their lives and the lives of their families than the pollution problem Robert raised. Frame alignment theory suggests Robert needed to figure out ways to build bridges between their understanding and his. He did not. Therefore, he received an unsympathetic hearing.

NEW SOCIAL MOVEMENTS

We can now turn to this chapter's final goal: sketching the prospects of social movements in broad, rapid strokes.

Between 1700 and the 1950s, social movements became larger and generally less violent, and they extended their focus from local to national issues. Often, they struggled to expand the rights of citizens, fighting at first for the right to free speech, freedom of religion, and justice before the law; next for the right to vote and run for office; and then, in the twentieth century, for the right to a certain minimum level of economic security and full participation in social life (Marshall, 1965; Tilly, 1979a, 1979b). In the 1960s, so-called new social movements set still broader goals, attracted new kinds of participants, and became global in scope (Melucci, 1980, 1995). Let us consider each of these issues in turn.

Goals

Some new social movements promote the rights not of specific groups but of humanity as a whole to peace, security, and a clean environment. Such movements include the peace movement, the environmental movement, and the human rights movement. Other new social movements, such as the women's movement and the gay rights movement, promote the rights of particular groups that have been excluded from full social participation. Accordingly, gay rights groups have fought for laws that eliminate all forms of discrimination based on sexual orientation. They have also fought for the repeal of laws that discriminate on the basis of sexual orientation, such as anti-sodomy laws and laws that negatively affect parental custody of children (Adam, Duyvendak, and Krouwel, 1999). Since the 1960s, the women's movement has succeeded in getting admission practices altered in professional schools, winning more freedom of reproductive choice for women, and opening up opportunities for women in the political, religious, military, educational, medical, and business systems (Adamson, Briskin, and McPhail, 1988). The emer-

gence of the peace, environmental, human rights, gay rights, and women's movements involves the extension of citizenship rights to all adult members of society and to society as a whole (Roche, 1995; Turner, 1986: 85–105).

Membership

New social movements are also novel in that they attract a disproportionately large number of highly educated, relatively well-to-do people from the social, educational, and cultural fields. Such people include teachers, professors, journalists, social workers, artists, actors, writers, and student apprentices to these occupations. For several reasons, people in these occupations are more likely to participate in new social movements than are people in other occupations. Their higher education exposes them to radical ideas and makes those ideas appealing. They tend to hold jobs outside the business community, which often opposes their values. And they often become personally involved in the problems of their clients and audiences, sometimes even becoming their advocates (Brint, 1984; Rootes, 1995).

Globalization Potential

Finally, new social movements increase the scope of protest beyond the national level. For example, members of the peace movement viewed federal laws banning nuclear weapons as necessary. Environmentalists felt the same way about federal laws protecting the environment. However, environmentalists also recognized that the condition of the Brazilian rain forest affects climatic conditions worldwide. Similarly, peace activists understood that the spread of weapons of mass destruction could destroy all of humanity. Therefore, members of the peace and environmental movements pressed for *international* agreements binding all countries to protect the environment and stop the spread of nuclear weapons. Social movements went global.

Inexpensive international travel and communication facilitate the globalization of social movements. New technologies make it easier for people in various national movements to work with like-minded activists in other countries. In the age of CNN, inexpensive jet transportation, fax machines, websites, Skype, instant messaging, and e-mail, it is possible not only to see the connection between apparently local problems and their global sources but also to act both locally and globally.

Consider the case of Greenpeace. Greenpeace is a highly successful environmental movement that originated in Vancouver in the mid-1970s. It now has offices in 41 countries, with its international office in Amsterdam. Among many other initiatives, it has mounted a campaign to eliminate the international transportation and dumping of toxic wastes. Its representatives visited local environmental groups in Africa. They supplied the Africans with

Since 1994, protests have been staged wherever major international trade talks have been held. For example, when the Summit of the Americas took place in Quebec City in April 2001, more than 20 000 protesters took to the streets. They catapulted teddy bears, smoke bombs, and rocks at riot police and at one point breached the chain-link security fence surrounding the summit. Police responded with tear gas, water cannons, rubber bullets, and arrests.

organizing kits to help them tie their local concerns to global political efforts. They also published a newsletter to keep activists up to date on legal issues. Thus, Greenpeace coordinated a global campaign that enabled weak environmental organizations in developing countries to act more effectively. Their campaign also raised the costs of continuing the international trade in toxic waste.

Greenpeace is hardly alone in its efforts to go global. In 1953, 110 international social movement organizations spanned the globe. By 1993, there were 631. About a quarter were human rights organizations and about a seventh were environmental organizations. The latter are by far the fastest-growing organizational type (Smith, 1998: 97).

The globalization of social movements can be further illustrated by coming full circle and returning to the anecdote with which we began this chapter. In 1991, Robert Brym visited his hometown. He hadn't been back in years. As he entered the city he vaguely sensed that something was different. "I wasn't able to identify the change until I reached the pulp and paper mill," says Robert. "Suddenly, it was obvious. The rotten-egg smell was virtually gone. I discovered that in the 1970s a local woman whose son developed a serious case of asthma took legal action against the mill and eventually won. The mill owner was forced by law to install a 'scrubber' in the main smokestack to remove most of the sulphur dioxide emissions. Soon, the federal government was putting pressure on the mill owner to purify the polluted water that poured out of the plant and into the local river system." Apparently, local

citizens and the environmental movement had caused a deep change in the climate of opinion. This influenced the government to force the mill owner to spend millions of dollars to clean up his operation. It took decades, but what was political heresy in 1968 became established practice by 1991. That is because environmental concerns had been amplified by the voice of a movement that had grown to global proportions. In general, as this case illustrates, globalization helps ensure that many new social movements transcend local and national boundaries and promote universalistic goals.

Conclusion

For many thousands of years, humans have done well on this planet. That is because we have created cultural practices, including technologies, that allowed us to adapt to and thrive in our environment. Nonetheless, there have been some failures along the way. Many tribes and civilizations are extinct. And our success to date as a species is no warrant for the future. If we persist in using technologies that create an inhospitable environment, nature will deal with us in the same way it always deals with species that cannot adapt.

Broadly speaking, we have two survival strategies to cope with the challenges that lie ahead: competition and cooperation. Charles Darwin wrote famously about competition in *The Origin of Species* (1859). He observed that members of each species struggle against one another and against other species in their struggle to survive. Most of the quickest, the strongest, the best camouflaged, and the smartest live long enough to bear offspring. Most of the rest are killed off. Thus, the traits passed on to offspring are those most valuable for survival. Ruthless competition, it turns out, is a key survival strategy of all species, including humans.

In *The Descent of Man*, Darwin mentioned our second important survival strategy: cooperation. In some species mutual assistance is common. The species members that flourish are those that best learn to help one another (Darwin, 1871:163). The Russian geographer and naturalist Petr Kropotkin (1908 [1902]) elaborated this idea. After spending five years studying animal life in Siberia, he concluded that "mutual aid" is at least as important a survival strategy as competition. Competition takes place when members of the same species compete for limited resources, said Kropotkin. Cooperation occurs when species members struggle against adverse environmental circumstances. According to Kropotkin, survival in the face of environmental threat is best assured if species members help one another. Kropotkin also showed that the most advanced species in any group—ants among insects, mammals among vertebrates, humans among mammals—are the most cooperative. Many evolutionary biologists now accept Kropotkin's ideas (Gould, 1988; Nowak, May, and Sigmund, 1995: 81).

As we have seen, a strictly competitive approach to dealing with the environmental crisis—relying on the market alone to solve our problems—now seems inadequate. Instead, it appears we require more cooperation and self-sacrifice. This involves substantially reducing consumption, paying higher taxes for environmental cleanup and energy-efficient industrial processes, subsidizing the developing countries to industrialize in an environmentally friendly way, and so forth. Previously, we outlined some grave consequences of relying too little on a cooperative survival strategy at this historical juncture. But which strategy you emphasize in your own life is, of course, your choice.

Similarly, throughout this book—when we discussed families, gender inequality, crime, race, population, and many other topics—we raised social issues lying at the intersection of history, social structure, and biography. We arrayed these issues on our sociological com-

pass, set out alternative courses of action, and outlined their consequences. We thus followed our disciplinary mandate: helping people make informed choices based on sound sociological knowledge (Wilensky, 1997). In the context of the present chapter, however, we can make an even bolder claim for the discipline. Conceived at its broadest, sociology promises to help in the rational and equitable evolution of humankind.

Note

1. The European Patent Office revoked W. R. Grace's patent for the neem fungicide in 2005 after the Green Party in the European Parliament, the International Federation of Organic Agriculture, and the Research Foundation for Science, Technology and Ecology filed suit against the corporation.

NASA Goddard Space Flight Center

Abraham, Carolyn. 2003. "Hong Kong Hotel Is Focus of Pneumonia Investigation." *Globe and Mail* 20 March. On the World Wide Web at http://globeandmail.workopolis.com/servlet/Content/fasttrack/20030320/UBUGGN?section=Healthcare (16 June 2003).

Abraham, Laurie Kaye. 1993. *Mama Might Be Better Off Dead: The Failure of Health Care in Urban America.* Chicago: University of Chicago Press.

Adam, Barry, Jan Willem Duyvendak, and Andre Krouwel. 1999. *The Global Emergence of Gay and Lesbian Politics.* Philadelphia: Temple University Press.

Adams, Henry E., Lester W. Wright, Jr., and Bethany A. Lohr. 1998. "Is Homophobia Associated with Homosexual Arousal?" *Journal of Abnormal Psychology* 105: 440–45.

Adams, Michael. 1997. *Sex in the Snow: Canadian Social Values at the End of the Millennium.* Toronto: Penguin.

Adamson, Nancy, Linda Briskin, and Margaret McPhail. 1988. *Feminist Organizing for Change: The Contemporary Women's Movement in Canada.* Toronto: Oxford University Press.

Adherents.com. 2001. "Religion Statistics: Predominant Religions." On the World Wide Web at http://www.adherents.com/adh_predom.html (30 November 2001).

Adler, Patricia A., and Peter Adler. 1998. *Peer Power: Preadolescent Culture and Identity.* New Brunswick, NJ: Rutgers University Press.

Albas, Daniel, and Cheryl Albas. 1989. "Modern Magic: The Case of Examinations." *The Sociological Quarterly* 30: 603–13.

Albelda, Randy, and Chris Tilly. 1997. *Glass Ceilings and Bottomless Pits: Women's Work, Women's Poverty.* Boston: South End Press.

Almey, Marcia. 2007. "Women in Canada: Work Chapter Updates." On the World Wide Web at http://www.statcan.ca/english/freepub/89F0133XIE/89F0133XIE2006000.htm#10 (21 April 2007).

Amato, Paul R., and Bruce Keith. 1991. "Parental Divorce and the Well-Being of Children: A Meta-Analysis." *Psychological Bulletin* 110: 26–46.

Ambert, Anne-Marie. 1998. "Divorce: Facts, Figures and Consequences." Vanier Institute of the Family. On the World Wide Web at http://www.vifamily.ca/cft/divorce/divorcer.htm (17 February 2000).

American Psychological Association. 1998. "Answers to Your Questions about Sexual Orientation and Homosexuality." On the World Wide Web at http://www.apa.org/pubinfo/orient.html (14 June 2000).

American Society of Plastic Surgeons. 2007. "2000/2005/2006 National Plastic Surgery Statistics." On the World Wide Web at http://www.plasticsurgery.org/media/statistics/loader.cfm?url5/commonspot/security/getfile.cfm&PageID523628 (25 March 2007).

American Society of Plastic Surgeons. 2009. "2000/2007/2008 National Plastic Surgery Statistics." On the World Wide Web at http://www.plasticsurgery.org/Media/stats/2008-cosmetic-reconstructive-plastic-surgery-minimally-invasive-statistics.pdf (23 February 2010).

American Sociological Association. 1999. *Code of Ethics and Policies and Procedures of the ASA Committee on Professional Ethics.* Washington, DC: Author.

Anderson, Benedict O. 1991. *The Imagined Community,* rev. ed. London: Verso.

Anderson, Craig, and Brad J. Bushman. 2002. "The Effects of Media Violence on Society." *Science* 295, 5564: 2377–79.

Anderson, Gerald F., Uwe E. Reinhardt, Peter S. Hussey, and Varduhi Petrosyan. 2003. "It's the Prices, Stupid: Why the United States Is So Different from Other Countries." *Health Affairs* 22, 3: 89–105.

Anderson, Michael. 2003. "Reading Violence in Boys' Writing." *Language Arts* 80, 3: 223–31.

Anesi, Chuck. 1997. "The *Titanic* Casualty Figures." On the World Wide Web at http://www.anesi.com/titanic.htm (11 March 2010).

Angus Reid Global Monitor. 2009. "Views on Health Care Differ in Canada, U.S." On the World Wide Web at http://www.angus-reid.com/polls/view/33946 (2 April 2010).

Angus Reid Global Monitor. 2010. "U.S., Britain and Canada Endorse Death Penalty." On the World Wide Web at http://www.angus-reid.com/polls/view/us_britain_and_canada_endorse_death_penalty/ (8 March 2010).

Arace, Michael. 2000. "Oft-injured Forward Feels OK." *Columbus Dispatch* 17 September. On the World Wide Web at http://www.dispatch.com/news/sports00/sept00/424238.html (22 July 2002).

Ariès, Phillipe. 1962 [1960]. *Centuries of Childhood: A Social History of Family Life,* Robert Baldick, trans. New York: Knopf.

Arnett, Jeffrey Jensen. 1995. "Adolescents' Uses of Media for Self-Socialization." *Journal of Youth and Adolescence* 24: 519–33.

Asch, Solomon. 1955. "Opinion and Social Pressure." *Scientific American* July: 31–35.

Associated Press. 2010. "Iran's Leader Introduces Plan to Encourage Population Growth by Paying Families." *New York Times* 27 July. On the World Wide Web at www.nytimes.com/2010/07/28/world/middleeast/28iran.html (3 August 2010).

Averett, Susan, and Sanders Korenman. 1996. "The Economic Reality of The Beauty Myth." *Journal of Human Resources* 31: 304–30.

Baer, Doug. 1999. "Educational Credentials and the Changing Occupational Structure." Pp. 92–106 in James Curtis, Edward Grabb, and Neil Guppy, eds. *Social Inequality in Canada: Patterns, Problems, Policies,* 3rd ed. Scarborough, ON: Prentice Hall Allyn and Bacon Canada.

Baran, Paul A. 1957. *The Political Economy of Growth.* New York: Monthly Review Press.

Barlow, Maude, and Elizabeth May. 2000. *Frederick Street: Life and Death on Canada's Love Canal.* Toronto: HarperCollins.

Barna, G. 2002. *Grow Your Church from the Outside In: Understanding the Unchurched and How to Reach Them.* Ventura, CA: Regal Books.

Bar-On, Dan. 1999. *The Indescribable and the Undiscussable: Reconstructing Human Discourse after Trauma.* Ithaca, NY: Cornell University Press.

Barth, Fredrik, ed. 1969. *Ethnic Groups and Boundaries: The Social Organization of Cultural Difference.* Boston: Little, Brown.

Baudrillard, Jean. 1988 [1986]. *America,* Chris Turner, trans. London: Verso.

Bauman, Zygmunt. 1989. *Modernity and the Holocaust.* Ithaca, NY: Cornell University Press.

Beaupré, Pascale, Pierre Turcotte, and Anne Milan. 2007. "When Is Junior Moving Out? Transitions from the Parental Home to Independence." *Canadian Social Trends* 82: 9–15. Statistics Canada Catalogue no. 11-008-XPE. On the World Wide Web at http://www.statcan.ca/english/ freepub/11-008-XIE/2006002/pdf/11-008-XIE20060029274.pdf (26 March 2007).

Beck, Ulrich. 1992 [1986]. *Risk Society: Towards a New Modernity,* Mark Ritter, trans. London, UK: Sage.

Becker, Howard S. 1963. *Outsiders: Studies in the Sociology of Deviance.* New York: Free Press.

Beil, Laura. 2007. "For Struggling Black Colleges, Hopes of a Big-Screen Revival." *New York Times* 5 December. On the World Wide Web at http://www.nytimes.com (5 December 2007).

Bell, Daniel. 1973. *The Coming of Post-Industrial Society: A Venture in Social Forecasting.* New York: Basic Books.

Belluck, Pam. 2008. "Strangers May Cheer You Up, Study Says." *New York Times* 4 December. On the World Wide Web at http://www.nytimes. com/2008/12/05/health/05happy-web. html?ref=sociology (8 August 2010).

Belluz, Julia. 2010. "Religion, No; Magic, Yes." *Maclean's* 19 July: 4.

Benford, Robert D. 1997. "An Insider's Critique of the Social Movement Framing Perspective." *Sociological Inquiry* 67: 409–39.

Berens, Michael J. 2002. "Infection Epidemic Carves Deadly Path." *Chicago Tribune* 21 July. On the World Wide Web at http://www.chicagotribune.com/news/ specials/chi-0207210272jul21.story (16 June 2003).

Berger, Peter L., and Thomas Luckmann. 1966. *The Social Construction of Reality:*

A Treatise in the Sociology of Knowledge. Garden City, NY: Doubleday.

Berk, Sarah Fenstermaker. 1985. *The Gender Factory: The Apportionment of Work in American Households.* New York: Plenum.

Berliner, Wendy. 2004. "Where Have All the Young Men Gone?" *Manchester Guardian* 18 May: 8.

Besserer, Sandra. 2002. "Criminal Victimization: An International Perspective: Results of the 2000 International Crime Victimization Survey." *Juristat* 22, 4 (May). Catalogue no. 85-002-XPE. Ottawa: Canadian Centre for Justice Statistics and Statistics Canada.

Betcherman, Gordon, and Graham Lowe. 1997. *The Future of Work in Canada: A Synthesis Report.* Ottawa: Canadian Policy Research Networks Inc.

Bianchi, Suzanne M., and Daphne Spain. 1996. "Women, Work, and Family in America." *Population Bulletin* 51, 3: 2–48.

Bibby, Reginald W. 1987. *Fragmented Gods: The Poverty and Potential of Religion in Canada.* Toronto: Irwin.

_____. 2001. *Canada's Teens: Today, Yesterday, and Tomorrow.* Toronto: Stoddart.

_____. 2002. *Restless Gods: The Renaissance of Religion in Canada.* Toronto: Stoddart.

———. 2004. *Restless Churches: How Canada's Churches Can Contribute to the Emerging Religious Renaissance.* Ottawa: Novalis.

———. 2005. *Project Canada National Survey Series.* Lethbridge, AB: University of Lethbridge.

———. 2006. *The Boomer Factor: What Canada's Most Famous Generation Is Leaving Behind.* Toronto: Bastian.

_____. 2007. "Religion." Pp. 334–62 in Robert J. Brym, ed. *New Society,* 5th ed. Toronto: Nelson.

_____. 2011. "Religion." Pp. 309–34 in Robert J. Brym, ed. *New Society,* 6th ed. Toronto: Nelson.

Biegler, Rebecca S. 1999. "Psychological Interventions Designed to Counter Sexism in Children: Empirical Limitations and Theoretical Foundations." Pp. 129–52 in William B. Swann, Jr., Judith H. Langlois, and Lucia A. Gilbert, eds. *Sexism and Stereotypes in Modern Society: The Gender Science of Janet Taylor Spence.* Washington, DC: American Psychological Association.

Bierstedt, Robert. 1974. "An Analysis of Social Power." Pp. 220–41 in *Power*

and Progress: Essays in Sociological Theory. New York: McGraw-Hill.

Bittman, Michael, and Judy Wajcman. 2000. "The Rush Hour: The Character of Leisure Time and Gender Equity." *Social Forces* 79: 165–89.

Blau, Peter M. 1964. *Exchange and Power in Social Life.* New York: Wiley.

Blauner, Robert. 1972. *Racial Oppression in America.* New York: Harper & Row.

Blazer, Dan G., Ronald C. Kessler, Katherine A. McGonagle, and Marvin S. Swartz. 1994. "The Prevalence and Distribution of Major Depression in a National Community Sample: The National Comorbidity Survey." *American Journal of Psychiatry* 151: 979–86.

Blossfeld, Hans-Peter, and Yossi Shavit, eds. 1993. *Persistent Inequality: Changing Educational Attainment in Thirteen Countries.* Boulder, CO: Westview Press.

Blum, Deborah. 1997. *Sex on the Brain: The Biological Differences Between Men and Women.* New York: Penguin.

Blumer, Herbert. 1969. *Symbolic Interactionism: Perspective and Method.* Englewood Cliffs, NJ: Prentice-Hall.

Blumberg, Paul. 1989. *The Predatory Society: Deception in the American Marketplace.* New York: Oxford University Press.

Boal, Mark. 1998. "Spycam City." *The Village Voice* (30 September–6 October). On the World Wide Web at http://www. villagevoice.com/ issues/9840/boal. shtml (26 March 2001).

Boles, Sharon, and Patrick Johnson. 2001. "Gender, Weight Concerns and Adolescent Smoking." *Journal of Addictive Diseases* 20, 2: 5–14.

Bonacich, Edna. 1972. "A Theory of Ethnic Antagonism: The Split Labor Market." *American Sociological Review* 37: 547–59.

Bornholt, Laurel. 2001. "Self-Concepts, Usefulness and Behavioural Intentions on the Social Context of Schooling." *Educational Psychology* 21, 1 (March): 67–78.

Boston Women's Health Book Collective, ed. 1998. *Our Bodies, Our Selves for the New Century: A Book by and for Women.* New York: Simon & Schuster.

Boswell, A. Ayres, and Joan Z. Spade. 1996. "Fraternities and Collegiate Rape Culture: Why Are Some Fraternities More Dangerous Places for Women?" *Gender and Society* 10: 133–47.

Bourdieu, Pierre. 1977 [1972]. *Outline of a Theory of Practice,* Richard Nice, trans. Cambridge, UK: Cambridge University Press.

Bourdieu, Pierre, and Jean-Claude Passeron. 1990. *Reproduction in Education, Society and Culture,* 2nd ed., Richard Nice, trans. London: Sage.

Bowles, Samuel, and Herbert Gintis. 1976. *Schooling in Capitalist America: Educational Reform and the Contradictions of Economic Life.* New York: Basic Books.

Boychuk, Gerard W. 2002. "Federal Spending in Health: Why Here? Why Now?" Pp. 121–36 in G. Bruce Doern, ed. *How Ottawa Spends 2002–2003: The Security Aftermath and National Priorities.* Toronto: Oxford University Press.

Boyd, Danah. 2008. "Facebook's Privacy Trainwreck: Exposure, Invasion, and Social Convergence." *Convergence* 14, 1: 13–20.

Boyd, Monica. 1997. "Feminizing Paid Work." *Current Sociology* 45, 2 (April): 49–73.

Braithwaite, John. 1981. "The Myth of Social Class and Criminality Revisited." *American Sociological Review* 46: 36–57.

_____. 1989. *Crime, Shame and Reintegration.* New York: Cambridge University Press.

Braver, Sanford L., Pamela J. Fitzpatrick, and R. Curtis Bay. 1991. "Noncustodial Parent's Report of Child Support Payments." *Family Relations* 40, 2 (April): 180–85.

Brechin, Steven R., and Willett Kempton. 1994. "Global Environmentalism: A Challenge to the Postmaterialism Thesis." *Social Science Quarterly* 75: 245–69.

Bricker, Darrell, and Edward Greenspon. 2001. *Searching for Certainty: Inside the New Canadian Mindset.* Toronto: Doubleday Canada.

Brint, Stephen. 1984. "New Class and Cumulative Trend Explanations of the Liberal Political Attitudes of Professionals." *American Journal of Sociology* 90: 30–71.

Brower, David. 1975. *Training the Nihilists: Education and Radicalism in Tsarist Russia.* Ithaca, NY: Cornell University Press.

Brown, Lyn Mikel, and Carol Gilligan. 1992. *Meeting at the Crossroads: Women's Psychology and Girls' Development.* Cambridge, MA: Harvard University Press.

Brown, Peter. 1996. *The Rise of Western Christendom: Triumph and Diversity, A.D. 200–1000.* Oxford: Blackwell.

Browne, Kevin D., and Catherine Hamilton-Giachritsis. 2005. "The Influence of Violent Media on Children and Adolescents: A Public-Health Approach." *The Lancet* 365, 9460: 702–10.

Browning, Christopher R. 1992. *Ordinary Men: Reserve Police Battalion 101 and the Final Solution in Poland.* New York: HarperCollins.

Bruce, Steve. 1988. *The Rise and Fall of the New Christian Right: Conservative Protestant Politics in America 1978–1988.* Oxford, UK: Clarendon Press.

Bryant, Marian E. 1999. "Sentencing Aboriginal Offenders." *Law Now,* October/November: 20–21.

Brym, Robert J. 1979. "Political Conservatism in Atlantic Canada." Pp. 59–79 in Robert J. Brym and R. James Sacouman, eds. *Underdevelopment and Social Movements in Atlantic Canada.* Toronto: New Hogtown Press.

_____. 1980. *Intellectuals and Politics.* London, UK: George Allen and Unwin.

_____. 2001. "Jewish Immigrants from the Former Soviet Union in Canada, 1996." *East European Jewish Affairs* 31: 36–43.

_____. 2003. "Affluence, Strikes, and Power in Canada, 1973–2000." Pp. 243–53 in James Curtis, Edward Grabb, and Neil Guppy, eds. *Social Inequality in Canada: Patterns, Problems, Policies,* 4th ed. Scarborough, ON: Prentice-Hall.

_____. 2006. "How High School Drama Helped Me to Become a Sociologist: An Essay in the Sociology of Autobiography." *Canadian Journal of Sociology* 31: 245–57.

_____. 2007a. "Hip Hop from Caps to Bling." Pp. 13–31 in *Sociology as a Life or Death Issue.* Toronto: Penguin.

_____. 2007b. "The Six Lessons of Suicide Bombers." *Contexts* 6, 4: 37–43.

_____. 2008. "Religion, Politics, and Suicide Bombing: An Interpretative Essay." *Canadian Journal of Sociology* 33. On the World Wide Web at http://ejournals.library.ualberta.ca/index.php/CJS/ (31 January 2008).

Brym, Robert J., and Bader Araj. 2006. "Suicide Bombing as Strategy and Interaction: The Case of the Second Intifada." *Social Forces* 84: 165–82.

Brym, Robert J., et al. 2005. "In Faint Praise of the World Bank's Gender Development Policy." *Canadian Journal of Sociology* 30: 95–111.

Brym, Robert J., and John Lie. 2009. *Sociology: The Points of the Compass.* Toronto: Nelson.

Brym, Robert J., John Lie, and Steven Rytina. 2010. *Sociology: Your Compass for a New World* (3rd ed.). Toronto: Nelson.

Brym, Robert J., Michael Gillespie, and A. Ron Gillis. 1985. "Anomie, Opportunity, and the Density of Ethnic Ties: Another View of Jewish Outmarriage in Canada." *Canadian Review of Sociology and Anthropology* 22: 102–12.

Brym, Robert J., and Rhonda Lenton. 2001. *Love Online: A Report on Digital Dating in Canada.* Toronto: MSN.CA. On the World Wide Web at http://www.nelson.com/nelson/harcourt/sociology/newsociety3e/loveonline.pdf (20 December 2001).

Brym, Robert J., with Rozalina Ryvkina. 1994. *The Jews of Moscow, Kiev and Minsk: Identity, Antisemitism, Emigration.* New York: New York University Press.

Brym, Robert J., William Shaffir, and Morton Weinfeld, eds. 1993. *The Jews in Canada.* Toronto: Oxford University Press.

Brzezinski, Zbigniew. 2002. "Confronting Anti-American Grievances." *New York Times* 1 September. On the World Wide Web at http://www.nytimes.com (1 September 2002).

Bullough, Vern L. 2000. "Transgenderism and the Concept of Gender." *International Journal of Transgenderism,* Special Issue 4, 3 (July–Sept).

Bunge, Valerie Pottie. 2000. "Spousal Violence." Pp. 11–21 in Statistics Canada, *Family Violence in Canada: A Statistical Profile 2000.* Catalogue no. 85-224-XIE. Ottawa: Minister of Industry.

Burns, Tom, and George M. Stalker. 1961. *The Management of Innovation.* London, UK: Tavistock.

"Business of Touch, The." 2006. On the World Wide Web at http://www.businessoftouch.com/index2.html (7 April 2006).

Buss, David M. 2000. *Dangerous Passion: Why Jealousy Is As Necessary As Love and Sex.* New York: Free Press.

Campbell, Donald, and Julian Stanley. 1963. *Experimental and Quasi-experimental Designs for Research*. Chicago: Rand McNally.

Campbell, Frances A., and Craig T. Ramey. 1994. "Effects of Early Intervention on Intellectual and Academic Achievement: A Follow-up Study of Children from Low-income Families." *Child Development* 65: 684–99.

Campion, Edward W. 1993. "Why Unconventional Medicine?" *New England Journal of Medicine* 328: 282.

"Canada Hosts the World: G8 and G20 Summits." 2010. *CBC News* 26 May. On the World Wide Web at http://www.cbc.ca/canada/story/2010/05/26/f-g8-huntsville-g20-toronto.html (2 November 2010).

Canadian Aboriginal News. 2001. "Innu, Health Officials Settle Differences over Treatment for Gas Sniffers." On the World Wide Web at http://www.candianaboriginal.com/health/health26b.htm (16 June 2006).

Canadian Council on Social Development. 2001. *The Progress of Canada's Children 2001—Highlights*. On the World Wide Web at http://www.ccsd.ca/pubs/2-1/pcc2001.hl.htm (17 February 2002).

_____. 2007. "Families: A Canadian Profile." On the World Wide Web at http://www.ccsd.ca/factsheets/family/ (24 April 2007).

Canadian Institute for Health Information. 2004. *Improving the Health of Canadians*. Ottawa: Author.

Cancer Care Nova Scotia. 2004. "Cancer Statistics in Nova Scotia." On the World Wide Web at http://cancercare.ns.ca/media/documents/CancerinNS_Overview.pdf (27 February 2008)

Cancio, A. Silvia, T. David Evans, and David J. Maume. 1996. "Reconsidering the Declining Significance of Race: Racial Differences in Early Career Wages." *American Sociological Review* 61: 541–56.

Carbon Dioxide Information Analysis Center. 1998. "Historical CO_2 Records from the Law Dome DE08, DE08-2, and DSS Ice Cores." On the World Wide Web at http://cdiac.ornl.gov/trends/co2/lawdome.html (29 March 2010).

Cardinal, Harold. 1977. *The Rebirth of Canada's Indians*. Edmonton: Hurtig Publishers.

Cardoso, Fernando Henrique, and Enzo Faletto. 1979. *Dependency and Development in Latin America,* Marjory Mattingly Urquidi, trans. Berkeley: University of California Press.

Caron, Roger. 1979. *Go-Boy! The True Story of a Life Behind Bars*. London, UK: Arrow Books.

Carrier, Roch. 1979. *The Hockey Sweater and Other Stories,* Sheila Fischman, trans. Toronto: Anansi.

Cassidy, Barbara, Robina Lord, and Nancy Mandell. 1998. "Silenced and Forgotten Women: Race, Poverty and Disability." Pp. 26–54 in Nancy Mandell, ed. *Race, Class and Sexuality,* 2nd ed. Scarborough: Prentice-Hall Allyn and Bacon.

Cavalli-Sforza, L. Luca, Paola Menozzi, and Alberto Piazza. 1994. *The History and Geography of Human Genes*. Princeton, NJ: Princeton University Press.

Central Intelligence Agency. 2001. *The World Factbook 2001*. On the World Wide Web at http://www.cia.gov/cia/publications/factbook/ (January 10, 2002).

_____. 2010. *The World Factbook*. On the World Wide Web at https://www.cia.gov/library/publications/the-world-factbook/ (11 March 2010).

Chagnon, Napoleon. 1992. *Yanomamö: The Last Days of Eden*. New York: Harcourt, Brace Yovanovich.

Chard, Jennifer. 2000. "Women in a Visible Minority." Pp. 219–44 in *Women in Canada, 2000: A Gender-Based Statistical Report*. Ottawa: Statistics Canada.

Charlton, James I. 1998. *Nothing about Us without Us: Disability Oppression and Empowerment*. Berkeley, CA: University of California Press.

Chauncey, George. 2005. *Why Marriage? The History Shaping Today's Debate over Gay Equality*. New York: Basic Books.

Chaves, Mark. 1994. "Secularization as Declining Religious Authority." *Social Forces* 72: 749–74.

Cherlin, Andrew J. 1992. *Marriage, Divorce, Remarriage,* revised and enlarged ed. Cambridge, MA: Harvard University Press.

Chesley, Laurie, Donna MacAulay, and Janice L. Ristock. 1991. *Abuse in Lesbian Relationships: A Handbook of Information and Resources*. Toronto: Counselling Centre for Lesbians and Gays.

Cicourel, Aaron. 1968. *The Social Organization of Juvenile Justice*. New York: Wiley.

Citizenship and Immigration Canada. 2005. *Annual Report to Parliament on Immigration 2005*. Ottawa. On the World Wide Web at http://www.cic.gc.ca/english/pdf/pub/immigration2005_e.pdf (22 March 2007).

Clairmont, Donald H., and Dennis W. Magill. 1999. *Africville: The Life and Death of a Canadian Black Community,* 3rd ed. Toronto: Canadian Scholars' Press.

Clark, Warren. 2003. "Pockets of Belief: Religious Attendance Patterns in Canada." *Canadian Social Trends* 68 (Spring): 2–5. Statistics Canada Catalogue no. 11-008-XPE.

Clarke, Harold D., Jane Jenson, Lawrence LeDuc, and Jon H. Pammett. 1996. *Absolute Mandate: Canadian Electoral Politics in an Era of Restructuring,* 3rd ed. Toronto: Gage.

Clarke-Stewart, K. Alison, Christian P. Gruber, and Linda May Fitzgerald. 1994. *Children at Home and in Day Care*. Hillsdale, NJ: Lawrence Erlbaum.

Clement, Wallace H. P. 1897. *The History of the Dominion of Canada*. Toronto: William Briggs.

Cleveland, Gordon, and Michael Krashinsky. 1998. *The Benefits and Costs of Good Child Care: The Economic Rationale for Public Investment in Young Children*. Toronto: University of Toronto.

Clinard, Marshall B., and Peter C. Yeager. 1980. *Corporate Crime*. New York: Free Press.

Cloward, Richard A., and Lloyd E. Ohlin. 1960. *Delinquency and Opportunity: A Theory of Delinquent Gangs*. New York: Free Press.

Cockerham, William C. 1998. *Medical Sociology,* 7th ed. Upper Saddle River, NJ: Prentice-Hall.

Cohen, Albert. 1955. *Delinquent Boys: The Subculture of a Gang*. New York: Free Press.

Cohen, Lynne. 1999. "Suing the Alternative Health-Care Provider." *Canadian Lawyer* November/December: 47–51.

Cohen, Patricia. 2010. "The Long Road to Adulthood is Growing Even Longer." *New York Times* 11 June. On the World Wide Web at http://www.nytimes.com/2010/06/13/us/13generations.html?scp=1&sq=long%20road%20to%20adulthood%20is%20growing%20even%20longer&st=cse (8 August 2010).

Cohen, Stanley. 1972. *Folk Devils and Moral Panics: The Creation of the Mods and Rockers*. London: MacGibbon and Kee.

Colapinto, John. 1997. "The True Story of John/Joan." *Rolling Stone* 11 December: 54–73, 92–97.

_____. 2001. *As Nature Made Him: The Boy Who Was Raised as a Girl.* Toronto: HarperCollins.

Cole, Michael. 1995. *Cultural Psychology.* Cambridge, MA: Harvard University Press.

Coleman, J. 1988. "Social Capital in the Creation of Human Capital." *American Journal of Sociology* 94: 95–120.

Coleman, James S. 1990. *Foundations of Social Theory.* Cambridge, MA: Harvard University Press.

Coleman, James, Ernest Q. Campbell, and Carol J. Hobson. 1966. *Equality of Educational Opportunity.* Washington, DC: United States Department of Health, Education, and Welfare, Office of Education.

Collins, Randall. 1979. *The Credential Society: An Historical Sociology of Education.* New York: Academic Press.

_____. 1982. *Sociological Insight: An Introduction to Nonobvious Sociology.* New York: Oxford University Press.

_____. 1993. "Review of *A Theory of Religion* by Rodney Stark and William S. Bainbridge." *Journal for the Scientific Study of Religion* 32, 4: 402–04, 406.

Collins, Randall, and Scott Coltrane. 1991. *Sociology of Marriage and the Family: Gender, Love, and Property,* 3rd ed. Chicago: Nelson-Hall.

_____. 1995. *Sociology of Marriage and the Family.* Chicago: Nelson-Hall.

Comte, Auguste. 1975. *Auguste Comte: The Foundation of Sociology,* Kenneth Thompson, ed. New York: Wiley.

Condry, John, and Sandra Condry. 1976. "Sex Differences: A Study of The Eye of the Beholder." *Child Development* 47: 812–19.

Conrad, Peter, and Joseph W. Schneider. 1992. *Deviance and Medicalization: From Badness to Sickness,* expanded ed. Philadelphia: Temple University Press.

Contenta, Sandro. 2010. "Canadian Health Care Has a Dirty Secret." *GlobalPost* 3 March. On the World Wide Web at http://www.globalpost.com/dispatch/canada/100302/health-care-danny-williams (3 August 2010).

Converse, Jean M., and Stanley Presser. 1986. *Survey Questions: Handcrafting the Standardized Questionnaire.* Newbury Park, CA: Sage.

Cooley, Charles Horton. 1902. *Human Nature and the Social Order.* New York: Scribner's.

Coontz, Stephanie. 1992. *The Way We Never Were: American Families and the Nostalgia Trap.* New York: Basic Books.

Costanzo, Mark. 1997. *Just Revenge: Costs and Consequences of the Death Penalty.* New York: St. Martin's Press.

Creedon, Jeremiah. 1998. "God with a Million Faces." *Utne Reader* July–August: 42–48.

Creighton, Sarah, and Catherine Mihto. 2001. "Managing Intersex." *BMJ: British Medical Journal* 323, 7324 (December): 1264–65.

Crozier, Michel. 1964. *The Bureaucratic Phenomenon.* Chicago: University of Chicago Press.

Culver, John H. 1992. "Capital Punishment, 1997–1998: Characteristics of the 143 Executed." *Sociology and Social Research* 76, 2 (January): 59–61.

Cureatz, Ryan. 2005. "Gossiping to Get Ahead." *New Media Journalism* December. On the World Wide Web at http://www.fims.uwo.ca/NewMedia2006/default.asp?id=324 (3 August 2010).

Curtis, Bruce. 1988. *Building the Educational State: Canada West, 1836–1871.* London, ON: Althouse Press.

Curtis, James, John Loy, and Wally Karnilowicz. 1986. "A Comparison of Suicide-Dip Effects of Major Sport Events and Civil Holidays." *Sociology of Sport Journal* 3: 1–14.

CyberPress. 2001. "The Recidivist Roger Caron Stopped Once Again" (translated from the French), 14 October. On the World Wide Web at http://216.239.37.120/transl (1 October 2003).

Dalphonse, Sherri. 1997. "Childfree by Choice." *The Washingtonian* 32, 5: 48–57.

Darwin, Charles. 1859. *On the Origin of Species by Means of Natural Selection.* London: John Murray.

_____. 1871. *The Descent of Man.* London: John Murray.

Davies, James B. 1999. "Distribution of Wealth and Economic Inequality." Pp. 138–50 in James Curtis, Edward Grabb, and Neil Guppy, eds. *Social Inequality in Canada: Patterns, Problems, Policies,* 3rd ed. Scarborough, ON: Prentice Hall Allyn and Bacon Canada.

Davies, James C. 1969. "Toward a Theory of Revolution." Pp. 85–108 in Barry McLaughlin, ed. *Studies in Social Movements: A Social Psychological Perspective.* New York: Free Press.

Davies, Mark, and Denise B. Kandel. 1981. "Parental and Peer Influences on Adolescents' Educational Plans: Some Further Evidence." *American Journal of Sociology* 87: 363–87.

Davis, Fred. 1992. *Fashion, Culture, and Identity.* Chicago: University of Chicago Press.

Davis, Kingsley, and Wilbert E. Moore. 1945. "Some Principles of Stratification." *American Sociological Review* 10: 242–49.

Dawson, S. E. 1906. "Principal Causes of Death." Table IV. *Fourth Census of Canada, 1901, volume IV.* Ottawa: Library and Archives Canada.

DeKeseredy, Walter S., and Katherine Kelly. 1993. "The Incidence and Prevalence of Woman Abuse in Canadian University and College Dating Relationships." *Canadian Journal of Sociology* 18: 137–59.

Demo, David H., Mark A. Fine, and Lawrence H. Ganong. 2000. "Divorce as a Family Stressor." Pp. 279–302 in P. C. McKenry and S. J. Price, eds. *Families & Change: Coping with Stressful Events and Transitions,* 2nd ed. Thousand Oaks, CA: Sage.

Derber, Charles. 1979. *The Pursuit of Attention: Power and Individualism in Everyday Life.* New York: Oxford University Press.

DeSteno, David, and Peter Salovey. 2001. "Evolutionary Origins of Sex Differences in Jealousy: Questioning the 'Fitness' of the Model." Pp. 150–56 in W. Gerrod Parrott, ed. *Emotions in Social Psychology: Essential Readings.* Philadelphia: Psychology Press.

de Villiers, Marq. 1999. *Water.* Toronto: Stoddart Publishing.

Diamond, Milton. 1982. "Sexual Identity: Monozygotic Twins Reared in Discordant Sex Roles and a BBC Follow-up." *Archives of Sexual Behavior* 11: 181–86.

Diamond, Milton, and H. Keith Sigmundson. 1999. "Sex Reassignment at Birth." Pp. 55–75 in Stephen J. Ceci and Wendy W. Williams, eds. *The Nature–Nurture Debate: The Essential Readings.* Maldan, MA: Blackwell.

Dietz, Tracy L. 1998. "An Examination of Violence and Gender Role Portrayals in Video Games: Implications for Gender Socialization and Aggressive Behavior." *Sex Roles* 38: 425–42.

DiMaggio, Paul. 1982. "Cultural Capital and School Success: The Impact of Status Culture Participation on the Grades of U.S. High School Students." *American Sociological Review* 47: 189–201.

Donahue III, John J., and Steven D. Levitt. 2001. "The Impact of Legalized Abortion on Crime." *Quarterly Journal of Economics* 116: 379–420.

Douglas, Emily M., and Murray A. Straus. 2006. "Assault and Injury of Dating Partners by University Students in 19 Nations and Its Relation to Corporal Punishment Experienced as a Child." *European Journal of Criminology* 3: 293–318.

Doyle, Aaron, Brian Elliott, and David Tindall. 1997. "Framing the Forests: Corporations, the B.C. Forest Alliance, and the Media." Pp. 240–68 in William Carroll, ed. *Organizing Dissent: Contemporary Social Movements in Theory and Practice,* 2nd ed. Toronto: Garamond Press.

Dranoff, Linda Silver. 2001. *Everyone's Guide to the Law.* Toronto: HarperCollins.

Duffy, Ann, and Nancy Mandell. 2011. "Poverty in Canada." Pp. 125–44 in Robert J. Brym, ed. *Society in Question,* 6th ed. Toronto: Nelson.

Dugger, Karen. 1996. "Social Location and Gender-Role Attitudes: A Comparison of Black and White Women." Pp. 32–51 in Esther Ngan-Ling Chow, Doris Wilkinson, and Maxine Baca Zinn, eds. *Race, Class, and Gender.* Newbury Park, CA: Sage.

Dumas, Jean, and Yves Perron. 1992. *Current Demographic Analysis: Marriage and Conjugal Life in Canada.* Catalogue no. 91-534. Ottawa: Statistics Canada.

Duncan, Greg, W. Jean Yeung, Jeanne Brooks-Gunn, and Judith Smith. 1998. "How Much Does Childhood Poverty Affect the Life Chance of Children?" *American Sociological Review* 63: 402–23.

Durkheim, Émile. 1938 [1895]. *The Rules of Sociological Method,* G.E.G. Catlin, ed., Solovay and J. Mueller, trans. Chicago: University of Chicago Press.

_____. 1951 [1897]. *Suicide: A Study in Sociology,* G. Simpson, ed., J. Spaulding and G. Simpson, trans. New York: Free Press.

_____. 1956. *Education and Sociology,* Sherwood D. Fox, trans. New York: Free Press.

_____. 1961 [1925]. *Moral Education: A Study in the Theory and Application of the Sociology of Education,* Everett K. Wilson and Herman Schnurer, trans. New York: Free Press.

_____. 1973 [1899–1900]. "Two Laws of Penal Evolution." *Economy and Society* 2: 285–308.

_____. 1976 [1915/1912]. *The Elementary Forms of the Religious Life,* Joseph Ward Swain, trans. New York: Free Press.

_____. 1997 [1893]. *The Division of Labor in Society.* New York: Free Press.

Dutton, Judy. 2000. "Detect His Lies Every Time." *Cosmopolitan* April: 126.

Eagley, Alice H., and Wendy Wood. 1999. "The Origins of Sex Differences in Human Behaviour: Evolved Dispositions versus Social Roles." *American Psychologist* 54: 408–23.

Eccles, Jacquelynne S., Janis E. Jacobs, and Rena D. Harold. 1990. "Gender Role Stereotypes, Expectancy Effects and Parents' Socialization of Gender Differences." *Journal of Social Issues* 46: 183–201.

Edmundson, Mark. 2003. "How Teachers Can Stop Cheaters." *New York Times* 9 September. On the World Wide Web at http://www.nytimes.com (9 September 2003).

Eichler, Margrit. 1987. *Nonsexist Research Methods.* Boston: Allen and Unwin.

_____. 1988. *Families in Canada Today,* 2nd ed. Toronto: Gage.

Ekman, Paul. 1978. *Facial Action Coding System.* New York: Consulting Psychologists Press.

Elliott, H. L. 1995. "Living Vicariously through Barbie." On the World Wide Web at http://ziris.syr.edu/path/public_html/barbie/main.html (19 November 1998).

Ellis, Lee, Brian Robb, and Donald Burke. 2005. "Sexual Orientation in United States and Canadian College Students." *Archives of Sexual Behavior* 34: 569–81.

Ellison, Nicole B., Charles Steinfeld, and Cliffe Lampe. 2007. "The Benefits of Facebook 'Friends': Social Capital and College Students' Use of Online Social Network Sites." *Journal of Computer-Mediated Communication* 12, 4. On the World Wide Web at http://jcmc.indiana.edu/vol12/issue4/ellison.html (21 September 2010).

Ellul, Jacques. 1964 [1954]. *The Technological Society,* John Wilkinson, trans. New York: Vintage.

Engels, Frederick. 1970 [1884]. *The Origins of the Family, Private Property and the State,* Eleanor Burke Leacock, ed., Alec West, trans. New York: International Publishers.

England, Paula. 1992. *Comparable Worth: Theories and Evidence.* Hawthorne, NY: Aldine de Gruyter.

Entine, J. 2000. *Taboo: Why Black Athletes Dominate Sports and Why We Are Afraid to Talk about It.* New York: Public Affairs.

Epstein, Helen. 1998. "Life and Death on the Social Ladder." *New York Review of Books* 45, 12 (16 July): 26–30.

Epstein, Steven. 1996. *Impure Science: AIDS, Activism, and the Politics of Knowledge.* Berkeley, CA: University of California Press.

Estrich, Susan. 1987. *Real Rape.* Cambridge, MA: Harvard University Press.

"Ethnic Groups in the World." 1998. *Scientific American.* On the World Wide Web at http://www.sciam.com/1998/0998issue/0998numbers.html (4 December 2001).

Evans, Robert G. 1999. "Social Inequalities in Health." *Horizons* (Policy Research Secretariat, Government of Canada) 2, 3: 6–7.

"Face of the Web Study Pegs Global Internet Population at More than 300 Million." 2000. On the World Wide Web at http://www.angusreid.com/media/content/displaypr.cfm?idto_view51001 (2 October 2000).

Fagot, Berly I., Caire S. Rodgers, and Mary D. Leinbach. 2000. "Theories of Gender Socialization." Pp. 65–89 in Thomas Eckes, ed. *The Developmental Social Psychology of Gender.* Mahwah, NJ: Lawrence Erlbaum Associates.

Families Against Deadbeats. 2000. On the World Wide Web at http://www.wantedposters.com (9 September 2003).

Fattah, Ezzat A. 1991. *Understanding Criminal Victimization: An Introduction to Theoretical Victimology.* Scarborough, ON: Prentice Hall.

Fekete, John. 1994. *Moral Panics: Biopolitics Rising.* Toronto: Robert Davies.

Fellegi, Ivan. 2000. "On Poverty and Low Income." In Statistics Canada. *Income in Canada 1998.* Ottawa: Ministry of Industry.

Felson, Richard B. 1996. "Mass Media Effects on Violent Behavior." *Annual Review of Sociology* 22: 103–28.

Fernandez-Dols, Jose-Miguel, Flor Sanchez, Pilar Carrera, and Maria-Angeles Ruiz-Belda. 1997. "Are Spontaneous Expressions and Emotions Linked? An Experimental Test of Coherence." *Journal of Nonverbal Behavior* 21: 163–77.

Fields, Jason, and Kristin Smith. 1998. "Poverty, Family Structure, and Child Well-Being." Population Division. Washington, DC: U.S. Bureau of Census.

Figart, Deborah M., and June Lapidus. 1996. "The Impact of Comparable Worth on Earnings Inequality." *Work and Occupations* 23: 297–318.

Finke, Roger, and Rodney Starke. 1992. *The Churching of America, 1776–1990: Winners and Losers in Our Religious Economy.* New Brunswick, NJ: Rutgers University Press.

Finnie, Ross. 1993. "Women, Men and the Economic Consequences of Divorce: Evidence from Canadian Longitudinal Data." *Canadian Review of Sociology and Anthropology* 30, 2: 205–41.

Fischer, Claude S., Michael Hout, Martín Sánchez Jankowski, Samuel R. Lucas, Ann Swidler, and Kim Voss. 1996. *Inequality by Design: Cracking the Bell Curve Myth.* Princeton, NJ: Princeton University Press.

Fisher, John. 1999. *A Report on Lesbian, Gay and Bisexual Youth.* Ottawa: EGALE.

Flood, Gavin D. 1996. *An Introduction to Hinduism.* Cambridge: Cambridge University Press.

Forbes.com. 2010. "The World's Billionaires." On the World Wide Web at http://www.forbes.com/lists/2010/10/billionaires-2010_The-Worlds-Billionaires_Rank.html (11 March 2010).

Forrest, C. B., and A. W. Riley. 2004. "Childhood Origins of Adult Health: A Basis for Life-Course Health Policy." *Health Affairs* 23, 5: 155–64.

Förster, Michael, and Michele Pellizzari. 2000. *Trends and Driving Factors in Income Distribution and Poverty in the OECD Area.* Labour Market and Social Policy Occasional Papers No. 42. Paris: OECD.

Foucault, Michel. 1977 [1975]. *Discipline and Punish: The Birth of the Prison,* Alan Sheridan, trans. New York: Pantheon.

_____. 1990 [1978]. *The History of Sexuality: An Introduction,* vol. 1. Robert Hurley, trans. New York: Vintage.

Franco, Zeno, and Philip Zimbardo. 2006–2007. "The Banality of Heroism." *Greater Good* 3, 2: 33–4. On the World Wide Web at http://greatergood.berkeley.edu/greatergood/archive/2006fallwinter/francozimbardo.html (3 January 2008).

Frank Porter Graham Child Development Center. 1999. "Early Learning, Later Success: The Abecedarian Study." On the World Wide Web at http://www.fpg.unc.edu/~abc/abcedarianWeb/index.htm (10 August 2000).

Frank, Thomas, and Matt Weiland, eds. 1997. *Commodify Your Dissent: Salvos from the Baffler.* New York: W. W. Norton.

Franklin, Karen. 1998. "Psychosocial Motivations of Hate Crime Perpetrators." Paper presented at the annual meetings of the American Psychological Association (San Francisco: 16 August).

_____. 2000. "Antigay Behaviors Among Young Adults." *Journal of Interpersonal Violence* 15, 4: 339–62.

Freedman, Jonathan L. 2002. *Media Violence and Its Effect on Aggression: Assessing the Scientific Evidence.* Toronto: University of Toronto Press.

Freidson, Eliot. 1986. *Professional Powers: A Study of the Institutionalization of Formal Knowledge.* Chicago: University of Chicago Press.

Freire, Paolo. 1972. *The Pedagogy of the Oppressed.* New York: Herder and Herder.

Frenette, Marc. 2007. "Why Are Youth from Lower-Income Families Less Likely to Attend University? Evidence from Academic Abilities, Parental Influences, and Financial Constraints." Catalogue no. 11F0019MIE. Ottawa: Statistics Canada. On the World Wide Web at http://www.statcan.ca/english/research/11F0019MIE/11F0019MIE2007295.pdf (26 April 2007).

Freud, Sigmund. 1962 [1930]. *Civilization and Its Discontents,* James Strachey, trans. New York: W. W. Norton.

_____. 1973 [1915–17]. *Introductory Lectures on Psychoanalysis,* James Strachey, trans., James Strachey and Angela Richards, eds. Harmondsworth, UK: Penguin.

Freudenburg, William R. 1997. "Contamination, Corrosion and the Social Order: An Overview." *Current Sociology* 45, 3: 19–39.

Friedenberg, Edgar Z. 1959. *The Vanishing Adolescent.* Boston: Beacon Press.

Galabuzi, G.-E. 2004. *Social Inclusion as a Determinant of Health.* Ottawa: Public Health Agency of Canada. On the World Wide Web at http://www.phac-aspc.gc.ca/ph-sp/phdd/overview_implications/03_inclusion.html (2 July 2005).

Galper, Joseph. 1998. "Schooling for Society." *American Demographics* 20, 3: 33–34.

Gamson, William A., Bruce Fireman, and Steven Rytina. 1982. *Encounters with Unjust Authority.* Homewood, IL: Dorsey Press.

Gans, Herbert. 1991. "Symbolic Ethnicity: The Future of Ethnic Groups and Cultures in America." Pp. 430–43 in Norman R. Yetman, ed. *Majority and Minority: The Dynamics of Race and Ethnicity in American Life,* 5th ed. Boston, MA: Allyn and Bacon.

Garland, David. 1990. *Punishment and Modern Society: A Study in Social Theory.* Chicago: University of Chicago Press.

Garner, David M. 1997. "The 1997 Body Image Survey Results." *Psychology Today* 30, 1: 30–44.

Gaskell, Jane, Arlene McLaren, and Myra Novogrodsky. 1995. "What's Worth Knowing? Defining the Feminist Curriculum." Pp. 100–18 in Adie D. Nelson and Barrie W. Robinson, eds. *Gender in the 1990s: Images, Realities, and Issues.* Scarborough: Nelson Canada.

Gauvain, Mary, Beverly I. Fagot, Craig Leve, and Kate Kavanagh. 2002. "Instruction by Mothers and Fathers During Problem Solving with Their Young Children." *Journal of Family Psychology* 6, 1 (March): 81–90.

Gegax, T. Trent, and Lynette Clemetson. 1998. "The Abortion Wars Come Home." *Newsweek* 9 November: 34–35.

Gelbspan, Ross. 1999. "Trading Away Our Chances to End Global Warming." *Boston Globe* 16 May: E2.

Gelles, Richard J. 1997. *Intimate Violence in Families,* 3rd ed. Thousand Oaks, CA: Sage.

Geohive.com. 2005. "The Demographical Status of the World's Population." On the World Wide Web at http://www.geohive.com/global/geo.php?xml=world&xsl=pop_data (26 June 2005).

Ghalam, Nancy Z. 1997. "Attitudes Towards Women, Work and Family." *Canadian*

Social Trends 46: 13–17. Statistics Canada Catalogue no. 11-008-XPE.

Giddens, Anthony. 1987. *Sociology: A Brief but Critical Introduction,* 2nd ed. New York: Harcourt Brace Jovanovich.

_____. 1990. *The Consequences of Modernity.* Stanford, CA: Stanford University Press.

Gilman, Sander L. 1991. *The Jew's Body.* New York: Routledge.

Gleick, James. 2000. *Faster: The Acceleration of Just About Everything.* New York: Vintage.

Glendon, Mary Ann. 1981. *The New Family and the New Property.* Toronto: Butterworths.

Glenn, Norval D. 1990. "Quantitative Research on Marital Quality in the 1980s: A Critical Review." *Journal of Marriage and the Family* 52 (November): 818–31.

Glock, Charles Y. 1962. "On the Study of Religious Commitment." *Religious Education* 62, 4: 98–110.

Goddard Institute for Space Studies. 2010. "GLOBAL Land-Ocean Temperature Index in 0.01 Degrees Celsius." On the World Wide Web at http://data. giss.nasa.gov/gistemp/tabledata/GLB. Ts+dSST.txt (29 March 2010).

Goffman, Erving. 1959. *The Presentation of Self in Everyday Life,* reprinted ed. Garden City, NY: Anchor.

_____. 1961. *Asylums: Essays on the Social Situation of Mental Patients and Other Inmates.* Garden City, NY: Anchor Books.

_____. 1963. *Stigma: Notes on the Management of Spoiled Identity.* Englewood Cliffs, NJ: Prentice-Hall.

_____. 1974. *Frame Analysis.* Cambridge, MA: Harvard University Press.

Goldberg, Andy. 2010. "As Facebook Lures 500 Millionth User—What's Next?" *Earth Times* 20 July. On the World Wide Web at http://www.earthtimes. org/articles/news/335578,-next-feature.html (21 September 2010).

Goldie, Terry. 2001. *In a Queer Country: Gay & Lesbian Studies in the Canadian Context.* Vancouver: Arsenal Pulp Press.

Gombrich, Richard Francis. 1996. *How Buddhism Began: The Conditioned Genesis of the Early Teachings.* London: Athlone.

Goode, Erich, and Nachman Ben-Yehuda. 1994. *Moral Panics: The Social Construction of Deviance.* Cambridge, MA: Blackwell.

Google Public Data. 2010. "Canada Fertility Rate." On the World Wide Web at http://www.google.com/ publicdata?ds=wb-wdi&met=sp_ dyn_tfrt_in&idim=country:CAN&dl =en&hl=en&q=canada+fertility+rate (22 March 2010).

Gordon, Sarah. 1984. *Hitler, Germans, and the Jewish Question.* Princeton, NJ: Princeton University Press.

Gorman, Christine. 1997. "A Boy without a Penis." *Time* 24 March: 83.

Gottfredson, Michael, and Travis Hirschi. 1990. *A General Theory of Crime.* Stanford, CA: Stanford University Press.

Gottwald, Norman K. 1979. *The Tribes of Yahweh: A Sociology of the Religion of Liberated Israel, 1250–1050 B.C.E.* Maryknoll, NY: Orbis.

Goubert, Jean-Pierre. 1989 [1986]. *The Conquest of Water,* Andrew Wilson, trans. Princeton, NJ: Princeton University Press.

Gould, Stephen J. 1988. "Kropotkin Was No Crackpot." *Natural History* 97, 7: 12–18.

_____. 1996. *The Mismeasure of Man,* rev. ed. New York: W. W. Norton.

Government of Canada. 2002. "Study Released on Firearms in Canada." On the World Wide Web at http:// www .cfc-ccaf.gc.ca/media/news_ releases/2002/ survey-08202002_ e.asp (29 December 2005).

Granovetter, Mark. 1973. "The Strength of Weak Ties." *American Sociological Review* 78: 1360–80.

Greenhill, Pauline. 2001. "Can You See the Difference: Queerying the Nation, Ethnicity, Festival, and Culture in Winnipeg." Pp. 103–21 in Terry Goldie, ed. *In a Queer Country: Gay & Lesbian Studies in the Canadian Context.* Vancouver: Arsenal Pulp Press.

Greenstein, Theodore. 1996. "Husbands' Participation in Domestic Labor: Interactive Effects of Wives' and Husbands' Gender Ideologies." *Journal of Marriage and the Family* 58: 585–95.

Grimes, Craig. 1997. "Adult Criminal Court Statistics, 1995–96." *Juristat* 17, 6 (May). Catalogue no. 85-002-XPE. Ottawa: Canadian Centre for Justice Statistics and Statistics Canada. On the World Wide Web at http:// dsp-psd.pwgsc.gc.ca/Collection-R/ Statcan/85-002-XIE/0069785-002-XIE.pdf (23 August 2007).

Groopman, Jerome. 2008. "Superbugs." *The New Yorker* 11 August 2008. On the World Wide Web at http://www.newyorker.com/ reporting/2008/08/11/080811fa_fact_ groopman (2 April 2010).

"G20 Thugs Don't Deserve a Break." 2010. *Maclean's* 19 July: 4–5.

Guillén, Mauro F. 2001. "Is Globalization Civilizing, Destructive or Feeble? A Critique of Five Key Debates in the Social Science Literature." *Annual Review of Sociology* 27. On the World Wide Web at http://knowledge.wharton.upenn. edu/PDFs/938.pdf (6 February 2003).

Gundersen, Edna, Bill Keveney, and Ann Oldenburg. 2002. "The Osbournes Find a Home in America's Living Rooms." *USA Today* 19 April: 1A–2A.

Guppy, Neil and Scott Davies. 1998. *Education in Canada: Recent Trends and Future Challenges.* Ottawa: Ministry of Industry.

Gurr, Ted Robert. 1970. *Why Men Rebel.* Princeton, NJ: Princeton University Press.

Haas, Jack, and William Shaffir. 1987. *Becoming Doctors: The Adoption of a Cloak of Competence.* Greenwich, CT: JAI Press.

Haas, Jennifer. 1998. "The Cost of Being a Woman." *New England Journal of Medicine* 338: 1694–95.

Hagan, John. 1989. *Structuralist Criminology.* New Brunswick, NJ: Rutgers University Press.

_____. 1994. *Crime and Disrepute.* Thousand Oaks, CA: Pine Forge Press.

Hagan, John, John Simpson, and A. R. Gillis. 1987. "Class in the Household: A Power-Control Theory of Gender and Delinquency." *American Journal of Sociology* 92: 788–816.

Haines, Herbert H. 1996. *Against Capital Punishment: The Anti-Death Penalty Movement in America, 1972–1994.* New York: Oxford University Press.

Hall, Edward. 1959. *The Silent Language.* New York: Doubleday.

_____. 1966. *The Hidden Dimension.* New York: Doubleday.

Halstead, Jason. 2010. "Husband Faces Charges in Wife's Death." *Edmonton Sun.* On the World Wide Web at http://www.edmontonsun.com/news/ canada/2010/03/21/13311596.html (22 March 2010).

Hamachek, D. 1995. "Self-concept and School Achievement: Interaction Dynamics and a Tool for Assessing the Self-concept Component." *Journal of Counseling and Development* 73: 419–25.

Hamilton, Roberta. 1996. *Gendering the Vertical Mosaic: Feminist Perspectives on Canadian Society.* Toronto: Copp-Clark.

Hancock, Lynnell. 1994. "In Defiance of Darwin: How a Public School in the Bronx Turns Dropouts into Scholars." *Newsweek* 24 October: 61.

Haney, Craig, W. Curtis Banks, and Philip G. Zimbardo. 1973. "Interpersonal Dynamics in a Simulated Prison." *International Journal of Criminology and Penology* 1: 69–97.

Hanke, Robert. 1998. "'Yo Quiero Mi MTV!' Making Music Television for Latin America." Pp. 219–45 in Thomas Swiss, Andrew Herman, and John M. Sloop, eds. *Mapping the Beat: Popular Music and Contemporary Theory.* Oxford, UK: Blackwell.

Hannigan, John. 1995. "The Postmodern City: A New Urbanization?" *Current Sociology* 43, 1: 151–217.

Hannon, Roseann, David S. Hall, Todd Kuntz, Van Laar, and Jennifer Williams. 1995. "Dating Characteristics Leading to Unwanted vs. Wanted Sexual Behavior." *Sex Roles* 33: 767–83.

Harding, David J., Cybelle Fox, and Jal D. Mehta. 2002. "Studying Rare Events through Qualitative Case Studies: Lessons from a Study of Rampage School Shootings." *Sociological Methods and Research* 31, 2: 174–217.

Harlequin. 2006. "About eHarlequin.com." On the World Wide Web at http://www.eharlequin.com/articlepage.html;jsessionid588F358D3D78BC869CC43E64EDA5987F8?articleId536&chapter50 (24 August 2007).

Harris, Marvin. 1974. *Cows, Pigs, Wars and Witches: The Riddles of Culture.* New York: Random House.

Hartnagel, Timothy F. 2000. "Correlates of Criminal Behaviour." Pp. 94–136 in Rick Linden, ed. *Criminology: A Canadian Perspective,* 4th ed. Toronto: Harcourt Canada.

Harvey, Andrew S., Katherine Marshall, and Judith A. Frederick. 1991. *Where Does the Time Go?* Ottawa: Statistics Canada.

Harvey, Elizabeth. 1999. "Short-Term and Long-Term Effects of Early Parental Employment on Children of the National Longitudinal Survey of Youth." *Developmental Psychology* 35: 445–49.

Hastings, Arthur C., James Fadiman, and James C. Gordon, eds. 1980. *Health for the Whole Person: The Complete Guide to Holistic Medicine.* Boulder, CO: Westview Press.

Haythornwaite, Caroline, and Barry Wellman. 2002. "The Internet in Everyday Life: An Introduction." Pp. 3–41 in Caroline Haythornwaite and Barry Wellman, eds. *The Internet in Everyday Life.* Oxford: Blackwell.

Health Canada. 1999a. *Statistical Report on the Health of Canadians.* Available on the World Wide Web at http://www.hc-sc.gc.ca/hppb/phdd/report/state/englover.html (25 December 1999).

_____. 1999b. *Toward a Healthy Future: Second Report on the Health of Canadians.* Prepared by the Federal, Provincial, and Territorial Advisory Committee on Population Health for the Meeting of Ministers of Health, Charlottetown, PEI. September. On the World Wide Web at http://www.hc-sc.gc.ca (4 April 2000).

_____. 2003. "Canadian Cancer Statistics, 2003." On the World Wide Web at http://www.cancer.ca/Canada-wide/About%20cancer/Cancer%20statistics/Canadian%20Cancer%20Statistics.aspx?sc_lang=en (30 March 2010).

_____. 2009. "Healthy Canadians: A Federal Report on Comparable Health Indicators 2008." On the World Wide Web at http://www.hc-sc.gc.ca/hcs-sss/pubs/system-regime/2008-fed-comp-indicat/index-eng.php (2 April 2010).

"Health Care Systems: An International Comparison." 2001. Ottawa: Strategic Policy and Research, Intergovernmental Affairs. On the World Wide Web at http://www.pnrec.org/2001papers/DaigneaultLajoie.pdf (13 June 2003).

Hechter, Michael. 1974. *Internal Colonialism: The Celtic Fringe in British National Development, 1536–1966.* Berkeley, CA: University of California Press.

_____. 1987. *Principles of Group Solidarity.* Berkeley, CA: University of California Press.

Helsing, Knud J., Moyses Szklo, and George W. Comstock. 1981. "Factors Associated with Mortality after Widowhood." *American Journal of Public Health* 71: 802–09.

Hendrick, Dianne. 1997. "Youth Court Statistics Highlights, 1995–96." *Juristat* 17, 10 (October). Catalogue no. 85-002-XPE. Ottawa: Canadian Centre for Justice Statistics and Statistics Canada. On the World Wide Web at http://dsp-psd.pwgsc.gc.ca/Collection-R/Statcan/85-002-XIE/0109785-002-XIE.pdf (23 August 2007).

Hendrick, Dianne, and Lee Farmer. 2002. "Adult Correctional Services in Canada, 2000/01." *Juristat* 22, 10 (October). Catalogue no. 85-002-XPE. Ottawa: Canadian Centre for Justice Statistics and Statistics Canada.

Henry, Frances, Carol Tator, Winston Mattis, and Tim Rees. 2001. "The Victimization of Racial Minorities in Canada." Pp. 145–60 in Robert J. Brym, ed. *Society in Question: Sociological Readings for the 21st Century,* 3rd ed. Toronto: Harcourt Canada.

Herlihy, David. 1998. *The Black Death and the Transformation of the West.* Cambridge, MA: Harvard University Press.

Herrnstein, Richard J. and Charles Murray. 1994. *The Bell Curve: Intelligence and Class Structure in American Life.* New York: Free Press.

Hersch, Patricia. 1998. *A Tribe Apart: A Journey into the Heart of American Adolescence.* New York: Ballantine Books.

Hesse-Biber, Sharlene, and Gregg Lee Carter. 2000. *Working Women in America: Split Dreams.* New York: Oxford University Press.

Hirschi, Travis. 1969. *Causes of Delinquency.* Berkeley, CA: University of California Press.

Hobbes, Thomas. 1968 [1651]. *Leviathan.* Middlesex, UK: Penguin.

Hoberman, John. 1997. *Darwin's Athletes: How Sport Has Damaged Black America and Preserved the Myth of Race.* Boston: Houghton Mifflin.

Hobsbawm, Eric. 1994. *Age of Extremes: The Short Twentieth Century, 1914–1991.* London: Abacus.

Hochschild, Arlie Russell. 1979. "Emotion Work, Feeling Rules, and Social Structure." *American Journal of Sociology* 85: 551–75.

_____. 1983. *The Managed Heart: Commercialization of Human Feeling.* Berkeley: University of California Press.

Hochschild, Arlie Russell, with Anne Machung. 1989. *The Second Shift: Working Parents and the Revolution at Home.* New York: Viking.

Hodgson, Marshall G. S. 1974. *The Venture of Islam: Conscience and History in a World Civilization,* 3 vols. Chicago: University of Chicago Press.

Homans, George Caspar. 1961. *Social Behavior: Its Elementary Forms.* New York: Harcourt, Brace and World.

hooks, bell. 1984. *Feminist Theory: From Margin to Center.* Boston: South End Press.

Houpt, Simon. 2004. "Pass the Popcorn, Save the World." *Globe and Mail* 29 May: R1, R13.

Houseknecht, Sharon K., and Jaya Sastry. 1996. "Family 'Decline' and Child Well-Being: A Comparative Assessment." *Journal of Marriage and the Family* 58: 726–39.

Huesmann, L. Rowell, Jessica Moise-Titus, Cheryl-Lynn Podolski, and Leonard D. Eron. 2003. "Longitudinal Relations between Children's Exposure to TV Violence and their Aggressive and Violent Behavior in Young Adulthood: 1977–1992." *Developmental Psychology* 39, 2: 201–21.

Hughes, Diane, Ellen Galinsky, and Anne Morris. 1992. "The Effects of Job Characteristics on Marital Quality: Specifying Linking Mechanisms." *Journal of Marriage and the Family* 54, 1 (February): 31–42.

Hughes, Fergus P. 1995. *Children, Play and Development,* 2nd ed. Boston: Allyn and Bacon.

Human Resources Development Canada. 1999. "Chronological Perspective on Work Stoppages in Canada." On the World Wide Web at http://labour. hrdc-drhc.gc.ca/doc/wid-dimt/eng/wsat/table.cfm (30 June 2003).

_____. 2001a. "Chronological Perspective on Work Stoppages in Canada." On the World Wide Web at http://labour. hrdc-drhc.gc.ca/doc/wid-dimt/eng/wsat/table.cfm (22 March 2003).

_____. 2001b. "Chronological Perspective on Work Stoppages in Canada (Work Stoppages Involving One or More Workers), 1976–2000." On the World Wide Web at http://labour-travail. hrdc-drhc.gc.ca/doc/wid-dimt/eng/wsat/table.cfm (27 March 2001).

Human Resources and Social Development Canada. 2006. "Database on Minimum Wages." On the World Wide Web at http://srv116.services.gc.ca/wid-dimt/mwa/menu.aspx (1 April 2007).

Human Rights Watch. 1995. *The Human Rights Watch Global Report on Women's Human Rights.* New York: Human Rights Watch.

Hunter, James Davison. 1991. *Culture Wars: The Struggle to Define America.* New York: Basic Books.

Hunter, Shireen T. 1998. *The Future of Islam and the West: Clash of Civilizations or Peaceful Coexistence?* Westport, CT: Praeger.

Ignatieff, Michael. 2000. *The Rights Revolution.* Toronto: Anansi.

Ignatiev, Noel. 1995. *How the Irish Became White.* New York: Routledge.

Infocom. 2003. "Bureaucracy." On the World Wide Web at http://infocom. elsewhere.org/gallery/bureaucracy. bureaucracy.html (14 March 2003).

Ingram, Gordon Brent. 2001. "Redesigning Wreck: Beach Meets Forest as Location of Male Homoerotic Culture in Placemaking in Pacific Canada." Pp. 188–208 in Terry Goldie, ed. *In a Queer Country: Gay & Lesbian Studies in the Canadian Context.* Vancouver: Arsenal Pulp Press.

Inkeles, Alex, and David H. Smith. 1976. *Becoming Modern: Individual Change in Six Developing Countries.* Cambridge, MA: Harvard University Press.

Intergovernmental Panel on Climate Change. 2007. On the World Wide Web at http://www.ipcc.ch/ (2 May 2007).

International Labour Organization. 2008. "Yearly Data." On the World Wide Web at http://laborsta.ilo.org (9 January 2008).

International Monetary Fund. 2009. "World Economic and Financial Surveys: World Economic Outlook Database." On the World Wide Web at http://www. imf.org/external/pubs/ft/weo/2009/02/weodata/index.aspx (2 January 2010).

Internet World Stats. 2010. "World Internet Users and Population Stats." On the World Wide Web at http://www. internetworldstats.com/stats.htm (22 February 2010).

Isaacs, Larry. 2002. "To Counter 'The Very Devil' and More: The Making of Independent Capitalist Militias in the Gilded Age." *American Journal of Sociology* 108: 353–405.

Isajiw, Wsevolod W. 1978. "Olga in Wonderland: Ethnicity in a Technological Society." Pp. 29–39 in L. Driedger, ed. *The Canadian Ethnic Mosaic: A Quest for Identity.* Toronto: McClelland & Stewart.

Jackson, Carolyn, and Ian David Smith. 2000. "Poles Apart? An Exploration of Single-Sex and Mixed-Sex Educational Environments in Australia and England." *Educational Studies* 26, 4 (December): 409–22.

James, Carl E. 2003. *Seeing Ourselves: Exploring Race, Ethnicity and Culture,* 3rd ed. Toronto: Thompson Educational Publishing.

James, William. 1976 [1902]. *The Varieties of Religious Experience: A Study in Human Nature.* New York: Collier Books.

Janis, Irving. 1972. *Victims of Groupthink.* Boston: Houghton Mifflin.

Jekielek, Susan M. 1998. "Parental Conflict, Marital Disruption and Children's Emotional Well-Being." *Social Forces* 76: 905–35.

Jencks, Christopher, Marshall Smith, Henry Acland, Mary Jo Bane, David Cohen, Herbert Gintis, Barbara Heyns, and Stephan Michelson. 1972. *Inequality: A Reassessment of the Effect of Family and Schooling in America.* New York: Basic Books.

Jenkins, J. Craig. 1983. "Resource Mobilization Theory and the Study of Social Movements." *Annual Review of Sociology* 9: 527–53.

"Jim Crow Laws: Texas." 2008. On the World Wide Web at http://www. jimcrowhistory.org/scripts/jimcrow/insidesouth.cgi?state=Texas (19 August 2008).

John Howard Society. 1999. *Fact Sheet: Population Trends and Crime.* Toronto: John Howard Society of Ontario.

Johnson, Jeffrey G., Patricia Cohen, Elizbaeth M. Smailes, Stephanie Kasen, and Judith S. Brook. 2002. "Television Viewing and Aggressive Behavior during Adolescence and Adulthood." *Science* 295, 5564: 2468–71.

Johnson, Michael P., and Kathleeen J. Ferraro. 2000. "Research on Domestic Violence in the 1990s: Making Distinctions." *Journal of Marriage and the Family* 62: 948–63.

Johnson, Sara. 2004. "Adult Correctional Services in Canada, 2002/03." *Juristat* 24, 10: 16. Catalogue no. 85-002-XPE. Ottawa: Canadian Centre for Justice Statistics and Statistics Canada. On the World Wide Web at http://www. statcan.ca/bsolc/english/bsolc?catno5 85-002-X20040108409 (8 May 2005).

Johnson, Terence J. 1972. *Professions and Power.* London: Macmillan.

Johnson, Tracy L., and Elizabeth Fee. 1997. "Women's Health Research: An Introduction." Pp. 3–26 in Florence P. Haseltine and Beverly Greenberg Jacobson, eds. *Women's Health Research: A Medical and Policy Primer.* Washington, DC: Health Press International.

Jones, Frank. 2000. "Are Children Going to Religious Services?" Pp. 202–25 in *Canadian Social Trends* 54 (Fall): 3–13. Catalogue no. 11-008-XPE.

Jones, Laura. 1997. "Global Warming Is All the Rage These Days . . . Which Enrages Many Doubting Scientists." The Fraser Institute. On the World Wide Web at http://oldfraser.lexi.net/media/media_releases/1997/19971201a.html (5 May 2002).

Joyce, Terrence, and Lloyd Keigwin. 2004. "Abrupt Climate Change: Are We on the Brink of a New Little Ice Age?" Ocean and Climate Change Institute, Woods Hole Oceanographic Institution. On the World Wide Web at http://www.whoi.edu/institutes/occi/currenttopics/abruptclimate_joyce_keigwin.html (29 May 2004).

Juergensmeyer, Mark. 2000. *Terror in the Mind of God: The Global Rise of Religious Violence.* Berkeley, CA: University of California Press.

Kalbach, Madeline A. 2000. "Ethnicity and the Altar." Pp. 111–21 in Madeline A. Kalbach and Warren E. Kalbach, eds. *Perspectives on Ethnicity in Canada: A Reader.* Toronto: Harcourt Canada.

Kalbach, Madeline A., and Warren E. Kalbach. 1998. "Becoming Canadian: Problems of an Emerging Identity." *Canadian Ethnic Studies* 31, 2: 1–17.

Kalmijn, Matthijs. 1998. "Intermarriage and Homogamy: Causes, Patterns, Trends." *Annual Review of Sociology* 24: 395–421.

Kanter, Rosabeth Moss. 1989. *When Giants Learn to Dance: Mastering the Challenges of Strategy, Management, and Careers in the 1990s.* New York: Simon and Schuster.

Karabel, Jerome. 1986. "Community Colleges and Social Stratification in the 1980s." In L. S. Zwerling, ed. *The Community College and Its Critics.* San Francisco: Jossey-Bass.

Katayama, Lisa. 2009. "Love in 2-D." *New York Times* 21 July. On the World Wide Web at http://www.nytimes.com/2009/07/26/magazine/26FOB-2DLove-t.html (8 August 2010).

Kay, Fiona, and John Hagan. 1998. "Raising the Bar: The Gender Stratification of Law Firm Capitalization." *American Sociological Review* 63: 728–43.

Kennedy, Paul. 1993. *Preparing for the Twenty-First Century.* New York: HarperCollins.

Kepel, Gilles. 1994 [1991]. *The Revenge of God: The Resurgence of Islam, Christianity and Judaism in the Modern World,* Alan Braley, trans. University Park, PA: Pennsylvania State University Press.

Kerig, Patricia K., Philip A. Cowan, and Carolyn Pape Cowan. 1993. "Marital Quality and Gender Differences in Parent–Child Interaction." *Developmental Psychology* 29: 931–39.

Kessler, Ronald C., Katherine A. McGonagle, Shanyang Zhao, Christopher B. Nelson, Michael Hughes, Suzann Eshleman, Hans Ulrich Wittchen, and Kenneth S. Kendler. 1994. "Life-time and 12-Month Prevalence of DSM-III-R Psychiatric Disorders in the United States." *Archives of General Psychiatry* 51: 8–19.

Kimmerling, Baruch. 2001. *The Invention and Decline of Israeliness: State, Society, and the Military.* Berkeley, CA: University of California Press.

King, Martin Luther. 1967. *Conscience for Change.* Toronto: CBC Learning Systems.

Kingsbury, Nancy, and John Scanzoni. 1993. "Structural-Functionalism." Pp. 195–217 in Pauline G. Boss, William J. Doherty, Ralph LaRossa, Walter R. Schumm, and Suzanne K. Steinmetz, eds. *Sourcebook of Family Theories and Methods: A Contextual Approach.* New York: Plenum.

Kingston, Anne. 2010. "Outraged Moms, Trashy Daughters." *Maclean's* 16 August: 51–53.

Kingston, Paul W. 2001. "The Unfulfilled Promise of Cultural Capital Theory." *Sociology of Education* Supplement: 88–91.

Kinsey, Alfred C., Wardell B. Pomeroy, and Clyde E. Martin. 1948. *Sexual Behavior in the Human Male.* Philadelphia: W. B. Saunders.

Kinsey, Alfred, Wardell Pomeroy, Clyde Martin, and Paul Gebhard. 1953. *Sexual Behavior in the Human Female.* Philadelphia: W. B. Saunders.

Kitano, Harry, and Roger Daniels. 1995. *Asian Americans: Emerging Minorities,* 2nd ed. Englewood Cliffs, NJ: Prentice-Hall.

Kling, Kristen C., Janet Shibley Hyde, Carolin J. Showers, and Brenda N. Buswell. 1999. "Gender Differences in Self-Esteem: A Meta-Analysis." *Psychological Bulletin* 125, 4: 470–500.

Koepke, Leslie, Jan Hare, and Patricia B. Moran. 1992. "Relationship Quality in a Sample of Lesbian Couples with Children and Child-Free Lesbian Couples." *Family Relations* 41: 224–29.

Kohlberg, Lawrence. 1981. *The Psychology of Moral Development: The Nature and Validity of Moral Stages.* New York: Harper and Row.

Köhler, Nicholas, and Stephanie Findlay. 2010. "Life after the G20 Protests." *Maclean's* 16 August: 26–27.

Kong, Rebecca. 1997. "Canadian Crime Statistics, 1996." *Juristat* 17, 8 (July). Catalogue no. 85-002-XPE. Ottawa: Canadian Centre for Justice Statistics and Statistics Canada. On the World Wide Web at http://dsp-psd.pwgsc.gc.ca/Collection-R/Statcan/85-002-XIE/0089785-002-XIE.pdf (23 August 2007).

Kong, Rebecca, and Kathy AuCoin. 2009. "Female Offenders in Canada." *Juristat* 28, 1. Statistics Canada. On the World Wide Web at http://www.statcan.gc.ca/pub/85-002-x/2008001/article/10509-eng.htm (21 August 2010).

Kornblum, William. 1997. *Sociology in a Changing World,* 4th ed. Fort Worth, TX: Harcourt Brace.

Kosmin, Barry A. 1991. *Research Report of the National Survey of Religious Identification.* New York: CUNY Graduate Center.

Kropotkin, Petr. 1908 [1902]. *Mutual Aid: A Factor of Evolution,* rev. ed. London: W. Heinemann.

Kurdek, Lawrence A. 1996. "The Deterioration of Relationship Quality for Gay and Lesbian Cohabiting Couples: A Five-Year Prospective Longitudinal Study." *Personal Relationships* 3: 417–42.

Kurzweil, Ray. 1999. *The Age of Spiritual Machines: When Computers Exceed Human Intelligence.* New York: Viking Penguin.

Labour Organizations in Canada 1972. 1973. Ottawa: Economics and Research Branch, Canada Department of Labour. Cat. No. L2-2-1972.

LaFeber, Walter. 1993. *Inevitable Revolutions: The United States in Central America,* 2nd ed. New York: W. W. Norton.

Lamanna, Mary Ann, and Agnes Riedmann. 2003. *Marriages and Families: Making Choices in a Diverse Society,* 8th ed. Belmont, CA: Wadsworth.

Lamont, Michele, and Annette Lareau. 1988. "Cultural Capital: Allusions,

Gaps, and Glissandos in Recent Theoretical Developments." *Sociological Theory* 6: 153–68.

Lapchick, Richard. 2004. *2004 Racial and Gender Report Card.* Orlando, FL: University of Central Florida. On the World Wide Web at http://www.bus.ucf.edu/sport/public/downloads/2004_Racial_Gender_Report_Card.pdf (29 April 2006).

Lapidus, Gail Warshofsky. 1978. *Women in Soviet Society: Equality, Development, and Social Change.* Berkeley, CA: University of California Press.

Lapidus, Ira M. 2002. *A History of Islamic Societies,* 2nd ed. Cambridge: Cambridge University Press.

Lautard, Hugh, and Neil Guppy. 2008. "Multiculturalism or Vertical Mosaic? Occupational Stratification among Canadian Ethnic Groups." Pp. 120–29 in Robert J. Brym, ed. *Society in Question,* 5th ed. Toronto: Nelson.

Lautard, Hugh, and Neil Guppy. 2011. "Multiculturalism or Ethnic Mosaic? Occupational Stratification among Canadian Ethnic Groups." Pp. 163–77 in Robert J. Brym, ed. *Society in Question,* 6th ed. Toronto: Nelson.

Lavoie, Yolande, and Jillian Oderkirk. 2000. "Social Consequences of Demographic Change." Pp. 2–5 in *Canadian Social Trends,* Volume 3. Toronto: Thompson Educational Publishing.

Leidner, Robin. 1993. *Fast Food, Fast Talk: Service Work and the Routinization of Everyday Life.* Berkeley, CA: University of California Press.

Lenton, Rhonda L. 1989. "Homicide in Canada and the U.S.A." *Canadian Journal of Sociology* 14: 163–78.

Levine, R. A., and D. T. Campbell. 1972. *Ethnocentrism: Theories of Conflict, Ethnic Attitudes, and Group Behavior.* New York: Wiley.

Levine, Robert, Suguru Sato, Tsukasa Hashimoto, and Jyoti Verma. 1995. "Love and Marriage in Eleven Cultures." *Journal of Cross-Cultural Psychology* 26, 5: 554–71.

Lewis, Bernard. 2002. *What Went Wrong? Western Impact and Middle Eastern Response.* New York: Oxford University Press.

Li, Peter. 1995. "Racial Supremacism under Social Democracy." *Canadian Ethnic Studies* 27, 1: 1–17.

———. 1998. *The Chinese in Canada,* 2nd ed. Toronto: Oxford University Press.

Lian, Jason Z., and David R. Matthews. 1998. "Does the Vertical Mosaic Still Exist? Ethnicity and Income in Canada, 1991." *Canadian Review of Sociology and Anthropology* 35: 461–81.

Lie, John. 1998. *Han Unbound: The Political Economy of South Korea.* Stanford, CA: Stanford University Press.

———. 2001. *Multiethnic Japan.* Cambridge, MA: Harvard University Press.

Light, Ivan. 1991. "Immigrant and Ethnic Enterprise in North America." Pp. 307–18 in Norman R. Yetman, ed. *Majority and Minority: The Dynamics of Race and Ethnicity in American Life,* 5th ed. Boston: Allyn and Bacon.

Lightfoot-Klein, Hanny, Cheryl Chase, Tim Hammond, and Ronald Goldman. 2000. "Genital Surgery on Children Below the Age of Consent." Pp. 440–79 in Lenore T. Szuchman and Frank Muscarella, eds. *Psychological Perspectives on Human Sexuality.* New York: Wiley.

Lips, Hilary M. 1999. *A New Psychology of Women: Gender, Culture and Ethnicity.* Mountain View, CA: Mayfield.

Lipset, Seymour Martin. 1963. "Value Differences, Absolute or Relative: The English-Speaking Democracies." Pp. 248–73 in *The First New Nation: The United States in Historical Perspective.* New York: Basic Books.

———. 1971. *Agrarian Socialism: The Cooperative Commonwealth Federation in Saskatchewan,* rev. ed. Berkeley: University of California Press.

Lisak, David. 1992. "Sexual Aggression, Masculinity, and Fathers." *Signs* 16: 238–62.

Livernash, Robert, and Eric Rodenburg. 1998. "Population Change, Resources, and the Environment." *Population Bulletin* 53, 1. On the World Wide Web at http://www.prb.org/pubs/population_bulletin/bu53-1.htm (25 August 2000).

Livingstone, David W. 1999. *The Education-Jobs Gap: Underemployment or Economic Democracy.* Toronto: Garamond Press.

Lofland, John, and Lyn H. Lofland. 1995. *Analyzing Social Settings: A Guide to Qualitative Observation and Analysis,* 3rd ed. Belmont, CA: Wadsworth.

Logan, Ron. 2001. "Crime Statistics in Canada, 2000." *Juristat* 21, 8 (July). Catalogue no. 85-002-XPE. Ottawa: Canadian Centre for Justice Statistics and Statistics Canada.

"Longitudinal U.S. Public Opinion Polls on Same-Sex Marriage and Civil Unions." 2010. ReligiousTolerance. org. On the World Wide Web at http://www.religioustolerance.org/hom_poll5d.htm (25 March 2010).

Lopez, Donald S. 2001. *The Story of Buddhism: A Concise Guide to Its History and Teachings.* San Francisco: Harper.

Lowman, John, Robert T. Menzies, and Ted S. Palys. 1987. *Transcarceration: Essays in the Sociology of Social Control.* Aldershot, ON: Gower.

Lucas, Samuel Roundfield. 1999. *Tracking Inequality: Stratification and Mobility in American High Schools.* New York: Teachers College Press.

Lupri, Eugen, and James Frideres. 1988. "Marital Satisfaction over the Life Cycle." Pp. 436–48 in Lorne Tepperman and James Curtis, eds. *Readings in Sociology: An Introduction.* Toronto: McGraw-Hill Ryerson.

Lyon, David, and Elia Zureik, eds. 1996. *Computers, Surveillance, and Privacy.* Minneapolis: University of Minnesota Press.

Mackie, Marlene. 1991. *Gender Relations in Canada: Further Explorations.* Toronto: Butterworths.

MacKinnon, Catharine A. 1979. *Sexual Harassment of Working Women.* New Haven, CT: Yale University Press.

Macklin, Eleanor D. 1980. "Nontraditional Family Forms: A Decade of Research." *Journal of Marriage and the Family* 42: 905–22.

MacLennan, Hugh. 1945. *Two Solitudes.* Toronto: Collins.

"Mad about Hockey: Superstitions." 2002. On the World Wide Web at http://www.mcg.org/societe/hockey/pages/aa-superstitions_2. html (20 June 2002).

Makomaski Illing, E. M., and M. J. Kaiserman. 2004. "Mortality Attributable to Tobacco Use in Canada and Its Regions, 1998." *Canadian Journal of Public Health* 95: 38–44.

Manga, Pran, Douglas E. Angus, and William R. Swan. 1993. "Effective Management of Low Back Pain: It's Time to Accept the Evidence." *Journal of the Canadian Chiropractic Association* 37: 221–29.

Mann, Susan A., Michael D. Grimes, Alice Abel Kemp, and Pamela J. Jenkins. 1997. "Paradigm Shifts in Family Sociology? Evidence from Three Decades of Family Textbooks." *Journal of Family Issues* 18: 315–49.

Markowitz, Fran. 1993. *A Community in Spite of Itself: Soviet Jewish Émigrés in New York.* Washington, DC: Smithsonian Institute Press.

Marshall, S. L. A. 1947. *Men Against Fire: The Problem of Battle Command in Future War.* New York: Morrow.

Marshall, Thomas H. 1965. "Citizenship and Social Class." Pp. 71–134 in Thomas H. Marshall, ed. *Class, Citizenship, and Social Development: Essays by T. H. Marshall.* Garden City, NY: Anchor.

Martineau, Harriet. 1985. *Harriet Martineau on Women,* Gayle Graham Yates, ed. New Brunswick, NJ: Rutgers University Press.

Marx, Karl. 1904 [1859]. *A Contribution to the Critique of Political Economy,* N. Stone, trans. Chicago: Charles H. Kerr.

_____. 1967 [1867–94]. *Capital,* 3 vols. New York: International Publishers.

_____. 1970 [1843]. *Critique of Hegel's "Philosophy of Right,"* Annette Jolin and Joseph O'Malley, trans. Cambridge, MA: Harvard University Press.

Marx, Karl, and Friedrich Engels. 1972 [1848]. "Manifesto of the Communist Party." Pp. 331–62 in R. Tucker, ed. *The Marx-Engels Reader.* New York: Norton.

Massey, Douglas S., Camille Z. Charles, Garvey F. Lundy, and Mary J. Fischer. 2003. *The Source of the River: The Social Origins of Freshmen at America's Selective Colleges and Universities.* Princeton, NJ: Princeton University Press.

Matalon, Jean-Marc. 1997. "Jeanne Calment, World's Oldest Person, Dead at 122." *The Shawnee News-Star* 5 August. On the World Wide Web at http://www.news-star.com/ stories/080597/life1.html (2 May 2000).

"Maternal Mortality: A Preventable Tragedy." 1998. *Popline* 20: 4.

Matsueda, Ross L. 1988. "The Current State of Differential Association Theory." *Crime and Delinquency* 34: 277–306.

_____. 1992. "Reflected Appraisals, Parental Labeling, and Delinquency: Specifying a Symbolic Interactionist Theory." *American Journal of Sociology* 97: 1577–611.

McAdam, Doug. 1982. *Political Process and the Development of Black Insurgency, 1930–1970.* Chicago: University of Chicago Press.

McClelland, W. R. 1931. "Precautions for Workers in the Treating of Radium Ores." *Investigations in Ore Dressing and Metallurgy.* Ottawa: Bureau of Mines. On the World Wide Web at http://www.ccnr.org/radium_warning. html (8 October 2000).

McCormick, Chris, ed. 1999. *The Westray Chronicles: A Case Study in Corporate Crime.* Halifax: Fernwood.

McLaren, Angus. 1990. *Our Own Master Race: Eugenics in Canada, 1885–1945.* Toronto: McClelland & Stewart.

McLuhan, Marshall. 1964. *Understanding Media: The Extensions of Man.* New York: McGraw-Hill.

McMahon, Maeve W. 1992. *The Persistent Prison? Rethinking Decarceration and Penal Reform.* Toronto: University of Toronto Press.

McManners, John, ed. 1990. *Oxford Illustrated History of Christianity.* Oxford: Oxford University Press.

McNeill, William H. 1976. *Plagues and Peoples.* Garden City, NY: Anchor Press.

McPhail, Clark. 1994. "The Dark Side of Purpose: Individual and Collective Violence in Riots." *Sociological Quarterly* 35: 1–32.

McRoberts, Kenneth. 1988. *Quebec: Social Change and Political Crisis,* 3rd ed. Toronto: McClelland & Stewart.

McVey, Wayne W., Jr., and Warren E. Kalbach. 1995. *Canadian Population.* Scarborough, ON: Nelson.

Mead, George H. 1934. *Mind, Self and Society.* Chicago: University of Chicago Press.

Melton, J. Gordon. 1996. *Encyclopedia of American Religions,* 5th ed. Detroit: Gale.

Melucci, Alberto. 1980. "The New Social Movements: A Theoretical Approach." *Social Science Information* 19: 199–226.

_____. 1995. "The New Social Movements Revisited: Reflections on a Sociological Misunderstanding." Pp. 107–19 in Louis Maheu, ed. *Social Classes and Social Movements: The Future of Collective Action.* London, UK: Sage.

Menzies, C. R. 1999. "First Nations, Inequality and the Legacy of Colonialism." Pp. 236–44 in J. Curtis, E. Grabb, and N. Guppy, eds. *Social Inequality in Canada,* 3rd ed. Scarborough, ON: Prentice Hall Allyn and Bacon Canada Inc.

Merton, Robert K. 1938. "Social Structure and Anomie." *American Sociological Review* 3: 672–82.

_____. 1968 [1949]. *Social Theory and Social Structure,* enlarged ed. New York: Free Press.

Messerschmidt, James W. 1993. *Masculinities and Crime: Critique and Reconceptualization of Theory.* Lanham, MD: Roman and Littlefield.

Messner, Michael. 1995. "Boyhood, Organized Sports, and the Construction of Masculinities." Pp. 102–14 in Michael S. Kimmel and Michael A. Messner. *Men's Lives,* 3rd ed. Boston: Allyn and Bacon.

_____. 2000. "Barbie Girls versus Sea Monsters: Children Constructing Gender." *Gender & Society, Special Issue* 14, 6 (December): 765–84.

Meyer, David R., and Judi Bartfield. 1996. "Compliance with Child Support Orders in Divorce Cases." *Journal of Marriage and the Family* 58, 1: 201–12.

Meyer, John W., Francisco O. Ramirez, and Yasemin Nuhoglu Soysal. 1992. "World Expansion of Mass Education, 1870–1980." *Sociology of Education* 65: 128–49.

Meyer, Thomas. 1984. "'Date Rape': A Serious Campus Problem that Few Talk About." *Chronicle of Higher Education* 5 December: 1, 12.

Milanovic, Branko. 2005. *Worlds Apart: Measuring International and Global Inequality.* Princeton, NJ: Princeton University Press.

Milem, Jeffrey F. 1998. "Attitude Change in College Students: Examining the Effect of College Peer Groups and Faculty Normative Groups." *Journal of Higher Education* 69: 117–40.

Miles, Robert. 1989. *Racism.* London: Routledge.

Milgram, Stanley. 1974. *Obedience to Authority: An Experimental View.* New York: Harper.

Miller, Ted R., and Mark A. Cohen. 1997. "Costs of Gunshot and Cut/ Stab Wounds in the United States, with Some Canadian Comparisons." *Accident Analysis and Prevention* 29: 329–41.

Milloy, John S. 1999. *A National Crime: The Canadian Government and the Residential School System, 1879 to 1986.* Winnipeg: University of Manitoba Press.

Mills, C. Wright. 1959. *The Sociological Imagination.* New York: Oxford University Press.

Minkel, J. R. 2002. "A Way with Words." *Scientific American* 25 March. On the World Wide Web at http://www.mit. edu/~lera/sciam (21 January 2003).

Mitchinson, Wendy. 1993. "The Medical Treatment of Women." Pp. 391–421 in Sandra Burt, Lorraine Code, and Lindsay Dorney, eds. *Changing Patterns: Women in Canada,* 2nd ed. Toronto: McClelland & Stewart.

Mohr, Johann W., and Keith Spencer. 1999. "Crime." Pp. 587–89 in James H. Marsh, ed. *The Canadian Encyclopedia,* Year 2000 Edition. Toronto: McClelland & Stewart.

Money, John, and Anke Ehrhardt. 1972. *Man and Woman, Boy and Girl.* Boston: Little Brown.

Montgomery, Malcolm. 1965. "The Six Nations and the Macdonald Franchise." *Ontario History* 57: 13.

Mooney, Linda A., David Knox, Caroline Schacht, and Adie Nelson. 2001. *Understanding Social Problems.* Toronto: Nelson Thomson Learning.

Mooney, Linda, Caroline Schacht, David Knox, and Adie Nelson. 2003. *Understanding Social Problems,* 2nd ed. Toronto: Nelson Thomson Learning.

Morris, Aldon D. 1984. *The Origins of the Civil Rights Movement: Black Communities Organizing for Change.* New York: Free Press.

Morris, Norval, and David J. Rothman, eds. 1995. *The Oxford History of the Prison: The Practice of Punishment in Western Society.* New York: Oxford University Press.

Morrison, Nancy. 1987. "Separation and Divorce." Pp. 125–43 in M. J. Dymond, ed. *The Canadian Woman's Legal Guide.* Toronto: Doubleday.

Mortimer, Jeylan T., and Roberta G. Simmons. 1978. "Adult Socialization." *Annual Review of Sociology* 4: 421–54.

Mundell, Helen. 1993. "How the Color Mafia Chooses Your Clothes." *American Demographics* November. On the World Wide Web at http://www.demographics.com/publications/ad/93_ad/9311_ad/ad281.htm (2 May 2000).

Murdock, George Peter. 1937. "Comparative Data on the Division of Labor by Sex." *Social Forces* 15: 551–53.

_____. 1949. *Social Structure.* New York: Macmillan.

Murray, Jane Lothian, Rick Linden, and Diana Kendall. 2011. *Sociology in Our Times,* 5th ed. Toronto: Nelson Education.

National Council of Welfare. 1999a. "A New Poverty Line: New, No or Maybe?" On the World Wide Web at http://www.ncwcnbes.net/htmdocument/reportnewpovline/newpovline.html (9 April 2000).

_____. 1999b. *Children First: A Pre-Budget Report by the National Council of Welfare.* On the World Wide Web at http://www.ncwcnbes.net/htmdocument/reportchildfirst.htm (9 April 2000).

_____. 2004. *Poverty Profile 2001.* Catalogue no. SD25-1/2001E. Ottawa: Minister of Public Works and Government Services Canada.

National Oceanic and Atmospheric Administration. 2010. "Use of NOAA ESRL Data." On the World Wide Web at ftp://ftp.cmdl.noaa.gov/ccg/co2/trends/co2_annmean_mlo.txt (29 March 2010).

National Opinion Research Center. 2006. *General Social Survey, 1972–2004.* Chicago: University of Chicago. Machine readable file.

National Rifle Association. 2005. "Guns, Gun Ownership, & RTC at All-Time Highs, Less 'Gun Control,' and Violent Crime at 30-Year Low." On the World Wide Web at http://www.nraila.org/Issues/FactSheets/Read.aspx?ID5126 (29 December 2005).

Nelson, Adie and Barrie W. Robinson. 2002. *Gender in Canada,* 2nd ed. Toronto: Prentice Hall.

Nelson, Dean, and Barney Henderson. 2009. "Slumdog Child Stars Miss Out on the Movie Millions." *Telegraph.co.uk* 26 January. On the World Wide Web at http://www.telegraph.co.uk/news/worldnews/asia/4347472/Poor-parents-of-Slumdog-millionaire-stars-say-children-were-exploited.html (2 January 2010).

Neubert, Amy Patterson. 2009. "Playing Favourites: Parents Still Involved after Children Are Grown." *Purdue University News* 7 December. On the World Wide Web at http://news.uns.purdue.edu/x/2009b/091207FingermanSupport.html (20 August 2010).

Nevitte, Neil. 1996. *The Decline of Deference.* Peterborough, ON: Broadview Press.

"New York Knicks History." 2000. On the World Wide Web at http://www.nba.com/knicks/news/00400499.html?nav5ArticleList#2 (9 May 2000).

Nicolaiedis, Nicos. 1998. "Pierre Marty's 'Doll' and Today's Barbies." *Revue française de psychanalyse, Special Issue: Psychosomatique et pulsionnalité* 62, 5 (Nov/Dec): 1579–81.

Nielsen, Linda. 1999. "College Aged Students with Divorced Parents: Facts and Fiction." *College Student Journal* 33: 543–72.

Nikiforuk, Andrew. 1998. "Echoes of the Atomic Age: Cancer Kills Fourteen Aboriginal Uranium Workers." *Calgary Herald* 14 March: A1, A4. On the World Wide Web at http://www.ccnr.org/deline_deaths.html (8 October 2000).

_____. 1999. "A Question of Style." *Time* 31 May: 58–59.

1994–1995 Directory of Labour Organizations in Canada. 1995. Catalogue no. L2-2-1995. Ottawa: Minister of Supply and Services Canada.

1998 Directory of Labour Organizations in Canada. 1998. Ottawa: Workplace Information Directorate.

Nisbett, Richard E., Kaiping Peng, Incheol Choi, and Ara Norenzayan. 2001. "Culture and Systems of Thought: Holistic versus Analytic Cognition." *Psychological Review* 108: 291–310.

Nolen, Stephanie. 1999. "Gender: The Third Way." *Globe and Mail* 25 September: D1, D4.

Norton, Kevin I., Timothy S. Olds, Scott Olive, and Stephen Dank. 1996. "Ken and Barbie at Life Size." *Sex Roles* 34, 3–4 (February): 287–94.

Nowak, Martin A., Robert M. May, and Karl Sigmund. 1995. "The Arithmetics of Mutual Help." *Scientific American* 272, 6: 76–81.

Nowell, Amy, and Larry V. Hedges. 1998. "Trends in Gender Differences in Academic Achievement from 1960 to 1994: An Analysis of Differences in Mean, Variance, and Extreme Scores." *Sex Roles* 39: 21–43.

Oberschall, Anthony. 1973. *Social Conflict and Social Movements.* Englewood Cliffs, NJ: Prentice-Hall.

Oderkirk, Jillian, and Clarence Lochhead. 1992. "Lone Parenthood: Gender Differences." *Canadian Social Trends* 27, Spring: 16–19. Catalogue no. 11-008-XPE.

Oeppen, Jim, and James W. Vaupel. 2002. "Demography: Enhanced: Broken Limits to Life Expectancy." *Science* 296: 1029–31.

Ogbu, John U. 2003. *Black American Students in an Affluent Suburb: A Study of Academic Disengagement.* Mahwah, NJ: Erlbaum.

O'Malley, Kady. 2007. "Under the Microscope: The UN Takes Aim at Canada's Treatment of Minorities on

Everything from the Arar Case to the Term 'Visible Minorities.'" *Maclean's* 21 February. On the World Wide Web at http://www.macleans.ca/canada/national/article.jsp?content=20070221_100909_12800 (6 August 2010).

Omi, Michael, and Howard Winant. 1986. *Racial Formation in the United States.* New York: Routledge.

Ontario Consultants on Religious Tolerance. 2000. "Homosexual (Same-Sex) Marriages." On the World Wide Web at http://www.religioustolerance.org/hom_marr.htm (20 August 2000).

_____. 2005. "Information about Religion in Canada." On the World Wide Web at http://www.religioustolerance.org/can_rel.htm (14 November 2005).

Ore, Timothy, and Astrid Birgden. 2003. "Does Prison Work: A View from Criminology." *Policy* 19, 2. On the World Wide Web at http://www.cis.org.au/policy/winter03/polwin03-9.pdf (8 March 2010).

Organisation for Economic Co-operation and Development (OECD). 2004. "Statistical Annex." *OECD Employment Outlook 2004.* On the World Wide Web at http://www.oecd.org/dataoecd/42/55/32494755.pdf (1 December 2005).

Organization of African Unity. 2000. *Rwanda: the Preventable Genocide.* New York. On the World Wide Web at http://www.visiontv.ca/RememberRwanda/Report.pdf (15 January 2005).

Ornstein, Michael D. 1998. "Survey Research." *Current Sociology* 46, 4: 1–87.

Ossowski, Stanislaw. 1963. *Class Structure in the Social Consciousness,* S. Patterson, trans. London: Routledge and Kegan Paul.

Owen, Michelle K. 2001. "'Family' as a Site of Contestation: Queering the Normal or Normalizing the Queer?" Pp. 86–102 in Terry Goldie, ed. *In a Queer Country: Gay and Lesbian Studies in the Canadian Context.* Vancouver: Arsenal Pulp Press.

Pacey, Arnold. 1983. *The Culture of Technology.* Cambridge, MA: MIT Press.

Pammett, Jon H. 1997. "Getting Ahead Around the World." Pp. 67–86 in Alan Frizzell and Jon H. Pammett, eds. *Social Inequality in Canada.* Ottawa: Carleton University Press.

Pape, Robert A. 2003. "The Strategic Logic of Suicide Terrorism." *American Political Science Review* 97: 343–61.

_____. 2005. *Dying to Win: The Strategic Logic of Suicide Terrorism.* New York: Random House.

Paperny, Anna Mehler. 2010. "Ontario Watchdog Launching New Review of Police Action during G20 Summit." *Globe and Mail* 22 July. On the World Wide Web at http://www.theglobeandmail.com/news/national/toronto/ontario-watchdog-launching-new-review-of-police-action-during-g20-summit/article1648886/ (6 August 2010).

Park, Jungwee. 2005. "Use of Alternative Health Care." *Health Reports* 16, 2: 39–43.

Parke, Ross D. 2001. "Paternal Involvement in Infancy: The Role of Maternal and Paternal Attitudes." *Journal of Family Psychology* 15, 4 (December): 555–58.

_____. 2002. "Parenting in the New Millennium: Prospects, Promises and Pitfalls." Pp. 65–93 in James P. McHale and Wendy S. Grolnick, eds. *Retrospect and Prospect in the Psychological Study of Families.* Mahwah, NJ: Lawrence Erlbaum Associates, Inc.

Parshall, Gerald. 1998. "Brotherhood of the Bomb." *US News and World Report* 125, 7 (17–24 August): 64–68.

Parsons, Talcott. 1942. "Age and Sex in the Social Structure of the United States." *American Sociological Review* 7: 04–616.

_____. 1951. *The Social System.* New York: Free Press.

_____. 1955. "The American Family: Its Relation to Personality and to the Social Structure." Pp. 3–33 in Talcott Parsons and Robert F. Bales, eds. *Family, Socialization and Interaction Process.* New York: Free Press.

Pascual, Brian. 2002. "Avril Lavigne Hates Britney Spears." *ChartAttack* 19 April. On the World Wide Web at http://www.chartattack.com/damn/2002/04/1901.cfm (15 January 2003).

Pasley, Kay, and Carmelle Minton. 2001. "Generative Fathering After Divorce and Remarriage: Beyond the 'Disappearing Dad.'" Pp. 239–48 in Theodore F. Cohen, ed. *Men and Masculinity: A Text Reader.* Belmont, CA: Wadsworth.

Pendakur, Krishna, and Ravi Pendakur. 1998. "The Colour of Money: Earnings Differentials among Ethnic Groups in Canada." *Canadian Journal of Economics* 31: 518–48.

Pendakur, R. 2000. *Immigrants and the Labour Force: Policy, Regulation and Impact.* Montreal: McGill-Queen's University Press.

Perrow, Charles B. 1984. *Normal Accidents.* New York: Basic Books.

Peters, John F. 1994. "Gender Socialization of Adolescents in the Home: Research and Discussion." *Adolescence* 29: 913–34.

Pew Research Center. 2002. *The Pew Global Attitudes Project: How Global Publics View Their Lives, Their Countries, the World, America.* On the World Wide Web at http://www.people-press.org (12 April 2003).

Piaget, Jean, and Bärbel Inhelder. 1969. *The Psychology of the Child,* Helen Weaver, trans. New York: Basic Books.

Piven, Frances Fox, and Richard A. Cloward. 1977. *Poor People's Movements: Why They Succeed, How They Fail.* New York: Vintage.

Place, Skyler, Peter Todd, Lars Penke, and Jens Asendorpf. 2010. "Humans Show Mate Copying after Observing Real Mate Choices." *Evolution & Human Behavior* 31: 320–25.

Plummer, Kenneth. 1995. *Telling Sexual Stories: Power, Change and Social Worlds.* London, UK: Routledge.

Pool, Robert. 1997. *Beyond Engineering: How Society Shapes Technology.* New York: Oxford University Press.

Popenoe, David. 1988. *Disturbing the Nest: Family Change and Decline in Modern Societies.* New York: Aldine de Gruyter.

_____. 1996. *Life without Father: Compelling New Evidence that Fatherhood and Marriage Are Indispensable for the Good of Children and Society.* New York: Martin Kessler Books.

_____. 1998. "The Decline of Marriage and Fatherhood." Pp. 312–19 in John J. Macionis and Nijole V. Benokraitis, eds. *Seeing Ourselves: Classic, Contemporary and Cross-Cultural Readings in Sociology,* 4th ed. Upper Saddle River, NJ: Prentice Hall.

Population Reference Bureau. 2009. *2009 World Population Data Sheet.* On the World Wide Web at http://www.prb.org/pdf09/09wpds_eng.pdf (1 April 2010).

Porter, John. 1965. *The Vertical Mosaic: An Analysis of Social Class and Power in Canada.* Toronto: University of Toronto Press.

_____. 1979. *The Measure of Canadian Society: Education, Equality, and Opportunity.* Toronto: Gage.

Portes, Alejandro, and Robert D. Manning. 1991. "The Immigrant Enclave: Theory and Empirical Examples." Pp. 319–32 in Norman R. Yetman, ed. *Majority and Minority: The Dynamics of Race and Ethnicity in American Life,* 5th ed. Boston: Allyn and Bacon.

Postel, Sandra. 1994. "Carrying Capacity: Earth's Bottom Line." Pp. 3–21 in Linda Starke, ed. *State of the World 1994.* New York: W. W. Norton.

Postman, Neil. 1982. *The Disappearance of Childhood.* New York: Delacorte.

Potts, Richard. 2008. "Summary Article: Religion and Politics in the Czech Republic from Daniel Raus and Hanka Rausova's Presentation to the Oxford Centre's Course on Religion & Politics." On the World Wide Web at http://www.ocrpl.org/?p=120 (3 August 2010).

Province of Nova Scotia. 2010. "Counties of Nova Scotia." On the World Wide Web at http://www.gov.ns.ca/snsmr/muns/info/mapping/counties.asp (30 March 2010).

Provine, Robert R. 2000. *Laughter: A Scientific Investigation.* New York: Penguin.

Raag, Tarja, and Christine L. Rackliff. 1998. "Preschoolers' Awareness of Social Expectations of Gender: Relationships to Toy Choices." *Sex Roles* 38: 685–700.

Raphael, D. 2004. *Social Determinants of Health: Canadian Perspectives.* Toronto: Canadian Scholars' Press.

Rapp, Rayna, and Ellen Ross. 1986. "The 1920s: Feminism, Consumerism and Political Backlash in the United States." Pp. 52–62 in J. Friedlander, B. Cook, A. Kessler-Harris, and C. Smith-Rosenberg, eds. *Women in Culture and Politics.* Bloomington, IN: Indiana University Press.

Reimann, Renate. 1997. "Does Biology Matter? Lesbian Couples' Transition to Parenthood and Their Division of Labor." *Qualitative Sociology* 20, 2: 153–85.

Reiter, Ester. 1991. *Making Fast Food: From the Frying Pan into the Fryer.* Montreal: McGill-Queen's University Press.

Reitz, Jeffrey G. 2011. "Tapping Immigrants' Skills." Pp. 178–93 in. Robert J. Brym, ed. *Society in Question,* 6th ed. Toronto: Nelson.

Resnick, Michael, Peter S. Bearman, Robert W. Blum, Karl E. Bauman, Kathleen M. Harris, Jo Jones, Joyce Tabor, Trish Beubring, Renee E. Sieving, Marcia Shew, Marjoie Ireland, Linda H. Beringer, and J. Richard Udry. 1997. "Protecting Adolescents from Harm." *Journal of the American Medical Association* 278: 823–32.

Richler, Mordecai. 1959. *The Apprenticeship of Duddy Kravitz.* Don Mills, ON: A. Deutsch.

Rifkin, Jeremy. 1998. *The Biotech Century: Harnessing the Gene and Remaking the World.* New York: Jeremy P. Tarcher/Putnam.

Risman, Barbara J., and Danette Johnson-Sumerford. 1998. "Doing It Fairly: A Study of Postgender Marriages." *Journal of Marriage and the Family* 60: 23–40.

Ritzer, George. 1993. *The McDonaldization of Society.* Thousand Oaks, CA: Pine Forge Press.

_____. 1996. "The McDonaldization Thesis: Is Expansion Inevitable?" *International Sociology* 11: 291–307.

Robbins, Liz. 2005. "Nash Displays Polished Look: On the Court, of Course." *New York Times* January 19. On the World Wide Web at http://www.nytimes.com (19 January 2005).

Roberts, Julian, and Thomas Gabor. 1990. "Race and Crime: A Critique." *Canadian Journal of Criminology* 92, 2 (April): 291–313.

Robertson, Ian. 1977. *Sociology.* New York: Worth Publishing.

Robinson, Richard H., and Willard L. Johnson. 1997. *The Buddhist Religion: A Historical Introduction,* 4th ed. Belmont, CA: Wadsworth.

Roche, Maurice. 1995. "Rethinking Citizenship and Social Movements: Themes in Contemporary Sociology and Neoconservative Ideology." Pp. 186–219 in Louis Maheu, ed. *Social Classes and Social Movements: The Future of Collective Action.* London, UK: Sage.

Rodinson, Maxime. 1996. *Muhammad,* 2nd ed. Anne Carter, trans. London: Penguin.

Roediger, David R. 1991. *The Wages of Whiteness: Race and the Making of the American Working Class.* London: Verso.

Rollins, Boyd C., and Kenneth L. Cannon. 1974. "Marital Satisfaction over the Family Life Cycle." *Journal of Marriage and the Family* 36: 271–84.

Romaniuc, Anatole. 1984. "Fertility in Canada: From Baby-Boom to Baby-Bust." *Current Demographic Analysis.* Ottawa: Statistics Canada.

Rootes, Chris. 1995. "A New Class? The Higher Educated and the New Politics." Pp. 220–35 in Louis Maheu, ed. *Social Classes and Social Movements: The Future of Collective Action.* London, UK: Sage.

Rose, Michael S. 2001. "The Facts Behind the Massacre." *Catholic World News* 17 October. On the World Wide Web at http://www.cwnews.com/news/viewstory.cfm?recnum520654 (15 January 2005).

Rosenbluth, Susan C. 1997. "Is Sexual Orientation a Matter of Choice?" *Psychology of Women Quarterly* 21: 595–610.

Rosenbluth, Susan C., Janice M. Steil, and Juliet H. Whitcomb. 1998. "Marital Equality: What Does It Mean?" *Journal of Family Issues* 19, 3: 227–44.

Rosenthal, Robert, and Lenore Jacobson. 1968. *Pygmalion in the Classroom: Teacher Expectation and Pupils' Intellectual Development.* New York: Holt, Rinehart, and Winston.

Rostow, Walt W. 1960. *The Stages of Economic Growth: A Non-Communist Manifesto.* New York: Cambridge University Press.

Roth, Cecil. 1961. *A History of the Jews.* New York: Schocken.

Rothman, Barbara Katz. 1982. *In Labor: Women and Power in the Birthplace.* New York: W. W. Norton.

———. 1989. *Recreating Motherhood: Ideology and Technology in a Patriarchal Society.* New York: W. W. Norton.

Rothman, David J. 1991. *Strangers at the Bedside: A History of How Law and Bioethics Transformed Medical Decision Making.* New York: Basic Books.

———. 1998. "The International Organ Traffic." *New York Review of Books* 45, 5: 14–17.

Rubin, Jeffrey Z., Frank J. Provenzano, and Zella Lurra. 1974. "The Eye of the Beholder: Parents' Views on Sex of Newborns." *American Journal of Orthopsychiatry* 44: 512–19.

Rural Advancement Foundation International. 1999. "The Gene Giants." On the World Wide Web at http://www.rafi.org/web/allpub-one.shtml?dfl5allpub.db&tfl5allpub-one-frag.ptml&operation5display&ro15recNo&rf1534&rt1534&usebrs5true (2 May 2000).

Rural Communities Impact Policy Project. 2003. "Painting the Landscape of Rural Nova Scotia." 2003. On the World Wide Web at http://www.ruralnovascotia.ca/RCIP/PDF/RR_final_full.pdf (30 March 2010).

Ryan, Kathryn M., and Jeanne Kanjorski. 1998. "The Enjoyment of Sexist Humor, Rape Attitudes, and Relationship

Aggression in College Students." *Sex Roles* 38: 743–56.

Sager, Eric. 2000. "Canadian Families—A Historian's Perspective." Pp. vii–xi in *Profiling Canada's Families II.* Nepean, ON: Vanier Institute for the Family.

Sampson, Robert, and John H. Laub. 1993. *Crime in the Making: Pathways and Turning Points through Life.* Cambridge, MA: Harvard University Press.

Samuda, R. J., D. Crawford, C. Philip, and W. Tinglen. 1980. *Testing, Assessment, and Counselling of Minority Students: Current Methods in Ontario.* Toronto: Ontario Ministry of Education.

Samuelsson, Kurt. 1961 [1957]. *Religion and Economic Action,* E. French, trans. Stockholm: Scandinavian University Books.

Sandqvist, Karin, and Bengt-Erik Andersson. 1992. "Thriving Families in the Swedish Welfare State." *Public Interest* 109: 114–16.

Sarlo, Christopher. 2001. *Measuring Poverty in Canada.* Vancouver: The Fraser Institute.

Sartre, Jean-Paul. 1965 [1948]. *Anti-Semite and Jew,* George. J. Becker, trans. New York: Schocken.

Sauve, Roger. 2002. "Job, Family and Stress among Husbands, Wives and Lone-Parents 15–64 from 1990 to 2000." On the World Wide Web at http://www.vifamily.ca/cft/connect.htm (3 March 2003).

Savoie, Josée. 2002. "Crime Statistics in Canada, 2001." *Juristat* 22, 6. Catalogue no. 85-002-XPE. Ottawa: Canadian Centre for Justice Statistics and Statistics Canada.

Saxton, Lloyd. 1990. *The Individual, Marriage, and the Family,* 9th ed. Belmont, CA: Wadsworth.

Schiebinger, Londa L. 1993. *Nature's Body: Gender in the Making of Modern Science.* Boston: Beacon Press.

Schippers, Mimi. 2002. *Rockin' Out of the Box: Gender Maneuvering in Alternative Hard Rock.* New Brunswick, NJ: Rutgers University Press.

Schoen, Cathy, Robin Osborn, Phuong Trang Huynh, Michelle Doty, Karen Davis, Kinga Zapert, and Jordan Peugh. 2004. "Primary Care And Health System Performance: Adults' Experiences In Five Countries." *Health Affairs* (Web Exclusive) 4.487. On the World Wide Web at http://content.healthaffairs.org/cgi/content/abstract/hlthaff.w4.487v1 (4 September 2008).

Schor, Juliet B. 1992. *The Overworked American: The Unexpected Decline of Leisure.* New York: Basic Books.

_____. 1999. *The Overspent American: Why We Want What We Don't Need.* New York: Harper.

Schwartz, Stephen. 2003. *The Two Faces of Islam: The House of Sa'ud from Tradition to Terror.* New York: Doubleday.

Scott, James C. 1998. *Seeing Like a State: How Certain Schemes to Improve the Human Condition Have Failed.* New Haven, CT: Yale University Press.

Scott, K. 1997. "Indigenous Canadians." Pp. 133–64 in D. McKenzie, R. Williams, and E. Single, eds. *Canadian Profile: Alcohol, Tobacco and Other Drugs, 1997.* Ottawa: Canadian Centre on Substance Abuse.

Scott, Wilbur J. 1990. "PTSD in *DSM-III*: A Case in the Politics of Diagnosis and Disease." *Social Problems* 37: 294–310.

Sedgh, Gilda, Stanley K.Henshaw, Susheela Singh, Akinrinola Bankole, and Joanna Drescher. 2007. "Legal Abortion Worldwide: Incidence and Recent Trends." *Perspectives on Sexual and Reproductive Health* 39, 4: 216–25.

Senn, Charlene Y., Serge Desmarais, Norine Veryberg, and Eileen Wood. 2000. "Predicting Coercive Sexual Behavior Across the Lifespan in a Random Sample of Canadian Men." *Journal of Social and Personal Relationships* 17, 1 (February): 95–113.

Sev'er, Aysan. 1999. "Sexual Harassment: Where We Were, Where We Are and Prospects for the New Millennium." *Canadian Review of Sociology and Anthropology* 36, 4: 460–97.

Shain, A. 1995. "Employment of People with Disabilities." *Canadian Social Trends* 38: 8–13. Catalogue no. 11-008-XPE.

Shakur, Sanyika (a.k.a. Monster Kody Scott). 1993. *Monster: The Autobiography of an L.A. Gang Member.* New York: Penguin.

Shattuck, Roger. 1980. *The Forbidden Experiment: The Story of the Wild Boy of Aveyron.* New York: Farrar, Straus, and Giroux.

Shea, Sarah E., Kevin Gordon, Ann Hawkins, Janet Kawchuk, and Donna Smith. 2000. "Pathology in the Hundred Acre Wood: A Neurodevelopmental Perspective on A. A. Milne." *Canadian Medical Association Journal* 163, 12: 1557–59. On the World Wide Web at http://www.cma.ca/cmaj/vol-163/issue-12/1557.htm (12 December 2000).

Sheehy, Elizabeth. 2003. "From Women's Duty to Resist to Men's Duty to Ask: How Far Have We Come?" Pp. 576–81 in T. Brettel Dawson, ed. *Women, Law and Social Change: Core Readings and Current Issues,* 4th ed. Concord, ON: Captus Press.

Shekelle, Paul G. 1998. "What Role for Chiropractic in Health Care?" *New England Journal of Medicine* 339: 1074–75.

Sherif, Muzafer, L. J. Harvey, B. Jack White, William R. Hood, and Carolyn W. Sherif. 1988. *The Robber's Cave Experiment: Intergroup Conflict and Cooperation,* reprinted ed. Middletown, CT: Wesleyan University Press.

Sherkat, Darren E., and Christopher G. Ellison. 1999. "Recent Developments and Current Controversies in the Sociology of Religion." *Annual Review of Sociology* 25: 363–94.

Sherrill, Robert. 1997. "A Year in Corporate Crime." *The Nation* 7 April: 11–20.

Shkilnyk, Anastasia. 1985. *A Poison Stronger than Love: The Destruction of an Ojibway Community.* New Haven, CT: Yale University Press.

Shorter, Edward. 1997. *A History of Psychiatry: From the Era of the Asylum to the Age of Prozac.* New York: John Wiley and Sons.

Signorielli, Nancy. 1998. "Reflections of Girls in the Media: A Content Analysis Across Six Media Overview." On the World Wide Web at http://childrennow.org/media/mc97/Reflect-Summary.html (2 May 2000).

Silberman, Steve. 2000. "Talking to Strangers." *Wired* 8, 5: 225–33, 288–96. On the World Wide Web at http://www.wired.com/wired/archive/8.05/translation.html (23 May 2002).

"Silent Boom, The." 1997. *Forbes* 7 July: 170–71.

Simon, Jonathan. 1993. *Poor Discipline: Parole and the Social Control of the Underclass, 1890–1990.* Chicago: University of Chicago Press.

Simons, Ronald L., Chyi-In Wu, Christine Johnson, and Rand D. Conger. 1995. "A Test of Various Perspectives on the Intergenerational Transmission of Domestic Violence." *Criminology* 33: 141–60.

Sissing, T. W. 1996. "Some Missing Pages: The Black Community in the History of Québec and Canada." On the World Wide Web at http://www.qesnrecit.qc.ca/mpages/title.htm (14 June 2002).

Skolnick, Arlene. 1991. *Embattled Paradise: The American Family in an Age of Uncertainty.* New York: Basic Books.

Smith, Christian. 1991. *The Emergence of Liberation Theology: Radical Religion and Social Movement Theory.* Chicago: University of Chicago Press.

Smith, Jackie. 1998. "Global Civil Society? Transnational Social Movement Organizations and Social Capital." *American Behavioral Scientist* 42: 93–107.

Smith, Michael. 1990. "Patriarchal Ideology and Wife Beating: A Test of a Feminist Hypothesis." *Violence and Victims* 5: 257–73.

Smyth, Julie. 2003. "Sweden Ranked as Best Place to Have a Baby: Canada Places Fifth on Maternity Leave, 15th for Benefits." *National Post* 17 January. On the World Wide Web at http://www.childcarecanada.org/ccin/2003/ccin1_17_03.html (27 June 2004).

Snider, Laureen. 1999. "White-Collar Crime." P. 2504 in James H. Marsh, ed. *The Canadian Encyclopedia,* Year 2000 Edition. Toronto: McClelland & Stewart.

Snow, David A., E. Burke Rochford, Jr., Steven K. Worden, and Robert D. Benford. 1986. "Frame Alignment Processes, Micromobilization, and Movement Participation." *American Sociological Review* 51: 464–81.

Sofsky, Wolfgang. 1997 [1993]. *The Order of Terror: The Concentration Camp,* William Templer, trans. Princeton, NJ: Princeton University Press.

Sokoloff, Heather. 2001. "Wealth Affects Test Scores." *National Post* 5 December: A17.

Solicitor General Canada. 2002. "Factsheets." On the World Wide Web at http://www.sgc.ca/Efact/emyths.htm (22 January 2004).

Sorenson, Elaine. 1994. *Comparable Worth: Is It a Worthy Policy?* Princeton, NJ: Princeton University Press.

Spade, Joan Z. 2001. "Gender and Education in the United States." Pp. 270–78 in Jeanne H. Ballantine and Joan Z. Spade, eds. *Schools and Society: A Sociological Approach to Education.* Belmont, CA: Wadsworth.

Spitz, René A. 1945. "Hospitalism: An Inquiry into the Genesis of Psychiatric Conditions in Early Childhood." Pp. 53–74 in *The Psychoanalytic Study of the Child,* vol. 1. New York: International Universities Press.

_____. 1962. "Autoerotism Re-examined: The Role of Early Sexual Behavior Patterns in Personality Formation." Pp. 283–315 in *The Psychoanalytic Study of the Child,* vol. 17. New York: International Universities Press.

Spitzer, Steven. 1980. "Toward a Marxian Theory of Deviance." Pp. 175–91 in Delos H. Kelly, ed. *Criminal Behavior: Readings in Criminology.* New York: St. Martin's Press.

Stacey, Judith. 1996. *Brave New Families: Stories of Domestic Upheaval in Late Twentieth Century America.* New York: Basic Books.

Stack, Stephen, and J. Ross Eshleman. 1998. "Marital Status and Happiness: A 17-Nation Study." *Journal of Marriage and the Family* 60: 527–36.

Stark, Rodney. 1985. *Sociology.* Belmont, CA: Wadsworth.

Stark, Rodney, and William Sims Bainbridge. 1979. "Of Churches, Sects, and Cults: Preliminary Concepts for a Theory of Religious Movements." *Journal for the Scientific Study of Religion* 18: 117–31.

———. 1987. *A Theory of Religion.* New York: P. Lang.

———. 1997. *Religion, Deviance, and Social Control.* New York: Routledge.

Starr, Paul. 1982. *The Social Transformation of American Medicine.* New York: Basic Books.

———. 1994. *The Logic of Health Care Reform: Why and How the President's Plan Will Work,* rev. ed. New York: Penguin.

Statistics Canada. n.d. "Census families—time series." On the world Wide Web at http://www12.statcan.ca/english/census01/products/analytic/companion/fam/family.cfm (22 April 2007).

_____. 1992. *Selected Marriage Statistics 1921–1990.* Catalogue No. 82-552. Ottawa: Ministry of Industry.

_____. 1998a. *Canada Yearbook 1999.* Catalogue no. 11-402-XPE. Ottawa: Minister of Industry.

_____. 1998b. "Marriages and Divorces, 1996." *The Daily* 29 January. On the World Wide Web at http://www.statcan.ca/Daily/English/980129/d980129.htm#ART1 (26 May 2006).

_____. 1999a. "Historical Statistics of Canada," 1983, Catalogue No. 11-516, July 29, 1999, Series D160-174. On the World Wide Web at http://www.statcan.

ca/english/freepub/11-516-XIE/sectiond/sectiond/.htm (2 May 2008).

_____. 1999b. "National Longitudinal Survey of Children and Youth: Transition into Adolescence 1996/97." *The Daily* 6 July. On the World Wide Web at http://www.statcan.ca/Daily/English/990706/d990706a.htm (10 May 2001).

———. 1999c. "Principal Religious Denominations of the Population, Census Dates, 1871 to 1971. Series A 164–184." *Historical Statistics of Canada.* Ottawa: Ministry of Industry. Catalogue No. 11-516-XIE. On the World Wide Web at http://www.statcan.ca/english/freepub/11-516-XIE/sectiona/A164_184.csv (15 October 2005).

_____. 2000a. "Population by Aboriginal Group, 1996 Census." On the World Wide Web at http://www.statcan.ca/english/Pgdb/People/Population/demo39a.htm (7 October 2000).

_____. 2000b. "Household Environmental Practices." On the World Wide Web at http://www.statcan.ca/english/Pgdb/Land/Environment/envir01a.htm (7 October 2000).

_____. 2000c. *Income in Canada 1998.* Ottawa: Ministry of Industry.

_____. 2000d. "Divorces, 1998." *The Daily* 28 September. On the World Wide Web at http://www.statcan.ca/Daily/English/000928/d000926.htm (10 May 2001).

_____. 2001. "Television Viewing: Fall 1999." *The Daily* 25 January. On the World Wide Web at http://www.statcan.ca/Daily/English/010125/d010125a.htm (23 July 2002).

_____. 2002. *Profile of the Canadian Population by Age and Sex: Canada Ages.* Catalogue no. 96F0030XIE2001002. Ottawa: Minister of Industry. Analysis Series, 2001 Census. On the World Wide Web at http://www12.statcan.ca/english/census01/Products/Analytic/Index.cfm (23 August 2007).

_____. 2003a. "Census of Population: Immigration, Birthplace and Birthplace of Parents, Citizenship, Ethnic Origin, Visible Minorities and Aboriginal Peoples." *The Daily* 21 January. On the World Wide Web at http://www.statcan.ca/Daily/English/030121/d030121a.htm (15 September 2004).

_____. 2003b. "Education in Canada: Raising the Standard." Catalogue no. 96F0030XIE2001012. On the World Wide Web at http://www12.statcan.

ca/english/census01/products/ Analytic/companion/educ/contents. cfm (15 September 2004).

———. 2003c. *Earnings of Canadians: Making a Living in the New Economy.* Catalogue no. 96F0030XIE2001014. On the World Wide Web at http:// www.statcan.ca/census01/products/ analytic/companion/earn/contents. cfm (15 September 2004).

———. 2003d. "Marriages, 1999." *The Daily* 6 February. On the World Wide Web at http://www.statcan.ca/Daily/ English/030206/d030206c.htm (15 September 2004).

———. 2003e. *Religions in Canada.* Catalogue no. 96F0030XIE2001015. Ottawa: Minister of Industry. http://www12. statcan.ca/english/census01/Products/ Analytic/companion/rel/canada.cfm (24 January 2004).

———. 2003f. "Non-Wage Job Benefits, 2000." *The Daily* 21 May. On the World Wide Web at http://www. statcan.ca/Daily/English/030521/ d030521c.htm (15 September 2004).

———. 2004. "Marriages, 2002." *The Daily* 21 December. On the World Wide Web at http://www.statcan.ca/Daily/ English/041221/d041221d.htm (26 May 2006).

———. 2005a. CANSIM (database). Using CHASS (distributor). Version updated August 16, 2005. On the World Wide Web at http://dc1.chass.utoronto. ca.myaccess.library.utoronto.ca/census/ mainmicro.html

———. 2005b. "Child Care, 1994/95 and 2000/01." *The Daily* 7 February. On the World Wide Web at http://www. statcan.ca/Daily/English/050207/ d050207b.htm (14 March 2006).

———. 2006a. "Access to Health Care Services in Canada, 2005." On the World Wide Web at http://www. statcan.gc.ca/pub/82-575-x/82-575-x2006002-eng.htm (2 April 2010).

———. 2006b. "Households and the Environment 2006." On the World Wide Web at http://www.statcan.ca/ english/freepub/11-526-XIE/11-526-XIE2007001.pdf (22 September 2007).

———. 2006c. "Study: Inequality in Wealth." *The Daily* 13 December. On the World Wide Web at http://www. statcan.ca/Daily/English/061213/ d061213c.htm (3 April 2007).

———. 2007a. "Consumer Price Index, Historical Summary, by Province or Territory." On the World Wide Web

at http://www40.statcan.ca/l01/cst01/ econ46a.htm (1 April 2007).

———. 2007b. "Market, Total and After-Tax Income, by Economic Family Type and Income Quintiles, 2005 Constant Dollars, Annual," CANSIM (database), Table 202-0701. Version updated April 30, 2007. On the World Wide Web at http://cansim2.statcan.ca (23 August 2007).

———. 2007c. "Marriages, 2003." *The Daily* 17 January. On the World Wide Web at http://www.statcan.ca/Daily/ English/070117/d070117a.htm (22 April 2007).

———. 2008a. "Labour Force Indicators by Age Groups for Males, Participation Rate (2006), for Canada, Provinces and Territories—20% sample data." On the World Wide Web at http:// www12.statcan.ca/english/census06/ data/highlights/Labour/Table601. cfm?SR=1 (2 May 2008)

———. 2008b. "Labour Force Survey Estimates (LFS), by Sex and Detailed Age Group, Annual (persons unless otherwise noted)." CANSIM database, Table 282-0002. On the World Wide Web at http://estat.statcan.ca/cgi-win/ CNSMCGI.EXE?CANSIMFILE-Estat\ English\CII_1_E.htm (2 May 2008)

———. 2008c. "Labour Markets." On the World Wide Web at http://www45. statcan.gc.ca/2009/cgco_2009_008-eng.htm (21 March 2010).

———. 2008d. "Screen Time among Canadian Adults: A Profile." *Health Reports* 19, 2: 31–43. On the World Wide Web at http://www.statcan.gc.ca/ pub/82-003-x/2008002/article/10600-eng.pdf (22 February 2010).

———. 2008e. "Sexual Assault in Canada 2004 and 2007." On the World Wide Web at http://www.statcan.gc.ca/ pub/85f0033m/85f0033m2008019-eng.pdf (21 March 2010).

———. 2009a. "Average Earnings of the Population 15 Years and Over by Highest Level of Schooling, by Province and Territory (2006 Census)." On the World Wide Web at http:// www40.statcan.gc.ca/l01/cst01/ labor50a-eng.htm (26 March 2010).

———. 2009b. "Couple Families by Presence of Children of all Ages in Private Households, 2006 Counts, for Canada, Provinces and Territories—20% Sample Data." On the World Wide Web at http://www12. statcan.ca/census-recensement/2006/

dp-pd/hlt/97-553/pages/page.cfm?L ang=E&Geo=PR&Code=01&Table= 1&Data=Count&Age=1&StartRec= 1&Sort=2&Display=Page (25 March 2010).

———. 2009c. "Ethnic Origins, 2006 Counts, for Canada, Provinces and Territories—20% Sample Data." On the World Wide Web at http:// www12.statcan.ca/census-recensement/2006/dp-pd/hlt/97-562/ pages/page.cfm?Lang=E&Geo=PR& Code=01&Data=Count&Table=2& StartRec=1&Sort=3&Display=All& CSDFilter=5000 (12 March 2010).

———. 2009d. *Family Violence in Canada: A Statistical Profile.* On the World Wide Web at http://www.phac-aspc.gc.ca/ ncfv-cnivf/pdfs/fv-85-224-XWE-eng. pdf (25 March 2010).

———. 2009e. *Health Indicators,* Vol. 1, No 1. On the World Wide Web at http:// www.statcan.gc.ca/pub/82-221-x/82-221-x2009001-eng.htm (23 February 2010).

———. 2009f. "Highest Level of Educational Attainment for the Population Aged 25 to 64, 2006 Counts for Both Sexes, for Canada, Provinces and Territories—20% Sample Data." On the World Wide Web at http://www12.statcan.ca/ census-recensement/2006/dp-pd/ hlt/97-560/pages/page.cfm?Lang=E& Geo=PR&Code=01&Table=1&Data =Count&Sex=1&StartRec=1&Sort=2 &Display=Page (21 February 2010).

———. 2009g. "Population by Immigrant Status and Period of Immigration, 2006 Counts, for Canada, Provinces and Territories—20% Sample Data." On the World Wide Web at http:// www12.statcan.gc.ca/census-recensement/2006/dp-pd/hlt/97-557/ T403-eng.cfm?Lang=E&T=403& GH=4&SC=1&S=99&O=A (12 March 2010).

———. 2009h. "Same-Sex Couples by Type of Union (Married, Common-Law) and Sex, 2006 Census—20% Sample Data." On the World Wide Web at http://www12.statcan.ca/census-recensement/2006/dp-pd/hlt/97-553/ tables/Table4.cfm?Lang=E (22 March 2010).

———. 2010a. "Average Female and Male Earnings, and Female-to-Male Earnings Ratio, by Work Activity, 2007 Constant Dollars, Annually." CANSIM Table 202-0102. On the World Wide

Web at http://www.chass.utoronto.ca (19 March 2010).

_____. 2010b. "Contact with Alternative Health Care Providers in the Past 12 Months, by Age Group and Sex, Household Population Aged 12 and Over, Canada, Provinces, Territories, Health Regions (June 2005 Boundaries) and Peer Groups, every 2 Years." CANSIM Table 1050462. On the World Wide Web at http://dc2.chass.utoronto.ca.myaccess.library.utoronto.ca/cgi-bin/cansimdim/c2_getArrayDim.pl (2 April 2010).

_____. 2010c. "Crude Marriage Rates, All Marriages, Canada, Provinces and Territories, Annually (rates per 1,000 population)." CANSIM Table 1011004. On the World Wide Web at http://dc1.chass.utoronto.ca.myaccess.library.utoronto.ca/cgi-bin/cansimdim/c2_getArray.pl (22 March 2010).

_____. 2010d. "Highest Level of Educational Attainment for the Population Aged 25 to 64, Percentage Distribution for Both Sexes, for Canada, Provinces and Territories—20% Sample Data." On the World Wide Web at http://www12.statcan.ca/census-recensement/2006/dp-pd/hlt/97-560/pages/page.cfm?Lang=E&Geo=PR&Code=01&Table=1&Data=Dist&Sex=1&StartRec=1&Sort=2&Display=Page (27 March 2010).

_____. 2010e. "Homicide Survey, Number of Solved Homicides, by Type of Accused-Victim Relationship, Canada, Annually (Number)." CANSIM Table 2530006. On the World Wide Web at http://dc1.chass.utoronto.ca.myaccess.library.utoronto.ca/cgi-bin/cansimdim/c2_getArray.pl (22 March 2010).

_____. 2010f. "Induced Abortions by Province and Territory of Report (Hospitals and Clinics)." On the World Wide Web at http://www40.statcan.gc.ca/l01/cst01/health40a-eng.htm (25 March 2010).

_____. 2010g. "Labour Force Characteristics by Age and Sex: Table 1." On the World Wide Web at http://www.statcan.gc.ca/subjects-sujets/labour-travail/lfs-epa/t100806a1-eng.htm (20 August 2010).

_____. 2010h. "Labour Force Survey Estimates (LFS), Wages of Employees by Type of Work, National Occupational Classification for Statistics (NOC-S), Sex and Age Group, Annually (current

dollars unless specified)." CANSIM Table 2820070. On the World Wide Web at http://www.chass.utoronto.ca (11 March 2010).

_____. 2010i. "Leading Causes of Death, Total Population, by Sex, Canada, Provinces and Territories, Annual." CANSIM Table 102-0563. On the World Wide Web at http://cansim2.statcan.gc.ca/cgi-win/cnsmcgi.exe?Lang=E&RootDir=CII/&ResultTemplate=CII/CII___&Array_Pick=1&ArrayId=1020563 (1 April 2010).

_____. 2010j. "Life Expectancy at Birth." On the World Wide Web at http://www40.statcan.gc.ca/l01/cst01/health72a-eng.htm (1 April 2010).

_____. 2010k. "Low Income Cut-Offs before and after TAX for Rural and Urban Areas, by Family Size, Current Dollars, Annually (Dollars)." CANSIM Table 2020801. On the World Wide Web at http://www.chass.utoronto.ca (11 March 2010).

_____. 2010l. "Major Field of Study—Classification of Instructional Programs, 2000 (13), Highest Postsecondary Certificate, Diploma or Degree (12), Age Groups (10A) and Sex (3) for the Population 15 Years and Over With Postsecondary Studies of Canada, Provinces, Territories, Census Metropolitan Areas and Census Agglomerations, 2006 Census—20% Sample Data." On the World Wide Web at http://www12.statcan.gc.ca/census-recensement/2006/dp-pd/tbt/Rp-eng.cfm?TABID=1&LANG=E&APATH=3&DETAIL=0&DIM=0&FL=A&FREE=0&GC=0&GK=0&GRP=1&PID=93582&PRID=0&PTYPE=88971,97154&S=0&SHOWALL=0&SUB=751&Temporal=2006&THEME=75&VID=0&VNAMEE=&VNAMEF= (19 March 2010).

_____. 2010m. "Number of Children at Home (8) and Census Family Structure (7) for the Census Families in Private Households of Canada, Provinces, Territories, Census Metropolitan Areas and Census Agglomerations, 2001 and 2006 Censuses—20% Sample Data." On the World Wide Web at http://www12.statcan.gc.ca/census-recensement/2006/dp-pd/tbt/Rp eng.cfm?LANG=E&APATH=3&DETAIL=0&DIM=0&FL=A&FREE=0&G

C=0&GID=0&GK=0&GRP=1&PID=89016&PRID=0&PTYPE=88971,97154&S=0&SHOWALL=0&SUB=689&Temporal=2006&THEME=-68&VID=0&VNAMEE=&VNAMEF= (22 March 2010).

_____. 2010n. "Persistence of Low Income, by Selected Characteristics, Every 3 Years." CANSIM Table 202087. On the World Wide Web at http://www.chass.utoronto.ca (11 March 2010).

_____. 2010o. "Persons in low Income, Annually." CANSIM Table 2020802. On the World Wide Web at http://www.chass.utoronto.ca (11 March 2010.)

_____. 2010p. "Population by Mother Tongue and Age Groups, 2006 Counts, for Canada, Provinces and Territories—20% Sample Data." On the World Wide Web at http://www12.statcan.gc.ca/census-recensement/2006/dp-pd/hlt/97-555/T401-eng.cfm?Lang=E&T=401&GH=4&SC=1&S=99&O=A (14 March 2010).

_____. 2010q. "Projections of the Diversity of the Canadian Population." On the World Wide Web at http://www.statcan.gc.ca/pub/91-551-x/91-551-x2010001-eng.pdf (13 March 2010).

_____. 2010r. "Suicides and Suicide Rate, by Sex and by Age Group." On the World Wide Web at http://www40.statcan.gc.ca/l01/cst01/hlth66a-eng.htm (16 February 2010).

_____. 2010s. "University Degrees, Diplomas and Certificates Granted, by Program Level, Classification of Instructional Programs, Primary Grouping (CIP_PG) and Sex, Annually (Number)." CANSIM Table 4770014. On the World Wide Web at http://dc2.chass.utoronto.ca.myaccess.library.utoronto.ca/cgi-bin/cansimdim/c2_getArrayDim.pl (26 March 2010)

_____. 2010t. "Unpaid Work (20), Age Groups (9) and Sex (3) for the Population 15 Years and Over of Canada, Provinces, Territories, Census Divisions and Census Subdivisions, 2006 Census—20% Sample Data." On the World Wide Web at http://www12.statcan.gc.ca/census-recensement/2006/dp-pd/tbt/Rp-eng.cfm?LANG=E&APATH=3&DETAIL=0&DIM=0&FL=A&FREE=0&GC=0&GID=0&GK=0&GRP=1&PID=

92108&PRID=0&PTYPE=88971, 97154&S=0&SHOWALL=0&SUB= 745&Temporal=2006&THEME= 74&VID=0&VNAMEE=&VNAMEF= (22 March 2010).

Steel, Freda M. 1987. "Alimony and Maintenance Orders." Pp. 155–67 in Sheilah L. Martin and Kathleen E. Mahoney, eds. *Equality and Judicial Neutrality*. Toronto: Carswell.

Steele, Claude M. 1992. "Race and the Schooling of Black Americans." *Atlantic Monthly* April. On the World Wide Web at http://www.theatlantic.com/ unbound/flashbks/blacked/steele.htm (2 May 2000).

_____. 1997. "A Threat in the Air: How Stereotypes Shape the Intellectual Identities and Performance of Women and African-Americans." *American Psychologist* 52: 613–29.

Sterling, Jim. 2009. "Man Falls in Love with Ten-Year-Old Videogame Girl." *Destructoid* 23 July. On the World Wide Web at http://www.destructoid. com/man-falls-in-love-with-ten-year- old-video-game-girl-141142.phtml (19 August 2010).

Sternberg, Robert J. 1998. *In Search of the Human Mind,* 2nd ed. Fort Worth, TX: Harcourt Brace.

Stewart, Abigail, Anne P. Copeland, Nia Lane Chester, Janet E. Malley, and Nicole B. Barenbaum. 1997. *Separating Together: How Divorce Transforms Families*. New York: The Guilford Press.

Stipp, David. 2003. "The Pentagon's Weather Nightmare." *Fortune* 26 January. On the World Wide Web at http://paxhumana.info/article. php3?id_article=400 (29 May 2004).

Stone, Lawrence. 1977. *The Family, Sex and Marriage in England, 1500–1800*. New York: Harper and Row.

Stouffer, Samuel A. et al. 1949. *The American Soldier,* 4 vols. Princeton, NJ: Princeton University Press.

Straus, Murray A. 1994. *Beating the Devil Out of Them: Corporal Punishment in American Families*. New York: Lexington Books.

Strauss, Anselm L. 1993. *Continual Permutations of Action*. New York: Aldine de Gruyter.

Strikes and Lockouts in Canada 1968. 1970. Catalogue no. L2-1/1968. Ottawa: Economic and Research Branch, Canada Department of Labour.

Strikes and Lockouts in Canada 1985. 1985. Catalogue no. L160-2999/85B.

Ottawa: Minister of Supply and Services Canada.

Subrahmanyam, Kaveri, and Patricia M. Greenfield. 1998. "Computer Games for Girls: What Makes Them Play?" Pp. 46–71 in Justine Cassell and Henry Jenkins, eds. *From Barbie to Mortal Kombat: Gender and Computer Games*. Cambridge, MA: MIT Press.

Sullivan, Mercer L. 2002. "Exploring Layers: Extended Case Method as a Tool for Multilevel Analysis of School Violence." *Sociological Methods and Research* 31, 2: 255–85.

Sumner, William Graham. 1940 [1907]. *Folkways*. Boston: Ginn.

Sutherland, Edwin H. 1939. *Principles of Criminology*. Philadelphia: Lippincott.

_____. 1949. *White Collar Crime*. New York: Dryden.

Swiss Re. 2005. "Sigma: Natural Catastrophes and Man-Made Disasters in 2004." On the World Wide Web at http:// www.swissre.com (2 March 2005).

_____. 2007. "Natural Catastrophes and Man-Made Disasters in 2006." On the World Wide Web at http://www. swissre.com/internet/pwswpspr.nsf/ fmBookMarkFrameSet?ReadForm &BM5../vwAllbyIDKeyLu/mpdl- 6z2krc?OpenDocument (30 April 2007).

_____. 2008. "Natural Catastrophes and Man-Made Disasters in 2007." On the World Wide Web at http:// www.swissre.com/resources/678 bb7004159bbdaa92ced3638166 fb1-Sigma_1_2008_e.pdf (29 March 2010).

_____. 2009. "Natural Catastrophes and Man-Made Disasters in 2008." On the World Wide Web at http:// www.swissre.com/resources/ dd6346004d4e9669ac76eeced- d316cf3-sigma2_2009_e.pdf (29 March 2010)

_____. 2010. "Natural Catastrophes and Man-Made Disasters in 2009." On the World Wide Web at http:// www.swissre.com/resources/6552 260041b90e4aac79fc55ef9dd899- sigma1_2010_e_rev.pdf (29 March 2010).

Sykes, Gresham, and David Matza. 1957. "Techniques of Neutralization: A Theory of Delinquency." *American Sociological Review* 22: 664–70.

Tait, Robert. 2006. "Ahmadinejad Urges Iranian Baby Boom to Challenge West." *The Guardian* 23 October. On

the World Wide Web at http://www. guardian.co.uk/world/2006/oct/23/ iran.roberttait (3 August 2010).

Tajfel, Henri. 1981. *Human Groups and Social Categories: Studies in Social Psychology*. Cambridge, UK: Cambridge University Press.

Tannen, Deborah. 1990. *You Just Don't Understand Me: Women and Men in Conversation*. New York: William Morrow.

_____. 1994a. *Talking from 9 to 5: How Women's and Men's Conversational Styles Affect Who Gets Heard, Who Gets Credit, and What Gets Done at Work*. New York: William Morrow.

_____. 1994b. *Gender and Discourse*. New York: Oxford University Press.

Tarrow, Sidney. 1994. *Power in Movement: Social Movements, Collective Action and Politics*. Cambridge, UK: Cambridge University Press.

Tasker, Fiona L., and Susan Golombok. 1997. *Growing Up in a Lesbian Family: Effects on Child Development*. New York: The Guilford Press.

Tec, Nechama. 1986. *When Light Pierced the Darkness: Christian Rescue of Jews in Nazi-Occupied Poland*. New York: Oxford University Press.

Thoits, Peggy A. 1989. "The Sociology of Emotions." *Annual Review of Sociology* 15: 317–42.

Thomas, Keith. 1971. *Religion and the Decline of Magic*. London: Weidenfeld and Nicolson.

Thomas, Mikhail. 2002. "Adult Criminal Court Statistics, 2000/01." *Juristat* 22, 2 (March). Catalogue no. 85-002-XPE. Ottawa: Canadian Centre for Justice Statistics and Statistics Canada.

_____. 2004. "Adult Criminal Court Statistics, 2003–04." *Juristat* 24, 12. Catalogue no. 85-002-XPE. Ottawa: Canadian Centre for Justice Statistics and Statistics Canada.

Thomas, William Isaac. 1966 [1931]. "The Relation of Research to the Social Process." Pp. 289–305 in Morris Janowitz, ed. *W.I. Thomas on Social Organization and Social Personality*. Chicago: University of Chicago Press.

Thompson, E. P. 1967. "Time, Work Discipline, and Industrial Capitalism." *Past and Present* 38: 59–67.

Thompson, Ross A., and Paul R. Amato. 1999. "The Postdivorce Family: An Introduction to the Issues." Pp. xi–xxiii in Ross A. Thompson and Paul R. Amato, eds. *The Postdivorce*

Family: Children, Parenting and Society. Thousand Oaks, CA: Sage Publications.

Thorne, Barrie. 1993. *Gender Play: Girls and Boys in School.* New Brunswick, NJ: Rutgers University Press.

Tierney, John. 2009. "Can You Believe How Mean Gossip Can Be?" *New York Times* 2 November. On the World Wide Web at http://www.nytimes.com/2009/11/03/science/03tier.html?ref=sociology (3 August 2010).

Tilly, Charles. 1979a. "Collective Violence in European Perspective." Pp. 83–118 in H. Graham and T. Gurr, eds. *Violence in America: Historical and Comparative Perspective,* 2nd ed. Beverly Hills: Sage.

_____. 1979b. "Repertoires of Contention in America and Britain, 1750–1830." Pp. 126–55 in Mayer N. Zald and John D. McCarthy, eds. *The Dynamics of Social Movements: Resource Mobilization, Social Control, and Tactics.* Cambridge, MA: Winthrop Publishers.

Tilly, Charles, Louise Tilly, and Richard Tilly. 1975. *The Rebellious Century, 1830–1930.* Cambridge, MA: Harvard University Press.

Tkacik, Maureen. 2002. "The Return of Grunge." *Wall Street Journal* 11 December: B1, B10.

Todd, Peter M., Lars Penke, and Jens B. Asendorpf. 2010. "Strangers Influence Our Dating Preferences." Indiana University. On the World Wide Web at http://newsinfo.iu.edu/news/page/normal/14650.html (8 August 2010).

Toffler, Alvin. 1990. *Powershift: Knowledge, Wealth, and Violence at the Edge of the 21st Century.* New York: Bantam.

Tong, Rosemarie. 1989. *Feminist Thought: A Comprehensive Introduction.* Boulder, CO: Westview.

Tönnies, Ferdinand. 1988 [1887]. *Community and Society (Gemeinschaft und Gesselschaft).* New Brunswick, NJ: Transaction.

Toronto Board of Education. 1993. *The 1991 Every Secondary Student Survey. Part II: Detailed Profiles of Toronto's Secondary School Students.* Toronto: Toronto Board of Education Research Services.

Torrance, Judy M. 1986. *Public Violence in Canada.* Toronto: University of Toronto Press.

Troeltsch, Ernst. 1931 [1923]. *The Social Teaching of the Christian Churches,* Olive Wyon, trans. 2 vols. London, UK: George Allen and Unwin.

Trovato, Frank. 1998. "The Stanley Cup of Hockey and Suicide in Quebec, 1951–1992." *Social Forces* 77: 105–27.

Tschannen, Olivier. 1991. "The Secularization Paradigm: A Systematization." *Journal for the Scientific Study of Religion* 30: 395–415.

Tufts, Jennifer. 2000. "Public Attitudes Toward the Criminal Justice System." *Juristat* 20, 12 (December). Catalogue no. 85-002-XPE. Ottawa: Canadian Centre for Justice Statistics and Statistics Canada.

Tuljapurkar, Shripad, Nan Li, and Carl Boe. 2000. "A Universal Pattern of Mortality Decline in the G7 Countries." *Nature* 405: 789–92.

Tumin, M. 1953. "Some Principles of Stratification: A Critical Analysis." *American Sociological Review* 18: 387–94.

Turcotte, Martin. 2007. "Time Spent with Family During a Typical Workday, 1986 to 2005." *Canadian Social Trends* 82: 2–11. Catalogue no. 11-008-XPE. On the World Wide Web at http://www.statcan.ca/english/freepub/11-008-XIE/2006007/pdf/11-008-XIE20060079574.pdf (26 March 2007).

Turkel, Ann Ruth. 1998. "All about Barbie: Distortions of a Transitional Object." *Journal of the American Academy of Psychoanalysis* 26, 1 (Spring): 165–77.

Turkle, Sherry. 1995. *Life on the Screen: Identity in the Age of the Internet.* New York: Simon & Schuster.

Turner, Bryan S. 1986. *Citizenship and Capitalism: The Debate over Reformism.* London, UK: Allen and Unwin.

UNAIDS. 2009. "09 AIDS Epidemic Update." Geneva. On the World Wide Web at http://data.unaids.org/pub/Report/2009/JC1700_Epi_Update_2009_en.pdf (1 April 2010).

Ungar, Sheldon. 1992. "The Rise and (Relative) Decline of Global Warming as a Social Problem." *Sociological Quarterly* 33: 483–501.

_____. 1999. "Is Strange Weather in the Air? A Study of U.S. National Network News Coverage of Extreme Weather Events." *Climatic Change* 41: 133–50.

"U. K. Panel Calls Climate Data Valid." 2010. *New York Times* 30 March.

On the World Wide Web at http://www.nytimes.com (1 April 2010).

United Nations. 1998a. "Universal Declaration of Human Rights." On the World Wide Web at http://www.un.org/Overview/rights.html (25 January 2003).

United Nations. 1998b. *Human Development Report 1998.* New York: Oxford University Press.

_____. 2002. *Human Development Report 2002.* New York: Oxford University Press. On the World Wide Web at http://hdr.undp.org/reports/global/2002/en (16 April 2003).

_____. 2004. *Human Development Report 2004.* On the World Wide Web at http://hdr.undp.org/reports/global/2004/ (1 February 2005).

_____. 2006. *Human Development Report 2006.* On the World Wide Web at http://hdr.undp.org/hdr2006/pdfs/report/HDR06-complete.pdf (21 April 2007).

_____. 2009. "Gender Empowerment Measure and Its Components." *Human Development Report 2009.* On the World Wide Web at http://hdrstats.undp.org/en/indicators/126.html (19 March 2010).

United Nations Educational, Scientific, and Cultural Organization (UNESCO). 2008. "International Literacy Statistics: A Review of Concepts, Methodology and Current Data." On the World Wide Web at http://www.uis.unesco.org/template/pdf/Literacy/LiteracyReport2008.pdf (27 March 2010).

_____. 2010. "Table 7. Measures of Children Out of School." On the World Wide Web at http://stats.uis.unesco.org/unesco/TableViewer/tableView.aspx?ReportId=184 (27 March 2010).

Unschuld, Paul. 1985. *Medicine in China.* Berkeley, CA: University of California Press.

U.S. Department of Commerce. 1998. "Statistical Abstract of the United States: 1998." On the World Wide Web at http://www.census.gov/prod/3/98pubs/98statab/sasec1.pdf (8 October 2000).

U.S. Department of Labor. 2010. "CPI Inflation Calculator." On the World Wide Web at http://www.bls.gov/data/inflation_calculator.htm (29 March 2010).

U.S. Environmental Protection Agency, Office of Air Quality Planning and Standards. 2000. *National Air Pollutant Emission Trends, 1900–1998.* On the World Wide Web at http://www.epa.gov/ttn/chief/trends98/emtrnd.html (3 August 2000).

Useem, Bert. 1998. "Breakdown Theories of Collective Action." *Annual Review of Sociology* 24: 215–38.

Vago, Stephen, and Adie Nelson. 2003. *Law and Society.* Don Mills, ON: Pearson Educational Publishing.

Vincent, David. 2000. *The Rise of Mass Literacy: Reading and Writing in Modern Europe.* Cambridge, England: Polity Press.

Vygotsky, Lev S. 1987. *The Collected Works of L. S. Vygotsky,* vol. 1, N. Minick, trans. New York: Plenum.

Wald, Matthew L., and John Schwartz. 2003. "Alerts Were Lacking, NASA Shuttle Manager Says." *New York Times* 23 July. On the World Wide Web at http://www.nytimes.com (23 July 2003).

Waldfogel, Jane. 1997. "The Effect of Children on Women's Wages." *American Sociological Review* 62: 209–17.

Wallace, James, and Jim Erickson. 1992. *Hard Drive: Bill Gates and the Making of the Microsoft Empire.* New York: John Wiley.

Wallace, Marnie. 2009. "Police-Reported Crime Statistics in Canada, 2008." *Juristat* 29, 3. On the World Wide Web at http://www.statcan.gc.ca/pub/85-002-x/2009003/article/10902-eng.htm (14 October 2010).

Wallerstein, Immanuel. 1974–89. *The Modern World-System,* 3 vols. New York: Academic Press.

Wallerstein, Judith S., Julia Lewis, and Sandra Blakeslee. 2000. *The Unexpected Legacy of Divorce: A 25 Year Landmark Study.* New York: Hyperion.

Walmsley, Roy. 2009. "World Prison Population List (eighth edition)." On the World Wide Web at http://www.kcl.ac.uk/depsta/law/research/icps/downloads/wppl-8th_41.pdf (7 March 2010).

Wanner, R. 1999. "Expansion and Ascription: Trends in Educational Opportunity in Canada, 1920–1994." *Canadian Review of Sociology and Anthropology* 36 (August): 409–42.

Wasserman, Stanley, and Katherine Faust. 1994. *Social Network Analysis: Methods and Applications.* Cambridge: Cambridge University Press.

Webb, Eugene J., Donald T. Campbell, Richard D. Schwartz, and Lee Sechrest. 1966. *Unobtrusive Measures: Nonreactive Research in the Social Sciences.* Chicago: Rand McNally.

Weber, Max. 1946. *From Max Weber: Essays in Sociology,* rev. ed., H. Gerth and C. W. Mills, eds. and trans. New York: Oxford University Press.

———. 1947. *The Theory of Social and Economic Organization,* T. Parsons, ed., A. M. Henderson and T. Parsons, trans. New York: Free Press.

———. 1958 [1904–5]. *The Protestant Ethic and the Spirit of Capitalism.* New York: Scribner.

———. 1968 [1914]. *Economy and Society,* Guenther Roth and Claus Wittich, eds. Berkeley, CA: University of California Press.

Weeks, Jeffrey. 1986. *Sexuality.* London: Routledge.

Weinstein, Rhona S. 2002. *Reaching Higher: The Power of Expectations in Schooling.* Cambridge, MA: Harvard University Press.

Weis, Joseph G. 1987. "Class and Crime." Pp. 71–90 in Michael Gottfredson and Travis Hirschi, eds. *Positive Criminology.* Beverly Hills, CA: Sage.

Welch, Michael. 1997. "Violence Against Women by Professional Football Players: A Gender Analysis of Hypermasculinity, Positional Status, Narcissism, and Entitlement." *Journal of Sport and Social Issues* 21: 392–411.

Wellman, Barry, and Stephen Berkowitz, eds. 1997. *Social Structures: A Network Approach,* updated ed. Greenwich, CT: JAI Press.

Wellman, Barry, Peter J. Carrington, and Alan Hall. 1997. "Networks as Personal Communities." Pp. 130–84 in Barry Wellman and Stephen D. Berkowitz, eds., *Social Structures: A Network Approach,* updated ed. Greenwich, CT: JAI Press.

Welsh, Sandy. 1999. "Gender and Sexual Harassment." *Annual Review of Sociology* 25: 169–90.

West, Candace, and Don Zimmerman. 1987. "Doing Gender." *Gender and Society* 1: 125–51.

Wheeler, Stanton. 1961. "Socialization in Correctional Communities." *American Sociological Review* 26: 697–712.

Whitaker, Reg. 1987. *Double Standard.* Toronto: Lester and Orpen Dennys.

Whorf, Benjamin Lee. 1956. *Language, Thought, and Reality,* John B. Carroll, ed. Cambridge, MA: MIT Press.

"Why Britney Spears Matters." 2001. *The Laughing Medusa.* On the World Wide Web at http://www.gwu.edu/~medusa/2001/britney.html (18 April 2006).

Whyte, William F. 1981. *Street Corner Society: The Social Structure of an Italian Slum,* 3rd ed. Chicago: University of Chicago Press.

Wilensky, Harold L. 1967. *Organizational Intelligence: Knowledge and Policy in Government and Industry.* New York: Basic Books.

———. 1997. "Social Science and the Public Agenda: Reflections on the Relation of Knowledge to Policy in the United States and Abroad." *Journal of Health Politics, Policy and Law* 22: 1241–65.

Wiley College. 2007 "History of Wiley College." On the World Wide Web at http://www.wileyc.edu/wly_content/departments/administrative/history.php (7 March 2008).

Wilkinson, Richard G. 1996. *Unhealthy Societies: The Afflictions of Inequality.* London: Routledge.

Wilkinson, Richard, and Michael Marmot, eds. 2003. *Social Determinants of Health: The Solid Facts.* Copenhagen: World Health Organization Regional Office for Europe.

Willardt, Kenneth. 2000. "The Gaze He'll Go Gaga For." *Cosmopolitan* April: 232–37.

Williams, David R., and Chiquita Collins. 1995. "U.S. Socioeconomic and Racial Differences in Health: Patterns and Explanations." *Annual Review of Sociology* 21: 349–86.

Willis, Paul. 1984. *Learning to Labour: How Working-Class Kids Get Working-Class Jobs,* reprinted ed. New York: Columbia University Press.

Wolf, Naomi. 1997. *Promiscuities: The Secret Struggle for Womanhood.* New York: Vintage.

"Woman Soldier in Abuse Spotlight." 2004. *BBC News World Edition* 7 May. On the World Wide Web at http://news.bbc.co.uk/2/hi/americas/3691753.stm (3 March 2005).

Wong, Lloyd, and Michele Ng. 1998. "Chinese Immigrant Entrepreneurs in Vancouver: A Case Study of

Ethnic Business Development."
Canadian Ethnic Studies 30: 64–85.

Wood, Julia. 1999. *Everyday Encounters: An Introduction to Interpersonal Communication*, 2nd ed. Belmont, CA: Wadsworth.

Woodrow Federal Reserve Bank of Minneapolis. 2000. "What's a Dollar Worth?" On the World Wide Web at http://woodrow.mpls.frb.fed.us/economy/calc/cpihome.html (8 October 2000).

Workplace Information Directorate. 1996. *Special Tabulation of Strikes Statistics for 1986–95*. Ottawa: Human Resources Development Canada.

World Health Organization. 2003. "Cumulative Number of Reported Probable Cases." On the World Wide Web at http://www.who.int/csr/sars/country/2003_06_16/en (16 June 2003).

_____. 2010a. "Suicide Rates per 100,000 by Country, Year and Sex." On the World Wide Web at http://www.who.int/mental_health/prevention/suicide_rates/en/index.html (16 February 2010).

_____. 2010b. *WHO Statistical Information System (WHOSIS)*. On the World Wide Web at http://www.who.int/whosis/en/index.html (1 April 2010).

World Values Survey. 2003. Machine readable data set. On the World Wide Web at http://www.worldvaluessurvey.org (1 May 2004).

World Values Survey. 2010. On the World Wide Web at http://www.wvsevsdb.

com/wvs/WVSAnalizeSample.jsp (20 October 2010).

Wortley, Scot, David Brownfield, and John Hagan. 1996. "The Usual Suspects: Race, Age and Gender Differences in Police Contact." Paper presented at the 48th Annual Conference of the American Society of Criminology, Chicago: November.

Wortley, Scot, and Julian Tanner. 2011. "The Racial Profiling Debate: Data, Denials, and Confusion." Pp. 295–302 in Robert J. Brym, ed. *Society in Question*. Toronto: Nelson.

Wu, Zheng. 2000. *Cohabitation: An Alternative Form of Family Living*. Don Mills, ON: Oxford University Press.

X, Malcolm. 1965. *The Autobiography of Malcolm X*. New York: Grove.

Yamane, David. 1997. "Secularization on Trial: In Defense of a Neosecularization Paradigm." *Journal for the Scientific Study of Religion* 36: 109–22.

Yancey, William L., Eugene P. Ericksen, and George H. Leon. 1979. "Emergent Ethnicity: A Review and Reformulation." *American Sociological Review* 41: 391–403.

Younge, Gary. 2009. "Are Black Rights Campaigners Still Relevant?" *BBC News* 3 August. On the World Wide Web at http://news.bbc.co.uk/2/hi/americas/8181127.stm (6 August 2010).

Zald, Meyer N., and John D. McCarthy. 1979. *The Dynamics of Social Movements*. Cambridge, MA: Winthrop.

Zimbardo, Philip G. 1972. "Pathology of Imprisonment." *Society* 9, 6: 4–8.

Zimmermann, Francis. 1987 [1982]. *The Jungle and the Aroma of Meats: An Ecological Theme in Hindu Medicine*, Janet Lloyd, trans. Berkeley, CA: University of California Press.

Zimring, Franklin E., and Gordon Hawkins. 1995. *Incapacitation: Penal Confinement and the Restraint of Crime*. New York: Oxford University Press.

Zinsser, Hans. 1935. *Rats, Lice and History*. Boston: Little, Brown.

Zogby International. 2001. "Arab American Institute Polls Results: Arab Americans Are Strong Advocates of War Against Terrorism; Overwhelmingly Endorse President Bush's Actions; Significant Numbers Have Experienced Discrimination since Sept. 11." On the World Wide Web at http://www.zogby.com/news/ReadNews.dbm?ID487 (21 December 2002).

Zola, Irving Kenneth. 1982. *Missing Pieces: A Chronicle of Living with a Disability*. Philadelphia: Temple University Press.

Zoutman, D. E., B. D. Ford, E. Bryce, M. Gourdeau, G. Hebert, E. Henderson, S. Paton, Canadian Hospital Epidemiology Committee, Canadian Nosocomial Infection Surveillance Program, Health Canada. 2003. "The State of Infection Surveillance and Control in Canadian Acute Care Hospitals." *American Journal of Infection Control* 31, 5: 266–73.

Note: Entries in **boldface** are key terms.